THE RIGHTS OF WASHINGTON PUBLIC SAFETY EMPLOYEES

2ND EDITION

AUTHOR

JAMES CLINE

ISBN-13: 978-0-9967645-0-6

DEDICATION

To the Cops, Firefighters, Dispatchers, Corrections Officers and First Response Support Personnel of our State — you offer calmness under pressure, courage in the face of danger, comfort to the hurt and troubled, perseverance in the face of endless challenge, integrity in your honest service, and a commitment to the common good.

ACKNOWLEDGMENTS

While only my name is on this book's cover, in truth there are many other people who have stood behind me and offered extensive assistance, in many forms, and that made this vastly expanded Second Edition a reality. Authors John Donne and Thomas Merton have explained that "No Man is an Island" and nowhere do I know that to be truer than when I reflect on this book's creation.

For one, this book could have not have been written without my clients. They not only helped contribute many of the problems considered here (sometimes repeatedly), but they also asked me the probing questions that this book tries to address. I have been very fortunate to have a challenging and interesting law practice, one that provides repeated opportunities to serve individuals who are service providers themselves.

Credit is in order for the many current and former law clerks who have worked for me over the years. They provided detailed and insightful legal research that I was able to use in drafting the book. Kate Acheson, Kasey Burton, Jennifer Campbell, Joe Chapman, Oliver Enquist, Jordan Jones, Geoff Kiernan, Brennen Johnson, Harrison Owens, Tony Rice, Brittany Torrence, Mitch Wilson, and David Worley have all contributed significant pieces of research to this book. In particular, Kasey Burton, Jordan Jones, Brennen Johnson, Geoff Kiernan, Harrison Owens, Tony Rice, and Brittany Torrence made significant contributions to the case tables that you see presented in this Second Edition.

Office support staff also made important contributions. Office Clerk Erica Graham helped in document production. Silvia Bass and Paul Diaz kept the office running smoothly while all this work was done in the background. Support Staff Darrah Hinton, Marga Bueno, Anneke Lee also deserve thanks for their contributions during the three year this revised edition was being written.

A particular callout also is owed to Donna Steinmetz. Not only did Donna make major contributions to law firm operations while the drafting proceeded, she was heavily involved in the final and important book production steps.

My longtime friend and graphic designer Steve Pillitu (https://p2graphicdesign.com/) worked closely with us to get this book to its final stage. Steve provided solid and steady advice in the production process but also was involved in the book formatting and redesign. It is our hope that the updated look and feel of this new edition will make it more accessible to the readers.

Attorneys Tristan Brown, Chris Casillas, Phillip Chandler, Sarah Derry, Karyl Elinski, Aaron Jeide, Kate Kremer, George Merker, Cynthia McNabb, Therese Norton, Erica Shelley Nelson, Mitch Riese, Christina Sherman, Jim Smith, Kelly Turner, and Reba Weiss are all owed thanks both large and small for presenting challenging questions and insights over the past dozen years. Their efforts contributed to my ability to prepare these materials and in many cases they produced substantive legal analysis that I was able to directly use. Special thanks goes to attorneys Tristan Brown, Kelly Turner, and Therese Norton who provided an in-depth analysis of PERC cases.

Sarah Derry also deserves a special callout. Her detailed and focused proofreading and editing of the final drafts helped spot many now eradicated errors and helped produce what we believe (hopefully) is a virtually error free final Second Edition.

This book would not be possible separate from a successful law practice that generated its raw materials. While I owe many thanks to many individuals for that success, there are two people in particular who I owe a special debt of gratitude.

For over 20 years Kate Kremer has practiced law with me. I greatly value her loyalty and friendship. Her contributions to the firm have alternated between those highly visible and stealth, but they have always been significant. She has worked in the background, sometimes from a distance, creating and maintaining the extensive resources used in our law practices. I cannot imagine our law firm being the success it is without her contributions.

I also must extend particular thanks to my loyal law partner Chris Casillas. As with Kate Kremer, I cannot imagine the law firm being the success that it is without Chris. His elevated standards and dedication made the firm what it is. His vast intellect and penetrating legal insights have contributed to this book in ways both large and small.

Finally, thanks are due to my family. Thank you, Sarah, Katherine, Rachel, and Eric for your love and support. And the most special thanks that remain is for my wife Lauren. She not only was constantly supportive of my law practice and the extensive periods away I needed for drafting this updated edition, she makes my time away from work rich and rewarding.

Chapter 1

Forums for Enforcing Legal Rights

A. Introduction

This chapter *could* have been presented as the final chapter but it seemed to make the most sense to present it first as the first chapter, even though it involves subjects dealt with in great depth only in the later chapters. Some readers might find it more effective to read this chapter quickly now and then re-read it again *after* covering all the other chapters. It addresses *how* to apply the rights covered by the rest of the book. To some readers it may simply seem more comprehensible after reviewing the chapters discussing those rights in depth.

This book addresses the wide-ranging rights of Washington public safety employees *and* their labor organizations, including the right to collectively bargain, the right to be paid the proper wage, and the right to be free from discrimination. Washington public safety employees and their unions are often presented with a *myriad* of sometimes bewildering choices on *how* to enforce these rights — there are different "forums" to have these rights vindicated *and* sometimes often more than one eligible forum for the *same* right. Courts, arbitrations, administrative agencies, and other entities have some jurisdiction over labor and employment law rights. This chapter is designed to provide a general framework of those different available legal forums, the pros and cons of each forum, and an overview of whether to elect one forum over another.

No doubt, *the final decision concerning the appropriate forum for a given case should be made in consultation with legal counsel.* But this chapter provides a basis for at least identifying the decisions union representatives and employees may ultimately have to make concerning electing remedies and allocating resources.

B. The Primary Forums for Enforcing the Rights of Washington Public Safety Employees

For every law violation, there is a means of redress. But sometimes there is *more than one* means of redress. In other words, some legal rights may be enforceable in more than one forum. Between where there exists more than one available forum, *choices* are forced — perhaps because of an "election of remedies" provision in a labor agreement or sometimes simply because of limits on resources.

Some fairly complex concepts are raised now and then discussed again later in this chapter:

- "Election of remedies" — usually the creature of the labor agreement with a clause which restricts an employee from arbitrating grievances when it is also being *simultaneously* litigated in another forum.

- "Res judicata" and "collateral estoppel" — legal principles that sometimes bar a party from "relitigating" an issue *already* decided elsewhere.

- "Deferral" — the practice of the Public Employment Relations Commission to "defer" an Unfair Labor Practices charge to assign to arbitrator under the Collective Bargaining Agreement what is otherwise a violation of the collective bargaining law.

These somewhat complex legal principles may restrict a party's freedom to elect the forum of its choice or may limit the ability to bring claims in one forum after another forum has already been selected.

There are innumerable — and sometimes overlapping — statutes, regulations, constitutional rights, common law doctrines and contract agreements that define public safety rights. And for each of these laws, there may be more than one way to enforce those rights.

Each forum presents its own advantages and disadvantages. Sometimes identical claims *may* be brought in multiple forums. The question is then presented whether all forums *should* be pursued in light of tactical and resource constraints. Other times, only *a portion* of a claim may be brought in each of the different available forums and the unfortunate question of an "election of remedies" or "collateral estoppel" may, therefore, force the foregoing of some available relief that might be available elsewhere.

There are innumerable — and sometimes overlapping — statutes, regulations, constitutional rights, common law doctrines and contract agreements that define public safety rights. And for each of these laws, there may be more than one way to enforce those rights. Just consider for a minute the vast array of the sources of legal rights:

The United States Constitution and all of its Amendments, the source of the right to freedom of speech, religion, Association, and due process, and a source of prohibition against discrimination, compelled self-incrimination, unreasonable searches, as well as the source of innumerable other rights.

- The Washington State Constitution and its Amendments which sometimes expand or add to the rights identified in the federal Constitution.
- The state collective bargaining law, administered and enforced by the Public Employment Relations Commission (PERC), which confers a right to engage in collective bargaining and to be free of unlawful retaliation and discrimination for the exercise of that right.
- Contract law — and the terms of the parties' Collective Bargaining Agreement (CBA), usually enforceable through final and binding arbitration.
- State and federal statutes prohibiting discrimination.
- State and federal statutes protecting family leave, medical privacy, and requiring the accommodation of various medical conditions.
- State and federal laws veteran and military leave laws, governing the right of those engaged in military service and even their families.
- State and federal wage and hour laws, defining a minimum wage and mandating that excess hours be paid as overtime.
- State and federal statutes associated with miscellaneous and numerous unfair employment practices.
- The State civil service law governing the selection, promotion and retention of law enforcement personnel and city firefighters.

- Regulations issued by various administrative agencies further defining of establishing enforcement schemes for many of the above rights.

- Court interpretations of common law, including interpretations regarding wrongful discharge and other forms of retaliation.

- Miscellaneous general laws governing all citizens, but that may also impact or define the rights of employees and their labor organizations.

There are different places to go to see that employment and labor rights are vindicated. In this chapter we will highlight and evaluate the four primary forums for obtaining legal relief for Washington public safety employees and their unions: Labor arbitration, local civil service commissions, the Public Employment Relations Commission (PERC), and the courts. We will closely review each of these forums and their limitations and benefits.

An appreciation of the limitations and benefits of each forum is important in choosing the proper forum. We will also discuss how the exercise of *one forum* can impact the rights available in *another.*

1. Labor Arbitration

Labor arbitration is a means by which the collective bargaining agreement between the union and the employer is enforced. At its core, a collective bargaining agreement (CBA) is a legal contract. Like any contract, there is a means to enforce it. Generally, contracts are enforced in court. But under a longstanding tradition in labor relations, labor and management almost uniformly agree to submit labor contract disputes to a private arbitration process rather than to the courts.

The right to enforce the labor agreement through the labor arbitration process does not exist as a matter of statute. It exists purely because the parties to the labor agreement — the union and the employer — agreed to waive their right to seek court enforcement of the agreement in favor of the private arbitration process. The nature of that agreement to arbitrate controls the extent of an arbitrator's authority and jurisdiction.

As indicated, provisions to resolve collective bargaining disputes through arbitration are a nearly universal element of collective bargaining agreements. The agreement to arbitrate is typically located in the grievance procedure section of the contract. Labor agreements generally require that grievances be filed and processed through a sequence of steps as a precondition to submission to arbitration.

Adherence to those steps — both as to the type of information required to be presented and the timing of the steps — is important. Failure to comply with the initial grievance step requirements can result in a loss of the right to enforce the contract through arbitration. Since the agreement to arbitrate generally includes a waiver of the right to enforce the legal claims through the courts, failure to properly process a grievance means a loss of the ability to enforce a legal claim at all.

The contract grievance procedures specify the manner in which an arbitrator is to be selected. It usually indicates that a "list" of arbitrators is to be obtained from one of the various arbitrator referral services. The parties can and often do reach a mutual agreement for the selection of an arbitrator without striking names on the list.

As indicated, an arbitrator's authority is purely a function of the labor agreement. Therefore, *an arbitrator has jurisdiction only to take those actions which the labor agreement gives him authority to do.* Arbitrators who act outside the authority vested in them by the labor agreement run the risk of having their decisions overturned by a court.

Often, though, this "arbitral" authority is *implied.* For example, where the CBA provides, as is typical, that the arbitrator has the authority to resolve disputes arising from the CBA, the arbitrator can issue any award "which draws its essence" from the agreement. Not every term of the CBA, as we will see later, is made explicit. Many may be implied by the parties, for example, adopted and adhered "past practices."

Furthermore, the arbitral authority to hear the dispute implies arbitral authority to grant a remedy. Even where the "remedy" authority is not defined in the CBA, courts have found implied authority for arbitrators to redress breaches of the CBA. But that "remedial" authority is not boundless — Washington arbitrators are prohibited by the courts to impose "punitive" awards.[1]

---

1 *Kennewick Education Association v. Kennewick School District,* 35 Wn. App. 280, 666 P.2d 928 (1983).

The primary advantages of labor arbitration are its speed, finality, and informality.

Grievance arbitration has a number of advantages for both parties. This is why it is such a common feature of mutually agreed upon labor agreements. In fact, the success that the labor relations field has had with arbitration is so pervasive that it has inspired the "alternative dispute resolution" movement within the broader legal field. Increasingly, parties to other types of contractual agreements have seen the advantage of submitting contract disputes to the private arbitration process.

The primary advantages of labor arbitration are its speed, finality, and informality. Parties are required to move CBA disputes through the grievance procedure on a timely basis, as dictated by the agreement. Arbitrators are usually scheduled within months of disputes arising, and labor agreements usually contain a provision requiring arbitrators to issue their awards within 30 days of the close of the hearing. Except in those unusual cases where arbitrators have exceeded the authority conferred on them by the parties or have issued an award in violation of "public policy," arbitrations are not subject to appeal and are final and binding upon the parties.[2]

A note on those "public policy" claims is in order. Generally parties honor the results of arbitration. Occasionally they don't. Most court challenges to arbitration decisions are brought by employers, not the unions. Sometimes a "headline grabbing" reinstatement is ordered, causing a stir among the public not familiar with all the nuances and fine points involved in any given grievance decision. On those occasions, some public employers have been tempted to attack the otherwise "final and binding" arbitration decision in court.

The 2009 Supreme Court decision in *Kitsap County Deputy Sheriff's Guild v. Kitsap County*[3] has served to squelch the number of these challenges. In *Kitsap*, the Supreme Court at least addressed some of the conflicting rules from the lower courts and its own and finally made clear that an employer cannot refuse on

---

[2] This depends, though, on the parties including a clause in their labor agreement specifically identifying the arbitrator's result as "final and binding." This is a stock provision in nearly all grievance arbitration clauses and is an essential one if the advantages of arbitration are to be obtained.

[3] 167.Wn.2d 428, 219 P.3d 657 (2009).

"public policy" grounds to abide by an award because the conduct of the employee at issue violates public policy. Instead, it ruled that the relevant public policy concerned whether there was a policy prohibition on the *reinstatement* of the employee.

An arguable example of a public policy challenge relating to reinstatement occur if arbitrators reinstated allegedly flagrant and repeat sexual harassers; the return of such employees to the workplace has been deemed by courts to be a violation of the public policy concerning nondiscrimination. This distinction is important since virtually any employee discipline, at some level, concerned misconduct touching on a violation of some type of public policy.

Arbitrations are informal both as to the hearing and the prehearing discovery. There is no right to take depositions or to propound lengthy or burdensome interrogatories. While there is an obligation — which PERC will enforce — to provide "bargaining information," including any information that may be relevant to the processing of a particular grievance, such discovery is informal and is satisfied simply by producing the papers requested. This "discovery" does not include more formal civil litigation methods like depositions.

Another advantage of arbitration is that the parties have some input on the choice of who the "judge" is. As indicated, often arbitrators are selected by mutual agreement. And even when the parties simply strike names off of a list, at least there is an opportunity to strike those arbitrators a party feels are least likely to give them a fair hearing. The ability to control the selection of an arbitrator is a means of ensuring the expertise of the decision-maker. Labor arbitrators always have experience in labor relations and are often labor lawyers. Their experience and training often produce higher quality result than could be obtained in other forums.

The "finality" of an arbitrator's award is usually seen as an advantage to the parties, but certainly could be a disadvantage in a given case. Under most circumstances, as discussed above, there is no right to "appeal" an arbitrator's award in Superior Court. *This is true even if an arbitrator is claimed to have incorrectly applied the law or blundered on the facts.* When parties agree to submit a matter to arbitration, they are agreeing not only to have the arbitrator decide the facts of a given case but also to decide the law — and to be bound by those decisions.

One disadvantage of arbitration, because it is a private means of obtaining legal recourse, is that the burden falls upon the parties to pay for the arbitrator. Generally, the parties' agreement includes an arrangement to divide the arbitrator's cost, but some agreements include a "loser pays" provision, which imposes the burden entirely on the losing party. "Loser pays" provisions can prove disadvantageous to unions, whose pockets are usually not as deep as those of the employer and who must carefully justify all expenditures to the membership.

Another potential pitfall of arbitration is that even with an experienced, expert arbitrator it can be difficult to predict the result. Arbitrators are not bound by case precedent — *stare decisis* — as courts are.

One alternative which exists to the private hiring of an arbitrator is utilizing PERC to provide arbitration services. PERC has a statutory mandate to assign PERC staff examiners to serve as arbitrators where the parties' collective bargaining agreement makes such an arrangement.[4] The primary problem with utilizing PERC arbitrators is delay. PERC case handling rules assign the lowest priority to such arbitration cases and it can sometimes up to a year to have such a grievance resolved. Further, PERC does not provide a list of staff members to select from, but simply randomly assigns a staff member. A party dissatisfied with the choice of assigned arbitrator is without recourse. Yet for small bargaining units with finite resources, this is an arbitration avenue to consider.

Another potential pitfall of arbitration is that even with an experienced, expert arbitrator it can be difficult to predict the result. Arbitrators are not bound by case precedent — *stare decisis* — as courts are. They are free to fashion their own notion of what the result ought to be. Often arbitrators will look to prior published decisions to guide their judgment, but there is no legal mandate that they do so.

Another disadvantage of arbitration is the limitation on an arbitrator's authority to issue a remedy. Although arbitrators have some authority to craft an appropriate remedy, their authority is not as broad as that of the courts. In particular, arbitrators can decide only the case before them and *cannot* grant a general injunction against an employer. Where an employer repeatedly violates a labor agreement, the union is forced to grieve repeatedly

---

[4] RCW 41.56.125.

and arbitrate on a case-by-case basis. Forcing unions into arbitration is certainly one means employers have available to tax the resources of unions. As a practical matter, however, public employers in Washington rarely adopt such a strategy because they have budget limitations of their own and because the political system provides its own checks and balances against public employers who repeatedly and flagrantly violate labor agreements.

2. Civil Service Commissions

State law mandates civil service coverage for a wide range of public safety employees in the State of Washington. Municipal police and fire departments, and county sheriff's offices are subject to civil service protection under the state law. The legislature has *not* mandated civil service coverage to fire districts, although they may opt into coverage on a voluntary basis.[5] (A challenge to the optional nature of this coverage on "equal protection grounds" was rejected by the Ninth Circuit in *Roley v. Pierce County Fire Protection District No. 4.*[6])

The scope of employees covered under civil service laws is broad. The municipal police and fire laws require initially required *all* employees except for the chief to be covered under civil service system. It has subsequently been amended to allow some additional exemptions for "unclassified appointments" for command staff and administrative assistants on a formula corresponding to the size of the Department.[7] The civil service law pertaining to county sheriffs makes exemptions corresponding to Department size.[8]

The state civil service laws constitute the *framework* that local governments must follow. But they are free to create their own local civil service rules, provided those local rule "substantially accomplish the purpose" of the state law.[9]

Sometimes public employers have argued that excluding certain categories of employees — typically civilian employees — is a permissible local variation under the civil service laws. Courts have generally disagreed with this claim, and it is generally understood now that the coverage of local civil service systems must be at least as broad as that under state law.[10]

---

[5] *See* RCW 52.30.040.

[6] 869 F.2d 491 (9th Cir. 1989).

[7] RCW 41.12.050.

[8] RCW 41.14.070.

[9] *Seattle Police Guild v. City of Seattle*, 151 Wn.2d 823, 92 P.3d 234 (2004).

[10] *Teamsters v. City of Moses Lake*, 70 Wn. App. 404, 853, P.2d 851 (1993).

The ultimate power in a civil service system resides with the local civil service commission. The civil service commission's authority is not to enforce labor laws in general, but simply to hear appeals from particular violations of local civil service rules. In order for a party to present a matter to a civil service commission for review, it must be able to cite a rule which it claims is violated.

Civil service commissions have the authority under the state law to craft their own rules. Again, this authority is limited by the statutory restriction that any such local rules must "substantially accomplish the purpose" of the state law. To change its rules, a civil service commission must go through a proper rulemaking process.

But the most significant restriction on the authority of a civil service commission to change its rules is the mandate imposed upon it from the collective bargaining law. Civil service commissions do not have the authority to circumvent the collective bargaining process.[11] A rule that would affect a mandatory subject of bargaining must first be negotiated between the employer and the union. And where an employer and a union have reached an agreement about a particular working condition, including the civil service process itself, the Civil Service Commission must abide by that agreement.[12]

The civil service system is in some ways a throwback to a period long before public employee collective bargaining rights were available. The civil service system was never conceived as a means of granting widespread employee rights in the workplace. Its initial goal was more limited. The original state civil service laws were passed in the late 1930s as a means of restricting unbridled political patronage. The primary purpose of the original civil service laws was to protect employees from political retaliation and bad faith employment decisions of the more extreme kind.

With the passage of time and the enactment of the collective bargaining statute, civil service commissions, unfortunately, have become less a means of protecting employee rights and more a means of advancing management's agenda. Most civil service commissioners are directly appointed by management and often have a background in management.

---

[11] *City of Yakima v. IAFF Local 469*, 117 Wn.2d 655, 818 P.2d 1076 (1991).

[12] *City of Spokane v. Spokane Civil Service Commission*, 98 Wn. App. 574, 989 P.2d 1245 (1999).

Civil service laws define their aim as the restriction of political patronage and arbitrary employment decisions. The laws contain certain elements mandating that discipline decisions be made for just cause and requiring that hiring and promotion decisions be based on merit and objective testing procedures. (This includes a prohibition on department management interference in the testing process that seems widely violated despite court decisions proscribing such interference.[13]) Local civil service rules which attempt to avoid these requirements are likely to be void under state law.

Although not required by the state law, local civil service rules often include additional provisions allowing for reinstatement of employees under certain circumstances. For example, civil service rules sometimes permit reinstatement after a resignation or sometimes after a period of medical disability.

The civil service system does have its advantages. The primary advantage is that of all the available forums it is undoubtedly the speediest. Local civil service rules typically call for a hearing to be set within 30 days of an appeal being filed, and generally civil service commissions attempt to stick to that deadline. Also, civil service commissions typically make a decision very quickly after conducting a hearing.

In most locales, civil service commissions simply do not provide a meaningful check against unfair management decision-making.

Civil service commissions usually proceed in an informal manner with relaxed rules of evidence and very limited discovery. These informalities, though, can also be seen as a disadvantage. For example, sometimes civil service commissions attempt to uphold employer action while relying on hearsay statements and other evidence which might be inadmissible or provided limited weight elsewhere.

The overwhelming disadvantage of a civil service system is that it is neutral only in the most superficial sense. By law, civil service commissions are intended to be "independent," but the reality is that civil service commissions are handpicked by management.[14] In most locales, civil service commissions simply

---

[13] *Simonds v. City of Kennewick*, 41 Wn.App 851, 706, P.2d 1080 (1985).

[14] RCW 41.12.030 provides for appointment by city officers of the

do not provide a meaningful check against unfair management decision-making.

And the informality of the procedures can also create fairness problems. Procedures are often so relaxed that they lead to procedural irregularities. Sometimes civil service commissions fail to retain independent attorneys to advise them and instead will simply rely on the City Attorney's office for advice. Thus, someone challenging the City on a civil service appeal will sometimes face one member of the law department in the hearing, while another member of the law department advises the commission. Civil service law allows civil service commissions to hire a secretary/examiner to help it do its work, but the tradition within cities, which has been upheld by the courts, is to hire someone who is already on the city's payroll.[15] Unfortunately, this individual often is the personnel director or an assistant to the personnel director.

Another disadvantage of the civil service system is the limited ability to appeal the decisions. Although technically there is a right to appeal any decision of a civil service commission in the superior court, such appeals are difficult to win. The "standard of review" the courts apply to such civil service decisions is generally the very narrow "arbitrary and capricious" standard. Courts have allowed a number of questionable civil service commission decisions to stand and have generally overturned civil service commissions in only the most extreme of cases.[16]

3. The Public Employment Relations Commission

The Public Employees Collective Bargaining Act (PECBA), RCW Chapter 41.56, calls for the creation of an administrative agency to hear labor law violations. That agency is the Public Employment Relations Commission.

PERC also has supervision over some other collective bargaining laws, including notably the law governing most employees of State Government defined in RCW Chapter 41.80.

---

commissioners.

[15] RCW 41.08.110 mandates competitive testing for the examiner. In at least one unpublished case, involving the City of Seatac, an improperly hand-selected appointment was determined to have be invalid. *Wieland v. City of Seatac*, 1997 Wash. App. Lexis 920 (1997).

[16] *See, e.g., Steve ex re. Perry v. City of Seattle*, 69 Wn.2d 816, 420 Pd.2d 704 (1966) (Supreme court, citing deferential standard of review, overturned Superior Court that had vacated a civil service decision upholding discharge for some traffic violations combined with the Chief's opinion that the officer was a "marginal" officer).

State troopers are actually covered under RCW 41.56, though.

PERC is a three-member commission appointed by the Governor. But most of the work of PERC is done through an Executive Director, which the Commission has hired and an entire staff of hearing examiners. Initial case decisions are made either by the executive director or an assigned hearing examiner. An appeal to the full three-person Commission is almost always the second step in the administrative process.

By statute, PERC is given wide-ranging labor relations responsibility, including mediating labor contract negotiations, but one of its primary responsibilities is to hear and decide unfair labor practice (ULP) complaints. The collective bargaining statute specifies a list of employer or union activities which are deemed to be "unfair labor practices."[17] The method for pursuing a ULP is to bring an administrative complaint to PERC alleging a violation of the state labor law.

If a party is claiming that the employer is failing to abide by the labor agreement, this complaint should be pursued through the grievance procedure, not through the ULP procedure. On the other hand, as will be discussed below, some types of labor law violations *may* also be ULPs

Such ULP complaints must be brought within six months of the violation. A narrow exception to the six-month limitation applies where the violation was concealed from a party so that it had no reasonable opportunity to know of the violation.[18] For example, when an employer makes a particular arrangement with an employee of which the union is unaware, the six-month period does not begin to run until the union learns of the arrangement.

It should be understood that a ULP process is an action to enforce the collective bargaining statute, *not the labor agreement.* If a party is claiming that the employer is failing to abide by the labor agreement, this complaint should be pursued through the grievance procedure, not through the ULP procedure. On the other hand, as will be discussed below, some types of labor law violations *may* also be ULPs, depending on the circumstances.

The strongest advantage of the PERC process over other

---

[17] RCW 41.56.140 (employer ULPs); RCW 41.56.150 (union ULPs).

[18] *King County*, Decision 9204-A (PECB, 2007); *citing City of Pasco*, Decision 4197-A (PECB, 1994).

forums is the expertise of the personnel assigned to decide ULP disputes. PERC examiners are very experienced labor relations personnel, often labor lawyers and are trained and experienced in applying labor law principles.

PERC publishes its decisions and, for the most part, attempts to adhere closely to the precedent set in previous decisions. The practice of PERC generally to follow its own case precedents lends itself to predictability in results. And that predictability in itself often resolves disputes on its own once the parties recognize the applicable law. Many an unfair labor practice complaint has been resolved by one party or the other simply being shown a prior PERC decision with similar facts. Advocates know that PERC generally takes a dim view of parties who insist on proceeding on unfair labor practice complaints in the face of clearly established precedent. This affects the nature of remedies at issue.[19]

Another advantage of the PERC process is its informality, compared to court litigation. Similar in informality to labor arbitrations, evidence rules are not strictly adhered to, although they are sometimes used as a basis to the judge whether or not evidence is reliable. For example, hearsay evidence is generally admissible, but PERC will give it less weight and will even decline to admit hearsay which becomes too attenuated.

The lack of formality can also be a disadvantage. PERC has very limited means to enforce discovery in its own proceedings. Parties who need to obtain necessary information to prosecute a ULP complaint can obtain a PERC subpoena order, but they must go to Superior Court to enforce it. Generally, though, simply a PERC order induces opponents to turn over requested information when they knows that the examiner who ordered the production of the information will also be deciding the case.

One significant disadvantage in the PERC system is the amount of time it takes to get a final decision. PERC rarely maintains adequate staffing and examiners carry heavy workloads, not only of conducting multiple hearings at a time, but also serving other agency roles such as mediator. And at least at this time, appeals to the Commission often face a backlogged docket.

Before a party can proceed to a hearing, it must first obtain a "preliminary ruling," giving it permission to pursue a complaint to a hearing. Although the Administrative Procedures Act requires

---

[19] For example, PERC is more likely to impose attorney fees where the defense lacks merit. But they do so infrequently.

such a decision to be issued within 30 days, at times in the past, PERC has not always adhered to that 30 day deadline. Over the past several years, though, PERC has improved this initial screening part of its case management.

After a preliminary ruling is granted, it often takes a few months before a hearing is held. And employers can obtain even further delay by then appealing the matter to the full Commission. It is common for ULP complaints to take a year to two for PERC to resolve. And that is even before a party decides to file an appeal to Superior Court.

The delay in PERC proceedings exists even when the legal rules are clear-cut. Unlike courts, which give parties the *right* to pursue clear-cut matters on a "summary judgment" basis, PERC will entertain summary judgment on a permissive basis but infrequently does so. Thus, unions are often forced into ULP hearings, even when there is little or no serious defense available to an employer in a given case.

Employers often use these delays for their own purposes. Employers will sometimes seem indifferent, engaging in activities which they suspect might violate the statute, with the knowledge that any order that might be issued is far into the future. Moreover, PERC has limited remedial authority. It is able to issue "make whole remedies" in certain cases, but it is barred from issuing any remedy which might be seen as punitive in nature. Therefore, PERC orders have a limited deterrent effect on employers.

4. The Courts

Traditionally, courts are where people would go to obtain legal relief. But between statutes which confer authority on administrative agencies and private agreements which confer authority on arbitrators, the original jurisdiction of courts in deciding public employee rights is limited. Often courts are involved in labor issues only on an appeal basis, and even then those appeals may be on a very restricted "standard of review."

Nonetheless, there are a number of claims over which courts have "original" jurisdiction. Although it rarely happens, courts do share original jurisdiction over ULP with PERC.[20] And PERC itself has the authority to bring Superior Courts into ULP proceedings when it seeks to enjoin employers from committing ULPs.[21]

---

20 *Northshore School District*, 99 Wn.2d 232, 662 P.2d 38 (1983).

21 RCW 41.56.160(3).

There are other types of legal rights claims, though, that courts are the primary forum. For example, civil rights and Fair Labor Standards Act claims usually start at the trial court level.

The most significant advantage of bringing a matter before a court is the extensive authority courts have to issue appropriate remedies. First and foremost, this includes the right to issue injunctions which restrain employers from repeating unlawful conduct. For most law violations, an injunction is an element of a final order. And often courts will even assert their authority to issue "preliminary injunctions" while a matter is still proceeding through court.

Other aspects of court proceedings which may be either an advantage or disadvantage, depending on the particular situation, are the rights of appeal and the formality of discovery. A party which is dissatisfied with a trial court decision always has a right to have at least the legal issues reconsidered by an appellate court. These appeals produce delay, but the right of an appeal is often valuable to unions simply because trial courts, frankly, frequently misapply the various statutes which apply to labor and employment situations. Appellate courts have more time and more staff and are more likely to arrive at a legally "correct" decision.

On the one hand, the discovery which is a mandatory part of any trial court litigation can be a disadvantage because of the expense involved. On the other hand, there are certain circumstances under which formal discovery, including the ability to depose an employer representative, can have some great value.

The chief disadvantages of using courts as a forum for resolving employee rights issues are the expense and delay involved in such procedures. Another significant problem with superior courts as a forum is the relative lack of expertise of trial court judges in labor law matters. Generally, trial court judges come from law practices other than labor and employment law. And many of the legal principles which apply in labor law are contrary to the "common law" principles governing contracts which judges may have previously been exposed to in their legal education or in their law practices. Much of the collective bargaining law was written to counter the common law approach to property and contract law.

For these reasons, the right to be able to pursue a trial court ruling to an appellate court is especially important. On a number of occasions, the court of appeals ruled in a union's favor *after* an unfavorable trial court decision. Appellate courts have staff, resources, and time that often allow them to take a closer look at cases and tend to adhere their rulings more commonly to case precedent than do trial courts.

C. Competition and Conflict Between the Available Legal Forums

There are a number of circumstances under which a given case may be pursued in more than one legal forum. There are a number of rules that apply which may determine the appropriate forum to begin such an action in. These rules also create a degree of competition and conflict between these forums and the decisions that might result. As indicated earlier, there are three different legal concepts that bear directly on forum conflict: deferral, election of remedy requirements and bars on relitigation ("collateral estoppel" and "res judicata").

Deferral to arbitration. Following a policy previous adopted by the National Labor Relations Board (NLRB), PERC has adopted a "deferral to arbitration" policy.[22] Under this policy, where a unilateral change which might be a ULP is also governed by the CBA, PERC has a policy of requiring the parties to submit the matter first to an arbitrator. PERC, though, refuses to "defer" on statutory ULP claims such as discrimination and retaliation.

This can marginally increase a union's expense because this "deferred" hearing in front of an arbitrator is paid for by the parties and not PERC. The most significant problem with "deferral" is that an arbitrator's narrow duty is to enforce the labor agreement, not the collective bargaining statute. Arbitrators enforcing labor agreements do not necessarily feel bound by the collective bargaining statute or PERC's prior cases and have developed their own notions of how labor agreements ought to be enforced.

The primary conflict arises when an employer argues that it may make a unilateral change because of a "waiver" in the collective bargaining agreement. PERC has historically adopted a much narrower view of what constitutes a "waiver" under the statute than most arbitrators do under contract arbitration law. Nonetheless, where an arbitrator follows this broader waiver standard in direct conflict to PERC standards, PERC nonetheless generally rubber stamps these awards. Although after an arbitrator has issued a decision PERC will review it for conformity to the statute, the practice is that PERC generally follows arbitrators' awards except in the cases involving the grossest

---

[22] WAC 391-45-110.

deviations from proper procedures, or where it is clear that the arbitrator simply did not consider the issue which PERC had deferred.[23]

One advantage to unions of the "deferral" process is that it is one way of reviving what might otherwise be a dead grievance. Where an employee or union has failed to process a grievance in a timely manner as required by the CBA grievance procedure and that conduct also would be a unilateral change in working conditions, the union can simply file an unfair labor practice complaint before PERC. Employers will often rather have the arbitrator than PERC decide the issue, and PERC insists that employers agree to waive any objection as to the timeliness of the grievance before it will grant any deferral order.

Discipline remedy elections. Another example of where a conflict of available forums arises is in the context of discipline cases. Where a labor agreement has a just cause provision and a civil service commission has a rule requiring discipline be only for just cause, there are two alternative forums available for appealing discipline. Generally, labor agreements contain an "election of remedies" clause which requires employees and unions to abandon a discipline grievance where the matter has also been submitted to the civil service commission. But where the contract contains no explicit election of remedies clause, unions are free to pursue a second appeal through the arbitration process *even after obtaining an adverse decision from the civil service commission.*[24] This "two bites out of the apple" approach particularly distresses employers, which is why they typically will insist upon an election of remedies clause as a condition of a grievance procedure.

Employers will sometimes try to insist on an election of remedies provisions pertaining to other statutory rights such as discrimination law, for example. Although a union is generally free to give up its own right to pursue a grievance under a collective bargaining agreement, often employers seek a clause which purports to deny the *employee* a right to pursue the matter later, after the union *submits* the matter to arbitration. These types of election of remedies clauses are likely void, if not illegal, as generally unions have no authority to waive their members' statutory rights. The right to pursue a grievance may be

---

[23] *See* WAC 391-45-110(b)(ii).

[24] *The Civil Service Commission of the City of Kelso v. City of Kelso*, 137 Wn.2d 166, 969 P.2d 474 (1999).

contracted away, since the union is one of the two "signatory" parties to the CBA, but the *statutory* rights are not controlled by the parties to a CBA.

"Res Judicata." Another issue that comes up when labor and employment law claims are brought up in more than one forum are rules barring relitigation of claims, referenced earlier as "res judicata" and "collateral estoppel" principles. The res judicata doctrine prohibits the same lawsuit from being tried twice. The closely related collateral estoppel doctrine may not bar the entire litigation, but binds a party to *rulings* of law or *findings* fact in a subsequent proceeding, thereby narrowing the possible arguments that might be raised in a separate legal action.

These "preclusion" principles are not always well understood and are even confusing to the judges and to labor and employment attorneys. But those unions and employees bringing legal challenges in more than one place on a related issue need to be aware of these preclusion principles and they should discuss with their legal counsel the tactical effect these rules can have on their multiple claims. A few cases demonstrate the involved principles.

Courts have often rejected employer arguments that the principles of *res judicata* apply where a case which has already been arbitrated is also pursued in court. The legal doctrine of *res judicata* is that, once a matter has been litigated in one forum, the parties are bound by it, and the matter may not be relitigated in another forum. As the State Supreme Court has recognized, a labor arbitration over a just cause standard not to be identical to a statutory discrimination claim, even if elements of the discrimination claim were considered in the arbitration, and have, therefore, declined to apply this doctrine.[25]

In fact, the Supreme Court indicates that even a civil service hearing does not bar a later arbitration on the issue of whether the discipline was for just cause because the just cause standards applied by an arbitrator and a civil service panel are not perceived as equivalent. So in a case involving a suspension of an officer in Kelso for a car accident, the court allowed the guild to bring a grievance before an arbitrator even after the officer had lost in front of the civil service commission.[26]

And in an arbitration enforcement action concerning a Yakima

---

25 *The Civil Service Commission of the City of Kelso v. City of Kelso*, 137 Wn.2d 166, 969 P.2d 474 (1999).

26 *Id.* (As noted earlier, this case involved a labor contract without an election of remedy clause.).

County deputy, brought by the Guild, the Court of appeals rejected the County's argument that the deputies failed employment discrimination claims barred the Guild from pursuing her discharge grievance under the labor contract.[27] Noting that the Guild was not in "privity" with the deputy (was not represented by her) and determining that the statutory discrimination and contractual just cause legal claims were not "identical," the court declined to apply the preclusion rule.

On the other hand in *Christensen v. Grant County Hospital District No. 1* the court held that a union's failed PERC ULP complaint alleging a union retaliation claim on behalf of a discharged union advocate *did* preclude a subsequent lawsuit by the advocate in his own civil retaliation lawsuit.[28] The Court ruled that Christensen was "in privity" with the union that had standing and had fully argued his claim before PERC and further ruled that the PERC findings could be applied to preclude his retaliation lawsuit, giving the overlap of the legal claims.

Because of these principles — deferral, election of remedies, and collateral estoppel — thought and careful decision-making needs to be made before a forum is selected. In the next section, we will examine the pros and cons of different forums for different types of claims.

Where more than one forum might be available for a given claim, the union should consult with legal counsel concerning the best strategy to follow in selecting a forum.

D. The Choice of Legal Forums for Particular Types of Cases

This section considers which forums might be appropriate for particular types of labor law issues. Where more than one forum might be available for a given claim, the union should consult with legal counsel concerning the best strategy to follow in selecting a forum. As just discussed, bringing a claim in one forum might limit the ability to bring a related claim in another forum. If the risk of preclusion exists, strategic decisions need to be made to select the best possible forum for that type of claim.

---

[27] *Yakima County v. Yakima County Law Enforcement Officers Guild*, 157 Wn. App. 304, 237 P.3d 216 (2010).

[28] 152 Wn.2d 299, 96 P.3d 957 (2004).

COMPARISON OF LEGAL FORUMS

Forum	Advantages	Disadvantages	Generally Best Forum for this Type of Claim
Arbitration	1) Relatively Quick 2) Expertise 3) Neutrality 4) Finality	1) Default for Failure to Process on Time 2) Cost of Arbitration and Attorney Fees 3) Not Bound by Case Precedent 4) Limited Authority on Remedies	Discipline
PERC	1) Expertise 2) Predictability	1) Limited Discovery Rights 2) Slow	Union Retaliation Unilateral Change in Working Conditions
Courts	1) Strong Authority to Issue Remedies, Including Preliminary Relief 2) Ability to Resolve on Summary Judgmcnt 3) Able to Recover Attorney Fees	1) Lack of Labor Law Expertise 2) Occasional Bias in Favor of Employers	Discrimination Unpaid Wages Civil Rights
Civil Service	1) Available to Employees Lacking Union Support 2) Fast Decisions	1) Appointed by Management 2) Subject to Manipulation by Management Representatives	Promotion Issues

1. Discipline and Discharge Cases

Labor agreements almost uniformly require that discipline and discharge be only for "just cause." But the just cause mandate also protects most Washington public safety employers through the civil service system. Most public safety labor agreements in Washington contain an "election of remedies" clause, which requires that an employee must choose whether to pursue an appeal before civil service or the grievance procedure.

The difficulty in making this election, though, is that while an employee can choose to go to civil service, it is not up to the employee to determine whether to go to arbitration. An employee may file a grievance, but it can only request a union to pursue the grievance to arbitration. It is ultimately up to the union to decide whether the matter has sufficient merit to warrant arbitration.

Therefore, from the employee's perspective, these election of remedies provisions can create a dilemma. Agreements can be crafted which defer the decision-making deadline concerning the election of remedies until after the union has had an adequate opportunity to make its decision whether or not to arbitrate a claim. This would prevent the employee from being put in the position of having to submit prematurely the matter to civil service, thereby foregoing the preferred forum of arbitration.

As has already been emphasized, for discipline and discharge cases, arbitration is almost always a better forum for employees and unions than civil service. Civil service commissioners are handpicked by management, whereas arbitrators are mutually selected by the parties. And as even understood by the Supreme Court in its *City of Kelso* decision,[29] arbitrators generally apply a much broader test for "just cause" then do civil service panels.

Even where arbitration is unsuccessful, employees still may be able to pursue their discipline cases through the courts. If, for example, the discharge involved a violation of some other type of employment law violation such as discrimination or retaliation, employees have legal recourse separate and apart from arbitration.

Unions are under no obligation to financially support such court litigation. A union's duty of fair representation, as will be discussed later, only applies to the forums over which the union has exclusive access — labor arbitration.

2. Discipline Procedure Issues

As will be discussed later, employers are bound to follow a number of procedures in investigating discipline cases. Where an employer fails to follow these procedures, these issues may be pursued in arbitration but may also be presented in other forums as well. For example, where an employer denies an employee his or her right to a union representative, this is deemed to be a *Weingarten* violation over which PERC asserts jurisdiction. PERC views the denial of a union representative as an unlawful

[29] *The Civil Service Commission of the City of Kelso v. City of Kelso*, 137 Wn.2d 166, 969 P.2d 474 (1999).

interference in the union's ability to represent its members.

Another disciplinary procedural requirement facing employers is that of providing a predisciplinary hearing. Before an employer can impose disciplinary action which involves the loss of an economic benefit, it must extend the employee a right to a "hearing." Although arbitrators will entertain such violations as a basis to set aside the discipline, the primary forum for presenting a pure *Loudermill* violation is in court. A *Loudermill* violation is a violation of the employee's civil rights and may be pursued as a Section 1983 claim.

As will become more evident when we turn to the later chapter on discipline appeals, usually arbitration is a better forum for these procedural objections then either PERC or a court. As will be discussed, much of this has to do with the potential remedies that might be available.

3. Wage and Hour Disputes

"Wage and hour" laws which apply to Washington public safety employees include the Washington State Minimum Wage Act (MWA) and the Federal Fair Labor Standards Act (FLSA). These Acts both require that certain minimum wages be maintained and that, under certain circumstances, overtime be paid.

Where an employer has failed to provide minimum wage or the proper overtime wage, such a claim would normally be pursued in court. Under some circumstances, the failure to pay the proper wage may also be a violation of the CBA. Generally, though, employees and their unions are better advised to pursue such claims through the courts.

FLSA remedies are superior to arbitration remedies. Wage statutes require that the prevailing party in court be paid their attorney's fees, whereas, in arbitration, the parties are responsible for their own attorney's fees.

Also, where an unlawful practice has continued for some time, an arbitrator may conclude that it is not a violation of the CBA, but is, instead, a "past practice." Arbitrators do *not* have general jurisdiction to ensure that all labor and employment laws are followed. Instead, their narrow jurisdiction is to see only that the agreement is enforced *as written*. So if the parties have developed a labor agreement which is defective or even contains unlawful provisions, arbitrators likely will believe themselves to be bound by such provisions and will leave it to the parties to pursue additional statutory claims in court.

When an established working condition is no longer followed, it may be a grievance or it may simply be a ULP. Or it may be both.

Where the amount of money involved in an overtime dispute is small, it may be advantageous to at least submit a grievance on the issue first. Judges, especially federal judges certainly do not like to see small wage claims presented to them in court when the matter should have been handled less formally and less expensively elsewhere. And employers will sometimes capitulate to such overtime grievances, when seemingly valid, knowing that the expensive litigation, including statutory attorney's fees, may easily dwarf the cost of the wage claim at issue.

4. Changes in Working Conditions

When an established working condition is no longer followed, it may be a grievance or it may simply be a ULP. Or it may be both. If the labor agreement expressly indicates the manner in which a certain working condition is defined and the employer deviates from that set of rules, it is likely that there is both a grievance *and* a ULP. But, as discussed above, PERC may issue a deferral order, at least when the contract is ambiguous or contains a claimed "waiver," and such an order would mandate that the matter be decided by an arbitrator. (PERC applies deferral when the unilateral conduct is arguably "protected or prohibited" by the labor contract.) Under other circumstances, such as when the contract has expired, or the contract is silent, a deferral order is not available and PERC is the only forum to decide the matter.

But PERC has been adamant in insisting that it is not a forum for enforcing the labor agreement. A party who pursues a ULP must establish more than a violation of the labor agreement, as PERC has *repeatedly* stated that it exercises no jurisdiction over the CBA. Instead, PERC is looking at whether there exists a well-established course of conduct — a "past practice" — which was unilaterally changed without negotiations. At most, the collective bargaining agreement is simply *evidence* of what the past practice is; *it is not conclusive in defining the past practice.*

There are a number of advantages of pursuing changes in working conditions before PERC rather than an arbitrator. First and foremost, PERC takes a much narrower view of what constitutes "inherent" management rights than do many arbitrators. PERC has seemingly taken seriously its statutory mandate that employers negotiate with the unions over any proposed change in "wages, hours and working conditions." It has interpreted restrictively management rights clauses which purport to confer on the employer the right to make unilateral changes. Arbitrators, on the other hand, have sometimes read management rights clauses more generously to management and thereby effectively confer on management the ability to avoid its statutory mandate to bargain — even when that result was not specifically intended by the union.

The key in determining whether a change in working condition is properly before PERC or an arbitrator is the nature of the change and law violation. If the change violates the terms of the labor agreement, a grievance exists. If the change is contrary to a well-established past practice, an unfair labor practice exists. If the change involves a violation of the labor agreement *and* a change in past practice, *both forums are available*, although as discussed above, PERC will often issue a deferral order nonetheless sending the matter to arbitration. So confusion often exists as to where to file claims that might be both changes and contract violations and determining the ultimate forum for a decision is not always straightforward.

Even if you have a case that most appropriately belongs in front of PERC for the ultimate decision, filing a grievance is a very useful *discovery tool.*

Sometimes CBAs have a "past practice," "maintenance of benefits" or similar clauses which allow a change in working conditions to be grieved without regard to whether it violates any other term of the agreement. If the CBA contains a clause requiring past practices to be maintained, the union may grieve what is otherwise just a ULP. This is sometimes a way to present issues in dispute without having to file a ULP. Usually the best ultimate forum for such claims is actually PERC on a ULP complaint, but a grievance can be a useful tool to try to resolve the issue and to try to collect information on the employer's position.

The last point is especially worth remembering. Even if you have a case that most appropriately belongs in front of PERC for the ultimate decision, filing a grievance is a very useful *discovery tool.* As indicated earlier, PERC's discovery provisions are extremely limited. They have modest authority to order discovery, and they do not usually even use that authority. But under a CBA grievance, a party has the right to collect information in the form of an "information request." So often it is recommended to *first* pursue unilateral change contract breaches as a grievance, if for no other reason than to conveniently gather information about your potential case that you might make before PERC. (Refusal to supply such information in a reasonably manner, as we will see later, is itself a potential separate ULP.)

5. Gender and Race Discrimination Claims

Labor agreements frequently will contain a "nondiscrimination" clause. Although these nondiscrimination clauses provide a means to present race and gender discrimination claims, most plaintiffs' attorneys and union labor attorneys would generally agree that labor arbitration is *not* the best forum to decide such issues. Labor arbitrators are reluctant to find affirmatively that management has engaged in race or gender discrimination. After all, arbitrators are selected through a mutual selection process of the parties.

But these nondiscrimination clauses may be useful in a grievance when there is another issue presented and the discrimination claim is simply associated with another broader claim for a breach of the labor agreement. For example, if a member of a protected class is disciplined arguably without cause, both the discrimination claims and just cause claims can be presented in tandem to an arbitrator. Even if the arbitrator does not acknowledge the sufficiency of the discrimination claim, such claims can cause the arbitrator to carefully assess the just cause issues, especially where arguments exist as to proportion or progressive discipline.

6. Disability Discrimination Claims

Like race and gender discrimination claims, there is usually more than one forum in which to bring disability discrimination claim. But unlike gender and race discrimination claims, arbitration is sometimes a more favorable forum for resolving these issues.

Arbitrators are seemingly less reluctant to find that employers have violated disability discrimination laws than they are as to race and gender discrimination laws. This is likely because a finding of disability discrimination is less stigmatizing to the employer and the employer's representatives than would be a finding of race or gender discrimination. Often, disability discrimination issues arise in the context of a failure to make a specific requested accommodation because of a disagreement about what is "reasonable" in a situation, not necessarily because of animosity to the disabled as a class.

Federal Courts previously have not been as favorable of a forum for disability discrimination claims as disability discrimination advocates had hoped. The disability discrimination statutes are subject to conflicting and sometimes bewildering interpretations by courts. This seems to be shifting now because the Americans with Disabilities Act has been amended to reinstate its original apparent Congressional purpose. The Washington state disability discrimination statute, though, has been favorably applied for employees, for the most part.

Often, labor arbitrators have extensive experience in interpreting these disability statutes and frequently can produce a sound result. Discharge issues often exist at the crossroads between the contract and the disability laws, such as when an employee has difficulty in fulfilling all claimed job functions. Arbitrators often are able to craft a middle ground on disability issues which satisfy the interests of all involved. And litigation in the courts often becomes protracted and lengthy, whereas labor arbitration can get the issue behind the parties much more quickly.

7. Civil Rights Claims

Civil rights claims are those claims which have a basis either in statute or under the Constitution. Typically, such claims are enforced in court.

But where the treatment of an employee, particularly in a discipline case, has involved a violation of the employee's civil rights, relief may be attainable under the CBA grievance procedure. For example, if an employee is discharged and the union can prove that it is in retaliation for the employees' exercise of their free speech rights or their right to participate in union activity, the arbitrator may set aside the action. Most arbitrators, as will be discussed later, agree that the notion of "just cause," among other things, requires that the employer not violate an employee's civil rights in the process of imposing discipline.

On the other hand, just as with race and gender discrimination claims, arbitrators are often reluctant to affirmatively find that the employer violated civil rights. Nonetheless, the issues can be presented in that form and arbitrators will sometimes set aside discipline, perhaps actually believing that a civil rights violation was a contributing factor, yet set out in the written decision a less provocative (albeit satisfactory) rationale for setting aside the discipline.

Chapter 2

The Right of Public Safety Unions to Organize Employees

A. Introduction

The collective bargaining statute provides employees the right to organize and to select representatives of their choosing. Both the collective bargaining statute and PERC rules provide guidelines for the process of organizing employees. The process of organizing employees involves competing interests of employers, unions, and employees. PERC has attempted to adopt a balanced set of principles, mostly borrowed from the National Labor Relations Board (NLRB), to guide the process.

This Chapter covers the process of acquiring union representation, or changing an existing representative. It describes the petition process, the rules for determining which employees belong in or out of a bargaining unit, and what the employee rights are during the election process.

B. Initiation of a Representation Petition

Election rules. Petitions seeking representation are generally in one of two forms — a petition seeking to organize a new group or a petition seeking to change representation. There are some similarities but also differences in the rules that apply to these two different types of petitions.

Under PECBA, the right to acquire a representation election is defined in RCW 41.56.070. (The election rights of state government employees are defined in RCW 41.80.080.) PECBA outlines the process only generally and most the details are spelled out, instead, in PERC's rules. WAC Chapter 391-25 provides detailed election procedures.

Petition cards. Either type of petition is commenced by filing papers with PERC indicating the desire to petition for representation, the makeup of the proposed bargaining unit, and a "showing of interest." A showing of interest is simply a set of individual employee "cards" indicating the desire of an individual employee to be represented in collective bargaining by that union.

Petition Window. When employees are currently unrepresented, a petition may be filed at any time. The only exception to that ability to file for representation is that PERC does apply an "election bar" rule which prohibits a new petition within one year of a previous representation election involving that bargaining unit.

But where a group of employees is already represented by another union, a different set of rules applies to the timing of a petition. A petition to *change* representation may only be filed only during a defined "window period." Once a bargaining relationship has been established with one union, that union is not subject to a decertification petition *except during these window periods.*

There are two open window periods during which a challenging union may file its change of representation petition: (1) *during* the defined statutory window period, which is the first 30 days of the last 90 days of a CBA; or (2) *after* the CBA has expired, *but before* the signing of a new agreement. (Under the State employee collective bargaining law this window period arises during the first 30 days of the last *120 days* of the CBA, and also after the contract expires.)

The window period near the end of the agreement provides employees a chance to file a petition. But also leaves the last 60 days of the contract as an "insulated period" in which the existing union can attempt to negotiate an agreement with the employer. Where a contract expires, as is common, on December 31, the open window period for filing a change of representation period for that contract is that thirty-day period between October 3 and November 2.

A *second* open window period arises after the contract has expired, but before a new contract is put in place. It does not matter whether the parties have a tentative agreement for a new agreement or not. *Until the contract is fully executed, a change of representation petition may be filed.*

For purposes of interest arbitration groups, PERC treats the issuance of an interest arbitration award as tantamount to a signed agreement. Once an interest arbitrator has issued a decision, the parties are bound by that order and are required to place the arbitrator's ordered language into their successor agreement. Therefore, PERC has concluded that a petition that was filed after the issuance of an award, but before the agreement was formally signed, was untimely.[1]

[1] *Kitsap County*, Decision 4961 (PECB 1995).

C. Creation of an Appropriate Unit

1. General Principles Followed by PERC in Determining Bargaining Units

After a petition is filed, PERC determines whether the proposed bargaining unit is an "appropriate" one. PERC's authority to determine bargaining units is set forth in RCW 41.56.060:

> The commission, after hearing upon reasonable notice, shall decide in each application for certification as an exclusive bargaining representative, the unit appropriate for the purpose of collective bargaining. In determining, modifying, or combining the bargaining unit, the commission shall consider the duties, skills, and working conditions of the public employees; the history of collective bargaining by the public employees and their bargaining representatives; the extent of organization among the public employees; and the desire of the public employees. The commission shall determine the bargaining representative by (1) examination of organization membership rolls, (2) comparison of signatures on organization bargaining authorization cards, or (3) by conducting an election specifically therefor.

PERC has repeatedly ruled that the ultimate issue is not whether there are other appropriate units — even other units that might be *more* appropriate.

The overriding principle followed by PERC in unit determination cases is the "community of interest." PERC rulings closely track the principles that have been adopted by the NLRB in assessing a "community of interest." Those factors include:

> A difference in method of wages or compensation; different hours of work; different employment benefits; separate supervision; the degree of dissimilar qualifications, training and skills; differences in job functions and amount of working time spent away from the employment or plant site. . .the infrequency

> or lack of contact with other employees; lack of integration with the work functions of other employees or interchange with them; and history of bargaining.[2]

PERC has repeatedly ruled that the ultimate issue is not whether there are other appropriate units — even other units that might be *more* appropriate. Instead, the issue is whether or not the unit proposed by the petitioning organization is *an* appropriate unit.[3] Employer concerns about the costs of bargaining due to fragmentation of bargaining units are not factors to be considered.[4] Concerns over whether the unit contains an appropriate "community of interest" generally overrides employers' desires to organize bargaining units along existing management structure lines.[5]

When PERC approves a bargaining unit, the defined unit typically includes not only all full-time employees in the included job classifications but also all "regular part-time employees." Seasonal employees or "temporary employees" are typically not part of the bargaining unit. PERC's guidelines define "regular part time employees" as those employees who regularly work at least 1/6 time (as defined in the preceding 12 months).

Use of seasonal or temporary or employees doing bargaining unit work is subject to a duty to bargain as covered in the next chapter. Exclusion of these short term employees from the bargaining unit sets up the issue of skimming bargaining unit work. It is up to the labor organization to negotiate with the employer over what work will be done by employees within the bargaining unit and what work will be assigned outside the unit.

2. Unit Determination Issues Particular to Public Safety Bargaining Units

There are a number of unit determination issues that affect public safety bargaining units in particular ways. This section discusses some of those public safety bargaining units' specific issues, including how interest arbitration eligibility affects bargaining unit scope, and the eligibility of supervisors for bargaining unit representation.

---

[2] Hardin (Editor), THE DEVELOPING LABOR LAW, 451 (1992) (quoting *Kalamazoo Paper Box Corp.*, 136 NLRB 134, 48 LRRM 1715 (1962)).

[3] *City of Dupont*, Decision 4959 (PECB 1995); *City of Winslow*, Decision 3520-A (PECB 1990).

[4] *Grays Harbor County*, Decision 3067 (PECB 1988).

[5] *Pierce County, supra.*

a. The Impact of Interest Arbitration Eligibility on Bargaining Unit Form

PERC has consistently followed a policy prohibiting the formation of what it calls "mixed units." "Mixed units" are bargaining units consisting of both interest arbitration eligible and non-interest arbitration eligible employees.

It is PERC's view that while it may be appropriate to form bargaining units along department lines when public safety employees are involved, those employees with interest arbitration eligibility should be placed in a separate bargaining unit from those without that eligibility.[6] Whenever certain classifications within a bargaining unit acquire interest arbitration rights, either through the amendment of the interest arbitration statute or an increase of the population in the jurisdiction, PERC has mandated that those newly eligible employees be separated from the non-interest arbitration eligible group and placed in a different bargaining unit.

Therefore, in a typical public safety department there will be commissioned and noncommissioned bargaining units. PERC has generally allowed, except with the smaller employers, the formation of noncommissioned bargaining units separate and apart from bargaining units for the general government employees.[7] In approving the maintenance of a noncommissioned bargaining unit, PERC has required those noncommissioned bargaining units to remain intact, not fragmenting into separate classifications. Therefore, PERC has disapproved efforts to separate out dispatchers from other noncommissioned personnel.[8]

b. The Rights of Public Safety Supervisors and Managers to be Represented

This section covers whether those supervisors and managers have representation rights, and if so, what bargaining unit is "appropriate" for them. The collective bargaining statute, unlike the National Labor Relations Act, contains no explicit exemption for supervisors and managers. PERC has consistently upheld the right of supervisors and mid-level managers to be represented in

---

6 *See, e.g., Clallam County*, Decision 4805 (PECB 1994).

7 *But see City of Snoqualmie*, Decision 11343 (PECB, 2012) in which PERC determined that the two noncommissioned members of the Snoqualmie Police Department belonged in the citywide bargaining unit.

8 *See, e.g., Okanagon County*, Decision 2000 (PECB 1987); *Cowlitz County*, Decision 4960 (PECB 1995); *Yakima County*, Decision 5566 (PECB 1996).

collective bargaining.[9]

"Confidential" exemption. The statute does, though, contain an exemption for what are called "confidential" employees. RCW 41.56.030(2) excludes persons having a "confidential" relationship to the executive head or body of the applicable bargaining unit from the definition of public employees, thus excluding them from coverage of PECBA. This exclusion from the definition of public employees is to be construed narrowly,[10] and the party proposing a "confidential" exclusion bears the heavy burden of proving the necessity of excluding the employee from the rights of the statute.[11] Employers are permitted to exempt from the otherwise broad definition of "public employee" in the statute, "a reasonable number of personnel from the rights of the collective bargaining statute in order to perform the functions of the employer in the collective bargaining process."[12]

The legal statutory definition of a "confidential" employee is set forth in RCW 41.56.030(2)(c) which states:

> "Public Employee" means any employee of a public employer except any person... (c) whose duties as deputy, administrative assistant or secretary necessarily imply a confidential relationship to the executive head or body of the applicable bargaining unit, or any person elected by popular vote or appointed to office pursuant to statute, ordinance or resolution for a specified term of office by the executive head or body of the public employer. The Courts as well as decisions from the Public Employment Relations Commission have further refined the statutory definition.

As the Supreme Court held in *Municipality of Seattle v. Department of Labor & Industries,*[13] it is not simply *the title* of "deputy" which excludes an employee from the coverage of the statute: "[E]ven if they fit one or more of the categories named in the statute, the persons holding them are never the less [sic] public employees if their duties do not

---

[9] *See, e.g., City of Richland,* Decision 2647 (PECB 1987) (affirming right of battalion chiefs to form own bargaining unit).

[10] *City of Mercer Island,* Decision 725-3 (PECB 1970).

[11] *Snohomish County,* Decision 4027-11 (PECB 1992).

[12] *City of Deer Park,* Decision 4237-C (PECB 1993).

[13] 88 Wn.2d 925, 568 P.2d 775 (1977).

necessarily imply a confidential relationship...."[14] And as the Court added: "The importance of the confidential relationship is obvious, for in its absence even the designated employees are not denied the right to engage in collective bargaining."[15]

Later, in *International Association of Firefighters, Local 469 v. Yakima,*[16] the Supreme Court took on the task of defining "confidential" status under PECBA and concluded that a "labor nexus" was required. First, the Court noted that the term "confidential" is a term of art in labor law.[17] The Court indicated that the legislature incorporated this exclusion from the statute because of the concern that those involved in formulating labor relations policy would have a conflict of interest.[18] The Court then noted that the Education Relations Act in RCW 41.59 provided a more detailed definition of confidential employee and the existence of this provision supported PERC's decision to apply the same standard of confidentiality to both statutes.[19]

But the court expressed concern about the conflict of interest that could occur should an employee be closely involved with both the development of labor relations policy as well as negotiations concerning the application of that policy that could also apply to themselves. The court identified that this conflict of interest arises when:

> An employee is in a fiduciary relationship with the employer and must act for the benefit of the employer. Such an employee could participate in the "formulation of labor relations policy" and should therefore not be in situations where they are negotiating with the employer on their own behalf.[20]

The Court then described the test to apply to determine when an employee might be excluded from an otherwise appropriate bargaining unit due to their status as confidential employees:

---

[14] *Id.* at 928.
[15] *Id.* at 930.
[16] 91 Wn.2d 101, 587 P.2d 165 (1978).
[17] *Id.* at 106.
[18] *Id.* at 105.
[19] *Id.* at 105-06.
[20] *Id.* at 105.

> We hold that in order for an employee to come within the exception of RCW 41.56.030(2), the duties which imply the confidential relationship must flow from an official intimate fiduciary relationship with the executive head of the bargaining unit or public official. The nature of this close association must concern the official and policy responsibilities of the public officer or executive head of the bargaining unit, including formulation of labor relations policy. General supervisory responsibility is insufficient to place an employee within the exclusion.[21]

The Court held that in order for the confidential exception to apply, the duties of the employee "must flow from an official intimate fiduciary relationship with the executive head of the bargaining unit or public official."[22] The court further explained, "The nature of this close association must concern the official and policy responsibilities of the public officer or executive head of the bargaining unit, *including the formulation of labor relations policy.*"[23]

Applying the "confidential" exception. PERC has followed *Yakima,* indicating that to effect the purpose of RCW 41.56 — establishing the right of public employees to collective bargaining — one must *narrowly construe* any exception to this right. Thus, *both* a confidential relationship and participation in labor relations policy are required to meet the "confidential employee" exception.[24] *Mere possession of confidential information is not sufficient to meet this test.* And the confidential information must directly relate to *labor relations policies* of the employer "which if improperly disclosed to the bargaining representative, would damage the collective bargaining relationship."[25] Further, the confidential employee must have an intimate fiduciary relationship with a department head or other management official responsible for labor policy matters, and the "confidential" assignments must be "necessary," "regular," and "ongoing."[26]

---

21 *Id.* at 106-107.

22 *International Association of Firefighters v. City of Yakima*, 91 Wn.2d 101, 587 P.2d 165 (1978).

23 *Id.*

24 *City of Yakima*, 91 Wn.2d at 109.

25 *Town of Granger*, Decision 2634 (PECB 1987); *see, also, Granite Falls*, Decision 2617 (PECB, 1987); *Bellingham Housing Authority*, Decision 2140-B (PECB 1985); *Richland School District*, Decision 2208 (PECB 1985).

26 *City of Cheney*, Decision 3693 (PECB 1991); *City of Mountlake Terrace*, Decision 4637 (PECB 1994); *City of Deer Park*, Decision 4237-C (PECB 1993).

PERC has since repeatedly and consistently applied a "labor nexus" test in determining confidential status.[27] PERC has also held: "Because status as a confidential employee deprives the individual of all collective bargaining rights under Chapter 41.56 RCW, the party proposing a confidential exclusion bears a heavy burden."[28]

Not only must the exception be narrowly construed, but PERC requires the party proposing a "confidential" exclusion to bear a heavy burden of proof. This heavy burden is required because the stakes are high — a determination that a position is "confidential" deprives the individuals holding the position of all collective bargaining rights under the statute.[29]

Very few cases have found supervisory positions to fall within the confidential employee exception. In *City of Seattle*,[30] the Director of Communications for the Seattle Police Department was found to be excluded from coverage because of his involvement on behalf of the employer at the bargaining table and in negotiations. His involvement exposed him to confidential information.[31]

But most cases have found an insufficient amount of involvement in labor relations to warrant exclusion. The *City of Seattle* decision also concluded that majors and the Director of Community Services were not confidential employees because "the evidence falls far short of indicating that the majors all are privy to bargaining information of a type where disclosure would be destructive of the collective bargaining process," and the employer failed to demonstrate "that the director has any role in the formulation of labor relations policy."[32] PERC has generally chosen not to apply the exception even when there has been some direct involvement with labor relations.

For example, in *City of Mercer Island and Mercer Island Police Association*,[33] PERC held that the lieutenants were not confidential employees despite their involvement in labor relations matters. One lieutenant had five or six meetings with the city's negotiator and the Association to discuss an educational incentive program.

---

27 *See, e.g., City of Puyallup,* Decision 5460 (PECB 1996) and cases cited therein.

28 *City of Puyallup, supra.*

29 *City of Seattle,* Decision 689-A (PECB 1979); *City of Winslow,* Decision 3520-A (PECB 1990); *City of Mountlake Terrace,* Decision 4637 (PECB 1994).

30 *City of Seattle,* Decision 689-C (1981).

31 *Id.*; *see, also, Town of Granger,* where the town clerk-treasurer was ruled a confidential employee.

32 *Id.*

33 Decision 725 (PECB 1979).

Another lieutenant suggested a shift schedule change that was implemented in the next labor agreement.

In *City of Seattle and Seattle Fire Chiefs Association,*[34] the confidentiality claim center on negotiations input. The deputy chiefs had been asked to comment on the employer's bargaining proposals and they were invited to present ideas and concepts that might included in their employer's bargaining position. But the Commission found this contact to be sporadic and not warranting exclusion.

In *Snohomish County and Teamsters Union Local 763,*[35] lieutenants and sergeants were included in a meeting where they discussed negotiations and were invited to comment on what issues should be raised. At another meeting, they discussed one of the union's proposals. The Commission found this was not sufficient:

> The limited evaluative/advisory role of the sergeants in collective bargaining is too remote to justify a finding that there is an intimate fiduciary relationship between the corrections sergeants and the employer's bargainers. The sergeants do not participate in executive-level discussions regarding management strategy, or bargaining positions, or attend executive-level policy making meetings. Corrections sergeants are not members of the employer's negotiating team, and do not have knowledge of confidential information concerning areas of potential compromise, 'bottom-line' bargaining positions, or other critical policies.[36]

In *King County and DAD Management Association,*[37] the Commission again ruled that the corrections managers at issue were not excluded from the Act. This finding is significant because the employees were quite involved with labor relations matters. One employee "participate[d] in the hiring process," "made effective recommendations on disciplinary matters, and has access to personnel and investigative files kept by the employer."[38] He also was assigned "to participate on behalf of the employer in collective bargaining negotiations with organizations representing DAD

---

[34] Decision 1797-A (PECB1985).
[35] Decision 4027 (PECB 1992).
[36] Decision 4027 (PECB 1992).
[37] PD-4004-A (PECB 1992).
[38] 4004-A (PECB 1992).

employees." He did so on two or three occasions.[39] Another employee also had participated on behalf of the employer in one contract negotiations.[40] Another employee was a supervisor, did employee performance evaluations, recommended hiring and discharge decisions, and had authority to take disciplinary actions. He also sat in on three collective bargaining sessions, serving as a technical resource.[41]

The Commission found that none of these employees were confidential employees because they did not participate in the formulation of labor policy, and were not "made privy to the employer's 'strategy' or 'policy' in any meaningful way."[42] Rather, these employees acted as a resource for operational issues which was a natural outgrowth of their supervisor roles.[43]

PERC has generally allowed public safety employees to exclude one or sometimes more secretarial personnel as "confidential." Therefore, the Secretary to the police or fire chief will generally be exempt from bargaining as a confidential employee. PERC has reasoned that where these chief secretaries are involved in preparing sensitive labor relations notes or disciplinary documents, the labor relations nexus is satisfied.

Mid-level managers and supervisors. PERC has had frequent occasion to visit the issue of how supervisors and mid-managers should be placed within bargaining unit structures. PERC cases indicate a degree of flexibility in this placement and bargaining units may take different forms.

Employer efforts to remove sergeants from bargaining units from line officers have been consistently unsuccessful.

Typically, PERC has allowed the placement of first level supervisors (e.g., law enforcement sergeants/fire lieutenants) in the bargaining unit with employees they supervise. PERC's reasoning is that these personnel are "working leads" and do much of the same work as the people they supervise. On at least one occasion, PERC even allowed lieutenants in the bargaining unit with deputy sheriffs and sergeants, where the lieutenants had

---

[39] *Id.*
[40] *Id.*
[41] *Id.*
[42] *Id.*
[43] *Id.*

limited supervisory discretion and fulfilled patrol functions with the others they supervised.[44] Employer efforts to remove sergeants from bargaining units from line officers have been consistently unsuccessful.[45]

But PERC also recognizes mid-manager bargaining units as appropriate and will generally permit more than one level of supervisors in a single bargaining unit. In *City of Seattle*,[46] for example, the Executive Director rejected the claim that the strict chain of authority in a Fire Department paramilitary structure required a separate level of bargaining units for each supervisory level:

> The para-military structure used in the uniformed services is often argued as a major distinction from the supervision arrangements commonly used in non-uniform public employment. No case is cited or found, however, where paramilitary ranks structure has been taken as absolute....The title is not controlling. It is the nature and scope of authority which must be evaluated. [Citations omitted.] In such cases, the Commission has determined that the community of interest and the avoidance of fragmentation of bargaining structures have weighed in favor of inclusion of two or more paramilitary ranks in the same bargaining unit.[47]

Although an existing bargaining unit shape is not beyond challenge, PERC generally rejects efforts to change bargaining units already established.

The Executive Director discounted the employer's evidence that Deputy Chiefs in the Seattle Fire Department had authority to discipline and evaluate Battalion Chiefs. He observed that "in actual practice, by the time an individual becomes a Battalion Chief in the Seattle Fire Department, he or she is a seasoned and

---

44 *Klickitat County,* Decision 5462 (PECB 1996).

45 *See, e.g., City of Pasco,* 12212-A (PECB 2015); *Okanagon County,* Decisions 6142-A and 6143-A (PECB 1998); *Adams County,* Decision 6005B (PECB 1998); *Franklin County,* Decision 5192 (PECB 1995).

46 Decision 1797-A (PECB 1985).

47 *Id.* at 9.

tested employee. No one who testified could recall any instance in which a Battalion Chief was brought up on disciplinary charges."[48] Since this decision, PERC has repeatedly approved petitions proposing more than one level of employees in the same bargaining unit.[49]

c. *Changes in Existing Bargaining Units*

Although an existing bargaining unit shape is not beyond challenge, PERC generally rejects efforts to change bargaining units already established. Parties seeking to challenge an existing bargaining unit form must either show that the bargaining unit was defective at its inception, or that there has been some change in circumstances which makes the bargaining unit no longer appropriate.[50] Efforts to carve off groups of employees from an otherwise appropriate unit have been generally been rejected by PERC.

Unit challenges must also be brought at an appropriate time. Challenges to a bargaining unit can either occur as part of a change of representation petition or as a unit clarification petition. A unit clarification petition may not be filed mid-contract. Instead, PERC has established a procedure that requires the parties to give the other side notice of its intent to seek a change in the bargaining unit. The parties can then negotiate such a change — although this is a permissive, not a mandatory subject of bargaining. But if they are unsuccessful in reaching an agreement, the party seeking the change must file the petition prior to the execution of the successor agreement.[51]

Still, a party seeking a severance of an existing bargaining unit faces a stiff challenge before PERC. PERC has generally dismissed petitions seeking to separate out one classification of public safety employees from others.[52]

---

48 *Id.* at 10.

49 *See, e.g., Snohomish County,* Decision 5375 (PECB 1995) (approving bargaining unit made up of both corrections lieutenants and corrections sergeants).

50 *See Island County,* Decision 2572 (PECB, 1986); *City of Bellingham,* Decision 7322 (PECB, 2001).

51 WAC 391-35-020; *Topenish School District,* Decision 1143-B (PECB 1981).

52 *See, e.g., Okanagon County,* Decision 2000 (PECB 1987) (rejecting effort to separate out dispatchers and corrections officers from other sheriff's department noncommissioned personnel); *Cowlitz County,* Decision 4960 (PECB (1995) (rejecting separation of dispatchers from other noncommissioned sheriff's department employees); *Yakima County,* Decision 5566 (PECB 1996) (rejecting petition seeking to separate dispatchers from

Conversely, once employees have been separated or formed into a bargaining unit on their own, PERC has rejected efforts to consolidate those employees. For example, in *City of Mill Creek,*[53] PERC rejected the effort of the Mill Creek Police Officers Guild to consolidate separate sergeant and patrol officer bargaining units.

An exception to PERC's resistance to allow changes in a bargaining unit is when there has been a significant change in employer operations. For example, in *City of Mount Vernon*, PERC mandated the consolidation of separate police and fire dispatcher bargaining units after the City of Mount Vernon changed their dispatch operations from separate department-based operations into a single city-wide operation.[54]

An exception to the "notice and file" rule outlined above exists as to confidential employees. An employer's right to exclude confidential employees is explicitly defined in the statute, and PERC allows this to be raised at any time.[55]

D. The Bargaining Representative Election Process

PERC has adopted a number of rules to make the election process regular. There many ways in which an employer (or unions) might try to interfere with the free choice of employees, and PERC has generally found these efforts to constitute unfair labor practices.

Although an employer need not remain neutral on the issue of unionization, it must not unduly impede the free choice of employees. PERC disallows employer activities that will impede that free choice.

Requirement to maintain the "status quo." One requirement that can prove cumbersome — especially for an employer — is the mandate to maintain the *status quo* on all wages, hours and working conditions while a representation petition is pending. PERC prohibits a change in working conditions at this time. It views removing benefits to be a form of retaliation or the appearance of retaliation. And, conversely, it views conferring additional benefits as undercuting the future role a union is seeking to have by petitioning for representation.[56]

An exception to the *status quo* requirement is a doctrine PERC has applied concerning what it calls the "dynamic status quo."

---

other noncommissioned police department employees).

[53] Decision 5952 (PECB 1997).

[54] *City of Mount Vernon*, Decision 5199-B (PECB 1992).

[55] WAC 391-35-020.

[56] *See, e.g., Central Washington University*, Decision 10967-A (PECB 2012).

Therefore, changes that have been previously decided but not yet implemented are considered to be part of the "dynamic status quo" and employers are permitted to go forward with their plans.[57] PERC does not view this as unlawful interference because employees are expected to understand that the change is part of a prior plan and was not an attempt to inhibit the formation of a union. PERC recently explained their doctrine:

> While some situations involve a "static" status quo, Commission precedent recognizes that in other situations employers are required to maintain the "dynamic" status quo. This concept recognizes that occasionally circumstances exist where changes determined and *set in motion by the employer prior to the filing of a representation petition* do not disrupt a bargaining relationship or undermine support for a union because the petitioned-for employees expect the changes to occur. [Citations omitted.]
>
> For example, where wage increases are previously scheduled, they are part of the dynamic status quo, and it would be unlawful to withhold them just because a representation petition was later filed. [Citations omitted.] Step increases have been considered part of the dynamic status quo because the employer has no discretion about granting the annual award and the employees expect those increases. [Citations omitted.]
>
> However, general wage increases have not been considered part of the dynamic status quo because they are usually far less concrete, do not follow an established or fixed formula, and allow the employer discretion as to whether to grant an increase at all. [Citations omitted.] Conversely, if changes the employees may view as negative merely carry out a dynamic status quo no violation will be found.[58]

In one controversial application of the "dynamic status quo" doctrine, PERC allowed Clark County to change the schedule of its corrections officers while a petition was pending because the

---

[57] *Id.*

[58] Id. (emphasis supplied.).

contract language from the county contract with the existing union provided it the right to change the work schedule upon notice.[59] As we will see in the next Chapter, bargaining waivers, by law, are to encumber only the incumbent union, not a union petition for a representation change. Although the language of the contract waivers was existent, the employer was allowed to implement a change that it could not have implemented once the petition was successful. This PERC result could effectively invite employers to utilize waivers to implement changes once a petition is filed, something contrary to what PERC claims it is seeking when it states "laboratory conditions" are to be maintained during an election.

PERC views the promise of benefits to employees during a unionization effort to constitute a ULP.[60] PERC also considers it to be an unfair labor practice to threaten employees or in any way retaliate against them for their efforts to unionize. Employee and union rights to be free of retaliation are discussed extensively (with detailed case tables) in Chapter 13.

Employer "free speech" rights. As indicated, employers are not required to remain neutral on the issue of unionization. PERC has recognized certain "free speech" rights employers have to express their viewpoint. But employers who exercise these "free speech" rights must be careful to provide accurate, fact-based information. PERC has found it a ULP for employers to make statements of fact which involve "substantial misrepresentations."[61] And employers are prohibited from engaging in "captive audience" speeches within 24 hours of an election. That is, employers may not hold meetings on the workplace premises within that 24-hour period to discuss the union election.[62]

And certain prohibitions on election propaganda and tactics *also apply to unions*. In one case, a union that threw a party in the 24 hours preceding the election, providing free food and beverages to attendees (and as to one lucky voter a financial gift) was found to have committed a ULP.[63]

This 24 hour meeting ban can be a trap for elections that are conducted by mail ballot, which at this point is the overwhelming number. In-person meetings must be made conducted not less

---

[59] *Clark County*, Decision 537-A (PECB 1996).
[60] *See, e.g., Quilalauyute Valley School District*, Decision 2809-A (PECB 1988).
[61] *Tacoma School District*, Decision 4216-A (PECB 1993).
[62] WAC 391-250-470(G); *City of Tukwila*, Decision 2434 (PECB 1986).
[63] *Lake Stevens-Granite Falls Transportation Cooperative*, Decision 2462 (PECB 1986).

than 24 hours before the ballots are issued. Following that, electioneering needs to be conducted via writing or email.

"Blocking charge" ULP. When one of the parties in an election proceeding has committed a ULP, it is generally treated as a "blocking charge."[64] *A blocking charge must be resolved before the election may proceed.* But PERC does allow the charging party to file "request to proceed" to an election, provided that party also agrees to waive an election set aside as a potential remedy.[65]

The issues concerning the formation of the bargaining unit generally are also to be decided preceding the election. One exception exists, though, where the number of positions in dispute is small in relation to the overall bargaining unit. In these cases, where it is determined that these positions will not likely affect the outcome for the rest of the bargaining unit, PERC allows the election to proceed for the major part of the unit and will issue an "interim certification."

Balloting. PERC typically conducts union elections by mail balloting. Where there is only one union involved and seeking representation, PERC will allow the union to proceed by means of a "cross-check." Under a cross-check method, no mail ballot is conducted. Instead the "showing of interest" cards that the union has filed are used to determine support, and if the union can present cards from 70% or more of the bargaining unit it will be certified as the representative.

64 WAC 391-25-370.
65 WAC 391-25-370(2).

Chapter 3

The Right to Collectively Bargain

A. The Statutory Right to Bargain

Labor organizations certified as exclusive bargaining representatives have a special status under Washington law. By statute and case law, they have been assigned the responsibility to represent their members — on an exclusive basis — in their employment relationship with the employer. This exclusivity includes the sole right to negotiate the workplace rules.

The Public Employees Collective Bargaining Act (PECBA) (RCW 41.56.140) provides that a public employer commits an unfair labor practice when it refuses to "engage in collective bargaining." The statute also provides that the scope of collective bargaining extends to "grievance procedures and collective negotiations on personnel matters, including *wages, hours and working conditions*, which may be peculiar to an appropriate bargaining unit."[1]

it is a ULP for a party to "refuse" to engage in collective bargaining on a subject which is within the scope of bargaining. But no express statement of "refusal" is required — PERC considers it a "refusal" to engage in collective bargaining whenever the employer makes a change unilaterally in a subject of bargaining without fully discharging its bargaining obligations.

PERC classifies the failure of a party to negotiate properly to be a "refusal to bargain" ULP. A "refusal to bargain" ULP typically occurs in one of two ways: (1) the employer makes a unilateral change in a subject over which it had a legal obligation to negotiate; or (2) negotiations occurred concerning the change, but the process was in some way defective so that it is charged that the party did not operate in negotiations "in good faith." This chapter will separately address these two types of "refusal to bargain" ULPs.

[1] RCW 41.56.030.

B. The Statutory Prohibition on Unilateral Changes

As indicated, it is a ULP for a party to "refuse" to engage in collective bargaining on a subject which is within the scope of bargaining. But no express statement of "refusal" is required — PERC considers it a "refusal" to engage in collective bargaining whenever the employer makes a change unilaterally in a subject of bargaining without fully discharging its bargaining obligations.

When defending against a ULP charge, employers typically present one of the following eight defenses:

1) The union was notified of the change but waived its right to negotiate by itself failing to engage in collective bargaining;

2) The union "waived" its right to bargain the subject in the CBA by conferring upon management through the CBA the authority to make the change;

3) There was no change — that the rule or policy announced by the employer was already a "past practice";

4) The subject at issue is outside the statutory scope of collective bargaining;

5) The employer had already negotiated and then had a statutory right to unilaterally implement the change;

6) The nature of the change was *de minimus*;

7) There was no change affecting the bargaining unit, but merely a dispute as to the application of past practice to a given individual; and

8) An emergency or business necessity existed which warranted immediate employer unilateral action.

In this Chapter, we shall examine each of these defenses, discussing the law that applies to these defenses and the appropriate union response.

PRIMARY EMPLOYER ULP DEFENSES

- Waiver by Conduct
- Waiver by Contract
- Status Quo
- Outside Scope of Bargaining
- Exhausted Bargaining Obligation
- De Minimis Change
- Involves Only Application to an Individual
- Emergency

1. The "Waiver" Defense

a. Nature of a Waiver

"Waivers" do not automatically exist by operation of law; they are created by *actions* of the labor organization. Waivers are created *either* when the labor organization has *expressly agreed* to a waiver of its bargaining rights (usually through contract language) *or* when the union, by its conduct, has *implied* a willingness to waive its right to bargain (usually through its inaction).

There are general principles regarding "waivers" that apply to *both* "waivers by contract" *and* "waivers by conduct." Legally speaking, a waiver has been defined as "an intentional relinquishment of a known right."[2] PERC has acknowledged a waiver to occur *only* where its existence is "clear and unmistakable."[3] For a waiver to be created, the decision to waive was "knowingly or consciously made."[4] Even if made, written waivers do not last indefinitely but end with the expiration of the CBA in which they were created.[5]

---

[2] *Spokane County*, Decision 2377 (PECB, 1986).

[3] *Snohomish County*, Decision 2234 (PECB, 1985).

[4] *Goldendale School District No. 404*, Decision 1634 (PECB, 1983); *Spokane County*, Decision 2377 (PECB, 1986).

[5] *Seattle School District*, Decision 2079 (1984).

Waivers by conduct have been found where a labor organization failed to act even though it was aware of an impending unilateral change.

PERC generally takes a skeptical view of waiver claims and has stated that it is hesitant to find that a waiver of collective bargaining rights has actually been made.[6] Consistent with that approach, PERC has stated that where waivers are not obvious they will not be "lightly inferred."[7] Because a legal presumption exists against a waiver claim, PERC has placed the burden of proof on the employer that claims a waiver occurred.[8]

b. "Waiver by Conduct"

Waivers by conduct have been found where a labor organization failed to act even though it was aware of an impending unilateral change. That knowledge, though, must be *actual*, not "imputed." In other words, the "should have known" concept that applies elsewhere in labor law does not apply to waiver arguments. Therefore, PERC will not find a waiver unless the employer gave *actual notice* to the labor organization,[9] *or* the labor organization otherwise acquired *actual knowledge* of the impending change.[10]

When notice is given to a union, it must be timely so that meaningful negotiations can occur before the change is implemented.[11] Where the employer does not clearly communicate exactly what proposed action it intends, no waiver will be inferred by the union's inaction.[12] Therefore, the employer is obligated to make it clear that there is a pending proposal to make a change, not simply suggest the theoretical possibility of a change.[13]

---

6 *City of Wenatchee*, Decision 2216 (PECB, 1985).

7 *Snohomish County*, Decision 2234 (PECB, 1985); *Spokane County*, Decision 2167 (PECB, 1985).

8 *City of Wenatchee*, Decision 2194 (PECB, 1985); *City of Yakima*, Decisions 3564 and 3564-A (PECB, 1990); *Spokane County*, Decision 2167 (PECB, 1985).

9 *City of Pasco*, Decision 2603 (PECB, 1987).

10 *City of Yakima*, Decision 1124-A (PECB, 1981); *Olympia School District*, Decision 1366 (PECB, 1982); *Pierce County*, Decision 1845 (1984); *Goldendale School District*, Decision 1634 (PECB, 1983); *Clover Park School District*, Decision 3266 (PECB, 1989).

11 *Clover Park School District*, Decision 3266 (PECB, 1989).

12 *Royal School District*, Decision 1419-A (PECB, 1982).

Communications directed at the individual employees do not give rise to a waiver by conduct where the responsible union officers do not acquire actual notice of the intended change.[14]

An employer commits a ULP if it fails to give notice of a change in a mandatory subject of bargaining prior to its implementation *or* presents the other party with what is called a "*fait accompli.*"[15] A "*fait accompli*" occurs where the change is announced at the same time as the notice. It is the duty of the employer proposing a change to give notice and to provide an opportunity for bargaining *before* the decision is made.[16] That notice must be given sufficiently in advance of the intended implementation of the change so as to allow a reasonable opportunity for bargaining.[17] In deciding whether a change was presented as a *fait accompli*, PERC's focus will be on the circumstances as a whole, including whether a meaningful opportunity for bargaining existed.[18]

Once a union is presented with a *fait accompli*, it is legally excused from its normal obligation to request bargaining.[19] The union generally cannot, absent special circumstances, be found to have waived its bargaining rights by inaction when the decision was already being implemented. As one examiner has aptly noted: "A union cannot be found to have waived its bargaining rights when it never had an opportunity to bargain."[20]

To put it another way, a "*fait accompli*" and "waiver by inaction" are mutually exclusive. A determination that a *fait accompli* occurred requires the finding that the employer provided the bargaining unit with ineffective notice. A waiver by inaction, on the other hand, requires finding first, the employer provided the union with effective notice and second, the union then failed to act upon that notice.

As indicated, a union has no particular obligation to request bargaining once presented with a true *fait accompli*. A union's filing

---

[13] *Port of Edmonds*, Decisions 844 and 844-B (PECB, 1980).

[14] *Royal School District*, Decision 1419-A (PECB, 1982).

[15] *City of Wenatchee*, Decision 6517-A (PECB, 1999); *Seattle School District*, Decision 5755-A (PECB, 1998).

[16] *City of Moses Lake*, Decision 6328 (PECB, 1998).

[17] *Washington Public Power Supply System*, Decision 6058-A (PECB, 1998); *Clover Park School District*, Decision 3266 (PECB, 1989).

[18] *Seattle School District*, Decision 5733-B (PECB, 1998).

[19] *City of Tukwila*, Decision 2424-A (PECB, 1986); *City of Bellevue*, Decision 839 (PECB, 1980); *Lakewood School District*, Decision 755-A (PECB, 1980); *Royal School District*, Decision 1419-A (PECB, 1982); *Spokane County*, Decision 2167 (PECB, 1985).

[20] *Clover Park School District*, Decision 3266 (PECB, 1989).

of a ULP complaint within the six month period of limitations set forth in RCW 41.56.160 is all that is needed to constitute a timely and proper response by the union to the employer's fait accompli.[21]

Also, where an employer does not clearly communicate what specific action it intends, no waiver should be inferred by the union's inaction.[22] Therefore, the employer is obligated to make it clear that there is a specific intent to make a change rather than simply inviting a discussion about the abstract possibility of change.[23]

ELEMENTS OF WAIVER BY CONDUCT

- Clear Notice to Union
- Opportunity to Bargain
- Not Presented as a *Fait Accompli*
- Failure by Union to Respond

When the union asserts its right to bargain the proposed change, a waiver does not arise from its failure to make a vigorous presentation of its position; it is incumbent on the *employer* not to make changes where there is no impasse.[24] On the other hand, a union's failure to make a simple request to negotiate when it has knowledge of an impending change does give rise to a waiver.[25] Another decision, though questionable, holds that the union's failure to provide counterproposals constitutes a waiver of its right to bargain.[26]

A labor organization does not waive its right to engage in collective bargaining by participating in civil service or city council hearings because these forums do not constitute a substitute for collective bargaining.[27] But if the union becomes aware that the employer is attempting to adopt a new rule or policy through civil service or ordinance on a mandatory subject of bargaining, it should assert its bargaining rights.

A waiver by conduct arises only where the union has failed to act in reference to a particular change. Therefore, a union's

---

[21] *Clover Park School District*, Decision 3266 (PECB, 1989).

[22] *Royal School District*, Decision 1419-A (PECB, 1982).

[23] *Port of Edmonds*, Decisions 844 (PECB, 1980) and 844-B (PECB, 1980).

[24] *City of Sumner*, Decisions 1839 and 1839-A (PECB, 1984); *Mukilteo School District*, Decision 3795-A (PECB, 1992).

[25] *City of Pasco*, Decision 2603 (PECB, 1987).

[26] *Willapa Valley School District*, Decision 4374 (PECB, 1993).

[27] *Kitsap County Fire District No. 7*, Decision 2872 (PECB, 1988); *City of Bellevue*, Decisions 3156 and 3156-A (PECB, 1989).

inaction resulting in waivers in the past does not create an ongoing waiver of its bargaining rights over similar future changes.[28] To put it another way, the union's past lax enforcement of its rights does not excuse the employer from complying with the statute in the future.

Practice Pointers:

- Train your Board members in the broad scope of bargaining (discussed below) so that they can recognize when a duty to bargain a change exists.

- Train your Board members to review various notices and memos that the employer generates and to bring issues to the attention of the responsible union officer.

- If the employer announces a change in a wage, hour or working condition, make a *written* demand to bargain. You want the demand well-documented and writing is the best way to do that. And while it might seem tempting to overlook minor and otherwise acceptable changes, you want to train the employer to recognize its continuous duty to provide you advance notice of all proposed changes.

- Even if the change is presented in an apparent "fait accompli" manner, make a written demand to bargain anyway. While a true fait accompli technically removes the requirement to make such a demand, it is better to err on the side of caution. The fait accompli doctrine is well-established in PERC case law but whether advance notice was given can still be subject to some dispute. And being able to offer evidence that you clearly objected is the best possible evidence that no waiver occurred.

[28] *City of Wenatchee*, Decision 2194 (PECB, 1985); *Kitsap County Fire District No. 7*, Decision 2872 (PECB, 1988).

A "waiver by contract" occurs when the union has agreed to specific contract language that confers upon management a right to take some action in a certain area.

c. *Waiver by Contract*

Besides "waiver by conduct" A labor organization may waive its right to engage in collective bargaining by contract. A "waiver by contract" occurs when the union has agreed to specific contract language that confers upon management a right to take some action in a certain area. As with all waivers, in order for a waiver by contract to exist, the waiver language must be clear and unmistakable, and the waiver must have been knowingly made.[29] PERC will find a waiver to exist in contract language in one of two circumstances:

1) The express terms of the agreement explicitly set forth a waiver; *or*

2) The terms of the agreement are ambiguous as to a waiver but the existence of the waiver is unequivocally corroborated by extrinsic evidence.[30]

PERC has consistently and repeatedly held that general management rights language contained in a contract does not constitute a waiver of bargaining rights.[31] Because waivers must be consciously and knowingly made, *management rights language will only be construed to be a waiver when specific as to the subject that is being waived.*[32] To put this another way, it is often said that

---

29 *City of Wenatchee*, Decision 2216 (PECB, 1985).

30 *Id.*

31 *City of Kennewick*, Decision 482-B (PECB, 1978); *City of Sumner*, Decisions 1839 and 1839-A (PECB, 1984); *City of Wenatchee*, Decision 2194 (PECB, 1985); *Kitsap County Fire District No. 7*, Decision 2872 (PECB, 1988); *Kennewick School District*, Decision 3330 (PECB, 1989); *City of Yakima*, Decisions 3564 and 3564-A (PECB, 1990); *City of Clarkston*, Decision 3286 (PECB, 1989); *Pierce County Fire District No. 3*, Decision 4146 (PECB, 1992); *City of Seattle*, Decision 4163 (PECB, 1992).

32 *City of Yakima*, Decisions 3564 and 3564-A (PECB, 1990); *Mukilteo School District No. 6*, Decision 3795 (PECB, 1991); *City of Wenatchee*, Decision 2194 (PECB, 1985).

purported waivers have to be "subject specific" to be effective.

PERC has consistently and repeatedly held that general management rights language contained in a contract does not constitute a waiver of bargaining rights. Because waivers must be consciously and knowingly made, *management rights language will only be construed to be a waiver when specific as to the subject that is being waived.*

Predicting when PERC will find language to be sufficiently specific to rise to the level of a waiver is often difficult. The first appendix to this chapter provides a table listing various cases in which PERC has examined whether specific contract language constitutes a waiver. A review of those PERC cases in this area indicates some degree of inconsistency as to how specific language must be to constitute a waiver.

At the very least, though, it is clear some type of specific subject must be referenced in the alleged waiver clause. But even language that mentions a subject will not normally be stretched too far to beyond its narrow meaning to be interpreted as a waiver.

PERC had previously indicated that waivers themselves were not mandatory subjects of bargaining. Therefore, while an employer was free to propose a management rights clause that might contain some type of waiver, it could not lawfully insist to impasse on its waiver. In *City of Pasco,*[33] PERC reversed course and found waivers bargaining. The matter was appealed to the State Supreme Court and the court affirmed.[34] But since that time PERC has modified its course again, finding that some proposed waivers that were overbroad in scope fell outside the union's duty to bargain.

Waivers eliminate your right to engage in collective bargaining in the future on that topic.

---

[33] *City of Pasco*, Decisions 4694-A and 4695-A (PECB, 1994).

[34] *Pasco Police Officers Association v. City of Pasco*, 132 Wn.2d 450, 938 P.2d 827 (1997).

Practice Pointers:

- During contract negotiations, be mindful and highly resistant to any employer proposals that could potentially be "waivers." Waivers eliminate your right to engage in collective bargaining in the future on that topic. Experience indicates that once management has placed waiver language in the CBA, they are extremely reluctant to relinquish it.

- The extent to which employers can insist that you negotiate away your bargaining rights through waivers is unclear and the case law is inconsistent, but you should put the employer on notice during bargaining that their proposed waivers (inclusive of ones from the existing CBA) fall outside the mandatory scope of bargaining and must be relinquished as permissive subjects.

- In the face of employer resistance to relinquishing waivers, you can blunt the impact of such waivers by adding new language in the CBA that covers the topic. As just one example of this method of blunting existing waivers, a waiver of the employer's "right to schedule work" can be partially limited by inserting a shift bidding clause in the CBA.

- During negotiations, have your legal counsel review existing and proposed language in the CBA closely to determine if current or proposed waivers exist. Most waivers are found in the management rights clause, but they can arise anywhere in the CBA.

- Acquire training in the scope of bargaining. This subject is a complex and confusing area, but a bit of training goes a long ways towards defending your bargaining rights.

2. The "*Status Quo*" Defense

A common employer defense to a union's ULP charge is that no actual change in working conditions occurred. As PERC has indicated:

> In order for there to be a unilateral change, there must have been some change in the *status quo*. No duty to bargain arises from a reiteration of an established policy, or from a change that has no material effect on employee wages, hours or working conditions.[35]

In other words, when the employer demonstrates a preexisting past practice, no duty to bargain arises from the mere application of the preexisting practice.

In a ULP hearing, the charging party bears the burden of proof. Therefore, when a union asserts that the employer has unlawfully made a unilateral change in a subject of bargaining, the union must establish proof as to the nature of the relevant past practice. A leading treatise discusses this obligation:

> The party asserting a past practice has the burden of proving that the past practice exists largely because a past practice represents implied agreement by mutual conduct. An approach that readily inferred mutuality without strong evidence would undermine the significance of written collective bargaining agreements.[36]

Moreover, "the party asserting a past practice bears the burden of proving not only the existence, *but also the scope*, of any alleged past practice."[37]

The generally accepted elements of a past practice include the requirement that the practice be unequivocal, clearly enunciated and acted upon, readily ascertainable, fixed for a certain period of time, and established through *mutual acceptance by both parties*.[38] Mutual acceptance does not require explicit agreement; acceptance is demonstrated by mere acquiescence. Past practices involve "those working conditions that are mandatory subjects of bargaining and cannot be changed unilaterally, whether they are established in writing or by custom."[39]

---

[35] *Walla Walla County*, Decision 11751 (PECB, 2013) (emphasis in original) (citations omitted).

[36] Bornstein and Gosline, *supra*, at § 18.02[1].

[37] *Id.* (emphasis added).

[38] *See* Bornstein and Gosline, *supra*, at § 18.01[1].

[39] *City of Burlington*, Decisions 5840, 5841, 5842, and 5843 (PECB, 1997).

Past practice can be created by the actions of responsible supervisors.

In *City of Pasco*, PERC defined a "past practice" as "a course of dealing acknowledged by the parties over an extended period of time, becoming so well understood that its inclusion in a collective bargaining agreement is deemed superfluous."[40] And in a *Washington State Ferry System*[41] arbitration decision a PERC examiner observed that for a union to establish a past practice, it "must prove that the action was consistent and all parties had knowledge."

ELEMENTS OF AN ESTABLISHED "PAST PRACTICE"

- Clear and Unequivocal
- Readily Definable
- Fixed for a Period of Time
- Mutually Known and Understood

To establish knowledge, a union need not demonstrate the practice was known and agreed by the highest circles of management. Past practice can be created by the actions of responsible supervisors. As PERC indicated in *City of Wenatchee*:

> We are not persuaded by the employer's argument that a past practice cannot be based on the practices or beliefs of non-management employees, and that one sergeant...liberally granted light duty requests without management approval. Anyone who granted the light duty requests which form the background to this case acted within their apparent scope of authority. Even if higher management was unaware of the sergeant's liberal practice of allowing light duty assignments, unfair labor practices committed by a superior serving in an official capacity are considered to be the responsibility of the public employer as an entity.[42]

Therefore, first-line supervisors — even though they are in the

[40] *City of Pasco*, Decisions 4197 and 4198 (PECB, 1992).
[41] Decision 1325 (PECB, 1982).
[42] Decision 6517-A (PECB, 1999).

bargaining unit — may create past practices through acquiescence or manner of enforcement of rules. Not every action of a supervisor leads to the creation of past practices. The question turns on the scope of their authority over particular working conditions. But even if outside their defined authority, consistent actions of supervisors can lead to the creation of past practices when management would have had knowledge of them.

---

a past practice is the actual custom between the parties *whether written* or not

---

It is important to bear in mind that what one is enforcing with a past practice is the actual custom between the parties *whether written* or not. A written document — whether in a CBA, a Policies and Procedures manual, or even a written memorandum — is not conclusive as to what constitutes a past practice. Those written documents may, though, serve as *best evidence* of a past practice.

When the parties have failed to adhere to the terms of these written documents, it will not be permissible for the employer simply to resume enforcing lapsed policies.[43] If an employer has failed to follow a written policy and now wishes to do so, it must commence new negotiations with the union concerning the issue.

An exception to the renewed bargaining obligation sometimes exists, though, when the topic is already specifically addressed in the CBA. If a collective bargaining agreement unequivocally confers upon management right to apply a certain working condition, PERC will not hold the employer to its obligation to renegotiate what it has already bargained. To put this another way, the union in this situation has essentially provided a "waiver" of its rights to further negotiate the topic with the employer. By defining a working condition in a specific way in the contract, the union has authorized the application of that working condition as it is written and even if the employer has lapsed in its enforcement of its rights, it is entitled to enforce the terms of that agreement.

On the other hand, this right to renew its enforcement of the labor agreement exists *only* during the term of an agreement. If the agreement has expired and the parties are not yet in agreement on a successor agreement, the employer has no ability to enforce its old rights under the expired labor agreement. This is especially true of contract waivers which PERC has specifically held expire with the

---

[43] *Pierce County Fire District 3*, Decision 4146 (PECB, 1992).

expiration of the CBA. (An exception applies here to groups not eligible for interest arbitration; under the statutory 12-month extension, discussed below, all the terms of the CBA, including contract waivers, remain intact.)

To put it another way, once the labor agreement has lapsed, all that remains for the parties is the past practice. If the past practice was not in conformity with the agreement, the past practice still prevails until such time as the new agreement is put in place.

Often at issue in ULPs is not just what the past practices have been but the "relevant status quo" is.[44] The practices that may have existed in years past may be interesting but not controlling. What matters is what the established practice was in place *at the time the union claims a change was made.*

Another "status quo" issue that arises is the inconsistent enforcement of working conditions. Especially when work groups are not well integrated, it is a common problem that different supervisors will enforce policies differently. Divergent practices develop, and this divergence is especially a problem for the union because PERC then will likely hold that the union cannot *prove* that a consistently followed established past practice exists, even one PERC thought existed.[45]

Practice Pointers:

- Train your board members to monitor establish working conditions and report when those are changed.

- As much as possible, document favorable existing practices in writing. Everything need not be in the CBA. But writing is whether inside or outside the CBA specifically detailing the nature of the past practice is the best evidence that the practice exists.

- When a potential change occurs, challenge it immediately.

- If a grievance or ULP hearing ensues, be prepared to locate as much evidence as possible, written and otherwise, regarding the disputed practice.

---

44 *See* Val Vue Sewer District, Decision 8963 (PECB, 2005).

45 *See, e.g., Kitsap County*, Decision 10669 (PECB, 2010).

3. The "Outside the Scope of Mandatory Bargaining" Defense

The most significant (and most common) defense raised by management is that they had no particular duty to bargain the change. This section discussions the particular duty to bargain both generally and in reference to particular subjects.

a. The General Nature of the Scope of Bargaining

The collective bargaining statute indicates that the obligation to engage in collective bargaining shall extend to "grievance procedures and collective negotiations on personnel matters, including wages, hours and working conditions..." PERC has the primary authority to determine whether a subject falls within the scope of collective bargaining. PERC determinations are subject to court appeals, but the courts generally defer to PERC's expertise in classifying subjects as bargainable or not bargainable.

PERC may determine in a given case that management's right to act freely outweighs the union's right to negotiate the issue even though it appears to be a "wage, hour or working condition."

Simply because a matter may appear to fall within the literal language "wages, hours and working conditions" does not necessarily make it a subject of bargaining. PERC may conclude for a variety of policy reasons to find that something does not fall within the scope of bargaining even though it does relate to your day-to-day work conditions.

PERC's first step is to look at whether an issue is literally something that involves a "wage, hour or working condition." But then PERC looks at whether even though something is in these categories, it ought to be bargainable because it is an inherent management right. In other words, PERC may determine in a given case that management's right to act freely outweighs the union's right to negotiate the issue even though it appears to be a "wage, hour or working condition." This is the "balancing process PERC undertakes.

PERC purports to make subject of bargaining determinations on a case-by-case basis. PERC classifies bargaining subjects into one of three categories:

1) Mandatory subjects of bargaining;

2) Permissive subjects of bargaining; or

3) Illegal subjects of bargaining.

Few subjects have been labeled as an illegal subject of bargaining. An illegal subject would be, for example, a proposal that employees could not communicate with union officers; that would be illegal because it would contradict the statutory prohibition on union interference. So most discussions regarding the scope of collective bargaining revolve around whether a matter is a mandatory or permissive subject of bargaining.

PERC views the determination of a subject of bargaining to be a matter of both fact and law. It is a specific inquiry that is applied to the particular proposal. Although previous PERC decisions are quite helpful in understanding how PERC will rule in the future on "scope of bargaining" cases, PERC insists that each particular proposal has to be assessed on its own terms.

The classification of subjects of bargaining is of great importance to the parties engaged in collective bargaining. Whether a subject is classified as a mandatory or permissive topic has extensive legal ramifications on the rights of the parties. First of all, the employer may make unilateral changes in subjects that have been deemed permissive by PERC. On the other hand, there are some matters that the employer would rather avoid having to talk about and a classification of these subjects as mandatory gives the union some leverage in its relationship with the employer.

PERC has recognized as legitimate the employer's interest in determining which services and programs it should offer to the public and at which level.

PERC is well aware the impact is subject of bargaining classification decisions have, especially as to the relative "balance of power" between the parties. PERC usually expressly weighs the competing interests involved. PERC has recognized that both sides have certain legitimate interests at stake which should be considered in defining the scope of collective bargaining.

On the one hand, PERC has recognized as legitimate the employer's interest in determining which services and programs it should offer to the public and at which level.[46] It has also held that public employers should have the right to establish their own budgets without interference by labor organizations.[47] PERC has also stated that public employers should have a free hand in determining which capital investments to make.[48]

On the other hand, PERC has found management's desire to maintain "flexibility" and control over the workplace not to be a valid consideration classifying subject of bargaining.[49] Similarly, PERC has not credited employers' claims that it found a labor organization's proposal to be offensive or burdensome.

PERC is quite aware that labor organizations have an interest in the broadest possible construction of the scope of collective bargaining. Nonetheless, PERC has stated that it will not define the scope of bargaining so broadly so as to include any subject that a union wishes to bargain.[50] PERC has recognized, though, that labor organizations have an especially strong interest in those working rules that directly relate to the continuation and security of employment.[51]

In balancing these competing interests, PERC has set forth a number of policy positions. These general factors guide its determinations and can be used to predict whether they will find something as mandatory or permissive:

- PERC generally will not require an employer to bargain over which services to offer or the level of such services.
- PERC also does not require employers to bargain over the budgeting to support such services.
- PERC has recognized a distinction, however, between the decision as to *whether* or not to offer a service and the *methods* of how that service will be delivered.[52]
- PERC will allow employers to determine which capital investments to make in furtherance of delivering

---

[46] *Federal Way School District*, Decision 232-A (PECB, 1977); *King County*, Decision 1957 (PECB, 1984).
[47] *Federal Way School District, supra.*
[48] *Seattle School District*, Decision 2079 (PECB, 1984).
[49] *City of Auburn*, Decision 901 (PECB, 1980).
[50] *City of Richland*, Decision 2486 (PECB, 1986).
[51] *City of Bellevue*, Decision 839 (PECB, 1980); *King County*, Decision 1957 (PECB, 1984).
[52] *King County*, Decision 1957 (PECB, 1984).

services, even when those capital investments directly affect working conditions, but it still requires employers to bargain the effects of such decision on the employees.[53]

- PERC will likely find something to be a mandatory subject of bargaining when it *directly* relates to a wage, hour or working condition

The more directly the issue impacts "wages, hours and working conditions," the greater likelihood it will be found to be a subject of bargaining

On the other hand, if something does touch on a "wage, hour or working condition, but management can show it impinges on a management operational interest, PERC then commences its "balancing test." Under this "balancing" analysis, PERC will weigh, on the one hand, *how directly* the issue relates to wages, hours and working conditions. Then, on the other hand, PERC weighs the extent to which management needs a free hand on that subject to deliver its public services.

The more directly the issue impacts "wages, hours and working conditions," the greater likelihood it will be found to be a subject of bargaining even in the face of a strong management rationale for flexibility. The less directly the subject impacts "wages, hours and working conditions," the greater likelihood it will be found to be a management prerogative.

In 1989, the State Supreme Court ordered PERC to make these determinations on a case-by-case basis.[54] This order followed a decision in which PERC had categorically ruled that all staffing issues fell outside the scope of bargaining. PERC has since taken the Supreme Court's directive seriously, and each ULP decision involves a balancing analysis even where PERC has previously made a clear ruling on a given subject.

Despite PERC's stated "case by case" approach, knowledgeable advocates can usually predict with fair accuracy the likelihood that PERC will deem a given issue to fall inside or outside the scope of bargaining. The primary factor an advocate would look to is how

---

53 *Seattle School District*, Decision 2079 (PECB, 1984); *King County Fire District No. 16*, Decision 3714 (PECB, 1991).

54 *IAFF Local 1052 v. PERC*, 113 Wn.2d 197, 778 P.2d 32 (1989).

PERC has ruled on the same *or similar* issues in the past, as PERC also takes its precedent quite seriously. We next turn to a review of that case precedent.

b. Classification of Particular Subjects of Bargaining

The appendix to this chapter provides an exhaustive catalog of how PERC has ruled on prior subject to bargaining cases. This list covers not only cases involving public safety employees, but all public sector classifications. As indicated, the best predictor of what PERC will do in future cases, is how it has ruled on similar cases in the past. While PERC purports to do a "case by case" analysis, it also takes its case precedent fairly seriously. Therefore, one can use this table as a guide for how PERC will likely rule on similar issues in the future.

This table presents all known PERC "subject of bargaining" decision through the date of the publication of this book. To review the table, turn to the appendix following this chapter. What follows is a written description of the patterns that emerge from the table.

i. Wages and Benefits

In the area of wages and benefits, PERC has recognized a very strong interest for labor organizations. PERC has consistently held wages in all of its various forms constitute a mandatory subject of bargaining. This extends even to the timing of when pay is received. Incidental pay issues such as special duty pay and the distribution and computation of overtime have been found negotiable.

Even more incidental benefits such as shower access, water, and locker have been found negotiable.

PERC has determined that the statutory term "wages" extends to all forms of compensation. Therefore, various forms of health and welfare benefits have been uniformly recognized to be mandatory subjects of bargaining. PERC has also recognized as within the scope of bargaining incidental fringe benefits such as clothing allowances, parking and take-home vehicles. Even more incidental benefits such as shower access, water, and locker have been found negotiable.

ii. Scheduling Work Hours and Leave

PERC has recognized the vital interest labor organizations have in hours of work as well as the express statutory mandate that "hours" be negotiated. Therefore, PERC has uniformly held that the manner in which work is scheduled is a mandatory subject of bargaining. It also deems the length of the workday and even starting and ending times to be bargainable. Shift bidding is bargainable. So too are shift rotation practices.

PERC has also labeled as a mandatory subject of bargaining employees' rest and meal breaks. PERC has even had occasion to find that access to bathrooms is bargainable.

Leave time, "Kelly" time and compensatory time and how they are scheduled are also considered mandatory subjects of bargaining. Light duty is a subject of bargaining.

---

discipline and the procedures for imposing discipline constitute mandatory subjects of bargaining

---

iii. Discipline and Discipline Procedures

PERC has given great weight to the employees' interest in job preservation and the rules and conditions under which they preserve their employment. For example, PERC has consistently ruled that discipline and the procedures for imposing discipline constitute mandatory subjects of bargaining. The creation or elimination of internal Discipline Review Boards are also negotiable. PERC examiners have rendered split decisions, though, concerning Citizen Review Boards. The length of probation periods is a mandatory subject of bargaining.

Procedural incidental to the discipline process like the use of surveillance cameras, drug testing and polygraphs has been found negotiable. The employer Code of Conduct or like rules are also subject to a duty to bargain.

iv. Conditions of Employment

PERC also generally recognizes that work rules that constitute conditions by which employees may maintain their jobs are subject to collective bargaining. The statute expressly says, after all, that "working conditions" are a subject of bargaining. So rules around physical fitness, tobacco and alcohol use, off-duty employment, and residency requirements have all been found bargainable.

PERC, however, has drawn a distinction between conditions of employment for employees and non-employees. PERC has held that pre-employment conditions or qualifications are not subject to collective bargaining as the labor organization has no standing to represent non-employees. The continuation of these conditions after employment, however, would constitute a mandatory subject of bargaining.

v. Promotions

As to promotions, PERC has drawn a distinction between promotions inside the bargaining unit and outside the bargaining unit. Promotions, and the rules for making those promotions, are considered mandatory subjects of bargaining where the promotion is inside the bargaining unit. Promotions to be made outside the bargaining unit are not considered a mandatory subject of bargaining. Rules regarding how specialty assignments are made may also be bargainable, although PERC cases are in conflict on this issue.

The employer is not permitted to avoid its bargaining obligation by having the change made by the Civil Service Commission. The Supreme Court has ruled that the civil service process is subordinate to the collective bargaining process. If the parties bargain for a change in a civil service rule, the Civil Service Commission is legally bound to adopt the change.

vi. Job Security

In the general area of job security, the cases are less clear-cut. PERC has frequently been compelled to consider the competing interests of the employer in operational efficiency and the employees in secure employment.

PERC has generally resolved these matters in favor of the employees. For example, PERC has held that subcontracting and layoffs constitute mandatory subjects of bargaining. "Furloughing" employees by reducing their work time (and associated pay) is a mandatory subject of bargaining.

However, PERC has found the decision by an employer to cease operations and allow the public service to be provided by another governmental agency to be a permissive subject. Rulings around "skimming" or "contracting out" are complex and conflicted but generally tilt towards finding a duty to bargain.

PERC has also held that the implementation of technology is not a mandatory subject of bargaining even if it directly results in a loss of jobs. Nonetheless, the effects of such a decision are a mandatory subject of bargaining.

vii. Workplace Operations

PERC has also balanced competing interests in the area of workplace procedures and standards. In general, PERC has been more inclined to find a matter to be a outside the scope of bargaining where it relates to how public services are delivered on a day-to-day basis. Employers are generally given a free hand to determine which services to offer and how to organize the workforce. Safety matters are generally deemed to be a mandatory subject of bargaining.

PERC has been more inclined to find a matter to be a outside the scope of bargaining where it relates to how public services are delivered on a day-to-day basis.

For example, PERC has generally held that minimum staffing levels will not be considered a mandatory subject of bargaining, although there may be some exceptions to this general rule, especially when safety is directly impinged. These rulings have been controversial. What is also not widely understood by employers is that changes in the minimum staffing formula that directly changes the ability to take paid leave time is negotiable.

Controversy exists concerning work standards. PERC has also held that the performance standards employees are required to meet are not a mandatory subject of bargaining, although the effects of implementing such standards are a mandatory subject of bargaining. PERC has found work quotas and time performances standards to be bargainable. But evaluations have been held not to be bargainable. PERC has yet to address it, but an evaluation procedure that was directly linked to pay would probably be negotiable.

The introduction of new technologies, equipment or tools is generally a management right. Building design is a management right. But there may be a duty to bargain identified “impacts” of such workplace changes. Workplace position reorganization is usually deemed a management right, but there are impacts that likely have to be negotiated with such reorganizations (and potential skimming issues to address).

Employee authority such as the “commission” authority of Park Rangers has been found a non-negotiable management right. Revised job descriptions that merely restate existing duties are not bargainable. A minor change in job duties is not bargainable, but substantial revisions likely are bargainable. The PERC decisions concerning when or whether the addition of new duties is negotiable is somewhat conflicted.

Practice Pointers:

- Train you Board to recognize the scope of bargaining issues.
- Recognize that the distinction between mandatory and permissive subjects is not always black and white. PERC has ruled on the scope of bargaining many times, but issues remain unresolved.
- Carefully craft your contract proposals so that they are presented in the form of a mandatory subject. If the employer objects to a proposal claiming it is permissive, carefully review the wording of your proposal, confer with legal counsel, and, if appropriate, revise the wording to bring it within the scope of bargaining.
- Generally avoid refusing to negotiate because you believe an employer proposal is "permissive." You are within your rights to refuse if you are correct as to the scope of bargaining, but if you are wrong you have committed a ULP.
- If there is a dispute over whether something is negotiable and it results in a ULP, you will need to be ready to prepare and present evidence as to how the issue impacts the bargaining unit members.

4. Other Employer Defenses to a Unilateral Change ULP

a. The Statutory Right to "Unilaterally Implement" Defense

This is one issue in which there is a great divergence between groups which have interest arbitration and those which do not. For both groups the statute requires both the union and the employer to engage in good faith bargaining. But once the parties reach the point in negotiations where no agreement is made and an "impasse" occurs, possible employer remedies to break the impasse diverge.

For non-interest arbitration groups, the impasse resolution process is defined in RCW 41.56.123. This section provides that even after the collective bargaining agreement expires, if the parties have not reached an agreement on a successor agreement, "all of the terms and conditions specified in the collective bargaining agreement shall remain in effect until the effective date of a subsequent agreement, *not to exceed one year from the termination date stated in the agreement.*"[55] But the statute then adds: "Thereafter, the employer may unilaterally implement according to law."[56]

Under this section, then, the employer has the following rights and obligations:

1) The employer may not make such changes until at least one year after a contract expires;

2) During that year, the employer must be engaging in good faith bargaining;

3) Whatever implementation is made at the end of the year has to be consistent with the employer's "last best offer"; and

4) The implementation may only consist of those items that constitute mandatory subjects of bargaining.

In many senses, the employer has a strong bargaining tool available when it ultimately can resort to unilateral implementation. While the union can insist that the employer go through the process of meeting with it and engaging in good faith negotiations over the union's proposals, ultimately the employer has the ability to say "no" to whatever it does not wish to agree to and make that binding.

But the statutory right to unilaterally implement has several drawbacks. And these drawbacks are serious enough that most employers have found it simply more productive to complete negotiations and reach a mutual agreement rather than force a non-agreed resolution upon the employees.

First, a union dissatisfied with the results of a unilateral implementation will predictably file a ULP complaint and may even win the complaint. As indicated above, to be able to unilaterally

---

[55] RCW 41.56.123.

[56] *Id.*

implement, the employer must show that throughout the year after the expiration of the agreement it engaged in good faith bargaining. If the union can show that the employer failed to engage in good faith bargaining, the implemented settlement will be set aside, and the employer will be directed to renew negotiations.[57]

Second, the implementation has to be fully consistent with the employer's "last best offer." In other words, the employer may not simply selectively implement the elements of its package it finds most desirable — it must also implement on those concessions it has made to the employees during the bargaining process as well. PERC has yet to clearly resolve exactly what constitutes the "last best offer," but presumably if the employer has made some compromise movement, even in the context of a "what if" package, it will be required to implement the total package, or whatever total package the union deems to have been the most desirable.

Third, the employer is *not* allowed to implement the aspects of its proposal that impair union statutory bargaining rights. Although PERC has ruled that "waivers" are a mandatory subject of bargaining in the context of interest arbitration group negotiations, it has yet to make this ruling as to non-interest arbitration groups. Even if PERC deems waivers to be a bargainable subject for non-interest arbitration groups, it seems unlikely that PERC would allow an employer to unilaterally implement its management rights clause. Therefore, an employer who implements its settlement offer will have to walk away from whatever contractual waivers it may have acquired in the prior agreement.

Fourth, implementation may not entirely conclude all bargaining. If a change in circumstances or change in the union position arises, the union may renew its demand to bargain.

Fifth, the unilateral implementation technique does not rapidly resolve the issue. The employer must wait *at least* one year before implementing, and even then not until bargaining has been sufficiently exhausted so the parties might be deemed to be "at impasse."

PERC takes seriously the obligation of the parties to engage in good faith collective bargaining. Unilateral implementations have been rare precisely because most advocates expect that PERC will closely scrutinize any unilaterally implemented offer. Given the substantial risk that the union will find one way or another to

---

57 *See Morton General Hospital*, Decision 2217 (PECB, 1985); *Fort Vancouver Regional Library*, Decision 2350-C (PECB, 1988).

challenge the implemented offer, most employers have found it more prudent to exhaust the bargaining process and arrive at a new contract which is *mutually* agreeable. Nonetheless, the right to unilaterally implement leaves in the employer's hands the strongest card in the collective bargaining process.

an employer may never implement on a mandatory subject of bargaining with a group that is covered by the interest arbitration provisions of PECBA

As indicated above, RCW 41.56.123 concerns unilateral implementation for non-interest arbitration groups and has *no application* to interest arbitration groups. In fact, the legislature has made clear that for interest arbitration groups, an employer is *never* able to unilaterally implement a mandatory subject of bargaining:

> During the pendency of the proceedings before the arbitration panel, existing wages, hours and other conditions of employment shall not be changed by action of either party without the consent of the other party....[58]

In short, an employer may never implement on a mandatory subject of bargaining with a group that is covered by the interest arbitration provisions of PECBA. Instead, employers must negotiate, mediate and — if still unsuccessful — arbitrate.

Given these stringent conditions, it is understandable why then there would be so much focus on whether an issue falls within the scope of bargaining. If an issue falls within the scope of bargaining, an employer must either reach an agreement or go through each of these steps, and *even then* it has no guaranty whatsoever that an arbitrator will agree to allow it to make the change. On the other hand, if the subject falls outside the scope of bargaining, the employer has no obligation whatsoever to even discuss the issue with the union and may unilaterally implement at its pleasure.

---

[58] RCW 41.56.470.

Practice Pointers:

- As to non-interest arbitration groups, maintain good records on the history of your bargaining efforts. You will need them if the employer unilaterally implements and you want to demonstrate it was premature or that bargaining occurred in bad faith.

- As to non-interest arbitration groups, recognize that ultimately it is very difficult to block an employer determined to unilaterally implement. Calibrate into your negotiations strategy the recognition that the employer has this ability.

- As to interest arbitration eligible groups, recognize any employer claim that they can implement after they have exhausted bargaining with you has no basis in law.

b. The De Minimus Defense

PERC has recognized a defense to a unilateral change ULP that the change was *de minimus*. The *de minimus* defense is available in cases where the change at issue technically involves a mandatory subject of bargaining, but the nature of the change is so insubstantial it does not incur a bargaining obligation. PERC finds a ULP to be committed when a change in working conditions has a "substantial" impact on the bargaining unit and

PERC cases in this area have not shed too much light on what actually would constitute a *de minimus* change. Their approach might fairly be characterized as one in which "they know it when they see it." In reality, the judgment of whether a matter is or is not *de minimus* tends to be a practical one. PERC balances the interests of the union in being able to negotiate something that truly affects its employees against management's interest in not being tied up in negotiations over small matters.

The *de minimus* defense is available in cases where the change at issue technically involves a mandatory subject of bargaining, but the nature of the change is so insubstantial it does not incur a bargaining obligation.

PERC has rejected employer arguments that a matter is *de minimus* simply because it only affects a few employees.[59] The test,

PERC has indicated, is not how many employees might be affected by a given change but how substantially it affects those employees.

A case that provides a good illustration of the *de minimus* doctrine is the Commission's decision in *Lake Chelan School District.*[60] Technically, the scope of an employee's duties are a mandatory subject of bargaining, and in this case the union filed a ULP when the school district ordered teachers to go outside before and after school and monitor the parking lot. But PERC deemed the change not to be significant enough to mandate negotiations.

Practice Pointers:

- Be realistic in evaluating whether a change really impacts the bargaining unit. Confer with legal counsel to assist as needed.

- If you believe it does and the employer disagrees, be prepared to document the way it impacts employees.

c. *The "No Change to the Bargaining Unit, Only the Application of a Rule to an Individual" Defense*

In the past few years, PERC has selectively applied a controversial exemption to bargaining. In a handful of cases, PERC has found that where the issue involved is whether a policy is applied properly to a given individual there is no ULP.[61] PERC's reasoning is that these cases do not involve a change in past practice, but merely the application of the past practice to a given individual.

Although there might be some logic in the notion that there is a distinction between a change in past practice and the application of the past practice, this line is a fuzzy one and this test will likely ultimately prove not to be workable. In other contexts, PERC has required unions to assert its bargaining rights when a rule is applied in a different manner or risk a later claim that the employer has already made the change in a past practice. PERC's cases in this area provide no guidance as to when or how a union is to raise an issue in which the employer is not following its past practices or how a union can avoid creating a new adverse past practice by not filing a ULP.

---

59 *See Richland School District*, Decision 6269 (PECB, 1998).
60 Decision 4940 (EDUC, 1994).
61 *Asotin County*, Decision 9549-A (PECB, 2007).

Practice Pointers:

- At a minimum, there should be a written objection and a grievance filed over any deviation from past practice.
- You should confer with counsel as to whether the pursuit of a grievance or ULP is the best recourse in the situation of a change impacting only one individual.
- If you do end up resolving the individual issue, you should strongly consider having the resolution in the form of an MOU that indicates that settlement is non-precedential.

d. The "Emergency" or Business Necessity Defense

Particularly in times of fiscal distress, employers may assert that they will avoid an obligation to bargain or even refuse to continue abiding by the collective bargaining agreement because of financial "emergencies." PERC has only considered the "emergency" defense in a limited number of occasions, but those cases indicate that it is not likely to view sympathetically such a defense absent truly extraordinary circumstances. Sometimes the defense is raised as a "business necessity" — usually where an employer asserts that events from third parties compelled the change at issue.

PERC Hearing Examiners have ruled on a *very limited* number of occasions that emergencies or business necessity did exist which created a defense to a refusal-to-bargain charge. In *Green River Community College*,[62] Hearing Examiner Martin Smith held that a "sickout" was tantamount to a strike and permitted the employer to reactivate a sick leave notification policy. In *Evergreen School District*, Hearing Examiner Mark Downing held there to be an emergency that permitted temporary skimming in order to deliver school books for which students had waited weeks.[63]

On the other hand, in *City of Sumner*,[64] the hearing examiner declined to find an "emergency" permitted the city to change paydays simply because the paydays did not conform to general accounting principles. The examiner noted that the city had failed to take all the available opportunities presented to it to engage in collective

[62] Decision 4008-A (PECB,1993).

[63] The facts of this case appear to more accurately belong in the category of "*de minimis* change."

[64] Decision 1839 (PECB,1984).

bargaining.

And in the *City of Tacoma,* the Commission rejected the claim that the emergency doctrine allowed the City to order a police officer to submit to a drug test after the parties had dragged their feet for years on drug testing and had reached no agreement as to a formal drug testing policy. (But perhaps aware of political ramifications, the Commission still dismissed the ULP, reasoning that the employer's past practice to perform medical fitness for duty examinations permitted the drug test.)

PERC has so infrequently addressed the "emergency" defense that a review of how other jurisdictions view the defense is useful to predict how PERC may respond to future issues. Other jurisdictions have recognized a defense tantamount to the emergency doctrine, normally referred to as the "business necessity" defense. A thorough discussion of this defense under Oregon and National Labor Relations Board law is set forth in Chicoine, *Business Necessity as a Defense to an Employer's Breach of Its Bargaining Duty Under the PECBA.*[65] Chicoine describes the employer's obligation under the defense:

> Even if the employer establishes a business necessity that warrants a unilateral change, the employer remains obligated to "engage....in as much good faith bargaining as circumstances allow." The business necessity defense modifies, but does not relieve, the employer's obligation to bargain.
>
> To comply fully with the bargaining obligation, the employer should be prepared to commence bargaining as soon as it becomes aware of exigent circumstances requiring a change in the status quo. Even if it takes some time for the employer to formulate its proposed change, the employer should consider notifying the union about the subject matter that the employer wishes to address.[66]

Under the National Labor Relations Act, only actions of a temporary nature have been allowed under the business necessity defense. For example, in *NLRB v. Powell Electric Mfg. Co.,*[67] the arbitrator allowed temporary rule changes so as to allow the company to continue operation during a strike, while in *American*

---

[65] 28 WILLAMETTE L. REV. 259 (1992).

[66] *Id.* at 277.

[67] 906 F.2d 1007 (5th Cir. 1990).

Cyanamid Co.[68] the arbitrator determined the employer commmitted a ULP when it used the strike to contract out work permanently. The NLRB has not allowed employers to use the economic necessity defense to repudiate collective bargaining agreements.[69]

A review of case law by PERC and other jurisdictions suggests five principles or tests to be applied to a claimed "emergency" or "business necessity" defense:

1) The employer has the burden to establish the defense;

2) The employer must give the union notice of the emergency situation as soon as possible;

3) The employer must engage in every reasonable opportunity to negotiate the matter as the circumstances of the emergency allow;

4) Whatever change the emergency requires must be made only on a temporary basis;

5) The defense is not available where employers have had prior opportunities to bargain the subject matter but have failed to complete such negotiations.

Only more recently PERC has not had occasion to assess an emergency defense under circumstances involving fiscal distress. In 2009, PERC considered three difference cases in which employers argued that their fiscal constraints forced them to furlough employees. The wage reductions caused by the reduced hours of work were intended to balance the budget. In each case, the argument was rejected.[70] Something tantamount to a bankruptcy or potential bankruptcy would likely be required before PERC would be persuaded a sufficient business necessity existed warranting unilateral employer action.

Practice Pointers:

---

[68] 592 F.2d 356 (7th Cir. 1979).

[69] *See, e.g., Willis Electric*, 116 LRRM 1045, 1046 (1984).

[70] *Griffin School District*, Decision 10489-A (PECB, 2010); *King County*, Decision 10576-A (PECB, 2010); *King County*, Decision 10547-A (PECB, 2010).

- Emergency/Necessity claims are frequently made and seldom proven.

- In the face of such claims, be prepared to present detailed information requests inquiring about the underlying circumstances, including available options.

- Don't refuse employer requests to bargain predicated on an "emergency" even if the matter is settled by your CBA. While many of these claims are misplaced, hear out the employer and use that as an opportunity to evaluate their claim.

- If the union is aware of potential options, at least identify those to the employer, even if you are not prepared to propose that as a solution. Evidence that an employer took more extreme action when more moderate option existed is good evidence they were not acting in response to the emergency at all.

C. The Obligation to Engage in Bargaining in Good Faith

The last section addressed *when* the parties have a duty to bargain. This section addresses *how* the parties must bargain.

1. The General Nature of the Obligation to Bargain in Good Faith

The statutory definition of "collective bargaining" provides some insight into the nature of the obligation of parties to bargain in "good faith." That section of the statute provides:

> [T]he performance of the mutual obligation of the public employer and the exclusive bargaining representative to meet at reasonable times, to confer, negotiate in good faith, and to execute a written agreement...except that by such obligation *neither party shall be compelled to agree to a proposal or be required to make a concession unless otherwise provided in this chapter.*[71]

[71] RCW 41.56.030(4).

PERC assesses good faith questions and procedural objections by a "totality of the circumstances" standard

An employer that unilaterally changes working conditions has committed what PERC calls a *per se* — automatic — violation of the statute. When the issue is not whether a unilateral change was made but whether the parties' negotiations were in good faith and followed proper procedures, PERC rarely finds a *per se* violation. Instead, PERC assesses good faith questions and procedural objections by a "totality of the circumstances" standard.[72]

This "totality of the circumstances" approach is consistent with how other labor boards have addressed "good faith" bargaining issues and is probably consistent with PERC's statutory mandate. Nonetheless, it makes it difficult to predict in any given case whether PERC will actually find the party's conduct to rise to the level of a ULP.

The uncertainty about whether bad faith bargaining will be found is further aggravated by limited remedies for established violations. PERC's remedies for such violations have generally been so limited so as not to create much of a deterrent for those who shirk their bargaining obligations. This problem is endemic in a system which effectively rewards employers who engage in delaying tactics: Such employers not only keep the interest they accrue on the higher wage they would otherwise be paying, but they also acquire greater bargaining leverage. In reality, frustrated members often are willing to make greater concessions as the size of the retroactive payment grows ever larger, and the history of the last wage increase grows dimmer.

The uncertainty about whether bad faith bargaining will be found is further aggravated by limited remedies for established violations.

Union bargaining teams that grow restless with stalled negotiations are often frustrated with PERC's approach. Given the relatively few times in which PERC has actually found that an employer committed a ULP through failure to bargain in good faith,

[72] *See Mansfield School District*, Decision 4552 (EDUC, 1993); *Fort Vancouver Regional Library*, Decision 2396 (PECB, 1986).

their frustration is warranted. At least one option is to *threaten* to file the ULP and then follow through when it fails to produce necessary results. Even though PERC's remedies have been limited in this area, the *pursuit* of such a ULP may have both internal and external political benefits that might kick-start the bargaining process again.

In assessing whether a party is bargaining in good faith, it is important to bear in mind that the statute explicitly indicates that in creating the obligation to bargain it was the legislature's intent that "by such obligation neither party shall be compelled to agree to a proposal or be required to make a concession unless otherwise provided in this chapter."[73] (The reference to "unless otherwise provided in this chapter" is an obvious reference to the interest arbitration provisions by which parties can, in fact, be compelled to submit to changes in their contract.)

This relates to a key misunderstanding employees often having regarding the term "good faith": Both the union and the employer have a right to say "no" to whatever proposal they do not wish to agree to. Just because a party is being hard-nosed or unreasonable does equate to bargaining in "bad faith." The statute protects the parties' rights to be difficult as long as they engage in communications as to why they are being difficult. Therefore, PERC will not find a ULP simply because a party is not giving the other side what it wants.

On the other hand, a close review of PERC precedent indicates that where parties have engaged in "hard bargaining" tactics, accompanied by other procedural violations, PERC is much more likely to find a violation of a duty to bargain. True, a party does not have an obligation to make specific concessions. But it cannot use tactics of evasion and avoidance to prevent *discussing* why it is justified in its rigid proposals. Therefore, while a party has a right to stake out a tough bargaining position, with it does so it should tread carefully because that conduct could be cited with other indicia of bad faith under the "totality of circumstances" test.

It is true that PECBA does not *compel* either party to make concessions. But a party must be willing to *consider alternatives and discuss them.* The obligation to bargain in good faith "encompasses a duty to engage in full and frank discussions on disputed issues, and to explore possible alternatives, if any, that may achieve a mutually satisfactory accommodation of the interests of both the employer and employee."[74]

---

[73] RCW 41.56.030.

PERC has said that a party may not "reduce collective bargaining to an exercise in futility."[75] Parties must enter negotiations "with a view towards reaching agreement.[76]" It has also said that "[g]ood faith is inconsistent with a predetermined resolve not to budge from an initial position."[77] Although this view is controversial and not consistently applied, PERC has ruled that it is bad faith bargaining for an employer to present "proposals which it knew were consistently and predictably unpalatable to the union and by failing to exert every reasonable effort to reach agreement."[78]

PERC has elaborated on the need for communication:

> Good faith bargaining requires full and frank discussions on disputed issues. There is no requirement that agreement be reached on every issue but an employer is expected to evidence some willingness to address a union's legitimate concerns. In rejecting union proposals the employer considered such matters as management rights, reduction in force, past practices, and supplemental contracts, to be the responsibility of management. It is not enough to repetitively invoke "management rights" without engaging in meaningful attempts to see if mutual accommodation is possible.[79]

There are several ways in which a party can breach defined standards for good faith bargaining. This section will review a number of tactics that have been found unlawful. Generally, though, the "totality of circumstances" approach indicates that PERC is unlikely to find a ULP where the procedural violations have been isolated. When PERC has found a breach of the obligation to bargain in good faith, there has usually been a continued use of improper bargaining tactics.

2. Tactics of Evasion

Both parties have a mutual obligation to meet and negotiate. PERC has repeatedly found it to be a ULP for parties to place

---

[74] *Mansfield School District*, Decision 4552-B (EDUC, 1995).
[75] *Mason County*, Decision 2706-A (PECB, 1991).
[76] *Snohomish County*, Decision 1661-A (PECB, 1984)
[77] *Yakima Valley Community College*, Decision 11.326-A (PECB, 2013). See also, *Kennewick General Hospital*, Decision 4815-A (PECB, 1996).
[78] *Mansfield School District*, Decision 4552-B (EDUC, 1995).
[79] *Id.*

preconditions on negotiations. For example, PERC has found it to be a ULP for an employer to refuse to meet with a union until there is an agreement concerning the ground rules over the meeting.[80] Ground rules are a permissive subject of bargaining, and if the parties cannot reach an agreement on the ground rules they have to forego the ground rules and proceed to discuss the issues.

While that is the stated standard, the "no preconditions" rule sets up some practical challenges. PERC has yet to address the situation, for example, where the inability of the parties to agree on the procedures for the meeting actually kept them physically apart. It is an open and interesting question what PERC would do when the parties were unable to reach an agreement on questions such as the time and location of the actual meeting or the length of the bargaining session. Likely, PERC would approach this question from its "totality of the circumstances" approach in determining whether a party or the other was actually trying to avoid negotiations. As a practical matter, if a party faces an impasse at the outset over such meeting conditions, the best approach is simply to file immediately for mediation with PERC and the mediator will surely direct one party or the other to appear at a certain place or time.

Certainly the obligation to bargain in good faith means to be willing to discuss *any and all* proposals that are put forth by one side or the other whenever those proposals fall within the scope of bargaining. Therefore, PERC found it an unfair labor practice when one employer declared impasse in contract negotiations simply because the union insisted on presenting its proposal concerning the single item — a union security clause — which the employer was adamantly opposed to.[81] Again, a party has a right to *refuse to agree* to a party's proposal, but it has no right to *refuse to discuss* the proposal.

Another common tactic of avoidance — particularly for certain negotiators — is to refuse to meet on a prompt and frequent basis. PERC has established no clear rule for when the delay between meetings is too long. PERC likely would look at the "totality of the circumstances." PERC has found that the refusal or failure to meet with a union for a period of three months during negotiations constituted bad faith bargaining.[82] And in another case, PERC found a delay for even as brief of a period as one month between

---

80 *City of Sumner*; *Adams County*, Decision 4006 (PECB, 1992).
81 *Walla Walla County*, Decision 2932 (PECB, 1998).
82 *Fort Vancouver Regional Library*, Decision 2396 (PECB, 1986).

negotiation sessions was a ULP — where it occurred at a critical time in negotiations.[83]

PERC has found that the unilateral cancelation of bargaining meetings by an employer is an "example of its intention to delay and frustrate bargaining."[84] An employer canceling a negotiating session is "another example of a pattern on the part of the employer designed to frustrate and delay bargaining with the union in violation of its good faith bargaining obligation."[85]

As suggested earlier, where an employer refuses to meet on a sufficiently frequent basis, the best approach is simply to file for mediation and let the mediator tell the employer when and where they will appear for negotiations.

Practice Pointers:

- You are allowed to propose ground rules. But be careful not to insist on "preconditions" on meeting.
- PERC has not clarified how to respond when the parties cannot even mutually agree on when or where to meet. Try to be flexible as possible. Document the employer's difficult response.
- If disagreement about the meeting process continues, invoke mediation. The mediator will find likely a way over the precondition hurdles.

---

the failure to vest the negotiator with sufficient authority to reach agreement is a ULP

---

3. Superficial or Regressive Bargaining

Employers have invented and apply a whole range of other tactics that can be used to defeat the reaching of an agreement. The most commonly employed tactic is simply to send a management representative to the table who has little or no authority. PERC has said on a number of occasions that the failure to vest the negotiator with sufficient authority to reach agreement is a ULP.

[83] *Morton General Hospital*, Decision 2217 (PECB, 1985).
[84] *Snohomish County*, Decision 9834 (PECB, 2007).
[85] *Snohomish County*, Decision 9834-B (PECB, 2008).

Unfortunately, PERC has not been clear on how much authority that might require. In at least one case, for example, PERC indicated that it was appropriate for a negotiator to be bargaining only within defined parameters so long as the negotiator had a willingness to discuss proposals outside those parameters.[86] Yet in other cases PERC has indicated that the negotiator must have full authority to enter into at least a tentative agreement.[87]

Unfortunately, PERC has not been clear on how much authority that might require.

Sometimes conflicts over the authority of the negotiator arise during county negotiations. In counties, where there are multiple independent elected officials, all have a right to participate in the process. Where, for example, there is a sheriff and a set of county commissioners that both insist on certain proposals as a condition of a contract, there is a possibility that the county's chief negotiator might not have clear authority. PERC has found it a ULP for county elected officials to insist that unions enter into separate agreements with each set of officials. Instead, PERC requires that the county officials themselves coalesce into a single bargaining team with a single bargaining strategy.[88]

It is an unfair labor practice to engage in what has been labeled "surface bargaining." Surface bargaining again is hard to define, and this is another example where PERC tends to use a "we'll know it when we see it" approach. In general, though, surface bargaining occurs where the party conveys the superficial appearance of being engaged in the process but in reality is not.

A good example of unlawful surface bargaining is found in PERC's decision in *Mansfield School District*[89] There, PERC noted that the obligation to bargain in good faith "encompasses a duty to engage in full and frank discussions on disputed issues, and to explore possible alternatives, if any, that may achieve a mutually satisfactory accommodation of the interests of both the employer and employee."[90]PERC elaborated further:

---

[86] *Mansfield School District*, Decision 4552 (EDUC, 1993).
[87] *See, e.g., City of Poulsbo*, Decision 2068 (PECB, 1984).
[88] *See, e.g., Lewis County*, Decision 2957 (PECB, 1988).
[89] Decision 4552 (EDUC, 1995).
[90] *Mansfield School District*, Decision 4552-B (EDUC, 1995).

> Good faith bargaining requires full and frank discussions on disputed issues. There is no requirement that agreement be reached on every issue but an employer is expected to evidence some willingness to address a union's legitimate concerns. In rejecting union proposals the employer considered such matters as management rights, reduction in force, past practices, and supplemental contracts, to be the responsibility of management. It is not enough to repetitively invoke "management rights" without engaging in meaningful attempts to see if mutual accommodation is possible.[91]

PERC has also said that a party may not reduce collective bargaining to "an exercise in futility."[92]

PERC has found other conduct to constitute bad faith bargaining:

- Coming to the bargaining table with a preconceived position and being unwilling to reconsider it.[93]
- Cancelling negotiations because management officials were angry about newspaper coverage on their poor labor relations.[94]
- "Exploding" angrily and storming out of negotiations.[95]
- Refusing to negotiate further and retrenching from potential offers because the union had served management officials with subpoenas in different proceeding.[96]
- Refusing to undertake calculations needed to determine payments owed to employees.[97]
- Threatening layoffs late in the bargaining process in response to a union proposal.[98]

---

[91] *Id.*
[92] *Mason County,* Decision 2706-A (PECB, 1991).
[93] *Yakima Valley Community College,* Decision 11326-A (PECB, 2013).
[94] *Snohomish County,* Decision 9834 (PSRA, 2007).
[95] *Colfax School District,* Decisions 9940-41 (PECB, 2007).
[96] *Grant County Public Hospital Dist. 1,* Decision 8378-A (PECB, 2004).
[97] *Spokane County,* Decision 8154 (PECB, 2003).
[98] *Public Utility District No.1 of Clark County,* Decision 2045-A (PECB,1989).

- Refusing to agree to a proposal on one item to "punish" the union for not promptly accepting an employer wage proposal.[99]

All of these type of conduct, though, will be judged under a "totality of circumstances" test and does not necessarily constitute a "per se" ULP.

A more clear-cut example of bad faith bargaining occurs when a party is actually "regressive." "Regressive bargaining" occurs when a party moves away from a proposal that it has previously presented to a less favorable position without a clear justification for doing so. Withdrawing from tentative agreements can also be unlawful regressive bargaining.[100] Withdrawing a proposal because you have "changed your mind" is also considered regressive.[101]

One recognized justification for a change in a proposal occurs when a proposal has been made as part of a "package." PERC permits "what if" packages as a way for a party, particularly those involved in interest arbitration, to preserve a "protected position" which could later be submitted to an arbitrator. But even a package approach can land a party in a ULP where the subsequent packages move further away, not closer to, an agreement. PERC has generally found it to be a ULP where a party — without justification — either withdraws certain proposals or escalates its bargaining demands.[102]

Unions can also be guilty of regressive bargaining. When a police union made a last minute escalation after a verbal agreement had been reached on a program that was due to expire, PERC found it had committed a ULP.[103]

Public employers are obligated to provide reasonably prompt responses to relevant information requested by the union.

---

[99] *Western Washington University*, Decision 9309 (PSRA, 2006).

[100] *Seattle School District*, Decision 10037 (PECB, 2008).

[101] *City of Redmond*, Decision 8879-A (PECB, 2006).

[102] *City of Milton*, Decision 4512 (PECB, 1993); *Skagit County*, Decision 6348 (PECB, 1998); *Asotin County*, Decision 4568-C (PECB, 1996); *Spokane County Fire Protection District No. 1*, Decision 3447A (PECB, 1990).

[103] *City of Vancouver*, Decision 10616 (PECB, 2009).

4. Refusal to Provide Bargaining Information

The Commission has held that a refusal to provide relevant information is a "refusal to bargain" ULP under RCW 41.56.140(4).[104] Public employers are obligated to provide reasonably prompt responses to relevant information requested by the union.[105]

Refusal to provide information is deemed to be a "refusal to bargain" in recognition that, without requested relevant information, it will often be difficult, if not impossible, for the parties to reach an agreement. For example, where an employer is insisting it has no ability to pay for a union's wage proposal, it has the obligation to provide extensive fiscal information — when requested — which the union could use to evaluate such a claim. An employer's failure to produce that information would only leave the union puzzled as to how to respond to the claims of poverty.

A party has the obligation to provide virtually any item of evidence which might be relevant to an issue in bargaining. Although the "burdensome" nature of the bargaining request might be a factor in permitting a party not to respond at least in full, PERC has yet to issue a ruling where it found the requested information to be too burdensome to produce. Instead, PERC has repeatedly mandated a party to produce information once it is deemed relevant.[106]

But there is at least one case when PERC, although requiring the employer to provide a response that was "large and complex," nonetheless refused the union's demand that the information be provided in less than three months. The employer had justified to PERC that it would simply take more than three months to fulfill the request.[107] The keystone is "reasonableness, both as to the nature of the request and the requested timetable for production.

Practice pointers:

- Parties requesting such information should put the request in writing so that it is clear and a record is made.

---

[104] *State of Washington*, Decision 4710 (PECB, 1994).
[105] *City of Bellevue*, Decision 432-A (PECB, 1994).
[106] *See City of Seattle*, Decision 3066-A (PECB, 1989); *Public Utility District No. 1 of Clark County*, Decision 3815-A (PECB, 1992).
[107] *Port of Seattle*, Decision 4989 (PECB, 1995).

- When the employer makes proposals or takes positions that are difficult to assess on what they have provided, exercise your right to request information.

- Frame your request in a reasonable way both as to the scope of the request and the timetable. But request that records be produced on a "rolling" (as available) basis, especially on a detailed request, so you get some of the documents sooner.

- Invoke the Public Records Act in your request. The PRA remedies are quite a bit more robust than PERC's remedies and include attorney fees. The reality of PRA remedies often persuades more prompt responses from employers than the potential PERC remedies.

5. Refusal to Create a Contract

There are a number of ways in which parties can frustrate the process so that an agreement is never reached, even after they *appear* otherwise to be engaged in bargaining. PERC has deemed such roadblocks to constitute bad faith bargaining.

PERC has found insisting to impasse on a permissive subject of bargaining — for either the employer or the union — to be a *per se* unfair labor practice.

One way to impede an agreement is for one party or another to insist on a "permissive" subject of bargaining as a precondition to an agreement. As addressed above, PERC has found insisting to impasse on a permissive subject of bargaining — for either the employer or the union — to be a *per se* unfair labor practice. In other words, a party may not "hold hostage" a contract to a concession on issues over which the other party is not obligated to negotiate. PERC's *per se* approach to this issue is necessary to prevent parties from circumventing the defined statutory scope of bargaining.

In reality, unfortunately, PERC's mandatory/permissive dichotomy rules have had limited success in curtailing permissive proposals. The parties are *allowed* to make proposals that are permissive; they simply are not allowed to pursue all the way to impasse on such proposals. PERC takes a very narrow view of what constitutes an actual "impasse." Therefore, in reality, if the contract is actually being held up over some permissive issue, it may be difficult for the party not willing to bargain that issue to avoid addressing it.

On the other hand, for those parties who have interest arbitration, the rule is clear — permissive subjects of bargaining may not be submitted to interest arbitration and it is a ULP to insist on doing so. In short, the parties are required to withdraw their permissive proposals at the time they are certified for arbitration or else they will be committing a ULP.

The collective bargaining statute requires parties to work towards a "written agreement."[108] PERC has yet to address the question of whether the obligation to work towards a written agreement also mandates that parties place their *proposals* in writing. One tactic parties sometimes use to avoid bargaining is to make the proposals verbally, in which event it is not clear to the other party exactly how the proposal would work. Likely, if PERC were to address this issue, it would mandate that all proposals be put in writing upon request but that has yet to occur.

PERC has been clear, though, that failure to make counterproposals can be seen — as part of a "totality of circumstances" approach — to be bad faith bargaining.[109] Granted, the statute does not compel agreement and parties are not *required* to make concessions, but the absence of a counterproposal might be seen as at least one indication that the party is not working towards an agreement. Certainly the parties have to put forward *some type* of proposal, because without a proposal — even if it is only for the *status quo* — there will never be an agreement.

Once an agreement is reached between the parties at the table, the road toward final execution can sometimes have some bumps. And PERC's cases have provided some inconsistent guidance on how those "bumps" are addressed.

First, it is generally understood that parties at the table, even when they have actual authority, have *limited* authority. In other words, chief negotiators usually come to the table with authority to enter "tentative agreements," but with the understanding that *those agreements are subject to ratification by the parties they represent.* Therefore, generally, it is not a ULP for a party to come back after a ratification meeting and indicate that the proposal was

---

[108] RCW 41.56.030(4).

[109] *See Marietta Water District No. 2*, Decision 937 (PECB, 1980); *but see Fort Vancouver Regional Library District*, Decision 2396 (PECB, 1986) (parties are not specifically required to make counterproposals); *Mansfield School District*, Decision 4552 (EDUC, 1993) (same).

rejected.[110]

But there are even exceptions to this approach. Where a party extracted concessions from the other side, for example, by indicating that it had full authority by the actual decisionmaker, and then later that decisionmaker did not ratify the agreement, a ULP could be found.[111] Certainly, city council or county commissioners generally remain free to reject the tentative agreement that was reached by their negotiator; but they are not free to reject an agreement that they had already specifically authorized in advance without some justification beyond having simply changed their minds.

An example of this occurred in *Kitsap County.*[112] During negotiations the parties had on-going discussions regarding compensatory time. Finally, the County generated a compromise proposal. The Guild accepted it. It had been a challenging issue and agreement on that point cleared the way for a contract. Later a civil deputy prosecutor reviewed it and found it unacceptable, erroneously claiming that the agreement violated federal law. She persuaded the commissioners to vote down the contract *because of* the proposal the County had made. The union filed a ULP and PERC agreed that it was a ULP for the County to refuse to ratify a contract that based on language they had proposed.

The rules are even clearer where both parties have actually ratified the agreement. Once an agreement is ratified by both parties, the obligation to execute a written agreement controls.[113] And this is true even where a party learns after ratification that a mistake has been made in the drafting of the agreement.[114]

Complications sometimes arise in the context of interest arbitration. A party faced with a final order by an arbitrator is not free to reject the arbitrator's order in a "ratification" meeting. The order is an order and, unless the parties mutually agree to renegotiate the ordered language, that language must be incorporated into the agreement. And that agreement needs to include all the prior tentative agreements that have been reached, even if they were not ratified.

A party submitting a matter to arbitration who wishes to have their principals pass on the tentative agreements not being forwarded to arbitration need to do that prior to the time in which

---

110 *Mason County v. PERC*, 54 Wn. App. 36, 771 P.2d 1185 (1989).

111 *See, e.g., City of Fife*, Decision 5645 (PECB, 1986).

112 *Kitsap County*, Decision 11675 (PECB, 2013).

113 *Kiona-Benton School District*, Decision 4312 (PECB, 1993).

114 *See Kitsap Transit Authority*, Decision 5143 (PECB, 1995).

the other issues are certified for arbitration. If a party fails to do so, PERC will have deemed the right to reject the proposals as having been waived, as it will not accept a party's refusal to execute an agreement after interest arbitration award by rejecting previously reached tentative agreements.

Direct dealing is *per se* unlawful, but direct communications may or may not be unlawful, depending upon the circumstances.

On the other hand, a party is not required to execute a partial agreement for those matters tentatively agreed upon when other matters are submitted to arbitration.[115] PERC has found it lawful for a party to hold those tentative agreements in abeyance until an entire successor agreement is reached.

6. Circumvention of the Bargaining Representative

There are two primary means in which an employer can "circumvent" the union and directly deal in negotiations with employees: direct dealing and direct communications. Direct dealing is *per se* unlawful, but direct communications may or may not be unlawful, depending upon the circumstances.

When a union is certified as the collective bargaining representative, the statute clearly requires *collective* bargaining. In other words, there will only be a single agreement with the union absent a union's acquiescence to individual side agreements.

Individual agreements between an employer and an employee are generally disallowed where a union has an exclusive bargaining relationship.[116] Such individual agreements are unlawful, and rescission of the contract is usually ordered.[117]

For example, in *Washington State Patrol*,[118] PERC ordered set aside a "last chance agreement" that the Patrol signed with a trooper over the union's objection. PERC emphasized that it was not ruling that the employer had to negotiate with the union over what discipline it imposed. Instead, it was pointing out that the agreement — which would have waived the just cause provisions in a subsequent infraction — constituted an alteration to the parties'

[115] *Snohomish County*, Decision 5578-A (PECB, 1996).
[116] *See, e.g., J.I. Case Co. v. NLRB*, 321 U.S. 332, 64 S.Ct. 576, 88 L.Ed. 762 (1944).
[117] *See, e.g., North Coast Cleaning Service*, 272 NLRB 1343 (1984).
[118] Decision 4757 (PECB, 1994).

CBA which the individual was not authorized to waive.

In other contexts, PERC has also found direct negotiations with employees to be unlawful.[119] And in perhaps the most egregious violation, the employer made an offer directly to the employees, told the employees that they needed to vote on the offer on the spot, and also told them they were not going to make the same offer later to their union. PERC had no difficulty in finding this to be a ULP.[120]

PERC has distinguished, though, between direct communications with employees about negotiations versus direct negotiations. An employer has certain "free speech" rights which allow it — within certain parameters — to communicate directly with employees concerning those negotiations.[121] There are two primary rules that govern such communications. First, the materials must be substantially truthful and may not misrepresent facts about what has been proposed.[122] Second, in making these communications, an employer is not allowed to present to the employees a new proposal that it has not previously presented to the union. The reason for this is clear: It frustrates the bargaining process for the employer to fail to make a proposal to the union which it is willing to make while at the same time confusing the employees into thinking that the union itself has not communicated the status of contract negotiations correctly.

7. "Me Too" Clauses

A "me too" clause is a contract provision whereby one bargaining unit has a condition in their contract that if *another* bargaining unit acquires a certain benefit or working condition such benefit or working condition will be automatically passed along to the other union, without any further negotiations. A thoughtful consideration of this practice clearly indicates the insidious impact this has on contract negotiations.

For example, if an employer places a "me too" agreement in its other contracts that if any other union acquires orthodontia

---

[119] *See, e.g., Shelton School District*, Decision 579 (EDUC, 1984).

[120] *Wellpinit School District*, Decision 5083 (PECB, 1992).

[121] *See, e.g., Seattle School District*, Decision 2079 (PECB 1984); *City of Seattle*, Decision 3566-A (PECB 1991); *METRO*, Decision 2197 (PECB, 1985); *Lake Washington School District*, Decision 2483 (EDUC, 1986); *Centralia School District*, Decision 2757 (PECB, 1987).

[122] *Lake Washington School District*, Decision 2483 (EDUC, 1986); *Spokane County*, Decision 2793 (PECB, 1987); Vancouver School District, Decision 10561 (EDUC, 2009).

benefits that union will as well, it makes it difficult — indeed unlikely — that it will agree to extend that benefit to another union which might be seeking to negotiate it. The impact of "me too" clauses is that one union ends up negotiating for other unions. It is particularly onerous for groups that have the right to interest arbitration — they end up carrying the weight of other bargaining units on their backs.

Despite the impact these clauses have on bargaining PERC has yet to rule that they are "per se" unlawful, contrary to the holdings of most other public labor boards. PERC has held that the union must show the clause has specifically prevented an agreement. Contrary to other labor board rulings, impeding the agreement is considered insufficient.[123]

D. Other Issues with the Execution of an Agreement

1. Public Meetings Act

The Public Meetings Act requires that governing bodies of public agencies, such as city councils or county commissioners, conduct open meetings when they adopt ordinances and resolutions.[124] Because contract ratifications are always presented in the form of an ordinance, this chapter applies to such ratifications. This requirement can contain a pitfall for the ratification of labor agreements.

The Public Meetings Act also allows the governing bodies to go into executive session for key confidential discussions, including information related to the ratification of a labor agreement. Generally, governing bodies will go into executive session while they review the terms of an agreement and obtain advice on whether or not to ratify. Under the Public Meetings Act, these bodies are required, at the least, to go back out on the record in an open meeting before they formally ratify the agreement.

When they fail to do so, this can lead to complications. Mason County was involved in extensive litigation, both before PERC and the courts, which finally resulted in a once-ratified labor agreement being thrown out.

In *Mason County*, the Commissioners met in a private meeting to review the labor agreement and ratified it there. Later,

---

[123] *City of Kelso*, Decision 11672 (PECB, 2013); *Whatcom County*, Decision 8512-A (PECB, 2005).

[124] *See* RCW 42.30.060.

apparently, they got cold feet, and the issue of whether the ratification was proper under the Public Meetings Act was raised. They concluded it was not proper and held a public meeting, at which point they voted down the contract.

The union filed a ULP with PERC. PERC ruled for the union, holding that while there was a defect in the Public Meetings Act requirements, it was "curable" and that Mason County meet its obligation to bargain in good faith by refusing to cure.[125]

Mason County appealed through the courts. Ultimately, the Court of Appeals ruled for Mason County. They held that it was not a ULP for an employer to change its vote after it went through a public vote on a contract. The court reasoned that the prior agreement was "void."

The case should be understood in its limited context. The union was trying to insist that essentially the county was bound by its prior improper ratification. There is nothing in the *Mason County* decision which holds that the county commissioners cannot ratify a contract; it simply holds that they have a right in the public meeting to make an independent decision. As frustrating as this may be for a union which has an ratified agreement disappear, this is probably consistent with the purpose of the Public Meetings Act, which is to require that governing bodies are held accountable by making decisions in public.

Another aspect of the Public Meetings Act is of interest to labor negotiators. The Public Meetings Act makes a specific exclusion in the public meeting requirement for contract negotiations.[126] But this is different than the process of ratifying a contract.

2. The Requirement to Make Timely Retroactive Wage Payments

The rules concerning whether and how collective bargaining agreements are retroactive are fairly clear cut, but frequently misunderstood.

The general principle that applies to the question of retroactivity of collective bargaining agreements is clear: *Economic terms are presumed retroactive and non- economic terms are presumed to be non-retroactive.* The presumption is a "rebuttable" one. In other words, if by the terms of the labor agreement the parties explicitly rewrite the rules concerning retroactivity, those rules will apply. But when the contract is silent, the presumption

---

125 *See Mason County*, Decision 2307-A (PECB, 1986).

126 RCW 42.30.140(4)(a).

controls.[127]

The requirement to pay retroactive wages applies not only to increases in the base monthly wage or salary but also to overtime payments. The best way to determine whether the employer has fully paid the retroactive wage owed is not simply to calculate the amount of the base monthly salary. Instead, you should take your total earnings for each year and measure your retroactivity owed against that. It also applies to other economic terms that might be changed. For example, if you increase the "callout" minimum from 3 hours to 4, the payroll department will need to go through the overtime slips and make those corrections retroactively so that every callout time was computed at not less than 4 hours.

Non-economic terms, on the other hand, by their nature are difficult to apply retroactively, and arbitrators generally will not do so. For example, if a new labor agreement includes an employee's bill of rights, the employer is not bound to have followed the new rules on prior discipline matters handled before the execution of the agreement.

The presumption of retroactivity also applies to those employees who have terminated their employment during the period of the expiration of the prior agreement and the execution of the new agreement.

Some contract items create problematic retroactivity issues. This is particularly the case for medical benefits. Even though medical benefits are an economic term, arbitrators not generally not require retroactive application of a newly agreed enhancement to the medical plan. But this point is at least arguable, so it ought to be entertained by the parties during negotiations. An increase in the employer pickup of the medical premium, on the other hand, is more purely an economic term and it is easy to calculate what the retroactive cost would be and arbitrators, therefore, will generally apply such an enhancement on a retroactive basis.

The presumption of retroactivity also applies to those employees who have terminated their employment during the period of the expiration of the prior agreement and the execution of the new agreement. Therefore, unless the CBA explicitly excludes such departing employees from the benefits of the agreement, they

---

[127] *Kitsap County v, Kitsap County Deputy Sheriff's Guild*, 148 Wn.App. 907, 201 P.2d 396 (2009).

are entitled to all retroactive economic enhancements through the last date of their employment.[128]

Questions sometimes arise concerning enforcing such rights for departed employees. Arbitrators and courts have generally acknowledged that there are two means to enforce such retroactivity rights: The union can pursue retroactivity for departing employees through the grievance and arbitration process or the former may bring their own action in court on an "intended beneficiary" theory.

A union's "duty of fair representation" does not mandate that the union pursue such issues to arbitration because the employee has an alternative forum in which to pursue the claim. But unions might want to pursue such claims on the notion that it is a benefit to all the continuing employees to know that they will be covered in the future if they depart between the expiration of an old agreement and the execution of a new agreement.

And, an even more compelling reason for pursuing this issue, is the long-term impact on negotiations. Allowing employers not to pay retroactivity to departing employees provides the employer an incentive to drag out negotiations, knowing that it will get to keep the otherwise payable wages of any employee who leaves in the interim. Some management negotiators even pride themselves on being able to withhold this money as they explain to their client that the retroactive savings paid the negotiator's fees.

Some employers like to tell employees that the employees will receive the "retro" checks when the payroll staff gets around to it. Such an approach is in violation of the law. The law has sufficient teeth in it that once an employer makes this mistake, they are unlikely to do it again.

RCW Chapter 39.76 requires that public entities that owe a debt must make the payment within 30 days of the execution of the debt. If an employer fails to make a timely payment within 30 days, it owes interest on the total sum owed. And the amount of the interest owed is simply not back to the 30th day, *but back to the first day on which the debt was incurred.*

The FLSA also requires that overtime owed be promptly paid, and it requires that overtime be recalculated under a retroactive labor agreement.

---

[128] *Barclay v. City of Spokane*, 83 Wn.2d 698, 700, 521 P.2d 937 (1974).

And the law provides a further vehicle for enforcing the right to interest on an untimely payment: The statute provides for attorney fees for prevailing parties in such a dispute.[129] Given that the interest payments are nominal, but the attorney fees are not, it is unlikely that the employer would make the mistake more than once of not making payments on time.

The FLSA also requires that overtime owed be promptly paid, and it requires that overtime be recalculated under a retroactive labor agreement.[130] What is common not understood or uniformly applied is that the FLSA requires that the retroactive overtime be paid at the time the wages under the contract are increased.[131] Therefore, an employer who fails to pay promptly retroactive overtime owed also faces a potential FLSA lawsuit.

[129] RCW 39.76.040.
[130] 29 C.F.R. § 778.303.
[131] 29 C.F.R. § 778.106

WAIVER BY CONTRACT TABLE

This table lists cases in which PERC has evaluated whether the union waived its right to bargain various topics.

Citation: *City of Lynnwood*, Decision 11614 (PECB, 2013) **Waiver Found: Yes**

Contract Language: Appendix E clearly states that the union cannot appeal how the employer uses the results of a compensation study.

Explanation: Examiner Nickleberry found that the employer did not breach its good faith bargaining obligations regarding the compensation study because the union had waived its right to bargain the outcome of the compensation study in its CBA. Examiner Nickleberry cited the entire relevant language of the CBA and found that the language was clear and unambiguous. Furthermore, it very specifically restricted which elements could not be grieved or arbitrated.

Citation: *Yakima County*, Decision 11621-A (PECB, 2013) **Waiver Found**: **No (Effects)** **Yes (Layoff)**

Contract Language: "The Sheriff and/or the Board of County Commissioners shall be the sole determiner of when layoffs are necessary. The Board may lay off employees when such action is determined to be necessary by reason of lack of work; lack of funds, and/or reorganization of the department. Each employee affected by a reduction in force/lay-off shall be notified in writing of the layoff and the reasons therefore at least fifteen days prior to the effective date of the layoff."

Explanation: The Commission stated that "[t]he union demanded to bargain both the decision and effects of the decision to lay off and reduce the rank of bargaining unit employees. While the union waived by contract its right to bargain the decision to lay off, the employer remained obligated to bargain, upon request, with the union over the effects of the decision to lay off employees." However, the Commission held that the "union did not waive, by contract, the right to bargain the effects of the employer's decision to lay off employees. The employer refused to bargain when it did not engage in effects bargaining with the union." The Commission held that "[t]he union maintained the right to raise and request to bargain other potential effects not addressed in the collective bargaining agreement." The Commission explained that the "parties anticipated and negotiated about, and included in the collective bargaining agreement, some of the potential effects of a decision to lay off. The collective bargaining agreement does not address all possible effects of such decisions."

Citation: *City of Mountlake Terrace*, Decision 11702 (PECB, 2013), *aff'd in part and rev'd in part*, Decision 11702-A (PECB, 2014)

Waiver Found: No

Contract Language: Section 9.3 of the parties' current collective bargaining agreement provides that officers' advance from one pay group to the next on the anniversary of their appointment. The advancement is "dependent upon confirmation by the Chief of Police that the employee has demonstrated his ability to satisfactorily perform the requirements of the position." It is referred to as experience achievement pay or step increases and represents an increase in salary. The language in the contract granting the increases dates back to at least 1985.

Explanation: Examiner Romeo found that the employer refused to bargain with the union by unilaterally changing when step increases are granted. The examiner rejected the employer's argument that the union contractually waived its right to bargain stating, "[w]hile the contract gives the chief the discretion to deny an increase, it has not been the practice to delay a step increase because someone had been previously disciplined. That is not a clear and unmistakable waiver by the union of the practice of an automatic step increase on an employee's anniversary date."

Citation: *University of Washington*, Decision 11600-A (PSRA, 2013)

Waiver Found:
No (Effects)
Yes (Schedule Change)

Contract Language:
"Hours of work for regular monthly employees in the bargaining units listed in Appendix 1 shall be established by the employing official....The Employer agrees to provide a minimum of fourteen (14) calendar days' notice to an employee in the event of an Employer-directed permanent change in the employee's shift assignment or work schedule."

"The Employer through its designated management personnel or agents has the right and responsibility, except as expressly modified by this Agreement, to control, change, and supervise all operations and to direct and assign work to all working forces. Such rights and responsibilities shall include by way of illustration but not be limited to: the selection and hiring; training; discipline and discharge; classification; reclassification; layoff; promotion and demotion or transfer of employees; the establishment of work schedules; the allocation of all financial and other resources; the control and regulation of the use of all equipment and other property of the Employer. The Employer shall determine the methods, technological means and qualifications of personnel by and for which operations are to be carried out. The Employer shall take whatever action as may be necessary to carry out its rights in any emergency situation."

Explanation: The Commission held that the "employer was not obligated to bargain the decision to change from fixed shift schedules to rotating shift schedules because the union waived by contract its right to bargain the decision. The obligation to bargain the effects of the decision remained." This is because "[t]he parties clearly and unmistakably agreed to allow the employer to change employee work schedules, including change from fixed to rotating shifts, and removed the assignment of hours from the scope of mandatory subjects of bargaining for the life of the agreement." The Commission explained that the "language in [various articles] is clear and specific enough to give the employer the right to establish work shifts, and to conclude that the union waived its right to bargain changes to work shifts. [One article] gives the employer the right to determine hours of work. [Another article] requires advanced notice of 'employer-directed' changes to employee shift assignment. [A third article] gives the employer the right to establish work schedules. The assignment of employees to shifts 'shall be determined by the employing official' clearly gives the employer the right to change from fixed to rotating shift schedules. [The articles] clearly contemplate the employer unilaterally establishing and changing employees' work schedules."

Citation: *City of Yakima*, Decision 11352-A (PECB, 2013), *aff'g* Decision 11352 (PECB, 2012) **Waiver Found: No**

Contract Language: Article 4.1(b) provides the employer "the right to determine reasonable schedules of work, overtime and all methods and processes by which said work is to be performed in a manner most advantageous to the Employer. . ."

Explanation: The Commission affirmed the Examiner's finding that the union did not contractually waive its right to bargain changes to the continuous duty policy. The employer argued that a management rights clause constituted a waiver. The Commission distinguished the management rights clause at issue in *City of Everett,* which reserved to the employer the right "to assign work and determine the location and the number of personnel to be assigned duty at any time," and the contract language at issue here, which only gave the employer, "the right to determine overtime." The Commission stated, "[w]hile the employer retained the right to determine when overtime is necessary, the employer must bargain other aspects of overtime" such as when employees are eligible to work overtime or how many hours an employee may continuously work.

Citation: *State – Employment Security*, Decision 11962 (PSRA, 2013) **Waiver Found: No**

Contract Language: "The Employer will maintain bulletin board(s) or space on existing bulletin boards currently provided to the Union for union communication. In bargaining units where no bulletin board or space on existing bulletin boards has been provided, the Employer will supply the Union with adequate bulletin board space in convenient places. Material posted on the bulletin board will be appropriate to the workplace, politically nonpartisan, in compliance with state ethic laws, and identified as union literature. Union communications will not be posted in any other location in the agency. If requested by the Union, the Employer will identify areas where Union provided newsstands can be located in their offices/facilities."

Explanation: Examiner Garcia determined that the union had not contractually waived its right to post union-related materials because the employer failed to show that the union understood, or reasonably could have been presumed to have known, what was intended when it accepted the contract language relied upon by the employer. In this case, the examiner concluded that "[g]iven the established past practice of allowing employees to post non-work items in their cubicles, including union posters and other items with union insignia, the employer has not established a waiver by contract defense."

Citation: *Seattle School District*, Decision 10983-B (PECB, 2013), *aff'g* Decision 10983-A (PECB, 2012) **Waiver Found: Yes**

Contract Language: The collective bargaining agreement, Article XII Section C 1, grants the Nutrition Services Director the ability to adjust hours. "Hours are assigned based on the number of meals served. However, hours may be adjusted by the Director of Nutrition Services when justified by program requirements." Further, in Article XII Section C 2, "[h]ourly time is assigned by school building Food Service Managers with approval by the Nutrition Services Director." While the Food Service Managers assign hours, the right of approval is retained by the employer.

Explanation: The Commission rejected the union's argument that the union did not contractually waive the right to bargain over the application of the meal per labor hour (MPLH) standard to the assignment of hours because the collective bargaining agreement grants the Nutrition Services Director the ability to adjust hours.

Citation: *University of Washington*, Decision 11600 (PSRA, 2012) **Waiver Found: Yes**

Contract Language: "The Employer agrees to provide a minimum of fourteen (14) calendar days' notice to an employee in the event of an Employer-directed permanent change in the employee's shift assignment or work schedule . . . . The assignment of employees in various shifts within each work group or department shall be determined by the employing official, provided that when qualifications are substantially equal in the judgment of the employing department, seniority shall be a factor in determining shift assignment. This criteria does not apply to positions deemed by the employer to require a rotational shift."

Explanation: Examiner Hartrich explained that to effectively waive a union's statutory right to bargain over a mandatory subject, the union and employer must consciously agree to the waiver and the waiver must be clear and unmistakable. A general management rights clause typically does not meet this standard; in contrast, a management rights clause that contains an itemized list of specific subjects that are waived likely would meet this standard. Here the language in the CBA is sufficiently specific to demonstrate that the union waived its right to bargain.

Citation: *Cowlitz County*, Decision 11515 (PECB, 2012) **Waiver Found: Yes**

Contract Language: [The analysis is in the underlying arbitration, not the ULP, and the arbitration could not be found]

Explanation: ULP Manager Gedrose dismissed the union's complaint that the employer refused to bargain by its unilateral change to the location and duration of forced assignments for court security positions, without an opportunity for bargaining. Here, the employer requested deferral to arbitration and the arbitrator denied the union's grievance finding that the employer's actions were permitted under the CBA. Thus, the union waived its right to bargain the disputed issue.

Citation: *Washington State Ferries*, Decision 11242 (MRNE, 2011) **Waiver Found: No**

Contract Language: "Except as modified by this Agreement, the Employer retains all rights of management, which, in addition to all powers, duties and rights established by constitutional provision or statute, will include but not limited to, the right to: . . . . (c) Direct and supervise employees; (d) And all other rights to manage and operate the Ferries Division in an effective, efficient, safe, and fiscally prudent manner within the Ferries Division fiscal budget."

Explanation: Examiner Latsch found that the union did not waive its right to challenge the employer's actions through a general management rights clause because it did not contain specific language. The employer "may not rely on a general management rights clause to prevent [the union] from negotiating the effect of the key box system and take the issue to interest arbitration if agreement cannot be reached."

Citation: *State – Corrections, Decision* 10842-A (PSRA, 2011*), aff'd,* Decision 10842-B (PSRA, 2012) **Waiver Found: Yes**

Contract Language: Article 41 of the parties' collective bargaining agreement provides a detailed description of the employer's responsibilities with reclassifications and reallocations. Article 41.1(B) 12 states: "The Employer will allocate or reallocate positions, including newly created positions, to the appropriate classification within the classification plan." Article 41.2 provides a review procedure employees may follow when they believe their position is improperly classified. Article 41.3 is titled "Effect of Reallocation" and 41.4 is titled "Salary Impact of Reallocation." Article 41.5 states: "The Employer will notify the Union when a position is being reallocated to a job classification that is excluded from a bargaining unit covered by this agreement."

Explanation: Examiner Siegel dismissed the union's charge finding that the employer did not commit a refusal to bargain unfair labor practice when it reallocated positions finding that the union had waived the right to engage in impact bargaining in the parties' collective bargaining agreement. Here, language in the CBA "clearly and unequivocally confers upon the employer the right to reallocate positions within the classification plan."

Citation: *Southwest Snohomish County Public Safety Communications Agency*, Decision 11149 (PECB, 2011), *aff'd*, Decision 11149-C (PECB, 2013) **Waiver Found: No**

Contract Language: "With reasonable advance notice, a representative of the Association may visit the work location of the employees covered by this Agreement at any reasonable time for the purpose of investigating grievances.

Said representative shall limit his activities during such investigations to matters relating to this Agreement. Work hours shall not be used by employees or Association representatives for the promotion of Association affairs other than stated above."

Explanation: Hearing Examiner Bradley determined that the parties had developed a past practice of allowing union-related discussions between employees in the work-place even though a provision in the CBA imposed certain limitations. The examiner explained, "Ambiguous contract language can be construed or defined through the development of past practice. The language in section 3.3 of the CBA was interpreted through past practice to allow employees to have conversations with their co-workers in the workplace about union-related matters."
Furthermore, the Examiner also evaluated the employer's argument that the union had waived its collective bargaining rights under the CBA using standard contract interpretation theories. PERC adheres to the 'objective manifestation' theory of contracts and 'subsequent conduct of contracting parties' may be examined in determining the intent of the parties and the 'reasonableness of the parties' respective interpretations.'

Citation: *City of Everett,* Decision 11241 (PECB, 2011), *aff'd in part; rev'd in part, order VACATED by* Decision 11241-A (PECB, 2013) **Waiver Found: No**

Contract Language: The Management Rights provision stated: 'Examples of such rights include the right: . . . D. to assign work and determine the location and the number of personnel to be assigned duty at any time.' The employer acknowledged that the article does subject itself to other terms of the agreement.

Explanation: Examiner Boedecker rejected the employer's waiver by contract defense. The employer argued that when it expanded the list of fire stations that the dispatch would automatically search to find the geographically closest available equipment for a call coming from the employer (allowed under the quoted language of the CBA), the union must allow bargaining unit work to be performed by non-bargaining unit employees. The employer argued that the Management Rights clause of the parties' CBA gave the employer the right "to assign work and determine the location and the number of personnel to be assigned duty at any time" but Examiner Boedecker explained that this clause is subject to the other terms of the contract including the minimum staffing requirements and prevailing rights, including overtime, and duration provisions. The Examiner explained, "[t]he general language of the Management Rights Article is subject to more specific language in other articles."

Citation: *Seattle School District*, Decision 11044 (PECB, 2011) **Waiver Found: Yes**

Contract Language: "The Council [union] recognizes the District's inherent and traditional right to manage its business and operations. Accordingly, except to the extent specifically covered and controlled by the express terms of this Agreement, the Council recognizes the right of the District to hire, transfer, promote, demote, assign and retain employees and to discipline, suspend or discharge employees for just cause and to maintain the discipline and efficiency of its employees; the right to lay off; the right to establish, change and direct the methods and processes of doing work, to introduce new and improved work methods or equipment and to assign work to outside contractors; the right to determine the starting and quitting times and the number of hours to be worked; and the right to make and amend such reasonable rules and regulations as it may deem necessary for the conduct of its business and to require their observance."

Explanation: Examiner Irvin dismissed the union's unilateral change complaint finding that the employer was acting consistent with its managerial right to assign work as contained in the parties' CBA and specifically the management rights clause of the contract; however the examiner did not conduct a waiver analysis in reaching his conclusion.

Citation: *Griffin School District*, Decision 10489 (PECB, 2009) **Waiver Found: No**

Contract Language: Under the management rights clause of the collective bargaining agreement, there are no limits upon the employer's ability "to lay off employees because of lack of work or other legitimate reasons."

Explanation: Hearing Examiner Boedecker dismissed the District's assertion of waiver by contract where the defense was based upon the District's novel interpretation of what constituted a 'layoff' which included furloughs. "In order to prove waiver, the evidence must be clear and unmistakable. The contract language claimed to constitute waiver must be specific, or it must be shown that the parties fully discussed the matter and that the party alleged to have waived its rights consciously yielded its interest in the matter." "The record does not support a finding that when the union agreed to this lay off reference in the management's rights article, that the union was also agreeing to include furlough days."

Citation: ***Mason General Hospital*****, Decision 9996 (PECB, 2008)** **Waiver Found: No**

Contract Language: "[T]he employer reserves the exclusive right to exercise the customary functions of management, including, but not limited to . . . the right to select, hire, promote, dismiss, assign and reassign, supervise and discipline nurses, to determine hours of employment . . . to establish, change, modify and abolish its policies, practices, rules and regulations; to determine, modify and change methods and means by which Hospital operations are to be carried on, and to determine the appropriate duties of nurses in meeting those needs and requirements, and do those things necessary to carry out all ordinary functions of management except as these matters are specifically referred to in this Agreement."

Explanation: Hearing Examiner Hartrich found that the employer failed to support the defense of waiver by contract where the language of the contract did not show a "clear and unmistakable" intent by the union to waive the right. "The management rights clause does not constitute a waiver of the Union's statutory bargaining rights because the clause is modified by other sections of the collective bargaining agreement."

Citation: ***City of Tukwila*****, Decision 9691A (PECB, 2008)** **Waiver Found: No**

Contract Language: "The Employer shall continue to pay the full premium for medical coverage under the Self-Insured Medical Plan up to a maximum increase of twelve percent (12%) in 2004. The twelve percent (12%) shall be changed to eleven percent (11%) in 2005, and to ten percent (10%) in 2006 and 2007. In the event the monthly premiums increase more than the stated amount in a year, the Employer or the Guild has the right to reopen the Agreement to negotiate changes in the Self-Insurance Medical Plan benefits so that the increase in premium costs does not exceed the stated amount."

Explanation: The Commission affirmed the Hearing Examiner's finding that, although the contract language gave management a right to cap their payment towards insurance premiums, it did not alleviate the duty to bargain where the language also explicitly allowed for a request to renew bargaining. "This language unambiguously allows either party to request bargaining, provided the triggering event occurs. Had the collective bargaining agreement only discussed the amount that the employer would contribute ... then an argument could be made that the language placed a hard 'cap' on the employer's contribution to health premiums, and the employees would have been obligated to pay the excess amounts for the life of the contract."

Citation: *State-Social and Health Services*, Decision 9551- A (PRSA, 2008) **Waiver Found: No**

Contract Language: The Commission examined three clauses, but the most relevant portions were: "The Employer will satisfy its collective bargaining obligation before making a change with respect to a matter that is a mandatory subject"; "This Agreement constitutes the entire agreement and any past practice or past agreement between the parties whether written or oral is null and void, unless specifically preserved in this Agreement": and in particular: "Nothing herein will be construed as a waiver of the Union's collective bargaining rights with respect to matters that are mandatory subjects/topics under the law."

Explanation: The Commission reversed the Examiner's finding in Decision 9551 (PRSA, 2007) that the union contractually waived its right to negotiate the impacts of contracting out bargaining unit work. The Commission found that the union did not waive their right to bargain subcontracting because the collective bargaining agreement "clearly and unequivocally states that the employer will satisfy its collective bargaining obligation before making changes to mandatory subjects of bargaining."

Citation: *Island County Fire District 1*, Decision 9867 (PECB, 2007) **Waiver Found: No**

Contract Language: "The Employer shall pay one hundred percent (100%) of those premiums necessary to maintain coverage under the Washington Fire Commissioners' Association (WFCA) medical benefit plan for enrolled employees during the term of this Agreement." The issue of the dispute turned on language the Union wanted, but failed to obtain.

Explanation: Examiner Yoshitomi found that the Union had not waived its right to bargain where in the previous contract negotiations the Union had sought more restrictive language around healthcare provisions and failed to get their language. "A party's unsuccessful effort to obtain contract revisions in the collective bargaining agreement during the course of negotiating for a successor contract is not tantamount to a 'conscious yielding.'" *Equitable Gas Company*, 245 NLRB 260 (1979).

Citation: *King County Fire District 43*, Decision 9236 (PECB, 2006), *aff'd in part*, Decision 9236-A (PECB, **Waiver Found: No**

2007)

Contract Language: "Subject to the specific provisions of this Agreement or applicable law, the Employer shall retain whatever rights and authority are necessary for it to operate and direct the affairs of the Employer in all of its various aspects; including, but not limited to: the right to manage all manpower, . . . to establish work schedules within the recognized hours of work and work schedules . . ."

Explanation: Examiner Carpenter disagreed with the employer's contention that the union waived its right to bargain a change in the use of Kelly days based on a general management rights clause in the collective bargaining agreement. "A party to a collective bargaining agreement may waive its right to bargain a subject if the waiver is demonstrated by clear, specific, and unmistakable language in the contract." However, here, the employer failed to meet the "high standard concerning specificity of language that would constitute a waiver by contract" because nothing in the management rights clause indicated the union intended to waive its right to bargain the use of Kelly days.

Citation: *Community College District 17*, Decision 9379 Waiver Found: Yes (PSRA, 2006)

Contract Language: The parties had two agreements about subcontracting. The first required the employer to orally inform the unit that it intended to subcontract. The second was much more detailed, but incorporated RCW 28B10.350. The waiver issue was whether the Union waived its right to object to the employer's interpretation of RCW 28B10.350. The decision does not analyze contract language.

Explanation: Hearing Examiner Gedrose found that a "union can waive its bargaining rights if it understood what the contract intended when it accepted contract language relied upon by the employer." *City of Yakima*, Decision 3564-A (PECB, 1991). Here, even though the union only agreed to allow the employer to subcontract public works projects based on the employer's misunderstanding that RCW 28B10.350 mandated open bidding for public works project, Hearing Examiner Gedrose found that the union had waived its right to object to the employer's interpretation of the law when it agreed to the waiver. The union did not negate the waiver by merely refusing to sign a form produced by the employer that classified a future project as subject to subcontracting. Instead, the union needed to produce evidence refuting the employer's determination that the project at issue was a public works project.

Citation: ***State – Corrections*, Decision 9421 (PSRA, 2006)** **Waiver Found: Yes**

Contract Language: "[W]orkweek and work shifts of different numbers of hours may be established by the Employer in order to meet business and customer service needs…"

Explanation: Hearing Examiner Stuteville found that where the union agreed to the collective bargaining agreement language "workweek and work shifts of different numbers of hours may be established by the Employer in order to meet business and customer service needs…," the union clearly and unambiguously agreed that the changes to schedule, workweek, work period, and assigned hours may take place.

Citation: ***Skagit County*, Decision 8746-A (PECB, 2006)** **Waiver Found: No**

Contract Language: Establishing that the ferry service is a management prerogative, "[f]or the purpose of monthly shift scheduling, the published sailing schedule will be used to prepare the monthly shift schedule. This is to include one half (1/2) hour prior to the first scheduled run and one-half (1/2) past the last scheduled run for the purpose of preparing and securing the vessel for service." Another provision was summarized by the Commission as: "Rule 23.01 states that the employer has the right to unilaterally modify any employment condition not covered by the terms of the agreement without bargaining the decision or its impact on the bargaining unit. Rule 23.01(1) grants the employer the exclusive right to determine the specific programs and services offered and how such programs are offered."

Explanation: The Commission pointed out it has "consistently evaluated waiver by contract claims under a 'clear and unmistakable' standard, so that the contract language being relied upon must be specific, or it must be shown that parties fully discussed the matter and that the party alleged to have waived its rights consciously yielded its interest in the matter." *Lakewood School District*, Decision 755-A (PECB, 1980). The contract language at issue fell short of waiving the union's right to bargain the shifts actually worked by as-needed employees. Even though the parties' collective bargaining agreement provided that the level of ferry service provided by the employer was a management prerogative, and therefore, not bargainable, such language did not limit or waive the union's right to bargain the employees' work shifts to provide the level of service established by the employer. Simply that a management prerogative correlates with a mandatory subject of bargaining does not reduce the mandatory subject to a management prerogative.

Citation: ***City of Wenatchee*****, Decision 8802-A (PECB, 2006)** **Waiver Found: Yes**

Contract Language: "Any and all rights concerned with the management and operation of the Department are exclusively that of the City unless otherwise provided for by the terms of the agreement. The City has the authority to adopt rules for the operation of the Department and the conduct of its employees, provided such rules are not in conflict with the provision of this Agreement or applicable law. The City has the right, among other actions, to discipline and discharge for just cause; to lay employees off; to assign work and determine the duties of employees; to schedule hours of work; to determine the number of personnel assigned to duty at any time; and to perform all other functions not expressly limited by this agreement."

Explanation: The Commission discussed the standard for construing words of the contract in order to determine whether a waiver exists. "Emphasizing the outward manifestation of assent by each party to the other, courts have found the subjective intention of the parties irrelevant." The Commission clarified that "contract provisions are not ambiguous merely because the parties disagree about their particular meaning," and that when the contract terms evidence a meeting of the minds, the Commission need not determine what was intended. Here, the Commission reversed the Hearing Examiner and interpreted a management rights provision which listed several actions the employer has the right to unilaterally make, specifically, to determine the number of personnel assigned to duty at any time, unequivocally granted the employer the determine the minimum staffing levels.

Citation: ***City of Pasco*****, Decision 9181 (PECB, 2005),** ***aff'd*****,** ***City of Pasco*****, Decision 9181-A (PECB, 2008)** **Waiver Found: No**

Contract Language: [The exact management rights clause is not given; the employer also issued a memo about compensatory time, which did not explicitly reserve rights for management]

Explanation: Hearing Examiner Helm discussed the impact of management rights clauses, pointing out that precedent indicates a strong presumption exists that management rights clauses do not give an employer the right to take unilateral action on a mandatory subject unless the right was specifically waived in the labor agreement. "In order to show a contractual waiver, the party must show the exact subject matter of the change was discussed in negotiations. Where the employer action involves a major change in policy, the employer is required to show an express written contractual waiver with respect to the changes at issue. The fact that prior minor changes in policy had not been objected to by the union does not foreclose the union from later contesting a major change in policy." "As noted earlier, no waiver by contract can be established by vague provisions of management rights clauses in collective bargaining agreements. If the employer cannot show express language in the labor agreement conferring upon it the right to act unilaterally with respect to the matter at issue, it acts at its peril. No such express language is found in the parties' labor agreement."

Citation: *City of Seattle*, Decision 9173 (PECB, 2005) **Waiver Found: No**

Contract Language: The collective bargaining agreement provides, under "Management Rights," section 4.2, that the employer may "determine the number of shifts and the number of personnel assigned to such shifts."

Explanation: Hearing Examiner Carpenter found the employer did not meet its burden of establishing that its management clause, which states that it may determine the number of shifts and number of personnel assigned to such shifts, constituted a contractual waiver that enabled it to unilaterally change minimum staffing levels.

Citation: *City of Edmonds*, Decision 8798 (PECB, 2004), *aff'd*, *City of Edmonds*, Decision 8798-A (PECB, 2005) **Waiver Found: Yes**

Contract Language: "The employer shall provide health, vision, life and disability plans for all employees in the bargaining unit. The selection of insurance providers shall be at the sole discretion of the Employer: provided that the benefit levels shall be substantially the same as those in effect as of the signing of this agreement. Furthermore, there shall be no increase in deductibles, percentage of premium co-payments and of stop loss limits in effect as of the signing of this agreement."

Explanation: Hearing Examiner Romeo explained that in order to prove a waiver by contract, it must be shown that the matter was fully discussed by the parties and that the party relinquishing its rights did so consciously. Because the contract language in question stated that "the benefits shall be substantially the same as those in place at the time the contract was signed," and because the increased cost to health insurance benefits was small, the parties bargained to allow for small changes in health insurance benefits, and therefore, the union waived its right to demand bargaining over small changes.

Citation: *Whatcom County*, Decision 7643 (PECB, 2002) **Waiver Found: No**

Contract Language: ". . . adopt reasonable rules for the operation of the Department and the conduct of its employees; provided such rules are not in conflict with the provisions of this Agreement, or applicable law," but the contract was not interpreted.

Explanation: Hearing Examiner Lacy pointed out that a waiver by contract must be knowingly made, and such a defense to a unilateral implementation is valid and appropriate when the parties have negotiated a subject matter and have incorporated controlling provisions on that subject matter into their contract. However, here, Hearing Examiner Lacy found that a waiver by contract defense was not applicable because the employer's unilateral implementation did not occur until after the contract with the alleged waiver clause had expired.

Citation: *Whitman County*, Decision 7735 (PECB, 2002) **Waiver Found: Yes**

Contract Language: "11.05 During the term of this Agreement the Association shall have the option to exercise a reopener on health care issues if the Association shops health care and finds a plan or plans that provide(s) substantially comparable benefits to Association members for less cost than the County is currently paying."

Explanation: Hearing Examiner Stuteville found that because the re-opener language in the parties' contract only requires that the employer bargain over health care coverage if the union presents an alternative health care plan that would be for less cost than the employer was currently paying, it waived its bargaining rights on more costly insurance plans for the term of the contract. As such, the employer was never placed under a statutory duty to re-open the health care issue and did not commit an unfair labor practice by refusing to bargain.

Citation: *Skagit County*, Decision 7554 (PECB, 2001) **Waiver Found: Yes**

Contract Language: "The Employer shall have the authority to alter the weekly work schedule in a manner consistent with providing all regular employees their fair share of regularly scheduled available work hours. Any such schedule change shall be posted not less than three (3) days in advance of a change."

Explanation: Hearing Examiner Cowan explained that "a union waives its bargaining rights by contract language," and, therefore, employer actions in conformity with the parties' contract will not constitute an unlawful unilateral change. Here, because the contract specifically allowed the employer to "alter the weekly work schedule in a manner consistent with providing all regular employees their fair share of regularly scheduled available work hours" the union waived its right to demand bargaining over changes in employee schedules.

Citation: *Chelan County*, Decision 5469 (PECB, 1996) Waiver Found: Yes

Contract Language: "[N]othing herein shall be construed as a waiver of the Association's right to engage in collective bargaining, pursuant to RCW 41.56...." The CBA also stated the work schedule "shall be five consecutive eight hour days ... or four consecutive ten hour days ...."

Explanation: Hearing Examiner Lacy disagreed with the union's claim that a management rights provision limited the ability of the employer to make any change in any contractual provision that falls under the mantle of mandatory subjects of bargaining. Hearing Examiner Lacy dismissed the union's notion, stating that "[g]eneral management rights provisions are often asserted by employers as waivers of union bargaining rights, and are often found insufficient under the high standards for finding a waiver." Hearing Examiner Lacy found that language in the parties' collective bargaining agreement, which stated the work schedule "shall be five consecutive eight hour days ..., or four consecutive ten hour days...," constituted an unambiguous and intentional relinquishment of its right to bargain concerning work schedule changes within a narrow zone limited to two specific choices. In a statement that seems to impose a requirement that a waiver be actually discussed in negotiations, Hearing Examiner Lacy pointed out that "it matters not that a unilateral change affects a mandatory subject of bargaining if the issue was negotiated and codified in a contract."

Citation: *City of Yakima*, Decision 3564-A (PECB, 1991) Waiver Found: No

Contract Language: In the words of the Commission: "Article XXX of the parties' 1988-89 contract is titled: 'Municipal Code Sections Pertaining to Fire Department LEOFF Employees.' The text of that article consists of only a list of section numbers and section titles. The employer argues that the ordinances referred to in Article XXX are incorporated into the parties' contract, and are not negotiable." Another section stated, "[n]o ordinances existing at the time of execution of this Agreement relating to wages, hours and working conditions for members of the bargaining unit shall be amended or repealed during the term of this Agreement without written concurrence of both parties."

Explanation: The Commission found that a clause in the collective bargaining agreement which made reference to Yakima City Code did not constitute a waiver of bargaining rights as to matters covered by the listed ordinances. Particularly persuading to the Commission was the fact that neither the language of the collective bargaining agreement nor the hearing testimony gave "any indication of the original intent of the parties."

PERC CLASSIFICATION OF BARGAINING SUBJECTS TABLE

The following table lists how the Public Employment Relations Commission (PERC) has ruled on prior subject to bargaining cases. This exhaustive list covers not only cases involving public safety employees but all public sector classifications.

Categories:

Wages
Benefits
Hours
Leave
Uniform and Equipment
Job Security
Discipline and Discipline Procedures
Workplace Procedures and Standards
Conditions of Employment
Miscellaneous Contract Clause
Promotions
Union Rights

Issue	Mandatory?	Case Citation
WAGES		
Wages	Yes	*City of Tukwila*, Decisions 2434 (1986) & 2434-A (PECB, 1987). *Ridgefield School District*, Decision 102-A (PECB, 1977). *Federal Way School District*, Decision 232-A (PECB, 1977). *Franklin County*, Decision 1890 (PECB, 1984). *City of Centralia*, Decision 3232 (PECB, 1989). *Shelton School District*, Decisions 579-A (1983) & 579-

		B (PECB, 1984). *Clover Park School District*, Decision 6072-A (EDUC, 1998). *King County Library System*, Decision 9039 (PECB, 2005). *Community College District 14*, Decision 9009 (CCOL, 2005). *Val Vue Sewer District*, Decision 8963 (PECB, 2005). *University of Washington*, Decision 10726 (PSRA, 2010), *aff'd*, Decision 10726-A (PSRA, 2012). *City of Tacoma,* Decision 11097 (PECB, 2011).
Temporary Reduction in Salary	Yes	*Yakima Valley Community College,* Decision 11326 (PECB, 2012), *aff'd*, Decision 11326-A (PECB, 2013).
Payroll Schedule	Yes	*City of Auburn*, Decision 455 (PECB, 1979). *City of Anacortes*, Decision 1493 (PECB, 1982). *Lewis County*, Decision 2957 (PECB, 1988). *Snohomish County*, Decision 9196 (PECB, 2005); *aff'd*, Decision 9196-A (PECB, 2007).
Retroactivity Prior to Certification of Bargaining Units	No	*King County*, Decision 4236 (PECB, 1992). *Snohomish County*, Decision 9607 (PECB, 2007).
Wage Reopener for Changes in Staffing Levels	Yes	*City of Richland*, Decision 1997 (PECB, 1984). *City of Bellevue*, Decision 9343 (PECB, 2006).

Reclassification Affecting Wages	Yes	*Seattle School District*, Decision 2079-B (PECB, 1986). *City of Hoquiam*, Decision 745 (PECB, 1979). *City of Tukwila*, Decision 2434-A (PECB, 1987). *Lake Washington Technical College*, Decision 4721 (PECB, 1994).
Wages of a Supervisor Reverting to Bargaining Unit	Yes	*City of Dayton*, Decisions 2111 & 2111-A (PECB, 1985).
Denial of Step Increases Because of Performance	Yes	*City of Mountlake Terrace,* Decision 11702 (PECB, 2013) *aff'd in part and rev'd in part,* Decision 11702-A (PECB, 2014).
Distribution of Overtime	Yes	*City of Clarkston*, Decision 3286 (PECB, 1989). *City of Wenatchee*, Decision 2194 (PECB, 1985). *Snohomish County*, Decision 9291-A (PECB, 2007).
Computation of Overtime Pay	Yes	*City of Clarkston*, Decision 3289 (PECB, 1989). *City of White Salmon*, Decision 4502 (PECB, 1993).
Overtime Rate	Yes	*City of Seattle*, Decision 787 (PECB, 1979).
Alternative Compensation for Overtime Work	Yes	*City of Pasco*, Decision 9181-A (PECB, 2008).
Opportunity for Overtime	Yes	*City of Everett,* Decision 11241-A (PECB, 2013); *aff'g in part and rev'g in part* Decision 11241 (PECB, 2011). *Skagit County,* Decision 7554 (PECB, 2001). *City of Yakima,* Decision 11352 (PECB, 2012); *aff'd*, Decision 11352-A (PECB, 2013.
Continuous Duty policy & Eligibility for OT or Shift	Yes	*City of Yakima,* Decision 11352 (PECB, 2012); *aff'd* Decision

Trades		11352-A (PECB, 2013).
Shift Trade Policy	Yes	*City of Vancouver*, Decision 11276, (PECB, 2012).
Unanticipated Funds Allocation	No	*Federal Way School District*, Decision 323-A (PECB, 1977).
Cost of Living Increase	Yes	*City of Seattle,* Decision 9938 (PECB, 2007).
Recoupment of Wages Paid	Yes	*City of Tacoma,* Decision 11097-A (PECB, 2012).
Stipend for Auxiliary Duties	Yes	*Wenatchee School District,* Decision 11138 (PECB, 2011), *aff'd*, Decision 11138-A (PECB, 2012).
Pay for Lunch on Training Days	Maybe	*Walla Walla County,* Decision 11877 (PECB, 2013).
Budget	No	*Anacortes School District*, Decision 2544 (PECB, 1986). *King County Library System*, Decision 9039 (PECB, 2005). *Western Washington University*, Decision 9309-A (PSRA, 2008). *King County*, Decision 10576-A (PECB, 2010).
Decision to Reduce Budget	No	*Spokane Education Association v. Barnes*, 83 Wn.2d 366, 374 (1974). *City of Bainbridge Island,* Decision 11465 (PECB, 2012).
Effects of Decision to Reduce Budget	Yes	*Spokane Education Association v. Barnes*, 83 Wn.2d 366, 374 (1974). *City of Bainbridge Island,* Decision 11465 (PECB, 2012).
BENEFITS		

Health Benefits	Yes	*City of Seattle*, Decision 651 (PECB, 1979). *Morton General Hospital*, Decision 2217 (PECB, 1985). *City of Dayton*, Decisions 1990 & 2234 (PECB, 1984). *Bates Technical College*, Decision 5140 (PECB, 1995). *Snohomish County*, Decision 9834-B (PECB, 2008). *City of Mukilteo*, Decision 9452-A (PECB, 2008). *City of Tukwila,* Decision 9691-A (PECB, 2008). *Island County Fire District 1,* Decision 9867 (PECB, 2007). *Lewis County,* Decision 10571 (PECB, 2009). *Yakima County,* Decision 9338 (PECB, 2006). *East Valley School District*, Decision 9256 (PECB, 2006). *King County Library System*, Decision 9039 (PECB, 2005). *City of Anacortes*, Decision 9004-A (PECB, 2007). *Val Vue Sewer District*, Decision 8963 (PECB, 2005). *Skagit County*, Decision 8886 (PECB, 2005); *aff'd*, Decision 8886-A (PECB, 2007). *Kitsap Transit*, Decision 11098-A (PECB, 2012); *aff'd*, Decision 11098-B (PECB, 2013). *Port of Anacortes*, Decision 12225 (PORT, 2014).
Health Insurance Premiums	Yes	*Snohomish County*, Decision 2234 (PECB, 1985). *City of Poulsbo*, Decision 2068 (PECB, 1984). *City of Kalama*, Decisions 6739, 6740 & 6741 (PECB, 1999).

		City of Tukwila, Decision 9691-A (PECB, 2008).
Prescription Drug Co-Payments	Yes	*City of Anacortes*, Decision 9004 (PECB, 2005); *aff'd,* Decision 9004-A (PECB, 2007).
Insurance Carrier	No	*City of Dayton*, Decisions 1990 & 1990-A (PECB, 1984). *Lewis County,* Decision 11521 (PECB, 2012).
	Maybe	*University of Washington,* Decision 10771 (PECB, 2010). *Kitsap County,* Decisions 11610-13 (PECB, 2012), *aff'd,* Decisions 11610-A-11613-A (PECB, 2013).
Elimination of Insurance Plan	Yes	*Kitsap Transit,* Decision 11098-A (PECB, 2012), *aff'd,* Decision 11098-B (PECB, 2013).
Financial Incentive to Move Insurance Plan	Yes	*Kitsap Transit,* Decision 11098-A (PECB, 2012), *aff'd,* Decision 11098-B (PECB, 2013).
Setting Premium Rates for Self-Insurance	No	*Kitsap County,* Decisions 11610-13 (PECB, 2012), *aff'd,* Decisions 11610-A-11613-A (PECB, 2013).
Employee Contribution Rates for Self-Insurance	Yes	*Kitsap County,* Decisions 11610-13 (PECB, 2012), *aff'd,* Decisions 11610-A-11613-A (PECB, 2013).
Use of Premiums and Reserve Funds in Self-Funded Insurance That are Collected from Employee Contributions	No	*Kitsap County,* Decisions 11610-13 (PECB, 2012), *aff'd,* Decisions 11610-A-11613-A (PECB, 2013).
Use of Health Insurance Rate Stabilization & Self-Insurance Reserve Funds	No	*Spokane County,* Decision 11627 (PECB, 2013).
Verification Employee	No	*King County,* Decision 11616

Dependent(s) Eligibility for Health Benefits		(PECB, 2013).
Who Qualifies as "Dependent" Eligible for Health Benefits and Appeals Process	Yes	*King County,* Decision 11616 (PECB, 2013).
Dental Benefits	Yes	*Skagit County*, Decision 8886 (PECB, 2005), *aff'd*, Decision 8886-A (PECB, 2007).
Parking	Yes	*Port of Pasco*, Decision 4021 (PECB, 1992). *King County,* Decision 11319 (PECB, 2012), *aff'd*, Decision 11319-A (PECB, 2013).
	Maybe	*Western Washington University*, Decision 9010 (PSRA, 2005).
Take Home Vehicles	Yes	*Pierce County*, Decision 1710 (PECB, 1983). *City of Brier*, Decisions 5089 & 5089-A (PECB, 1995). *City of Burlington*, Decisions 5840, 5841, 5842 & 5843 (PECB 1997). *City of Kalama*, Decision 6853 (PECB, 1999). *Lake Stevens School District*, Decision 9840-A (PECB, 2009). *City of Sunnyside,* Decision 11629 (PECB, 2013).
LEOFF Plan Supplements	No	*City of Seattle*, Decisions 4687-A, 4687-A, 4687-B, 4688-B (PECB, 1997), *aff'd,* 93 Wn. App. 235 (1998).
Life Insurance	Yes	*Lewis County*, Decision 3418 (PECB, 1990).
Employee Assistance Program	Yes	*City of Tukwila*, Decision 2434 (PECB, 1986).
Physical Fitness	Yes	*City of Tukwila*, Decision 2434 (PECB, 1986).
Potable Water	Yes	*Snohomish County*, Decision 9291-A (PECB, 2007).
Lockers	Yes	*Snohomish County*, Decision 9291-A (PECB, 2007).

Shower Facilities	Yes	*Snohomish County*, Decision 9291-A (PECB, 2007).
Use of Personal Digital Assistants	Yes	*Snohomish County*, Decision 9291-A (PECB, 2007).
Uniform Cleaning Allowance	Yes	*Snohomish County*, Decision 9291-A (PECB, 2007).
HOURS		
Shift Starting and Ending Time	Yes	*Chelan County*, Decisions 5559 & 5559-A (PECB, 1996).
Number of Hours Worked During Scheduled Day	Yes	*Seattle School District*, Decisions 5733-A & 5733-B (PECB, 1998).

Shift Schedule	Yes	*City of Yakima*, Decision 767 (PECB, 1979). *City of Auburn*, Decision 901 (PECB, 1991). *Seattle School District*, Decision 2079 (PECB, 1984). *City of Clarkston*, Decision 3286 (PECB, 1989). *Morton General Hospital*, Decision 2217 (PECB, 1985). *Chelan County,* Decision 5469-A (PECB, 1996). *Spokane County*, Decision 5698 (PECB, 1996). *Skagit County,* Decision 7554 (PECB, 2001). *State - Social and Health Services,* Decision 9690-A (PSRA, 2008). *Snohomish County,* Decision 9770 (PECB, 2007). *City of Seattle,* Decision 9938 (PECB, 2007). *City of Vancouver,* Decision 10616 (PECB, 2009). *City of Tukwila*, Decision 10536 (PECB, 2009).
Shift Bidding	Yes	*Val Vue Sewer District*, Decision 8963 (PECB, 2005). *City of Bremerton*, Decisions 2733 & 2733-A (PECB, 1987). *City of Moses Lake*, Decision

		6328 (PECB, 1998).
Fixed/Rotating Shifts	Yes	*University of Washington*, Decision 11600 (PSRA, 2012).
Shift Trade Policy	Yes	*City of Vancouver*, Decision 11276, (PECB, 2012).
Duration of a Specialty Assignment	Yes	*City of Yakima*, Decision 10270 (PECB, 2009).
Posting of Specialty Assignments	Yes	*City of Yakima*, Decision 10270 (PECB, 2009).
Rest and Meal Breaks	Yes	*City of Bellevue*, Decision 2788 (PECB, 1987). *City of Clarkston*, Decision 3286 (PECB, 1989). *Snohomish County,* Decision 9770 (PECB, 2007).
Access to Bathrooms	Yes	*Snohomish County*, Decision 9291-A (PECB, 2007).
Access to Break Room	Yes	*Washington State Ferries,* Decision 11825 (MRNE, 2013); Decision 11825-A (MRNE, 2014).
Standby Time	Yes	*City of Clarkston*, Decision 3286 (PECB, 1989). *King County*, Decision 3448 (PECB, 1990). *Pierce County Fire District*, Decision 4146 (PECB, 1992).
Callback	Yes	*City of Clarkston*, Decision 3286 (PECB, 1989).
Jobsharing	Yes	*City of Marysville*, Decision 5306 (PECB, 1995).
LEAVE		
Scheduling Leave Time	Yes	*City of Yakima*, Decisions 3564 (PECB, 1990) & Decision 3564-A (PECB, 1991). *Snohomish County,* Decision 9770 (PECB, 2007).

Scheduling Leave Time for Training	Yes	*City of Mountlake Terrace,* Decision 10734 (PECB, 2010).
Setting of Holiday Schedules	Yes	*Western Washington University*, Decision 9309 (PSRA, 2006).
Accrual of Sick Leave	Yes	*Snohomish County*, Decision 9291-A (PECB, 2007).
Reduction in the Availability of Leave Use	Yes	*City of Seattle*, Decision 9173 (PECB, 2005).
Forfeiture of Accrued Vacation	Yes	*Walla Walla County,* Decision 11751 (PECB, 2013).
Use of Sick Leave During Vacation	Yes	*City of Yakima*, Decision 3564-A (PECB, 1991).
Use of Kelly Days	Yes	*King County Fire District 43*, Decision 9236 (PECB, 2006).
Scheduling Kelly Days	Yes	*Port of Walla Walla*, Decision 9061-A (PECB, 2006).
Requiring Use of Accrued Paid Leave Before Use of Unpaid Leave	Yes	*Mason General Hospital*, Decision 9996 (PECB, 2008).
Sick Leave Accrual Cap	Yes	*Sunnyside Valley Irrigation District*, Decision 314 (PECB, 1977). *Snohomish County,* Decision 9770 (PECB, 2007).
Comp Time Off	Yes	*Spokane County*, Decision 4973 (PECB, 1995). *Kitsap County,* Decision 10669 (PECB, 2010). *King County,* Decision 11597-A (PECB, 2014).
Scheduling of Comp Time Light Duty	Yes	*Kitsap County,* Decision 10669 (PECB, 2010). *Port of Anacortes*, Decision 12160-A (PORT, 2015). *City of Wenatchee*, Decisions 6517 & 6517-A (PECB, 1998).
Sick Leave	Yes	*City of Wenatchee*, Decisions 6517-A (PECB, 1998).

"Earned Time" (Combines Traditional Sick Leave and Annual Leave)	Yes	*Mason General Hospital*, Decision 9996 (PECB, 2008).
Authorization Procedure of Requesting Leave Without Pay	No	*East Valley School District*, Decision 9256 (PECB, 2006).
Leave Use During Inclement Weather Closures	Yes	*Pierce County*, Decision 11818 (PECB, 2013).
Paid Release Time	Maybe	*State – Fish and Wildlife*, Decision 11394-A (PSRA, 2012), *aff'd*, Decision 11394-B (PSRA, 2013).
UNIFORM AND EQUIPMENT		
Wear Uniform Union Insignia On Uniform	Yes	*State – Washington State Patrol*, Decision 11283 (PECB, 2012). *City of Clarkston*, Decision 3286 (PECB, 1989).
Identification Badge	Yes	*King County*, Decisions 5810 & 5810-A (PECB, 1997); *aff'd*, 94 Wn. App. 431 (1999). *State – Washington State Patrol*, Decision 11283 (PECB, 2012).
Possess Service Weapon	Yes	*State – Washington State Patrol*, Decision 11283 (PECB, 2012).
JOB SECURITY		
Subcontracting	Yes	*Community College District 17*, Decision 9379 (PSRA, 2006). *State-Social and Health Services*, Decision 9551–A (PRSA, 2008). *City of Vancouver*, Decision 808 (PECB, 1980). *Port of Edmonds*, Decision 844 (PECB, 1980). *Newport School District*, Decision 2153 (PECB, 1985). *Clover Park School District*, Decision 3069 (PECB, 1988).

		City of Tacoma, Decision 5634 (PECB, 1996). *Camas School District*, Decision 6603 (PECB, 1999). *City of Seattle*, Decisions 5391-B & 5391-C (PECB, 1997). *Peninsula School District*, Decision 5929 (PECB, 1997). *North Franklin School District*, Decisions 3980 (PECB, 1992) & 3980-A (PECB, 1993). *City of Seattle*, Decision 4163 (PECB, 1972). *Battleground School District*, Decision 2449 (PECB, 1986). *City of Auburn*, Decision 10062 (PECB, 2008).
Subcontracting Required by Law	Yes	*Hoquiam School District*, Decision 2489 (PECB, 1986).
Temporary Subcontracting	Yes	*City of Seattle*, Decisions 4163-B and 4988 (PECB, 1995).
Subcontracting New Duties	No	*Pierce County Fire District 9*, Decision 4547 (PECB, 1993). *City of Tacoma*, Decision 6601 (PECB, 1999).
Contracting Out	Depends	*Evergreen School District,* Decision 10546 (PECB, 2009).
	Yes	*City of Kelso,* Decision 2120 (PECB, 1985).
Contracting Out Non-Bargaining Unit Work	No	*Washington State University,* Decision 11498 (PSRA, 2012), *aff'd*, Decision 11498-A (PSRA, 2013).
Creation of New Positions	No	*City of Snohomish,* Decision 9569 (PECB, 2007).
Transfer of Bargaining Unit Employees to Vacant Already Existing Positions Outside Bargaining Unit	No	*Community College District 5 – Everett,* Decision 10177 (PECB, 2008).
Termination of Services as Part of Regional Consolidation	No	*City of Anacortes*, Decision 6830 (PECB, 1999).
Consolidation of Services and	No	*University of Washington,*

Operations		Decision 11075 (PSRA, 2011), *aff'd*, Decision 11075-A (PSRA, 2011).
Layoffs	Yes	*Tacoma-Pierce County Employment and Training Consortium,* Decision 10280 (PECB, 2009). *Snohomish County*, Decision 9540-A (PECB, 2007). *City of Kelso*, Decisions 2633 & 2633-A (PECB, 1988), *aff'd in part and reversed in part*, 57 Wn. App. 721 (1990), *rev. denied*, 115 Wn.2d 1010 (1990). *Federal Way School District,* Decision 232-A (EDUC, 1977). *South Kitsap School District,* Decision 472 (PECB, 1978). *Stevens County*, Decision 2602 (PECB, 1987). *City of Mercer Island,* Decision 1026-A (PECB, 1981). *City of Centralia,* Decision 1534-A (PECB, 1982). *King County*, Decision 10576-A (PECB, 2010). *Yakima County,* Decision 11621 (PECB, 2013).
	No	*Washington State University,* Decision 11704 (PSRA, 2013), *aff'd*, Decision 11704-A (PSRA, 2013).
Effects of Layoffs	Yes	*Tacoma-Pierce County Employment and Training Consortium,* Decision 10280 (PECB, 2009). *Washington State University,* Decision 11704 (PSRA, 2013), *aff'd,* Decision 11704-A (PSRA, 2013).
Effects of Layoffs and Reorganization	Yes	*City of Bainbridge Island,* Decision 11465 (PECB, 2012).

Effects of Consolidating Services	Yes	*University of Washington,* Decision 11075 (PSRA, 2011) *aff'd,* Decision 11075-A (PSRA, 2011).
Furloughs	Yes	*Griffin School District,* Decision 10489 (PECB, 2009). *King County,* Decision 10547 (PECB, 2009). *King County,* Decisions 10576-8 (PECB, 2009), *aff'd*, Decision 10576-A (PECB 2010).
Transfer of Work	Yes	*Snohomish County*, Decision 9540-A (PECB, 2007). *Lakewood School District,* Decision 755 (PECB, 1979), *aff'd,* Decision 755-A (PECB, 1980).
Skimming	Yes	*Community College District 17,* Decision 9379 (PRSA, 2006). *Colville School District,* Decision 9836 (EDUC, 2007). *Community Transit,* Decision 9783 (PECB, 2007). *City of Snoqualmie,* Decision 9892-A (PECB, 2009). *Seattle School District,* Decision 10028 (PECB, 2008). *Snohomish County*, Decision 9291-A (PECB, 2007). *Snohomish County*, Decision 9180 (PECB, 2005). *City of Seattle*, Decision 9173 (PECB, 2005). *Western Washington University*, Decision 9010 (PSRA, 2005). *State – Corrections,* Decision 11060 (PSRA, 2011). *University of Washington,* Decision 11075 (PSRA, 2011), *aff'd*, Decision 11075-A (PSRA, 2012). *Central Washington University,* Decision 11630 (PSRA, 2013).

Decision to Train Non-Bargaining Unit Employees to Perform Bargaining Unit Work	No	*Port of Walla Walla*, Decision 9061-A (PECB, 2006).
Collective Bargaining Provisions That Allow Workers to Transfer to Positions in Another Bargaining Unit	No	*Energy Northwest*, Decision 9424 (PECB, 2006).
Annexation	No	*City of Kelso*, Decisions 2633 & 2633-A (PECB, 1988).
Effect of Annexation	Yes	*City of Kelso*, Decisions 2633 & 2633-A (PECB, 1988).
Seniority Protection	Yes	*City of Pasco*, Decisions 3368 (PECB, 1989) & 3368-A (PECB, 1990). *City of Walla Walla*, Decision 1989 (PECB, 1984).
Seniority, Bumping and Recall	Yes	*City of Bainbridge Island*, Decision 11465 (PECB, 2012).
Scope of Bargaining Unit	No	*Snohomish County*, Decision 9540-A (PECB, 2007).
Successorship Clause	Yes	*City of Richland*, Decision 2486 (PECB, 1986).
Elimination of Positions	Yes	*Seattle School District*, Decision 2079 (PECB, 1984).
Use of Volunteers for Standby	Yes	*Spokane County Fire Protection District No. 9*, Decision 3021-A (PECB, 1990).
Implementations of Computer Technology Causing Loss of Positions	No	*Seattle School District*, Decision 2079-B (PECB, 1986). *City of Seattle*, Decision 9173 (PECB, 2005).
Use of Volunteers for Work Not Normally Performed	No	*City of Seattle*, Decision 2435 (PECB, 1988).
Work Performed by Confidential Employee Previously within Bargaining Unit	No	*Wishkaw Valley School District*, Decisions 4093 & 4093-A (PECB, 1993).
Elimination of Job Classification	Yes	*Morton General Hospital*, Decision 2217 (PECB, 1985).

Allocation or Reallocation of Employees to Job Classifications	No	*University of Washington*, Decision 10490-C (PSRA, 2011). *State – Corrections*, Decision 10842-A (PSRA, 2011), *aff'd,* Decision 10842-B (PSRA, 2012).
Decision To Not Rehire a Position and Disburse Job Duties	Yes	*Central Washington University,* Decision 10413 (PSRA, 2009).
	No	*Washington State University,* Decision 11704 (PSRA, 2013), *aff'd,* Decision 11704-A (PSRA, 2013).
Decision to Cease Operations	No	*Port of Seattle*, Decision 4989 (PECB, 1995).
Effect of Decision to Cease Operations	Yes	*Port of Seattle*, Decision 4989 (PECB, 1995).
Decision to Cease Operations Which Results in Layoffs	No	*City of Bellevue,* Decision 10830-A (PECB, 2012). *City of Kirkland,* Decision 10883-A (PECB, 2012). *City of Anacortes,* Decision 6830-A (PECB, 2000).
Effects of Ceasing Operations Which Results in Layoffs	Yes	*City of Bellevue,* Decision 10830-A (PECB, 2012).
Decision to Move Employee Work Stations	No	*City of Seattle,* Decision 9956 (PECB, 2008).
Changing of Job Titles	No	*Community College District 5 – Everett,* Decision 10177 (PECB, 2008).
Size of Work Force	No	*Central Washington University,* Decision 10413 (PSRA, 2009). *Washington State University,* Decision 11704 (PSRA, 2013), *aff'd,* Decision 11704-A (PSRA, 2013).
Effects of Change of Size of Work Force	Yes	*Central Washington University,* Decision 10413 (PSRA, 2009). *Washington State University,* Decision 11704 (PSRA, 2013), *aff'd,* Decision 11704-A (PSRA, 2013).

		City of Kirkland, Decision 10883-A (PECB, 2012).
Additional Duties on Job Description	Depends	*Snohomish County*, Decision 9291-A (PECB, 2007).
Reassignment or Change in Duties	Yes	*Port of Walla Walla*, Decision 9061-A (PECB, 2006).
Updated Job Description but No Change to Substance of Work Expected	No	*Clark County,* Decision 11065 (PECB, 2011).
Assign Work To Employees Within Budget Constraints	No	*Seattle School District,* Decision 11044 (PECB, 2011).
Workload Audit	No	*Washington State University,* Decision 11704 (PSRA, 2013), *aff'd*, Decision 11704-A (PSRA, 2013).
DISCIPLINE AND DISCIPLINE PROCEDURES		
Installation of Cameras for Disciplinary Purposes	Yes	*King County*, Decision 9495-A (PECB, 2008).
Installation of Cameras for Safety and Security	No	*Snohomish Fire District 3*, Decision 12273 (PECB, 2015).
Use of Cameras for Discipline	Yes	*City of Mountlake Terrace,* Decision 11702 (PECB, 2013) *aff'd* in part; *rev'd* in part Decision 11702-A (PECB, 2014).
Arbitration of Discipline	Yes	*City of Pasco*, 119 Wn.2d 504 (1992).
Discipline in General	Yes	*City of Yakima*, Decision 9062-B (PECB, 2008).
Drug Testing	Yes	*City of Yakima*, Decision 9062-A (PECB, 2006); *aff'd*, Decision 9062-B (PECB, 2008).
Representational Rights	Yes	*City of Pasco*, Decision 3368 (PECB, 1989) & Decision 3368-A (PECB, 1990).

Rules of Conduct	Yes	*City of Olympia*, Decision 3194 (PECB, 1989).
Polygraph Tests	Yes	*City of Olympia*, Decision 3194 (PECB, 1989).
Citation for Violation of State Law	No	*City of Tukwila*, Decision 4084 (PECB, 1992).
Accident Review Board	Yes	*City of Pasco*, Decisions 4197-A & 4198-A (PECB, 1994).
Make-Up of Collision Review Board	Yes	*City of Mountlake Terrace*, Decision 11702 (PECB, 2013) *aff'd*, in part; *rev'd* in part Decision 11702-A (PECB, 2014).
Collisions Subject to Collison Review Board	Yes	*City of Mountlake Terrace*, Decision 11702 (PECB, 2013), *aff'd in part*; *rev'd in part*, Decision 11702-A (PECB, 2014).
Citizen Review Board	Yes	*City of Spokane*, Decision 5054 (PECB, 1995).
	Depends	*City of Seattle*, Decision 6662 & 6034-B (PECB, 1999).
Denial of Step Increases Because of Performance	Yes	*City of Mountlake Terrace*, Decision 11702 (PECB, 2013), *aff'd in part, rev'd in* part, Decision 11702-A (PECB, 2014).
Individual Last Change Agreement	Yes	*Washington State Patrol*, Decision 4757-A (PECB, 1995).
Performance Plan	No	*King County*, Decision 4893-A (PECB, 1995).
Discharge	Yes	*City of Seattle*, Decision 9938-A (PECB, 2009).
Changing a City Ordinance Altering the Procedures of a Professional Accountability Review Board to Include Previously Redacted Information	Yes	*City of Seattle*, Decision 9957 (PECB, 2008).
Second Disciplinary Procedure (Monetary Fine)	Yes	*City of Seattle*, Decision 12060 (PECB, 2014).

Disciplinary Procedure for Same Infraction	Yes	*City of Mountlake Terrace,* Decision 11702 (PECB, 2013), *aff'd in part, rev'd in* part, Decision 11702-A (PECB, 2014).
Duration of Employee's Probationary Period	Yes	*King County,* Decision 9979 (PECB, 2008).
Limitations of Employee's Probationary Period	Yes	*King County,* Decision 9979 (PECB, 2008).
Employer's Use of Administrative Leave During Investigation	No	*Southwest Snohomish County Public Safety Communications Agency*, Decision 11149 (PECB, 2011), *aff'd*, Decision 11149-C (PECB, 2013).
Employer Placing Restrictions on Employee Communications Who are on Administrative Leave During Investigation of Employee Misconduct	No	*Southwest Snohomish County Public Safety Communications Agency,* Decision 11149 (PECB, 2011), *aff'd*, Decision 11149-C (PECB, 2013).
"Consequential Discipline" Authority	Yes	*City of Spokane,* Decision 11263 (PECB, 2011).
WORKPLACE PROCEDURES AND STANDARDS		
Participation in Advisory Committees	No	*Kent School District*, Decision 595-A (PECB, 1979).
Assignment of Duties	Possibly	*City of Clarkston*, Decision 3286 (PECB, 1989)
Assignment of Work	Yes	*Snohomish County*, Decision 9540-A (PECB, 2007). *Seattle School District,* Decision 10983-A (PECB, 2012), *aff'd*, Decision 10983-B (PECB, 2013).
Change in Job Description	Depends	*City of Richland*, Decision 1957 (PECB, 1984).
Additional Job Duties	Yes	*City of Seattle*, Decisions 5391-B & 5391-C (PECB, 1997).
	No	*Lake Chelan School District 129,* Decision 4940 (EDUC, 1994).

Additional Disciplinary Authority	Yes	*City of Spokane,* Decision 11263 (PECB, 2011).
Revocation of Commission Powers of Park Managers	No	*King County*, Decision 1957 (PECB, 1984).
Introduction of Computers	No	*Spokane Fire District No. 9*, Decision 3021-A (PECB, 1990).
Implementation of New Technology	No	*King County Fire District No. 16*, Decision 3714 (PECB, 1991). *Washington State Ferries*, 282-MEC (2001). *Seattle Community College,* Decision 12014 (CCOL, 2014).
Effects of Implementation of New Technology	Yes	*King County Fire District No. 16*, Decision 3714 (PECB, 1991). *Seattle Community College,* Decision 12014 (CCOL, 2014).
Employee Evaluations	No	*Pierce County Fire District*, Decision 4146 (PECB, 1992). *Spokane County*, Decision 6073-A (PECB, 1998). *City of Seattle*, Decision 6357 (PECB, 1998).
Change in Performance Evaluations	Yes	*City of Yakima*, Decision 10270 (PECB, 2009).
Effect of Employee Evaluations	Yes	*Pierce County Fire District*, Decision 4146 (PECB, 1992).
Performance Standards	No	*Spokane Fire Protection District No. 9*, Decision 3661 (PECB, 1990).
	Yes	*City of Bremerton*, Decisions 5898-A & 5898-B (PECB, 1997).
Effects of Performance Standards	Yes	*Spokane Fire Protection District No. 9*, Decision 3661 (PECB, 1990).
Time Allocation Standard	Yes	*Seattle School District*, Decision 2079 (PECB, 1984).
Reorganization which Increases Number of Positions	No	*City of Bellevue*, Decision 3343-A (PECB, 1990).

Reorganization which Affects Hours, Leave and Bargaining Unit Work	Yes	*City of Kalama*, Decisions 6739, 6740 & 6741 (PECB, 1999).
Safety Rules	Yes	*City of Olympia*, Decision 3194 (PECB, 1989).
Key Box System that Affects Employee Safety	Yes	*Washington State Ferries*, Decision 11242 (MRNE, 2011).
Services Offered by Employer	No	*Federal Way School District*, Decision 232-A (PECB, 1977).
Smoking Restrictions	Yes	*Mason County*, Decisions 3108 & 3108-A (PECB, 1989). *Clover Park School District*, Decision 3266 (PECB, 1989). *Kitsap County Fire District No. 7*, Decisions 2872 & 2872-A (PECB, 1988). *City of Seattle*, Decisions 3051-3054 & 3051-A - 3054-A (PECB, 1988).
Staffing Levels	No	*City of Yakima*, Decision 1130 (PECB, 1981). *Pierce County*, Decision 1710 (PECB, 1983). *City of Bellevue*, Decision 3343-A (PECB, 1990). *City of Spokane*, Decision 4746 (PECB, 1994). *Energy Northwest*, Decision 9424 (PECB, 2006). *City of Kelso,* Decision 11321 (PECB, 2012).
	Yes	*City of Seattle*, Decision 9173 (PECB, 2005). *City of Centralia*, Decision 5282-A (PECB, 1996).
	Maybe	*City of Richland*, 113 Wn.2d 197 (1989).
Change in Staffing Levels	No	*Port of Seattle,* Decision 11763 (PECB, 2013), *aff'd and modified*, Decision 11763-A (PORT, 2014).

Effects of Decision to Change Staffing Levels When Overtime is Required	Yes	*Port of Seattle,* Decision 11763 (PECB, 2013), *aff'd and modified,* Decision 11763-A (PORT, 2014).
Employee Suggestion System	No	*Spokane School District,* Decision 310 (PECB, 1977).
Training Standards	No	*King County Fire District No. 16,* Decision 3714 (PECB, 1991).
Work Rules	Yes	*Town of Granite Falls,* Decision 2692 (PECB, 1987). *Community Transit,* Decision 10647-A (PECB, 2011).
Use of Employer's Structural Facility and Effects on Working Conditions	Maybe	*Snohomish County,* Decision 9770-A (PECB, 2008).
Overall Design of Building Structure	No	*Snohomish County,* Decision 9770-A (PECB, 2008).
Effects of Overall Design of Building Structure on Working Conditions	Yes	*Snohomish County,* Decision 9770-A (PECB, 2008).
Substance of Training	No	*State - Individual Providers,* Decision 10193 (PECB, 2008).
Changes in Requirements for Requests for Information	Yes	*Community College District 17,* Decision 9379 (PSRA, 2006).
Mutual Aid Policy	No	*City of Everett,* Decision 11241-A (PECB, 2013), *aff'g in part and rev'g in part* Decision 11241 (PECB, 2011).
Effects of Changes to Mutual Aid Policy	Yes	*City of Everett,* Decision 11241-A (PECB, 2013), *aff'g in part and rev'g in part* Decision 11241 (PECB, 2011).
CONDITIONS OF EMPLOYMENT		
Off-Duty Employment Policy	Yes	*City of Bellevue,* Decision 893 (PECB, 1980).
Physical Fitness Standards	Yes	*City of Olympia,* Decision 3194 (PECB, 1989).
Tobacco Rules	Yes	*City of Olympia,* Decision 3194 (PECB, 1989). *WPPSS,* Decisions 6058 &

		6058-A (PECB, 1997). *Pierce County Fire District*, Decision 4146 (PECB, 1992). *Kitsap County Fire District 7*, Decisions 2872 & 2872-A (PECB, 1988). *Clover Park School District*, Decision 3266 (PECB, 1989).
Drug and Alcohol Use	Yes	*City of Tacoma*, Decision 4539-A (PECB, 1994).
Employment Qualification Standards	No	*King County Fire Protection District No. 39*, Decision 2160-A (PECB, 1985).
Residency Requirements	Yes	*Kitsap County Fire District 7*, Decisions 2872 & 2872-A (PECB, 1988). *Pierce County Fire District*, Decision 4146 (PECB, 1992).
Substance Abuse Testing	Yes	*City of Olympia*, Decision 3194 (PECB, 1989). *City of Tacoma*, Decision 4539-A (PECB, 1994).
Pre-Hire Conditions	Yes	*Kitsap County Fire District 7*, Decisions 2872 & 2872-A (PECB, 1988).
	Maybe	*City of Seattle*, Decision 8916 (PECB, 2005).
Application of Pre-Hire Conditions After Hiring	Yes	*Kitsap County Fire District 7*, Decisions 2872 & 2872-A (PECB, 1988).
Pre-Employment Minimum Qualifications Affecting Safety	Possibly	*King County Fire Protection District No. 39*, Decision 2160-B (PECB, 1986).
Establishment of Requirement to be Qualified to Operate Automatic Defibrillator	No	*King County Fire District 16*, Decision 3714 (PECB, 1991).
Requirement to Attend Radio Training and Become Qualified as a Radio Dispatcher	Yes	*City of Seattle*, Decision 8916 (PECB, 2005).
MISCELLANEOUS CONTRACT CLAUSE		

Grievance Procedures	Yes	*Clark County*, 3451 (PECB, 1990). *United Electrical, Radio, and Machine Workers of America v. NLRB*, 409 F.2d 150 (D.C. cir. 1969). *City of Pasco v. Public Employment Relations Commission*, 119 Wn.2d 504 (1992). *Community Transit,* Decision 10267-B (PECB, 2013). *City of Bellevue*, Decision 11435 (PECB, 2012). *King County Fire District 36*, Decision 11120 (PECB, 2011), *aff'd,* Decision 11120-A (PECB, 2013).
Cost of Representation at Grievance Arbitration	Yes	*King County Fire District 36*, Decision 11120 (PECB, 2011), *aff'd,* Decision 11120-A (PECB, 2013).
Attorneys' Fees Related to Grievance Arbitration	Yes	*King County Fire District 36*, Decision 11120 (PECB, 2011), *aff'd,* Decision 11120-A (PECB, 2013). *City of Bellevue,* Decision 11435 (PECB, 2012).
Restricting Union Access to Grievance Procedure	No	*City of Bellevue*, Decision 3129 (PECB, 1989).
Successorship Clause	Yes	*City of Richland*, Decision 2486 (PECB, 1986).
Interest Arbitration	No	*San Juan County*, 107 Wn.2d 338 (PECB, 1986).
Binding Arbitration of Grievance Clause	Yes	*Community Transit*, Decision 10267-B (PECB, 2013).
Contractual Waivers	No	*Seattle School District*, Decision 2079 (PECB, 1984). *City of Yakima*, Decision 3564-A (PECB, 1991). *City of Bellevue,* Decision 11435 (PECB, 2012).

	Yes	*City of Pasco*, Decision 4197-A, 4198-A (PECB, 1994), *aff'd*, 132 Wn.2d 450 (1997).
Legal Liability for Contractual Breaches	No	*Port of Ilwaco*, Decision 970 (PECB, 1980).
Agency Shop Clause	Yes	*University of Washington*, Decision 4668-A (PECB, 1994).
Dates and Times of Bargaining Sessions	No	*Kitsap Transit*, Decision 10206 (PECB, 2008).
Ratification Procedures	No	*Community College 19*, Decision 9210-A (PSRA, 2006). *Community College 7*, Decision 9094-A (PSRA, 2006).
Collective Bargaining Procedures	Maybe	*City of Tukwila*, Decision 1975 (PECB, 1984).
	No	*Seattle School District*, Decision 10732 (PECB, 2010), *aff'd*, Decision 10732-A (PECB, 2012). *State – Office of Financial Management,* Decision 11084 (PSRA, 2011).
Ground Rules	No	*State – Fish and Wildlife*, Decision 11394-A (PSRA, 2012), *aff'd*, Decision 11394-B (PSRA, 2013).
Legal Rights Enumerated in Management Rights Clause	No	*City of Bellevue*, Decision 11435 (PECB, 2012).
Use of In-house Attorneys to Represent Police Officers	No	*City of Seattle*, Decision 11588 (PECB, 2012), *aff'd*, Decision 11588-A (PECB, 2013).
Use of a Legal Representation Agreement	No	*City of Seattle,* Decision 11588 (PECB, 2012), *aff'd*, Decision 11588-A (PECB, 2013).
PROMOTIONS		

Promotion Procedures	Yes	*City of Wenatchee*, Decision 2216 (PECB, 1985). *Spokane County Fire Protection District No. 9*, Decision 2860 (PECB, 1988). *City of Tacoma*, Decision 9287 (PECB, 2006). *City of Vancouver*, Decision 10616 (PECB, 2009).
Promotion Standards for Positions Outside Bargaining Unit	No	*City of Tacoma*, Decision 9287 (PECB, 2006).
	Maybe	*City of Seattle,* Decision 12102 (PECB, 2014), *vacated by* Decision 12012-A (PECB, 2014).
Effects of Promotion Standards for Positions Outside Bargaining Unit	Probably	*City of Seattle*, Decision 12102 (PECB, 2014).
Rule of Three	Yes	*Spokane County Fire Protection District No. 9*, Decision 2860 (PECB, 1988).
Acting Assignments Outside Unit	Yes	*City of Yakima*, Decision 3564 (PECB, 1990) & Decision 3564-A (PECB, 1991).
Promotion Qualifications	Yes	*City of Yakima*, Decisions 3053-A & 3054-A (PECB, 1990).
Physical Agility Test for Promotion	Yes	*City of Anacortes*, Decision 5668 (PECB, 1996).
Assignment of Specialty Positions	Yes	*City of Auburn*, Decision 4896 (PECB, 1984). *City of Bremerton*, Decisions 4738 & 4739 (PECB, 1994). *Yakima County*, Decisions 6594-A & 6595-C (PECB, 1996).
UNION RIGHTS		
Union Leave	Yes	*Seattle School District*, Decisions 2079-B & C (PECB, 1986). *County of Yakima*, Decision 10204 (PECB, 2008).

	No	*City of Burlington*, Decisions 5840, 5841, 5842 & 5843 (PECB, 1997).
Leave to Conduct Union Business	Yes	*County of Yakima*, Decision 10204 (PECB, 2008).
Employer's Rule Prohibiting Where Union-Related Discussions Can Occur	Yes	*Southwest Snohomish County Public Safety Communications Agency*, Decision 11149 (PECB, 2011), *aff'd*, Decision 11149-C (PECB, 2013).
Union Use of Employer Bulletin Boards	Yes	*Snohomish County*, Decision 9291-A (PECB, 2007). *Kittitas County Public Hospital District 1*, Decision 11992 (PECB, 2014).
Employees Posting Personal Materials in Their Cubicles, Including Union Materials	Yes	*State-Employment Security*, Decision 11962 (PSRA, 2013).
Copying Charges Imposed on Information Requests in ULP Case	No	*Snohomish County*, Decision 9570 (PECB, 2007).
Procedural Motions to Arbitrator to Determine Scope of Grievance	No	*City of Mountlake Terrace*, Decision 11605 (PECB, 2012), *aff'd*, Decision 11605-A (PECB, 2013).

Chapter 4

Resolution of Collective Bargaining Disputes: Impasse and Arbitration

A. Introduction

This chapter covers the rights and responsibilities of the parties when the collective bargaining process breaks down. It explains how the negotiation process moves from contract negotiations through mediation to interest arbitration. It discusses the rules concerning the resolution of the impasse for those bargaining units who do not have interest arbitration. It discusses alternative means of pressuring the employer to halt the impasse, including the legality of those means. It discusses the process of preparing and presenting an interest arbitration case and the standards used by arbitrators to decide interest arbitration issues.

B. Negotiating to Impasse

Invoking mediation. When parties reach the juncture in their negotiations where they are unable to come to an agreement, they can obtain the assistance of PERC. Upon request, PERC will appoint a mediator.

The mediator will not "decide" the issue for the parties or make any "order." Mediation should be simply seen as an extension of the collective bargaining negotiation process.

Upon appointment, the mediator will want to ensure that the parties have made a good faith effort on their own to resolve the dispute without prematurely invoking mediation. Nonetheless, the statutory provisions applicable to interest arbitration groups permit a party as a matter of right to invoke the mediation process "if no agreement has been reached 60 days after the commencement" of negotiations.[1] Having the ability to invoke mediation when faced with a stalling employer is one technique for advancing the negotiations process.

Limits of mediation. It is important to bear in mind that mediation is quite different from arbitration. Frequently, there are misunderstandings as to the limits on a mediator's authority. The

[1] RCW 41.56.440.

mediator will not "decide" the issue for the parties or make any "order." Mediation should be simply seen as an extension of the collective bargaining negotiation process. The role of the mediator is not to judge the "fairness" or the "justice" of a party's proposal or position, no matter how much one party or other might want that.

Mediators may volunteer their insights into the "reasonableness" of the proposals, and for those groups subject to interest arbitration, likely will. Where interest arbitration is the final step in impasse resolution, mediators will draw the parties' attention to those factors arbitrators could reasonably be expected to use in resolving the issues in dispute. But ultimately whatever mediators do, they can only encourage voluntary settlement, not impose an agreement.

Preparation and team discipline in the face of mediator persuasion is important.

Mediator techniques. Mediation is usually performed through a combination of joint bargaining sessions and separate sessions with each party. During these sessions, PERC mediators will encourage the parties to set forth revised proposals in a continual process of bringing the parties closer and closer together toward an agreement.

Stylistically mediators vary widely, often reflecting their personalities. Some arbitrators apply soft pressure, in hopes the parties will be persuaded on their own to develop new proposals. Other arbitrators apply intense pressures, sometimes either acquiring concessions never intended or galvanizing stubborn resistance. Most mediators combine some clever persuasion with subtle pressure in hopes of inducing an agreement.

Preparation and team discipline in the face of mediator persuasion is important. Certainly compromise is necessary if an agreement is to be reached. But concessions made during mediation should reflect a team consensus developed through careful assessment and thorough team dialog, not spontaneous concessions.

Mediation is a necessary preliminary to the submission of a matter to interest arbitration. Before a party could have an interest arbitrator hear its negotiation dispute, the parties must first be "certified" by PERC's Executive Director as having reached impasse.[2] The Executive Director will generally not make this finding unless it is the determination of the mediator that negotiations have been exhausted and that the matters are ripe for interest arbitration.

The reality that negotiations might be certified is about the only real power a mediator has. If a mediator is convinced that one party or the other has not completed its concessions, the mediator can decline to declare an impasse and insist on further mediation sessions. This action sometimes continues the process for months and months.

This possibility again points to the need for preparation and team discipline. Mediators will often respond to the "weakest link" in the bargaining team. If a mediator perceives that more concession will dribble out with further pressure, or that the bargaining team is divided, they will be unlikely to declare an impasse. With proper preparation, union teams should have already evaluated the strengths and weakness of their position and that of the employer. Bargaining priorities and potential concessions should be fully discussed in caucus preceding negotiation sessions, including meetings with the mediator.

Concessions should be made tactically and with the goal of achieving reciprocal concessions by the other side. Erratic unplanned concessions do not advance the goal of reaching an overall agreement. Spontaneous concessions induced by mediation pressure do not necessarily lead to a strong agreement. While compromise is necessary and the mediator is a resource in achieving that, teams should insist on their ability to caucus over potential compromises outside the presence of the mediator.

C. Unilateral Implementation for Non-interest Arbitration Bargaining Units

As indicated in the last chapter, the statute grants the employer the right to unilaterally implement after negotiations have been exhausted. And as also discussed in the last chapter, the statute places strict parameters on the employer as to how they implement. Non-interest arbitration groups are not necessarily powerless, though, even in the face of a threatened implementation. The restrictions on employer implementation rights provide at least some incentive for an employer to negotiate to a contract. The next section discusses ways in which a union can respond to a difficult employer and still reach a mutual agreement.

---

[2] RCW 51.56.450.

D. Other Weapons Available to Break an Impasse

This section applies to both interest arbitration and non-interest arbitration groups. Both parties overlook these available tools but for different reasons. Non-interest arbitration groups often conclude that they have no means available for pressing further bargaining demands. But interest arbitration groups, on the other hand, think only of interest arbitration as the means for resolving their impasses. Both groups are overlooking other opportunities for bringing pressure to bear on their public employers — pressure that might lead to a voluntary agreement without resort to either unilateral implementation or arbitration.

The tools for breaking public sector impasses are much different from the tools available to private sector unions. The ultimate economic weapon of a private sector union — the right to strike — is either limited or nonexistent for Washington public sector unions. Whatever arguable right to strike might exist — discussed in greater detail below — it is even more circumscribed for those public employees fulfilling public safety functions.

On the other hand, public sector unions must always bear in mind that public sector contract negotiations are ultimately a political process. Appealing through the political process might well be a potential method of resolving a contract dispute short of interest arbitration. While the recent shifts in politics have made such appeals more challenging, these public communication rights still exist.

This section discusses the legality of strikes and other work stoppages. It also discusses the rights of public safety labor organizations in Washington to invoke political or public pressure as a method of acquiring an agreement.

1. Limitations on the Right to Engage in Strikes and Other Drawbacks

Although union arguments have been attempted that there is a "right" of public employees to strike, the prevailing view of Washington courts is that *there is no such "right."* But it should be borne in mind that the absence of a right to strike does not necessarily mean that every strike will necessarily be "enjoinable" — that is, stopped by a court through the means of an injunction. Many Washington public employees have struck successfully, especially teachers, despite the supposed absence of any "right" to strike. On the other hand, under most circumstances, it is likely that a court will quickly enjoin a strike involving public safety employees. The issue is a complex one and frequently misunderstood.

To the extent that there is any ambiguity concerning the "right to strike," it stems from the "common law" history of this issue. Prior to there being a collective bargaining statute, there were public sector labor organizations and these organizations often argued that they had the right to strike. Courts relied on "common law" holdings from other states which held that there was no such right. This case law, therefore, allowed public employers any reasonable means to bring the strike to an end, including obtaining injunctions and terminating employees.

When PECBA was being enacted, the question of whether employees would have the right to strike was hotly debated. The unions wanted an affirmative right to strike, and the public employers wanted an affirmative prohibition on strikes. Instead, the legislature enacted the following compromise provision: "Nothing contained in this chapter shall permit or grant any public employee the right to strike or refuse to perform his official duties."[3]

This provision did not confer upon unions the right to strike it sought. But it also did not go as far as the public employers wanted. The provision simply provided that the statute does not affirmatively grant the right to strike. This ambiguity left room for the unions to argue that there is still some inherent common law right to strike. Nonetheless, this union argument has been rejected by the courts for a number of reasons.

A deeper look at labor history is needed. The PECBA statute should be understood against the backdrop of the National Labor Relations Act (NLRA) that governs the private sector. The NLRA and PECBA are different in one key respect concerning strike rights: The NLRA contains a specific "concerted activity" clause, while PECBA does not. The NLRA's concerted action clause makes it unlawful for an employer to discriminate against employees for engaging in concerted activity. And concerted activity includes strikes. Under the NLRA, employers are allowed to utilize certain economic weapons of their own, including lockouts, and are allowed to hire replacements. But they may not discriminate against strikers when the strike is over. Therefore, generally, private sector strikers are returned to their former jobs at the end of a strike.

PERC, on the other hand, has noted that there is no affirmative right to strike granted in the collective bargaining statute, nor are

[3] RCW 41.56.120.

there any legal protection of employees engaging in a strike. While PECBA does contain a provision prohibiting "interference" or "discrimination" for employees engaging in protected union activity, this has never been interpreted nearly as broadly as the NLRA's "concerted activity" clause.

The Washington State Supreme Court was well aware of this judicial and legislative history when it first considered, following the enactment of Chapter RCW 41.56, union arguments that public employees had a "right to strike." The court adopted an interpretation of PECBA as reinforcing the common law restriction on the right of public employee strikes. In *Roza Irrigation District*,[4] the court reasoned:

> The legislature must have been aware that this court had held that public employees, while they have the right to organize, do not have the right to strike. It preserved that ruling in the provisions of [RCW 41.56]. The right to organize is protected by RCW 41.56.040 and the legislature expressly disavowed any grant of the right to strike in RCW 41.56.120. By way of compensation for the refusal to grant this right, however, are the provisions defining unfair labor practices and providing remedies therefor.[5]

And then two years later in *International Union of Operating Engineers v. Sand Point Country Club*, in *dicta*,[6] the court further discussed its view concerning the right of public employees to strike:

> In 1967 after the decision in *Port of Seattle v. I.L.W.U.* holding that public employees may not strike if the public health and safety are involved, the legislature enacted RCW 41.56 governing public employee collective bargaining, and imposing on the employer a duty to engage in bargaining. At the same time it expressly refrained from granting the right to strike.
>
> Thus it appears that where the legislature has seen fit to impose upon the employer a duty to bargain with the designated representative of his employees, it has at the same time either restricted the right to strike and to

[4] 80 Wn.2d 633, 497 P.2d 1967, 169 (1972).

[5] *Id. (citing Port of Seattle v. International Longshoremen's & Warehousemen's Union*, 52 Wn.2d 317, 324 P.2d 1099 (1958)).

[6] 83 Wn.2d 498, 519 P.2d 985, 988 (1974).

picket or has recognized that the right to strike is not available to employees covered by the act. In other words, the imposition of the duty has been compensatory.[7]

Unions still make arguments that since the ultimate question of whether there is a right to strike or not rests on "common law" and since the common law is judge-made law, it can be altered. But virtually all states, except for Wisconsin (which has not limited most public sector bargaining rights[8]), have ruled that the common law prohibits public employee strikes. Therefore, it is unlikely that the State Supreme Court will change its view any time soon.

Participants in an illegal strike *face the danger of losing their job.* As indicated, nothing in RCW 41.56 protects "concerted activity" like the NLRA. PERC cites this omission as the reason it will not get involved in strike situations through ULP cases.[9] In one PERC case, employees had engaged in a sick-out that was listed as a contributing cause of an employee's discharge. The examiner stated that the sick-out did not fall within the type of activity protected by RCW 41.56.[10]

While PERC has held that it will not involve itself in strike situations, there is one exception. If the employer hires permanent replacements during the strike, these employees become part of the bargaining unit and are subject to the existing wage, hours and working conditions.[11] Any pay differences for replacements from the regular pay of the current unit members who are on strike will constitute a unilateral change in working conditions. This unilateral change in working conditions will constitute a ULP for refusing to bargain to an impasse and the employer will be forced to bargain with the union.[12] This principle places an effective statutory restriction on an employer during a strike. No changes in working conditions can be made outside the restrictive statutory implementation process that requires employers to implement only their last best offer.

---

[7] *Id.*

[8] Ironic, given the position on unions of Wisconsin Governor Scott Walker.

[9] *Concrete School District,* Decision 1059 (EDUC 1980); *Lake Washington School District,* Decision 2327 (EDUC 1985). Both of these cases dealt with issues under the educational employee collective bargaining act (RCW 41.59). However, according to the examiner in each case, the proposition for which they are cited also applies to RCW 41.56.

[10] *City of Westport,* Decision 1194 at 6 (PECB, 1981).

[11] *Spokane School District,* Decision 310-B (PECB, 1977).

[12] *Id.*

And another circumstance under which PERC might find a ULP is if union leaders were treated more harshly in the return to work process than other employees. Although PERC will not acknowledge a categorical right of strikers to return to their former jobs, if an employer did accept workers back, it is quite possible that PERC would require the employer to do this is in a nondiscriminatory manner. Union activities cannot properly be relied on as a basis to treat employees selectively. But no case on these facts has yet been presented to PERC.

In the case of a public employee strike, injunctive relief may be available upon application by the state to prevent substantial injury to the public.[13] Also, adversely affected community members may demand that the Attorney General seek injunctive relief and initiate their own suit if the Attorney General refuses to do so.[14]

Therefore, in a public safety employee strike, it would appear that an injunction would be almost automatic, particularly given the possible dangerous situation that could be created. While injunctions are always possible in a public employee strike situation, the courts have also espoused a doctrine of judicial restraint and neutrality when it comes to labor relations matters.

In *Burke*, the Supreme Court's other two cases where restraint was practiced while injunctions were sought by public employers against employees. According to the court, for an injunction to be issued, there needs to be a showing under all the circumstances that an injunction is necessary to prevent violence, irreparable injury, or breach of the peace. The court explained:

> The delicate balance of labor relations is now primarily the province of the legislature and the schemes created must be allowed to function as intended without the added coercive power of the courts being thrown into the balance of one side or another. This could make the judiciary an unwitting third party at the bargaining table and a potential coercive force in the collective bargaining process.[15]

Thus, we have a peculiar combination of a court that believes that public employee strikes are illegal while also determined to practice restraint when it comes to issuing injunctions to stop illegal strikes.

---

13 *Burke & Thomas*, 92 Wn. 762, 600 P.2d 1282, 1290 (1979).

14 *Id.*

15 *Id.* at 1288.

Another limitation on the likelihood an injunction will be issued is the "clean hands" doctrine. An injunction is a request for "equitable" relief. A basic judicial concept is that equity will only be extended to those who "do equity." This notion — sometimes called the "clean hands" notion — *requires courts to consider whether the employer's own unlawful activities have contributed to the strike.* If they have, the court might choose to deny an injunction, even if public safety employees are involved.

Although the court decisions thus far have addressed the issue of actual strikes, it seems likely the court would extend these principles to other types of job actions that were tantamount to a work stoppage. The "blue flu" would seem to be one such type of work stoppage which would be deemed unlawful.

Less clear, though, is the legality of other activities that fall short of an outright work stoppage. For example, some public safety unions, especially correction officer units, have made use of "work to rule" procedure where work slows by means of conforming to written policies to the letter. "Work to rule" actions would prove difficult for an employer to resist, given that the employees are following the rules that the employer has provided them. To counter this maneuver, the employer would have to set forth a new set of expectations and make it clear that refusal to conform to those expectations would be considered insubordination. At that point, continuing with a "work to rule" action might be considered grounds for discharge.

2. Legally Protected Means of Pressure: Politics, the Public, and the Press

As will be discussed in greater detail later, public sector unions and their employees have broad constitutional rights to appeal to public officials, the media, and the citizens at large. Many public safety labor organizations have found that a well-planned and well-executed campaign of political and public pressure may facilitate a more positive collective bargaining outcome.

Clearly though the recent political winds have shifted in a direction adverse to public employees and their unions. Increasing resistance to employee collective bargaining rights has reduced the ability to of public unions to appeal to the public. While there is still a role for such tactics, care is needed to avoid unconstructive pushback.

There is also a constitutional right to appeal directly to public officials under the constitutional right to "petition" elected representatives.

As will be discussed in Chapter 9, the right to make public statements on matters of public concern is well established under the First Amendment. The condition of contract negotiations involving public safety employees is certainly a matter of public concern. While some departments have broad rules prohibiting employees from speaking out on matters of department business (or alternatively requiring "prior approval" for such speech), these types of rules have almost uniformly been stricken by courts as a violation of the First Amendment.

There is also a constitutional right to appeal directly to public officials under the constitutional right to "petition" elected representatives. Even though PERC's rules require the parties to engage in good faith bargaining through designated representatives, even PERC has acknowledged that the statutory requirement for good faith bargaining cannot override First Amendment rights to petition elected officials. Nonetheless, parties contemplating such direct appeals should do so only in a well-planned and tactical manner; such appeals risks destroying what little good will that existed at the table.

Finally, the public can be a great ally in support of public safety union demands. On the other hand, the public may not be as sympathetic as hoped, especially in these times with greater expression of hostility to collective bargaining rights. Whether or not an appeal to the public will be useful depends on the nature of the issues that might be presented. Some claims are simply more appealing to the public who are generally supportive of a fair salary for their public safety employees, but also are opposed to more taxes. Appeals have proven most successful when public safety unions can demonstrate that their claim has a strong equitable basis and that the local government is misallocating its existing budgetary dollars, thereby diverting dollars that could fulfill those demands. Relating contract negotiations to failed employer recruitment and retention issues is also a means of invoking the public's own interest in proper staffing and public safety.

E. Interest Arbitration Preliminaries

As indicated above, the biggest preliminary to proceeding to interest arbitration is the completion of the mediation process. Until mediation has been exhausted and PERC deems the parties to be at an impasse, there will be no "certification." And without a certification, the parties cannot proceed to arbitration.

the filing of a ULP by one party or another may result in the issue being "blocked" from arbitration

Once the certification is issued, a number of procedural steps — defined in the administrative regulations — must be fulfilled. These involve the process of selecting an arbitrator, formulating issue proposals and others. Between the time of certification and the hearing, several months may pass, which is, in any event, usually necessary for proper preparation.

There are other issues that may arise during this interim period. First, the filing of a ULP by one party or another may result in the issue being "blocked" from arbitration. This blocking charge commonly occurs when one party has alleged that the other either did not negotiate in good faith or has persisted to impasse on a permissive subject of bargaining. If PERC issues a "preliminary ruling" indicating that a cause of action exists as stated, it will pull that issue from the interest arbitration proceeding until it can be resolved. And if the issue is a major one, such as wages, it is likely that the entire interest arbitration proceeding will be put on hold.[16]

Such ULP complaints are required to be handled on an expedited basis, but with PERC this is a relative term. PERC rarely utilizes its "summary judgment" process, thereby requiring parties to go to hearings even on relatively weak ULP complaints. The result is that employers are sometimes able to drag out the process by presenting questionable ULPs, which take months and months to resolve. When this occurs, it is important to bear in mind the discussion just above concerning the exertion of political pressure. If the employer representatives are engaging in tactical maneuvers to avoid a quick hearing on the merits of union contract proposals, the union can certainly make that known to the public.

The certification of a dispute to interest arbitration does not put an end to the obligation to engage in good faith bargaining. Although parties cannot be compelled to continue to bargain, they can be required to continue producing information in support of their proposals. In this phase of negotiations, this typically

[16] *See* WAC 391-55-255.

requires the parties to exchange current information regarding comparability and wages as well as anything else that may have a bearing on their interest arbitration proposals. PERC has held,[17] and the State Supreme Court has affirmed,[18] that the failure to produce such information during the pendency of an interest arbitration dispute is itself a ULP.

F. Preparation for Interest Arbitration

Properly done, interest arbitration is an involved, complex matter requiring *significant* preparation. Sometimes a party tries to take shortcuts in their presentations but such sloppy efforts, usually done to save money, can prove to be quite expensive in the long run. Generally management will come to the hearing very well prepared and armed with substantial data; a failure to effectively respond to their case can set your contract back years.

Extensive data need to be gathered concerning comparables, including demographic characteristics and wage and benefits information. Information concerning the current fiscal conditions facing the employer must collected and evaluated. And the list goes on and on. (A detailed identified of the proper steps in preparing for arbitration is outside the scope of this chapter.)

Properly done, interest arbitration is an involved, complex matter requiring *significant* preparation.

The course of this preparation can often be useful in the collective bargaining process itself. Often, the internal discussions concerning the support and merits of a proposal will lead a party to discard a proposal or to think of other alternatives. It can also lead a party to take a more critical eye toward what may have been an overoptimistic assessment of the likelihood of a given result being achieved. To put it another way, the optimism that existed during mediation may be confronted with the new reality that an arbitrator will be weighing how both parties proposals are actually supported by comparability.

G. The Interest Arbitration Process

The interest arbitration process is designed to be fairly informal. The rules of evidence that apply to a grievance arbitration (even loosely there) are generally all waived in an interest

---

17 *See City of Bellevue*, Decision 3085-A (PECB, 1989).

18 *City of Bellevue v. IAFF Local 1604*, 119 Wn.2d 373, 831 P.2d 738 (1992).

arbitration. The interest PECBA provision describing such hearings provides:

> The rules of evidence prevailing in judicial proceedings may be considered, but are not binding, and any oral testimony or documentary evidence or other data deemed relevant by the chairman of the arbitration panel may be received in evidence.[19]

If all the foundational and hearsay requirements of a normal hearing had to be fulfilled, an interest arbitration panel would be deprived of the most valuable types of information. Interest arbitration proceedings generally require consideration of wide-ranging demographic and economic information which is typically produced by various government agencies. The practicalities of the interest arbitration hearing do not allow for calling representatives from each of those various agencies as witnesses. As Arbitrator Alan Krebs noted in a *Snohomish County Deputy Sheriff*'s interest arbitration, hearsay evidence is not only admissible, but it is "often necessary."[20]

One procedural rule that does apply to such evidence, though, is that it needs to be considered and offered during the actual arbitration hearing. While the parties may submit post-hearing briefs, which often involves a reanalysis of data already presented, the post-hearing brief is *not* an opportunity to interject new materials into the proceeding, absent permission having been granted by an arbitrator to "reopen" the hearing.[21] Once again, there is a premium on being prepared *before* the hearing, anticipating rather than reacting to what management will argue.

In a typical case, when a party puts on their "evidence" through a mix of documents and live witnesses, the live witnesses are subject to cross-examination. For the most part though, the evidence is efficiently placed into evidence by the parties' advocates without time-consuming questioning.

Even though parties have an obligation to produce requested information prior to a hearing, interest arbitration proceedings often involve an abundant amount of evidence which one side or the other is seeing for the first time at the hearing. There is an obligation to present information but often the parties' information is only turned into presentation charts and graphs immediately

---

[19] RCW 51.56.450.

[20] *Snohomish County* (Deputy Sheriff) (Krebs, 1987) at 13.

[21] *See, e.g., City of Pasco* (Police) (Krebs, 1990) at 16.

before the hearing.

Under these circumstances, the post-hearing briefs become critical because it is the first opportunity the parties have for analyzing and criticizing the data offered by the opposing party. Such post-hearing briefs are usually not filed for at least 30 days after the close of an arbitration hearing. And after the post-hearing briefs are submitted, interest arbitration decisions are due within another 30 days, but by common practice the parties agree to allow the arbitrator to extend this deadline to at least 60 days.

H. Issues in Interest Arbitration

1. Introduction

The interest arbitration statute sets forth guidelines for arbitrators to follow in issuing their awards. But these are *only* guidelines. And as one arbitrator has indicated, they are not to be applied with "surgical precision."[22] This approach leaves arbitrators with a tremendous range of discretion in deciding interest arbitration cases.

At best, experienced advocates can come up with only an educated guess when predicting the possible outcome of a given arbitration case. Interest arbitrators do have a tendency to give a great deal of weight to the approaches prior arbitrators have taken under similar circumstances. So these awards provide a great deal of insight. But there is a lot of room for creativity in arbitration, both by the advocates and the arbitrators, so that no two cases are alike.

The goal of this section is to set forth an explanation of the factors and considerations arbitrators have used previously in rendering interest arbitration awards.

2. The Relation of Interest Arbitration to Collective Bargaining

A number of arbitrators have observed that interest arbitration is not a substitute for collective bargaining, but rather is an extension of it. Some arbitrators have indicated that the parties should not be able to obtain through interest arbitration what they would not have been able to have obtained in collective bargaining.

But it is difficult to discern exactly what that statement means because the parties *were* unable to reach any agreement if they are in arbitration. A different way of wording that principle is to say

[22] *City of Pullman* (Police) (Axon, 1992) at 18.

that the parties should not be able to acquire anything through interest arbitration that they could reasonably have expected to have obtained through collective bargaining *had the parties negotiated a result consistent with other parties under similar circumstances where the parties were bargaining in good faith with an intent to reach an agreement.*

What arbitrators are really expressing here is that a party is not going to get everything it wants in arbitration. Arbitrators view the interest arbitration process, like the collective bargaining process, to be one of principled compromise. It is a "conservative," incremental process, just as is collective bargaining. If you are unwilling to compromise, you cannot expect that the arbitrator will just gift you all your wishes and wants.

But the likelihood of arbitral-imposed compromise raises another problem in the arbitration process. Some parties arbitrate, just hoping for a "split the difference" approach that might reward the less reasonable party. Fortunately, though, a number of arbitrators have explicitly rejected the "split the difference" approach as contrary to the purpose of the statute.[23]

As Arbitrator Bill Reeves explained in a Mount Vernon police decision, the goal of arbitrators in applying the statutory factors is to:

> [F]ashion an acceptable and workable bargain. Interest arbitration is not an exact science. However, the arbitrator uses principled reasoning to arrive at a bargain approximating *what the parties themselves would have reached if they had continued to bargain with determination and good faith.* Thus, the award should reflect the relative bargaining strength of the parties and *should not be a mere 'compromise' between the parties' positions because such a compromise would favor the party with the more extreme or intransigent position.*[24]

Although a number of arbitration awards are marked by what *appears* to be a compromise, this often is the same compromise reasonable parties would have reached had the collective bargaining process functioned properly.

There are other arbitration awards where the arbitrators clearly

[23] *See City of Kent* (Police) (LaCugna, 1980) at 4; *Pierce County Fire District No. 9* (Kienast, 1979) at 3.

[24] *City of Mount Vernon* (Police) (Reeves, 2007) at 2.

came down on the side of one party with very little imposed compromise. These awards can be explained by seeing this as a rejection of an unreasonable posture taken by the other party. And sometimes arbitrators even seem to "punish" those parties who appear to be taking unreasonable or extreme positions, giving them less than they would have obtained if their proposals were more reasonable.

Employers sometimes present a clever recharacterization of these principles in arbitration. They cite the arbitrator language that arbitration is an extension of collective bargaining and should place the parties in the position that they would have reached through agreement and then note that the employer never did agree to the union proposals. They then argue that because the employer was unwilling to reach a mutual agreement on the union agreement and then conclude that, therefore, these union proposals cannot represent an extension of the collective bargaining process.

Of course, acceptance of these cleverly worded arguments would frustrate the very purposes of interest arbitration. Arbitrator Howell Lankford dissected the logic of this management argument and provided an effective restatement of what arbitrators have meant all along in their references to the collective bargaining process:

> Both parties recognize that the Washington courts have held quite clearly that interest arbitration is not a substitute for collective bargaining but only "an extension" of the collective bargaining process. *City of Bellevue v. Int'l Ass'n of Firefighters, Local 1604*, 119 Wn.2d 373 (1992). But, although they hold hands at the beginning of the analytical journey, the parties almost immediately find different paths leading from the Court's holding in *City of Bellevue*. The County, essentially, stresses that an interest arbitrator should not impose on an employer a contract which it would never, never accept in two party negotiations; and the Association stresses that an interest-arbitrable bargaining unit is not just another bargaining unit, because the theoretical consequences of a work stoppage in interest-arbitrable units has been recognized by the legislature to be unacceptable.
>
> I submit that interest arbitration is properly viewed as

> "an extension of the collective bargaining process" not in the sense of collective bargaining as economic warfare—based on "the mutual ability to do one another harm"—but in the sense of a good faith exchange of reasons and arguments. It is undoubtedly true that the economic warfare model played an important role in the history of collective bargaining. But the fundamental right of unions—in the private sector and certainly in the public sector in Washington—is not simply the right to strike but the right to *bargain*, the right to engage in the good faith exchange of reasons and argument. Both in the private sector and in the public sector in Washington the right to bargain was soon recognized as including the right to have access to the information relied on by the other side; and so the fundamental right to bargain became the right to look at the data and to analyze and argue about it. In two-party negotiations, that exchange is convincing or not depending only on whether the parties come to agree. *Interest arbitration is an extension of the collective bargaining process in the sense that it provides a neutral third party to be convinced—or not—by the same sort of data, analyses and arguments the parties traditionally exchange in two-party negotiations.*

Therefore, contrary to this clever employer argument, the employer does not win just by pointing out that they never offered the terms proposals by the union. Or as Arbitrator Janet Gaunt explained this principle: "[I]nterest arbitration is an extension of the collective bargaining process.... With the reality of the bargaining table in mind, this Arbitrator tries to frame the type of award it seems likely the parties would have ultimately reached through good faith negotiations *if the Union's right to strike had been unfettered.*"[25]

3. Burden of Proof

In general, the burden of proof is upon the party who sets forth the proposal. But the reality in interest arbitration is much more complex than that. Different types of issues involve different approaches by arbitrators as to the burden of proof. Arbitrators

---

[25] *City of Tacoma* (Police) (Gaunt, 2008) at 3.

tend to adjust the burden of proof, depending on the type of issue.

Although it would seem that the union is the moving party on economic issues, in reality both sides are the moving party. Even if the employer is proposing a percentage of CPI or less, it is still a proponent of a specific proposal. On questions of the basic wage increase, arbitrators have not typically imposed a heavy burden of proof or any burden of proof on the parties. Instead, arbitrators simply take whatever available evidence there is and arrive at the solution they deem best.

The issue of burden of proof arises most frequently where a proposal is presented to insert new language into the contract. Under these circumstances, the burden of proof is generally on the party who is making the proposed change. But even the nature of that burden varies by issue.

For example, where the issue is an economic one, the burden is not unusually heavy. Although arbitrators are reluctant to add additional new benefits into a collective bargaining agreement, the burden on a party proposing such a change is simply to demonstrate that the weight of the comparable support of such a proposal. The arbitrator may not grant the award at that time in light of the total package. But many arbitrators have inserted new economic benefits into a contract simply by observing that the majority of comparables already have that benefit available. As to new economic benefits, there is a weighing and balancing of the strength of the comparability data against the fact that arbitration is fundamentally a conservative process.

Arbitrator Jane Wilkinson once noted this resistance to adding new premiums, explaining that her "predilection is to leave premium pay to the parties' negotiations, a forum that is more suited to fine tuning the division of the compensation 'pie,' so to speak." She added: "The parties themselves are in a better position than an arbitrator to place a relative value on the specialized skills and training for which special compensation is suited."[26]

---

[26] *City of Tacoma* (Fire) (Wilkinson, 2007) at 13.

When it comes to non-economic issues, the burden of proof is generally even higher upon a party. It is often not enough simply to show that the comparables support a proposal. Arbitrators usually also look to determine if there is an *actual problem* that the proposal is designed to address.

There is a problem, though, when this argument is taken to its logical extension. Some employers simply refuse to add premiums, not matter what the comparability evidence supports. In reality, arbitrators *do* add new premiums, but the burden on the union to support those proposals is often a high one. The union needs to be prepared to present very strong comparability evidence when adding new premiums to the contract.

When it comes to non-economic issues, the burden of proof is generally even higher upon a party. It is often not enough simply to show that the comparables support a proposal. Arbitrators usually also look to determine if there is an *actual problem* that the proposal is designed to address. As Arbitrator Lankford pithily explained: "When it comes to the 'language' portions of a collective bargaining agreement, the party proposing the 'fix it' should have to show just why it is 'broke'."[27] And as Arbitrator Gary Axon stated: "Arbitral authority teaches the moving party must establish a compelling need for a major change in the status quo and the past practice established by previous Collective Bargaining Agreements."[28]

Again, arbitration should be viewed as a conservative process. Arbitrators are reluctant to rewrite the collective bargaining agreement simply to add a clause that other jurisdictions might have. The party proposing such a clause must explain why there is a compelling need to change the parties' existing collective bargaining agreement.

In reality, as non-economic terms the burden of proof appears to be different depending on the type of non-economic issue at stake. In public safety labor agreements, there are certain "boilerplate" clauses that one would simply expect to have. For example, one would ordinarily have a "just cause" provision in a

---

[27] *City of Longview* (Police) (Lankford, 2008) at 9-10.
[28] *King County* (Transit) (Axon, 2006) at 7.

contract as a means of protecting employees from unreasonable discipline. Most arbitrators would not require a union to put on compelling proof of a "problem" before agreeing to add such language to a contract, although the extent of a problem might be a factor to be considered. It is understood that the absence of certain clauses will prove to be a problem in the future even if they have not been yet and that they should simply be part of the agreement. On these types of issues, therefore, comparability evidence alone might carry the day.

On the other hand, with contract language outside the common boilerplate, the proponent of the language would typically be held to a high standard of evidence. Most arbitrators have an inherent resistance to rewriting the CBA language. They fear, with some justification, that such a redrafting can have unforeseen consequences and place the parties in a worse position than before. So parties advocating for such changes have to be ready to present strong evidence not just of the problem but also equally strong evidence that their proposed solution is workable and will solve the problem.

4. The Statutory Criteria

In enacting the interest arbitration provisions of the collective bargaining agreement, the legislature primarily adopted language from other state interest arbitration statutes. In so doing, they indicated to arbitrators that they could rely on the traditional approaches that interest arbitrators had taken in deciding cases.

The criteria arbitrators are defined in RCW 41.56.465:

> (1) In making its determination, the panel shall be mindful of the legislative purpose enumerated in RCW 41.56.430 and, as additional standards or guidelines to aid it in reaching a decision, the panel shall consider:
>
> (a) The constitutional and statutory authority of the employer;
>
> (b) Stipulations of the parties;
>
> (c) The average consumer prices for goods and services, commonly known as the cost of living;

(d) Changes in any of the circumstances under (a) through (c) of this subsection during the pendency of the proceedings; and

(e) Such other factors, not confined to the factors under (a) through (d) of this subsection, that are normally or traditionally taken into consideration in the determination of wages, hours, and conditions of employment. For those employees listed in *RCW 41.56.030(7)(a) who are employed by the governing body of a city or town with a population of less than fifteen thousand, or a county with a population of less than seventy thousand, consideration must also be given to regional differences in the cost of living.

(2) For employees listed in RCW 41.56.030(7) (a) through (d) [law enforcement and corrections], the panel shall also consider a comparison of the wages, hours, and conditions of employment of personnel involved in the proceedings with the wages, hours, and conditions of employment of like personnel of like employers of similar size on the west coast of the United States.

(3) For employees listed in *RCW 41.56.030(7) (e) through (h) [fire personnel], the panel shall also consider a comparison of the wages, hours, and conditions of employment of personnel involved in the proceedings with the wages, hours, and conditions of employment of like personnel of public fire departments of similar size on the west coast of the United States. However, when an adequate number of comparable employers exists within the state of Washington, other west coast employers may not be considered.

As indicated, the statute indicates the arbitrator being "mindful" of the purposes in RCW 41.56.430. That provision states:

The intent and purpose of chapter 131, Laws of 1973 is to recognize that there exists a public policy in the

> state of Washington against strikes by uniformed personnel as a means of settling their labor disputes; that the uninterrupted and dedicated service of these classes of employees is vital to the welfare and public safety of the state of Washington; that to promote such dedicated and uninterrupted public service there should exist an effective and adequate alternative means of settling disputes.

Essentially, the legislature if substituting arbitration for any strike rights to ensure that these public safety services are "uninterrupted." Arbitration decisions that estimate what the outcome would be, were the union to strike, appear to be consistent with this policy.

Next we will consider how arbitrators have interpreted and applied these various statutory criteria.

5. Comparability

a. The Importance of Comparability

Without a doubt, "comparability" is the most important factor in an interest arbitration proceeding. The requirement under RCW 41.56.465(e)(ii) to make a "comparison of the wages, hours and conditions of employment" has *consistently* been interpreted to require an examination of "comparable" jurisdictions in the rendering of an award.

Comparability has been recognized as the predominant criteria used in interest arbitration proceedings.[29] Comparability is seen as a "rational" principle to apply because it furthers the interest of all concerned. Arbitrators have cited the reasoning of Professor Irving Bornstein:

> Comparisons are preeminent in wage determinations because all parties at interest derive benefit from them. To the worker they permit a decision on the adequacy of his income. He feels no discrimination if he stays abreast of other workers in his industry, his locality, his neighborhood. They are vital to the Union because they provide guidance to its officials upon what must be insisted upon and a yardstick for measuring their bargaining skill. In the presence of

[29] *See* Bornstein, Gosline, and Greenbaum, LABOR AND EMPLOYMENT ARBITRATION, § 48.05[2] (2d Ed. 1998).

> internal factionalism or arrival unionism, the power of comparisons is enhanced. The employer is drawn to them because they assure him that competitors will not gain a wage-cost advantage and that he will be able to recruit in the local labor market. Small firms (and unions) profit administratively by accepting a ready-made solution; they avoid the expenditure of time and money needed for working out one themselves. Arbitrators benefit no less from comparisons. They have "the appeal of precedent and...awards based thereon are apt to satisfy the normal expectations of the parties and to appear just to the public.[30]

Comparability is often fiercely contested in interest arbitration hearings. The parties usually recognize that defining which jurisdictions are comparables will largely control the outcome.

One explanation for the overwhelming reliance on comparability data is that such a comparison allows a "presumptive test to the fairness of a wage."[31] As Arbitrator Snow notes:

> The purpose of comparisons is to provide a rational standard and not to create a method for splitting the difference in interest arbitration. The parties do not seek the weighted average of an arbitrator's notion of equity but, rather, a principled basis for resolving their impasse.[32]

Because these comparisons seem inherently fair, they are presumed to be more likely to produce a result acceptable to those

---

[30] Bornstein, ARBITRATION OF WAGES at 54 (1954) (*quoting* Note, "Factors Relied Upon by Arbitrators in Determining Wage Rates", 47 COLUMBIA LAW REVIEW, 1028 (1947)).

[31] *City of Moses Lake* (Fire) (Snow, 1991) at 5 (*quoting* Fies, PRINCIPLES OF WAGE SETTLEMENT, 339) (1924); *see also, City of Ellensburg* (Fire) (Snow, 1992) at 5 (same effect).

[32] *City of Moses Lake, supra* at 6.

affected.[33]

Although it is easy to see why "comparability" would be important, it is less easy to resolve disputes over defining comparability. Comparability is often fiercely contested in interest arbitration hearings. The parties usually recognize that defining which jurisdictions are comparables will largely control the outcome. Often, parties end up in interest arbitration *because* they had widely divergent views on what constituted "comparable" jurisdictions.

Although the statute provides some guidance, it also gives room for both parties to make dueling arguments about comparability. In reality, there are a number of competing considerations that go into determining what is a "comparable."

In interest arbitration, the parties set forth what they believe are their best arguments and allow the arbitrator to decide and balance these competing factors. Next we will look at a number of the most important factors in measuring comparability.

b. *Defining Comparability*

There are usually two threshold questions toward defining comparability. First, which factors (including how many) factors should an arbitrator use? Second, as to the quantitative demographic data, what type of numeric selection "range" should an arbitrator impose on the data.

Advocates and arbitrators have taken divergent approaches to how complex determination should be. The "traditional" approach has been relatively simple. Generally, the parties come in with data on population and probably assessed valuation. They then usually offer some type of "geographic screen" over the data. But with the increasing availability of computerized databases and the increased sophistication of advocates, there have been a number of cases where arbitrators have been presented with a "multi-factor" approach toward selecting comparables.

Arbitrators have had differing views toward this more complex approach. Some have criticized the multi-factor approach as involving "esoteric demographics."[34] These arbitrators have indicated that the simpler approach is what arbitrators have followed in the past, and it is what they think is most acceptable to the parties themselves.

---

[33] *See Whatcom County* (Police) (Snow, 1986) at 6-8 (Appendix 23).

[34] *See City of Walla Walla* (Police) (Levak, 1986) at 23.

While arbitrators sometimes rely only on population and assessed valuation for selecting comparables, this is more of a reflection of the approach of the advocates than anything based either in fact or in the statute.

On the other hand, a number of arbitrators have been convinced that there is merit to the more complex "multi-factor" approach. In a number of arbitration cases, the advocates have convinced the arbitrator that these other factors have a stronger relationship to actual comparability and warrant consideration.

While arbitrators sometimes rely only on population and assessed valuation for selecting comparables, this is more of a reflection of the approach of the advocates than anything based either in fact or in the statute. Objective, scholarly studies on wage determination indicate many factors than just population and assessed valuation are predictive of wage rates. Demographic data such as population density, hourly wage earnings and income inequality, and other demographic factors have been determined by economists to be highly predictive of public safety employee wages.

Arguably, factors that are predictive of wages should be used in selecting comparables because such factors reflect actual market forces. The use of multiple factors using concrete demographic data lends a greater degree of objectivity and a lower degree of subjectivity to the process. Jurisdictions are identified as "comparable" not because they "seem" comparable but because statistical studies confirm certain demographic factors that are known to be predictive of wages and which are shared in common.

One of the most frequently contested questions in defining comparability is how "close" jurisdictions need to be in demographic characteristics in order to be considered "comparable." Because most of the demographic criteria is quantitative in nature, it is easy enough for the parties to spell out simple numeric formulas for selecting comparables.

Early on in the statute, some arbitrators have selected comparables if they were within "x" number of thousands of the target jurisdiction. This approach never fully caught on much because it is fairly arbitrary and does not lend itself to much predictability. Instead, the parties have advocated, and arbitrators began agreeing, that comparables should be selected by imposing a certain *percentage* range upon the data and determining if the jurisdictions fell within that range.

In the early use of this percentage approach, it was common to impose a range in which jurisdictions were selected which were 50% larger or 50% smaller than the target jurisdiction. But despite the superficial appeal this approach might have, as a matter of mathematical logic, it actually proves to be unfair to the target jurisdiction. In reality, it can be shown that this method is borne out of an error both in logic and language grammar.

The key is understanding that what logically should be used is a "ratio" between the jurisdictions. A common ratio selected is 2:1. In percentage terms, this actually ends up being 100% above and 50% below. Because 100% above and 50% below does not "sound" symmetrical, employers generally criticize this approach as being unfair and result-oriented. In fact, a rigorous statistical analysis of the data indicates it produces a more fair result than the 50/50 approach generally argued by employers.

Most union advocates apply the 2-1 (+100%/-50%) formula but, surprisingly, a small number of union advocates unnecessarily concede this point.

Over time, the 2:1 ratio approach has caught on, although it is still controversial. The leading case adopting this approach is a *City of Bellevue* Fire decision by Arbitrator Janet Gaunt in 1988. In that award, she stated:

> In this regard, the Chair finds the reasoning of union expert David Knowles regarding the law of large numbers, i.e., that a decrease in numeric amount has a much larger impact than an increase in the same numeric amount. It stands to reason that if a department 50% the size of Bellevue is deemed similar, then a department *to which Bellevue stands in the same ratio should also be deemed similar on the upper end.*[35]

This same range has since been approved by a number of other arbitrators.[36] Most union advocates apply the 2-1 (+100%/-50%)

---

35 *City of Bellevue* (Fire) (Gaunt, 1988) at 15 (emphasis supplied).

36 *See, e.g., City of Yakima* (Police) (Abernathy, 1980) at 14; *City of Pullman* (Police) (Lumley, 1981) at 10; *City of Pasco* (Police) (Wilkinson, 1994) at 15-16.

formula but, surprisingly, a small number of union advocates unnecessarily concede this point.

The best statement discussing this issue may be that in Arbitrator Jane Wilkinson's decision in a *City of Pasco* police arbitration:

> In my view, the screen utilized is the one needed to produce an adequate number of (usually in-state or local labor market) comparators. The objective, in addition to a sufficient number, is balance. One does not 'fine tune' the screen for the sole purpose of adding or omitting a desirable or undesirable (in terms of pay) jurisdiction. In questionable cases, one should initially err on the side of inclusion. The final list should be balanced in terms of population, wealth, degree of rural isolation and the like. *The best argument for using the Association-preferred approach (minus 50% to plus 100%) for the population screen is that in almost all cases, there are fewer large jurisdictions from which to choose than there are smaller.* Therefore, this approach is necessary to obtain population balance. On the other hand, the debate is academic when the balance can be obtained without that approach.[37]

The point made by Arbitrator Wilkinson is the bottom line on this question. What one seeks in selecting comparables is *balance* on the given criteria.

c. *The Importance of Location*

The statute. Location is important in a number of respects. First of all, the statute specifies the geographic range from which comparables are to be drawn.[38]

The Collective Bargaining Statute sets forth the criteria to be used in selecting comparables. The interest arbitration provision covering law enforcement officers requires a "comparison of the wages, hours, and conditions of employment of personnel involved in the proceedings with the wages, hours and conditions of employment of like personnel of like employers of similar size *on the West Coast of the United States*."[39]

---

[37] *City of Pasco, supra*, at 16 (emphasis added).

[38] Here there is some divergence in the statute between firefighters and others subject to arbitration.

That the legislature intended to mandate out-of-state comparisons under certain circumstances is made even more apparent when the interest arbitration provisions governing firefighters is compared. These provisions are worded identically in terms of how comparisons are made, *except* that the firefighter interest arbitration statute contains an additional proviso: "However, when an adequate number of comparable employers exist within the State of Washington, other West Coast employers may not be considered."[40] In short, firefighter comparables are to be selected within the state except for those larger jurisdictions for which there are few comparables, such as Seattle or Tacoma.

As to law enforcement officers, however, no such out-of-state restriction exists. Numerous arbitrators have interpreted and applied RCW 41.56.465 to mandate at least the consideration of out-of-state comparables.[41]

Case developments over time. In the early years of the interest arbitration statute (from the late 1970s to the early 1980s), a number of arbitrators concluded that they were required to look at out-of-state comparables, even for smaller-to-medium size jurisdictions for which there were ample in-state comparables.[42] Within a few years, though, arbitrators' consensus evolved to include some commonsense considerations about labor markets and the number of comparables. The new consensus was that if there were a sufficient number of comparables within the state or a "readily identifiable labor market," the selection of out-of-state comparables was not mandatory.[43]

A couple of arbitration cases offer a good representative of the current mainstream arbitrator thinking on this issue. In a *City of Pasco* police case, Arbitrator Jane Wilkinson held for the Association that the comparables should be selected entirely within the State of Washington and rejected the employer's attempt to go out-of-state. She reasoned:

> I do not favor out of state comparators, particularly California jurisdictions *when there are a sufficient*

---

[39] RCW 41.56.465(e)(2) (emphasis added).

[40] RCW 41.56.465(e)(3).

[41] *See, e.g., City of Kent* (LaCugna, 1979); *City of Renton* (Snow, 1978); *City of Bellevue* (Block, 1982); *City of Olympia* (DeGrasse, 1984); *City of Kennewick* (LaCugna, 1985); *City of Walla Walla* (Levak, 1986); *Kitsap County* (Tinning, 1986); *Cowlitz County* (Beck, 1987).

[42] *See, e.g., City of Renton* (Snow, 1978); *City of Kent* (LaCugna, 1979).

[43] *See, e.g., City of Bellevue* (Block, 1982); *City of Edmonds* (Lindauer, 1983); *City of Bothell* (Beck, 1983); *City of Walla Walla* (Levak, 1986).

> *number of comparators in state.* Although the interest arbitration statute permits an arbitrator to consider "West Coast" jurisdictions, I believe *the legislature intended out of state comparisons for larger jurisdictions having an insufficient number of in state comparators.* Several arbitrators have discussed this view or some variation thereon.[44]

Another case that demonstrates this principle is a *City of Vancouver* police decision by Arbitrator Michael Beck. *Vancouver* presented some interesting comparative questions because of its location on the Oregon-Washington border. The City urged consideration of comparators from Oregon, Washington and California. Arbitrator Beck ruled for the union on this issue.

Beck noted the statutory mandate to consider the "West Coast" and then stated:

> While it is possible as the employer suggests to first consider and then reject California as a source of comparable employers, there must be a significant reasons [sic] to do so in light of the statutory language. Thus, for example, if an arbitrator is looking at comparators for a small city located along the I-5 corridor between Seattle and Olympia, and the arbitrator finds there are a sufficient number of comparators located along that I-5 corridor, the arbitrator might appropriately limit consideration of comparators to that area based on well recognized concepts of labor markets.

Beck also considered the distinction between the police and fire arbitration statutes to be significant. He reasoned:

> Thus, as the Union points out, while the legislature thought it was appropriate to limit comparable employers to the State of Washington when an adequate number of such employers existed for firefighters, it did not make the same determination with respect to law enforcement officers. This suggests to the arbitrator that *it would be contrary to the legislative intent to limit the selection of comparable employers to state or regional areas merely because*

---

[44] *City of Pasco* (Wilkinson, 1994) (emphasis added).

> *there was an adequate number of such comparable employers in that state or regional area with respect to law enforcement officers.*[45]

California jurisdictions. Because of its sheer size and number of cities and counties, data runs often produce far more California matches than Oregon or Washington matches. To avoid giving extensive weight to California, some arbitrators have ruled that the number of California jurisdictions to be selected should be limited so as not to distort the result.[46]

The other issue that arises in connection with the use of California jurisdictions is the alleged differential in the cost of living. Where West Coast jurisdictions have been mandated — because the jurisdiction at issue was large so that California comparables had to be used — employers have generally made cost of living arguments. Some of these arguments have become fairly technical and advanced. In a number of cases, cities have presented expert economic evidence purporting to show that the cost of living in California is substantially higher than the cost of living in Washington. Although arbitrators have generally rejected these arguments — usually because the economic evidence is insufficiently conclusive — it does appear that arbitrators have been reluctant to pull Washington wages up to exact parity with California wages. Whether or not arbitrators say so explicitly in their decisions, a close reading of the awards shows that arbitrators tend to give more attention to disparities of nearby jurisdictions and less weight to disparities with out-of-state jurisdictions.

Arbitrators have consistently held that close geographic proximity between jurisdictions warrants special consideration in the selection of comparables.

Geographic proximity and "labor market." Another factor given significant and sometimes controlling — weight is geographic proximity. Sometimes by geographic proximity arbitrators are looking at physical distance, whereas at other times they are looking at whether there is a definable common "labor market" among the available comparables.

---

[45] Emphasis added.

[46] *See, e.g., City of Kennewick* (LaCugna, 1985); *City of Seattle* (Kienast, 1984); *City of Everett* (Axon, 1997).

Arbitrators have consistently held that close geographic proximity between jurisdictions warrants special consideration in the selection of comparables.[47] In fact, some arbitrators have even ruled that close geographic proximity offsets dissimilarities in size.[48] Jurisdictions that share a defined labor market are often given special consideration in the determination of comparables.[49]

Another line of arbitration decisions has noted the significant impact proximity to major metropolitan areas has upon wages. These arbitrators have held that this metropolitan impact is entitled to special consideration in the selection of comparables.[50]

Yet another related argument concerning geographic proximity and urban location concerns comparability where the comparables are from a different labor market. This argument states that what ought to be given weight is how close the proposed comparables are to a large metropolitan area. The argument is that proximity to a large metropolitan area has a strong impact on wages.

Such arguments have been received on a mixed basis. Often, the notion is criticized because of the lack of available supporting economic data to make the concept meaningful or measurable.[51] But Arbitrator Levak in a leading arbitration decision out from the *City of Walla Walla* did claim that comparables should be selected based upon their belonging to an "ascertainable geo-political Washington labor market." Examples Levak gave of such separate "geo-political" labor markets were the isolated agricultural-based cities east of the Cascades and hub cities close to large metropolitan areas.[52]

And more recent arbitrator decisions do seem to give more weight to the urban-rural distinction. For example, in a Mount Vernon arbitration, Arbitrator Reeves followed the path of another recent Longview decision[53] in crediting an "Interstate 5" theory of comparability, rejecting Wenatchee and Port Angeles and comparables for Mount Vernon.[54]

---

[47] *See, e.g., Board of Supervisors, Sioux County, Iowa*, 87 LA 552, 553-56, (1986); *City of Ellensburg* (Fire) (Snow, 1992) at 12-13 (Appendix 4); *Whatcom County* (Police) (Snow, 1986) at 8.

[48] *See City of Renton,* 71 LA 271, 274 (Snow, 1978); *City of Pasco* (Police) (Krebs, 1990) at 10; *City of Seattle* (Police) (Kienast, 1984) at 4-5.

[49] *See City of Richland* (Fire) (Lehleitner, 1984) at 15-16.

[50] *See City of Richland* (Fire) (Lehleitner, 1984) at 15-16; *City of Pullman* (Police) (Lumbley, 1981) at 10.

[51] *See, e.g., City of Olympia* (Police) (DeGrasse, 1984) at 11-12.

[52] *City of Walla Walla* (Police) (Levak, 1986) at 23.

[53] *City of Longview* (Police) (Nelson, 2001).

[54] *City of Mount Vernon* (Police) (Reeves, 2007) at 4.

General principles. All these competing factors can probably be boiled down into a description of the *general arbitral tendencies* in applying labor market considerations:

- Defined labor markets should be the source of comparables whenever a sufficient number of comparables can be identified within that labor market.
- What constitutes a "sufficient number" of comparables is unclear, but it is usually a half dozen or more.
- For the largest jurisdictions, those for whom few in state comparables exist, arbitrators will reach out to the West Coast states of California and Oregon, sometimes limiting the number of California jurisdictions to be used.
- For jurisdictions in King, Pierce and Snohomish, comparables will usually be selected from this area as a defined labor market.
- For urban Central Puget Sound jurisdictions outside the three largest counties, such as Thurston and Kitsap Counties, there is a strong tendency to select comparables from the Central Puget Sound area; but arbitrators will sometimes go outside that immediate area especially if an insufficient number of comparables can be identified within the area, or if the jurisdiction is on the perimeter of the Central Puget Sound.
- For Western Washington jurisdictions outside the Central Puget Sound area, comparables will be selected within Western Washington, sometimes with a reduced emphasis on the greater Seattle area, but if an insufficient number of Western Washington exist, Eastern Washington will be used.
- But for those Western Washington jurisdictions on the I-5 corridor, some weight will be given to reducing the number of rural comparables with the selection of a greater number of comparables on or near I-5.
- For Eastern Washington jurisdictions, the a statewide labor market is usually applied, except that with smaller jurisdictions, where a sufficient number of Eastern

Washington comparables exist, the comparables might be selected exclusively from Eastern Washington.

Applying these labor market concepts is more art than science. Therefore, predicting the result is difficult. First of all, the concept of "labor market" is itself flexible and not well defined. Even economists cannot provide a clear definition of what constitutes a "labor market." Second, there is no strong consensus on what makes up an adequate number of comparables.

An Ellensburg Firefighter case well demonstrates this point.[55] The parties were quite divided on the question of the relevant labor market, the union arguing for a statewide market and the City arguing that the comparables should be drawn only from Eastern Washington. The union argued that because only three Eastern Washington fire departments matched Ellensburg and because Ellensburg was located near the center of the state, the arbitrator should give equal weight to the union's proposed Western Washington jurisdictions. Arbitrator Carlton rejected the union argument, finding that while three comparables was not very many it was enough and that Eastern Washington was more relevant to determining Ellensburg wages.

This case provides an example of one arbitrator's analysis, but this probably would *not* reflect a majority approach. Most arbitrators seem to be looking for at least a half dozen comparables and if the list of jurisdictions within the proposed labor market is less than that, they will usually broaden the geographic scope.

Another controversial consideration in selecting comparables is cost of living variability, discussed above in the context of California comparables. Often advocates argue that a jurisdiction is or is not comparable based on supposed distinctions in the relative cost of living. These applications are controversial because the underlying cost of living data is itself controversial.

Sometimes arbitrators will exclude as comparables those jurisdictions that it believes have a vastly different regional cost of living. A more recent trend of arbitrators is to select such jurisdictions as comparables but "weight" them differently. Arbitrator Lankford proposed this approach in a pair of recent Kitsap County decisions[56] but then never explained or applied his weighting methodology, finding it was not relevant to his award. But in an even more recent Spokane County case, Arbitrator

---

[55] *City of Ellensburg* (Fire) (Snow, 1992).

[56] *Kitsap County* (Corrections) (Lankford, 2012); *Kitsap County* (Deputies) (Lankford, 2013).

Wilkinson did apply a weighting factor, using BLS cost of living statistics.[57] Cost of living differences are a recognized factor in awards discussed in greater detail below.

d. *The "Like Employer" Mandate*

Numerous arguments have been made and much speculation has previously existed concerning the mandate in the statute to compare "like personnel of like employers." Nonetheless, a clear consensus has developed among arbitrators as what this mandate means.

arbitrators interpret this phrase to mean that cities should be compared to cities and counties should be compared to counties

First, the "like personnel" requires comparison of police officers to police officers and firefighters to firefighters. There has never existed much dispute concerning that requirement, although how alike personnel are as to the extent of their duties and the workloads can be considered a secondary factor, as will be discussed below.

At the outset of the statute, there was some controversy concerning what the "like employers" mandate was to mean, but this has largely been resolved. For the most part, arbitrators interpret this phrase to mean that cities should be compared to cities and counties should be compared to counties. Although in a handful of cases, arbitrators have allowed the comparison of cities and counties, this is a distinctly minority approach. The comparison between cities and counties seems more frequent when the county is highly urbanized and operates to some degree in the nature as a municipal police force.

The issue concerning firefighters and "like employers," though, was previously the subject of greater controversy. Early on, there was abundant argument about whether municipal fire departments and fire districts should be compared. A number of arbitrators had ruled that they should not, as they were not "like employers" as far as agency funding and governance. These disputes eventually resulted in a legislative fix in which the firefighter portion of the interest arbitration statute was amended to require comparison "of like personnel of public fire departments

---

[57] *Spokane County* (Deputies) (Wilkinson, 2015).

of similar size."[58]

e. Population

Without a doubt, population is the single most used criteria for selecting comparables. The statute specifies, after all, that comparables should be of "similar size."

Nonetheless, there has been some controversy concerning population for two reasons. First, there are different ways of measuring size, including population. Second, some parties have argued that population is the *only* criteria that should be used in selecting comparables.

population is the single most used criteria for selecting comparables

Another argument that have been made, with mixed success, is that size should take into account not simply the official residential population, which after all only measures nighttime population, but it should take into account other measures, such as the daytime population or the population of the actual service area. Those advocates can point to the language in the statute which specifies similar "size," not similar population. These advocates argue that if the legislature had intended to use population as the sole measure of size it would have simply specified population. The prevailing arbitrator view is to give great, if not conclusive, weight to the official nighttime population, consider other measures of size or population under particular circumstances, and consider population as a leading, but not sole, measure of comparability.

f. Tax Base

Beyond geographic proximity and population, assessed valuation is the next leading factor relied upon to measure comparability. A number of arbitrators have approved a methodology that simply uses population and assessed valuation as the sole demographic screen. As one arbitrator reasoned, considering assessed valuation was a means of determining if employers were "alike" so as to satisfy the statutory "like employer" criteria.[59]

Advocates utilizing the multi-factor approach have usually urged consideration of broader measures of tax base, including

---

[58] RCW 41.56.030(e)(3).

[59] *City of Pasco* (Police) (Krebs, 1990) at 5.

sales tax revenue and total retail activity. The logic of such an approach is sound, given that in a number of jurisdictions retail sales and business tax revenue equals or exceed the revenue derived from the property tax. Wholly focusing on assessed valuation can arguably produce a distorted result of a jurisdiction's tax base.

Advocates utilizing the multi-factor approach have usually urged consideration of broader measures of tax base, including sales tax revenue and total retail activity.

Despite this logic, advocates for this position have met with mixed success before arbitrators. In more recent years, when that data was actually presented, arbitrators have seemed open to considering sales tax revenue, especially when wide variance in sales tax revenue existed among the proposed comparables.[60]

g. *Other Measures of Comparability*

Advocates have also urged arbitrators to consider a wide range of additional and miscellaneous criteria. These sometimes creative and even logical arguments have met with mixed success.

Arbitrators, for example, have given more or less weight to considerations such as the size of a department (for example, number of commissioned or total personnel) and workload. Employees have often strenuously argued for consideration of workload as a factor in measuring comparability, but arbitrators have generally concluded the measures of workload not necessarily to be reliable indicators of what was occurring in a jurisdiction. When workload is considered, it is not for the purpose of selecting comparables but as an "other factor" for the purpose of evaluating wages.

6. Factors Other than Comparability

Although the statute suggests comparability is a criterion for determining arbitration issues, it is not the only guideline set forth in the statute. Arbitrators have considered other factors as well, some of which are specified in the statute and some of which are not.

a. *Cost of Living*

---

60 *See, e.g.*, *City of Omak* (Police) (Reeves, 2004).

As we discussed above, some arbitrators have evaluated supposed cost of living differences in selecting comparables. But cost of living considerations can also be used in determining the award.

Changes in the CPI in a relevant time period have been given great weight in arbitration proceedings.

The interest arbitration statute specifies as a factor to consider "the average consumer prices for goods and services, commonly known as the cost of living."[61] But the concept of "cost of living" can be and has been interpreted to mean two different things. The most common understanding of the notion of "cost of living" — and the most commonly used — is the measure of year-to-year adjustments in the supposed cost of living, commonly known as the CPI Index.

Changes in the CPI in a relevant time period have been given great weight in arbitration proceedings. Along with the "wage gap" identified by an analysis of the comparables and recent settlement trends, CPI appears to be a primary determinant of wage awards.

There has been some contention concerning the appropriate CPI Index to use. Clearly, the appropriate measure of CPI to use in the core Seattle metropolitan area is the Seattle CPI.[62] The further one moves away from Seattle, though, the more argument there has been overuse of the Seattle CPI versus other national or west coast measures of CPI.

There has also been some argument made on behalf of employers that the CPI Index "overstates" the amount of inflation occurring in the economy. Arbitrators have yet to accept this argument. In a recent Washington State Patrol case, Arbitrator Lankford rejected the State's argument that he should adopt the "Implicit Price Deflator" because the CPI overstated inflation.[63]

On the other hand, there has been consideration and some degree of acceptance of the employer arguments that some percentage of the CPI less than the full 100% is warranted. Employers have argued, for example, that the cost of living increase is not necessary each year because much of the CPI Index is based on rising housing costs and individuals do not replace their house each year. But arbitrators have given little or no weight

[61] RCW 41.56.430(d).
[62] *King County* (Transit) (Beck, 2008).
[63] *Washington State Patrol* (Troopers) (Lankford, 2008) at 6.

to this claim. Instead, arbitrators have often found persuasive the employer argument that where the employer maintains 100% coverage of health insurance premiums, a full 100% increase in CPI on top of benefit maintenance would result in total compensation increase greater than 100%. The logic is that the health insurance component makes up a large part of the CPI Index.[64] But where the employer is attempting to erode existing benefits, this argument could probably be flipped on them.

The other meaning the term "cost of living" that has been urged by some advocates is that of the actual cost of living in a given locale. Therefore, parties have sometimes argued that regional differences in the cost of living warrant some consideration in making wage comparisons.

For example, employers in cities which have California comparables have gone to great length — and apparent great expense — to present highly technical studies and to argue that the California wages should be discounted. Although some arbitrators seem to acknowledge the possibility of such regional differences, arbitrators in the past have been fairly consistent in rejecting these regional difference studies, often because of the inadequacy or unreliability of the presented evidence.[65] One arbitrator went so far as to refer to the studies as "patently flawed."[66]

A more recent Spokane County arbitration decision by Jane Wilkinson, though, adopts a recent BLS estimate of regional cost of living variance.[67] Due to the "official" nature of the source, as opposed to the previous proffered proprietary measures, the BLS method could gain some traction.

b. Prevailing Contract Settlements

"Settlement trends" have been frequently relied upon by arbitrators in rendering wage awards.[68] Often, arbitrators will consider the settlement trends among the selected comparables.

But arbitrators have also used non-comparables in assessing settlement trends.[69] Although, as discussed above, arbitrators have

---

[64] *See, e.g., City of Seattle* (Police) (Kienast, 1984) at 19.

[65] *See, e.g., City of Seattle* (Police) (Kienast, 1984) at 12-15; *City of Seattle (Police Management)* (Krebs, 1984); *King County* (Deputy Sheriffs) (Dorsey, 1985) at 14-15.

[66] *City of Walla Walla* (Police) (Levak, 1986) at 23-24.

[67] Spokane County (Deputies) (Wilkinson, 2015).

[68] *Spokane County* (Transit) (Torosian, 2006) at 15; *City of Omak* (Police) (Reeves, 2004); *City of Everett* (Police) (Axon, 1997); *City of Bremerton* (Police) (Axon, 1998); *City of Seattle* (Police) (Kienast, 1984) at 16-17; *City of Walla Walla* (Police) (Levak, 1986) at 28.

not selected comparables that were not of like type or like size even if in the same labor market, arbitrators have considered settlement trends within the labor market for that job classification.[70] For example, arbitrators will sometimes consider in a given county what the settlements have been among a wide range of jurisdictions, including both the municipal police departments and the sheriff's office.

"Settlement trends" have been frequently relied upon by arbitrators in rendering wage awards.

And parties sometimes argue that wages for the broader labor market outside that job classification should be considered. For example, where the general labor market is strong and wages are rising, or the economy is in recession and wages are falling or flat, parties have argued arbitrators should look at these other wage trends. A review of arbitration awards does not indicate much support for this approach, but it does appear to be something that arbitrators take into account.

c. *Internal Equities*

Parties have argued for consideration of "internal equity" — that is, within the employer — with a limited degree of success. Here again the notion of "internal equity" has different considerations. First, it can refer to agreed or imposed wage settlements in that jurisdiction in that given year. Second, it can refer to the overall wage gap between arguably similar job classifications.

Often, employers will argue that if, for example, the other bargaining units only receive 2%, then the interest arbitration group should also receive the same percentage. Some arbitrators have found this to be "relevant," but other arbitrators have given it limited weight.[71] And even those arbitrators who deem it relevant do not seem to give it too much weight.[72] Other arbitrators have distinguished between the settlements reached by other interest arbitration eligible bargaining units and those that lack binding

[69] *City of Tukwila* (Firefighters) (LaCugna, 1976).
[70] *City of Pullman* (Police) (Axon, 1992).
[71] *King County* (Transit) (Lankford, 2004); *Franklin County* (Deputies) (Wilkinson, 2007) at 9.
[72] *City of Camas* (Fire) (Abernathy 1996); *Whatcom County* (Deputies) (Gangle Smith, 2001).

arbitration.[73]

A policy reason for extending such a factor limited weight is that the group before the arbitrator has no control over what other unions agreed to, and the employer virtually dictates the wages of non-unionized employees. To the extent arbitrators have considered this at all, it usually is a factor when the employer argues that it lacks the ability to pay and is under financial distress.[74] In those circumstances, some arbitrators have extended internal equity significant weight.

Arbitrators have considered the wage relationship between different job classifications as another aspect of "internal equity." But these differences between classifications have not generally been given much consideration except for intra-departmental differentials.

As to the department differential between different ranks, arbitrators have considered "market" differential which should exist between classifications. On the other hand, arbitrators have given this consideration less weight where the employer has argued that the union's wage proposal would cause "wage compression," bumping up against (often non-unionized) mid-level managers. These arbitrators, while not stating this explicitly, probably recognize the higher ranking employees are underpaid relative to their market and are likely due for a raise of their own.

The issue of police and fire parity often arises in contract negotiations, but has received little discussion in Washington interest arbitration. But there is at least one published arbitration award out-of-state which criticized the notion that police and firefighters should be placed in lock step parity.[75]

d. Economic and Fiscal Conditions

Generally, arbitrators will thoroughly consider evidence concerning local economic conditions and a jurisdiction's fiscal situation, but these considerations have been given widely varied weight.

Where the general economic conditions are good, arbitrators will sometimes note it, but it certainly is not given any controlling weight. When the economic conditions are not as good, arbitrators

---

73 *City of Lynnwood* (Fire) (Beck, 2013); *City of Mount Vernon* (Reeves 2007); (Deputies) (Latsch 2011).

74 See *Kitsap County* (Corrections) (Lankford, 2012; *Yakima County* (Deputies) (Gangle Smith, 2004); *City of Redmond* (Police) (Wilkinson, 2004).

75 *District of Columbia Office of Labor Relations and Collective Bargaining*, 84 LA 809 (Rothschild, 1985).

will also consider that as well, particularly when it is presented in conjunction with arguments demonstrating low settlement trends and a jurisdiction's distressed fiscal conditions.

Arbitrator Gary Axon urged that wage awards not be "out of touch" with current economic conditions.[76] But this standard is ambiguous enough to leave room for both sides to make their arguments.

---

arbitrators will thoroughly consider evidence concerning local economic conditions and a jurisdiction's fiscal situation, but these considerations have been given widely varied weight

---

Where an employer can make a strong case concerning difficult fiscal conditions — the condition of their budget, this is extended great, and perhaps controlling, weight by an arbitrator. But arbitrators have often expressed skepticism employers' claims that they have an inability to pay. Arbitrators have created criteria to measure "inability to pay," which makes it difficult for employers to meet the test. Arbitrator Sandra Gangle Smith summarized many of these criteria in a 2004 Yakima County decision:

- "[A]n employer must produce evidence of a current precarious financial condition that mandates a conservative approach to salaries, not simply a fear of future uncertainties regarding revenue losses or adverse legislative action. The employer need not be bankrupt, however."

- "Evidence might include a dramatic downturn in regular revenue receipts, a showing of severely depressed economic conditions, or high unemployment."

- "Other evidence could include prior levy defeats, layoffs, program reductions, absence of a contingency fund or other discretionary fund in the budget, or achievement of a wage freeze with other bargaining units."

---

[76] *City of Pullman* (Police) (Axon, 1992) at 27.

- "The employer must offer clear, authoritative evidence, by experts...regarding the negative status of the budget."

- "The situation must be beyond the employer's control. The employer must convince the arbitrator that it is unable to raise sufficient revenues to meet an established need for a raise, especially where there is compelling evidence shown by comparability or cost of living factors."

Gangle Smith added that: "If the Union disagrees with the employer regarding the employer's stated limited ability to pay, the Union must produce credible expert testimony to support its refutation."[77]

Arbitrator Howell Lankford has criticized the concept of inability to pay, suggesting it does not fit the public sector financial system. He explained:

> *"Financial responsibility"* might be a better term for this traditional factor. The basic economic argument offered by public sector employers in interest arbitration cases amounts to a claim that the union's proposed allocation of the employer's financial resources would be irresponsible, i.e., that funding the union's proposal would deprive the employer of its ability to fund its other statutory responsibilities at a responsible level or would leave the employer in a fiscally irresponsible condition either immediately or in the future.[78]

Perhaps the most thoughtful and detailed discussion of the ability to pay, fiscal condition element, is an arbitration decision by Carlton Snow concerning Whatcom County Deputy Sheriffs.[79] In this decision, Arbitrator Snow created the concept of a "fiscal strain index" as a means of assessing whether a jurisdiction had an ability to pay. Snow proposed four *primary* factors for determining that ability:

1) The employer's long-term per capita debt;

---

[77] *Yakima County* (Deputies) (Gangle Smith, 2004).
[78] *Kitsap County* (Corrections) (Lankford, 2012).
[79] *Whatcom County* (Deputy Sheriffs) (Snow, 1986).

2) The employer's short-term per capita debt;

3) The employer's per capita expenditures for fundamental functions compared to those expenditures in other jurisdictions; and

4) The ratio of revenue to assessed valuation.

Traditionally, Snow proposed seven additional factors to be given *secondary* consideration:

1) The unemployment rate in the jurisdiction;

2) The percentage of residents on welfare;

3) Bond ratings;

4) The employer's unfunded pension liability;

5) Per capita income compared to comparables;

6) Percentage of per capita income expended on property taxes; and

7) The jurisdiction's financial situation, including employee layoffs, new revenues, and budgetary surpluses.[80]

Although other arbitrators have not been as elaborate in their analysis, the types of factors articulated by Snow are the types of factors arbitrators would predictably consider as evidence of a county's fiscal condition.

And though not mentioned in in Snow's list of factors, the employer's actual fund balance is a factor that normally gets a lot of attention whenever an employer claims an inability or limited ability to pay.[81] The factors identified by Snow can be used to supplement an analysis of the fund balance. Snow's factors address long-term fiscal capacity more than the immediate funding situation.

Even where jurisdictions have been in some level of fiscal distress, arbitrators have often still not found that there to an inability to pay. But they have acknowledged the claim and given the fiscal condition some secondary weight in assessing the

[80] *Id.* at 20-21.

[81] *Island County* (Corrections) (Boedeker, 2013); *Lewis County* (Corrections) (Gaba, 2011).

"reasonableness" of the union proposal.

An example of this approach is reflected in a *City of Pasco* case. The arbitration was held during the course of a Hanford economic downturn. Arbitrator Krebs did accept that the city lacked the ability to pay.[82] He cited the city's declining revenue, declining population, declining assessed valuation, maximum tax capacity, reduction in the number of employees on the payroll, and the loss of thousands of jobs in the local economy. In measuring all these factors, he labeled the local economy as "depressed" and indicated that it was a significant consideration to be taken into account in determining wages. And yet he still awarded some wage increases, although moderated ones.

e. *Work Load and Productivity*

It is frequently argued in interest arbitration that employees should receive a large wage increase because of high calls for service, a high number of emergency runs, or a high crime rate. Arbitrators have patiently considered such evidence and then generally given it minimal weight.

Although these factors bear some logic, arbitrators have been reluctant to assess whether the perceived workloads are, in fact, higher. Likewise, arbitrators have usually given little to no weight to employee arguments that there have been improvements or gains in employee productivity as indicated by such measures as clearance rate.

This approach is demonstrated in a Tacoma Fire decision issued by Arbitrator Jane Wilkinson:

> The Union presented evidence showing the increase in call volume from 1996 to 2006. According to that evidence ..., calls increased steadily from 27,995 calls in 1996 to 41,693 calls in 2006. It also presented evidence of changes in workload.
>
> This evidence is not helpful in setting wages for 2006 2008, in my opinion. One could argue that the annual wage increases enjoyed by the bargaining unit (which have outpaced changes in the CPI) reflected, at least in part, this increase in call volume or workload changes. In addition, there was no evidence of record showing a nexus between call volume and wages. Moreover, it is possible that personnel increases offset

---

[82] *City of Pasco* (Police) (Krebs, 1990) at 15-16.

> the impact of increased call volume on workload.
>
> Similarly, although the Union presented evidence that bargaining unit duties increased in scope, skill, and required training, it has not shown that these changes were not taken into account in past wage increases or personnel increases, and it has not shown the relationship between changed duties and compensation.[83]

On occasions, though, arbitrators have found workload claims to be persuasive. In a 2008 Washington State Patrol case, Arbitrator Lankford found convincing the Association's claim that they had to work harder due to understaffing, and concluded that factor should be taken into account in setting wages.[84] And in a Walla Walla Deputy case, Arbitrator Krebs indicated that the higher number of calls per deputy "provide justification for the above average wages the deputies receive."[85] Some arbitrators have at least acknowledged workload issues but have not clearly indicated how that affects their wage award.[86]

f. Employee Morale and Recruitment and Retention Issues

Arbitrators have generally stated that employee morale is an important factor, but it is certainly not clear how much weight they have given the factor. As explained by Arbitrator Levak:

> The Arbitrator has also considered the traditional factor of the "interest and welfare of the public." The Arbitrator has determined that it will serve those interests to pay a wage that is at least the average of the comparators. Payment of a lesser wage, in the face of a demonstrated ability to pay, can only have a significant effect on morale and a resultant decrease in the quality of police services.[87]

---

[83] *City of Tacoma* (Fire) (Wilkinson, 2007).
[84] *Washington State Patrol* (Troopers) (Lankford, 2008).
[85] *Walla Walla County* (Deputies) (Krebs, 2003).
[86] *City of Port Angeles* (Fire) (Gaunt, 2004).
[87] *City of Walla Walla* (Police) (Levak, 1986). *See also*, *City of Pullman* (Police) (Gaunt, 1997).

At least one arbitrator cited employee morale as an important factor in support of a union proposal to extend dependent insurance coverage.[88] But after stating that, the arbitrator rejected the union proposal anyway.

Parties have had greater success arguing recruitment or retention issues, at least where they had clear data to support the claim. Arbitrators have considered a period of either very high or very low turnover as a relevant factor.[89] Even emerging, but not yet fully materialized, recruitment issues can be taken into consideration.[90]

Advocates often will present evidence when there is either a high number or a low number of qualified applicants on recent civil service examinations. Anecdotal evidence might prove to be mildly persuasive where a union can show that the better-qualified candidates are being attracted away to other nearby jurisdictions by higher rates of pay.

Employers often present evidence on this subject as well, claiming that the wage is adequate because recruitment and retention is strong. Arbitrators have given these arguments some weight as well.

7. Determining Wages

After the arbitrator has determined what comparables and other factors to rely upon in setting the interest arbitration award, the important task of actually setting the wage remains. A review of arbitrator's awards indicates no single method or formula exists that one could use to predict with any high degree of accuracy what an arbitrator would actually do in a given case. But there is a general tendency for arbitrators to use the following approaches:

- Comparables that are particularly high or particularly low might be disregarded in setting the wage award.

- There is a strong tendency of arbitrators to at least maintain a jurisdiction placement on the overall list of comparables that existed at the end of the prior contract and, toward this end,

---

[88] *Kitsap County* (Deputy Sheriffs) (Tinning, 1986) at 29-30.

[89] *See, e.g., Snohomish County* (Deputy Sheriffs) (Krebs, 1987) at 16 (citing low turnover); *City of Pasco* (Police) (Krebs, 1990) at 17 (citing high turnover).

[90] *City of Wenatchee* (Police) (Savage, 2003).

recent settlements among the comparables are an important factor.

- Where jurisdictions are below the market, there is a tendency to push them toward, but not necessarily to, the average, particularly when the economic and fiscal conditions permit that type of wage enhancement.

- Jurisdictions that are far behind the average are not likely to be brought up to the average in one or even two agreements; interest arbitration, again, is an incremental, conservative process.

- Jurisdictions that are above the average for the comparables will not usually be denied, for example, a standard cost of living increase in order to bring them down to the average of the comparables; whether or not they receive the average settlement of the comparables that would maintain their place in the list will depend on the arbitrator's discretion and the economic conditions at the time.

- Where there has been a historic pattern of "parity" between two geographically close jurisdictions, those jurisdictions will be given special weight in setting the wage award.[91]

- There is a strong tendency for arbitrators not to pull jurisdictions out of the middle of the pack of comparables and grant them an award which would make them a "wage leader."[92]

The standard point of comparison in police awards and for other groups of employees who work a standard 2,080-hour annual schedule is to focus on base wages.

And if these principles seem vague, they certainly are much

[91] *King County* (Deputy Sheriffs) (Gillingham, 1983).

[92] *City of Pullman* (Police) (Axon, 1992) at 25-26; *City of Seattle* (Police) (Kienast, 1984) at 18-19.

more concrete than the description one arbitrator provided in explaining how wages should be awarded; he simply indicated that the wage award should simply be within "the range of reasonableness" compared with the other comparables.[93]

A frequent point of contention in interest arbitration in comparing wages is what actually should be counted as "wages." Different arbitrators have adopted and applied different models of wage comparison. Further, there is some divergence between the methods applied for setting firefighter awards with those of others subject to interest arbitration, including police.

The standard point of comparison in police awards and for other groups of employees who work a standard 2,080-hour annual schedule is to focus on base wages. Under these circumstances, most arbitrators will examine the "top step" wages from each of the comparables without an immediate comparison of the additional premiums, such as education, longevity and other types of specialty premiums.[94]

When comparisons are made to out-of-state jurisdictions, the issue of "retirement pickup" has arisen, given the practice in California and Oregon for employers to pick up a portion of the wages. (As this benefit is being phased out in these states, this will become less of a comparison issue in the future.) Arbitrators have almost uniformly concluded that such retirement pickup is simply another form of wages and have allowed that to be added to the base wage for purposes of making the top step wage comparison.[95]

In fire interest arbitrations, it has been common to use a "net wage" approach.

There has been more conflict over the concept of "total compensation" as a basis for comparing wages. Under the total compensation approach, virtually all forms of compensation are added to the base wage, not only various premiums, but also the cost of benefits as well.

Although some arbitrators have used this approach,[96] the

---

93 *City of Pullman* (Police) (Axon, 1992) at 28.

94 *See, e.g., City of Richland* (Police) (Beck, 1987) at 12-13; *City of Walla Walla* (Police) (Levak, 1986) at 24.

95 *See, e.g., City of Walla Walla* (Levak, 1986) at 23; *King County* (Deputy Sheriffs) (Dorsey, 1985) at 11-12.

96 *See, e.g., City of Seattle* (Waste Management) (Krebs, 1984) at 10-13; *Snohomish County* (Deputy Sheriffs) (Krebs, 1987) at 12-13.

majority of arbitration awards have declined to follow it. Generally arbitrators have indicated that those other wage-related and benefit-related matters should be evaluated separately in the arbitration decision.[97] Another reason given by arbitrators for not adopting a total compensation model is that arbitrators have claimed it is difficult to make accurate comparisons of the cost or value of different types of benefits.[98] But even where arbitrators have elected to adopt a full "total compensation" approach, they have often given significant weight to education and longevity premiums as part of a base wage comparison.[99]

In fire interest arbitrations, it has been common to use a "net wage" approach. The "net hours" are calculated where the total hours to be worked are measured by taking the total scheduled hours and subtracting out the paid leave such as holiday, vacation and Kelley time. The net hours are then divided by the total wage to determine the net hourly rate. This formula has become a quite common method of comparison in fire arbitration simply because there is a wide variability among fire contracts, based on most of the annual number of hours actually worked.

In non-fire contracts, there is much less variability in the annual hours of work, given the predominant pattern of the 2,080-hour work year. In police contracts, for example, even where the officers are assigned to an alternative schedule such as a "4/12" shift, hours are usually adjusted back to 2,080 annually by means of "Kelley time." Perhaps largely due to the limited variability in work hours, Arbitrators have been disinclined to accept a net wage analysis outside of the fire service.[100] As Arbitrator Greco explained in a Kitsap deputy sheriff case, the net wage analysis common to fire contracts is less applicable to law enforcement contracts:

> Those cited cases involved firefighters who, as the Guild points out, often have irregular work schedules which make it very different to compare their hourly wages with the hourly wages paid to other firefighters. Here, though, law enforcement personnel have more

[97] *See, e.g., Cowlitz County* (Deputy Sheriffs) (Beck, 1987) at 10; *City of Pasco* (Police) (Krebs, 1990).

[98] *See, e.g., King County* (Deputy Sheriffs) (Dorsey, 1985) at 13-14.

[99] *See, e.g., Cowlitz County* (Deputy Sheriffs) (Beck, 1987) at 11.

[100] *Pacific County* (Deputies) (Siegel, 2012); *City of Elma* (Police) (deGrasse, 2009) at 4-5; *City of Wenatchee* (Police) (Savage, 2003); Cowlitz County (Deputies) (Beck, 1987).

> regularized work schedules which make it much easier to compare hourly wage rates, and that is the way hourly wage rates have been traditionally determined for law enforcement groups. [101]

But some arbitrators have agreed to apply this net wage methodology.[102]

Where law enforcement agencies did have a differing work year lengths, there is a division among the arbitrators as to how to handle this issue. Some have said that such should be accounted for in setting wage awards,[103] while others have indicated that this issue should be addressed in the context of the hours of work article.[104]

Issues sometimes arise concerning the makeup of the pay system. Where the issue has related to changing the number of pay steps, arbitrators have been reluctant to alter the steps, stating this is probably better a matter left for collective bargaining.[105] On the other hand, especially where the adjustments are supported by comparability data, arbitrators have considered the existing differentials *between* classifications as a factor of internal equity which might warrant a change.

Occasionally, contracts have a provision that require some type of "satisfactory performance" element in order to move through the pay steps. Arbitrators have issued divided awards on whether these are warranted. And even if arbitrators do grant such language, they would likely be assessing whether the proposal was subject to the grievance procedure.[106]

As was discussed earlier, pay periods are a mandatory subject of bargaining. Sometimes employers acquire new payroll systems or computer systems which necessitate, from their perspective, a change in the timing of paychecks. Arbitrators have recognized that employers want to have county-wide payroll systems and have generally granted these proposals.[107]

---

101 *Kitsap County* (Deputies) (Greco, 2005).

102 *City of Vancouver* (Police) (Axon, 2013); *Franklin County* (Deputies) (Wilkinson, 2007); *City of Vancouver* (Police) (Beck, 1998).

103 *City of Seattle* (Police) (Kienast, 1984).

104 *City of Everett* (Axon, 1997).

105 *Mount Vernon* (Police) (Axon, 1994); *City of Seattle* (Police Management) (Krebs, 1984) at 23.

106 Compare *Cowlitz County* (Deputy Sheriffs) (Beck, 1987) at 19-21 with *City of Bremerton* (Police) (Axon, 1997).

107 *City of Pullman* (Police) (Axon, 1992) at 84-85.

8. Other Premiums and Pays

Because arbitration is a conservative, incremental approach, it is often difficult to win the addition of new premium plans in arbitration.

Typically, the issue of other types of premiums such as education, longevity, specialty assignment, shift differential will be determined by arbitrators largely by looking at the same type of factors they consider for wage awards, especially comparability. In assessing whether to add new premiums or enhance existing ones, arbitrators will certainly look at the overall wage, including all available premiums. Because arbitration is a conservative, incremental approach, it is often difficult to win the addition of new premium plans in arbitration. Arbitrators seem to be more likely to enhance existing premiums when they can be shown to be out of line with comparables rather than interjecting new premium proposals.

On the other hand, there have been a number of arbitration awards where arbitrators have provided strong comparability evidence as a basis to create a new premium. In general, it appears that arbitrators are more sympathetic with proposals for education premiums than with longevity premiums. In an Olympia Police case Arbitrator DeGrasse explained his award adding an education premium:

> Concerning educational attainment, the Guild introduced evidence that compels the conclusion that increased education contributes to good police work. Not only does education make an officer more effective in dealing with the public, but it also makes the officer a better employee by reducing absenteeism. I do not find that educational attainment in and of itself will insure better police work or that an officer without a college degree cannot be an effective police officer. Nonetheless, *I find that educational attainment is sufficiently correlated to good police work, that it should be encouraged and rewarded.*[108]

[108] *City of Olympia* (Police) (DeGrasse, 1984) (emphasis added).

Questions frequently arise in arbitration about whether premiums should be maintained on a flat dollar amount or a percentage amount. Arbitrators have generally ruled for unions on this issue, holding that premiums should be defined in percentage terms, which means that they rise automatically as the base wage rises. The general rationale arbitrators have offered for this position is that it will avoid the need for continual renegotiation of the issue.[109]

Issues concerning adding or enhancing deferred compensation benefits have arisen on a handful of occasions in arbitration. Arbitrators have demonstrated a fairly cautious approach toward increasing deferred compensation. The most significant unresolved issue arbitrators have yet to address fully is whether all comparisons ought to be made between jurisdictions which have social security versus those which do not. Given that agencies have been pursuing deferred compensation as a substitute for social security for the past 20 years, the continued lack of clarity on this issue is surprising.

9. Benefits

Health insurance benefits have been a frequently arbitrated issue. Arbitrators' awards have run the gamut on this issue and it is difficult to generalize. As with other economic enhancements, arbitrators place a strong emphasis on comparability data.

Arbitrators have been reluctant to impose caps on employer medical premium contributions except where it was strongly supported by comparability data. On the other hand, where a cap has been imposed by negotiations, they are reluctant to remove it.[110]

In the past, most of the emphasis in arbitration was over the relative employer-employee contribution as well as whether or not those contributions should be "capped." In more recent years, there has been an increasing emphasis on negotiating (and arbitrating) plan specifications. In those fights, arbitrators have been to some degree sympathetic to employer claims that uniformed personnel should be placed on the same plan as all other employers. The "internal equity" factor has a special force as to the insurance question.

In the years ahead, it remains an open question to what extent arbitrators will agree with employer "internal equity" interests.

---

109 *See, e.g., City of Olympia* (Police) (DeGrasse, 1984); *City of Pasco* (Police) (Krebs, 1990) at 53.

110 *See, e.g., City of Pasco* (Police) (Wilkinson, 1995).

With the diverging premium tax levels for first responders versus other public employees, it seems likely that a great divergence in plan specifications will open up between these two groups. Ultimately arbitrators tend to place a lot of weight on comparability on economic issues, including insurance so it seems unlikely that internal equity will gain controlling weight on insurance coverage issues.

As to leave benefits, such as vacation, sick leave, holidays, arbitrators again have followed a cautious, incremental approach, being reluctant to either increase or decrease existing benefits. But arbitrators have made changes where it was supported by clear comparability evidence.[111] As discussed above regarding net wage analysis, some of these questions are integral to wage resolution issues.

Arbitration awards are split on the issue of whether sick leave cash-out incentives should be added to a contract. The arbitration decisions seem to turn on how strong the comparability evidence supports such an enhancement.[112]

10. Hours of Work and Overtime

Hours of work are mandatory subjects of bargaining. Nonetheless, there is some tendency of arbitrators to defer to some extent to management's judgment concerning the best work schedule.[113] Arbitrators have indicated a reluctance to grant union proposals to change the fundamental work schedule, leaving that to collective bargaining.[114]

As to overtime questions, arbitrators give strong weight to comparability evidence. Issues such as callback and pay and court pay and compensatory time caps will largely turn on what benefits comparables have available to them.[115]

11. Legal Rights

Arbitrators have generally supported union proposals to grant

---

[111] *City of College Place* (Police) (Williams, 2009) at 20; *Spokane Transit Authority* (Transit) (Torosian, 2006).

[112] *Compare City of Pasco* (Police) (Krebs, 1990) at 33-34 and *City of Olympia* (Police) (DeGrasse, 1984) at 24-25 *with City of Everett (Police)* (Axon 1997); *City of Anacortes* (Police) (Parent, 2006); *City of Mount Vernon* (Police) (Reeves, 2007).

[113] *See, e.g., Whatcom County* (Deputies) (Gangle Smith, 2001).

[114] *See, e.g., Kitsap County* (Deputy Sheriffs) (Buchanan, 1998).

[115] *See, e.g., Kitsap County* (Deputy Sheriffs) (Buchanan, 1998) (increase in callback minimum based on support for union's proposal incomparability data).

the right to arbitrate discipline to employees. Arbitrators are more reluctant to add or enhance employee "bill of rights" absent strong evidence of a specific problem.

Questions have sometimes arisen in arbitration concerning "agency shop" clauses — those provisions that mandate payment of dues as a condition of employment. Arbitrators have generally approved such proposals.[116]

I. Implementation of Interest Arbitration Award

An interest arbitration award essentially removes the discretion from the parties as to the term of the agreement. When properly drafted, an interest arbitration award not only discusses the arbitrator's ruling, but grants specific language which is to be incorporated into the contract. It is then incumbent upon the parties to take that arbitrator order and incorporate the language into an executable agreement.

Interest arbitration awards are binding upon the parties. As the interest arbitration statute indicates:

> The determination shall be final and binding upon both parties, subject to review by the Superior Court upon application of either party solely upon the question of whether the decision of the panel was arbitrary or capricious.[117]

The arbitrary and capricious standard is a heightened standard of review, and it is very difficult to have an arbitrator's award set aside on that standard. Generally, challenges to arbitrators' awards have been unsuccessful and courts great deference provide those awards under the "arbitrary and capricious" standard.[118]

---

116 *See, e.g., City of Pullman* (Police) (Axon, 1992).

117 RCW 41.56.450.

118 *See City of Moses Lake v. IAFF Local 2052*, 68 Wn.2d 742, 847 P.2d 16 (1993), *reviewed denied*, 121 Wn.2d 1026 (1993).

Chapter 5

The Right of Employees to a Fair Predisciplinary Process

A. Introduction

Public safety employees have a number of constitutional and statutory rights which insure that the procedures used to investigate disciplinary charges against them are fair and proper. This chapter considers the various sources of these procedural rights. Many of these procedural rights also bear directly on the question of whether discipline was for "just cause," something covered in the next chapter.

B. *Weingarten* Rights: The Right to Union Representation

The *Weingarten* rule adopted by the NLRB and approved by the United States Supreme Court has also been adopted and applied by PERC.[1] It requires that an employee subject to discipline be permitted to have a union representative during any discipline investigation upon request. In this section, we will discuss two topics concerning Weingarten rights —how the rights are invoked and their scope.

In *NLRB v. Weingarten*, the United States Supreme Court held that it was an unfair labor practice to deny an employee's request for union representation during an investigatory interview. The Court based its finding on Section 8(a)(1) of the National Labor Relations Act which provides that it is an unfair labor practice for an employer "to interfere with, restrain, or coerce employees in the exercise of the rights guaranteed in section 157 of this title." The Court also cited Section 7 of the Act which gives employees the right "to engage in . . . concerted activities for . . . mutual aid or protection . . . ."

Although Washington state employees are not covered under the NLRA, and the Washington collective bargaining law does not contain the "concerted activity" clause of the NLRA, PERC has applied the union "interference" prohibition in the statute to confer Weingarten representational rights. Specifically, RCW 41.56.040[2]

---

[1] *See, e.g., King County*, Decision 4299-A (PECB 1994). The *Weingarten* principle was first adopted by PERC in *Okanogan County*, Decision 2252-A (PECB 1986).

[2] RCW 41.56.040 states: "No public employer, or other person, shall directly or

and 41.56.140(1)[3] have been cited as the basis of this right.[4]

PERC first adopted the federal *Weingarten* rule in a 1985 case involving the Okanogan County Sheriff's Office. PERC defined four threshold tests to invoke the right:

> (1) the employer must compel the employee to attend the investigatory meeting;
>
> (2) the main purpose of the meeting was investigatory in nature, meaning the employer was attempting to obtain facts upon which to base disciplinary action;
>
> (3) the employee must have made a request for union representation;
>
> (4) the employee must have had a reasonable belief that the meeting could result in a disciplinary action.

When these elements are met, the employer commits an unfair labor practice by denying the employee the right to a union representative.

Some issue still remains as to whether an investigation must be compelled to be an "investigatory interview" for *Weingarten* to apply. For example, in *Cowlitz County,*[5] *Weingarten* applied even without a specific order to answer questions. There the commission noted that the employer had "solicited answers" from the employee's "either directly or by strong implication. It was enough that the employee reasonably believed the questions could elicit information that could lead to discipline.[6]

Similarly, in *City of Seattle,*[7] PERC hearing examiner Fred Rosenberry found a Weingarten violation despite the lack of a

---

indirectly interfere with, restrain, coerce, or discriminate against any public employee or group of public employees in the free exercise of their right to organize and designate representatives of their own choosing for the purpose of collective bargaining, or in the free exercise of any other right under this chapter.

3 RCW 41.56.410(1) makes it an unfair labor practice for a public employer to "interfere with, restrain or coerce public employees in the exercise of their rights guaranteed by this chapter".

4 *See Teamsters, Food Processing Employees, Public Employees Warehousemen and Helpers Union Local 760* and *Okanogan County*, Decision 2252-11 (1985).

5 Decision 6832-A (PECB 2000).

6 See also, Whatcom Transportation Authority, Decision 5276 (PECB 1995).

7 Decision 3593 (PECB 1990).

specific order to answer questions. In this case, though, the employer had provided additional assurance, after a union representative had been requested, that that the meeting was merely informal and that no discipline would result. But in fact discipline later did get issued. Rosenberry placed the burden on the employer to explain to the employee that the interview was voluntary, which it had not done.

In *City of Puyallup*[8] the hearing examiner stated that a requisite element of Weingarten was at the interview be "compelled" but that this test could be made even without "any formal, written directive." He found it sufficient that the commander had invited an officer to meet with him to discuss an issue:

> Even without any formal, written directive, it would be difficult in any employment setting -- and even more difficult in context of the paramilitary rank structure of a police department -- to view this request as something less than compelling, in most supervisor - employee settings, but particularly in a police department, it would be difficult not to view this as something less than a "compelling" request to attend.

This distinction as to whether the right only applies to "compelled" interviews is especially important on the question of whether *Weingarten* rights apply in pre-disciplinary *Loudermill* hearings. In another decision involving Puyallup[9] the hearing examiner rejected a union argument that the denial of an employee's choice of representative during a Loudermill hearing constituted a *Weingarten* violation. One key distinction in *Loudermill* hearings versus other disciplinary interviews is that by their nature participation in such hearings is generally considered voluntary. Nonetheless, in such hearings employers do not usually refrain from asking questions, and consequently some continuing dispute continues concerning the nature of *Weingarten* rights during a *Loudermill* hearing.[10]

---

[8] decision 6784 (PECB 1999).

[9] *City of Puyallup* decisions 7490 and 7491 (PECB 2001).

[10] See *Okanogan County*, Decision 9980 (PECB 2008) (granting preliminary ruling to unions claim that pre-disciplinary hearings may be "investigatory" and thereby implicate *Weingarten*); Southwest Snohomish County Public Safety Communications Agency, Decision 11149-A (PECB 2013) (Commission decision affirming examiner ruling that *Weingarten* rights do not apply in

PERC has held that the employee must make an affirmative effort to request representation in order to invoke *Weingarten*. It is important that public safety unions make employees aware of the necessity to ask for representation. *The employer has no duty to inform the employee of this right*. But it is also true that once the representative right is invoked, the employer must either acknowledge that right or discontinue the interview.[11]

Even though *Weingarten* is a right of union representation, PERC has ruled that the right belongs to the employee, not the union. PERC has ruled that employers do not need to acknowledge union request to participate in disciplinary interviews when the employee has not made the request.[12]

the employee must make an affirmative effort to request representation in order to invoke *Weingarten*

PERC has specifically held that an employer may not deflect *Weingarten* rights by engaging in subterfuge. In *City of Seattle*,[13] discussed above, the Commission found a *Weingarten* violation where an employee had initially made arrangements for a union representative and was then told by the employer that it was not a disciplinary interview although later it proved to be one.

There has been some litigation concerning the *Weingarten* requirement that there be a "reasonable" belief that the interview will result in discipline. But PERC has been clear that it does not matter what the *employer* believes. The question is the reasonable perception of the *employee*. Furthermore, "under *Weingarten*, the existence of reasonable grounds is not predicated upon evaluating the subjective perceptions of individuals in each case, but upon objective standards based upon all the circumstances of the particular case."[14] Therefore, unlawful intent or motivation by the employer is not a prerequisite to a *Weingarten* violation.[15]

Loudermill hearing); *Mountlake Terrace Police Guild,* Decision 11702 (PECB 2013) (finding a Weingarten violation in pre-disciplinary hearing in which employee was compelled to attend).

11 *See, e.g., Washington State Patrol, supra*; *see, also,* Hardin, THE DEVELOPING LABOR LAW (3d 1992) 155-56.

12 See University of Washington, Decision 9929 (PSRA 2007); *Methow Valley School District,* decision 8400 (PECB 2004).

13 Decision 3593-A (PECB 1989).

14 *Cowlitz County,* Decision 6832 (PECB 1999).; *Snohomish County* Is, Decision 9291-A (PECB 2007).

15 *See City of Seattle,* Decision 2134 (PECB 1984).

WEINGARTEN RIGHTS

- Applies When Employee Reasonably Believes Discipline May Result
- Employee Must Affirmatively Request Representation
- Representative Has Right to Active, Yet Nondisruptive Participation
- Employee Has Right to Intermissions to Confer with Representative
- Once Invoked, Right Applies to All Subsequent Interviews

For these reasons, Weingarten rights may apply even when the employer does not believe it is undertaking a formal disciplinary interview. On the one hand, if it is clear that the purpose of the meeting is only to announce the predetermined discipline, *Weingarten* does not apply.[16] On the other hand, it is certainly enough that the meeting might be used to collect information that could be used for future discipline even if an immediate investigation is not underway.[17]

But an employee's "fear" of a supervisor does not mean that all meetings with that supervisor are considered disciplinary interviews.[18] Counseling sessions simply to announce a result are *not* considered disciplinary interviews.[19] Counseling sessions, though, involving discussion with the employee that can later be used for discipline do invoke the Weingarten rule.[20]

Weingarten rights may apply even when the employer does not believe it is undertaking a formal disciplinary interview

---

The Weingarten right is the right of an employee to have a reasonable opportunity to consult with the union. But the right is not unlimited:

> For example, an employer is not required to postpone a disciplinary interview because a particular union representative is unavailable for an unreasonable

---

[16] See e.g., *Seattle School District*, Decision 10066 (PECB 2008); *Pierce County Fire District Number* 9, Decision 3334 (PECB 1989).

[17] *Lewis Public Transportation Benefit Area*, Decision 9275 (PECB 2006).

[18] *University Of Washington*, Decision 8794 (PSRA 2004).

[19] *University Of Washington*, Decision 8794 (PSRA 2004).

[20] *Cowlitz County*, Decision 6832 (PECB 1999).

> period of time for reasons not attributable to the employer, provided another representative is available whose presence could have been requested by the employee in the absent representative's place. *See Coca-Cola Bottling Co. of Los Angeles*, 227 NLRB 1276 (1977). If the employee still asserts that no available union representative is satisfactory and continues to demand that the unavailable union representative be present, then the employer must either discontinue the interview or offer the employee the opportunity to continue the interview unrepresented.[21]

While the Weingarten right does not guarantee a break long enough to procure the attendance of the union attorney or other paid representatives, under some circumstances, failing to provide an opportunity to consult with legal counsel may be a ULP.[22]

Once the Weingarten right has been properly asserted, PERC has been quite clear that the role of a union representative is expansive. While the union representative may not fundamentally impede an employer's ability to perform the investigative interview,[23] it has rejected employer arguments that the union representative's role is limited to one of a quiet observer.[24]

The role of the union representative is to be not just a witness, although that is an important role, it is also to be an active participant at critical junctures. This includes:

- Making objections to improper or unlawful questions;
- Asking clarification of questions which are unclear;
- Offering additional evidence at an appropriate time in the proceeding; and

---

21 *Seattle School District,* Decision 10732-A (PECB 2012)

22 *Cowlitz County,* Decision 7037 (PECB 2000).

23 *Snohomish County,* Decision 9291-A (PECB 2007).

24 *King County* Decision 4299 (PECB 1993); *City of Bellevue* Decision 4324 (PECB 1993). On the other hand, an employee representatives identified as "confrontational and agitated" was found not to be acting within the proper boundaries of *Weingarten. Pierce County Fire District Number 9,* decision 3334 (PECB 1989).

- Requesting breaks for the employee when necessary.

An order that the union representative be passive or silent through the interview is itself a *Weingarten* violation.[25] In *City of Bellevue*[26] PERC noted there is a balance to be struck between the employer's ability to conduct the interview and the union's right to represent and defined some of those parameters:

> We thus agree with the view that an employer may achieve an orderly interview, by hearing the employee's account first.
>
> The balancing of interests changes, however, when an employer begins actively questioning an employee. It hardly makes sense to provide a right to representation and then force a union representative to sit idly by while the employer browbeats or intimidates an employee, or elicits damaging and unintended responses through the use of confusing or misleading questions. An employer cannot deny an employee the assistance a union representative can offer in alerting the employee to problems with the phrasing or scope of a question. Examples of the type of assistance which might be provided by a union representative include: Noting when questions are ambiguous or misleading; noting when questions invade a statutory privilege that the employee has the right to invoke; or interceding when questions become harassing or intimidating.[27]

But PERC also indicated the union representation role did not allow it to hinder the interview:

> The right to raise objections to questions is one which the union representative must exercise cautiously. As the NLRB has noted:

---

[25] *City of Bellevue*, Decision 4324-A (PECB 1994); *King County*, Decision 4299-A (PECB 1993).

[26] Decision 4324-A (PECB 1994).

[27] *Id.*

> The repetition of a question, or the phrasing of it in alternative ways, is a common and legitimate investigatory technique, which, in our view, cannot fairly or reasonably, be described as harassment. Consequently, the representative cannot act to preclude the employer from using this technique.

PERC indicated the right of consultation with the employee could also not be used to impede the interview:

> Thus, the right of a union representative to participate during the questioning process does not necessarily allow that representative to confer with the employee before every answer. When a statutory privilege is not at issue, the representative cannot delay an employee's responses while the representative advises an employee whether or how to answer a question. Likewise, the union representative is not free to interject comments whenever he/she wishes during the interview. Some input or assistance can rightfully be delayed. In the interest of maintaining an orderly process, an employer may reasonably require the union representative to wait until the conclusion of employer questioning before seeking clarification of previous employee answers, bringing to light favorable facts the employee might have overlooked, suggesting other individuals who may have relevant knowledge, describing relevant practices, or advancing extenuating circumstances for the employer to consider.

And as hearing examiner Karyl Elinski explained:

> The purpose of having a union representative present at such times is to assist employees who may be unfamiliar with and intimidated by the situation. When an employer questions an employee, a union representative might be able to point out ambiguous or misleading questions, intercede if the questioning invades a statutory privilege the employee has the right to invoke or, if the questioning becomes harassing or intimidating, keep the interviewer and/or employee on task, or bring out all of the facts (or at least facts unknown to or overlooked by the employer

official).[28]

One last issue which has concerned PERC is the type of remedy which should be awarded to the employee whose *Weingarten* rights are violated. In *Okanogan County*, PERC recognized that reinstatement and backpay is the presumed remedy for employees who are discharged in retaliation for exercising their rights under RCW 41.56.[29] But PERC feared that remedy would have put the employee in a better position than before because evidence showed he likely would have been disciplined despite the unlawful interview: "[T]he record here is devoid of evidence showing that any ill-gotten information was used by the employer in making its discharge decision."[30] PERC then concluded that make-whole relief would not be imposed "unless there is a showing that the affected employee was clearly discharged or disciplined for cause, and not for attempting to assert *Weingarten* rights."[31] The discharge in *Okanogan County* was then upheld despite the violation.

Applying this same rule, a different result was reached in *King County* and *City of Bellevue*. In those cases, the employer failed to meet its burden of proof that the information learned at the unlawful interview did not contribute to the disciplinary decision.[32] In *King County*, PERC observed: "The employer made no attempt at all in this proceeding to show that it had any independent grounds for its discharge decision that were unrelated to, and unaffected by, the unlawful interview."[33] Thus, the employer must make an affirmative showing that there is just cause to discipline an employee based on information outside of that learned from the interview in order to avoid this make-whole remedy.

In practice, it is usually very difficult to acquire meaningful Weingarten remedies, at least to the extent "meaningful" includes overturning the subsequent discipline. Without a link between the questioning and the ultimate discipline, usually the union's recourse is limited to "paper" remedies in front of PERC. But the violation of Weingarten rights can be a part of a basis to challenge discipline on a just cause arbitration appeal, something discussed in the next chapter.

---

[28] *City of Brier,* Decision 10013 (PECB 2008).
[29] PD-2252-16.
[30] PD-2252-A-10.
[31] *Id.*
[32] *King County,* PD-4299-21; *City of Bellevue,* PD-4324-14.
[33] *King County,* at 22.

C. *Garrity* Rights: Protection Against Involuntary Incrimination

1. Introduction

The Fifth Amendment of the United States Constitution protects individuals against self-incrimination. The right to avoid self-incrimination includes the right not to be coerced or compelled to give a statement against oneself which could be used in a criminal matter.

The issue arises with public employees as to how to balance their right not to incriminate themselves against the public employer's right to enforce standards of conduct. Enforcing such standards requires investigating alleged misconduct which might be criminal. This section addresses the approach the courts have developed in an attempt to respect both sets of rights.

2. The *Garrity* Case

Garrity v. New Jersey[34] is a criminal case concerning the admissibility of statements of police officers provided during an investigation. The officers had been accused of ticket-fixing and were advised that anything they said during the investigation could be used against them in a criminal proceeding, but if they refused to talk they would be fired. The officers talked. They were charged criminally, and the prosecutor sought to use their statements in a criminal proceeding. They were convicted, and they appealed their convictions.

The Supreme Court addressed the issue of whether the threat of job loss made their statements involuntary and, therefore, inadmissible. The Court concluded that the statements were inadmissible in a criminal proceeding because they were coerced:

> The choice given petitioners was either to forfeit their jobs or to incriminate themselves. The option to lose their means of livelihood or to pay the penalty of self-incrimination is the antithesis of free choice to speak out or remain silent. That practice, like in interrogation practices we reviewed in *Miranda v. Arizona*, 384 U.S. 436, 464-465, is "likely to exert just pressure upon an individual as to disable him from making a free and rational choice." We think the statements were infected by the coercion inherent in

---

[34] 385 U.S. 493 (1967).

> this scheme of questioning and cannot be sustained as voluntary under our prior decisions. [35]

The Court rejected the argument that public employees had a lesser Fifth Amendment right against self-incrimination: "We conclude that policemen, like teachers and lawyers, are not relegated to a watered-down version of constitutional rights."[36]

The next year, the Court addressed a slightly different variation of the same question. In *Gardner v. Broderick*,[37] the Court addressed the question of the legality of the termination of an employee who refused to waive privilege against self-incrimination and was dismissed as a result. Following *Garrity*, the Court found the termination to be unconstitutional:

> If appellant, a policeman, had refused to answer questions specifically, directly and narrowly relating to the performance of his official duties, without being required to waive his immunity with respect to the use of his answers or the fruits thereof in a criminal prosecution of himself, *Garrity v. New Jersey, supra*, the privilege against self-incrimination would not have been a bar to his dismissal. The facts of this case, however, do not present this issue. Here, petitioner was summoned to testify for a grand jury in an investigation of alleged criminal conduct. He was discharged from office not for failure to answer relevant questions about his official duties, but for refusal to waive a constitutional right. He was dismissed for failure to relinquish the protection of the privilege against self-incrimination.[38]

The principle then deduced from this pair of cases — *Garrity v. New Jersey* and *Gardner v. Broderick* — is that statements which are compelled upon threat of job loss cannot be admitted in a criminal proceeding. Also, an employee may not be fired for refusing to waive his Fifth Amendment right against self-incrimination, but he can be fired for refusal to answer questions when clearly ordered to do so.

---

[35] 385 U.S. at 499.
[36] *Id.*
[37] 392 U.S. 273 (1968).
[38] 392 U.S. at 278.

In order for a public safety employee to be protected by the *Garrity* rule, a proper "order" must be issued

3. Nature of a Proper *Garrity* Order

Questions frequently arise concerning the proper nature of a *Garrity* order. In order for a public safety employee to be protected by the *Garrity* rule, a proper "order" must be issued. A statement which is voluntarily provided is not given under the protection of *Garrity* and *may* be used in a criminal proceeding. Therefore, an important role for union representatives in this situation is to ensure that a proper *Garrity* order has been issued *before* an employee makes a statement in a disciplinary matter.

The question of the clarity of an "order" has arisen in two separate contexts. The first issue arises when an employee is subject to discipline for exercising their *Miranda* rights even though there is no clear *Garrity* order provided. This may seem like an anomalous situation, but these situations do occur as there seems to be no end to the creativity some employers will go to try to get employees to give up their Fifth Amendment right without providing a clear *Garrity* order.

GARRITY RIGHTS

- Apply to Any Interview Regardless of Whether Actual Criminal Investigation is Pending
- Must Obtain Clear Order for *Garrity* Protection to Apply
- Refusal to Comply with Clear *Garrity* Order is Considered Insubordination and is Grounds for Dismissal
- Statements Given in Response to *Garrity* Order May Not be Used in Any Criminal Proceeding

A good example of this type of situation arose in the Massachusetts case of *Carney v. City of Springfield*.[39] In this case, an officer was investigated in a criminal investigation and was provided a *Miranda* warning. *Immediately after* being *Mirandized*, the officer was then informed that he had to respond to questions as a part of a "departmental disciplinary proceeding." Given these simultaneous and seemingly conflicting orders, the officer sought clarification of what type of proceeding he was subject to. It was

[39] 532 N.E.2d 631 (1988).

merely repeated "that he would be subject to departmental discipline." Upon the advice of counsel, the officer refused to answer any questions. A week later, the employer again brought him in and gave him a *Miranda* warning and then asked him to answer questions at which point he again refused. He was later terminated.

There is a large body of somewhat conflicting case law regarding how clear the order must be.

The court had little trouble in finding that this treatment was improper:

> Where public employers compel answers in investigation, however, the employer, at the time of the interrogation, must specify to the employee the precise repercussions (i.e., suspension, discharge, or the exact form of discipline) that will result if the employee fails to respond. [Citation omitted.] Where, as here, economic sanctions threaten an individual's livelihood, a general warning that the employee may be subject to "departmental disciplinary proceedings" in insufficient.[40]

A different situation arises sometimes when an employee proceeds to give a statement even though it might be unclear whether or not an order has been issued. There is a large body of somewhat conflicting case law regarding how clear the order must be. Because neither Washington courts nor the Ninth Circuit have weighed in on this issue, the best guidance is outside case law. The majority of those cases hold that if the employee has an "objectively reasonable" belief that the statement is compelled, Garrity immunity attaches. This is sometimes referenced as "implied Garrity" and in this view, Garrity immunity can arise even without an express threat to discharge, but can be implied, for example, by Department rules or policies requiring the production of statements.

[40] 403 Mass. at 609-10.

the more prudent practice for union representatives is to obtain a *clear* order specifying that the employee is being compelled to provide a statement upon threat of an insubordination charge

But a minority view is that the employee no Garrity immunity attaches unless the order contains an "overt threat" of termination. Under this view, an officer, for example, who produces a statement with the belief that it is being ordered does not acquire Garrity immunity and the statement is available for later use by prosecutors.

In light of this ambiguity in the law, the more prudent practice for union representatives is to obtain a *clear* order specifying that the employee is being compelled to provide a statement upon threat of an insubordination charge. Many officer bill of rights contain a mandate that an affirmative Garrity order be issued at the outset of investigative interviews.

The practical point for union representatives is simply to insist on obtaining a clear order if the employer is being ambiguous about what is occurring. Employers sometimes try to use subterfuge to obtain a statement without taking the statement under the ambit of *Garrity* and the task of the union representative is to make sure that that does not happen.

It might be thought that a *Garrity* order is not always necessary because not all investigations will result in a criminal matter. There is a twofold response to that reasoning.

First, there is no harm in obtaining a *Garrity* order, and it is simply better to be safe, knowing one is operating under the *Garrity* protection. Second, the scope of the criminal laws that apply to public safety employees, particularly police officers, is much broader than one might ordinarily think. Investigations do not need to involve allegations of theft or other traditional criminal conduct to expose the officer to criminal liability.

For example, matters which involve a violation of a citizen's civil rights could — if the federal attorney's office chose to pursue them — result in criminal charges. The possibility of a criminal charge is quite remote, but it is certainly not outside the realm of possibility. So, too, there are statutes which make it a crime for a public officer or employee to engage in misfeasance or malfeasance. For example, several years ago a police supervisor in this state faced criminal charges for his failure to report on an alleged criminal conduct involving a subordinate.

In short, acquiring a *Garrity* order should be routine in any internal interview. If no *Garrity* order is given, not statement is required and, generally, none should be produced.

4. The Scope of the Interview Pursuant to *Garrity*

The *Garrity* rule provides the public employer a right to compel answers to bona fide internal investigations. It allows employers to ask questions that are "narrowly job related." Given the broad reach of agency conduct rules, including the ability to discipline for certain off-duty conduct, the "job relatedness" test still leaves the employer with a broad capacity to investigate. The requirement that the request be "narrowly" related to employment, only requires that they be focused on work rules violations. The *Garrity* rule does not allow a public employer to go on fishing expeditions for matters outside a valid internal investigation in order to permit them to become effectively an arm of another prosecutor's agency. A couple of cases demonstrate the limits on employer authority.

In *Cox v. City of Chattanooga*,[41] the court found the termination to be improper of a firefighter who refused to provide a statement to a fire department where the questions did not sufficiently relate to the scope of his employment. At issue in *Cox* was that his name and telephone number had surfaced during the course of a murder investigation. But he was not the suspect, and the department was not investigating him for any type of wrongdoing. Instead, simply it sought to compel him to give a statement which could assist the ongoing investigation that the police department was conducting. But the firefighter did not want to cooperate and refused to give a statement. He was then fired.

The court held the discharge to be improper:

> In this case, there is no claim or contention the investigation of the murder was in any way related to or within the scope of duties of Captain Cox. Thus, as distasteful as it may be to some, Captain Cox [the firefighter] had the constitutional right under the Fifth Amendment to remain silent. His discharge from his employment, as found by the Chancellor, is illegal and in violation of his rights under the Constitution.[42]

---

[41] 516 S.W.2d 94 (1973).

[42] 516 S.W.2d at 97.

A somewhat more questionable decision was issued by the Texas Supreme Court in *Talent v. City of Abilene.*[43] In this case, a firefighter refused to answer questions concerning how he came in possession of a car which was later determined to be stolen property. The Court found the dismissal of the firefighter for refusal to answer the questions improper, because the questions were not job-related. The Court reasoned that the fire chief was not a law enforcement official and "has not roving commission to detect crime or enforce the criminal law."[44] But as the dissent properly pointed out, the fire chief had a valid reason for knowing why one of his firefighters was in possession of stolen property, as this would be a violation of department rules.

The decision lacks some clarity as to why the court ruled as it did. But this likely stemmed from the confusion within the department as to whether it was formerly commencing an internal investigation. Generally agencies have rules that prohibit "criminal conduct" so virtually any allegation that an employee committed a crime could be the subject of a valid internal investigation.

The practice impact of this principle is that public employers need to be clear what they are investigating when they begin interviewing employees about wrongdoing, particularly when it could be criminal in nature. If is a criminal investigation, *Miranda* should be given. If it is work rule investigation, *Garrity* should be given, and the focus of the investigation should upon the alleged rule violation. A public employer has the right to commence an internal investigation to determine workplace misconduct, and it should make it clear to the employee that this is the purpose of the interview. If the purpose is a criminal investigation, the Fifth Amendment right of silence should be invoked and counsel should be obtained.

5. Nature of *Garrity* Immunity

As a general matter, statements given pursuant to a *Garrity* order cannot be used later in a criminal proceeding. But there has been some litigation concerning what it means to be "used" in a criminal proceeding.

In a traditional criminal prosecution where the defendant has been previously provided "use immunity," there is a process a prosecutor has to go through called a "*Kastigar*" hearing to establish that the evidence is not "derived" from a source subject to

---

[43] 508 S.W.2d 592 (1974).

[44] 508 S.W.2d at 597.

the immunity. The notion of "use immunity" is broad. It does not simply mean use of the actual direct evidence acquired but also anything *derived from that use*. This places a heavy — perhaps even onerous — burden upon the prosecutor to show that prior to granting immunity, the evidence to be used in the trial was either already acquired. If the evidence was later acquired, the prosecutor *must* show it came from an entirely independent source.

In *United States v. Koon*[45] — one of the prosecutions in the aftermath of the Rodney King incident — the Ninth Circuit issued its most definitive explanation as to the scope of immunity as a result of a *Garrity* order. First, the court concluded that a *Garrity* order produced an immunity that was precisely analogous to that traditionally provided by prosecutors under immunity agreements. That is, once a *Garrity* order is given, the prosecutor has an obligation to produce independent evidence and to demonstrate independence of that evidence through a *Kastigar* hearing.

The court then reviewed cases from other circuits which have placed an extremely heavy *Kastigar* burden on prosecutors. It rejected that approach, finding some of the other federal courts had read *Kastigar* too broadly and adopted the standard since applied in the Ninth Circuit:

> In sum, it is the law of our circuit that the prosecutors *Kastigar* burden is met if the substance of the exposed witnesses' testimony is based on a legitimate source that is independent of the immunized testimony. Ensuring that the content of a witness's testimony is based on personal knowledge provides the required Fifth Amendment protections and meets the *Kastigar* requirement that the defendant's compelled statement shall not be used against him in a subsequent criminal proceeding.[46]

These *Kastigar* principles, as interpreted by the Ninth Circuit, do not prevent the prosecutor from having *access* to the statements. Instead, when a prosecutor has access to a statement, it complicates, but does not prevent the prosecution; the prosecutor will have to show that there was no use or taint of any testimony from those statements.

In another Ninth Circuit decision, the court considered whether the prosecutor's use of a statement acquired pursuant to

[45] 34 F.3d 1416 (1994).
[46] 34 F.3d at 1432-33.

a *Garrity* order of a San Jose police officer violated the Constitution.[47] The issue arose in the context of a Section 1983 claim, not a criminal prosecution. The court held that it was not a *per se* violation for the statement to be transmitted to the prosecutor or for the prosecutor to show it to the complaining witness.

But the court did acknowledge that use of such a statement to "refresh the memory" of a witness has been held to be an improper use of a statement acquired pursuant to *Garrity*. Seemingly, had it proceeded to a criminal prosecutor, the prosecutor would have had tremendous difficulty proceeding once having shown the immunized statement to the complaining witness.

Another incidental issue about the nature of Garrity immunity which has come up a handful of times — and which has particular bearing on the in Washington — is the question of the scope of the immunity. The traditional scope of the immunity which is required under the *Garrity* rule is only "use immunity," but Washington law, like the laws of a handful of other states, requires that any immunity that is given by a prosecutor must be "transactional" in nature. "Transactional immunity" is much broader in that it completely bars the prosecutor from later bringing a criminal charge in that matter. So a question arises: Can an effective Garrity order be issued without the offer of transactional immunity?

Surprisingly, Washington courts have yet to address this matter, at least in a published appellate decision. But at least two other "transactional immunity" states that have addressed this question and they are split on the issue of whether the immunity must be transactional in nature to be effective.

In *Carney v. City of Springfield*,[48] the Massachusetts Supreme Court ruled that it was improper to discharge an officer without providing a promise of full transactional immunity. The court emphasized that it was relying on the Massachusetts Constitution for this interpretation as an independent source of authority from the United States Constitution. The same question was presented to the Oregon Court of Appeals in *Decker v. Mason*,[49], but the court declined to follow the approach set out by the Massachusetts Supreme Court. The Oregon court concluded: "There was nothing improper about proceeding with the disciplinary hearing despite

---

[47] *Gwillen v. City of San Jose*, 929 F.2d 465 (9th Cir. 1991).
[48] 403 Mass. 604, 532 N.E.2d 631 (1988).
[49] 95 Or. App. 320, 769 P.2d 228 (1988).

the failure to provide transactional immunity."

6. Necessity of a *Garrity* Order as Part of a Fair Investigation

employees participating in a *Loudermill* hearing while a cloud of a criminal charge simultaneously hangs overhead, proceed at their own risk

Typically, a *Garrity* order is part and parcel of any formal internal investigation. On the other hand, once an employer has acquired the employee's statement and has decided to sustain charges, the question sometimes arises as to the ability of an employee to provide an immunized statement at a *Loudermill* hearing. (The *Loudermill* requirement will be discussed later in this chapter.)

The courts which have reviewed this question have deemed the *Loudermill* process to be voluntary and have held that there is nothing that requires an employer to provide a *Garrity* order in order to fulfill the mandate of the *Loudermill* case.[50] Therefore, employees participating in a *Loudermill* hearing while a cloud of a criminal charge simultaneously hangs overhead, proceed at their own risk. It may be more prudent for the employee to have others, such as a union representative or an attorney, speak on their behalf.

Another question which may arise is whether an employer may conduct an internal investigation but never provides any "order" for an employer to give a statement. Such a failure would likely be challenged as a violation of "just cause" principle given the employer's obligation to acquire all relevant information before making a disciplinary decision. It is clear that a *Loudermill* hearing is voluntary on the employee's part, but the burden of conducting the *initial* internal investigation rests on the employer and, therefore, it is not clear that the employer may waive that obligation by simply advising the employee that their participation is voluntary and that no *Garrity* order will be provided. But because the authority on this point is sparse, and tips toward the employer, the better practice for labor organizations is to add to the Bill of Rights a provision mandating the issuance of a Garrity order as part of the investigation process.

---

[50] *See, e.g., Gniotek v. City of Philadelphia*, 808 F.2d 241 (3rd Cir. 1986).

D. The Right to a Fair and Legal Investigation

There are a number of statutes, constitutional rules, and arbitration decisions regulating the proper conduct of a disciplinary investigation. This section addresses these various rules.

1. Thorough Investigation

Though it will be discussed in a later chapter, it is a paramount principle of "just cause" that investigations be thorough and fair. This usually involves collecting all relevant information.

The obligation of an employer to perform a thorough investigation, however, does not give it license to perform an unlawful investigation. The remainder of this section will address the various ways in which employers violate the law in conducting investigations.

2. Polygraphs

RCW 49.44.120 states it is unlawful for an employer to require "directly or indirectly" that any employee be subjected to a polygraph. There is an exemption in this law for law enforcement agencies, but only to the extent the polygraph involves "the initial application for employment." Attorney General opinions,[51] and a court decision,[52] indicate that the "initial application" exemption from the polygraph ban applies to those employees from other law enforcement agencies who are transferring in to a new agency after a consolidation. The plain meaning of the statute would suggest polygraphs are not permitted for promotional processes.

The statutory prohibition on employers to "require, directly or indirectly," polygraphs, has not been interpreted by a court in the context of a situation where there is no direct "order," but where there is subtle coercion to take a polygraph. Presumably, the statute gives employers a fair degree of leeway to *request* a polygraph without *ordering* it. This conclusion is reached by contrasting state law with federal law.

The federal polygraph law, which is not applied to local agencies, makes it is unlawful even to request submission to a polygraph. Such a prohibition, if incorporated into state law, would address the problem which has occasionally arisen — public safety

---

[51] 87 Attorney General Opinion No. 15.

[52] *Stone v. Chelan County Sheriff's Department*, 110 Wn.2d 806, 756 P.2d 736 (1988).

employers implying to employees that if they do not take a polygraph, they will have to infer guilt. While such a course of conduct does not explicitly violate RCW 49.44.120, it is the type of tactic which many arbitrator would likely question under a just cause challenge.

It is a rare circumstance in which it would be advisable for an employee to submit voluntarily to a polygraph. A union representative should provide blanket advice to employees to decline the request to take a polygraph at least until the representative has had the opportunity to consult with union counsel to determine if unusual circumstances are present which might warrant a voluntary polygraph. A more cautious practice — when a polygraph might advance an employee's interest — is to have the employee first submit to a polygraph on a confidential basis from an outside polygrapher hired by the union.

3. Searches and Seizures

There are a number of means by which a public safety employer might acquire evidence. Any of these involve some intrusion in the personal space of the individual being investigated. A number of these search tactics have been found unlawful as a violation of either a statute or the Fourth Amendment. In assessing the validity of any search by a Washington public employer, one must also be mindful that Article 1, Section 7 of the State Constitution sometimes confers additional rights under its private affairs clause.

a. Offices, Desks and Lockers

The Supreme Court addressed the issue of when a public employer can search the work area of its employees in *O'Conner v. Ortega.*[53] In that 1987 decision, the Court set forth the following principles that still appear to stand:

1. Employees may have a "reasonable expectation of privacy" in their office space, but that determination needs to be made on a fact-by-fact basis and depends on the circumstances and the work environment;

---

[53] 480 U.S. 709, 107 S. Ct. 1492 (1987).

2. If the employer is investigating a matter which is work related, the constitutional requirement for a warrant in inapplicable;

3. Although waiving the warrant requirement for work related searches, the Court nonetheless holds an employer to a "reasonable suspicion" standard.

Shortly thereafter, the Ninth Circuit applied and interpreted the *Ortega* decision in *Schowengerdt v. General Dynamics.*[54] The Ninth Circuit found that *Ortega* is limited to (1) searches for violations of work rules, as criminal searches require more stringent procedure, and (2) work space that is private in nature, as open areas do not afford a reasonable expectation of privacy. It also rejected the contention that no reasonable expectation of privacy can exist if the item or space searched is owned by the employer.[55] Thus, in the Ninth Circuit, an employer's claim that office spaces owned by the employer, such as lockers, are subject to search at any time does not automatically remove an employee's reasonable expectation of privacy. criminal.

Another federal appellate court has extended the search principles of *Ortega* to workplace searches involving a state-owned police vehicle.[56] That same court, however, declined to rule on whether closed containers contained within that vehicle were covered by the *Ortega* rule.

Restrictions on an employer's ability to conduct searches of an office also extend surveillance. In *U.S. v. McIntyre,*[57] the Ninth Circuit found an Arizona police department had violated the Constitution when it placed a microphone inside of a briefcase in the office of an officer under investigation. The Court found there was still some reasonable expectation of privacy within the office,[58] and the police department had violated that expectation by bugging the office.

---

[54] *Schowengerdt v. General Dynamics Corp.*, 823 F.2d 1328, 91 A.L.R. Fed. 201 (1987).

[55] See *id.*; *but see Shields v. Burge*, 874 F.2d 1201,(7th Cir. 1989) (search of the officer's desk and of a briefcase in the officer's department-owned car was proper).

[56] *Shields v. Burge*, 4 IER Cases 623 (7th Cir. 1989).

[57] 582 F.2d 1221 (9th Cir. 1978).

[58] This aspect of the decision is in doubt due to *O'Connor v. Ortega* — issued 9 years later. In *McIntyre*, the office was open yet the court found a protective privacy interest. *O'Connor* indicates otherwise.

These Fourth Amendment limits on office surveillance are separate and apart from limits that arise from the collective bargaining statute. As will be discussed later, the collective bargaining law may mandate negotiations over office surveillance systems and any surveillance of union activity is probably a form of unlawful interference.

Since *Ortega* decision, there has been some renewed discussion regarding lockers searches. Many departments had issued guidelines declaring that the lockers are owned by the department and were, therefore, subject to search at any time. Apparently, the theory was that such a declaration removed the reasonable expectation of privacy that an employee might have.

Courts have yet to definitively determine whether such a declaration, in fact, has that effect, but it is doubtful that this unilateral declaration automatically removes an otherwise reasonable expectation of privacy. No doubt, though, such a declaration would be considered *one factor* as to whether the employees retained a reasonable expectation of privacy. Generally, the test under the "reasonable expectation of privacy" is whether the person reasonably believed the area was not subject to intrusion. If the only time an employer enters a locker is to investigate some misconduct, it may well be that these employees still retain a "reasonable expectation of privacy," the employer's declaration notwithstanding. If, on the other hand, where lockers are generally deemed openly accessible to coworkers, any reasonable expectation of privacy is likely eliminated.

b. Search of the Person

Courts have recognized that strip searches and body searches are extremely intrusive and that public employees have a constitutional right in connection with such searches. The test for determining whether such a search in the workplace is valid has generally been the "reasonable suspicion" standard.[59] Therefore, in one case where the employer had received a tip that a correctional officer would be bringing drugs into the workplace — a correctional institution — the court found the employer was justified in conducting a strip search which also extended to a body cavity search.[60]

In *Kirkpatrick v. Gates*,[61] the Ninth Circuit rejected the L.A.

---

[59] *Kirkpatrick v. City of Los Angeles*, 803 F.2d 485 (9th Cir. 1986).
[60] *Profitt v. District of Columbia*, 6 IER Cases 1319 (D.C.D.C. 1991).
[61] 803 F.2d 485 (1986).

Police Department's claim that it had a right to perform a strip search on its officers without reasonable suspicion. In *Kirkpatrick*, a sergeant had required the body search of a number of its officers after a citizen had complained that he might have lost money during the booking process even though he was uncertain when or even whether such a loss of cash had occurred. There were several officers with the possible access to the suspect and they were all ordered to be strip searched.

The Ninth Circuit rejected this search due to the lack of "reasonable suspicion" that any one of the officers had taken any money from the complaining trustee:

> The government has an interest in the integrity of its police force which may justify some intrusions on the privacy of police officers which the Fourth Amendment would not otherwise tolerate. However, because of their highly intrusive nature, investigative strip searches of police officers must be supported by a reasonable suspicion that the evidence will be found, despite the government's interest in police integrity.[62]

c. *Residential Searches*

In another Ninth Circuit case, the court ruled that a police department — again the L.A.P.D. — could not conduct a warrantless search on a police officer's home in violation of the Fourth Amendment.[63] In *L.A. Police Protective League v. Gates*, the Department was conducting the investigation of an officer who allegedly engaged in off-duty burglaries. The department had ordered the officer to submit to a search of his own home which he refused. He was then terminated for not consenting to the search.

The Ninth Circuit found the "ordered" search to be unconstitutional. The court further found it to be improper for L.A.P.D. to terminate the officer for not submitting to an unconstitutional search of his home:

> By the same token, Gibson [the officer] could not be disciplined when he refused to allow the appellants to violate his constitutional rights. As the Supreme Court has pointed out, it is not proper to discharge an officer from duty in order to punish that officer for exercising rights guaranteed to him under the Constitution.[64]

---

[62] 803 F.2d at 489.

[63] *Los Angeles Police Protective League v. Gates*, 907 F.2d 879 (1990).

d. Drug Testing

In 1989, the U.S. Supreme Court issued a pair of drug testing cases which only partially cleared up the confusion as to a public employer's right to undertake drug tests on its employees.[65] What was left unclear after the decision was how far the principles set forth in those decisions reach beyond the specific facts presented to the court. In these two cases, the court made the following rulings:

1. A federal regulation mandating drug testing without any reasonable suspicion of railroad employees involved in an accident is justified in light of the safety issues at stake;

2. The Customs Department is allowed to undertake drug testing of applicants without reasonable suspicion where the applicants are applying for positions involving either drug interdiction or the carrying of a weapon.

Prior to this pair of cases, many courts had held that public safety employees can only be tested where the employer had a "reasonable suspicion" that they were impaired or otherwise in possession of controlled substances. Since these decisions, courts have wrestled with which class of public safety employees might be subject to drug testing absent reasonable suspicion.

The Ninth Circuit has addressed the issue of drug testing of law enforcement personnel on at least two occasions since the Supreme Court rulings. In *Jackson v. Gates*, the court overturned the discharge of a police officer for refusal to submit to a drug test where the employer had no reasonable suspicion to justify the order of the test.[66] In another case involving a prison, the Ninth Circuit upheld random drug testing of prison employees who had actual contact with inmates or were otherwise responsible for prison security.[67] The court suggested that it was a close call which might indicate a reluctant to extend random testing to other public safety employees.

---

[64] 907 F.2d at 887.

[65] *Skinner v. Railway Labor Executives Ass'n*, 4 IER Cases 225 (1989); *National Treasury Employees Union v. Von Raab*, 4 IER Cases 247 (1989).

[66] *Jackson v. Gates*, 7 IER Cases 1249 (9th Cir. 1992).

[67] *American Federation of Government Employees v. Roberts*, 9 IER Cases 285 (9th Cir. 1993).

Against the backdrop of the larger body or federal case law, it appears that under the federal constitution (the state constitution is a separate matter) the constitutionality of employee classifications to random testing is as follows:

- Corrections officers, based on nearly uniform case law, are almost certainly subject to random testing;
- Law enforcement officers, based on the majority of cases, are probably subject to random testing;
- Other public safety employees, based on a divided body of case law may or may not be subject to random testing, although it seems likely that such testing would not survive approval of the Ninth Circuit.

The Ninth Circuit's ruling in *Jackson v. Gates* invalidating the suspicionless search of the officer is not necessarily an indicator of how it might stand on a random drug testing program. In that case, no random program was in place, and courts have generally invalidated suspicionless tests where they were not part of a properly designed and implemented program to ensure true randomness.

But in Washington State, the federal case law is not the end of the analysis. Public employees in Washington have a basis to argue that the Washington State Constitution requires a more stringent standard for mandatory drug testing. And it remains an open question.[68] State courts elsewhere with constitutional provisions similar to Washington have found random testing unconstitutional, including for police.[69]

---

68 One Division of the Washington Court of Appeals did uphold drug testing for law enforcement applicants challenged under the state constitution. *Robinson v. City of Seattle*, 102 Wash. App. 795 (2000).

69 *Anchorage Police Dept. Employees Ass'n v. Municipality of Anchorage*, 24 P.3d 547 (Alaska 2001)(random testing unconstitutional for police officers and firefighters); *Guiney v. Police Comm'n of Boston*, 582 N.E.2d 523 (Mass. 1991) (testing of police officers unconstitutional); *Petersen v. City of Mesa*, 83 P.3d 35 (Ariz. 2004) (random testing of firefighters unconstitutional but appears to distinguish public safety officers who carry weapons or are involved in narcotics interdiction). But see some court challenges based on state constitutions have failed: *New Jersey Transit PBA Local 304 v. New Jersey Transit Corp.*, 151 N.J. 531 (N.J. 1997) (random testing of officers not unconstitutional); *McCloskey v. Honolulu Police Dept.*, 799 P.2d 953 (Haw. 1990) (random testing of police officers not unconstitutional).

The ability of an employer to mandate other types of medical or psychological tests is severely circumscribed by the Americans with Disabilities Act

As was indicated above, drug testing is certainly a mandatory subject of bargaining. It is in the interest of both management and labor to negotiate testing policies with strong procedural protections: A number of courts have rejected drug testing programs which lack necessary safeguards without regard to the level of evidence that triggered the test.

e. *Other Tests*

The ability of an employer to mandate other types of medical or psychological tests is severely circumscribed by the Americans with Disabilities Act (ADA), which will be discussed in detail later. Under the ADA, an employer would only be allowed to compel such tests when it had a reasonable basis to conclude that there was a business necessity for the test. Prior to the enactment of the ADA, there were at least two cases where the courts had sustained public employer orders or its employees to be tested for HIV or Hepatitis B.[70]

In another case, a court addressed the issue of an employer's order to a police officer to submit to a penile plethysmograph examination after allegations of sexual misconduct arose. The court remanded to the lower trial court to make a determination about whether the test would violate the employee's "substantive due process." The court stated several serious concerns it had in the order of giving the test, and directed the trial court to make a factual determination on at least two questions: is the plethysmograph a reliable examination; and are there other reasonable alternatives to this test?[71]

There was no subsequent published decision as a followup to the court's order, and we are aware of no other published decision regarding plethysmograph examinations. Nonetheless, we believe the court's concerns regarding employee due process are valid and likely to be raised by other courts when facing similar employer orders for intrusive tests.

---

[70] *Anonymous Firefighter v. City of Willoughby*, 7 IER Cases 17 (N.D. Ohio 1991); *Glover v. Encor*, 3 IER Cases 135 (D.C. Neb. 1988).

[71] *Harrington v. Almy*, 977 F.2d 37, 8 IER Cases 449 (1st Cir. 1992).

f. Telephone Lines, Voice Mail and E-mail

The law recognizes as distinction between stored communications, such as computer email systems and telephone systems. But with the merging and changing of technologies, courts are having trouble keeping up, and the law in this area is less defined now then it was years ago.

Washington State law makes it generally illegal to intercept electronic communications without consent. The law does provide a limited exemption for incoming telephone calls to an emergency service center.[72] Previously, some police departments had recorded their incoming general business lines but this practice would appear to be unlawful under the revised exemptions in RCW 9.73.070.

Using a federal statute, the Electronic Communications Privacy Act (FECPA), employers have argued the right to intercept voicemails and emails. No challenge has been brought under the state law to the prevailing practice among employers to assert the right to inspect emails. It seems probable that such emails, once "stored" on the system which is owned by the employer, would by definition not be considered "intercepted" within the meaning of RCW 9.73.070.

The expansion of smartphones and other similar devices has created additional issues. In *Quon v. City of Ontario*, the Ontario, California Police Department had issued all of its SWAT team members pagers with text capacity. The City issued a written policy advising the officers it reserved the right to monitor and log all computer network activity, including emails and the internet. Text messages were not covered by the policy, but the officers were told the officers that texts would be treated the same as emails. In practice, the content of the messages were not audited

Officer Jeff Quon sent numerous emails on his account, a number sufficient to trigger an interest by the department in his usage. His high usage involved sending numerous emails of a sexual nature to his mistress. The City requested from the wireless provider and obtained the content of the messages.

A suit predictably followed. The Ninth Circuit upheld the suit of Quon (joined in my some of the recipients of his messages) finding a reasonable expectation of privacy existed.[73] The Supreme Court overturned the Ninth Circuit. Applying workplace search principles adopted in *O'Conner v. Ortega*, the Court found the review of the

---

[72] RCW 9.73.070.

[73] 529 F.3d 892 (9th Cir. 2008)

text transcripts was reasonable and had a "legitimate workplace rationale." The Court also found that Quon could have no reasonable expectation of privacy in texts transmitted over the City's pager.

The lack of clear privacy guarantees over the employer email system likely means that attorney client and union privileges are likely waived by the transmission of emails.

The Court expressed noticeable concern and constraint over the scope of its ruling. It noted that technologies were evolving rapidly and that adopted workplace search rules applicable to those technologies would have to wait another day.

Washington public sector employees should be mindful of the limitations of their privacy aspirations. Privacy expectations are not enforceable when they are not "reasonable." Given the repeated declarations employers have made concerning computer and email monitoring, claims that such emails cannot be inspected are unlikely to succeed.

Union leaders should especially take note. The lack of clear privacy guarantees over the employer email system likely means that attorney client and union privileges are likely waived by the transmission of emails. Employers have even claimed that such emails are public records. External email accounts should be established for such purposes.

E. *Loudermill* Rights: The Right to Predisciplinary Due Process

1. Introduction

Courts have held that under the United States Constitution, public employees are entitled to due process. The Fourteenth Amendment's guarantee of "procedural due process" protects individuals from erroneous or unjustified deprivation of life, liberty, or property.[74] This section discusses how due process entitlement is triggered and what process is "due."

In a procedural due process case, the court applies a two-step analysis. First, it is necessary to determine whether a protected "liberty" or "property" interest exists entitling the individual to due

[74] *Carey v. Piphus,* 435 U.S. 247, 259, 98 S.Ct. 1042, 1050, 55 L.Ed.2d 252 (1978).

process.[75] Second, *if* a protected interest exists, *then* the court will employ a balancing test to determine what process is due.[76]

Loudermill rights are named after the Supreme Court decision in "*Cleveland Board of Education v. Loudermill.*[77] In *Loudermill*, the United States Supreme Court held that public employees with tenure were entitled to a pretermination hearing before being fired. This 1985 ruling was unsurprising. In fact, it was fully consistent with a long line of Supreme Court cases that had held that before the government can remove a property or liberty interest from a citizen, it must provide that citizen due process. Following those general due process principles, federal courts had generally extended these due process rights to public sector employment decisions.

In this section, we will first review types of "interests" the courts have recognized as protectable "liberty" or "property" interests. Then we will turn to what "due process" is actually "due" before those protectable liberty or property interests may be taken away.

2. Protectable Property Interests

An individual has a property interest in a government job or benefit *only if he has a legitimate claim of entitlement to it.* A mere abstract need or desire for it is not enough.[78]

But if a city, for example, has established that a police officer will only be discharged for "cause," by virtue of that "cause" requirement that the police officer will be generally deemed to have a "property interest" in continued employment.[79] More specifically, those provisions of a CBA or civil service rule that prohibit the discharge of an employee without cause have been ruled sufficient to create a protected property interest.[80]

Although property interests are created and defined by existing rules or "understandings" that stem from independent sources such as state or local law, the minimum procedural protections

---

[75] *Hewitt v. Grabicki*, 794 F.2d 1373, 1380 (9th Cir. 1986).

[76] *Knudson v. City of Ellensburg*, 832 F.2d 1142, 1143 (9th Cir. 1987).

[77] 470 U.S. 532 (1985).

[78] *Board of Regents v. Roth*, 408 U.S. 564, 577, 92 S.Ct. 2701, 33 L.Ed.2d 548 (1972). While public employment alone does not create constitutionally protected property interests, protected property interests can arise from express or implied contracts for continued employment.

[79] *Hoflin v. City of Ocean Shores*, 121 Wash. 2d 113, 127 (1993).

[80] *Washington Education Association v.* State, 97 Wash. 2d 899, 908, 652 P.2d 1347 (1982); *Cleveland Board of Education v. Loudermill*, 470 U.S. 532, 546, 105 S.Ct. 1487, 1493, 84 L.Ed.29 194 (1985).

extended those interests are matters of federal law.[81] Put another way, although a state or city may elect not to confer a property interest in public employment, but *once conferred*, an employee owed that "property" may not be deprived of that interest without appropriate procedural safeguards.[82]

The actual source of the property interest can be "a statute, policy, practice, regulation, guideline, written contract, or contract implied from the 'mutually explicit understanding' of the parties."[83] So where a statute or agreement provides that the employee has the right to continued employment except where there is just cause to remove the employee from the position, a protectable "property interest" is established.[84]

The scope of protected "property interests" according to most courts, also extends to lesser forms of discipline, including suspensions and demotions.

And once this property interest is established, *Loudermill* requires a hearing be given *before* an employee is discharged.[85] As will be discussed later, the extent of this "hearing" need not be a full blown evidentiary hearing, although a "post deprivation" hearing likely would be of that more formal nature.

The scope of protected "property interests" according to most courts, also extends to lesser forms of discipline, including suspensions and demotions.[86] For example, a five-day suspension has been found to require due process,[87] and even a three-day suspension has been held not to be *de minimis*.[88] It is clear that "demotions" from a civil service rank involve the deprivation of a property interest.[89]

There is some division among the courts as to how far to reach

[81] *Loudermill*, 470 U.S. at 538.

[82] *Loudermill*, at 541 (quoting *Amett v. Kennedy*, 416 U.S. 134, 94 S.Ct. 1633, 40 L.Ed.2d 15 (1974)).

[83] *Pesek v. City of Brunswick*, 794 F. Supp. 768, 779 (N.D. Ohio 1992).

[84] *Jones v. Doria*, 767 F. Supp. 1432, 1436 (N.D. Ill. 1991).

[85] 105 S.Ct. at 1493.

[86] A Supreme Court decision made prior to *Loudermill* explained that "[t]he Court's view has been that as long as a property deprivation is *not* de minimis, its gravity is irrelevant to the question whether account must be taken of the Due Process Clause." *Goss v. Lopez*, 95 S.Ct. 729, 737 (1975).

[87] *Boals v. Gray*, 775 F.2d 686, 697 (6th Cir. 1985).

[88] *Golbeck v. City of Chicago*, 782 F. Supp. 381, 385 (N.D. Ill. 1992).

[89] Greene v. Barrett, 174 F.3d 1136 (10th Cir1999).

to protect property interests. For example, the courts are split as to whether specialty assignments are required the protection of due process. The prevailing rule appears to be that "disciplinary" transfers are accorded due process protection but operational transfers are not. Even this distinction, though, hinges on whether the CBA at issue allows a grievance to challenge the transfer as lacking cause; the source of the "property right" must be grounded in "law" such as the labor contract. Generally labor contracts allow that a discipline transfers be grievable,[90] but where that element is absent in a CBA, a *Loudermill* hearing need not precede such a transfer.

The courts have recognized a number of other employment property rights also to be protected by the due process clause. The linchpin of the "due process" concept is that it keeps the government from removing property, i.e, money from an individual without proper due process. The key questions to assess any "property interest" claim is first, whether an economic interest is at stake and second, whether those interests are grounded in a source of law, such as contract or statute so as to confer there is an enforceable "property interest."

Despite that money nexus, economically motivated layoffs or reorganizational position consolidations are generally *not* deemed encompassed by the Loudermill requirements.[91] If such reorganization is merely a pretext to remove a targeted employee, though, this exception does not apply and a hearing would be required.[92]

On the other hand, the right to a Loudermill hearing is *not* dependent on the removal being characterized a form of "discipline." Medical removals fall within the scope of the property

---

[90] Often the CBA will not expressly indicate that "disciplinary transfers" are grievable yet the right to grieve nonetheless exists. As will be discussed in the next chapter, if the CBA indicates that "discipline" must be for cause and no exemption is expressed for discipline transfers, the right to grieve transfers with a disciplinary purpose is encompassed in the term "discipline." Decisions that are bona fide operational in purpose are not grievable as discipline since their purpose is not disciplinary. (Whether the purpose is in fact operational or discipline can itself be the subject of a grievance.) This obligation is clear in the law yet often misunderstood and resisted by errant managers.

[91] See *Dwyer v. Regan*, 777 F.2d 825 (2nd Cir. 1985); Connolly v. City of Rutland, 2011 U.S. Distr. Lexis 94978 (U.S.Vt. 2011); Duffy v. Sarault, 892 F.2d 139 (1st Cir. 1989); Duncan v. Dept of Pern. Administration, 77 Cal.App.4th 1166 (2000).

[92] *Levine v. City of Alameda*, 525 F.3d 903 (9th Cir. 2008). *Dwyer v. Regan*, 777 F.2d 825 (2nd Cir. 1985); Ritz v. Town of East Hartford, 110 F.Supp.2d 94 (D.Conn. 2000).

interest that requires due process.[93] In *Ganley v. County of San Mateo,*[94] the court dismissed the County's argument that no due process hearing was required for someone it alleged was unable to perform required job duties. The court called the arguments "bizarre":

> This inverted reasoning assumes that there is "cause" to terminate Plaintiff -- the same fact of which she seeks a procedurally adequate determination *prior to* her removal. Under this logic, no disabled employee would be entitled to procedural due process, and a determination by human resources personnel that an employee is permanently disabled would divest an employee of her property interest in her job. Whether the County has cause to terminate an employee is not the same question as whether the employee has a property interest.

Although the U.S. Supreme Court and the courts of this state have not addressed the issue, other courts have held that status on an eligibility or promotion list is a protectable property interest within the meaning of the due process clause. In *Stana v. School District of the City of Pittsburg,*[95] the court ruled that an applicant who had achieved placement on an eligibility list for a teacher position had a property interest in her status on the eligibility list of which she can not be deprived without due process. Similarly, in *Drogan v. Ward,*[96] the court held that continued placement on an eligibility list constituted a property interest where the state civil service law provided that all applicants obtaining passing scores shall be placed on the eligibility list. The court reasoned that even if the applicant did not have the right to employment itself, *the opportunity to be considered was in itself an important interest.*[97]

This case is also consistent with a line of Ninth Circuit Court of Appeals holdings. The Ninth Circuit has repeatedly held that if an employee is transferred out of a protected civil service job and loses

---

[93] See, e.g, *Coffan v. Board of Trustees*, 842 F.Supp. 723 (S.D.N.Y. 1994); Gaines v. New York State Division for Youth, 213, A.D.2d 894, 623, N.Y.S.2d 936 (1995)

[94] 3007 U.S. Dist. Lexis 93489 (N.D.Cal. 2007)

[95] 775 F.2d. 122 (3rd Cir. 1985).

[96] 675 F. Supp. 832 (S.D.N.Y. 1987).

[97] *See, also, Norlander v. Schleck*, 345 F. Supp. 595 (1972) (due process right in placement on eligibility lists where cand*ida*te had achieved a qualifying score for placement on such a list).

reversion rights as a result of the transfer, the employee is entitled to notice *before* the loss of those reversion rights so that the employee may make an intelligent decision concerning whether to accept the transfer. Furthermore, an employee could not be compelled to take such a transfer which would result in a loss of that property right without a hearing.[98]

And in *McGraw v. City of Huntington Beach*,[99] the Ninth Circuit ruled that the fact that an individual had failed in a trial promotion in which he could be removed from the position during the probationary period did not remove from that individual the property rights in the *prior* position. Therefore, the employee could be demoted without a due process hearing, but the employee could not be terminated without a due process hearing.

3. Protectable Liberty Interests

Whenever a document is created that stigmatizes such employee, even though lacking an enforceable "property interest" a due process claim may yet arise under the "liberty" prong.

The United States Supreme Court has long indicated that interests in "liberty" are also protectable under the United States Constitution. In *Goss v. Lopez*, the Court stated:

> The Due Process Clause also forbids arbitrary deprivations of liberty. 'Where a person's good name, reputation, honor, or integrity is at stake because of what the government is doing to him,' the minimal requirements of the Clause must be satisfied.[100]

In my view, Washington public safety agencies currently seem to underestimate their exposure for liberty interest claims in that they misunderstand the murky nature of this interest. Discharged employees not covered by just cause requirements, such as appointees or probationers are still susceptible to a violation of their "liberty" interests. Whenever a document is created that

[98] *Alexander v. City of Menlo Park*, 787 F.2d 1371 (1986); *Bukwith v. County of Clark*, 827 F.2d 595 (1987).

[99] 82 F.2d 384 (9th Cir. 1988).

[100] 95 S.Ct. at 736, quoting *Wisconsin v. Constantineau*, 400 U.S. 433, 437, 91 S.Ct. 507 510 (1971).

stigmatizes such employee, even though lacking an enforceable "property interest" a due process claim may yet arise under the "liberty" prong. The risk, or even the likelihood, that the document will become public is what creates the risk of a liberty interest violation.

The general rule is that if the discharge involves allegations of misconduct and the misconduct is ever publicized then the employee's "good name" is called into question. And employees have a liberty interest in their good name. It should be stressed that this right to enforce the liberty interest has been generally limited to discharge cases. Courts have applied what is often called the "stigma plus" requirement, meaning that some significant impairment be suffered by the employee in addition to the negative publicity and usually that has meant a discharge.[101]

Employers are often under the misperception that a due process hearing would never be required for the termination of a probationary employee. While this may be true *if* the employee is quietly released due to the simple failure to meet standards set for probationary employees and no "misconduct" is alleged, there are a number of other circumstances which arise which *will* invoke a liberty interest.

A good case that demonstrates this point is *Heger v. City of Costa Mesa.*[102] Heger was a probationary officer who was discharged during his probationary period after it had been determined that he had been "discourteous" to a number of citizens. The court held that Heger had protectable liberty interests because discharge under these circumstances "might foreclose other employment opportunities."[103] Not all courts would reach as far as this court did to find that a liberty interest had been violated.

The second area of risk for an employer stems from discharge records for those employees who are regular but exempt from just cause requirements. The nature of this risk stems directly from the mandate of the state Public Records Act. The Act requires that the sustained discipline be treated as public records and it does not distinguish based on whether the records are subject to appeal. An example of this situation is a Ninth Circuit decision involve a Spokane County employee — Cox v. Roskelley.[104]

---

101 *Paul v. Davis*, 424 U.S. 693 (1976). This rule was cogently critiqued in Stern, *Defamed but Retained Public Employees: Addressing a Gap in Due Process Jurisprudence*, 31 HOFSTRA L. REV. 795 (2003).

102 231 Cal. 3d 42, 282 Cal. Rptr. 341 (1991).

103 282 Cal. Rptr. at 346.

Cox was the County's risk manager. After a dispute with other County officials, he was discharged. The termination letter, which was added to his personnel file, accused him of misconduct. No hearing was held preceding the discharge. The Ninth Circuit found this violated his due process rights. It hinged its analysis on the Washington state public records law, noting that, once placed in Cox's file, the discharge letter automatically become a public record and was subject to publication to a wider audience.

4. The Nature of the Process Which is Due

Once it has been established that the employee in question has a protected property interest in continued employment, the logical next step is to determine what process must be followed. The "root requirement" of the Due Process Clause is that the deprivation of property be preceded by notice and the opportunity for hearing appropriate to the nature of the case.[105] The specific dictates of due process are determined by *balancing* the competing interests at stake in a particular case.[106] In public employment cases, these identified interests are (1) employee' private interest in retaining their position of employment, (2) the employer's interest in expeditious removal or demotion of unsatisfactory employees and the avoidance of administrative burdens, and (3) the risk of an erroneous deprivation.[107] In balancing these competing employment interests, the Supreme Court arrived at the elements of due process set forth in the Loudermill case.

Due process, as applied by most courts, requires a formal *post*-discharge hearing where the employer must establish both the specific charges against the employee and the evidence on which the employer is basing his charges. This post discharge hearing is presumably required to be a full evidentiary hearing with cross examination of witnesses[108] although there is some dispute over the extent of the required formality.[109] As a practical matter, arbitration or civil service will involve an evidentiary hearing with cross-examination.

---

104 369 F.3d 1105 (9th Cir 2004).

105 *Loudermill*, at 1493.

106 *Mathews v. Eldridge*, 424 U.S. 319, 335, 96 S.Ct. 893, 903, 47 L.Ed.2d 18 (1976).

107 *Loudermill*, at 1493.

108 *See McClure v. Independent School District No. 16*, 228 F.3d 1205 (10th Cir. 2000); Tolson v. Sheridan School District, 703 F. Supp 755 (E.D.Ark. 1988)

109 *See Sutherland v. Tooele City Corp.*, 91 Fed. Appx. 632 (10th Cir. 2004) (Cross examination and confrontation of witnesses not always required).

It is not required that such a full hearing be conducted *prior* to the deprivation of the property right. The pre-deprivation process need only provide an "initial check" against mistaken decisions — essentially, a determination of whether there are reasonable grounds to believe that the charges against the employee are true and support the proposed action.[110] If the employer provides a prompt post-deprivation evidentiary hearing, pre-deprivation due process requires only that the employee be afforded notice of the charges, an explanation of the employer's evidence, and an opportunity to present "his side of the story".[111]

The rationale for requiring pre-termination hearings is stated in *Loudermill*:

> [S]ome opportunity for the employee to present his side of the case is recurringly of obvious value in reaching an accurate decision. Dismissals for cause will often involve factual disputes. [Citation omitted.] *Even where the facts are clear, the appropriateness or necessity of the discharge may not be; in such cases, the only meaningful opportunity to invoke the discretion of the decision maker is likely to be before the termination takes effect.*[112]

A *narrow exception* to this pre-termination requirement exists when an employee is placed on administrative leave due to a criminal charge. In *Gilbert v. Homar*,[113] the United States Supreme Court held that a public university could put a police officer who had been charged with a drug-related felony on an unpaid suspension pending the outcome of the criminal case. The court stressed that this was a suspension, not a termination, that the employee would eventually be provided due process. Applying *Homar*, the Ninth Circuit has held that after felony charges were presented, the employees still retained the right to a post discharge hearing.[114]

LOUDERMILL RIGHTS

- Apply Whenever a Public Employer Seeks to Remove a

[110] *Williams v. City of Seattle*, 607 F. Supp. 714, 720 (W.D. Wash. 1985); *see, also, Los Angeles Police Protective League v. Gates*, 995 F.2d 1469 (9th Cir. 1993).

[111] 470 U.S. at 546.

[112] 470 U.S. at 543 (Emphasis supplied).

[113] 520 U.S. 924 (1997).

[114] See Association for L.A. Deputy Sheriffs v. County of Los Angeles, 648 F.3d 986 (9th Cir 2011) (dissent opinion filed to the opposite effect).

Protected "Property Interest" or "Liberty Interest"
- Require "Notice" and "an Opportunity to be Heard" Prior to the Deprivation
- Require an Informal Conference, not an Elaborate Trial

Due process not only requires that a hearing occur but that it be with the person effectively empowered to make a decision.[115] The rationale for requiring a hearing with the decisionmaker was set forth long ago in *Goldberg v. Kelly.*[116] The Court noted:

> The second-hand presentation to the decision maker by the case worker has its own deficiencies; since the case worker usually gathers the facts upon which the charge of an eligibility rests, the presentation of the recipient's side of the controversy cannot safely be left to him."[117]

The notice must also make it clear that there is a specific intent to take disciplinary action. In *Matthews v. Harney County,*[118] the Ninth Circuit found a due process violation where an employee had been terminated without being specifically advised that termination was being contemplated. Although the employee knew there was an investigation underway, the employee was never advised what specific action was contemplated until just before a meeting that the employee was asked to either resign or be fired. The employee resigned but withdrew the resignation the following day. The court found that the employee had a right to withdraw the resignation and that her due process rights were violated because of the lack of specific advance notice.

There is some lack of clarity in the case law concerning how much evidence must be produced to the employee prior to the *Loudermill* hearing. While many courts have suggested that just a general description of the evidence will suffice, a few other courts have indicated that the employer must produce investigatory documents.[119] Given the importance of having the documents one

---

115 *See, e.g., Stretten v. Wordsworth Veterans Hospital*, 537 F.2d 361, 369 (9th Cir. 1976) (employee has the right to "present his side of the story to the decision maker" prior to termination).

116 397 U.S. 254, 25 L.Ed.2d 287, 90 S.Ct. 1011 (1970).

117 397 U.S. at 296.

118 819 F.2d 889 (9th Cir. 1987).

119 See *Gaines v New York State Division for Youth*, 213 A.D.2d 894 (1995) (due process violation to withhold some of the medical evidence from employee on medical discharge matter); *Hrbek v. City of Bellevue Civil Service Commission*, 2005 Neb. App. Lexis 179 (2005); *Martinez v. City of Loma Linda*

is attempting to rebut, it would be prudent to make production of these documents a contractual requirement in your Bill of Rights.

There is also a lack of clarity in the cases concerning who must preside over the hearing. There is abundant dicta in the case law that the hearing must be with the "decisionmaker." But there are also a number of cases in which the employee only met with a midlevel manager and then was later notified by the department head that he had been terminated. Despite the debatability of this point,[120] an employer who is subject to a "just cause" requirement proceeds at its own risk when it terminates an employee without a face-to-face meeting with the actual decisionmaker.

It should be stressed that the *Loudermill* requirement does not call for a formal trial in any sense. It would be more apt to describe the *Loudermill* "hearing" as a "conference." Employees are allowed to present evidence but in an informal sense. As one court noted, a hearing lasting only 30 minutes may suffice.[121]

5. Contractual Bill of Rights

Public safety employee contracts, especially police contracts, frequently contain a "Bill of Rights." These Bill of Rights frequently spell out specific procedural requirements an employer must fulfill before, during, and after the disciplinary investigative process. As will be discussed in the next chapter, the failure of an employer to comply with these procedures may be the basis for setting aside the discipline.

Often the parties are well-served by having a Bill of Rights even though it may expose the employer to greater risk of having a discipline decision overturned. An advantage to the parties is that the rules and procedures become clearer which may actually reduce the risk that the employer will inadvertently violate one of the many statutory or constitutional mandates during the course of an investigation.

The extent of "what process is due" during prediscipline hearings, as discussed above, is still evolving under the case law.

(Unpublished) 2003 WL 429505 (Cal.App.4th Dist. 2003); *Los Angeles Protective League v. Gates*, 907 F.2d 879 (9th Cir. 1990) (due process violation to withhold investigative information).

[120] There are conflicting Ninth Circuit decisions on this point. See *Stretten v. Wordsworth Veterans Hospital*, 537 F.2d 361, 369 (9th Cir. 1976) (employee has the right to "present his side of the story to the decision maker" prior to termination) and *Los Angeles Protective League v. Gates*, 907 F.2d 879 (9th Cir. 1990) (meeting with midlevel manager, not the decisionmaker suffices.

[121] *Browning v. City of Odessa*, 990 F.2d 842 (1993).

Defining procedures in the CBA could be useful for *both* parties. Later litigation could be avoided by ensuring that certain notice, discovery and representation rights are safeguarded well inside the ill-defined outer boundaries of the law. Employers who instead operate at the gray edge of the law do so at their peril. Prudent employers arrive at negotiated understandings as to prediscipline procedures and then adhere to them.

Chapter 6

Right of Employees to be Disciplined Only for Just Cause

A. Discipline Appeals Systems

The public safety personnel carry a high profile in their communities. Their failings and alleged failings will be dissected both by the public and their employers. While certainly not all discipline is unjust, sometimes this additional scrutiny leads to penalties that are unjustified or excessive. Consequently, having a stout discipline appeals system is of prime importance to public safety employees.

Most, but not all, Washington public safety personnel are covered by a dual discipline appeal system. Virtually all employees covered by a labor contract are also covered by a right to binding discipline arbitration. The second less used, but older appeals system is civil service.

Scope and purpose of Civil Service. Civil service was primarily adopted to prevent political patronage. The standard of review applied to civil service largely reflects that heritage; it often primarily focuses on whether there is a good faith basis for the employer's decision, not necessarily whether the discipline or discharge was avoidable. While a minimal check on employer discretion, at a time where no other effective protection against arbitrary and politically motivated personnel action existed, civil service appeal rights had value.

The civil service law covers most public safety employees in the state of Washington. It covers:

- All Sheriff's Departments[1]
- All Municipal police departments with 3 or more full-time commissioned personnel[2]
- All Municipal Fire Departments[3]

---

[1] RCW Chapter 41.14.

[2] RCW Chapter 41.12.010. *See also Jordan v. Oakville*, 106 Wn.2d 122, 720 P.2d 824 (1986).

[3] RCW 41.08.

- Fire Districts but only on opt-in basis[4]

The optional nature of fire district civil service coverage means district employees only have due process and tenure rights if they are covered by a labor contract assuring them.[5] The Ninth Circuit has held that Washington's system, even though it creates different civil service rights between city and fire district employees, does not violate equal protection.[6] Almost all employees within those other departments are covered. The protections extend to not only uniformed personnel but also to civilian employees. (Employers seem to have abandoned fighting claims that civilian employees are exempt following *Teamsters v. City of Moses Lake*,[7] which had rejected this argument.) The law enforcement civil service statutes permit an employer to exempt a limit number of appointees from civil service coverage. The number of exemptions is based on a sliding scale corresponding to department size.[8] All employees of city fire departments are covered, with the Fire Chief as the sole exemption.[9]

There is one subtle yet important impact that employer organization decisions might have on civil service rights. *State law civil service rights extend to law enforcement employees only when they are employed in a Sheriff or Municipal police department.* If County jail management is transferred from the Sheriff to the Commissioners, municipal fire service is transferred to an exempt district, or 911 services are consolidated into a stand-alone regional 911 center, civil service protection is lost. (City or county governments may voluntarily extend civil service coverage to other departments and some large governments, for example, Seattle, Tacoma, and King County, do so.)

Civil Service v. Arbitration. The other system of discipline appeals is the one that arises from a CBA — that of binding

---

4 RCW 52.30.040 ("A fire protection district with a fully-paid fire department *may*, by resolution of its board of fire commissioners, provide for civil service in its fire department in the same manner, with the same powers, and with the same force and effect as provided by chapter 41.08 RCW for cities, towns, and municipalities, including restrictions against the discharge of an employee because of residence outside the limits of the fire protection district.") (Emphasis added.).

5 *Roley v. Pierce County Fire Protection District No. 4*, 869 F.2d 491 (9th Cir. 1989).

6 *Id.*

7 70 Wn. App. 404, 853 P.2d 951 (1993).

8 See RCW 41.12.050 and RCW 41.14.070.

9 RCW 41.08.050.

arbitration by a neutral arbitrator. The overwhelming majority of public safety labor contracts contain a provision that employees be disciplined only for "just cause" and allow appeals to a neutral arbitrator.

Between Civil Service and contract arbitration, the later is a vastly superior method of appealing discipline cases. There are three principal reasons for this:

1. The civil service board is made up of individuals who are hand-picked by the employer, often with little experience in modern labor law principles and personnel rules; a neutral arbitrator is generally quite experienced in labor law and is quite capable of applying relevant legal principles;

2. Generally, the burden of proof in an arbitration is higher than the burden of proof followed by local civil boards in that arbitrators often follow a "clear and convincing" standard; civil service boards tend to follow a lesser "preponderance of evidence" standard (and some have been known to improperly impose the burden of proof upon the employee); and

3. Civil service boards tend to apply a more narrow definition of "just cause," namely that of whether the employer made the decision in good faith and with substantial evidence; arbitrators usually require the employer to meet a number of rigorous tests.

The opinion that Civil Service offers "watered down" appeal rights isn't just the opinion of those who have served as advocates within both systems. The State Supreme Court has weighed in on the relative inadequacies of the civil service standard. In *Civil Service v. City of Kelso*,[10] the Washington Supreme Court, in addressing a technical "res judicata" defense, rejected an argument that Civil Service was a sufficiently adequate substitute for arbitration:

> Thus, although at first blush the Commission and the

[10] 137 Wn.2d 166, 969 P.2d 474 (1999).

> arbitrator appear to be deciding the same issue (whether Officer Stair's suspension was valid), the civil service hearing was based on a statutory right, while the arbitration was based on a more expansive contractual right. The Kelso Police Department was constrained by the civil service ordinance not to suspend Officer Stair except "in good faith and for good cause." It was further constrained under the collective bargaining agreement because it voluntarily contracted not to suspend an officer without "just cause." *The evidence necessarily considered in applying each standard was not substantially the same. The Commission focused on whether Stair violated department regulations; the arbitrator examined whether the punishment was appropriate in proportion to his offense.* While the Commission may have correctly determined that the police department had cause to suspend Officer Stair under the civil service rules, this is not determinative of whether the police department had the authority to suspend him under the voluntary contract it had entered into with the Union.[11]

And in an even more informative footnote comment, the Court observed:

> The difference in the substance of the two analysis is underscored by the fact that the Commission's decision is a sparse document that lists nine findings of fact and four conclusions of law. In contract, the arbitrator's opinions is an in-depth examination of numbers factual and contractual issues.[12]

So you can appeal your discipline to a board that is hand-selected by the employer, applies a narrow "good faith" standard, sometimes improperly shifts the burden of proof to the employee, and writes up perfunctory explanations of their decisions. Or you can appeal to a professional labor arbitrator that is mutually selected by the parties, applies a robust just cause test, holds the employer to a high burden of proof, and documents his or her decision in a thorough written decision. It is your choice. But we

---

[11] *Id.* at 174-75 (emphasis added).

[12] *Id.* at 175, n.3.

will solely focus the rest of this Chapter on the "just cause" standard as applied by labor arbitrators.

B. The Just Cause Standard

A preliminary comment about arbitration case law is in order here. In other chapters of this book, there are extensive cites to legal authority to support or explain a point. In this chapter, there are as well. But to understand the law addressed in this chapter, the reader needs to be aware that *there is a difference in the significance of that cited authority.*

Courts[13] and most administrative agencies — including PERC,[14] operate under a doctrine called "stare decisis." Stare decisis is a fundamental principle of law which recognizes the "binding" nature of case precedent. It is so central to the rule of law that it is virtually the first topic covered in almost every law school.

Our State Supreme Court recently explained the principle: "Generally, under stare decisis, we will not overturn prior precedent unless there has been 'a clear showing that an established rule is incorrect and harmful.'"[15] In principle, an evolution away from existing case precedent occurs only when changes in circumstances or other intervening case interpretations make that precedent no longer viable.

The significance of precedent when discussing court and PERC rulings is that past cases rulings are the strongest indicator of what will happen in the future precisely because *those tribunals can be expected to adhere to those past rulings.* But in the circumstance as to arbitration case law, *there is no doctrine of "stare decisis."* To underscore that point, a computer search of published BNA cases produces not a single hit on the term "stare decisis."

What does this ultimately mean as to the significance of published arbitration decisions? Because previous decisions are not recognized "binding authority," each case can *only* be understood as that arbitrator's best effort to interpret the terms of that particular labor agreement.

---

[13] *W.G. Clark Construction Co. v. Pacific NW Regional Council of Carpenters,* 180 Wn.2d 54, 66, 322 P.3d 1207 (2014).

[14] *Grant County,* Decision 2233-A (PECB, 1986).

[15] *W.G. Clark Construction Co, supra.*

no single arbitration case can serve as a likely predictor over how future arbitrators will rule. Instead, to predict future arbitration results, one should evaluate the *broad body of arbitration cases.*

Most arbitrators see their role as *limited to interpreting the parties' mutual intent when they adopted their labor contract.* As to some contract terms, particularly the "just cause" language primarily discussed in this chapter, arbitrators recognize the language as a "term of art." They then conclude that the parties intended a particular meaning when they added the words to their CBA. Around such "terms of art," and especially one as common as the two words "just cause," arbitrators assume that the parties understood that the language would be applied to them as in had been usually applied in previous arbitration decisions to other parties.

In that context, it should be understood that *no single arbitration case can serve as a likely predictor over how future arbitrators will rule.* Instead, to predict future arbitration results, one should evaluate the *broad body of arbitration cases.* Arbitrators do not adhere to precedent, but they do respect and consider the consensus position reflected in those decisions.

With that qualifying comment, we can proceed to how arbitrators normally interpret the requirement that discipline be only for "just cause" and what those interpretations means for your labor contract.

1. An Overview of the Just Cause Standard

Employers and labor organizations have agree in most CBA's that discipline be only for "just cause." Yet it has taken many years and many arbitration decisions to clarify exactly what "just cause" means. In 1966, Arbitrator Carrol Daugherty issued a now famous "Enterprise Wire" decision setting forth the quoted definition of "just cause." After reviewing the body of pre-1966 arbitration decisions, Daughtery summarizes the existing consensus standard into "seven tests" of just cause:

1. Did the company give the employee forewarning or foreknowledge of the possible or probable disciplinary consequences of the employee's conduct?

2. Was the company's rule or managerial order reasonably related to (a) the orderly, efficient, and safe operation of the company's business and (b) the performance that the company might properly expect of the employee?

3. Did the company, before administering discipline to an employee, make an effort to discover whether the employee did in fact violate or disobey a rule or order of management?

4. Was the company's investigation conducted fairly and objectively?

5. At the investigation did the "judge" obtain substantial evidence or proof that the employee was guilty as charged?

6. Has the company applied its rules, orders, and penalties evenhandedly and without discrimination to all employees?

7. Was the degree of discipline administered by the company in a particular case reasonably related to: (a) the seriousness of the proven offense; and (b) the record of the employee in his service with the company?[16]

Under Daugherty's standard, *if one or more of these questions is answered in the negative, then normally the just cause requirement has not been satisfied.*[17]

Although Daugherty's seven tests have proven durable to a point, they do not precisely depict current arbitral decision-making. For starters, some the "seven tests" involve more than one test within a test. Properly applied, then, Daughtery's tests add up to more than 7. Moreover, cases in the nearly 35 years since *Enterprise Wire* have indicated a continued evolution in arbitral standards.

A close review of the current body of arbitration decisions indicates that *there are at least 19 factors that can be evaluated in determining whether the employer truly disciplined an employee for "just cause."* Those modern 19 just cause factors are as follows:

---

[16] *Enterprise Wire Co.*, 46 LA 359, 363-4 (1966).
[17] *Id.* at 362.

1. Did the employer provide a clear and precise statement of charges?

2. Did the employee have reasonable notice of the rule?

3. Did the employee have reasonable notice of the penalty for violating the rule?

4. Is the rule consistently enforced?

5. Is the rule reasonable and lawful?

6. Did the investigation comply with all legal and contractual due process requirements?

7. Were the methods used by the employer to gather evidence lawful?

8. Did the employee, in fact, violate the rule?

9. Was the penalty that was imposed consistent with the treatment of other employees?

10. When appropriate, did the employee receive progressive discipline?

11. Does the employer have a strong, legitimate interest in enforcement of the rule?

12. Did the employer conduct a thorough and fair investigation and consider all relevant evidence?

13. Is the penalty reasonable in light of the nature of the offense, the employee's length of service and the employee's discipline record?

14. Was the penalty reasonable in light of all the mitigating factors?

15. Was the discipline imposed the only disciplinary action taken concerning the alleged conduct?

16. Did the employer contribute in any way to the employee's conduct through its action or lack of

action?

17. Was the motivation and reasoning process of the employer in making the discipline decision proper?

18. Did the employer fulfill all legal obligations to accommodate the employee?

19. Did the discipline violate any legal or constitutional rights of the employee?

2. An Analysis of the 19 Just Cause Factors

The factors that make up "just cause" are not technically or legally complex. *They are basic common sense.* The fundamental requirement of "just cause" is that people be treated with due process and fundamental fairness. There is a large body of arbitration case law giving the parties guidance on how to fulfill the requirements of just cause. Those principles are discussed in detail in this section but for a sense of how arbitrators rule in various situations, you may find the appendix to this chapter useful. It contains a lengthy table how Northwest arbitrators have ruled in discipline arbitrations.

Precision in the nature and notice of the rule must exist both prior to the alleged occurrence of the infraction but also in the *statement of charges* to the employee at the time of the discipline.

---

a. (1) Notice of Charges

Due process requires notice as to what the employee is being charged with. Employees need to know *why* they are being disciplined. And unions also need to know exactly why, so they can prepare a proper defense.

Precision in the nature and notice of the rule must exist both prior to the alleged occurrence of the infraction but also in the *statement of charges* to the employee at the time of the discipline. The termination letter invariably serves as the "statement of charges."

A leading arbitration treatise explained the fundamental importance of a precise statement of charges:

> Any reason the employer intends to rely on for discharge must be either stated in writing or communicated to the employee, unless special grounds exist that excuse the failure to present reasons for management's action at the time discipline is imposed. Surprise and lack of adequate notice about the basis for disciplinary action generally prejudices the union and the employee in investigating the charges and preparing a defense. "The discharge...must stand or fall upon the reason given at the time of the discharge."
>
> The employer may not give the reasons for the discharge and then alter or add to them at the arbitration hearing.[18]

The notice must contain some degree of detail — there must be enough facts identified to explain the reason for the disciplinary action. *Merely listing cited rules without describing the conducted alleged is insufficient notice.*[19]

b. (2) Notice of Rule

Just cause does *not* mean "just because." The employer must demonstrate that an *actual* rule was violated.[20] But just cause also requires far more due process than proof of a rule violation. The employer must *also* prove that the employee knew, or reasonably should have known, about the existence of the rule.

It is a well-accepted arbitral principle that an employee should not be disciplined for a violation of a rule that the employee did not know about.

Publication requirement. The "rule" does not necessarily have to be in writing, although prudent employers will publish their rules to the extent feasible. Even in a policy-driven department, the workplace likely still operates on *unwritten rules* that employees

---

[18] Brand, DISCIPLINE AND DISCHARGE, at 43 (1998) (*quoting West Virginia Pulp & Paper Co.*, 10 LA 117 (Guthrie, 1947)).

[19] *Id.* at 43.

[20] *See e.g., Buckeye Local School District*, 127 LA 1560 (Lalka, 2010) (no just cause for termination of mechanic for watching dashboard camera of malfunctioning school bus when employer had no policy forbidding the viewing of that footage).

are bound to know. In other instances, discipline may still be predicated on an unstated or unwritten rule; when behavior is so egregious that *common sense* dictates the employee must have known, or at least should have known, their conduct was wrong, the employer may act.

It is a well-accepted arbitral principle that an employee should not be disciplined for a violation of a rule that the employee did not know about.[21] Regardless of *how* the rule is disseminated to employees, the employer must prove that the employee must had either actual or constructive notice of the rule.[22] Generally, publication of the rules is at least *evidence* that the employee knows what behavior will be subject to discipline.[23]

Constructive notice. Exceptions to the "formal notice" requirement exist. The employer's specific instruction provides actual notice, but common sense teaches employees that discipline can occur for certain conduct. Yet some arbitrators have ruled that the variety of conduct where knowledge will be "imputed" is *limited*:

> Only certain egregious conduct, such as stealing, intoxication while at work, or fighting with supervisors or co-workers is so evidently a violation of commonly accepted notions of work conduct that it will be presumed that the employee is on notice..."[24]

For example, an arbitrator upheld the demotion of a male police officer when he requested a female subordinate unbutton her shirt, and then he placed his hand inside her shirt and vest, touching her body.[25] The arbitrator rejected his union's argument

---

[21] *Bay Area Transit Dist.*, 80-2 ARB ¶ 8612, 5734 (Koven 1980); *Millcreek Township,* 128 LA 221 (Franckiewicz, 2010) (finding no just cause to discharge employees for violation of computer usage policy when there was no evidence that employees had been notified in any way); *Iowa-Ill. Gas & Elec. Co.*, 84 LA 868 (Keefe, 1985) (unpublicized rule applying greater penalty for misconduct); *Bekins Moving & Storage Co.*, 82 LA 642 (Daughton, 1984) (dissemination of rules could not be proven).

[22] LABOR AND EMPLOYMENT ARBITRATION, Bornstein & Gosline, eds., 19-8 (Matthew Bender & Co., 1991). *See also, Delta Air Lines*, 89 LA 408 (Kahn, 1987).

[23] *Bay Area Transit Dist.*, 80-2 ARB ¶ 8612, 5734 (Koven 1980).

[24] 80-2 ARB ¶ 8612, 5734.

[25] *City of Mission*, 126 LA 1372, (Jennings, 2009); *see also, Community Coll. Of Allegheny Cnty.*, 124 LA 1398 (Franckiewicz, 2008) (failure to follow explicit instructions); *MT Detroit, Inc.*, 118 LA 1777 (Allen, 2003) (racial epithets); *A. E. Staley Mfg. Co.*, 119 LA 1371 (Nathan, 2004) (disseminating pornography in the workplace). *But see Dynamet, Inc.*, 126 LA 903 (Fagan, 2009) (finding no just cause for termination for testing positive for cocaine as employee was

that there was no specific written description prohibiting this conduct. Instead, he cited the general prohibition of conduct unbecoming an officer (requiring only professional and courteous behavior) and the fact that this behavior was clearly egregious misconduct.[26]

But this "should have known" standard is fairly flexible and different arbitrators approach the notice obligation differently. Some arbitrators have found employees *should have known* their conduct was impermissible even when the conduct was *not* particularly egregious.

For example, a discharge was upheld for an employee who posted disparaging remarks about her employer on her Facebook page.[27] Even though the employer had no published or otherwise disseminated policy about that specific conduct, the arbitrator found that the nature of the activity *should have been known* to the employee as a dischargeable offense.[28]

Incorporated into the notice requirement is the requirement that the rule be articulated and *administered* in a clear and consistent manner so that employees may fairly be held accountable for violation of the rules.[29] It is especially important that the rules regarding off-duty expectations be clearly delineated.[30]

CBA notice requirements. It is possible that the CBA will specify the manner in which employees must be notified of new or modified rules. If so, the employer must follow the guidelines of the CBA. If the employer notifies employees contrary to the process defined in the CBA, that notice may be considered inadequate, even if it otherwise would have constituted adequate notice absent the CBA requirement.[31] For example, in *Costco Wholesale*, notice was ruled insufficient, even though the employer posted the

---

absent when new policy was implemented).

26 *Id.*

27 *Vista Nuevas Head Start*, 129 LA 1519 (VanDagens, 2011).

28 *See id*; *See also*, *City of Las Vegas*, 128 LA 596 (Staudohar, 2010) (upholding termination of guard for failing to file Use of Force report when he punched an inmate; guard was trained to file reports in such situations and therefore should have known better).

29 *Id.*

30 *See* Koven & Smith, *supra* at 31 (*citing Lamb Glass Co.*, 32 LA 420, 423 (Dworkin, 1959), ("[s]ince it is a matter of 'common law' applicable to industrial relations, what an employee does on his own time is not a subject of regulation by the employer, any qualifying restriction must be expressly set out in clear and unequivocal language.") (emphasis supplied).

31 *See Bayshore Concrete Prods. Co.*, 92 LA 311 (Hart, 1989) (finding employer did not provide sufficient notice of rules by adding a notice to paycheck envelopes).

policies on their website, informed the employees, and posted a notice on the bulletin board.[32] The arbitrator pointed out that the CBA required that all policies be sent to the union as well.

Because of the pervasiveness of computers and email, employers may be tempted to provide notice of rules electronically. But some decisions declare this is not sufficient even when it does not specifically violate a CBA notice obligation. For example, one arbitrator ruled that even when the employer informed employees that the policies in question were available online *and* emailed them, notice was insufficient.[33] He explained that because there was no mechanism to determine if the employee *actually read* the email, notice could not be proven.

Rule clarity. The rules also need to be drafted clearly. A labor arbitration treatise aptly summarizes precedent concerning the requirement of rule clarity:

> A rule must clearly and unambiguously establish the scope of prohibited conduct, as well as the consequences of violation, in order to be enforceable. Work rules may not be enforced if they are vague. Arbitrary rules have been overturned, as have overbroad rules. Arbitrators have found rules to be unreasonable where they provide no clear guidance as to what is expected of employees.[34]

c. (3) Notice as to the Penalty

It is not enough that the employer write a rule defining prohibited conduct. The employer must also communicate the *expected penalty* for violating the rule.

Absent some indication, either through communication or past practice, that a rule violation *will* result in discipline, the employee has not been provided reasonable notice that a penalty will attach for violating the rule. Due to insufficient notice of the penalty, an arbitrator may overturn the discipline.

Moreover, where the employer attempts to impose a more severe penalty for violation of the rule than in the past, employees should be put on notice that a more severe penalty will now be provided for that type of rule violation.[35] Unannounced penalty

---

[32] *Costco Wholesale, Inc.*, 118 LA 1626 (Hockenberry, 2003).

[33] *Campbell v. General Dynamics Gov't Systems Corp.*, 16 AD Cases 1361 (1st Cir. 2005).

[34] *See* Koven & Smith, *supra* at 79. *See also, Honolulu Police Dept., supra* n. 16 (rule unenforceable due to vagueness).

enhancements often cause discipline to be overturned by arbitrators.[36]

Therefore, an arbitrator may decline to uphold a termination *even though an employee might have been aware that his conduct violated a rule,* when the employee was unaware of the *seriousness* with which the employer considered the rule.[37] Employers often use boilerplate warnings or policy announcements that infractions can result in discipline "up to and including termination." But that has been held *not* to provide proper notice of the expected penalty. Language that an employee "may" be terminated or is "subject to" being terminated is deemed to be conditional language that does not put employees on notice that termination is the appropriate penalty.[38]

For example, in one case, an employee was reinstated after being terminated for theft when the employer had not notified employees that every instance of theft will result in termination.[39] (This theft example is unlikely to be applied in a law enforcement department where there the egregiousness of such conduct imputes constructive notice, but it demonstrates the principle.)

There are other limits on a union's ability to use the "notice of penalty" factor to attack discipline. Arbitrators generally hold that if the conduct is sufficiently egregious conduct, the employer is not necessarily required to state the penalty is termination. For example, a university employee with an otherwise unblemished record was discharged for fondling a female students panties in her dorm room while she lay sleeping. The University had not published a policy that specifically prohibited panty fondling, nor had it expressed the penalty for such conduct.[40] But the discharge was upheld as the conduct was found so egregious that any

---

35 *See Waste Connections of Neb., Inc.*, 120 LA 1357 (Remmes, 2004) (reinstating driver was not informed that failure to report accident would result in termination).

36 *See, e.g., Snohomish County,* 115 LA 1 (Levak, 2000) (reinstating employee terminated for sending inappropriate emails when manager had failed to enforce email guidelines previously and in fact participated in same behavior); *Champion Spark Plug Co.*, 93 LA 1277 (Dobry, 1989) ("[Employer's] lax enforcement was a signal that unacceptable behavior was tolerable. [Employer's] attempt to abruptly draw a line, without first giving a warning that a new infraction would result in discharge [is unacceptable].").

37 *See, e.g., Illinois-Iowa Gas & Elec. Co.*, 84 LA 868 (Keefe, 1985) (termination set aside when no notice was given that the penalty for the violation, for which the employee confessed, would amount to termination.)

38 Koven, *supra,* at 43.

39 *Buckeye Feed Mill, Inc.*, 122 LA 719 (Murphy, 2006).

40 *Adelphi Univ.*, 121 LA 1010 (Gregory, 2005).

reasonable employee would have recognized the penalty for such conduct would only be termination.

d. (4) Consistency in Rule Enforcement

It is not enough to simply publish a rule and then not enforce it. In fact, it is not enough to publish a rule and only occasionally enforce it. Intermittent enforcement of a rule may cause an arbitrator to conclude that employees have not truly been put on notice that the employer would see contravention of the rule as improper.

Arbitrators have, however, advised employers they have a mechanism for relief when facing a lax enforcement challenge: Though the pending discipline charge will likely fail because of lax enforcement, if the employer clearly communicates to the employees that it is reviving the rule, and it will thereafter be enforced, the employer may justifiably hold employees to that rule in the future. (The employer may well still have a duty to bargain such a rule change, though, with the union, a topic covered in Chapter 3.)

e. (5) Reasonableness of Rule

Employees should not be expected to follow absurd rules. The rules that employees should be held to follow should be those rules that bear some *rational relationship* to the employer's operations.

Nor should employees be required to follow unlawful rules. Rules that, for example, violate statutory or constitutional rights will not be enforced by an arbitrator.

f. (6) Thorough and Fair Investigation

When an employer contracts to a just cause standard, it is contracting not to make "knee jerk" personnel decisions. Arbitrators have consistently held that employers who seek to discipline employees must first acquire as much information as reasonably possible, including statements from all key witnesses, and especially a statement from the accused employee.

One of the significant requirements of the just cause standard is that the employer undertake a thorough investigation *before* imposition of discipline.[41] Included in this test is the requirement that the employer obtain all relevant evidence.[42] As one arbitration treatise notes:

---

[41] *See* Koven & Smith, JUST CAUSE: THE SEVEN TESTS (2d. ed. 1992) 159-236.
[42] *Id.* at 171-173.

> When such readily available and obvious evidence is overlooked or disregarded or perhaps in some cases consciously ignored, an arbitrator may conclude that the investigation was incomplete or shabby and consequently sustain the grievance in whole or in part.[43]

The investigation not only must be "thorough," it also needs to be "fair." Apparent investigator bias is a frequent case of discipline actions being set aside.

g. *(7) Legal and Contractual Due Process*
CBA requirements, legal due process, and "industrial due process."

> Employer violation of these procedural rights frequently is a basis for setting aside discipline that otherwise might be supported by the evidence of the charged infraction.

Both external law and the "just cause" mandate impose upon employers certain due process requirements they must fulfill during the discipline process. These obligations include complying with *Weingarten* and *Loudermill* requirements. Often there are also specific CBA mandates that define the required "due process." These dual sets of legal and contractual requirements embody the "industrial due process" standard that arbitrators will assess in determining if just cause exists.

It is common for public safety employees, especially law enforcement officers, to be covered by an employee "Bill of Rights" in the CBA. A Bill of Rights typically specifies detailed procedures governing the investigation and the prediscipline procedure. Employer violation of these procedural rights frequently is a basis for setting aside discipline that otherwise might be supported by the evidence of the charged infraction.

As discussed earlier in Chapter 5, the normal remedy issued by PERC for a *Weingarten* violation does not usually involve setting aside the discipline. Yet, many arbitrators have held that a *Weingarten* violation is a violation of "industrial due process" and is the basis for setting aside discipline in an arbitration proceeding.[44]

---

[43] *Id.* at 171.

[44] Discipline and Discharge in Arbitration, 52-53 (1998) (Brand Editor); JUST CAUSE: THE SEVEN TESTS, *supra*, at 214-15.

A competing line of arbitration cases holds that a *Weingarten* violation does not make the penalty *per se* void, but these arbitrators will sometimes try to develop some alternative remedy for the due process breach.

Arbitrators have consistently found that principles of just cause incorporate the concept of "industrial due process."[45] Arbitrators have also held that, in the public sector, the constitutional due process requirements (*Loudermill*) are also incorporated into the just cause standard.[46]

Separate and apart from the *Loudermill* due process requirements or the express terms of a "Bill of Rights" clause, arbitrators have held employers must provide a hearing as an element of a thorough investigation.[47] This "hearing" process requirement includes providing the employee the information in the employer's possession and extending the right to present witnesses.[48]

As noted previously, the constitutional requirements necessary to satisfy due process under *Loudermill* can be very informal.[49] However, to satisfy the procedural elements of just cause many decisions have held that far more structured steps are required. Employers' decisions can be overturned for their failure to follow very specific requirements, which arbitrators may consider as falling into the realm of "industrial due process."[50] Indeed, to fulfill the "industrial due process" elements of just cause for public employees, many procedural steps may be required. This requirement often, but not always, includes an employee's right to be heard, as well as the right to confront an accuser. [51] One decision reversed the discharge of an employee who was not given an interview prior to the discharge. The employer offered no mitigating factors that would have precluded an interview.

The procedure was a clear violation of a thoroughly

---

[45] *See* Koven & Smith, *supra*, 179-91, 197-98; Elkouri & Elkouri, *supra*, 673-75.

[46] *See, e.g.*, *City of Pembroke Pines*, 93 L.A. 365 (Cantor 1989) (the just cause provision of the contract "adopts by implication the rules ordinarily considered applicable under statute and case law with regard to the review of the facts on a discharge of a public employee"); *Merced Irrigation District*, 86 L.A. 851 (Riker 1986); *U.S. Customs Service*, 95 L.A. 1311 (Williams 1990).

[47] *See* Koven & Smith, *supra*, at 182-85.

[48] *Id.* at 183.

[49] *Coburn*, 2012 U.S. Dist. LEXIS 28834, 18-19 (*citing Browning v. City Odessa*, Texas, 990 F.2d 842, 844 (5th Cir. 1993)) (holding a thirty minute informal meeting fulfilled the *Loudermill* requirement).

[50] Koven & Smith, *supra*, n. 18 at 183.

[51] *Interstate Brands*, 97 LA 657 (Ellman, 1991).

> settled principle of industrial due process that a decision to discharge must be based on a fair and thorough investigation of the facts, and that this includes an opportunity for the employee to make such statement or explanation as he can in his own behalf. The requirement that no one shall be found guilty and sentenced without a hearing and opportunity to defend is drawn from the law, but its basis is common fairness.[52]

Arbitrators have also required employers furnish employees with any information in the company's possession that may be used in the investigation.[53]

Arbitration remedies. Especially when there exists express CBA mandates defining the prediscipline process, such as in a Bill of Rights, the remedies are likely to be more robust. One line of arbitration cases provides that "rescission" of the discipline is the only appropriate remedy for violation of contractual procedural rights.

For example, in *Areonca, Inc.*,[54] the arbitrator directed the reinstatement of an employee who had been discharged without being accorded the right to appear before the decision-maker prior to the termination, despite being required by the CBA. The arbitrator explained: "In the conduct of discipline it is as important to maintain the integrity of the process as it is to discipline for just cause."[55]

Another arbitrator was even more direct in *Huffman Mfg. Co.*[56] In *Huffman*, the company failed to follow CBA language requiring that the nature and reason for suspensions to be put in writing. The arbitrator overturned the discipline, stating:

> While to all practical intent, the purposes of Section 9, paragraph a, were served the fact remains that the language thereof makes it mandatory that the company notify the grievance in writing. It is expressly provided therein that the suspended employee 'shall' be notified. This arbitrator cannot ignore such a mandatory requirement, regardless of whether the purpose of the contractual provisions in question have been served.

---

52 *Gilman Paper Co.*, 61 LA 416, 420 (Murphy, 1973).

53 *Mobil Oil Corp.*, 63 LA 263 (Sinclitico, 1974) (holding employer must furnish information of any significant relevance to the investigation).

54 71 L.A. 452 (Smith, 1978).

55 *Id.* at 454.

56 31 L.A. 882 (Stouffer, 1962).

> It is, therefore, the finding of the Arbitrator that the suspension imposed the grievant on August 12, 1961, was voidable, and where, as here, its imposition was timely protested, the arbitrator has no alternative but to find the suspension to be improper and ineffective. If the Arbitrator were to decide otherwise, he would exceed his jurisdiction and authority.[57]

Moreover, arbitrators who have reviewed Bill of Rights clauses in Washington arbitration cases have also concluded that rescission of discipline is a required remedy where a Bill of Rights provision has been violated. In *City of Bremerton*,[58] Arbitrator Jack Calhoun reinstated the employee when the employer violated the provision requiring the employer to give all employees subject to disciplinary interviews the names of the complaining parties. And an unpublished Mount Vernon discipline decision Arbitrator Gordon Byrholdt reinstated an officer to a canine position where the department had violated the 48-hour rule provisions of the contractual bill of rights.

Competing view on remedies. But not all arbitrators will necessarily find that an employer's violation of procedural rights mandates setting aside the discipline. This resistance occurs especially when the violation may be a small or technical one. Arbitrators sometimes apply their own concepts of equity in arbitration, and some of those arbitrators are reluctant — simply because of what they might view as a "technicality" — to set aside a discipline, especially the misconduct is serious and the evidence is strong. This line of cases finds that a determinative factor is often whether the failure to follow the required procedure for the accused employee resulted in unfair prejudice; if no prejudice occurred then the discipline might still be upheld.[59] As Arbitrator Jane Wilkinson noted in a Renton School case: "The essential question for an arbitrator is not whether disciplinary action was totally free from procedural error, but rather whether the process was fundamentally fair."[60]

---

[57] 31 L.A. 885-86; *see also*, *Okonite Co.*, 75 L.A. 1053 (Monet, 1980) (contractual disciplinary procedures are to be "strictly interpreted"); *United States Steel Corp.*, 55 L.A. 677 (Wolff, 1970) (holding company's description of the charged offense was inadequate and violated the fundamental procedural fairness due under the contract.).

[58] 97 LA 937 (Calhoun, 1991).

[59] *See Southern Bell Tel. & Tel. Co.*, 75 LA 409 (Mikrut, 1980).

[60] *Renton School Dist.*, 102 LA 854 (Wilkinson, 1994) (right to confront an accuser will yield to a need to protect that accuser from retaliation and clear

Yet, the majority rule appears to be that where the parties have contracted to certain discipline procedures, those procedures are mandatory and *must be followed* as a prerequisite to any discipline. The legal requirements of *Weingarten* and *Loudermill* can be enhanced with a Bill of Rights to provide even more effective due process protections for your members.

h. (8) Lawful Evidence Gathering

An investigation must not only be thorough and fair, it must also be lawful. When the employer acquires the evidence through improper or unlawful investigative techniques, arbitrators will be inclined to set aside the discipline. For example, if a polygraph was improperly compelled[61] or an employee's home was unlawfully searched, this would be the basis for setting aside discipline. When the search of the employee's property is not unlawful but merely aggressive, the arbitrator has discretion to consider the evidence obtained from that search.[62]

The determinative factor in these situations can be the employee's reasonable expectation of privacy, or whether there was a reasonable basis for the search.[63] In one decision, an employee's lunchbox was searched while it was in his locker. In upholding the search, the arbitrator relied on the fact that the employee lockers were open to everyone, and therefore there was no reasonable expectation of privacy for the lockers.[64] Another arbitrator commented:

> Evidence obtained from an otherwise legal search has been excluded when the search had no reasonable basis to undertake the search. For example, evidence obtained from an employee's car was excluded when the information that led to the search was deemed unreliable.[65]

---

guilt of the accused negated any prejudice from improper hearing procedures).

[61] *See, e.g., Houston Lighting & Power Co.*, 87 LA 478 (Howell, 1986) (holding employee's refusal to submit to lie detector test is excused, and does not weigh against the employee); *International Minerals & Chem. Corp.*, 83 LA 593 (Kulkis, 1984) (refusal to submit to polygraph inadmissible to prove guilt).

[62] Elkouri & Elkouri, *supra* n. 31 at 400.

[63] *Id.*

[64] *American Welding and Mfg. Co.*, 89 LA 247 (Dworkin, 1987).

[65] *Kerr-McGee Chem. Corp.*, 90 LA 55 (Levin, 1987); *See also Ross-Meehan Foundries*, 55 LA 1078 (King, 1970) (search deemed impermissible where employer did not have sufficient cause to search employee's lunchbox).

i. (9) Employee Violation of a Rule

Undoubtedly this is the most important of all the tests. If the employee did not do the act that is alleged, no discipline should occur.

arbitrators are divided as to the extent of that burden

Burden of Proof. Collective bargaining agreements containing "just cause" provisions have been interpreted almost uniformly to impose a burden of proof upon the employer. Although there is some disagreement among arbitrators about the *quantum* of proof required, there is a consensus that the employer must carry the burden not only to prove the alleged defense but also the appropriateness of the penalty.[66]

But arbitrators are divided as to the extent of that burden. Nationally, a majority seems to apply the "mere preponderance" borrowed from civil law. But a large minority apply the heightened "clear and convincing" standard. In the Northwest, it appears a majority of arbitrators have opted for the more favorable "clear and convincing standard."

Credibility cases. Especially in a "credibility case" — a case that turns primarily on the believability of key witnesses — the choice of which burden to apply to the employer can make a significant difference to the ultimate outcome. In a one-on-one credibility case or a charge involving an allegation of dishonesty, the "clear and convincing" standard is particularly advantageous for the union because the arbitrator must be *clearly convinced* that the grievant is lying.

Under the "mere preponderance" standard involving "just more than 50%" threshold with a similar credibility case, an arbitrator would theoretically only need to be *slightly* more persuaded by the employer's witnesses. One leading commentator described the application of the "mere preponderance" standard": "Where the parties are adjudged to have presented equally persuasive evidence on each side of an issue, it is in equipoise, and the party asserting the claim has failed to meet its burden."[67]

Historically, a pervasive view of arbitrators, which has fallen out of favor, was that in the case of a credibility dispute, the

---

[66] *See*, Elkouri & Elkouri, HOW ARBITRATION WORKS, 906-08 (5th Ed., 1996) (Volz & Goggin, Editors); Koven & Smith, JUST CAUSE: THE SEVEN TESTS, 266-68 (2d Ed., *1992*) (Revised by Farwell).

[67] Elkouri & Elkouri, HOW ARBITRATION WORKS, at 190 (6th Ed. Supp. 2010).

arbitrator should lean to the employer in determining truthfulness. The primary rationale for this view was that the employee is motivated to protect his own interest with his testimony, and the supervisor (probably) has nothing to gain. Therefore, the employee, according to this rationale, is more likely to lie.[68] Some arbitrators continue to adopt this view.[69] Even for those arbitrators that do not openly express this view, it stands to reason that they are going to maintain a healthy skepticism of the testimony of a grievant seeking to save his job.

Serious offenses. Some arbitrators have also concluded that a sliding scale burden of proof is appropriate, in which more serious the alleged offense, the higher the burden to which the employer should be held.[70] And it has been observed:

> An arbitrator may require a high degree of proof in one discharge case and at the same recognize that a lesser degree may be required in others. Similarly, where the proof was not strong enough to support discharge, some arbitrators have, nonetheless, found it strong enough to justify a lesser penalty.[71]

The union argument for a high standard of proof is based on what is at stake for the employee in a termination case. Especially for public safety employees, what is at stake is usually not simply a job but an entire career. Applying too low a standard runs the risk of ruining a worthwhile career as one commentator has recognized:

> If the employer has not proven the infraction occurred, the employee is exonerated. The employee *may* have been guilty, but to punish an employee for a possible or even probable wrong, without convincing proof, runs the risk of penalizing an innocent employee. *That would violate just cause precepts.* If the employee is in fact guilty but guilt is unproven, the employee may profit from the scrape with discipline, and reform.[72]

---

68 *Ford Motor Co.*, 1 ALAA ¶67,224, p. 67620 (Shulman, 1954).

69 *See Smith's Food and Drug Centers*, 129 LA 1384 (Jennings, 2011); *Maui Pineapple Co.*, 86 LA 907 (Tsukiyama, 1986) (resolving credibility dispute in favor of the supervisor solely because supervisor had less incentive to lie).

70 Elkouri & Elkouri, *supra* n. 31 at 951.

71 *Id.* at 906-07.

72 Bornstein & Gosline, LABOR & EMPLOYMENT ARBITRATION, 19.03[2] (1991) (emphasis supplied).

In actual practice with public safety employee discharge cases, experience suggests arbitrators are aware of take seriously what is involved. There seems to be a recognition that a denial of the grievance usually means an end to a professional career. In such cases, whatever the stated burden of proof test they apply, most arbitrators seem to hold the employer to the full appropriate burden of proof.

Criminal and "moral turpitude" charges. Frequently, arbitrators will apply an *even higher* standard of proof for the most serious discipline cases. The criminal law standard of "proof beyond a reasonable doubt" may be imposed on the employer when the employee is being disciplined for conduct that is criminal or involves moral turpitude. The premise is that sustaining such a charge may have an enormous impact on the employee's reputation and employability.[73]

Therefore, there is significant, but not conclusive, authority for the union position in such cases that the proof be beyond a reasonable doubt.[74] As one arbitrator concluded:

> It seems reasonable and proper to hold that alleged misconduct of a kind which carries the stigma of general social disapproval...should be clearly and convincingly established by the evidence. Reasonable doubts raised by the proofs should be resolved in favor of the accused.[75]

One of the reasons for requiring a heightened burden of proof for such cases is the social stigma which attaches to a sustained discharge. But a related, yet more compelling reason exists for such a higher standard of proof: An employee who has a sustained discharge for such an offense is likely to have long-term employment prospects damaged even greater than would be the case in a typical discharge case.

These dynamics have been noted by arbitrators. For example, one arbitrator explained a rational for a heightened burden of proof in criminal cases:

---

[73] Elkouri & Elkouri, *supra*, at 662. *See also*, *Jefferson County Sherriff's Office, Steubenville, Ohio*, 114 LA 1508 (Klein, 2000) (sexual misconduct with inmates); *Yellow Freight Sys.*, 103 LA 731 (Stix, 1994) (theft); *Greyhound Food Mgmt.*, 89 LA 1138 (Grinstead, 1987) (theft of thirty-eight cent orange juice).

[74] *Dunlop Tire & Rubber Co.*, 64 LA 1099, 1102 (Mills, 1975); *see also*, *Iowa Department of General Services*, 79 LA 852, at 855 (Mikrut, 1982).

[75] Elkouri & Elkouri, *supra*, at 662 (*quoting Kroger Co.*, 25 LA 906, 908 (Smith, 19550).

> [A] discharge for theft has such catastrophic economic and social consequences to the accused that it should not be sustained unless supported by the overwhelming weight of the evidence...the accused must always be given the benefit of substantial doubts.[76]

Another interesting and practical perspective from one arbitrator is that *regardless* of whatever burden is identified:

> Beyond a reasonable doubt, arbitrators will often implicitly impose this burden because of the severity of the punishment. Most of us "consciously or unconsciously" require the highest degree of proof in discharge cases where the involved employee action . . . also constitutes a crime.[77]

Finally, as another arbitrator strongly stated, "the arbitrator must be completely convinced that the employee [is] guilty."[78]

"Deference to management" arguments. On the other end of the spectrum is the frequent employer argument that the arbitrator should "defer" to their "good faith" determination. A small minority of arbitrators have voiced this view. Otherwise, this claim has been widely rejected by arbitrators. One commentator offered strong criticism of this argument:

> The theory does afford a mechanical method for assessing truthfulness. But it is grossly unfair and contrary to the most fundamental precepts of what arbitration is, how it works, and what it is supposed to achieve.
>
> In short, this mechanism for finding "truth" is a canard which ought to be summarily dismissed from arbitral thinking. What it says to a union and a grievant is, "you are going to lose if your evidence and testimony differs from what the company presents." It makes that statement even before the employer's first witness testifies; before the controversy begins to enroll. It flies in the face of the universal understanding that management, not the bargaining unit, carries the burden of proof in a dispute over discipline. It

---

76 *Armour-Dial*, 76 LA 96, 99 (Aaron, 1980).
77 *American Air Filter Co.*, 64 LA 404, 406-07 (Hilpert, 1975).
78 *Columbia Presbyterian Hosp.*, 79 LA 24, 27 (Spencer, 1982).

> undermines arbitration as an impartial instrument for preserving industrial peace.[79]

While no two discipline cases are the same, arbitrators expect some rough equality in the discipline of employees committing similar infractions.

In short, in most cases the employer must present clear-cut evidence of wrongdoing. The arbitration advocates will frequently argue over which burden of proof should be applied because they recognize it is a consequential decision in many cases.

j. (10) Proportionality

While no two discipline cases are the same, arbitrators expect some rough equality in the discipline of employees committing similar infractions. Typically, arbitrators will carefully examine penalties for the same rule violation. As one commentator explained:

> [T]here must be reasonable rules and standards of conduct which are consistently applied and enforced in a non-discriminatory fashion. It is also generally accepted that enforcement of rules and assessment of discipline must be exercised in a consistent manner; thus all employees who engage in the same type of misconduct must be treated essentially the same.[80]

The difficulty in comparing different discipline is that often factors other than the nature of the violation itself warrant the treatment at hand. For example, such as the length of service of the employees involved, their record of discipline, and other mitigating factors may have been considered. While arbitrators especially scrutinize disparity in treatment when multiple employees are involved in the same but receive different discipline, arbitrators will also recognize varying degrees of fault. A common example is when a number of employees are involved in a work stoppage. The employer may permissibly discharge the instigating

---

[79] Koven & Smith, JUST CAUSE: THE SEVEN TESTS, 273 (1992) (*quoting Cincinnati Paperboard Corp.,* 93 L.A. 505 (Dworkin 1989)).

[80] Aaron, *The uses of the Past in Arbitration*, ARBITRATION TODAY, PROCEEDINGS OF THE 8TH ANNUAL MEETING OF NAA 1, 10 (McKelvey ed., BNA Books 1955).

employee, while providing lesser punishment for those that simply participated.[81] Similarly, arbitrators may find it unfair for employers to impose uniform discipline to employees who have varying degrees of fault.[82] As one arbitrator explained, "equality of penalties does not represent equal justice."[83]

When disparity in penalties is wide, arbitrators will expect the employer to justify such a disparity. The case law is unclear as to who bears the burden of proving proportionality claims but certainly once a union raises a colorable claim of disparate penalties, it forces the employer to respond.

An even more compelling expectation of relatively even penalties occurs when multiple employees are charged in the same incident. Arbitrators will especially scrutinize claims in such a situation.

k. (11) Progressive Discipline

One of the leading reasons for discipline being overturned is the failure of employers to follow standards of progressive discipline.

The primary purpose of employee discipline under a just cause standard is to correct, not to punish. Punitive measures are deemed appropriate only where corrective measures have been tried and failed. It is a rule that the penalty should be in keeping with the seriousness of the offense.[84] Discharge, which is arguably the only penalty not aimed at correcting the misconduct, is usually deemed appropriate only where punitive measures aimed at correction have been tried and failed.

One of the leading reasons for discipline being overturned is the failure of employers to follow standards of progressive discipline. Some employers forget that the primary purpose of discipline should be corrective, not punitive.

On the other hand, for unusually severe rule violations — sometimes known as "capital offenses" — arbitrators will excuse the requirement of progressive discipline or corrective discipline. If

---

81 *Lockheed Martin Missiles & Space*, 108 LA 482 (Gentile, 1997).

82 *See Cavalier Corp.*, 75 LA 258 (Haemmel, 1980) (different penalties for aggressor and victim involved in a fight); *Hooker Chem. Corp.*, 36 LA 857 (Kates, 1961).

83 *United States Steel Corp.*, 51 LA 464, 548 (Garrett, 1968).

84 *Capital Airlines*, 25 LA 13 (Stowe, 1955).

the arbitrator is persuaded that the misconduct is serious enough to rupture irreparably the employer-employee relationship, he or she will not be much impeded by a lack of documented previous discipline.

l. (12) Employer Interest in the Rule

The nature of the employer's interest in the enforcement of the rule has a strong bearing on the reasonableness of the discipline imposed. Violations of less significant rules may warrant less significant punishment, and violation of more significant rules may warrant more significant punishment. And "significant" has to be seen in the context of the industry and the workplace.

Put simply, if the misconduct causes a high level of liability for the employer, then a harsh penalty will be supported.[85] In a very illustrative case, an employer rightfully terminated an employee for a single negligent act, but one that may have had serious, potentially deadly consequences.[86] Here, the employee negligently failed to perform a crucial test on a gas line which resulted in a dangerous leak. Although the misconduct was simple negligence, the termination was upheld because of the severity of the risk of that misconduct. It is clear that in situations such as this, the employer has a very important interest in deterring even minor negligence.

m. (13) Reasonableness of the Penalty

Arbitrators recognize an employee's good and lengthy service record as an important mitigating factor.

This test requires a *balancing* of competing interests. Where the violation is of a more severe nature ("capital offenses"), immediate termination may be warranted despite lengthy service and a clean disciplinary record. On the other hand, an employee with a brief period of service marked by disciplinary infractions might be terminated for a less significant rule violation.
Generally, for employees with satisfactory work records, summary termination is considered justified only in the category of rule violations known as "capital offenses." Capital offenses are

[85] *See generally, Deluxe Saw and Tool*, supra.
[86] *BHP Petroleum/Gasco*, 102 LA 321 (Najita, 1994).

considered those rule violations so severe that the employer and employee relationship is considered irreparably destroyed. Even then, arbitrators have been known to reinstate employees for fairly serious violations where the employee has a lengthy service record without a significant record of disciplinary infractions.The general rule is that, absent a more serious offense, just cause requires that employers invoke the steps of progressive discipline prior to imposing the ultimate penalty of termination.

Arbitrators recognize an employee's good and lengthy service record as an important mitigating factor.[87] One arbitration treatise noted:

> Some consideration generally is given to the past record of any disciplined or discharged employee. An offense may be mitigated by a good past record and it may be aggravated by a poor one. Indeed, the employee's past record often is a major factor in the determination of the proper penalty for the offense.[88]

n. (14) Mitigating Factors

Often there are unusual circumstances that may explain the conduct at issue. An employer is obligated to hear from the employee and thoughtfully consider all these potential mitigating circumstances. Where personal or family circumstances exist that may partially explain the employer's conduct, this will be weighed. The primary notion of mitigation is that it may not necessary cause the arbitrator to entirely "excuse" the conduct but might persuade them to adopt a more lenient penalty.

The primary notion of mitigation is that it may not necessary cause the arbitrator to entirely "excuse" the conduct but might persuade them to adopt a more lenient penalty.

Arbitrators have generally recognized that employer or co-

---

[87] Elkouri & Elkouri, *supra*, at 918, 925-29. *See also, Franklin Cnty. Sherriff's Office*, 127 LA 283 (Felice, 2003); *Meijer*, 120 LA 700 (Obee, 2004) (15 years of service with no misconduct warranted reduction in discipline for dishonesty); *Bootz Mfg. Co.*, 119 LA 1803 (Lalka, 2004) (27 years of service without infraction required reinstatement after employee refused to work overtime).

[88] *Id.* at 925.

worker provocation is a mitigating factor warranting reducing the penalty.[89] This recognition is especially likely where the provocation presents itself in a racial context. One leading arbitration treatise notes:

> Arbitrators use the term racial slur to describe racial epithets and insulting reference to an employee's race, religion, or ethnic origin. Racial slurs are inherently provocative. Employees who react to racial slurs with violence are frequently reinstated. An unpaid suspension is often imposed as a deterrent to further violence. A racial slur may goad an employer into impulsive violence.

o. (15) Jeopardy

Once a penalty is imposed, it may not be increased.

The "double jeopardy" concept is generally applied by arbitrators to prohibit double punishment. Once a penalty is imposed, it may not be increased.[90] The concept is one of fairness borrowed from the constitutional prohibition on double criminal punishments, yet it lacks the compelling strength of a criminal right. Still, arbitrators can and often do set aside a second imposition of discipline.

However, simply because two different forms of discipline are present does not mean that double jeopardy has taken place, even when the discipline occur at different times. For example, an employee may be suspended with pay pending an investigation, and may be terminated when that investigation yields enough facts to justify a termination.[91]

Simply because an employee has been disciplined for misconduct in the past does not mean it is "double jeopardy" if that conduct leads to a harsher discipline for similar misconduct in the future. If an employee is frequently tardy, each subsequent punishment should increase in severity as the employee is not changing their behavior.[92] That employer response is "progressive

---

[89] *See* Bornstein & Goslin, *supra*, at § 1903; *Olin Corporation*, 103 LA 981 (Fowler, 1981).

[90] Elkouri & Elkouri, *supra*, at 923-35.

[91] *City of Coweta*, 119 LA 42 (Moore, 2003).

[92] *See Summit Cnty.*, 121 LA 1681, 1683-84 (Skulina, 2005) (noting CBA explicitly allowed progressive discipline that is based in part on previous

discipline," not "double jeopardy."

In cases where the delay in disciplining the employee is caused management, the delayed discipline may potentially be a form of double jeopardy applying a very expansive view of the term.[93] Delay in imposition of discipline will only be deemed "double jeopardy" in very unusual cases, and with an arbitrator who takes a very broad view of the concept. Likewise, in unusual cases where a prolonged delay in discipline is cause by *union* requests to delay determination and imposition of discipline, double jeopardy is not present.[94]

In most discipline cases involving double jeopardy, the unreasonableness of the discipline imposed will fairly be obvious. In one case, a whistle-blowing employee was suspended for insubordination, and then later transferred to a less significant position for the same incident.[95] In this case, double jeopardy is clearly present, as two distinct penalties have been imposed for one offense. The imposition of a later transfer is a common form of double jeopardy. But in such cases, the union, as will be discussed later, needs to demonstrate the transfer was a form of discipline.

As noted above, however, double jeopardy occur in other less obvious situations. Whenever two or more actions are taken against an employee in the aftermath of a misconduct investigation, the possibility of "double jeopardy" should be assessed.

p. (16) Fault of the Employer

It is appropriate to set aside discipline where management is also at fault in some respect in connection with an employee's conduct.[96] Arbitrators have sometimes identified inappropriate employee conduct as having been provoked by the actions of the employer or the employer's supervisors. In such instances, discipline has been overturned.

In other situations, it is the lack of resources, for example, training or equipment, that has led to the employee conduct at

---

misconduct).

93 *Titanium Metals Corp.*, 121 LA 1441 (Franckieiwicz, 2005) (holding discipline for tardiness 113 days after it occurred and 71 days after it was recorded is double jeopardy).

94 See *Bethlehem Steel Corp.*, 83 LA 833 (Sharnoff, 1984).

95 *City of Miami*, 122 LA 237 (Sergent, 2006).

96 Elkouri & Elkouri, *supra,* at 688; *Washington Hospital Center*, 73 LA 535, 538 (Seidenberg, 1979) (holding management failure to carry out appropriate supervisory responsibility constituted far greater breach of duty than grievant's alleged carelessness; discipline vacated).

issue. Arbitrators have set aside discipline when the cause was the employer's failure to adequately train or equip the employees. Arbitrators have also set aside discipline when the employer failed to identify and address employee problems stemming from personal or family situations.

q. (17) Employer's Motivation and Reasoning Process

Where an employer is unable to explain clearly what legitimate interests required it to discipline an employee, the arbitrator may well overturn the discipline. Also, when an employer relies upon inadmissible or unsubstantiated evidence, the arbitrator may overturn the discipline.

In a leading arbitration treatise, the authors cite a study of arbitration awards which reveals that the most common reasons arbitrators modify a termination penalty are the prior work record of the grievant and the motivation and reasoning of management.[97] Just cause, among other things, means to impose discipline in good faith and in a sensible, reasonable manner.

the most common reasons arbitrators modify a termination penalty are the prior work record of the grievant and the motivation and reasoning of management

r. (18) Obligation of Accommodation

Arbitrators generally recognize that principles of just cause incorporate statutes prohibiting discrimination,[98] especially when the collective bargaining agreement contains a non-discrimination clause.[99] This approach extends as well to the law regarding disabilities.[100]

Issues of gender and race may arise in discipline grievances. Separate and apart from the question of whether discrimination occurred, there may be some obligation to accommodate attributes inherently associated with a particular gender or race.

---

[97] Elkouri & Elkouri, *supra*, at 135.

[98] Elkouri & Elkouri, *supra*, at 85 (4th Ed. 1985-87 Supplement).

[99] *Id.*

[100] Bornstein & Gosline, *supra*, at § 21.11; *see also, Goodman v. Employment Security Dept.*, 69 Wn. App. 98 (1993) (Personnel Appeals Board should consider alleged breaches of collective bargaining agreements).

Addiction-related behaviors, even where arbitrators did not apply the standard under disability discrimination statutes, have been recognized to be mitigating factors justifying reinstatement.

In one case, the employer required that all male employees who were required to wear respirators be clean shaven to ensure a sufficient seal. One black employee had a skin condition prevalent in black males that caused severe irritation when shaving with a blade razor. The employee shaved with an electric razor, but management declared this was not adequate to ensure a proper respirator seal, and suspended the employee when he protested.[101] The arbitrator found that although there was a business necessity for ensuring adequate safety, the employer erred by not attempting to find out if the electric razor caused an inadequate seal.

Various discrimination laws may require some degree of "reasonable accommodation" for disabilities, religious practices and conditions directly linked to gender or race. Discipline entered without undertaking reasonable accommodations may be set aside.

Addiction-related behaviors, even where arbitrators did not apply the standard under disability discrimination statutes, have been recognized to be mitigating factors justifying reinstatement. In *Ohio State Highway Patrol*,[102] the arbitrator reinstated a state trooper who was convicted of a drunk driving charge where the trooper was making successful progress in an alcohol treatment program. While the arbitrator acknowledged that law enforcement personnel are held to a higher standard, she concluded that the employer had failed to give the employee's effort at rehabilitation the weight it deserved as "distinctive and crucial mitigating factors."[103] In *Phillips 66 Company*,[104] the arbitrator held that the grievant's gambling addicting which resulted in excessive absenteeism constituted a mitigating factor warranting reinstatement.

The question of how far employers must go to accommodate

---

[101] *Niagara Mohawk Power Corp.*, 74 LA 58 (Markowitz, 1980).

[102] 96 L.A. 613 (Bittel, 1991).

[103] 96 L.A. at 619; *see also, Ashland Petroleum Co.*, 90 L.A. 681 (Volz, 1988) (reinstating employee who participated in rehabilitation program for drug use after the discharge; arbitrator noting that addictive behaviors involve denials which are often only overcome in "crisis situation").

[104] 88 L.A. 617 (Weisbrod, 1987).

disabilities, including addictions such as alcoholism, will be covered in Chapter 11.

s. (19) Violation of Employee Civil Rights

Closely associated with the duty to accommodate discussed above, employees have a right to be free of discrimination. Furthermore employees, especially public employees, have numerable statutory and constitutional rights that cannot be violated —such as the right to free speech or the right to privacy. These rights are thoroughly discussed in other Chapters of this book. Disciplinary actions that violate these rights can be expected to be overturned by an arbitrator.

C. Common Discipline Issues

In this section we discuss the application of the 19 just cause factors to specific discipline situations. We emphasize the most common discipline situations facing public safety employees and discuss how arbitrators typically respond to those discipline grievances.[105]

1. Job Performance Problems

Is this discipline? Ironically, the first common discipline problem we discuss is the one for which the "19 factors" analysis is probably least useful. Arbitration of job performance grievances — issues regarding "unsatisfactory performance," "incompetency" and "neglect of duty" — often involves tremendous confusion.

The source of confusion is the threshold question of whether employer actions address incompetence *are even to be considered "discipline"* (at least as that term is generally understood). That important threshold question is frequently overlooked, generating quite a bit of confusion, not only among employers and unions, but also for labor lawyers and arbitrators. So we need to step back and understand how arbitrators view employer charges for unsatisfactory performance and incompetence in the context of the "just cause" requirement.

Arbitrators have differing views as to how to approach unsatisfactory performance or incompetency grievances, but the mainstream approach is *not* to treat these as misconduct cases involving fault. Instead, arbitrators usually proceed on the

---

[105] The table in the appendix to this chapter, which details how discipline has been treated in arbitration, is divided by the action for which the employee was disciplined, so it may be helpful to refer to it as you read this section.

common sense notion that management has the right to discharge an employee that is unable to perform the job *regardless of any employee fault or intention.*

In fact, *most arbitrators do not consider employer actions in response to an alleged incompetence to even be "discipline."* Consequently, they do not require the employer to meet all the "tests" of just cause. Instead, arbitrators require employers to prove that the employee is, in fact, incompetent. As a practical matter, though, establishing employee incompetence may, in many ways, be *more difficult* than establishing just cause for disciplinary action based on misconduct or rule violation.

Nature of Incompetence. An incompetent employee is one who *lacks the necessary skills to perform the essential job functions.* When an underperforming employee is removed, it is often difficult to determine whether the employer action constitutes "discharge" of an incompetent employee or "discipline." In fact, *employers are often themselves unaware of this distinction.*

Typically, in cases of alleged employee incompetence, there has been some rule violation, normally in a series, leading the employer to the ultimate conclusion that the employee cannot do the job and must go. Usually it is a particular incident that triggers the decision to demote or discharge, making the issue even more confusing.

Incompetence v. Negligence. Arbitrators tend to cut through the employer statements of what they believe did and assess what they are, in fact, did. When the action is essentially "incompetence," the employer must prove the employee lacks the required skills for the job *and* is unable to acquire them. And when the "triggering event" for an incompetence charge is a *specific mistake,* the just cause requirement that the employer prove the alleged act still exists.[106] On the other hand, when the discipline is essentially for "negligence," these charges are still subject to the progressive discipline requirement, as well as all the other just cause factors.[107]

Arbitrators have consistently acknowledged a distinction between "negligence" and "incompetence."[108] In *Copperweld Bimetallics Group v. Int'l Ass'n of Machinists & Aerospace Workers,* the arbitrator explained the distinction:

> A careless employee has the ability to efficiently

[106] Brand, *supra,* at 137.
[107] Brand, *supra,* at 143.
[108] *See* Bornstein & Gosline, *supra,* § 20.03.

> perform, but fails to do so because of inattentiveness to duty, or for some other reason. Because such behavior is willful, it is correctable through the application of progressive discipline. In contrast, an incompetent employee lacks the ability to do the assigned work usually because of some mental or physical limitations. Even if the incompetent employee approaches the task with the utmost care, the employee's innate inadequacies render the employee incapable of doing the work. *Incompetency is not correctable by disciplinary action because it is not willful in nature.*[109]

Proving Negligence. Proof of negligence typically involves some combination of the following:

- That the employee was under a clear obligation to carry out the omitted task or to refrain from committing the act charged as negligence;
- That the act or omission was unreasonable;
- That the damage or adverse consequences was reasonably foreseeable by the offending party;
- That the alleged negligence was the proximate cause of damage;
- That the company was substantially damaged or otherwise adversely affected in a significant way by the alleged negligence;
- That the employer received adequate training or instruction in the performance of tasks in question; and
- That the employee was on notice that the action or omission could lead to discipline.[110]

Proving Incompetence. Incumbency in a position creates a presumption of competence that the employer has the burden to overcome.[111] In other words, an employee has tenure rights under

---

[109] 83 LA 1025, 1028 (Denson, 1984).
[110] Bornstein & Gosline, *supra*, § 20.02[1][c] (1991).

the CBA and the employer must prove that tenure should be revoked because the employee cannot meet the minimal job requirements.

Employer evidence that the employee is *somewhat* unsatisfactory or deficient in productivity is usually insufficient to sustain a competency discharge. For example, in *American Fuel Cell & Coated Fabrics Co.*,[112] the arbitrator overturned the discharge of an employee when he concluded that the grievant "was not wholly unsatisfactory." He explained that while she was performing at a lower level of efficiency, she was not *so far* outside the bounds of what other employees were producing to conclude that she was truly "incompetent."

Because the principles of "just cause" do not apply to the discharge of an incompetent employee the principles of "progressive discipline," strictly speaking, also do not apply. But as a practical matter, *an employer who cannot offer extensive progressive discipline documentation, beginning with repeated correction and training will be unlikely not to prevail in an incompetency discharge grievance.*

Employers often find this surprising: In an incompetence grievance arbitration, it is generally insufficient for the employer to prove that the employee has been unable to fulfill the essential functions of the job. Instead, the employer is obligated to show that it has tried and failed through training and correction to make the employee competent *and conclusively has been unable to do so.*

---

an employer who cannot offer extensive progressive discipline documentation, beginning with repeated correction and training will be unlikely not to prevail in an incompetency discharge grievance

---

In short, employers who fail to train and provide corrective guidance to employees will be unlikely to prevail in a grievance on an incompetence discharge (or demotion). These critical proof elements normally must be met:

- Warnings of alleged incompetence
- Attempts at training

---

[111] *Marathon Oil Co.*, 97 LA 1145 (Massey, 1991).

[112] 97 LA 1045 (Nicholas, 1991).

- Communication of well-defined and consistent job standards

These standards make sense once you recognize that what is to be proven is not merely that the employee *has been incompetent* but rather that have *little reasonable likelihood of ever becoming competent.* For these reasons, while strictly speaking "just cause" is not the standard, wise employers approach incompetency as if it required, especially as to issuing and documenting progressive discipline.

Providing repeated warnings is essential. Employers are held to provide *specific forewarning* as to the *specific shortcomings* so that the employee has ample opportunity to correct the deficiencies.[113]

It is also an essential that the employer establish clear and repeated attempts at training the employee.[114] If an employer cannot demonstrate that it has attempted to train an employee to perform work in an improved manner, that employer cannot demonstrate that the employee is incapable of working in an improved manner.

The obligation to provide training also includes the obligation to maintain *firm and consistent* standards *and* to communicate clearly those standards to the employee. For example, in *Mead Co.,*[115] the arbitrator overturned the discipline of an employee who had been quite unsatisfactory and had even been insubordinate. But in sustained the grievance the arbitrator explained:

> If the company is to be faulted for any reason, this fault must lie in the fact that *they were far too lenient* and did not take a firm disciplinary approach to the problems much sooner and sometime within the troublesome four-month period.... The discharge of an individual is considered to be the capital punishment of the industrial society and Arbitrators are more inclined to sustain a discharge penalty in a 'last straw' situation if it is preceded by a positive form of progressive discipline, i.e., written warning and/or disciplinary suspension for offenses not serious enough to warrant discharge for a first occurrence.[116]

---

[113] *See, e.g., Papercraft Inc.*, 80 LA 13, 15 (Anderson, 1982) and *Mead Co.*, 80 LA 713, 716 (Milentz, 1983).

[114] *See, e.g., Leavenworth Times*, 71 LA 397, 402 (Bothwell, 1978).

[115] 80 LA 713 (Milentz, 1983).

[116] *Id.* (emphasis added.) *See also, Papercraft Inc.*, 80 LA 13, 15 (Anderson, 1982)

The employer's failure to properly train and supervise an employee is subject to special scrutiny whenever an employee qualifies for "protected class" status under employment discrimination laws. Discrimination claims are not limited to those where the employer or employer's agent act with discriminatory animus, but also extend to situations where those employer practices have a disparate impact. A discrimination plaintiff certainly need not show that the employer is an open racist in order to prove discrimination occurred. Instead, ironically, *acts of leniency — when motivated in any way by racial considerations — can themselves be discriminatory actions.*

This leniency problem was addressed in *Vaughn v. Edel*,[117] where the court reinstated an employee and stated:

> In neither criticizing Vaughn when her work was unsatisfactory, nor counseling her how to improve, Texaco treated Vaughn different than it did its other employees because she was black. As a result, Texaco did not afford Vaughn the same opportunity to improve her performance...as it did its white employees.

The law requires consistent treatment in all regards to all employees and *the failure to discipline may constitute discrimination.*

Incompetency grievances are often successful. Employees are frequently unable to show that a series of acts of simple negligence add up to an employee who is simply incapable of doing the job. Furthermore, employers often make the mistake of tolerating a substandard employee for a long period, waiting until their frustration grows to a high level, at which point they search for justification to take severe action. Those late efforts to acquire "evidence" may or may not be sufficient to support a charge of incompetence.

(overturning discipline where supervisor's unfamiliarity with discipline responsibilities resulted in grievant not having sufficient forewarning or being "officially notified of such performance shortcomings" and rejecting employer's reliance on supervisor's counseling in a "friend-to-friend basis" because it failed to provide grievant sufficient understanding his situation).

117 54 FEP 870, (5th Cir. 1990).

Incompetency grievances are often successful. Employees are frequently unable to show that a series of acts of simple negligence add up to an employee who is simply incapable of doing the job.

Types of Negligence: Gross versus Ordinary. When the employer fails to establish that the employee is truly incompetent, what remains is a sustained charge of negligence on particular acts. But arbitrators will rarely, if ever, sustain a termination based on ordinary negligence.

"Gross negligence," though, is a different matter. Gross and ordinary negligence are distinguishable with the former deemed "misconduct." When the employee's actions indicate a degree of *willfulness* and extraordinary disregard for the property or rights of others, arbitrators label the negligence as "gross" and have held that more serious discipline is warranted than would be the case with ordinary negligence. In such gross negligence situations, though, the employer is back to having to satisfy the rigorous just cause factors discussed earlier in this Chapter.

2. Off-Duty Conduct

Employers are allowed to discipline employees for off-duty conduct *but only if there exists a nexus between the off-duty misconduct and the workplace.*

There are two beliefs often expressed regarding off-duty conduct discipline. The first belief (usually expressed by employees) is that the employers may not regulate off-duty conduct whatsoever. The second belief (usually expressed by employers) is that employers may discipline for off-duty misconduct to the same extent as if the misconduct occurred on duty. Neither is true.

Instead, the truth lies in between these two myths. Employers are allowed to discipline employees for off-duty conduct *but only if there exists a nexus between the off-duty misconduct and the workplace.* To determine whether the "workplace nexus" exists, arbitrators have adopted a three-part test:

1. Did the employee's behavior harm the

employer's reputation or product;

2. Did the employee's behavior render the employee unable to perform job duties; or

3. Did the employee's behavior lead to a refusal, reluctance or inability of other employees to work with the employee.[118]

Generally, *satisfying any one of these three tests is sufficient* to allow the employer to exercise their management discipline rights (assuming all the other just cause requirements are met).

Employer efforts to regulate off-duty conduct, though, sometimes impermissibly violate the *constitutional rights* of public-sector employees, an issue we will discuss in a later Chapter. Work rules that prohibit certain off-duty conduct must be narrowly and rationally tailored to regulate only that conduct *that directly affects the employee's ability to effectively perform the job.*[119]

Two particular types of off-duty conduct have special rules that apply to them and warrant further discussion: "conduct unbecoming" and criminal conduct. Especially since these are recurrent issues in public safety employment, we will provide these discipline issues their own discussion immediately below.

3. Conduct Unbecoming an Officer

The charge of "conduct unbecoming an officer" traces its historic origins in the military service code of conduct. Public safety employers often use a conduct unbecoming charge as a "catch-all" category. They invoke it when an employer asserts that the employee has engaged in misconduct, but lack a *specific published rule* prohibiting the conduct asserted to be improper.

Most law enforcement agencies have a rule specifically called "conduct unbecoming an officer." But sometimes law enforcement agencies (or other paramilitary public safety departments) may also denominate their general discipline "catch-all" rule under a different name. Regardless of how an agency label its policy, this section addresses the wide variety of "catch all" rules — those rules that express a generalized (and often vague) standard that employees avoid stupid actions that embarrass the agency.

---

118 *State of Ohio*, 94 LA 533 (Sharpe, 1990).

119 *See Thorne v. City of El Segundo*, 726 F.2d 459 (9th Cir. 1983); *See also*, *Waters v. Chaffin*, 684 F.2d 833 (11th Cir. 1982); *Flanagan v. Munger*, 890 F.2d 1557 (10th Cir. 1989).

Constitutionality. Because the "conduct unbecoming" charge is inherently ambiguous, it has been subject to legal attack as being unconstitutionally vague. Yet these rules have usually sustained these attacks. Most courts have ultimately adopted the following approach to "conduct unbecoming an officer" rules: The rules themselves are not deemed to be *per se* unconstitutional, *but they will closely scrutinize how the rules are applied in specific situations to determine whether the conduct involved is conduct that the officer knew, or should have known, was improper.*

The court challenges to conduct unbecoming type rules were based on constitutional law. The chief principle used in these challenges is the generally recognized principle of constitutional law that "a statute which either forbids or requires the doing of an act in terms so vague that men of common intelligence must necessarily guess at its meaning and differ as to its application violates the first essential of due process of law."[120] Accordingly, some courts have found a conduct unbecoming rule to be void for vagueness for these reasons.[121] Most courts, however, uphold the constitutionality of the rule *if it is given a narrow interpretation.* Instead, under the doctrine established by these courts, a challenge to the rule's constitutionality can still be made *as applied to a particular case.*

To escape the "void for vagueness" objections, courts adopted a standard asking whether the alleged employee misconduct at issue could was "hard-core conduct." The purpose of this is to determine if the employee must have known that his or her conduct was subject to regulation. As one court explained:

> When a type of conduct has not been expressly said to fall within the conduct unbecoming rule, the officer will only be considered to have knowledge that his conduct is subject to discipline if it is "hard-core conduct."[122]

The court added further explained that hard-core conduct is conduct that "any reasonable person must know would be cause for discipline or dismissal."[123]

---

[120] *Connally v. General Construction Co.*, 269 U.S. 385, 391 (1926).
[121] *Bence v. Breier*, 501 F.2d 1185 (7th Cir. 1974); *Sponick v. City of Detroit Police Department*, 211 N.W.2d 674 (Mich. Ct. App. 1973).
[122] *Fabio v. Civil Service Commission*, 414 A.2d 82, 88 (Pa. 1980).
[123] *Id.*

The majority of courts have found conduct unbecoming rules constitutional, but narrowly restrict them in order as to address the constitutional vagueness problem.

Therefore, it is constitutional for a public safety employer to have a policy prohibiting "conduct unbecoming an officer." *The real issue is whether the rules may be applied as to particular types of conduct.*

The majority of courts have found conduct unbecoming rules constitutional, but narrowly restrict them in order as to address the constitutional vagueness problem. In assessing the constitutionality of such rules, courts generally ask three questions:

(1) How the conduct reflects on the officer's fitness to perform job functions;

(2) Whether the conduct is likely to destroy public respect and disrupt department operations; or

(3) Whether the officer has fair warning that their conduct will be subject to discipline, i.e. whether or not it is "hard-core conduct."

Application of the Constitutional Standard. Some courts restrict the reach of conduct unbecoming rules by only applying them when the officer's actions *reflect on their fitness to perform his or her duties*. California state courts, for example, extend the rule "to refer only to conduct which indicates a *lack of fitness* to perform the functions of a police officer."[124] These courts' rationale is that a police officer should be able to know whether his conduct compromises his fitness to perform.[125]

A *nexus* between the conduct and the officer's fitness to perform his duties is required under this standard. For example, in In *Cranston v. City of Richmond*, the court held that the police officer's reckless driving fulfilled this "nexus" requirement, finding that it exemplified carelessness, poor judgment, disregard for the safety of others and disregard for the laws the officer was supposed to enforce.[126]

---

124 *Cranston v. City of Richmond*, 710 P.2d 845, 854 (Cal. 1985).
125 *Id.*

Courts also evaluate the *impact of the officer's conduct on the public and fellow officers. Fabio v. Civil Service Commission,* exemplifies this approach.[127] *Fabio* involved adulterous activity in which Officer Fabio convinced his wife to sleep with another police officer. The court found this conduct to be "potentially disruptive and explosive" to the department and allowed the application of the conduct unbecoming rule.[128] The court explained:

> Unbecoming conduct...is any conduct which adversely affects the morale or efficiency of the bureau to which he is assigned....[It] is also any conduct which has a tendency to destroy public respect for municipal employees and confidence in the operation of municipal services."[129]

Arbitrators are divided as to whether public knowledge of misconduct justifies applying conduct unbecoming rules. Several arbitration cases have found the publicity of an officer's conduct to be an *insufficient* basis for severe punishment.

For example, in *City of New Britain* a police officer made remarks that patrons of a certain restaurant were "scum of the earth." The statement was reproduced in the media. The department imposed a one-day suspension, claiming that the "statement brought discredit and embarrassment to the entire police department...."[130] Despite the indisputable embarrassment, the arbitrator overturned the suspension. It reasoned the officer had not intended his comments to be quoted.[131]

City of Shawnee involved a firefighter arraigned for manslaughter following a boating accident.[132] He appeared in court in his uniform and pled "no contest" to the criminal charge. Later he was fired and appealed his discharge. The contested manslaughter provided grounds for discipline, but the city also relied on his published uniform depiction, which it argued embarrassed the city. The arbitrator extended limited weight to the city's embarrassment, found the suspension to be overly severe and imposed a 90-day suspension.[133]

---

[126] *Id.* at 856, n. 15.
[127] 414 A.2d 82, 86 (Pa. 1980).
[128] 414 A.2d at 88.
[129] *Id.*
[130] 82 LA 1196, 1197 (Blenner, 1984).
[131] *Id.*
[132] 91 LA 93 (Allen, 1988).
[133] *Id.* at 100.

Importance of Notice. In determining the constitutionality of the unbecoming conduct rule as applied to a particular set of facts, courts also focus on whether the officer has notice that his conduct is subject to discipline. If the officer has engaged in "hard-core" conduct that clearly is prohibited by the rule, then he has no ability to challenge its constitutionality.[134]

Hard-core conduct is conduct that "any reasonable person must know would be cause for discipline or dismissal."[135] Whether conduct is hard-core must be evaluated on the specific facts of the alleged misconduct.[136] An employer's assertions that conduct qualifies as "hard-core" may be rebutted with the testimony of other employees who testify they might have done the same thing.[137]

---

arbitrators will recognize conduct unbecoming an officer rules as valid, but will very closely scrutinize how those rules are applied to assess whether the application is fair in those circumstances

---

In finding that officers have had fair warning, courts have also considered the fact that other agency like rules or laws existed. For instance, in *Fabio*, the police department had a police code of ethics which included a provision addressing the private life of officers.[138] (Despite this holding citing to a code of ethics, the enforceability of the Law Enforcement Officers Canon of Ethics as a "rule" is unlikely and nor usually intended by the parties.) In other cases, officers engaged in unlawful or criminal conduct, and notice was a given.

Obviously, there is a balancing of interests whenever a conduct unbecoming an officer charge is applied. Realistically, an employer needs a "catch-all" category. Experience teaches that a public

---

[134] *Aiello v. City of Wilmington*, 623 F.2d 845, 849 (3d Cir. 1980).

[135] *Fabio*, 414 A.2d at 86.

[136] *See Parker v. Levy*, 417 U.S. 733 (1973) (finding similar military rule not void for vagueness. Where military physician attempted to persuade officers not to go to Vietnam, court found there was fair notice that the particular conduct was punishable); *Herbebrun v. Milwaukee County*, 504 F.2d 1189 (7th Cir. 1974) (sabotaging phone system was hard core conduct); *Aiudi v. Baillargeon*, 399 A.2d 1240 (R.I. 1979) (larceny and theft); *Aiello*, 623 F.2d (getting drunk and breaking into a store).

[137] *See City of Shawnee*, 91 LA 93 (Allen, 1988) (arbitrator holding that boating accident resulting in second degree manslaughter, where evidence of alcohol was involved, did not reflect on ability to perform firefighter duties).

[138] 414 A.2d at 88.

safety agency cannot reasonably contemplate in advance all forms of mischief that a public safety employee might engage in, including mischief of the sort that any reasonable person would recognize as warranting discipline. On the other hand, fundamental fairness requires that employees have *some* notice of what type of conduct might subject them to discipline.

In summary, arbitrators will recognize conduct unbecoming an officer rules as valid, but will very closely scrutinize how those rules are applied to assess whether the application is fair in those circumstances.

4. Criminal Conduct

Under the "just cause" standard public safety employers have broader authority to discipline employees for criminal conduct than would, for example, a construction company. Rules governing criminal misconduct involve a more specific application of the general right of employers to discipline for off-duty conduct. But it is subject to the same "nexus" tests.

This Chapter addresses the just cause standard across the broad swath of public safety employees. But certainly not all public safety employees are similarly situated when it comes to the just cause standards as to criminal misconduct. It is best to comprehend the standard on a continuum in this general descending order:

- Commissioned law enforcement officers
- Corrections officers and limited commission officers
- Noncommissioned law enforcement employees
- Firefighters and other emergency responders

This continuum provides you a framework to understand how arbitrators will most likely respond to criminal misconduct charges. It is clear that commissioned personnel are subject to the highest level of scrutiny in the context of criminal conduct. The further an employee's duties are removed from the enforcement of the law, the likelihood that arbitrators will uphold the most severe discipline is reduced.

> not all public safety employees are similarly situated when it comes to the just cause standards as to criminal misconduct

It is the "nexus" with law enforcement that matters. Under this continuum, for example, emergency dispatchers that work within a law enforcement would be predicted to be slightly less likely to successfully attack severe penalties for criminal misconduct than dispatchers working inside civilian 911 centers. That distinction might seem unfair, but it reflects arbitral thinking as to the relationship between the employer's business interests and the quantum of reasonable discipline. When you accept employment, you are expected not to damage your employer's interests.

Proof of Charges. The employer *need not wait for the completion of the criminal process to take employment action.* The employer need only prove that the employee *committed* misconduct, *not* that a court or jury actually convicted the employee of the crime. In fact, the burden of proof for the employer in an arbitration involving criminal conduct *might* be lower than a criminal case — that of the traditional clear and convincing standard. (Although, as discussed above, a minority of arbitrators hold that where the termination was for criminal conduct, the "beyond a reasonable doubt" standard should apply.)

> The employer *need not wait for the completion of the criminal process to take employment action.*

Discipline for just cause is based upon a violation of work rules. A rule that an employee not commit a crime can be demonstrably violated even if no conviction, or even criminal charge exists. Furthermore, in almost all cases where criminal misconduct is at issue, other potential work rule violations exist.

Therefore, prudent employers will usually proceed immediately to make an employment decision when criminal conduct is at issue without regard to the status of any criminal proceeding. Sometimes employers have hesitated to make a decision until after the trial, and the trial results in an acquittal. Then they are often hard-pressed to explain to the arbitrator why termination is now necessary after an acquittal when it was unnecessary before the acquittal.

On the other hand, there are instances when the criminal allegations are so perplexing and the accuser credibility so uncertain that it may be prudent to allow the criminal process to run its course. This interval may provide the employer "discovery" more powerful than it might be able to acquire through its own internal investigation.

Of course, either the express or implied terms of the CBA will likely require a prompt investigation. The employer cannot properly assert a unilateral ability to indefinitely place the investigation on hold. The employer must acquire the consent for such a delay from the union (which should confer with the affected employee) or risk a later claim that the charges are "stale" and now unenforceable. An employer that does otherwise, does so at its peril.

Law Enforcement Officers. Obviously, when law enforcement personnel commit crimes, this misconduct is much more likely to have a detrimental effect on the employer's operations. Law enforcement agencies are in the business of enforcing laws, so when the employees they have commissioned to enforce those laws violate them, the employer's credibility can be damaged. And even more damaging can be the credibility of the offending officer is damaged.

In the case of law enforcement personnel, especially commissioned officers, arbitrators will usually recognize serious criminal conduct as a basis for summary discharge, with or without progressive discipline. Clearly, conduct that is felonious is almost always going to be grounds for discharge, and if a long jail sentence is imposed, that creates an unavailability that renders the discipline question moot. As to less serious criminal conduct, the standards become murkier and depends entirely on context and the nature of the offense. We next turn to how arbitrators generally assess misdemeanor conduct.

In the case of law enforcement personnel, especially commissioned officers, arbitrators will usually recognize serious criminal conduct as a basis for summary discharge, with or without progressive discipline.

DUI. Arbitrators are divided over whether a DUI is a valid basis for summary discharge. At least one arbitrator has upheld the discharge of a state trooper for driving under the influence, despite an otherwise good employment record.[139] It is conceivable that some arbitrators might conclude that a DUI violation is a more serious matter for state troopers in light of their significant traffic enforcement responsibilities, than it would be for a deputy sheriff or police officer. Absent aggravating factors such as extreme intoxication or accompanying misconduct, or a poor service record, most employers (and arbitrators) recognize that a first time DUI is not grounds for summary discharge.

Domestic violence. Instances involving domestic violence might form the basis of a justified termination, although generally we would expect that arbitrators would require progressive discipline with this type of offense. The events stemming from a domestic violence charge, though, could lead to a weapons revocation under the *Brady* law, which almost surely would lead to employment disqualification.

Sexual offenses. Arbitrators are divided on whether solicitation of prostitution warrants summary discharge. Criminal sexual conduct of a hands-on nature, if proven, will almost invariably lead to discharge.

Crimes of dishonesty. When the offense is one which goes to the officer's veracity, arbitrators are much more likely to sustain a discharge. By crimes of veracity, we do not narrowly mean perjury or false swearing events, which almost surely will lead to discharge. It could be a type of crime that implies dishonesty. For example, one arbitrator upheld a termination of an officer who filed a fraudulent insurance claim.

Other public safety employees. For public safety employees other than commissioned officers, it is more difficult to predict serious an arbitrator will view a criminal conduct charge. Clearly, the highest standards will be those imposed on commissioned law enforcement personnel, as explained earlier under the "continuum" model.

With firefighters, there is a much weaker nexus between their job duties and the criminal code, and most arbitrators would take a closer look at whether criminal conduct justified termination. But the expectation would be that firefighters, like all public employees, are expected to comply with the law. The issue is not whether a criminal law violation would be grounds for discipline. The question is the magnitude of discipline that would be appropriate.

Other public safety employees, such as dispatchers, corrections officers, and records clerks, can still be subject to

---

[139] *State of Ohio*, 94 LA 533 (Sharpe, 1990).

serious discipline for criminal conduct. Most arbitrators would appreciate law enforcement employer arguments that there is a strong employer interest in penalizing criminal conduct, not just as to police officers, but as to any employee in the department.

In short, one would expect a range in the approaches arbitrators may bring when public safety employees are involved in alleged criminal conduct. Conduct that might not rise to the level of discharge might still warrant a long-term suspension. As with all misconduct, the complete context of the conduct and the employee's service record need to be considered.

Arbitrators recognize that every industry and every workplace has its own set of standards and that the standards of acceptable behavior may vary widely.

5. Offensive Conduct

Offensive conduct — that conduct that is rude, profane or disrespectful — is the type of conduct that arbitrators will especially scrutinize to determine if the employer is consistent in its treatment of employees and is following principles of progressive discipline. Arbitrators recognize that every industry and every workplace has its own set of standards and that the standards of acceptable behavior may vary widely.

As discussed above concerning the just cause factor "proportionality," when the employer has tolerated behavior, it cannot abruptly impose a penalty on one employee significant in excess of previous penalties, simply to make the employee an example. Instead, the employer, if it wishes to heighten the standards of the workplace, must announce to its employees that the standards are changing and new standards will be enforced. (As indicated above, if the enforcement of the rule has lapsed, there may be a duty to collectively bargaining bargain re-imposition of the policy, as it would be considered a "new rule," even if had been "on the books.")

Most arbitrators are wise enough to recognize that cops and firefighters, in particular, have their own sometimes "rough" standards of conduct, especially amongst themselves. In overturning an officer termination based upon profanity, one arbitrator aptly commented: "The prohibition of swearing in a police department strikes me as analogous to the prohibition of temper tantrums in a nursery school."[140]

Consequently, arbitrators will find the matter less serious where profanity used by law enforcement officers and firefighters is in-house and not conveyed to the public.[141] This approach may also apply *even when the comments are "over the top" even for internal consumption.* For example, one arbitrator overturned discipline against an officer who used profanity and ethnic slurs in reference to a fellow officer. Similarly, one officer, who received a one-day suspension for being quoted in a newspaper article as referring to the customers of a particular all-night restaurant as being "scum of the earth," had his suspension overturned where he demonstrated that he never intended his comments to be quoted by the newspaper.[142]

Provocation by others, including supervisors, may be a basis for overturning discipline. One arbitrator overturned the termination of a police sergeant who lost his temper and kicked a chair across the room when he learned that once again he would be shorthanded. The police chief had given employees permission to take the night off without consulting or informing the sergeant. The arbitrator weighed that to some extent the sergeant had a legitimate reason to be angry.[143]

Arbitrators are more likely to sustain the discipline imposed on employees who have been warned and trained regarding the use of certain profanity or other improper conduct. For example, one arbitrator upheld a written reprimand against an officer who referred to a certain neighborhood as the term "jungle" in a context in which the employer and others construed it to be racially derogatory. In sustaining the reprimand, the arbitrator gave great weight to the fact that his sergeant had previously warned the officer regarding this specific term.

In fact, documented progressive discipline is key in offensive conduct grievance arbitrations. Generally, most offensive conduct that that we are contemplating here is unlikely to constitute a "capital offense" justifying summary discharge.

For example, Northwest Arbitrator Gary Axon overturned a discharge of two Portland officers who had left opossum carcasses on the front steps of a restaurant.[144] There was a preceding context

---

140 *City of Balch Springs*, 84 LA 268 (Nelson, 1985).

141 *See City of Tampa*, 92 LA 256 (Rains, 1989) (finding comments "reprehensible" but setting aside the discipline because conduct was not "public" and was less serious than "conduct against citizens in the line of duty").

142 *City of New Britain*, 82 LA 1196, 1197 (Blenner, 1984).

143 *City of Balch Springs*, 84 LA 268 (Nelson, 1985).

to the incident that led the restaurant owner believe the officers' conduct was racially motivated. Extensive local publicity surrounded the incident, and the city terminated the officers. The union argued the termination was politically motivated. In overturning the terminations, the arbitrator rejected the city's argument that because an unhealed "wound" had been created in the community, progressive discipline could be bypassed.

6. Alcohol and Substance Abuse

Arbitrators will generally find these disability laws implied into the just cause standard.

Alcoholic employees have certain protections under various discrimination laws that will be discussed later. These laws, which will be discussed in greater detail in Chapter 11, offer employees extensive protection *if they are diagnosed alcoholics and seeking treatment*. Arbitrators usually find the "just cause" standard incorporates these legal requirements. Employees are who not alcoholics often have less protection for alcohol-related misconduct. And even employees who are alcoholics are not insulated from behavior that violates work rules. Though courts and arbitrators are divided on this point, most have held that disability discrimination laws do not require an accommodation that permits the violation of a reasonable work rule.

Disability discrimination laws offer little or no protection for employees who are current substance abuses of illegal narcotics. Therefore, those employees are not entitled to any accommodation, especially when they work in a law enforcement department.

Arbitrators will generally find these disability laws implied into the just cause standard. Often contracts also explicitly incorporate these provisions through an anti-discrimination clause. Even prior to the enactment of disability discrimination laws, the majority view of arbitrators which had developed is that alcoholics who are in recovery and treatment are entitled to some opportunity to demonstrate rehabilitation.

Where an employee engages in conduct that is alcohol-related, yet is not a diagnosed alcoholic, separate and apart from the "just cause" requirements, *such an employee has no particular protection under disability laws*. Experience indicates that this dichotomy

[144] *City of Portland*, 77 LA 820 (Axon, 1981).

under the law for those who declare their status as alcoholics and those that deny they are alcoholics — once clearly explained to employees caught in the cross-hairs of an alcohol-related misconduct investigation — is the most forceful inducement known to trigger a trip to rehabilitation, often overcoming years of denial.

Some employers have rules prohibiting off-duty public intoxication. It is questionable whether most arbitrators would find such rules to be reasonable or lawful, except to the extent to the extent there is a demonstrable impact on fitness for duty. But employees who engage in criminal conduct or other conduct rising to the level of "conduct unbecoming an officer" while intoxicated, as discussed above, may face serious discipline.

Separate from nondiscrimination statutes, most arbitrators have interpreted the just cause standard as an *independent source* of legal protection for recovering alcoholics. Even before disability discrimination laws were enacted, arbitrators had developed guidelines addressing the extent of accommodation required for the recovering alcoholic employee. There is no single consensus position on this controversial subject. One observer identified three distinct arbitral approaches to alcoholism:

> 1. Hold all employees to the same standards of conduct, without regard to the nature or severity of their substance abuse problems or their efforts to seek assistance.
>
> 2. Give special consideration to employees who have acknowledged to the employer that they have a substance abuse problem, and who actively seek help in resolving the problem before discharge.
>
> 3. Treat substance abuse as a "disease," and accommodate it like other diseases.[145]

The first hard line approach is a distinctly minority view. Most arbitrators approach alcohol problems with some blend of the second and third approaches. And this tendency to give treatment opportunities has accelerated in light of disability laws.

In *Phillip Morris*,[146] Arbitrator Volz set out five common sense principles that should be considered in handling alcoholism in the context of discipline. These provide a good framework for

---

[145] Bornstein & Gosline, *supra*, at § 18.10.

[146] 99 LA 1017 (Volz, 1992).

understanding how most arbitrators will treat this issue:

- First, progressive discipline is ineffective in improving employee reliability until the employee recognizes that he is an alcoholic.
- Second, an alcoholic will usually not recognize the disease until faced with a crisis such as termination.
- Third, post-discharge evidence is relevant and admissible in alcohol-related arbitrations to show the extent of the alcoholic's rehabilitation.
- Fourth, in assessing rehabilitation, the arbitrator should consider more than the alcoholic's word.
- Fifth, a return to employment is often part of the treatment, during which time the employer can determine the employee's progress through monitoring, attitude and adjustment to work.

As indicated, Chapter 11 contains an extensive discussion about how alcoholism is accommodated under disability discrimination laws. Because arbitrators generally find these legal standards implied into CBAs, the principles laid out in that discussion should be understood to integrate with the five principles described above by Arbitrator Volz.

7. Insubordination

Arbitrators generally will not sustain insubordination charges *except when the employee was specifically and clearly advised of the consequences for failing to abide by the order or rule.*

A charge of insubordination is one of the most serious discipline charges an employee in a public safety organization might face. Insubordination is serious in such an organization because it strikes at the core of how that entity functions. Because the consequences of a sustained insubordination charge are normally severe to employees, arbitrators have narrowly and carefully defined the standard for what is, in fact, "insubordination."

Contrary to common belief in some departments, especially about chiefs and other managers, *a mere failure to conform to a stated work standard or rule is not insubordination.* Instead, insubordination is the *deliberate* and *willful refusal* to follow a clear and specific order. Arbitrators generally will not sustain insubordination charges *except when the employee was specifically and clearly advised of the consequences for failing to abide by the order or rule.*

The broadly accepted arbitral meaning of the term "insubordination" is set forth in a leading arbitration treatise:[147]

> Insubordination has been defined as "a willful disregard of express or implied directions of the employer and refusal to obey reasonable orders." A broad meaning, however, derived from a reading of the arbitration decisions, would define insubordination as an improper response by an employee to management's exercise of authority in operating the enterprise.

Moreover, it recognizes that "[c]ommon to all forms of insubordination is a willful deliberate defiance of managerial or supervisory authority."[148]

The following are the normally the necessary elements to establish an insubordination charge:

- The person giving the order had authority to do so;
- The order was work-related;
- The order was clear and understood by the employee;
- The consequences of disobedience where known to the employee; and
- The employee has sufficient time to comply.[149]

The most problematic issues concerning insubordination are those situations relating to safety concerns or unlawful orders. Arbitrators generally will not find insubordination if employees refuse to follow an order that would truly endanger their safety or

---

[147] Bornstein & Gosline, *supra*, at § 20.04[1].
[148] *Id.*
[149] *Id.*

the safety of others. Similarly, refusing to abide by demonstrably unlawful or unconstitutional directive is not insubordination.

It is well established that employees must obey management's orders even if they violate a CBA and the employees, instead, should turn to grievance procedures for relief.[150] But if an unusual or abnormal safety or health hazard exists, an exception to the "obey now and grieve later" doctrine exists.[151]

Of course, an employee will not be allowed to make this claim if the hazard they are asserting exists is inherent to the job itself.[152] The employee must also show that the hazard was not merely a potential hazard, but that the safety risk asserted occurred at the time the refusal took place.[153]

The risk need not be one that impacts the entirely workforce identically. Employees are allowed to refuse an order in the face of an individualized risk, most often a health condition of the employee.[154]

The obvious question arises of whether the risk must have actually been present. Most arbitrators would find that the risk need not have been actually present. Hazards are, by definition, "potential," and the employee is therefore always refusing to complete a task for fear of some injury that *might* take place. Therefore, the ultimate question is *whether the hazard as perceived by the employee justified the employee's refusal to work, regardless of whether such hazard existed.*

Arbitrator decisions on this question have been quite varied.[155] Arbitrators have sometimes employed a purely subjective test of what the particular employee believes, noting that the hazard need not actually exist.[156] On the other hand, some arbitrators have require a factual showing that a real and imminent danger existed.[157]

---

150 Elkouri & Elkouri at 1023 (Reuben ed., 6th ed. 2003).

151 *See, e.g., US Department of the Army,* 125 LA 1287 (Gaba, 2008) (holding refusal to violate CBA by working overtime warranted reprimand because employee did not obey first and grieve later); *Leland Oil Mill,* 91 LA 905 (Nicholas, 1988); *West Penn Power Co.*, 89 LA 1227 (Hogler, 1987).

152 *See, e.g., Alliance Mach. Co.*, 48 LA 457 (Dworkin, 1967).

153 *City of Los Angeles, Cal.*, 111 LA 406 (Daly, 1998).

154 *Minnesota Mining and Mfg.*, 112 LA 1055 (Bankston, 1999); *Health Plus*, 110 LA 618 (Duff, 1998).

155 *See*, Elkouri & Elkouri, *supra*, n. 31 at 1025-26 (providing a large number of arbitration standards to measure the required employee belief).

156 *Leland Oil Mill*, 91 LA 905 (Nicholas, 1988); *A.M. Castle Co.*, 41 LA 666, 671 (Sembower, 1963) (holding employee protected in decision not to act, regardless of whether later on it is established that no hazard existed).

157 *See Consolidated Edison Co.*, 61 LA 607 (Turkus, 1973) (holding unless real danger can be proven at hearing, the employee is not immunized from

Some arbitrators have held that the employee must at some point to explain the reason for refusing an order.[158]

As a general rule, however, the employee's perceived risk must be based on objective evidence, and must, therefore, be *reasonable*.[159] Subjective belief alone is not sufficient to prove that the employee was acting with self-preservation in mind.

union representatives need to take great care when asked by employees whether they are obligated to follow a presumably unsafe or unlawful order

In one illustrative case, a telephone employee refused a request to work in a remote village, fearing that the plane trip to the village would be unsafe, and the inhabitants would harm him.[160] But there was no actual evidence that either of his fears were based on reality, and the termination was upheld. In another case, an employee was terminated when he refused to perform his duties alleging that they were incompatible with his medical condition.[161] Because there was no proof of any hazard to the employee, and his duties had been specifically tailored for his medical condition, the termination was upheld.

The difficulty, though, is that if an employee incorrectly perceives the safety stakes or the legality of an order, termination might be the consequence. The risks of refusing an order may be great. Consequently, union representatives need to take great care when asked by employees whether they are obligated to follow a presumably unsafe or unlawful order. Legal counsel should, whenever possible, be contacted when such a situation arises.

8. Dishonesty

Although matters involving dishonesty will certainly be grounds for discipline for any public safety employees, they are especially serious for commissioned police officers. By nature of their employment, officers are called upon to testify in court and fill out affidavits. Therefore, questions concerning their integrity can undermine their effectiveness and employability. As discussed previously in the context of criminal conduct charges, the

discipline for failure to obey order).

158 *A.M. Castle & Co.*, 41 LA 666 (Sembower, 1963).

159 *Bargar Metal Fabricating Co.*, 110 LA 119 (Oberdank, 1998).

160 *Alaska Communications Sys.*, 118 LA 1583 (Landau, 2003).

161 *United States Steel Corp.* 120 LA 1801 (Peterson, 2005).

predicted arbitral approach to public safety dishonesty charges can best be understood on a continuum with commissioned officers held to the most stringent standard.

Alleged "lying" is just one form of a dishonesty charge. Dishonesty issues arise in many other contexts. For example, a crime involving tax or insurance fraud is serious even if it "only" a misdemeanor. Such offenses are serious because this type of criminal conduct is viewed as having a direct related to someone's honesty. At least one arbitrator has upheld the termination of a police officer who was charged with filing a fraudulent insurance claim.[162] The dishonesty need not be in the form of an untruthful statement; any dishonest act may warrant termination.[163]

But most of the published arbitration cases concerning dishonesty have involved an accusation of untruthfulness. Untruthfulness will usually be grounds for serious discipline, but this also depends on the discipline standards established and *followed* within the department. Many public safety employers will claim that truthfulness is grounds for summary discharge, but few actually consistently follow such a policy. As a consequence, when an employer elects to discipline an employee for untruthfulness, and the discipline has been inconsistent an arbitrator may overturn it.

Arbitrators will almost surely sustain a termination of a police officer for dishonesty when the dishonesty is in the form of a testimonial statement.

There are numerable cases in which arbitrators have sustained terminations for untruthfulness, but many of these cases also involve other sustained misconduct. For example, one arbitrator sustained the termination of a correction officer who concocted an elaborate story regarding the theft of his weapon. It was later revealed that the gun was stolen during a gay liaison with a criminal the officer had met in the correctional facility; the conduct was violated a department rule that employees not associate with known criminals.[164]

Although some departments have attempted to set forth a claim standard that untruthfulness is an automatic basis for

---

[162] *City of Stamford*, 97 LA 261 (Pittocco, 1991).

[163] *See City of Galion*, 112 LA 771 (Talarico, 1999) (officer shoplifting while off duty requires termination of the officer).

[164] *Hamilton County Sheriff's Department*, 99 LA 6 (Duff, 1992).

discharge. But often when those standards are challenged in an arbitration proceeding, it sometimes develops that the standards have not been applied uniformly.

Arbitrators will almost surely sustain a termination of a police officer for dishonesty when the dishonesty is in the form of a testimonial statement.[165] Lying in a sworn testimonial statement is of course a crime, and, as one arbitrator explained, "[w]hen a Police Officer engages in criminal activity, not only does he violate his Oath of Office but, more importantly, he destroys the very fabric of the officer-community relationship."[166] Another arbitrator stated: "Dishonesty destroys the trust which is essential to the relationship between an employer and an employee.... [I]t is so obvious that dishonesty constitutes a dischargeable offense that no employee can claim ignorance of the rule or the consequences, even absent a published rule or policy."[167]

When dishonesty occurs in the course of internal investigations, it will usually warrant termination.[168] If the untruthfulness is not established by the appropriate evidence standard, however, termination may not be warranted.[169]

Confusion abounds regarding the status of a "*Brady* officer" and its implications for job tenure. *Brady v. Maryland* is a U.S. Supreme Court case that requires all potentially exculpatory evidence to be furnished to the defendant and his attorneys in a criminal trial.[170] Contrary to popular misconceptions, *Brady* does not involve an untruthful officer or the admissibility of evidence. The *Brady* case involves criminal discovery obligations.

claims made that *Brady* officers will be unable to testify effectively and must be barred from employment are based on a misreading of the law

---

165 *See City of Monclair*, 127 LA 32 (Gaba, 2009) (lying to court makes officer unemployable).

166 *City of Galion*, 112 LA 771 (Talarico, 1999).

167 *Huron Lime Co.*, 106 LA 997, (Bowers, 1996) (internal quotation marks omitted).

168 *City of Kitsap*, 118 LA 1173 (Gaba, 2003) (holding dishonesty about previous insurance fraud when asked by superiors warrants termination of officer).

169 See *City of Monclair*, 127 LA 32 (Gaba, 2009) (accuser must meet a preponderance standard to prove the accused committed the act). *See also Steen v. City of Cathedral City*, 31 Cal.2d 542, 547 (1948); *Parker v. City of Fountain Valley*, 127 Cal.App.3d 99, 113 (1981).

170 373 U.S. 83, (1963).

In *Brady*, the prosecution had a confession of a co-defendant that would have greatly reduced the penalty of the plaintiff. However, the prosecution did not furnish the confession to the plaintiff, and the plaintiff, upon learning of the confession, alleged a due process violation had occurred. Under *Brady*, all "arms" of "the state", including law enforcement agencies, have an affirmative duty, through the prosecutor, to disclose to the defendant any potentially favorable evidence. It is generally recognized that if a police officer has a record of untruthfulness, that record will have to be furnished to a criminal defendant.

As a result, local prosecutors must, and generally do, maintain a list of "*Brady* officers" — those officers with a sustained finding of having made an untruthful statement. An officer's *Brady* status and associated circumstances must be disclosed to the defendant in cases in which the officer might testify. But this obligation to produce such discovery, contrary to common misperception, does *not* mean that the officer will be impeached with that evidence. In fact, in nearly all cases, such evidence is unlikely to be admitted. Therefore, claims made that *Brady* officers will be unable to testify effectively and must be barred from employment are based on a misreading of the law.

This issue was addressed by the Washington State Supreme Court in *Kitsap County Deputy Sheriff's Guild v. Kitsap County.*[171] Kitsap County involved the employer's collateral attack on a binding arbitration award and the question of whether they could even present such a collateral attack.

In the underlying arbitration award, Arbitrator Gaba reinstated a deputy *even though he sustained the employer's untruthfulness charge*. Gaba declined to find that the deputy had intentionally lied, explaining that the deputies stress impinged on his mental fitness to a degree that it was unclear whether the deputy was aware of the truth content of his statements. He reinstated the deputy, subject to a condition that he pass a fitness for review.

The deputy passed the review, but the County refused to reinstate. Instead, it filed suit, challenging the validity of the award. Following conflicting lower court decisions, the case made its way to the Supreme Court. The narrow issue presented was whether an otherwise binding arbitration award could be set aside based on "public policy" when a commissioned officer had a sustained truthfulness charge. The court ruled it could not and enforced the award.

---

[171] 167 Wn.2d 428, 219 P.3d 675 (2009).

In so doing, the court discussed the County's claim that the deputy was "unemployable" due to the sustained charge. During oral argument the County had fatally conceded that witnesses who had a record of lying, officers included, were not automatically barred from testifying. In its decision, the court discussed and rejected the County's claim that the *Brady* rule precluded reinstatement of the deputy:

> The cases requiring disclosure of an officer's history of untruthfulness have not commented on whether such an officer could continue to be employed. As a result, there is no explicit (or even implicit) statement regarding the continued employment of an officer found to be untruthful.[172]

In short, untruthfulness is a serious matter, but not all arbitrators find each instance to be a "summary discharge" offense, warranting bypassing the progressive discipline requirements. Discipline is most likely to be severe when untruthfulness is coupled with some other misconduct. But discharges are likely to be upheld where lies are made during the internal investigation.

Whether and how much discipline should be imposed for such accidents is a frequent source of conflict between unions and management.

It is this reality that makes it prudent for union representatives to remind employees that being truthful in an internal investigation interview is paramount. Before any interview, employees should be diplomatically yet forcefully counseled about the formula for the loss of a career:

Minor misconduct + Lying about it = Termination

9. Vehicle Accidents

Law enforcement officers and firefighters drive vehicles extensively and in a variety of circumstances. As a consequence, vehicles are damaged. Whether and how much discipline should be imposed for such accidents is a frequent source of conflict between unions and management.

---

[172] *Id.*

A single accident, regardless of how severe, does not rise to the level of being a summary discharge case. Therefore, this is an area where employers are required to follow progressive discipline standards. Moreover, arbitrators will give great weight to the discipline imposed in like cases throughout the department.

It is common for public safety employers in evaluating accidents to classify them as "preventable" and "non-preventable." At least one arbitrator has questioned the logic of basing discipline on this type of distinction. The arbitrator rejected the application of the standard because it was "ambiguous." Instead, he adopted the tort standard from civil law: whether the employee failed to use the care that a reasonable person would have used in the circumstances.[173]

Employees who are repeatedly at fault in driving accidents could be subject to discharge on the grounds that they are incompetent to perform one of the essential functions of the job. Short of establishing actual incompetency to drive, an employer is unlikely to prevail in a termination case even with repeated vehicle accidents.

10. Attendance

Sick leave abuse is an area where progressive discipline is especially required. Isolated, improper use of sick leave is not the sort of offense that warrants summary discharge.

Although proof of abuse through attendance analysis is relevant, frequently these employer reports are flawed.

Often, discipline appeals regarding alleged sick leave "abuse" turn on issues of proof. In the face of a denial of any sick leave abuse, employers need to go to great lengths to prove their charge. Generally, this can be demonstrated by comparing sick usage pattern against adjacent holidays and weekends. As will be discussed later, employers also have a right in the face of rampant sick leave use, to obtain a medical examination as authorized by the terms of the CBA.

Although proof of abuse through attendance analysis is relevant, frequently these employer reports are flawed. Often an employer will press forward with claims such as "55% of all sick leave time off is adjacent to a weekend." Such evidence might

---

[173] *Ramsey County Sheriff's Department*, 100 LA 208 (Gallagher, 1992).

initially seem strong. But when it is pointed out that such a number the involved employee is on a 4/10 schedule, it then becomes clear that the "evidence of abuse" actually proves nothing since fully 50% of days off are adjacent to weekends.

Another way for a union to rebut accusations of sick leave abuse is to obtain the sick leave records of other employees to show that the pattern is not out of line. This evidence could be particularly effective where it can be shown that supervisors have similar absences without any discipline action incurred. Some high stress industries such as dispatching appear to have a higher volume of sick leave use.

Besides the fact that adoption of such a policy would be subject to a duty to bargain, the policies are also suspect under state and federal laws.

Some employers have attempted to shortcut these proof problems by creating "no fault" attendance policies. Such policies typically state a maximum number of sick leave absences an employee can incur before facing discipline.

Besides the fact that adoption of such a policy would be subject to a duty to bargain, the policies are also suspect under state and federal laws. At a minimum, to be lawful, such policies would have to exempt absences for statutorily protected leave, including FMLA leave, and State Family Care Act (FCA) leave. Under the State FCA, use of sick leave care for qualified dependents is a protected right, and any retaliation against the use of such leave is unlawful. Similarly, absences associated with disabilities cannot be the source of discipline. Particularly given the broad definition of "disability" under Washington law, employers need to tread carefully in applying a numeric attendance system.

On the other hand, employers have recently made significant headway in courts asserting that regular attendance is an "essential requirement" of the job. While these claims will be reviewed on an industry-specific basis, it is ultimately true that *if* regular attendance is essential for the job, an employee's irregular attendance could prove to be a disqualification from employment. This remains a complex and contentious area, and it competes with another line of cases that extend employees the right to "intermittent" FMLA absences.

Issues sometimes arise concerning whether an employee is

"abusing" sick leave by not quietly staying at home and recuperating. Surprisingly, some departments have such rules on the books. A requirement that the employee stay at home is patently unreasonable. On the other hand, if the nature of the medical condition for which one is calling in sick could only involve recuperation only at home, it certainly can be an indication of sick leave abuse if the employee is not staying at home.

But arbitrators have rejected employer claims that there is a *per se* requirement that employees stay at home. Arbitrators have consistently held that an employee does not engage in sick leave abuse by failing to remain at home during the sick leave period.[174] As the arbitrator noted:[175]

> To require an employee to be confined to his home or to a hospital during their waiting period and immediately discharge him if he violates such confinement, gives imposing authority to the company, such a managerial right cannot exist unless it is clearly spelled out in the contract.

Consumption of alcohol also does not necessarily constitute sick leave abuse, though it might be presented as evidence of abuse. In *City of Jeannette*,[176] the arbitrator overturned the discipline imposed on an employee where the employer had alleged that the employee had consumed alcohol at a local bar after he had called in sick. In overturning the discipline, the arbitrator reasoned that being in a bar while on sick leave does not constitute a *per se* abuse of sick leave. He stated:

> What is relevant here is whether employee's medical condition could reasonably be expected to excuse him from work, so that he could consume sick leave. The employer created a situation whereby the grievant, as well as others, could call of from work to an answering machine and appropriately charge such absence to whatever type of leave requested. It was an accepted practice that such action on the part of the employee

---

[174] *See, e.g.*, *North Worldwide Aircraft Srvcs.*, 75 LA 1059 1062 (Mewhinney, 1980) (holding participation in sports activities while on sick leave does not establish sick leave abuse); *Lilly Industrial Coatings*, 68 LA 1051 (Leahy, 1977) (holding playing golf while on sick leave is not sick leave abuse); *Central Illinois Public Srvcs. Co.*, 91 LA 127 (Hill, 1988).

[175] *Gen'l Telephone Co. of Florida*, 61 LA 1313, 1316 (Caraway, 1974).

[176] 10 LA 1045 (D'Eletto, 1993).

> established illness and was granted sick leave status. According to this practice, the grievant met the established threshold to establish illness and earn sick leave . . . . While I question, for a variety of reasons, the wisdom of the grievant's behavior, I cannot draw the inference the City has. It is my opinion that the grievant's behavior in going to a tavern was viewed by the City as both embarrassing and suspicious and, prompted by embarrassment, the City acted based upon suspicion rather than evidence that the grievant was not ill.[177]

On the other hand, there is at least one unpublished Washington case in which the arbitrator sustained the discharge of a police officer who consumed alcohol while out on a stress-related leave related to a divorce. The arbitrator concluded that, although the impairment did not require the employee to stay at home, it was not proper for him to be going to bars at night. The arbitrator reasoned that the officer should have been avoiding alcohol consumption as a way of recovering from his stress. The arbitrator was surprisingly impressed by management's testimony that officers had been "specially trained" in alcohol and knew they should avoid alcohol when depressed.

What is vital in any case involving sick leave abuse of this nature — where the employee is validly off work, but there is a question of what activities he is engaged in during sick leave — are the written department rules. It is incumbent upon departments to establish clear rules indicating what employees may or may not due under those circumstances. In the absence of clear rules, discipline for improper activities during sick leave are not likely to be sustained except where the nature of the activities engaged in demonstrate that the initial report of sickness was not truthful.

As with any misconduct investigation, employees should be warned that untruthfulness in the course of an investigation can be separate grounds for discipline. While sick leave abuse itself constitutes a form of deception, it has generally not been treated as dishonesty per se under truthfulness policies. But lying about an absence in the course of an internal investigation would be.

D. Issues With the Form of Discipline

This section addresses limitations on management's authority

---

[177] *Id.* at 1051.

to impose certain forms of discipline. These types of discipline often involve some unique applications of the just cause principles.

1. Termination

As discussed above, termination is typically the last step in the progressive discipline continuum. Employers are required to follow the progressive discipline steps absent extraordinary circumstances. As indicated, an extraordinary circumstance is where the nature of the conduct engaged in is considered a "summary discharge" offense — an offense so serious that it is deemed to rupture the employer-employee relationship.

Arbitrators tend to take a very close look at the basis for the employer action in a discharge case. Therefore, in discharge cases arbitrators tend to be less deferential to the employer's judgment than they might be as to less serious forms of discipline. Typically, arbitrators also will hold employers to a strict burden of proof in establishing that the misconduct occurred.

---

demotions as a form of discipline will be appropriate only a limited range of cases

---

2. Demotion

Some employers believe that they have a range of disciplinary options when disciplining supervisors including demotion. This view is often incorrect. In fact, *demotions as a form of discipline will be appropriate only a limited range of cases.*

Demotions are an appropriate measure when the employee has demonstrated a lack of ability to perform the job duties of the higher rank in a competent and qualified manner. Where the employee engages in misconduct, some form of discipline other than demotion should be applied, *unless the misconduct demonstrates that the employee inherently lacks the qualifications of the higher-ranked position.*

For example, one arbitrator overturned a demotion of an "investigator" to the police officer rank where the allegation was that the employee used profanity and was insubordinate.[178] While such conduct would subject the officer to potential discipline, it demonstrated little about his capacity to serve as an investigator.

In another case, an arbitrator overturned the demotion of a

---

[178] *Southern California Rapid Transit District*, 100 LA 701 (Brisco, 1992).

fire apparatus engineer to a firefighter position based on a charge of negligent driving of a fire truck. The arbitrator concluded that this single insurance of negligent driving did not demonstrate that the employee was incapable of driving the vehicle in the future.[179]

The arbitration decision in *Southern Calif. Rapid Transit District* is particularly illustrative.[180] A transit police officer with a history of conflict was demoted for using profanity to demean a supervisor. The Arbitrator overturned the demotion as a penalty. The union showed that the officer was competent to perform his duties, and while some penalty may be appropriate, an open-ended demotion was not.

Under generally accepted arbitration principles, the distinction to be made is that demotion must be related to an employee's *ability to perform the position.* Discipline, on the other hand, is properly related to misconduct. If an employee has the full capability of performing a job, but for reasons of wilful misconduct he does not properly carry out his duties, then progressive discipline must be applied. But if the reason for the employee's poor performance is due to incompetence, then disciplinary measures are not in order, a demotion may be appropriate.[181]

3. Transfers

Arbitration decisions regarding the issue of compelled transfers or reassignments have often reached inconsistent results regarding the rights of management to make such transfers. These wide-ranging results mean that it is difficult to predict with a close degree of accuracy what the result in a particular arbitration hearing will be. Nonetheless, there are certain general principles that guide decisions in this area.

There is a threshold issue to consider on a compelled transfer is the question: Is it "discipline?" Sometimes this is not easy to determine. For example, if an employee is in a rotating specialty assignment position and those rotations occur on an irregular basis, is it considered discipline where the employer cites minor performance concerns regarding the employee and reassigns the individual to a different position? Arbitrators have provided varying answers to this particular question.

---

[179] *City of Omaha*, 86 LA 142 (Thornall, 1985).
[180] 100 L.A. 701.
[181] *Id.* at 702-703.

Arbitration decisions regarding the issue of compelled transfers or reassignments have often reached inconsistent results regarding the rights of management to make such transfers.

It becomes more likely that the employer action will be deemed "discipline" when there was an investigation conducted over a specific rule violation or alleged act of misconduct. And a finding that it is "discipline" is even more likely when that investigation resulted in a document that connects the transfer with other formal disciplinary actions, such as a reprimand or suspension. Once threshold question is answered that the action constitutes "discipline," then it will subject to the "just cause" standard.

On the other end of the continuum is a reassignment of an employee at the end of a fixed rotation period and, in which, the civil service rules or contract provide no "tenure" for that particular assignment. In these case, arbitrators will almost always hold management has the right to make the reassignment without proof of "just cause."

The second question to consider in evaluating a compelled transfer is the specific contract language pertaining to that position. If the position at issue is treated in the CBA as a separate position "classification," then normally those employees have tenure in that position and can only be removed for just cause. Occasionally, though not commonly, contracts will treat specialty assignments as a separate "classification." If so, the employees in those classifications arguably have tenure protection equivalent to that of a civil service position.

Often CBA management rights clauses identify management as retaining the right to "transfer" or "reassign" employees. While arbitrators will give weight to such language in evaluating a transfer, they generally hold that, absent a more specific waiver, such a management right remains subject to the just cause provisions. On the other hand, some contracts contain language that is less equivocal about management's right to transfer — language such as management has "complete and unfettered discretion" to make reassignments out of specialty positions — and in these cases, arbitrators will generally conclude that reassignment from these specialty positions is not subject to a just cause limitation. (A practical point for your negotiation team —

evaluate your CBA language to ensure you have not waived your right to grieve disciplinary transfers.)

A third factor is whether the particular position carries with it any additional pay premiums or benefits such as a take-home vehicle or clothing allowance. The presence of such compensation is *a factor*, though not necessarily a controlling one, in determining whether an involuntary transfer is subject to a just cause standard. On the other hand, even if the specialty assignment carries no additional pay, arbitrators often will hold the employer to the just cause standard where the employer's action is otherwise clearly "disciplinary" in nature.

A common procedural error made by employers in the context of involuntary transfers is to fail to provide a *Loudermill* hearing. If an employer has incorrectly assumed its action is not "discipline" it often fails to extend a *Loudermill* opportunity. But if the specialty assignment provides extra pay or benefits, and the transfer is being made as a result of alleged misconduct or performance deficiencies, a *Loudermill* hearing is required *before* the transfer order is issued.

E. Non-disciplinary Discharge

Most Washington public safety union CBAs require employers "discipline or discharge" only for just cause. This clause requires just cause not only, then, for disciplinary actions in response to misconduct but other types of discharges as well. Thus far in this chapter we have dealt with disciplinary types of infractions. Although just cause requirement imposes a contractual restriction on all types of discharge, the just cause model discussed above does not apply in the same manner as to "non-disciplinary" discharges — those situations in which an employee is discharged for reasons other than misconduct. In this section, we will review the rules that apply to those different types of non-disciplinary discharges.

1. Inability to Satisfactorily Perform Job Duties

This issue was discussed in detail above. As indicated, there is extensive confusion among employers, union and even arbitrators about how to evaluate performance related "discipline" actions.

The prevailing arbitral view is not to treat these as "discipline" *per se*, unless the discipline is for isolated acts of negligence — in which case it should only lead to minor discipline. If the employer is attempting to discharge an employee because of an inability to perform the job, it is not "discipline" in a traditional sense. Instead, as discussed above, the focus is on whether the employer has proven *that the employee is fundamentally incapable of performing the job.* Such a finding requires evidence that its training and supervision efforts has been extensive and in good faith, that those efforts have been unsuccessful *and* that any future efforts will not likely ever become successful due to the employee's limitations.

2. Discharge Due to a Lack of Fitness for Duty

Employees with physical or mental conditions that interfere with their ability to perform the job functions are potentially protected under state and federal disability discrimination laws. The rights of employees under given circumstances is discussed in greater detail later in a chapter addressing the legal rights of injured and disabled employees.

Employees with physical or mental conditions that interfere with their ability to perform the job functions are potentially protected under state and federal disability discrimination laws.

Arbitrators generally hold that the "just cause" requirement implicitly incorporates the mandates of state and federal disability discrimination laws. Therefore, they will require employers to comply with any legal duty they may have to accommodate an employee.

General standard. Nonetheless, there sometimes comes a time where it is clear that the employee is not capable of performing the job because of physical or mental limitations. Arbitrators have held that where it is established that the employee cannot and will not be able to perform the job, this is in itself just cause for discharge.

The challenging situations arise where the employee is recovering, but the progress of recovery is uncertain. Employers will sometimes object to being compelled to maintain an opening for an employee. Arbitrators have approached this problem from a rule of reason: The employer will be required to maintain the employee on a leave status (unpaid, if paid leaves have been exhausted) *if there is a reasonable prospect that the employee can return in a reasonable amount of time.* But when either the prospects of recovery are low or in the distant future, an arbitrator will generally hold that the employer is justified in discharging the employee.[182]

One expedient way to address this challenge is through contract negotiations by adopting a provision of the civil service rules allowing for "medical reinstatement." Some jurisdictions have created civil service rights, placing medically disabled individuals on a medical reinstatement register, giving these individuals priority for reinstatement, up to a period of time, if there is a recovery.

Mental health. Arbitrators have occasionally had to address the issue of employees whose mental health difficulties created a potential hazard in the workplace. Employers are under an obligation to reasonably accommodate an employee with a disability, but not if such accommodation would create a safety hazard.[183] Before an employer can discharge or discipline an employee with mental health problems, it must conduct some type of investigation into the reasons for the employee's conduct.[184] As one leading arbitration treatise indicates:

> Most arbitrators have been less willing to uphold disciplinary action for violation of shop rules where the employee's conduct was caused by mental health problems that were treatable or in a state of remission, or where the employee had apparently recovered as a result of subsequent treatment.[185]

The treatise further indicates that:

> There is a general consensus that when medical evidence indicates that a worker's mental disability exposes that employee or others to serious risk of injury or harm, or, alternatively prevents that employee from performing his or her duties, dismissal may be justified.[186]

---

182 *Compare Fleet Combat Training Center, Pac. Agency*, 82-1 ARB ¶8099, 3482 (Ross, 1981) (holding employer required to accommodate employee who missed a third of work and needed to restructure hours when recovery uncertain, even though employee's missed work seriously burdened the employer) *with Packaging Corp. of Am.*, 105 LA 591 (Hewitt, 1995) (termination of combat-veteran employee with stress reaction upheld despite fact that employee was receiving treatment, but had not yet recovered).

183 *Johnson Am. Corp.*, 114 LA 577 (D'Eletto, 2000).

184 Bornstein & Gosline, *supra*, at § 23.09.

185 *Id.*

186 *Id.*

It then adds:

> In determining whether an employee represents a direct threat to the health or safety of the employee or others, the following factors should be considered:
>
> - The duration of the risk;
> - The nature and severity of the potential harm;
> - The likelihood that the potential harm will occur; and
> - The imminence of the potential harm.

"Direct threat" to safety. The determination of direct threat must rely on objective factual evidence and not on subjective perceptions, irrational fears, patronizing attitudes or stereotypes. Likewise, whether the employee poses a safety risk must be based on an individual evaluation, and not on generalizations about their medical conditions.[187] The determination must be based on the circumstances of the individual under consideration, and the evidence must be compelling and supported by expert opinion.[188] It is impermissible for an employer to simply *assume* that a mental or physical condition automatically makes an employee unfit for work.

Like the balancing test required when determining whether employers must accommodate disabilities, the ADA requires that employers conduct a similar balancing test when determining whether a disabled employee presents a significant safety hazard to warrant termination.[189] Therefore, employers are required to accommodate disabilities, but they need not create or prolong a safety hazard for their employees, including the one with the mental or physical condition. The employer must balance the interest of the disabled employee in continued employment with the interests of all parties that could potentially be affected by the safety risk posed by that disability, including the affected employee.

In an illustrative case, an employee was terminated because he had homicidal intentions towards many of his coworkers, which came to light during a review of his medical records.[190] The union

---

[187] *See* Elkouri & Elkouri, *supra*, n. 31.
[188] *Id.* (emphasis supplied).
[189] Elkouri & Elkouri, *supra*, n. 31.

argued that as the threats were not directed at anyone in particular, there was no real threat. But the arbitrator sided with the employer, stating that the employee appeared to be a "ticking time-bomb" and creates an undue risk to the district, as well as other employees.[191] In considering the balancing of interests, the arbitrator, concluded "[t]he consequences are too grave and the probability of such death threats being carried out is simply too high."

In another case, the employee had been fit for duty with medication, but when he went off his medication, he threatened and endangered co-workers.[192] The arbitrator agreed that the employee would work safely on the medication. But because he had already caused a hazard, the damage had been done, and the arbitrator concluded that an impermissible hazard existed that the employer no longer had to accommodate.[193]

Medical conditions. Many medical restrictions do not qualify as "disabilities" under the ADA, and, therefore, do not require accommodations by the employer. As we will discuss later, Washington law is somewhat more protective of employees with medical disabilities. The extent to which an arbitrator finds just cause to exist or to be lacking will often turn on their interpretation of these statutes.

In one case, an employee had a medical restriction that did not allow him to work more than 9.5 hours a week.[194] The employer eventually reassigned the employee to a lesser paid position, to the former position with shorter shifts. The employee grieved, requesting an accommodation. The arbitrator sided with the employer. Because the hour restriction would not qualify under the ADA as substantially limiting major life activities, the restriction does not have to be accommodated.[195] Following the expansion of the definition of "disability" under the ADAAA,[196] employers will have to accommodate a wider range of disabilities that before.[197]

---

[190] *Anchorage School Dist.*, 119 LA 1313 (DiFalco, 2004).

[191] *Id.* at 1320.

[192] *Anchor Hocking*, 125 LA 312 (Cohen, 2008).

[193] *Id.*

[194] *DelMonte Foods*, 121 LA 1100 (Miles, 2005).

[195] *Id. See also City of Minneapolis*, 125 LA 558 (Befort, 2008) (holding employee with 50lb lifting restriction does not have disability under ADA as lifting restrictions of no more than 25lbs have been recognized).

[196] 42 *U.S.C.* § 12102

[197] See generally *Paige v. Jefferson Transit Authority*, 2009 WL 2057045 (W.D.Wash. 2011), for a discussion of the expansion of the ADA under the ADAAA.

And a different result could occur in Washington more expansive definition of "disability."

> The degree of proof required by arbitrators in unfitness cases is conflicted and controversial.

Proving unfitness. Unless the employee admits to being unfit for duty, the burden of proof rests on the employer to establish the actual lack of fitness, though there are questions as to the extent of this burden. At a minimum, this burden typically requires a fitness for duty exam by an appropriate health professional. During this process, the employee or the union are allowed to obtain and present a second opinion. In the event there is a dispute, but the employer insists on proceeding to termination, it will ultimately be up to an arbitrator to make the determination.

The degree of proof required by arbitrators in unfitness cases is conflicted and controversial. Many arbitrators defer to management's determination on such issues and relax the burden of proof below what it would be under the traditional "just cause" standard. The majority approach on fitness discharge cases is to assess them under a deferential "arbitrary and capricious" standard. The arbitration cases applying this standard often focus on whether the employer had a "good faith" belief that medical evidence supported the employer action without regard to whether sufficient proof existed in fact. Especially in light of these cases it is important for the union to present any competing medical opinions before the discharge decision is made.

> It is a best practice to negotiate for CBA language that clearly states that both discipline and "discharges" are subject to just cause.

Some CBAs require medical arbitration proceedings in which the two health professionals agree on a third professional. This approach is not advisable, though. There may be a number of legal arguments the union may be able to bring which the medical professional would be inclined to overlook and not be in a meaningful position to assess. For example, often the issue concerning fitness for duty turns on whether an accommodation is reasonable, and arbitrators are better qualified to judge the "reasonableness" of such an accommodation than is a medical professional.

It is a best practice to negotiate for CBA language that clearly states that both discipline and "discharges" are subject to just cause. Absent such language, arbitrators will be more inclined to relieve employers of some of their burden of proof and apply a deferential "good faith" standard for determining whether the discharge was valid. Such a deferential standard weakens your tenure protection and could even bypass the important question of whether the actual medical evidence even establishes any actual unfitness.

3. Layoffs

Layoffs are a "no-fault" discharge, in most circumstances, and so the just cause elements discussed above would not apply. But there is one exception to this. Normally, layoffs are performed according to a seniority system. Although most clauses require a strict inverse seniority order in layoffs, some CBAs grant employers discretion to lay people off out of order based on different performance or qualification related criteria.

These clauses certainly seem to set up a troubling possibility that an employer will exercise favoritism in the layoff process. Should an employer exercise its supposed right to lay individuals off out of order, they could expect scrutiny of such a decision by an arbitrator. In an arbitration hearing they will have to carry a heavy burden to establish that the individual laid off out of order lacked sufficient qualifications or skills. Typically, the union response under such circumstances would be to ask why the individual is being terminated at that time if they were supposedly a poor performer when there had been no previous efforts to remove them.

If an employee is laid off and the employer takes into account non-seniority factors that make the layoff seemingly disciplinary, the employee may have a right to a *Loudermill* hearing.

Although arbitrators might assume that employers have an implicit right to lay off employees, PERC's view might be different. Although existing PERC cases have muddied the issue, there is some authority in those cases for the proposition that layoffs are a mandatory subject of bargaining. And even if the union has waived its right to bargain the layoff themselves, PERC has held that the "impacts" of layoffs, which could include such elements as the seniority principles and severance pay, are bargainable.[198] Seemingly if the parties have negotiated a specific layoff clause in the contract, both parties have then discharged their obligation to engage in collective bargaining on those issues identified in the CBA language. On the other hand, where the layoff rules are defined only in civil service rules, not in the labor agreement, there may be a requirement before any layoff for both parties to sit down and negotiate the rules for the layoffs.

As discussed in Chapter 5, when an employee is terminated for cause, they are allowed a *Loudermill* hearing to present their side of the story. But, in the context of layoffs, an employee is not being terminated for cause, but because of a presumed business necessity. So the question arises as to whether a Loudermill hearing would be required in a layoff situation.

If an employee is laid off and the employer takes into account non-seniority factors that make the layoff seemingly disciplinary, the employee may have a right to a *Loudermill* hearing. For example, the Federal First Circuit Court of Appeals has held that when an employee is laid off, and they are chosen for performance reasons, they are entitled to a *Loudermill* hearing.[199]

Similarly, the Ninth Circuit has also found a Loudermill right during a layoff but the extent of their holding is unclear. In *Levine v. City of Alameda*,[200] an employee who was faced with a layoff requested a pre-termination hearing because he thought the layoff was not seniority-based, but was because of a conflict with another employee. He was the sole person laid off. His request was denied.

The Ninth Circuit held that had had a right to *Loudermill* hearing. Interestingly, the court did not differentiate between layoffs in general, and layoffs for some pretextual reason, as was alleged by the plaintiff in the case. The court simply and briefly stated that because a property interest was at stake, a *Loudermill* hearing was required.

But other courts have held that layoffs for purely economic reasons that follow seniority rules do not require a *Loudermill* hearing.[201] Whether the Ninth Circuit will follow that law remains to be seen. But most employers do not extend Loudermill hearings

---

198 *Yakima County*, Decision 11621-A (PECB, 2013).

199 *Whalen v. Mass. Trial Ct.*, 397 F.3d 19 (1st Cir. 2005).

200 *Levine v. City of Alameda*, 525 F.3d 903 (9th Cir. 2008).

201 *See Mayfield v. Kelly*, 801 F.Supp. 795 (D.D.C.1992); *Franks v. Magnolia Hosp.*, 77 F.3d 478 (N.D. Miss. 1995).

in seniority-based layoff situations, and until a clear holding emerges that seniority-based layoffs require a hearing, that likely will not change. On the other hand, if an employer engages in individual layoffs or group layoffs that are not based strictly on seniority, it should probably extend a Loudermill hearing.

4. Constructive Resignations

Most public safety employers have a rule that states conditions under which someone is deemed to have "abandoned" their job. Such a rule provides, for example, that if the employee has not shown up for work without any word some defined period, it is presumed that the employee intends to abandon the job, and it will be treated as a resignation.[202]

There have been a number of arbitrations of such "resignations" where the surrounding circumstances of the failure to report have been considered. In one recent case, an employee was considered to have abandoned his job after missing three consecutive days of work without permission.[203] However, the employee had been caring for his wife, and then had his own health problems. He also submitted a doctor's note and informed the employer that he would be gone "until further notice."[204] The arbitrator found that although a work rule existed, it was being applied in an unnecessarily harsh manner and that termination was not warranted.

In another case, an employee missed work for three weeks following a miscarriage without giving notice to her employer, and only provided a hand-written sticky note to indicate the reason for her absence.[205] Although she did not actually provide a doctor's note as required, the arbitrator found that the circumstances did not warrant termination. The arbitrator explained that her manager knew that she was pregnant, and, therefore, had reason to rely on the self-written sticky-note.[206]

A discharge due to "job abandonment" or constructive resignation for a tenured employee constitutes a deprivation of a

---

202 *See Creamland Dairies*, 125 LA 1149 (DiFalco, 2008) (noting employer policy that two days consecutive unexcused absences is considered job abandonment); *Cooper Center*, 123 LA 193 (Gregory, 2006) (noting employer policy that three or more consecutive missed days without doctors note considered abandonment).

203 *Multi Packaging Solutions*, 127 LA 1377 (Brunner, 2010).

204 *Id.*

205 *Cooper Center, supra.*

206 *Id.*

property interest. Not surprisingly, there are a few court decisions that specifically hold that a *Loudermill* hearing is required by law before such an individual is removed from the position.[207]

It is probably "best practice" for an employer who believes a constructive resignation has occurred to offer an employee a *Loudermill* hearing, wherever they might be able to contact them.[208] After all, a "constructive resignation" is not a true resignation, but rather it is a termination where the employer *assumes* that the employee is abandoning the job and actually terminates based on that alone.

---

[207] *Hudson v. City of Chicago*, 175 LRRM 2140 (7th Cir. 2004) (Employer is required to take reasonable means to notify police officers who are absent without permission that they will be terminated so that officers may have an opportunity to challenge that termination); *Coleman v. Dept. Of Personnel Admin.*, 6 IER Cases 365 (Cal. 1991) (holding a statutory right under California law exists that requires notice and an opportunity to be heard once an employer determines that a constructive resignation has taken place).

[208] *Metropolitan Council Transit Operations*, BMS Case # 11-PA-0724 (Jacobs, 2011); *Cantwell v. City of Boise*, 28 IER Cases 471 (Idaho 2008).

DISCIPLINE ARBITRATION TABLE

This table lists reasons public sector union employees have been disciplined, what discipline they received, and whether the discipline was upheld or overturned in arbitration. This table is limited to Pacific Northwest arbitrators only. It includes rulings from Washington, Oregon, Alaska and Montana, but includes decisions those Northwest arbitrators have rendered involving agencies outside the Northwest.

Categories:

Criminal Conduct
Off-Duty Misconduct
Conduct Unbecoming
Offensive Conduct/Courtesy
Alcohol/Substance Abuse
Insubordination
Dishonesty
Attendance
Incompetence/Negligence
Vehicle Accidents
Other Policy Violations

ALCOHOL/SUBSTANCE ABUSE

Citation: *City of Bremerton*, 97 LA 937 (Calhoun, 1991)

Finding: Discharge overturned

Charge: Alcohol/Substance Abuse

Arbitrator's Explanation: Police officer was denied names of officers who had accused him of using marijuana. The arbitrator found that the collective bargaining agreement (CBA) required that all persons who accuse another be named. Violation of CBA in this way caused unfair prejudice.

ATTENDANCE

Citation: *State of Montana*, 116 LA 410 (Prayzich, 2001)

Finding: Discharge overturned

Charge: Attendance

Arbitrator's Explanation: Corrections officer habitually failed to attend safety and staff meetings and did not comply with work rules regarding time sheets. The arbitrator found that the grievant had failed to conform to work rules regarding attendance and time sheets for 17 months before being told that further noncompliance could result in termination and the action plan to remedy the situation was not followed through with by the employer.

Citation: *Lewis County*, 118 LA 685 (Ables, 2003)

Finding: Two-week suspension overturned

Charge: Attendance; Incompetence/Negligence; Other Policy Violations

Arbitrator's Explanation: Juvenile detention officer was suspended for being late to work one day, for leaving a secure area before notifying co-workers, for failing to do security checks by making sure locks were enabled, and for making personal phone calls during a workday to ensure that someone was home to watch his children after school. The arbitrator found the two-week suspension excessive when the grievant was not put on notice of possible discipline from being late.

CONDUCT UNBECOMING/OFFENSIVE CONDUCT/OFF-DUTY CONDUCT

Citation: *City of Portland*, 134 LA 389 (Vivenzio, 2014)

Finding: Indefinite demotion changed to temporary suspension

Charge: Conduct unbecoming; Offensive conduct; Off-duty conduct

Arbitrator's Explanation: This officer involved in an off duty incident where he flashed his gun at a motorist while on vacation. The investigation into this event led to the uncovering of several other incidents of improper behavior. However, the officer said these charges were negated by the officers 27 years of service without discipline. The arbitrator also felt that the demotion served no other purpose than to punish and therefore was not corrective as just cause demands.

CRIMINAL CONDUCT

Citation: *County of Monterey*, 127 LA 207 (Gaba, 2009)

Finding: Discharge upheld

Charge: Criminal Conduct; Alcohol/Substance Abuse; Off-Duty Misconduct; Dishonesty; Other Policy Violations

Arbitrator's Explanation: Deputy Sheriff was arrested for DUI while off-duty. Grievant had a 0.16 blood alcohol content concentration and was carrying his duty weapon at the time of his arrest. The arbitrator found that the grievant had lied to the arresting officer and had previously been disciplined for the same offense. In addition, the arbitrator found that the deputy had associated with a known felon after being warned not to do so.

Citation: *City of Centralia*, 102 LA 520 (Stuteville, 1994)

Finding: 30-day suspension upheld

Charge: Criminal Conduct; Dishonesty

Arbitrator's Explanation: Police officer committed theft and forgery when taking a memorandum off a superior's desk and photocopying that document. The arbitrator stated that although the document was returned, theft was still found to have occurred since the police officer appropriated the document to himself.

Citation: *Honolulu Police Dep't*, 127 LA 148 (Henner, 2009)

Finding: Discharge overturned

Charge: Criminal Conduct; Alcohol/Substance Abuse; Off Duty Misconduct

Arbitrator's Explanation: Police officer who was off-duty was involved in a single car accident and was charged with driving under the influence. The arbitrator found that the tests determining sobriety were insufficient and the department did not interview any independent witnesses regarding the incident.

DISHONESTY

Citation: *City of Montclair*, 127 LA 32 (Gaba 2009)

Finding: Discharge upheld

Charge: Dishonesty

Arbitrator's Explanation: A police officer, while off duty, was caught running a red light by a red-light camera. The officer admitted committing the infraction to the coworker who reviews the photos. However, the officer contested the traffic ticket in court and attested that it was not him driving the car but a dealership employee. The arbitrator found that this was a clear untruthful statement to the court and this conduct made the officer unable to testify in any future court issues.

Citation: *Virgin Islands Dep't of Justice*, 125 LA 626 (Henner, 2008)

Finding: Discharge reduced to a 45-day suspension

Charge: Dishonesty

Arbitrator's Explanation: Corrections officer brought his cell phone into the prison, allowed an inmate to use it, and subsequently lied about the incident to his employer.

Citation: *City of Port Orchard*, 123 LA 581 (Knutson, 2006)

Finding: Discharge upheld

Charge: Dishonesty

Arbitrator's Explanation: Civilian police employee was found to have lied about having an affair with the police chief and that he had threatened her. The grievant was also found to have lied that the police chief told her to falsify a log. The arbitrator found that the grievant had violated her employer's code of conduct to be truthful and that the grievant had been dishonest about another co-worker in the past.

Citation: *Kitsap County*, 118 LA 1173 (Gaba, 2003)

Finding: Termination upheld

Charge: Dishonesty

Arbitrator's Explanation: Police sergeant had committed insurance fraud before taking Sheriff's job and lied about it.

Citation: *Ore. Dept. of Corrections*, 113 LA 374 (Skratek, 1999)

Finding: Discharge reduced to 30- day suspension

Charge: Dishonesty

Arbitrator's Explanation: Corrections officer participated in offensive verbal conduct and did not immediately report a co-worker who exposed himself. When questioned, the officer was evasive and denied the incident occurred to protect the other employee. The arbitrator found that the dishonesty warranted discipline, but in light of over six years of a spotless work record, the officer to should get a reduced punishment.

Citation: *Solano County Sheriff's Dep't*, 129 LA 449 (Reeves, 2011)

Finding: Discharge upheld

Charge: Dishonesty; Incompetence/Negligence

Arbitrator's Explanation: Corrections officer used his cell phone in the jail which was against department policy. The arbitrator found that the grievant subsequently lied about the incident in reports to his supervisors and had received haircuts by an inmate using a banned razor.

Citation: *County of Yolo*, 129 LA 1249 (Reeves, 2011)

Finding: Discharge upheld

Charge: Dishonesty; Offensive Conduct/Courtesy

Arbitrator's Explanation: Deputy Sheriff assaulted an arrestee and knowingly made false statements in stating that the arrestee had assaulted her first. Grievant was subsequently convicted of assault by a public officer and filing a false police report. The arbitrator found that that the grievant had been provided proper training regarding use of force and the grievant knew that she always had to be truthful in reports submitted to her employer.

INCOMPETENCE/NEGLIGENCE

Citation: *Pacific County*, 132 LA 261 (Coss, 2013)

Finding: Suspension overturned

Charge: Incompetence/Negligence

Arbitrator's Explanation: Deputy Sheriff was suspended for not properly handling citizen complaint about their dog being attacked by another dog. The deputy failed to do a complete investigation when he did not contact the veterinarian who treated the dog. The arbitrator found that the county did not fully investigate the matter and did not consider mitigating factors such as the deputy's performance reviews.

Citation: *City of Livingston*, 124 LA 1516 (Calhoun, 2008)

Finding: Five-shift suspension upheld

Charge: Incompetence/Negligence

Arbitrator's Explanation: Fire captain made a number of negligent calls in responding to a call. He cancelled the second ambulance without knowing of the circumstances, improperly performed CPR, and violated HIPPA regulations.

Citation: *City of Napavine*, 128 LA 1134 (Romeo, 2011)

Finding: Discharge upheld

Charge: Incompetence/Negligence; Attendance

Arbitrator's Explanation: Police Department clerk consistently failed or refused to complete her monthly reports and did not process concealed pistol requests on time. Grievant also left a voicemail at work that she was taking off a work day that accounted for eight hours when she only had four hours of sick leave available.

INSUBORDINATION

Citation: *City of Sandy*, 129 LA 669 (Calhoun, 2011)

Charge: Insubordination

Finding: Discharge rescinded. Reinstated with full back pay and privileges

Arbitrator's Explanation: Police officer was involved in an investigation concerning a friend of his who was a former police officer. During one of the questioning periods, he "downplayed" some of the information he knew regarding the situation with his friend. The chief used this "downplaying" as the basis for termination, calling it insubordination. However, the arbitrator found that there was no other evidence of any insubordination, no investigation took place, no Loudermill hearing, and the chief clearly had ulterior motives.

Citation: *City of Raymond*, 121 LA 1168 (Romeo, 2005)

Charge: Insubordination

Finding: Discharge reduced to a written reprimand

Arbitrator's Explanation: Police officer committed a number of violations of policy, but every violation had a circumstance that was outside the control of the officer. However, the officer made errors in submitting evidence to a lab, and although there were mitigating circumstances to this also, he should have checked with a superior before making the errors. His supervising officer caused him to make the errors, but he could have prevented them with ease. There were indications that the investigations into the misconduct were unfair also.

Citation: *State of Alaska Dep't of Corrections*, 117 LA 674 (Henner, 2004)

Charge: Insubordination

Finding: 84-hour suspension upheld

Arbitrator's Explanation: Corrections officer refused to go to a specific training session when ordered. The arbitrator found that he committed insubordination, even when he was a well-trained, stellar employee who had already received the training in question, and he wanted to attend a different training session that was more useful.

Citation: *City of Sumner*, 115 LA 580 (Calhoun, 2001)

Finding: Letter of Reprimand overturned

Charge: Insubordination

Arbitrator's Explanation: Police department did not have just cause to reprimand officer who did not leave his other job early to come into work, when the request to come into work did not come in the form of an order, and the officer did not recognize it as an order.

Citation: *City of Bremerton*, 121 LA 915 (Reeves, 2005)

Finding: Suspension reduced to a written reprimand

Charge: Insubordination; Other Policy Violations

Arbitrator's Explanation: Grievant was a police officer who was told by his lieutenant not to "fraternize" with a 19-year old civilian explorer. The grievant disobeyed his superior's oral order and told the civilian explorer to keep the relationship a secret. The arbitrator found that the department did not have just cause to suspend the grievant because the officer was not properly notified along with the department of its "non-fraternization" rule.

USE OF FORCE

Citation: *City of Oakland,* 128 LA 1217, (Gaba, 2011)

Finding: Discharge overturned

Charge: Use of Force

Arbitrator's Explanation: Police officer shot and killed a civilian who posed a high risk and there was extensive public backlash and distrust of the police. However, the arbitrator found that there were circumstances of the shooting that indicated the suspect was high risk and he was running toward the officer's partner and looking as though he was pulling a gun from his waistband.

Citation: *State of Alaska*, 98 LA 545 (Levak, 1992)

Finding: Suspension upheld

Charge: Use of Force

Arbitrator's Explanation: Correctional officer hit a mentally ill inmate two times with a closed fist after the inmate became enraged and moved toward other staff members. The arbitrator found that the suspension had just cause because the officer was trained not to use closed fists and could have restrained the inmate without hitting him. In addition, the arbitrator stated that the officer appeared motivated by the demeanor and racially charged words of the inmate.

Citation: *Portland Police Bureau*, 104 LA 647 (Henner, 1995)

Finding: Discharge overturned

Charge: Use of Force

Arbitrator's Explanation: Police officer fired 13 shots at a suspect and was subsequently fired for "unjustified use of force." The arbitrator found that the officer's actions were justified given that in pursuing the suspect, the suspect indicated that he was going to grab his gun.

OTHER POLICY VIOLATIONS

Citation: *City of Sumner*, 123 LA 1249 (Coss, 2007)

Finding: Discharge reduced to demotion and a six-month suspension without pay

Charge: Other Policy Violations

Arbitrator's Explanation: Firefighter captain did not notify employer when he took position as sales rep for a fire engine company. Captain also took part in purchasing decision where he made commission from the sale of a fire engine that his precinct purchased. The arbitrator found termination improper because of the implied requirement for progressive discipline.

Chapter 7

The Rights of Officers Involved in a Use of Force Incident

A. The Legal and Human Context

Many law enforcement officers go through their careers harboring dual concerns about the use of lethal force. They ask themselves: Will I ever be in an officer involved shooting? And if I do, what how will I be treated?

Police unions have little ability to control the frequency of officer-involved shootings in an increasingly violent society. But they can do quite a bit to make the aftermath of an officer involved shooting for the affected officer better.

Obvious points still worth recalling. The seriousness context of lethal force is well-known and often well-covered in training, but still bears repeating. There are at least two factors present in particular that warrant that police unions allocate a high level attention to the issue.

The first context is the legal one. When an officer shoots and kills under color of law, *a homicide has occurred.* The *only* question the legal system poses is the whether the homicide is "justified" or "criminal." *The legal system offers no third option on this question.*

Experience in Washington law enforcement indicates nearly all officer involved shooting deaths have been ruled justified. But the *potential* legal consequences of use of lethal force remain serious, serious enough that police unions *need to have programs and protocols in place to safeguard their members' legal rights.*

The second context is the psychological and human one. Again, the general situation is well known, even if the precise data describing the magnitude varies from study to study: At the moment of decision and in the immediate aftermath, officers involved in lethal force are under *extraordinary* stress.

The psychological response. In handling over 150 officer involved shooting incidents, I have learned more than anything *the individualized nature of the officer response.* No two officers react the same way. And even when I have responded for officers with whom I had prior personal knowledge, their response is not necessarily what I would have anticipated. Until you are in the situation, you cannot predict who you will actually respond.

The other important fact I have learned first-hand is the extreme level of perceptual distortion that occurs in the overwhelming majority of officer involved shootings. And this distortion *does not entirely dissipate in the hours following the incident.* Memory impacts may last days or even be permanent.

Not only are the perceptional impacts dramatic, they are also sometimes difficult to comprehend in that officers sometimes had *opposite perceptual distortion simultaneously.*

Reviewing the academic literature has led me to conclude that my lay assessment of the psychology of shootings is well grounded in the actual science. Several psychologists have undertaken formal surveys of the officer involved in shootings. Those studies are consistent my own personal experience: Not only are the perceptional impacts dramatic, they are also sometimes difficult to comprehend in that officers sometimes had *opposite perceptual distortion simultaneously.*

This phenomenon was best revealed in a study by Dr. David Klinger. Klinger was personally involved in an officer involved shooting within months of completing the academy with the Los Angeles Police Department. A few years later he left the Department and pursued an academic career. He was commissioned by the NIJ to perform a study on officer shootings which he published in 2002.[1]

He studied 113 incidents. The results of his study are generally consistent with the data gathered from other like studies, but he also highlighted the *conflicting* nature of some responses:

- 15% of the officers had *both* tunnel vision *and* heightened visual detail.
- 9% perceived *both* blunted auditory *and* enhanced auditory.
- 2% perceived *both* slow motion *and* fast motion.

Dr. Alexis Artwohl is recognized as one of the leading forensic psychologists on the subject of officer involved shootings. Her clientele has consisted of many Northwest law enforcement agencies, including Portland P.D. As part of her work, she

[1] *David Klinger,* POLICE RESPONSES TO OFFICER-INVOLVED SHOOTINGS *(2002).*

performed a study of officers involved in shootings from 1994 to 1999.[2] Her results point to some of the same conflicting perception patterns. Her study of the officers showed:

- 84% perceived diminished sound
- 16% perceived intensified sounds
- 71% reported heightened visual clarity
- 79% reported tunnel vision
- 62% perceived slower motion time
- 17% perceived faster motion time
- 52% reported memory loss for part of the surrounding event
- 46% reported memory loss for part of their actions
- 21% reported a distorted memory —seeing, hearing or experiencing something that did not really happen
- 74% reported responding as if on "automatic pilot," with little or no conscious thought
- 26% reported having intrusive or distracting thoughts
- 39% reported a sense of detachment or unreality
- 7% reported temporary paralysis

Medical studies repeatedly identify stress as impacting memory creation and retention. And a lethal force situation is a stress overload event. Studies by Artwohl and others have identified the memory impairment that may following an incident. In her report, Artwohl describes several cases in which officers have discharged their weapons in the line of duty *yet have no recall of doing so.*[3] Her article discusses other scientific studies that have identified other like situations.

She explains the dynamic:

---

[2] Alexis Artwohl, "Perceptual and Memory Distortions During Officer-Involved Shootings," FBI LAW ENFORCEMENT BULLETIN (Oct. 2002).

[3] Artwohl, "No Recall of Weapon Discharge," LAW ENFORCEMENT EXECUTIVE FORUM (2003).

> Dissociation, defined as "a disruption in the usually integrated functions of consciousness, memory, identity or perception of the environment" (DSM-IV, 1994), is an experience people are prone toward experiencing in a high stress situation. Artwohl (2002) found that 39% of 157 officers involved in shootings experienced dissociation as defined by "there were moments when you had a strange sense of detachment, as if the event was a dream and not real, or like you were looking at yourself from the outside." Solomon (1986) reported that 9% of 44 officers involved in shootings reported dissociation to the extent of having out-of-body experiences. During dissociation, people can become psychologically detached from their bodies or aspects of the experience, resulting in lack of awareness of pain, loss of memory for parts of the event, feeling numb and detached from their emotions, and other strange experiences that can interfere with conscious awareness of their behavior and their ability to recall what they did.[4]

Artwohl also explains that many of these situations may also involve something else identified in the research — the unintentional discharge of a weapon. While uncommon, likely due to the intensive training on indexing, several research reports have identified a "fist reflex" action that has been known to occur "with a high stress confrontational situation."[5]

The psychological aftermath. Given such a disorientating event, it is little wonder that the psychological fallout is significant. Again, response and recovery seems to be individual in nature. But a review of how other officers have responded can be useful.

Klinger's NIJ study also details the physical and mental response by officers in the days, weeks and months following their shooting:

---

[4] *Id.*

[5] *Id.*

Table 2. Officers' response following a shooting[6]

Physical Response	At any time (n=113)	First 24 hours (n=112)	First week (n=113)	Within 3 months (n=111)	After 3 months (n=115)
Trouble sleeping	48%	46%	36%	16%	11%
Fatigue	46%	39%	26%	7%	5%
Crying	24%	17%	7%	2%	2%
Appetite loss	17%	16%	8%	2%	1%
Headache	7%	6%	4%	1%	1%
Nausea	4%	4%	4%	0%	0%
Other physical response	19%	18%	11%	12%	6%
Thoughts and feelings					
Recurrent thoughts	83%	82%	74%	52%	37%
Anxiety	40%	37%	28%	13%	10%
Fear of legal or administrative problems	34%	31%	25%	19%	11%
Elation	29%	26%	19%	11%	5%
Sadness	26%	18%	17%	5%	5%
Numbness	20%	18%	7%	4%	3%
Nightmares	18%	13%	13%	10%	6%
Fear for safety	18%	9%	10%	9%	8%
Guilt	12%	10%	5%	6%	2%
Other thoughts or feelings	42%	33%	23%	20%	14%

Because these reactions are self-reported, there is a distinct possibility that *actual* reactions of the individual officers are *even more* elevated than shown here. Regardless of the precise fallout, the potential for lingering impacts upon the officer is real and sometimes leads to a variety of personal problems, some which lead officers to abandon their careers.

[6] *David Klinger,* POLICE RESPONSES TO OFFICER-INVOLVED SHOOTINGS *(2002).*

The human reality involved here should point to a conclusion by police union representatives that something needs to be done. Guild officers and Guild attorneys have a role to play in establishing sound operational guidelines and otherwise protecting your members. The balance of this chapter covers the legal rights your members have regarding an officer involved shooting and what your Guild or Association can do to make a possibly difficult situation at least somewhat better.

B. Legal Rights

In Chapter 5 we covered extensively the rights that apply in a prediscipline context. For the purpose of this Chapter, this is what you need to know: *Everything we said applied in a prediscipline context also applies following an officer involved shooting.* But the context here is a bit different so we will turn to a detailed discussion of those rights in a lethal force reporting context.

Weingarten. *Weingarten* applies any time an interview could lead to discipline. It is only prudent to assume that any investigation regarding an officer-involved shooting *could* lead to discipline, although, in practice, discipline generally does not result. And your officers would, or should "reasonably perceive" that a threat of potential discipline is in the background. Therefore, under *Weingarten, an officer involved in a use of force situation has a right to a union representative.*

Although police union representatives typically will seek to have their attorney available for such a disciplinary investigation, the right to attorney access is *not* guaranteed under *Weingarten. Weingarten* does not require the employer to wait until any particular individual, including the association attorney, can be made available. Therefore, *absent a labor agreement to the contrary*, the employer *could* order the employee to give an immediate statement, providing the officer only a limited period to arrange for a union representative to be present. This legal reality is another example of an occasion in which the constitutional or statutory rights fall short of needed protection, and a well-negotiated labor contract needs to step into the gap.

***Miranda* and *Garrity*.** Anytime a law enforcement officer uses lethal force, it has the *potential* to be criminal in nature. *The only difference between criminal homicide and justifiable homicide is that in the latter, the elements of justification are met.* It would only be prudent for any law enforcement employee — before submitting a statement regarding their use of lethal force — to review that statement with an attorney to determine if the elements of justification are met.

Any officer involved in a use of force situation may invoke their constitutional rights under the Fifth Amendment and *Miranda*. Once invoked, it is incumbent upon the employer — if it wishes to obtain a statement — to *order* the employee to give a statement. Any statement given pursuant to such an order would then fall under the protection under the *Garrity* rule and could not be used against the officer in a later criminal proceeding. Of course, a *Garrity* order does not prevent the department from taking necessary disciplinary action.

Because an officer is only protected by the *Garrity* rule when an order is given, care should be taken by a union representative to ensure that an *actual Garrity* order has been made.

Where the employer does not give a *Garrity* order, *any statement provided by an officer is considered entirely voluntary, and the department, the prosecutor, and the courts may make unlimited use of it.* On the other hand, if the department does not give a *Garrity* order, the officer is in no way required to give a statement and is free to remain silent about the matter.

Because an officer is only protected by the *Garrity* rule when an order is given, care should be taken by a union representative to ensure that an *actual Garrity* order has been made. A simple "request" by an employer for a statement does *not* constitute a *Garrity* order. Therefore, the representative should make sure that the employee is *being specifically ordered* to provide a statement.

Often departments will be reluctant to issue a specific *Garrity* order. The chiefs and sheriffs are often urged by prosecutors not to issue a *Garrity* order. Their apparent concern (elected prosecutors are reluctant to express this openly) is that it might interfere with their ability to prosecute the officer later. That reality alone should serve as a reminder as to why an officer would want to invoke their *Garrity* rights.

It is unfortunate that *Garrity* orders are not forthcoming more freely. The message sent is that the officer should be viewed as suspect until they prove they are innocent of wrong-doing. And even more unfortunate is the degree of management manipulation which often follows the refusal to provide a *Garrity* order. Often chiefs and sheriffs suggest, more or less directly, that the officer should give a statement despite the lack of *Garrity* to clear the situation up or get this behind them.

Often the psychological pressures at the time, including the natural pressure to appear not to be hiding anything, leads a number of officers to waive their Fifth Amendment rights and proceed to provide a statement. But it should be clear to these officers when they do so, unlimited use may be made of that statement by any prosecutor.

One possible way to circumvent the failure of a chief to provide an explicit *Garrity* order is found in the department manual. Often the procedures manual will contain an explicit mandate that officers do, in fact, make a report. Unless the chief or sheriff specifically countermands that mandate, presumably it remains in effect. Although the case law, as discussed early, is somewhat divided on this question, there is at least a fairly strong prospect that a written policy that requires submission of a statement constitutes an "order" within the meaning of *Garrity.* If so, it extends a written statement protection of the Fifth Amendment privilege.

Officers should be advised to begin such statements with a brief introduction such as: "This is an involuntary statement provided pursuant to the department procedural manual..." Given that the case law is divided on this subject, operating under "implied *Garrity*" is not as secure as having an actual *Garrity* order. But if an officer is determined to submit a report, but it is better than the alternative of waiving all rights.

Legal privileges, generally. A legal privilege is the right of an individual to give a statement to someone who will maintain its confidentiality and which a court will not order to be disclosed. Washington law recognizes the following legal privileges relevant to an officer involved in a use of force situation:

- Spouse[7]
- Attorney[8]
- Psychologist/Psychotherapist[9]
- Priest or Clergy[10]

---

[7] RCW 5.60.060(1).
[8] RCW 5.60.060(2).
[9] RCW 18.83.110.
[10] RCW 5.60.060(3).

- Peer Support Counselor[11]

But it is important to understand the limitations on the scope of these privileges. While these privileges are virtually absolute in the circumstances to which they apply, *officers involved in a lethal force situation must ensure that they are only speaking when the privilege attaches.*

Spousal privilege. Any time one is talking to a spouse there is an evidentiary privilege. But, like other privileges, that privilege does *not* extend to third persons who might be present during the conversation where a separate privilege does not also cover their participation in the communication.

A common living arrangement without that registration will not allow for recognition of the spousal privilege.

Washington law has also been amended to allow the spousal privilege to extend to "domestic partners."[12] Since the original domestic partnership provisions were adopted in statutory law, court decisions extended the right the right of marriage to gays and lesbians. In recognition of that expansion of marriage rights, the domestic partnership definition was amended again. The amendment narrows the domestic partnership to apply only to senior couples, ones in which at least one member of the couple is 62 years of age or older.

A qualifying requirement for these senior couples is that a "domestic partners" must "share a common residence."[13] To confirm the domestic partnership, a declaration must be filed and registered with the Secretary of State.[14] A common living arrangement without that registration will *not* allow for recognition of the spousal privilege.

Attorney-client privilege. Some jurisdictions even have written policies *requiring* officers to talk to the Prosecutor or City Attorney. These rules are ill-conceived and have been revoked by most agencies because they created unintended civil consequences for the Department. If applied, such policies may be the equivalent of a *Garrity* "order," but this should be verified. As always with *Garrity* immunity, the officer or his or her advocate should ensure

[11] RCW 5.60.060(5).
[12] *Id.*
[13] RCW 26.60.020.
[14] RCW 26.60.040.

that what is intended is an actual "order."

If the discussions are indeed mandatory, then the statements could not be used in a criminal prosecution. But they would nonetheless *not* be privileged from use in a later civil action because the Prosecutor is *not* the officer's attorney. Twenty years ago Washington Departments commonly had such policies yet they were rarely invoked and ultimately most have now been repealed from the policy manuals.

But an officer is advised to speak with that civil attorney only when it is *clear* that the attorney is *also serving as the attorney for the officer.*

The confusion over these policies leads to a more important point: As to the attorney-client privilege, officers need to be clear that the attorney to whom the officers are communicating with are *their* attorney. There is the possibility of confusion arising in the aftermath of a shooting when the employer might rush in with its legal counsel and asks the officer to discuss the matter with that attorney. Generally, the attorney retained by the jurisdiction is not also the officer's attorney, at least at that juncture, and no privilege would attach.

There are some limited circumstances under which an attorney may be paid for by the city, or offered through their insurance carrier, and also serve as the officer's attorney. Public employers are obligated to defend and indemnify and, as a result, eventually they will provide an attorney to represent both the city and the involved-officer in any civil proceeding. But an officer is advised to speak with that civil attorney only when it is *clear* that the attorney is *also serving as the attorney for the officer.* Further, especially early on, the officer needs some assurance that he is not communicating with the attorney in a "joint client" situation in which the statements will be communicated back to the Department. Otherwise, the "joint client" arrangement will be the basis of a legal privilege but the statements made can still be used for discipline purposes.

Typically, police unions in this state make arrangements with law firms to serve as advisors for officer-involved shooting situations. Arrangements should be established so that under these circumstances the union retained attorney comes in, on that matter, as the officer's attorney and not the union's attorney.

Psychologist privilege. The psychologist privilege[15] is an important one that allows officers to speak freely about the incident they have gone through. Generally, the department is willing to pay for the psychologist. And often the departments wants and expects a fitness examination before the officer is released for full duty.

If the Department's expectation and directive are that this is a fitness for duty review for which they are the client, there is no privilege.

This process creates a potential trap, but one that is easy to address. Steps must be taken to ensure that when the officer goes into the psychologist in this situation, *it is privileged and not simply a fitness for duty examination in which the department is the actual client.* This challenge is easily resolved by verifying that the client relationship resides between the officer and the doctor, not between the department and the doctor. In practice, I have found little difficulty issue as departments have come to recognize their great risk management interests reside with allowing the officer to speak to a psychologist but without the loss of legal privilege.

If the Department's expectation and directive are that this is a fitness for duty review for which they are the client, there is no privilege.[16] So this expectation should be clarified in advance of any session with the psychologist. Any "waiver" form the officer is expected to sign for such a session should be reviewed with legal counsel in advance.

---

the privilege does *not* broadly encompass any and all statements they may make to personnel employed by church organizations

---

As an aside, a closely related medical privilege also exists.[17] Statements the officer makes to a physician in the course of acquiring medical treatment are recognized as legally privileged.

Priest/Clergy privilege. There has been some confusion and some litigation concerning the scope of the legal privileges applying

---

[15] RCW 18.83.110.

[16] *See J.N. ex rel. Hager v. Bellingham Sch. Dist. No. 501*, 74 Wn. App. 49, 871 P.2d 1106 (1994).

[17] RCW 5.60.060(4).

to priests and clergy. Officers should be clear that the privilege does *not* broadly encompass any and all statements they may make to personnel employed by church organizations. The statute defines the scope of the privilege to extend to:

> A member of the clergy, a Christian Science practitioner listed in the Christian Science Journal, or a priest shall not, without the consent of a person making the confession or sacred confidence, be examined as to any confession or sacred confidence made to him or her in his or her professional character, in the course of discipline enjoined by the church to which he or she belongs.[18]

In *State v. Martin*,[19] the State Supreme Court clarified the reach of this privilege. It ruled that the privilege *only* applies where: (1) the clergy member is ordained; (2) the statements are made as a "confession in the course of discipline enjoined by the church"; and (3) practice or rules of the church to which the clergy or member belongs require that confessions be maintained confidentially.

The historic origin of this privilege was the "priest-penitent" privilege long recognized in common law as an aspect of Roman Catholic sacramental practice. But in creating the statute, as the Supreme Court recognized that the legislature was intending to broaden the privilege to other denominations, while not leaving the privilege so open ended as to encompass any and all types of counseling sessions which were never mutually intended to be confidential.

> the greatest pitfall to avoid is the Department "chaplain"

In *Martin*, the court also made clear that it does not matter that the individual making the confession actually is a member of that church or is in any way an adherent to the beliefs relating to the "confession." The court said the focus is on the mandate governing the clergy and that if their church rules require confidentiality, then the statements are privileged. In *Martin*, the minister improperly related the comments to third persons without permission, but the court indicated that the privilege remained intact because only the penitent could waive it.

---

[18] RCW 5.60.060(3).

[19] 137 Wn.2d 774, 975 P.2d 1020 (1999).

In the law enforcement context, the greatest pitfall to avoid is the Department "chaplain." Some chaplains may not even be ordained. But even if a chaplain is an ordained minister, *statements made to them are likely not privileged.* As the Court explains in *Martin*, statements are privileged only when they occur within a "confession" session, *not* a counseling session. A competent clergy member will be trained in the parameters of this privilege and will able to establish the proper ground rules to ensure such talks are privileged.

---

informal peer counselor arrangements will not suffice to protect the interests of the officers involved in a shooting

---

Peer Support Counselor privilege. The newest statutory privilege, and perhaps the one most important in this situation, is the "peer support group counselor" privilege. It is important to understand that this privilege is not overbroad and that to fall under the umbrella of this privilege, *its terms must be strictly adhered to.* Those terms are defined in RCW 5.60.060(6)(a) which provides:

> A peer support group counselor shall not, without consent of the law enforcement officer making the communication, be compelled to testify about any communication made to the counselor by the officer while receiving counseling. The counselor must be designated as such by the sheriff, police chief, or chief of the Washington state patrol, prior to the incident that results in counseling. The privilege only applies when the communication was made to the counselor while acting in her or her capacity as a peer support group counselor. The privilege does not apply if the counselor was an initial responding officer, a witness, or a party to the incident which prompted the delivery of peer support group counseling services to the law enforcement officer.

The statute also further defines a peer support group counsel:

> Law enforcement officer, or civilian employee of a law enforcement agency, who has received training to provide emotional and moral support and counseling to an officer who needs those services as a result of an

incident in which the officer was involved while acting in his or her official capacity.[20]

Therefore, *informal peer counselor arrangements will not suffice to protect the interests of the officers involved in a shooting.* There are a number of formal conditions that *must* be satisfied for the privilege to attach:

- The individual purporting to be a counselor must receive training to provide emotional or moral support in counseling;
- The counselor must be designated by the departmental chief;
- The designation must occur *prior* to the incident; and
- Peer support counselors cannot fulfill that function when the counselor is an "initial responding officer, a witness, or a party to the incident."

Many departments, inexplicably, have failed to take the necessary steps to appoint peer support counselors. This inaction is an issue that should be addressed in negotiations. The preferred peer support language we recommend involves allowing Guild input into the peer support counselor designation process. For the appointment to be legally effective, the counselor needs to be appointed by the Chief or Sheriff, but your contract language can make the Guild's consent necessary for that appointment.

Although conversations between union members and union representatives in the context of representation have been recognized as generally confidential by PERC, this does not create the status of a statutory privilege.

The peer support counselor permits an opportunity to lend support for the officer, but this should occur *only* in the presence of other persons with whom a privilege attached. As with all privileges, *statements made in the presence of unprivileged third persons lose their privileged status.* But if the conditions of this

[20] RCW 5.60.060(b)(i).

privilege can be established, a peer support counselor can be an important ally for the period immediately after the use of a lethal force incident.

Limited nature of the "union privilege." It is also important to bear in mind a privilege that is *not* firmly recognized under Washington law. Although conversations between union members and union representatives in the context of representation have been recognized as generally confidential by PERC, this does not create the status of a statutory privilege. PERC has deemed these conversations to be confidential *as to the employer*, holding that for an employer to order a union representative to disclose these matters would constitute unlawful interference in internal union affairs. (And even then, as we shall cover later in the Chapter 13 interference discussion, this is not treated as an absolute bar to inquiry in the manner a legal privilege is.)

But there is nothing that keeps a *court* from compelling disclosure of these statements. The legislature to date has not chosen to add a union-member privilege to its permitted list of statutory privileges.

The union-member privilege has been recognized so far in only two states—New York and Alaska. These holdings are of relatively recent origin, New York first recognizing the privilege in 1979[21] and again 1991.[22] Alaska followed in 2012.[23] The Alaska Supreme Court found the privilege "implied" in the collective bargaining statute, which, like Washington's PECBA, prohibits employer interference. Union advocates have argued for a broader recognition of the privilege.[24] Federal courts have not recognized it yet.[25] Whether Washington courts will formally recognize such a privilege remains to be seen but at this point, no solid union privilege claim can be asserted.

---

[21] *City of Newburgh v. Newman*, 421 N.Y.S.2d 673 (N.Y. App. Div. 1979).

[22] *Seelig v. Shepard*, 152 Misc.2d 699, 578 N.Y.S.2d 965 (N.Y.Sup. 1991); Rubenstein, *A New York Court Recognizes a Labor Union Evidentiary Privilege*, 9 LAB. LAW. 595 (1993).

[23] *Peterson v. State of Alaska*, 280 P.3d 559 (Alaska 2012).

[24] *See, e.g.*, Muniz, *Bringing Jobs Back to the American People: The Need for a Recognized Labor Relations Privilege in the Aftermath of the Economic Recession*, 31 HOFSTRA LABOR & EMP. L.J. 237 (2013).

[25] *See Curry v. Contra Costa County*, 120 Fair Empl.Prac. Cas. (BNA) 1216 (N.D. Cal. 2013) and cases cited therein.

C. Practical Considerations

Numerous scientific reports have addressed this issue and virtually all reinforce the need for at least one complete sleep cycle, if not more.

Timing of Statement. Often an officer involved in a use of lethal force will not be psychologically ready to give an immediate detailed account of what occurred. As indicated above, shooting situations are often accompanied by great perceptional distortion. These distortions severally restrict many officers' abilities to relate accurately or recall all the necessary specifics. Often, with the passing of time an officer may become more capable of giving a detailed account of what occurred.

Numerous scientific reports have addressed this issue and virtually all reinforce the need for at least one complete sleep cycle, if not more. The evidence is strong that the lack of a solid sleep cycle prevents memory from congealing. And since there are many reports that in the first few days, quality sleep may be lacking, the best practice is to delay any statement for several days.

For all these reasons, both the employee *and* the department are better served if no immediate statement is required. An immediate statement is likely to contain inaccuracies that will expose both the employer and officer to greater civil liability.

The guidelines approved by the psychological services section of the International Association of Chiefs and Police concurs with our position on this.[26] It states:

> While officers may be asked to provide pertinent information soon after a shooting to aid the initial investigative process, whenever feasible, officers should have some recovery time before providing a full formal statement. Depending on the nature of the incident, the demands on the agency, and the emotional and physical status of the officers, this can range from a few hours to several days. An officer's memory will often benefit from at least one sleep cycle prior to being interviewed leading to more coherent and accurate statements.[27]

[26]http://www.theiacp.org/portals/0/documents/pdfs/Psych-OfficerInvolvedShooting.pdf.

Negotiated procedures. What every organization needs to do is negotiate with the department for policy guidelines — preferably placed in an enforceable collective bargaining agreement — that offer the officers involved in shootings real legal protection. IACP's Board of Psychologists has made solid recommendations to police managers which can form the basis of such agreement:

- "Immediately after an officer-involved shooting or other critical incident, involved personnel should be provided physical and psychological first aid (e.g., emotional support, reassurance to involved personnel, assignment of a companion officer to any officer who is directly involved in a shooting and is separated from others pending investigative procedures)."[28]

- Recognize that "'involved officers' may include not only those who fired their weapon, but also officers who were at the scene and either did not, or could not, fire their weapon. Such officers are often strongly impacted."[29]

- "After providing needed public safety information, officers who fired a weapon or were directly involved in a critical incident should be encouraged to step immediately away from the scene and be transported to a safe and supportive environment by a trusted peer or supervisor."[30]

- "To ensure officers are not isolated once transported from the scene, whenever possible the agency should ensure there is a companion officer of the officer's choice, a chaplain, or a supportive peer available. Often the best support person is a fellow officer who is trained in peer support (see *IACP PPSS Peer Support Guidelines)*, or has previously gone through an officer-involved shooting, who can be assigned to the officer immediately following the incident."[31]

---

[27] *Id.* at Section 5.2.
[28] *Id.* at Section 4.1.
[29] *Id.* at Section 4.1.1.
[30] *Id.* at Section 4.2.
[31] *Id.*

- The Guidelines also wisely note that "[i]f officers have an immediate need to talk about the incident, they should be encouraged to do so solely with individuals with whom they have privileged communication.[32]

- "Following a shooting incident, officers often feel vulnerable if unarmed. If an officer's firearm has been taken as evidence or simply pursuant to departmental policy, a replacement weapon should be immediately provided as a sign of support, confidence, and trust unless there is an articulable basis for deviating from this procedure. Officers should be kept informed of when their weapon is likely to be returned."[33]

- "Officers involved in a shooting or other critical incident should be provided with the opportunity and encouraged to personally contact their family members as soon as possible after the incident." The Guidelines also wisely add: "Officers should be instructed to limit information to their well-being and not the facts of the incident." [34]

- The first few hours after a shooting or other critical incident is a potentially emotional and confusing time so officers may wish to consult their union and legal counsel.[35]

A sound CBA provision will contain, at a minimum, the following:

- A provision requiring that no statement be given for at least 48 hours and longer if achievable.

---

[32]*Id.* (But the Guidelines erroneously identify "chaplains" as individuals covered by a privilege which they are not Washington state nor most states.

[33] *Id.* at Section 4.3.

[34] *Id.* at Section 4.4.

[35] *Id.* at Section 4.5. (This Guideline is watered down from a previous version of the Guidelines which had recommended that the Department remind the officers of these rights.).

- A provision guaranteeing access for the officer to individuals with whom the officer can speak in a privileged manner.

- A requirement that the department undertake a thorough and competent investigation.

- Access to any videotaping of the incident that might be available.

- A requirement that if the officer's weapon is removed it will be replaced.

- A provision providing guaranteed access to mental health providers, at the Department's expense.

- A provision spelling out the nature of the return to duty psychological review, especially including its privileged nature.

In the event you do not have a contract provision or other policy guidelines in place, you will be put in the position of doing on the spot negotiations. If this is your department's first officer-involved shooting, or first shooting for some time, and especially if there are no written guidelines, there is a good chance that the investigation will be led blindly. This novelty gives you an opportunity to contact whoever is leading the investigation and negotiate a reasonable set of ground rules. My experience in such situations indicates that those leading an investigation are often quite willing to consider the suggestions of the union or union attorney and work in a cooperative manner towards common ends.

Immediate actions. You should have made previous arrangements with your department to have the appropriate union representative contacted in the event of an officer-involved shooting. It is wise to retain legal counsel with 24-hour availability.

When an association representative arrives at the department, he or she should attempt to make the following determination:

- The physical and psychological condition of the officer;

- The status of the investigation;

- The department's immediate intentions as to interviewing the officers; and

- The location of an attorney for the officer.

After making those determinations, the representative should make contact with the officer to assess his well-being and determine what further resources he or she needs. As the IACP psychologists recommend, the officer should not be completely isolated. Therefore, it is best if the officer is placed in the room surrounded by a few fellow officers — especially any officers who have previously been involved in use of lethal force situations—with the specific directive that they not discuss the facts of the incident.

A written statement assures that the necessary elements of lawful use of force are clearly identified. And the written format assures that spontaneous or incomplete comments are eliminated, something investigator interrogations cannot guarantee.

Officer Statement. In almost all cases, my preference is for the submission of any statement by the officer, following the issuance of a *Garrity* order, be presented *in writing.* A written statement assures that the necessary elements of lawful use of force are clearly identified. And the written format assures that spontaneous or incomplete comments are eliminated, something investigator interrogations cannot guarantee.

A recent interrogation fad proposed by some is the "Cognitive Interview." While this process has been around for a while as a lay witness interview tactic, only more recently have some proposed extending this technique (often by using briefly trained investigators), to lethal force investigations. Based on my experience, I am not only unconvinced that the interview is as effective as advocates suggest, I also see such a relatively uncontrolled process as posting many dangers in the context of lethal force reporting.

Even the designer of this technique, Professor Edward Geiselman, indicates that an investigator lightly trained in this technique probably produces *weaker* results that by using conventional interrogation techniques.[36] Furthermore, the

[36] R. Geiselman, *Investigative Interviewing and the Detection of Deception*, PSYCHOLOGY IN ACTION, (June 3, 2011) , available at

purposes of such a tactic do pair up well with the ultimate purpose of the officer's reporting.

Whether the officer does or does not accurately perceive every motion is not what matters. Officer are entitled by law to use force when "objectively reasonable" *from the perspective of the involved officer.*

Geiselman, the designer of Cognitive Interviewing, suggests that for individuals with impaired memories, it brings further more detailed facts. He has compared it to hypnotism for that purpose.[37] But like hypnotism, the process is likely to a documented stream of information on response very possibly counterproductive to later court cross-examination.

Developing all the facts is an important aspect of a proper lethal force investigation. More often than not, the better fact witnesses are bystanders or fellow officers who generally observe many details outside the tunnel vision of the involved officer.The premise of this technique also misapprehends the relevant legal standard. Whether the officer does or does not accurately perceive every motion is not what matters. Officer are entitled by law to use force when "objectively reasonable" *from the perspective of the involved officer.*[38] As the Supreme Court explained in *Graham v. Connor*:

> The calculus of reasonableness must embody allowance for the fact that police officers are often forced to make split-second judgments — in circumstances that are tense, uncertain, and rapidly evolving — about the amount of force that is necessary in a particular situation.[39]

The court also explained: "The "reasonableness" of a particular use of force must be judged from the perspective of a reasonable officer on the scene, rather than with the 20/20 vision of

---

http://www.psychologyinaction.org/2011/06/03/investigative-interviewing-and-the-detection-of-deception-professor-r-edward-geiselman-ucla/

[37] Geiselman, "Eyewitness Memory Enhancement in the Police Interview: Cognitive Retrieval Mnemonics Versus Hypnosis" J. APPLIED PSYCH. 401 (1985).

[38] *Graham v. Connor*, 490 U.S. 386 (1989).

[39] *Id.* at 396-97.

hindsight."[40] Officer have a right and obligation to protect themselves and third parties from imminent threats. Their reasonable perceptions at the scene ultimately carry more weight than all the specific facts. A solid statement that articulates the basis for their decision is what is needed.

Not being overly precise about details for which an officer is not certain and may not be completely accurate is actually a better report writing practice.

Toward that end, a review of available evidence, and especially something as relevant as a video recording of the incident, can help the officer better congeal their memory of the incident. A *privileged* walk-through of the scene may also be useful for memory enhancement. Such walk-throughs are often the source of assistance as officers re-form their memories. But the process congealing those memories during a walk-through is not linear. Just as the original memories are fragmentary, the recall that occurs from a return to the scene is also often fragmentary. Recollections often flow back to officers randomly as the details of the scene are absorbed. Therefore, any recording or transcription of such a randomized recall process is unlikely to produce text helpful to the later cause in any court proceeding.

Officers often struggle to put together all possible details in their report, seeking to be as conscientious as possible. I don't always find this to be critical. They should report what they remember and not be anxious about what they cannot recall. Not being overly precise about details for which an officer is not certain and may not be completely accurate is actually a better report writing practice.

An effective legal advocate should be able to present such a report in the proper light. Ultimately what is most important is expressing the *reasonable basis* the officer had for exercising the level of force. The officer's then existent *state of mind* is more critical than all the surrounding details that they may or may not be able to recall accurately.

[40] *Id.* at 396.

Chapter 8

Public Safety Contract Interpretation and Enforcement Issues

A. Introduction

There are a number of contract interpretation issues that reoccur in public safety labor agreements. Often these issues end up before arbitrators, so we will discuss the common ways in which arbitrators approach these issues.

The chapter is divided roughly into two parts. The first part covers how arbitrators tend to approach issues generally, including what factors they rely upon to interpret labor contracts. You may find this information useful and informative especially if you have a pending grievance arbitration. It gives you insight into how arbitration advocates would argue a grievance. But you might also find it technical and less immediately practical, in which you case you might prefer to skip ahead to the second part of the chapter. The second part covers how arbitrators approach particular types of contract issues.

The Appendix to this chapter provides a table highlighting how Northwest arbitrators have interpreted various contract language. This table provides insight into how local arbitrators are likely to view certain CBA language and certain topics.

B. General Principles of Contract Interpretation

Labor agreements are like most other contracts; when it serves their interests, parties are capable of reaching conflicting views of what the seemingly simplest phrase or sentence might mean. There are certain rules of interpretation arbitrators use to help sort out these conflicting claims and arrive at a result the parties can live with into the future. In this section will delve into those factors and the arbitration decision-making process.

Nature of Arbitration Decision-making. We should start this discussion by restating the significant caveat that was presented in Chapter 6, our chapter addressing discipline arbitrations. As we explained there, the PERC and court decisions we cite from litigation are governed by the legal doctrine of "stare decisis" — the fundamental legal principle that says a tribunal should base its decisions, to the greatest extent possible, on previous rulings ("precedent") on similar issues. But as we also explained in Chapter 6, in arbitration *there is no doctrine of "stare decisis."*

Arbitrators have a strong tendency to consider the views of other arbitrators expressed in published arbitration decisions. But they are interpreting what they believe to be the parties' intent in the labor contract and are in no way bound by other arbitrators opinions.

To predict the outcome of your particular grievance issue, you would want to study the larger *pattern* of arbitrator awards.

Therefore, we study prior arbitration decision mostly to see the pattern of decision making in order to best predict the result on future arbitrations. No single decision can predict what another arbitrator will do on the same issue. Instead, a "consensus" among arbitrators has developed on various questions of the course of years. To predict the outcome of your particular grievance issue, you would want to study the larger *pattern* of arbitrator awards. As I indicated in Chapter 6: "Arbitrators do not adhere to precedent, but they do respect and consider the consensus position reflected in those decisions."

Therefore, when advocates are predicting the outcome of grievance arbitrations, they are engaging in as much "art" as "science." Litigation is always uncertain, but the arbitration process contains even greater variability in decision-making then that which occurs in court or before PERC.

Grievance arbitrators generally do not see their job as *producing a grievance resolution that is "fair" or "reasonable."* Rather, they see their core role as identify and *applying the "intent" of the parties' written contract when they adopted it.*

There is one point about arbitration decision-making that that especially strikes those new to the process as surprising: Grievance arbitrators generally do not see their job as *producing a grievance resolution that is "fair" or "reasonable."* Rather, they see their core role as identify and *applying the "intent" of the parties' written contract when they adopted it.* If the agreement parties settled on arguably unfair terms, the arbitrator would leave it up to the parties to make necessary adjustments later. "Fairness" and "reasonableness" may play a minor role in contract interpretation, but those equities are subordinate to the arbitrator's search for the parties' contracting "intent."

Much of this restraint is a product of the limitations of an arbitrator's authority. Although arbitration decisions are normally treated as "final and binding," they are subject court review on a single question — did the arbitrator exceed their authority. Most CBAs contain a provision in the arbitration clause expressly prohibiting arbitrators from "adding to, or modifying" the language. But even absent such an express clause, that is a constraint that has been a recognized limit in their authority.

So while fairness is a commendable goal, to be valid, an arbitration award must "draw its essence" from the contract.[1] The arbitrator will draw from many sources to make that determination, as is only natural to do. However, the "award is legitimate only so long as it draws its essence from the collective bargaining agreement."[2] If the arbitrator goes outside the "essence" of the agreement, the award will not be enforced by the courts.[3]

Most contract grievances that arise are fairly easy to resolve. Usually, there is something in the CBA language or bargaining history which indicates what the disputed language is "supposed" to mean. The cases that result in grievances submitted to an arbitrator, tend to be the cases that are closer calls, often the ones for which the parties could expect to reasonably "agree to disagree."

In order to make judgments in these "close call" cases, arbitrators have developed a number of somewhat technical rules of interpretation. Some of these rules are conflicting or competing, so it is not always easy to predict the outcome of a given case.

Principles of contract interpretation. As stated, the *primary goal* of most arbitrators is to determine the intent of the parties to the agreement.[4] In determining intent, arbitrators usually only consider the intent "manifested" by the parties to each other during negotiations, rather than their hidden intentions.[5]

---

[1] *Steelworkers v. Enterprise Wheel & Car Corp.*, 363 U.S. 593 (1960).

[2] *Id.* at 597.

[3] *See Coca-Cola Bottling Co., Consol., Inc. v. Teamsters*, 411 F. Supp. 2d 1338 (S.D. Ala. 2006).

[4] LABOR AND EMPLOYMENT ARBITRATION, Tim Bornstein & Ann Gosline, § 14.01[2] (Mathew Bender et. al eds., 1991); *Sunrise Medical*, 86 L.A. 798, 799 (Redel, 1985); *Independent School District No. 47*, 86 L.A. 97 (Gallagher, 1985).

[5] Bornstein & Gosline, *supra*, § 14.01[2].

In other words, what matters is not what each of the parties thought they were getting in the bargain, but what they communicated to each other, as well as the objective terms in the contract.

This approach is not too much different than how courts interpret contracts. Washington courts (and PERC) have adopted what is known as the "objective manifestation theory" of contract interpretation. Under this approach, the parties' mutual intent is inferred not from each of the parties' subjective intent but from what is "objectively manifested" in their communications during the creation of the contract.[6] This "objective manifestation" theory imputes to a person the intention that corresponds "to the reasonable meaning of his words and acts."[7]

In other words, what matters is not what each of the parties thought they were getting in the bargain, but what they communicated to each other, as well as the objective terms in the contract. But figuring out what those supposed "objective" contract words means is sometimes easier said than done.

"Plain meaning v. ambiguity. *The threshold question facing arbitrators is whether the contract is ambiguous or clear on its face.* If the contract words are clear, one set of rules guides their interpretation. If the language is ambiguous a whole different set of considerations apply.

A contract's language is considered "ambiguous" if it is "reasonably susceptible of more than one meaning."[8] Perhaps not surprisingly, parties often disagree as to whether the contract is actually ambiguous. That is, much of the time, why they are in front of the arbitrator.

Generally, arbitrators hold that under the "plain meaning rule," when CBA wording is plain and unambiguous, its meaning should be determined without reference to any "extrinsic" (outside) evidence.[9] A party seeking to establish a meaning *other than* what the plain meaning suggests must carry the burden of proof to

---

6 *Wells Trust v. Grand Central*, 62 Wn. App. 593, 603, 815 P.2d 284 (1991); *Dwelley v. Chesterfield*, 88 Wn.2d 331, 335, 560 P.2d 353. (1977).

7 *Dwelley, supra*, at 335; *Gilmore v. Hershaw*, 83 Wn.2d 701, 521 P.2d 934 (1974); *Weinerskirch v. Leander*, 52 Wn. App. 807, 813, 764 P.2d 663(1988).

8 Bornstein & Gosline, *supra*, at 14.01[3] (*citing Sunrise Medical*, 86 LA 798, 799 (Redel, 1985)).

9 *Id.* at § 14.02[1][a].

demonstrate to why the plain meaning rule should *not* apply.[10]

---

the preliminary question for most arbitrators is to determine whether the CBA language is clear on its face or if it is ambiguous, in which case it would be subject to additional interpretation

---

But one exception exists to the "plain meaning rule" that only a lawyer could love: Plainly clear language may nonetheless contain a "latent ambiguity" which thereby allows the introduction of the extrinsic evidence. A "latent ambiguity" exists when the language seems to be clear on its face, yet some fact outside the contract makes it susceptible to be reinterpreted to be ambiguous after all.[11]

Arbitrators consider such "latent ambiguity" claims seriously, but parties have varied degrees of success with such claims. No matter the logic, it usually is not an easy argument to make to say that, "yes the words seem quite clear, admittedly, but there's some other information that shows the words don't really mean what they say."

So the preliminary question for most arbitrators is to determine whether the CBA language is clear on its face or if it is ambiguous, in which case it would be subject to additional interpretation. More often than not in arbitration, arbitrators conclude the language is ambiguous and needs to be evaluated in light of language and evidence outside the "four corners" of the CBA. As a practical matter, usually parties don't get all the way to arbitration if the meaning is clear. Ambiguous language is that language that "reasonable people" could interpret differently, so an arbitrator that indicates there is no ambiguity, they are implied indicating that one of the parties was unreasonable.

But sometimes CBA language is undeniably clear and unambiguous. And if it is (and if no "latent ambiguity" exists), the arbitrator will decide just on its "plain meaning" alone.[12] Ironically, even if both parties argue that a term is ambiguous, an arbitrator may disagree and find the plain meaning to be sufficient.[13]

Arbitrators give serious consideration to "plain meaning"

---

[10] *Id.*

[11] *Id.*

[12] Bornstein & Gosline, *supra*, 14.02 [1] (*citing Mohawk Rubber Co.*, 83 LA 814, 816 (Flannagan, 1984)).

[13] *Andrew Williams Meat Co.,* 8 LA 518 (Cheney, 1947).

claims because they assume they that may not change the meaning of the contract when the terms are spelled out clearly. To do so would arguably be a misuse of their power.[14]

In during this threshold check on the CBA's "plain meaning," arbitrators apply certain interpretation principles:

- Where a writing is plain and unambiguous, its meaning should be determined without reference to extrinsic evidence.[15] (This is, unless a party can make a "latent ambiguity argument.")

- A party seeking to establish a meaning other than what the plain meaning of the document indicates has the burden of proof as demonstrate why the plain meaning rule should not apply.[16]

- Even where the parties have divergent understandings of what the contract language means, generally the party that indicates it intended the ordinary meaning of the language would likely prevail.[17]

- Words of the contract will be given their normal meaning absent any variant contract definition extrinsic evidence indicating another meaning.[18]

- Arbitrators need not always cite external authority in determining the meaning of words and phrases in a contract. In some cases, the arbitrators will rely on their own interpretations.[19]

Probably more often than not, the search for the "plain meaning" of the CBA fails, an arbitrator concludes that the contract is indeed ambiguous, and then, because it is susceptible to more than one "reasonable interpretation," they proceed to try to identify the parties' true intent. Once CBA language is found to be

---

[14] *City of Bainbridge Island, Wash.*, 115 LA 747 (Lacy, 2001).

[15] Bornstein & Gosline, *supra*, § 14.02[1][a].

[16] *Id.*

[17] *Id.* at § 14.02[1][b].

[18] *Quadcom 9-1-1 Pub. Safety Communication Syss.*, 113 LA 987 (Goldstein, 1999).

[19] *See Air Force Logistics Command*, 85 LA 735 (Dilts, 1985) (declaring the meaning of the word "illness" did not include intoxication or the following hangover).

ambiguous, an entirely different and additional set of interpretation principles come into play:

- Ambiguous terms should be construed in light of their context.[20]

- Ambiguous language should be given a reasonable and equitable construction.[21]

- A reasonable and lawful interpretation will be favored over unreasonable and unlawful interpretation.[22]

- Contracts should be interpreted so as to avoid harsh, absurd and nonsensical results.[23]

- Where contract language is ambiguous, arbitrators should adopt the interpretation that best carries out the objective of the contract.[24]

- Technical terms, including the terminology of labor relations, should be given their technical meaning "unless the context or usage indicates a different meaning."[25]

- Language common to collective bargaining agreements throughout an industry may be interpreted by reference to how those other parties have interpreted their agreements.[26]

- If the language of a contract is susceptible of two constructions, one that will carry out the objectives of the contract and the other that will not, the first construction should prevail.[27]

---

[20] Elkouri & Elkouri, HOW ARBITRATION WORKS (4th Ed. 1985), at 356.
[21] *Id.* at 365.
[22] Bornstein & Gosline, *supra*, § 14.02[3][b].
[23] *Id.* at § 14.02[3][c].
[24] Bornstein & Gosline, *supra*, at § 14.02[1][d].
[25] *Id.* at § 14.02[1][b][v].
[26] *Id.* at § 14.03[8].
[27] Bornstein & Gosline, *supra*, at § 14.02 [1].

- An interpretation that gives meaning to every part of the contract is preferred to one that gives no effect to one or more parts.[28]

- Therefore, effect should be given to every word, sentence and clause in the contract.[29]

- When one interpretation of an ambiguous contract would lead to harsh, absurd, or nonsensical results, and another alternative interpretation, equally consistent, would lead to just and reasonable results, the latter interpretation will be used.[30]

- Ambiguous contract language will be given a construction that is "reasonable and equitable to both parties rather than one that would give one party and unfair and unreasonable advantage."[31]

- Arbitrators should "look at the language in the light of experience and choose that course that does the least violence to the judgment of a reasonable man."[32]

Contract negotiations frequently are used in the interpretation of ambiguous provisions.

In addition to applying these contract interpretation principles, many of which are borrowed from civil law, labor arbitrators typically apply, often with great impact, two additional sources of authority particular to labor contracts: Bargaining history and "past practice."

Bargaining History. The context and history of contract negotiations is an important factor in contract interpretation.[33] Contract negotiations frequently are used in the interpretation of

---

28 *Id.*

29 *Id.*

30 Elkouri & Elkouri, *supra*, at 495 n.123. *See also Hertz corp.*, 119 LA 138 (Goldstein, 2004).

31 Elkouri & Elkouri, *supra*, at 513-14.

32 *Id.* at 514 n.241 (*quoting Clifton Paperboard Co.*, 11 LA 1019, 1020 (Stein, 1949)).

33 Bornstein & Gosline, *supra,* at § 14.03[3].

ambiguous provisions.[34]

One argued approach towards contract interpretation is to construe any ambiguities in contract language against the party that proposed the language.[35] While some have questioned this approach to collective bargaining where agreements were invariably arrived at jointly, other arbitrators have favored this approach because it requires disclosure of the drafter's intent.[36] A different way of describing this view — if one party talks another party to adopting unclear language, it suffers the risk that it may not achieve its bargaining goals on that topic.

Generally, though, the arbitrators do recognize that a deeper look at the bargaining history and context is needed to discern the parties' mutual intent. Generally any change in the *words* of contract strongly implies an intent to change the *meaning* of the contract.[37] Where the meaning of a term is unclear, it will be deemed that the parties intended it to have the same meaning given it during the negotiations, if there is no evidence to the contrary.[38]

If the language could be interpreted to mean different things, arbitrators will generally give heavy, if not controlling, weight to the practice of the parties that preceded the grievance.

CBA language was presumably changed for a reason, so the context of that change can be critically important. So too, under the "objective manifestation theory" would be the statements the parties made during the adoption of the language.

Past practice. Past practice is a very important factor used in interpreting contracts. Past practice generally only comes into play

---

[34] *Downingtown Sch. Dist.*, 88 LA 59 (Zirkel, 1986); *John F. Kennedy Ctr. For the Performing Arts*, 101 LA 174, 179 (Ables, 1993) ("Prior disputes in arbitration or in court, leave foot-prints on what is troubling parties in a collective bargaining relationship").

[35] *Id.* at § 14.03[3]; *Genova Pennsylvania*, 99 L.A. 475, 480 (DiLauro, 1992); *Independent School District, supra*, 86 L.A. at 103; *Low Engineering Co., Inc.*, 85 L.A. 581, 584 (Gallagher, 1985); *Bunny Bread Co.*, 85 L.A. 1118, 1121 (Krislov, 1985).

[36] Bornstein & Gosline, *supra*, at § 14.03[3]; *Independent School District, supra*, 86 L.A. at 103.

[37] *Id.* at § 14.03[3][i].

[38] Elkouri & Elkouri, *supra*, at 501 n.163; *see also Schnuck Mkts.*, 107 LA 739 (Cipolla, 1996); *Copper & Brass Sales*, 105 LA 730 (Nelson, 1995).

when language is determined to be "ambiguous." If the language could be interpreted to mean different things, arbitrators will generally give heavy, if not controlling, weight to the practice of the parties that preceded the grievance.[39]

As indicated in Chapter 3, past practice is used by PERC to determine the "status quo" from which parties operate under. This "past practice" concept under collective bargaining law is equally important in contract arbitration. It is built on a recognition that labor contracts, different from more precise commercial agreements, cannot possibly capture the hundreds and hundreds of variable working conditions that define workplace terms and conditions. The doctrine was recognized very early on in the history of labor law that parties reaching agreements were creating "gaps" as they described their understanding of mutually accepted working conditions.

The generally accepted elements of a past practice include the requirement that the practice be unequivocal, clearly enunciated and acted upon, readily ascertainable, fixed for a certain period of time, and established through *mutual acceptance by both parties.*[40] Mutual acceptance does not require explicit agreement; mere acquiescence demonstrates acceptance. Past practices involve "those working conditions that are mandatory subjects of bargaining and cannot be changed unilaterally, whether they are established in writing or by custom."[41]

Past practice may be so controlling in arbitrations that when a contract is silent on a matter, the past practice usually becomes the de facto missing contractual term that is to be enforced, though unwritten.[42] Depending on the nature and scope of the past practice, some arbitrators have held that a sufficiently established past practice can even represent a modification of the CBA, overriding express terms.[43] In one case, for example, the past practice was found to be more important than the provision in the contract that gave management an unqualified right to change the schedule.[44]

---

39 *Alcoa Printing Plant*, 119 LA 565 (Neigh, 2004); *Standard Furniture Mfg.*, 122 LA 986 (Howell, 2006) (discussing the use of past practice in prior awards).

40 *See* Bornstein & Gosline, *supra,* at § 18.01[1].

41 *City of Burlington*, Decisions 5840, 5841, 5842, and 5843 (PECB, 1997).

42 *Sturgis Foundry Corp.*, 120 LA 609 (Allen, 2004) (providing benefit for a period of time established expectation that benefit would continue to be provided.).

43 *Chicago Meat Auth.*, 126 LA 1213 (Wolff, 2009) ("clearly established past practice that has continued over many years and successive contracts, without grievances, objections, or efforts to change it, has resulted in mutual agreement to change the CBA.").

PRINCIPLES ARBITRATORS USE IN INTERPRETING CBAs

- Determine the mutual intent of the parties
- Hidden separate intentions of each party are not controlling
- Specific language trumps general language
- If language is not ambiguous, there is no need to resort to other evidence of the parties' intent
- If language is ambiguous, arbitrators resort to other evidence indicative of intent including past practice, bargaining history, industry practices, reasons and equity

The role of "management rights." Another important issue that arises in contract interpretation is the role of management rights clauses. Management rights clauses frequently come into play when it specifies one specific area in which management has an apparent right to operate unilaterally. Management rights clauses can be used by employers to deflect a claim of past practice by the union. Employers will argue that it has retained the right by contract to make certain changes notwithstanding "past practices" to the contrary, especially where the terms of the CBA are otherwise silent on the subject.[45]

Despite the frequent claim of employers that they can do certain actions solely because of the management rights clause, the issue is often not as clear as they would like to make it. First, management rights clauses are construed *narrowly* and must be related to the *specific action* at issue. Second, and even more important, *management rights clauses are subordinate to the specific terms of the agreement.*

In other words, management rights clauses only allow employers to act where the agreement is silent and their rights to act unilaterally are express and specific. If elsewhere in the agreement a specific provision describes how a matter is to be regulated, this other provision almost invariably controls over any purported waiver language from the management rights clause.

---

[44] *National Fuel Gas Distribution Corp.*, 130 LA 513 (D'Eletto, 2012)(schedule change did not deprive workers of any pay, but simply put a half-hour unpaid lunch break in the middle of their shift, yet was still improper).

[45] *Sealy Mattress*, 121 LA 883 (Paolucci, 2005) (When strong management rights language exists, caution must be used in implying binding past practices).

Without a doubt, some of the most complicated contract interpretation issues relate to the scheduling of work.

As we discussed earlier, in Chapter 3, concerning collective bargaining rights, if your contract has become watered down through "waivers" contained in management rights clauses, an alternative negotiations strategy to removing the waivers is to blunt the management rights clause by adding specific language addressing specific working conditions.

Contract interpretation is complicated and unpredictable. In the rest of this chapter, we will delve into how arbitrators typically rule as to particular types of issues.

C. Hours of Work, Scheduling, and Overtime

Without a doubt, some of the most complicated contract interpretation issues relate to the scheduling of work. This difficulties are even greater when the schedule issues appear to constitute an "avoidance of overtime" — that is, those changes in schedule that have the direct impact of depriving the employee of overtime pay they would otherwise have earned had the schedule not changed. Another contributor to the complexity is that public safety union CBAs contain multiple, and sometimes conflicting, clauses governing the scheduling of work.

Often the subject of hours of work and scheduling is described both in the management rights clause and in the hours of work clause. Management often seeks to retain the right to unilaterally change the hours of work or the schedule. As indicated earlier, though, specific language can, and often does appear in public safety CBAs that overrides the general management rights language in a management rights clause.

employers often misunderstand the difference between the right to determine "hours of work" and the right to determine "schedules"

Hours of work v. scheduling. The most frequent source of confusion in contract administration on this issue relates to terminology, specifically the misunderstanding of what some basic terms actually means. In my experience, employers often misunderstand the difference between the right to determine "hours of work" and the right to determine "schedules." They sound like they cover the same subject, but they do not.

It is PERC's view[46] — and the view of most arbitrators[47] — that the term hours of work refers to the fundamental *length* of the work day and work week. "Hours" may or may not also relate to the starting and ending times of that work day. This point is less clear.

Regardless, the right of management to change "hours" is not interpreted by most labor relations professionals to refer to the actual assignment of employees to a specific *assignment* day to work. In one arbitration decision, for example, the arbitrator explained that the employee "adjusts his life" to the normal routine, and absent some circumstance that made a change of the *hours of work* necessary, the change did not fall under the rights of the employer to change the *work schedule.*[48]

So, for example, a provision giving management the right to set hours of work would not give management the right to unilaterally change a long-established shift bidding process, *whether or not* it was specifically itemized in the contract; bidding relates to the *scheduling* of work, *not the work hours*. Nor would such a management rights clause it allow the employer to change when someone worked on a given day.

If the employer has retained the right to change the "work schedule," it may have a broader right to change the way it assigns employees. But again, even then, if the labor agreement contains a specific shift bidding provision, this clause will override management right to change the schedule, at least as to the shift bid process.[49]

Management rights language. This situation demonstrates a more universal point that is important to keep bearing in mind regarding management rights. To the extent that the employer insists on a broad range of management rights during negotiations, the union should be aware of what it might be giving up.[50]

---

[46] *See Clark County Deputy Sheriff's Guild*, PERC NO. 11845-1-95-252 (1996) ("hours of work" refers to the length of the shift).

[47] *See, e.g., JM Mfg. Co.*, 84 LA 679 (Sisk, 1985)(holding contractual provision allowing employer to change work *schedule* did not grant employer authority to change hours of work, as that related to a mandatory subject of bargaining (wages, hours, and working conditions)).

[48] *Aro, Inc.*, 34 LA 254 (Tatum, 1960). *See also Traylor Eng'g & Mfg. Div.*, 36 LA 687 (Crawford, 1961) (holding employer could not expand workweek where contract spoke of normal, 40 hour work week).

[49] *See, e.g., Wilson & Co.*, 1 LA 342 (Lohman, 1946) (holding other contract provisions override a general management right to control the work schedule).

Sometimes a middle ground can be found between the two parties in contract negotiation that accommodate the competing interests while still blunting the effect of the management rights clause with specific contractual provisions. The better practice, though, is to extend "waivers" of bargaining rights to management, rarely, if ever. As has been discussed previously, once such rights are embedded in the contract, like a bad weed, they are hard to remove.

By extending management rights language to the employer over certain areas, the employer acquires the right to make unilateral changes in these past practices *even though they are otherwise mandatory subjects of bargaining.*

There are a myriad of past practices which the parties live by which are not likely to even be added to the labor agreement, if for no other reason that the union did not think to propose language on them until after a problem materialized. By extending management rights language to the employer over certain areas, the employer acquires the right to make unilateral changes in these past practices *even though they are otherwise mandatory subjects of bargaining.*[51]

Overtime "avoidance." Issues concerning when management can change the schedule when such a change the *result* of depriving an employee of overtime have been among the most problematic hours of work interpretation questions. The majority approach on this issue is that even if the employer retains some inherent right to reschedule employees in certain situations,that does not necessarily allow them to use their right to schedule hours of work to reschedule employees as a method of avoiding overtime payment.

---

[50] *See Voss Steel Corp.*, 123 LA 1005 (Allen, 2006) (holding generic management rights clause gave employer right to set work schedule and hours of work in an arguably harsh way, as there was no contractual provision requiring otherwise).

[51] *See, e.g.*, *Calument & Hecla*, 42 LA 25 (Howlett, 1963).

Arbitrators will almost uniformly agree with the general notion that the employer cannot change their schedules to avoid overtime. But on closer examination, it becomes clear that arbitrators have different concepts of what it means to change the schedule "to avoid overtime."

For example, in *Hudson County Bus Owners Assoc.,*[52] the arbitrator rejected the employer's change of the employees' regular day off. He stated that the employer did not have the right to assign the employees to another day off just "because it happens to need them on their usual day off." He ordered the employees to be paid overtime for working on what should have been their day off.[53] But a minority view other arbitration decisions have held that the contractual language detailing rescheduling has greater authority than that which covers overtime, and rescheduling that results in avoiding overtime is allowed.[54]

Arbitrators will almost uniformly agree with the general notion that the employer cannot change their schedules to avoid overtime. But on closer examination, it becomes clear that arbitrators have different concepts of what it means to change the schedule "to avoid overtime." As to this complex issue, the specific contract language terms (including the absence of specific terms) is going to decide such an issue. Although arbitrators frown on "overtime avoidance" scheduling techniques as a general matter, it is the specific CBA language that will control the outcome in specific situations. So it is simply not possible to project a universal rule on this complicated subject.

An easier case to predict is when an employee works an overlong shift one day and then the employer "short shifts" the individual later in that work cycle so as not to pay the overtime. This issue might arise in contracts where the accrual of overtime is on a weekly and not a daily basis. Few arbitrators would have trouble with the notion that management does not have the right

---

[52] 5 L.A. 69 (1946).

[53] *See also Kennecott Copper Corp.*, 6 L.A. 820 (Kleinsorge, 1947); *Carnegie-Illinois Steel Corp.,* 5 L.A. 403 (Bloomer, 1946); *Inland Steel Corp.*, 12 L.A. 624 (Gilden, 1949); *United Carbon Co.*, 39 L.A. 10 (Hale, 1962).

[54] *See Tribune-Star Publi'g Co.*, 95 LA 210 (Whitney, 1990) (permitting employer changing shift length to avoid overtime payment is when contract states that employer may determine shift length).

to change the schedule for this purpose because it clearly is "avoiding overtime."[55]

PRINCIPLES APPLICABLE TO SCHEDULING ISSUES

- Specific contract language trumps general management rights language
- The right to "determine schedules" and the right to "set hours of work" are different rights
- Generally, there is no right to change an employee's schedule to avoid payment of overtime

The more difficult case arises when the employer wants to change the regularly assigned schedule to place an individual on a different day in which there is a peak demand for service. The employer will simply claim that they are simply changing the schedule to address service needs. But this clearly is also a form of avoidance of overtime — the employer could simply have an employee come in and work this as an extra shift while maintaining the employees' regular schedule.

Arbitrators are divided on whether this constitutes the type of "overtime avoidance" which management does not have a right to do. In one case, the arbitrator found for the employer, when the employer changed the schedule of the employees to match the demand for the product, and then subsequently reduced or eliminated overtime the employees would have received prior to the change.[56] Further, evidence of the intent of management may be gleaned from the length of the change, and the amount of notice that is given. One arbitrator held that when the schedule change is made with a full week's notice, the purpose of management is irrelevant.[57]

Shift bidding rights. The union will have a stronger argument that this is an improper schedule change if it has a shift bidding process built into the labor agreement. Then the union would be able to argue that the employees had bid for a certain schedule during the shift bidding process, and the schedule change was at

[55] *See, e.g., Kennecott Copper Corp., supra* at 91. Here, the arbitrator noted that the intent of the management was the determinative factor. If the management has a valid reason for the change, other than the avoidance of overtime, the change may be proper. However, management's right to change the schedule does not extend so far as to change specifically to avoid the paying of overtime.

[55] *Cooper Tire & Rubber Co.*, 122 LA 1345 (Abrams, 2006).

[56] *Cooper Tire & Rubber Co.*, 122 LA 1345 (Abrams, 2006).

[57] *Wilson & Co.*, 7 LA 601 (Lohman, 1947).

variance with that process. In another example, employees were denied overtime they had bid for and would have received if the employer had not changed the schedule.[58] The employer argued the schedule change was to allow more experienced, but no more qualified, employees to work the overtime shifts. The arbitrator sustained the grievance, finding the employer's reasoning deficient.

Occasionally, questions arise concerning the shift bidding assignment process itself. Some labor agreements allow employers to exempt certain individuals from their bid for a shift based on "good cause" or other reasons. If the employer exercises their limited discretion to interrupt an individual's bidding rights, they will have to be prepared to meet their burden of proof that the contractual requirement was met.

For example, in one arbitration decision, the Sheriff's department had a shift bidding procedure in place that prioritized seniority.[59] But the department, in attempting to reschedule a worker, argued that it reserved the right to reschedule in the interest of public safety and in emergencies. While the arbitrator agreed that the employer did indeed have this right, the arbitrator rejected the employer's broad definition of what constituted "in the interest of public safety." The arbitrator found that a broad definition of this term would essentially remove any meaning from the shift bidding process, and put all scheduling at the whim of the management.[60]

In another, similar case, the police department violated the shift bidding portion of the collective bargaining agreement when it reassigned a state trooper to a different shift.[61] Here, the employer cited a portion of the agreement that allowed changes when particular skills were needed for a certain shift. However, this trooper did not possess any specialized skills or training, so the change was found invalid.

The main takeaway should be that language matters, and it particularly matters in issues concerning hours and overtime issues. Predicting the outcome in a particular case depends upon an understanding of the varied contract language, often contained in different articles, bargaining history over how that language developed, and the parties past practice under that language.

---

[58] *Lockheed Space Operations Co.*, 91 LA 457 (Richard, 1988).

[59] *Lincoln Cnty.*, 118 LA 1340 (Calhoun, 2003).

[60] *Id.*

[61] *State of Michigan*, 116 LA 69 (Sugarman, 2001).

D. Leave Benefits

1. The Scheduling and Loss of Accrued Vacation

There are two types of issues that commonly arise related to vacations. The first issue concerns the process for obtaining approval for taking a vacation. The second issue concerns the loss or forfeiture of vacation time when it is not used on a timely basis.

Rights to use vacation. The predominant view of arbitrators is that the scheduling of vacation, as a general matter, is a management right. In other words, management can deny employees the right to take vacations at particular time periods.

But these denials must be done in good faith. There must be a reason for the denial of the vacation, such as the need to maintain proper staffing to address operational needs. After all, the vacation is a bargained for benefit and *some use* of the benefit must ultimately be allowed.

If the employer denies a certain vacation request, then the employer has the "burden to substantiate denial of vacation requests as being reasonable in light of business needs."

An argument sometimes arises in this situation when the employer blocks off such a large portion of the year, or is so stingy in allowing vacation slots, that as a practical matter it is difficult for employees to obtain vacation during any of the time periods that they would enjoy the vacation's use. For example, most employees are unlikely to be unhappy if they are told that the only time left for them to take their vacation is in the third week of February.

Indeed, arbitrators have held that unjustified prohibitions on vacations during certain times of the year are generally not allowed.[62] If the employer denies a certain vacation request, then the employer has the "burden to substantiate denial of vacation requests as being reasonable in light of business needs."[63] To illustrate, arbitrators have held that an employer may deny employees vacation requests during entire seasons if the employer shows that there will be a peak demand for the employee's work at

---

62 *See Multimedia of Ohio*, 87 LA 927 (Kindig, 1986); *Supreme Life Ins. Co. of Am.*, 85 LA 997 (Cox 1985).

63 *Stanwich Indus.*, 90 LA 895,898 (Roumell, Jr., 1988).

that time.[64]

Even on this issue, arbitrators have arrived at divided results, but still largely in support of management's right to restrict vacation usage.[65] The only requirement most arbitrators have placed on this right is that there will be at least some time during the year that employees be allowed to take their vacations. To put this another way, when the contract specifies that the employees will be granted some vacation time, it is a breach of that contract for the employer to restrict the scheduling of vacationing in a way that eliminates that bargained-for benefit.[66]

Shift bidding language. Because of situations like this, many unions have found it necessary to set the employees' rights on firmer ground by placing a vacation bidding clause in the labor agreement. Some CBAs go so far as to spell out the blocks of time available or unavailable for leave and even how many slots per week.

If bidding is the practice of the parties, it is wise to put this practice into the agreement, perhaps not into great details as to all the bidding procedures, but at least enough language to contractually "anchor" bidding rights. If the management rights clause indicates that management has the right to schedule leave and there is no vacation bidding written into the contract, the management rights clause is likely to prevail should there arise a conflict on this issue. If vacation bidding is included in the labor agreement, on the other hand, these specific bidding provisions will usually prevail over more general management rights provisions.

For example, in one case, an employer had a vacation bidding system that prioritized seniority (as most do), but the employer then tried to entirely prohibit vacations during holiday weeks.[67] The arbitrator, finding that no operational necessity existed, then concluded that the absence of language unambiguously allowed the employer to restrict vacations in such a way was determinative.

---

[64] *Westinghouse Elec. Corp.*, 40 LA 972 (Cahn, 1963).

[65] *See Deere & Co.*, 82 LA 1299 (Cox, 1984) (permitting employer to prohibit vacations during certain portion of the year, and reschedule those vacations to a different time, as vacations needed to match times of lower demand for workers).

[66] *National Linen Serv.*, 110 LA 476 (Frockt, 1998) (holding employer may only restrict vacation time for specific operational need. Because need cannot be ever-present, employee will at some point be afforded their vacation). *See also Schnuck's Baking Co.*, 73 LA 813 (Erbs, 1979) (holding employer may restrict vacations when substantial business interest requires it).

[67] *Id.*

If the employer wanted that right, the arbitrator concluded, it should have bargained for it.

In another case, a similar situation arose when vacation requests were evaluated based on seniority, and the contract provided that management would accommodate those requests "whenever possible."[68] The employer argued that the "whenever possible" language allowed it to schedule vacation as it pleased. But the arbitrator found that this "whenever possible" language merely meant that the employer would honor the vacation bidding *unless there was a specific operational need*, and the seniority-based bidding rights were held to prevail.

Management cannot unduly exercise their "management right" to schedule vacation by restricting reasonable access to vacation slots and then advising the individual that the time has been forfeited.

"Forfeiture" of leave. Occasionally, questions arise concerning forfeiture of accrued vacation time. Most agreements require that only a certain amount of vacation may be accrued and that vacation beyond the cap will be lost, typically at the end of the calendar year. It is then incumbent upon the parties to come to a reasonable accommodation for the scheduling of that vacation. For example, in one case, the management argued that accrued vacation time had been forfeited, even though the employee was injured and was unable to take that vacation time. The arbitrator found that, as per the contract, unless the employee voluntarily fails to use their vacation, they cannot be denied the vacation (or compensation for unused time).[69]

Management cannot unduly exercise their "management right" to schedule vacation by restricting reasonable access to vacation slots and then advising the individual that the time has been forfeited. Some jurisdictions have found a more reasonable compromise on this issue under these circumstances, is to allow a special carryover of the accrued vacation into the next year.[70]

---

68 *Baltimore Sun Co.*, 103 LA 363 (Cushman, 1994).

69 *City of Tulsa,* 116 LA 1192 (Jennings, 2001). *See also Comcast Cable Communications,* 123 LA 1206 (Kravit, 2007) (upholding accumulation of vacation time while employees are on worker's compensation).

70 *See City of Danbury,* 96 LA 1010 (Orlando, 1991) (Contractual provision requiring city to assign vacation time to employees who do not schedule their vacation is clearly intended to avoid loss of accrued vacation. Therefore,

2. Verification of Sick Leave

Contract disputes arise from time to time concerning management's ability to demand information verifying that sick leave usage is valid. These types of questions generally get intertwined with some legal questions that are discussed in other chapters in this book, including management's right to discipline for just cause (for alleged sick leave abuse), the Americans with Disabilities Act (ADA) (which regulates compelled medical examinations and the confidentiality of medical records), and various statutes that protect employees rights to use sick leave (including the federal Family Medical Leave Act (FMLA) and the state Family Care Act (FCA)). Grievances addressing whether management can insist on medical verification in any given situation turns on the facts that are presented, the specifics of the CBA language but also the interaction of that CBA language with these other requirements.

The ADA does not allow employers to decide randomly to send people in for a medical examination to determine if they are truly sick. But this right has been upheld under the ADA where there is some indication of the possibility of abuse.

As will be discussed later, the ADA greatly limits the ability of the employer to acquire and maintain sick leave information. The ADA limits the employer to acquiring information in those situations where it fulfills a "business necessity." The ADA restricts the employer's ability to compel medical examinations, as well. And it specifies that whatever "medical information" is obtained needs to be maintained confidentially, in separate medical files.

Most CBAs typically contain provisions that allow employers to require, to some extent or another, medical verification at management's discretion. These provisions very possibly are in violation of the ADA. The ADA does not allow employers to decide randomly to send people in for a medical examination to determine if they are truly sick. But this right has been upheld under the ADA where there is some indication of the possibility of abuse.[71]

---

employee who is unable to take vacation days is entitled to three days that were not taken in the specified period).

[71] *Newton Falls Exempted Vill.*, 121 LA 345 (Lalka, 2005) (reasonable inquiries are allowed when fraud is suspected).

The other way in which sick leave verification clauses in CBAs might violate the ADA concerns sick leave reporting is in the extent of the medical report required. The ADA does not seem to permit the employer to compel employees to disclose precisely *why* they were out on sick leave. Sick leave verification forms that provide for general categories such as illness, injury, care of dependents, would pass ADA muster, but forms that required employees to report their specific illness probably do not.

The ADA does not seem to permit the employer to compel employees to disclose precisely *why* they were out on sick leave.

Moreover, even if an employer can validly collect such information, under the ADA it is required to maintain these records in segregated, confidential medical files with greatly restricted access. It is likely unlawful to maintain records such as this in the payroll clerk's bottom drawer, at least if there is any indication of a medical condition. The overriding principle of the ADA rules concerning medical records is that the employer is entitled to no more information than actually needed and any information that is acquired must be stored in securely segregated files in which individuals without a "need to know" have no access.

Arbitration decisions vary widely concerning the extent of management right's to compel verification that sick leave use has been appropriate. Most of these contracts turn on the specifics of the particular CBA.

For example in *Kitsap County,*[72] Arbitrator Dave Gaba found the County had violated the CBA when in required an officer to provide a doctor's note whenever she called out where the contract stated that a doctor's note would be required for leaves greater than 3 days. The Guild did not contest that the Deputy had many absences but cited the CBA language and the past practice of not requiring doctor's notes for leave shorter than three days. Gaba held: "The past practice of the parties would indicate that the Sheriff's department has contractually limited itself to requiring doctors certification for using sick leave to the sole situation where an employee has been on sick leave for three or more consecutive days."[73]

---

[72] 119 LA 1753 (Gaba, 2004).

[73] *Id.*

Arbitrators have also blocked employer efforts to compel verification when done for an improper reason. For example in *Federal Corrections Institution,*[74] the arbitrator disallowed an employer order to a union representative to provide on-going verification that sick leave use was legitimate, when the arbitrator concluded that the Employer's demand for substantiated sick leave was connected to the Grievant' protected activity as Union representative." But arbitrators have sometimes concluded that management had rights to compel verification even in the absence of clear CBA language or a clear past practice.[75]

3. Holidays

An issue which often arises under holidays, and is often not well enforced by labor organizations, is the application of holiday pay in an overtime situation. The general (but not uniformly understood) rule that if an employee works *overtime on a holiday,* the employee is entitled to both the holiday and the overtime pay:

> Pyramiding of holiday pay and holiday premium pay for work on the holiday should be contrasted with the payment of holiday pay and overtime pay for work on the holiday. An employee otherwise entitled to overtime compensation for work performed on the holiday should receive both overtime pay and the designated holiday pay in the absence of a provision expressly prohibiting such payment.[76]

The overwhelming weight of arbiter authority on this issue is consistent with this position.[77]

---

[74] 96 LA 60 (Murphy, 1990).

[75] *See City of Detroit*, 68 LA 848 (Roumell, 1977).

[76] Bornstein & Gosline, LABOR AND EMPLOYMENT ARBITRATION, § 34.04[3], n.17.

[77] *See, e.g., Olin Conductors*, 68-1 Arb. ¶ 8076 (Hon, 1967) (denying employer's request for offset of holiday hours paid at premium rate for overtime liability for hours worked excess of 40 in the pay period); *J-M Poultry Packing Co.*, 67-1 Arb. § 8239 (Coffey, 1967); *Northwest Protective Service, Inc.*, 65 L.A. 931 (Short, 1975); *Ellicott-Brandt, Inc.*, 62-3 Arb., ¶ 9069 (Jaffee, 1962); *Hilo Transportation & Terminal Co.*, 33 L.A. 541 (Burr, 1959); *Hawaiian Pineapple Co., Ltd.*, 30 L.A. 324 (Cobb, 1958); *Butler County Mushroom Farms, Inc.*, 30 L.A. 117 (Duff, 1958); *Transparent Package Co.*, 24 L.A. 247 (Kelliher, 1955); *California Cotton Mills*, 16 L.A. 335 (Marshall, 1951); *L.A. Jewish Community Council*, 11 L.A. 869 (Warren, 1948); *Phelps Dodge Refining Corp.*, 9 L.A. 475 (Cahn, 1948); *Hooker Chemical Corp.*, 68-1 Arb. ¶ 8291 (Russell, 1968).

The leading rationale provided in arbitration decisions for requiring payment of overtime on top of the holiday premium is known as the "dual inconvenience" theory.

In fact, arbitrators have refused to allow the employer an offset against holiday premiums paid *even where the contract contained a bar against pyramiding overtime pay.*[78] These cases reason that overtime anti-pyramiding provisions only apply to various types of overtime pay and that holiday premiums are a different type of compensation.

The leading rationale provided in arbitration decisions for requiring payment of overtime on top of the holiday premium is known as the "dual inconvenience" theory. This theory is aptly set forth in *Transparent Package Co.*:[79]

> In the absence of clear and unambiguous language setting forth an absolute exception, it must be presumed that the Parties intended the reasonable result that employees would be paid at the rate of time and one-half for hours worked beyond forty (40) hours in one week as they are in every other week except that work is performed on a holiday in said week. The policy that gave rise to the Fair Labor Standards Act is to compensate employees for the "inconvenience" of performing work beyond the normal forty (40) hours work week. This payment is a matter of legal requirement. The policy of paying an employee at a rate higher than the straight time for actual work performed on a holiday is based upon the "inconvenience" of performing work on this holiday and thus not enjoying the social and family benefits of a holiday. To follow the company's interpretation would mean realistically that the employee was not being compensated for one of these "inconveniences" simply because of the occurrence of a holiday in the week, i.e., he would either be getting straight time for actual work on the holiday or only straight time for work beyond forty (40) hours.

---

[78] *See Hawaiian Pineapple, supra,* 30 L.A. at 325-26; *L.A. Jewish Community Council, supra,* 11 L.A. at 871; *California Cotton Mills, supra,* 16 L.A. at 337; *Olin Conductors, supra,* 68-1 Arb. At ¶ 3276.

[79] *Supra,* 24 L.A. at 249.

Another arbitrator has noted that permitting an offset of the holiday premium against overtime liability would render "nugatory [irrelevant] the overtime provisions of the contract."[80]

As to the method for calculating the wages owed, it appears the general approach taken by arbitrators is to permit the adding of the two premiums. In this event, the time and one-half for overtime and holiday work would become double time, with a half-time being the premium added from each. In at least one published case, however, the arbitrator awarded a remedy that involved multiplication of the holiday premium and the overtime premium.[81]

These arbitration decision presume, though, that there is no existing past practice. A different issue arises where the holiday premium rights have not been enforced for some period and then the union seeks to obtain the dual premiums. In these situations, some arbitrators will still follow the approach that these are separate premiums and that the employer should pay for the dual inconvenience. But the majority arbitrator approach in this context is to give weight to the past practice and to order no additional compensation when it has not been paid in the past.[82]

Sometimes, the question will arise as to whether a past practice has truly been established under these circumstances. If the issue of holiday and overtime pay has come up on only a limited number of occasions, and the union representatives had no notice as to how the contract was being administered, it can be said that there simply is no past practice. In this event, most arbitrators will go back to the prevailing principle that both premiums are due.

The practice pointer here for representatives is that when they successfully negotiate for premium pay on a holiday, you should be sure to immediately follow-up on the next holiday under the new CBA to ensure that any individual who worked overtime

---

[80] *Phelps Dodge Refining Corp., supra*, 9 L.A. at 478; *see also Hawaiian Pineapple Co., supra*, 30 L.A. at 325 ("[t]he additional hours of pay given [the grievant] by the change in the language on holiday pay would be illusory").

[81] *See Phelps Dodge Refining Corp., supra*, 9 L.A. at 475.

[82] *Folgers Coffee Co.*, 124 LA 1623 (Nicholas, Jr., 2008) (holding because past practice and contract did not allow pyramiding, employer was correct in paying straight time for eight hours of what would have been overtime worked when the previous hours contained holiday pay for Thanksgiving, paid at double time); *see also City and County of Denver*, 130 LA 837 (DiFalco, 2012) (holding no CBA violation when employee worked extra two hours at end of holiday shift, and employee was paid overtime for the two hours, and holiday pay for the normal hours, and past practice indicated that the two pay rates were mutually exclusive).

received both premiums. The failure to do so may cause this available benefit to lapse. On the other hand, if your existing overtime on a holiday arrangement has not been well enforced, you may need to gather records on past situations and determine if you have a valid grievance or if this is a benefit that you need to negotiate for.

E. Wages

1. Acting Pay and Classification Pay

Questions will sometimes arise concerning whether an individual is entitled to additional pay for performing duties outside their classification. As a general matter, management has the right to assign duties which are incidental to the classification.[83] Enhancement of the duties beyond incidental duties, though, likely will produce an obligation to bargain and may invoke the obligation to pay a higher rate of pay under the contract.

As a general rule, when a material increase is made in the workload of an hourly employee, the employer will be required to increase the hourly pay rate of that employee.[84] Some agreements will require bargaining as soon as the job description is substantially changed and before a new rate of pay is determined.[85] Finally, other CBAs will give discretion to the management to set a rate of pay when a new job is created.[86] But the overriding question in such a circumstance is whether an employer is creating a new job or whether they are modifying an existing job.

A complication arises when the employee is not actually assigned the acting duties formally but is merely given the job duties without the title. In this instance, an employer typically will have one or two obligations. If the employer has reassigned only a portion of the job duties, it PERC may hold that the employer had an obligation to bargain that reassignment *before* the change. Therefore, an employer that unilaterally shifts duties incidental (other than duties) to an existing classification commits a ULP. On

---

[83] *St. Joseph Lead Co.*, 20 LA 890 (Updegraff, 1953) ("It is assumed throughout the industry that the employer has the general right to make reasonable changes from time to time in the job duties of every individual. The employer may decrease or increase the duties as long as the total work load remains in reasonable bounds."). *See also Alabama Educ. Ass'n*, 113 LA 493 (Singer, Jr., 1999) (management has right to reassign and redistribute duties.).

[84] *Arizona Chem. Co.*, 107 LA 836 (Grooms, Jr., 1996).

[85] *Virginia-Carolina Chem. Corp.*, 23 LA 228 (Marshall, 1954).

[86] *Peerless Wire Goods Co.*, 49 LA 202 (Lewis, 1967).

the other hand, PERC's case law regarding assignment of new duties is not clear or consistent.

if a lower-paid employee is assigned the "core-duties" of a higher-paid employee, then the lower-paid employee is likely entitled to a higher rate of pay

Arbitration cases generally hold that any major change to job duties that "alters the basic characteristics of what employees are required to do," will require a wage adjustment.[87] Therefore, if a lower-paid employee is assigned the "core-duties" of a higher-paid employee, then the lower-paid employee is likely entitled to a higher rate of pay.[88]

This result is even more likely when the employer simply assigns the duties of an entire classification to an employee. In these situations it is clear that the employee is entitled to the pay for that classification. But an exception may exist where the parties have agreed on a contractual arrangement permitting limited acting pay assignments without additional pay. It is common in labor agreements, for example, to establish a threshold upon which the acting pay requirement will kick in. Under these conditions, the terms of the labor agreement will control.

The obligation to either reach an agreement or pay for out-of-class work applies as well when the work is outside the bargaining unit. Management does not have the inherent right to force employees to do the work, for example, of a captain, for a sergeant's wage.[89] In such a case, where the jobs are classified by titles, only work that is incidental to the regular duties of the designated classification may be assigned to the employee.[90] For example, only duties normally assigned to a sergeant may be assigned to sergeants; if a captain's duties are assigned as well, the reassignment will likely be improper.[91] Ultimately, though, the

---

87 *Tone Bros.*, 116 LA 1678 (Berger, 2002) (finding significant change when 6 to 8 hours of the workweek were affected).

88 *GTE Sw.*, 117 LA 292 (Schieber, 2002) (employee did not have training to perform higher paying job, but was nonetheless required to be paid a higher amount).

89 *See Kraft Foods, N.A.*, 121 LA 673 (Abrams, 2005) (any change in work that is significant requires the pay rate to be reevaluated.).

90 For example, see *City of Madison Heights*, 119 LA 390 (Sugerman, 2003), where the arbitrator found that assigning an EMT the task of administering flu shots to co-workers unreasonable, even when the EMT would be forced to administer shots in the course of treating patients.

union has the burden of proving that the reassignment of duties violates the contract.[92]

---

it is important for union representatives to monitor the assignment of duties

---

A union can waive these rights by nonenforcement of its practices. If an employer assigns extra duties to individuals without additional compensation and there is no objection, that likely will become the new past practice.[93] Therefore, it is important for union representatives to monitor the assignment of duties. And these issues often become inherently intertwined with obligations under PECBA to negotiate changes in job duties or skimming of bargaining unit work. Often different bargaining units can become allies in efforts to block such reassignments.

The more common problem is where there is a creeping redefinition of the classification and the duties are added incrementally over time. If the union is not careful, a number of small, incremental changes, over time, will lead to more significant changes that may effectively create a modification in the classification.[94] If the union has been lax in enforcing its rights to negotiate these types of changes, it will need to be addressed as a compensation issue at the collective bargaining table.

2. Retroactivity

As indicated earlier, there is a presumption that economic terms, including wages, are retroactive.[95] Unless retroactivity has been specifically waived in a labor agreement, the employer owes direct payment to the employees retroactive to the beginning of the labor agreement. The requirement to pay for that retroactivity extends, as well, to overtime.[96]

3. Overpayment

On occasion, a problem arises where the payroll department

---

[91] *American Zinc Co.*, 18 LA 827 (Updegraff, 1952).

[92] *V.T. Griffin Serv.*, 119 LA 1045 (Robinson, 2004).

[93] *See Southern Local Sch. Dist.*, 118 LA 314 (Murphy, 2003) (finding acceptable expansion of school custodian's duties to assign them to clean boiler room because that assignment had been given informally in the past without objection).

[94] *See Board of Educ., Twp High Sch. Dist. 211*, 118 LA 867 (Nathan, 2003).

[95] *Barclay v. City of Spokane*, 83 Wn.2d 698, 700, 521 P.2d 937 (1974).

[96] 29 CFR §778.106.

has miscalculated someone's pay in the employee's favor and then a demand for a refund is made. This obviously is a delicate situation. The employee is usually not entitled to keep wages that they were not supposed to receive under the labor agreement. If an inadvertent overpayment has been made, an arrangement will need to be entered to make the repayment.

Regardless of whether the claim of "overpayment" is valid or not, management will not be able to act unilaterally to deduct the overpayment out of wages.

But in the case of an intentional overpayment, the results can vary. In one case, an employee was paid more than was specified in the CBA for his classification. Here, the arbitrator found that the employer was in effect undermining the authority of the CBA, which stated that the employer "shall" pay the employee a set wage.[97] The union, not wanting to reduce the wage of the employee allegedly overpaid, argued that because the CBA had a uniform wage requirement for all employees of a certain classification, all employees should be paid the "overpayment" wage. The arbitrator agreed, finding the "overpayment" wage established a new base wage for the classification.[98]

Regardless of whether the claim of "overpayment" is valid or not, management will not be able to act unilaterally to deduct the overpayment out of wages. The State Wage and Hour Law makes it unlawful for employers to make deductions from paychecks that are not authorized. If the employee does not agree to a repayment schedule, the employer's only resort is to bring a civil claim.[99] State law also permits (and requires) employers to pursue such claims under the CBA grievance clause if, for example, a dispute exists that turns on the wording of the contract.[100]

If the employee truly owes the employer the money and an accommodation of both interests need to be made. Fortunately, the state wage law protects the employee. It restricts efforts to collect by limiting the repayment schedule to no more than five percent of the debt per paycheck.[101]

---

[97] *Interstate Brands Corp.*, 114 LA 334, 335 (Paolucci, 2000).
[98] *Id.*
[99] RCW 49.48.200.
[100] RCW 49.48.210.
[101] RCW 49.48.200.

4. Satisfactory Performance

Occasionally, labor agreements contain a requirement that for the employee to attain either longevity or a wage step increase, they must have "satisfactorily performed" the requirements of the job. Even where labor agreements contain such provisions, employers rarely seem to aggressively enforce these clauses.

The other potential pitfall for employers in this situation is the obligation to provide a *Loudermill* hearing.

The practical reason for that is, most employers would have a difficult time winning on a satisfactory performance claim absent thorough documentation. In order to show that the employee was not performing, the question would arise as to why the employer had not already engaged in some type of discipline. Since it is likely just as easy to establish just cause for discipline then to deny an employee a step increase, the traditional disciplinary system is more commonly used to address performance problems.

The other potential pitfall for employers in this situation is the obligation to provide a *Loudermill* hearing. Employees being denied a pay step are entitled to due process. In *City of Omaha and Nebraska Public Employees, AFSCME,*[102] the grievant was arguing that he was entitled to a wage increase as called for in the CBA. The employer argued he was not entitled to the merit increase because of alleged excessive use of sick leave. However, no notice was given to the employee warning him of the jeopardy of his merit increase, and no merit increases had been denied on these grounds in the past. The arbitrator ordered the grievant advanced one step in pay based on the reasoning that:

> The City, as a governmental employer, owes constitutional due process to its employees in matters affecting their pay...A governmental employer 'may not constitutionally authorize the deprivation of...and [public employment property] interest, once conferred, without appropriate procedural safeguards.'[103]
> Here, no prior notice was given to the employee....F*or that reason and for no other*, Grievant must be granted the merit pay increase.[104]

---

102 98 LA 931 (1992).

103 *Cleveland Board of Education v. Loudermill*, 470 U.S. 532 (1985).

104 *City of Omaha*, 98 LA at 938 (emphasis added).

F. Transfers and Assignments

As indicated previously, if an employee is transferred for the purpose of discipline, this will be subject to the just cause requirement of the contract. Often, an employer will not be able to establish that they have just cause for the transfer, either because there was not a sufficient basis to warrant a transfer or they failed to fulfill a necessary procedural requirement.

Then there are some confusing situations sitting between a pure operational transfer and a clear act of discipline.

But often there are many other operational reasons why employers would seek to transfer or reassign an employee that do not involve discipline. Just as in the case of hours of work, there is a great deal of confusion among arbitrators about how extensive the right to make "operational" transfers is. Most arbitrators, though, will acknowledge that the employee has the right to transfer between positions unless it is restricted by some other provision in the labor agreement, such as the just cause provision or a position bidding clause.

Then there are some confusing situations sitting between a pure operational transfer and a clear act of discipline. Sometimes, a transfer is warranted not as a disciplinary measure, but simply because the employee is unable to perform the job. Arbitrators usually do not deem this to be a form of discipline subject to the just cause requirement. Most arbitrators have held that if the employee is not capable of performing the job, management has the right to transfer them.[105]

G. Off-Duty Employment

Often, labor agreements will contain a provision establishing the process for approving off-duty employment. Often, these agreements will set forth the factors that management has to follow in approving or disapproving off-duty employment. Unless the contract gives management the specific authority to deny off-duty employment at their discretion, they will normally be bound to

---

[105] *Carnegie-Illinois Steel Corp.*, 17 LA 328 (Morgan, 1951) (transfer approved to protect safety); *Machine Products Co. Inc.*, 26 LA 245 (Hawley, 1956) (employer cannot use demotion for the purpose of vitiating other provisions of the agreement, but has the right to transfer to ensure efficiency and competence); *Ataco Steel Products Corp.*, 86 LA 470 (Grenig, 1986) (management has the right to expect reasonable standards of performance).

follow the factors set forth in the off-duty employment provision.

there is no constitutional right for public employees to engage in off-duty employment. But management power to restrict off-duty work is still controlled by collective bargaining requirements

As a general rule, absent some rule to the contrary, employees are permitted to have other employment outside their regular hours of work.[106] As discussed later in Chapter 9, there is no constitutional right for public employees to engage in off-duty employment. But management power to restrict off-duty work is still controlled by collective bargaining requirements.

Even if management has discretion to deny the off-duty permit, most arbitrators will hold that they cannot do this for arbitrary reasons.[107] This is an extension of the established principle that CBAs contain an implied condition of "good faith". Under this principle, even if management has the right to take an action, it may only do so where it operates in good faith and may not exercise its management rights arbitrarily.

H. Residency Requirements

Occasionally, contracts have residency requirements. Often, these requirements include a mandate that an employee live within "x" miles of the department. These types of agreements are not necessarily unlawful, except, as discussed later, it is a requirement that a municipal police officer or firefighter resides *within* a jurisdiction's boundaries. Those types of residency restrictions violate state civil service laws. To put it another way, city firefighters and cops cannot be compelled to reside within a city's boundaries, but agencies may lawfully create residency distance standards beyond those municipal boundaries — subject to the duty to bargain.

---

106 *Janitorial Serv.*, 33 LA 902 (Whelan, 1959).

107 *See Safeway Stores*, 49 LA 400 (Caraway, 1967) (Employee's hours were suffering); *Jacksonville Shipyards*, 74 LA 1066 (Taylor, 1980) (conflict of interest); *Cincinnati Tool Co.*, 52 LA 818 (Kates, 1969) (primary employer otherwise adversely affected).

A more common question that has arisen concerns what "residency" means.

When the employer does have a valid and lawfully adopted residency rule, questions can still arise concerning the interpretation of the rule. For example, one rule had a requirement that employees live a certain mileage distance from their police department. The employer attempted to implement the rule using a "driving distance" method.[108] The union argued that this could not be implemented fairly, and, therefore, the distance should be measured as a radius. In this case, the arbitrator sided with the union, although there was no contract language that indicated one way or the other. This arbitrator had concluded that fairness would not allow the driving distance method, but other arbitrators might take a different approach.

A more common question that has arisen concerns what "residency" means. Many courts and arbitrators who have looked at this issue have given the benefit of the doubt to employees and have found a distinction between the terms "residency" and "domicile." "Domicile" is the person's primary location, where they reside with their family. Sometimes employees will attempt to sidestep the residency requirement by setting up a second residence within the required area. There is strong legal authority for the proposition that someone can have more than one residency.

A clear example occurred in *City of Warren*,[109] where the firefighter had a residence outside the prescribed area, where his wife and children lived, and one inside the area, which he commuted from on weekdays. Here, the arbitrator found that modern living situations can clearly lead to multiple residences, and, therefore, the employer lacked just cause for the discharge.

In another case, a firefighter did not even own or rent a residence in the prescribed area, but argued that he was sleeping in his sister's basement rent free.[110] Even though the employee in question did, in fact, own a house outside the prescribed area with his estranged wife, there was no proof that he actually lived or spent any time at that house, and the discharge was overturned. Further, testimony indicated that the employee did in fact sleep at

---

[108] *City of Robinson*, 118 LA 1276 (Suntrup, 2003).
[109] 118 LA 129 (Duff, 2003).
[110] *City of Cicero*, 115 LA 740 (Nathan, 2001).

the sister's house. Thus, residency requirements do not even require a title or lease to a residence in the prescribed location, but simply that the employee sleep at least some of the time in that area.

Therefore, sometimes these attempts to circumvent the residency requirement are often successful. Since these rules can have a harsh impact on the private lives of employees, arbitrators tend to give the "benefit of the doubt" in these situations to the employee. It is then incumbent on the employer to negotiate newer, clearer rules concerning residency if it wishes to maintain strict residency rules. As indicated, such changes, as identified in Chapter 3, are subject to the duty to bargain under the collective bargaining law.

I. Reserves and Volunteers

It is most advisable under these circumstances to develop a negotiated set of rules that clearly defines what the permitted scope is for reserve/volunteer work. If there are no written guidelines, it will be easy for there to be a "creeping" skimming of the bargaining unit's work.

The presence of reserves and volunteers in the workforce presents a thorny problem for unions. Where there are no reserves doing work and the employer wishes to introduce them, it is clear that there is an obligation to bargain.[111] But once this occurs, there is a continual problem in enforcing the parameters of the bargaining unit work. In most cases when work is transferred out of the bargaining unit, including to volunteer or reserve employees, there is a duty to bargain.[112] Otherwise, impermissible skimming occurs.[113]

It is most advisable under these circumstances to develop a negotiated set of rules that clearly defines what the permitted scope is for reserve/volunteer work. If there are no written

[111] *Spokane Cnty. Fire Dist. 9*, Decision 3012-A (PECB, 1990) (holding employer has mandatory duty to give notice to exclusive bargaining representative of its employees prior to any transfer of bargaining unit work to employees outside of bargaining unit; employer is then obligated to bargain such matters upon request).

[112] *Kitsap County Fire District 7*, Decision 7064-A (PECB, 2001).

[113] *Id.*

guidelines, it will be easy for there to be a "creeping" skimming of the bargaining unit's work. When reserves or volunteers continue to encroach on the bargaining unit work, that encroachment will then become the new past practice, and that work will be lost as to belonging to the bargaining unit.

J. Union Release Time

Open-ended release time clauses that allow work for any and all union activities without parameters are likely to run afoul of PERC's prohibition of the employer's support of the union.

Labor agreements contain a variety of clauses permitting union representatives release time for union-related functions. There is a question under existing PERC law as to the permissible scope of such clauses. The prevailing view in PERC is that these clauses are lawful as long as they allow release time for work related to the collective bargaining process. PERC has moved to restrict the scope of such activities, in one Yakima County case claiming that release time for union board meetings was not a mandatory subject of bargaining. The Court of Appeals rejected PERC's conclusion, agreeing with the Guild that such release time was in further of the union's "duty of fair representation."[114] The court, though, agreed with PERC's assessment that release time for training and attendance at state law enforcement meetings fell outside the scope of bargaining.[115]

[114] *Yakima County v. Yakima County Law Enforcement Officer's Guild*, 174 Wn.App. 171, 297 P.2d 745 (2013).
[115] *Id.*

what the union sought was limited and that the training at the seminar directly related to the types of collective bargaining issues that release time had been agreed to. The arbitrator also noted the city's admission that having well-trained union representatives was in the interests of the city.

In another arbitration decision, the arbitrator generously held that paid "reasonable release time" for training also included pay for travel time to and from the training. Even though the CBA stated that the paid release time was for training (and not travel), the arbitrator concluded that as the travel was necessary for the training, it should also be compensated.

A similar decision held that when the employees are given paid time for union business, the employer does not get to restrict what constitutes union business when those restrictions are not discussed in the CBA.

Here, the employer did not way to pay leave time for an annual union "party" where official union business was being conducted. The arbitrator found that as it was normal union business, it clearly fell within the scope of the CBA clause.

But where the CBA does specifically enumerate what union business will be granted paid release time, the employer will be allowed to deny release time for union business that falls outside those enumerated tasks, even though it might appear legitimate.

Open-ended release time clauses that allow work for any and all union activities without parameters are likely to run afoul of PERC's prohibition of the employer's support of the union. A question arose, for example, off of a union law firm seminar that a local police union representative attended for training. Their CBA allowed "reasonable release time" for union activities. The arbitrator upheld the union's grievance that it was improper for the employer to deny permission to attend the seminar. The police chief had contended that he did not want to pay for the representative's training.

The arbitrator rejected the city's contention that the union's interpretation would run afoul of PERC's prohibition on employer support of unions. First, the arbitrator pointed out that that was an issue for the city to raise with PERC, not the arbitrator. Second, the arbitrator noted that the scope of what the union sought was limited and that the training at the seminar directly related to the types of collective bargaining issues that release time had been agreed to. The arbitrator also noted the city's admission that having well-trained union representatives was in the interests of the city.

In another arbitration decision, the arbitrator generously held that paid "reasonable release time" for training also included pay for travel time to and from the training.[116] Even though the CBA stated that the paid release time was for training (and not travel), the arbitrator concluded that as the travel was necessary for the training, it should also be compensated.[117]

A similar decision held that when the employees are given paid time for union business, the employer does not get to restrict what constitutes union business when those restrictions are not discussed in the CBA.[118] Here, the employer did not way to pay leave time for an annual union "party" where official union business was being conducted. The arbitrator found that as it was normal union business, it clearly fell within the scope of the CBA clause.

But where the CBA does specifically enumerate what union business will be granted paid release time, the employer will be allowed to deny release time for union business that falls outside those enumerated tasks, even though it might appear legitimate. For example, in *City of Sandusky*, the arbitrator held that the employer was correct in denying paid leave for the union representative when that representative attended workers compensation hearings.[119] The CBA, which specifically enumerated situations in which the employees would be granted paid leave, did

---

[116] *Univ. of California*, 122 LA 532 (Bogue, 2006).
[117] *Id.*
[118] *City of Sonoma*, 113 LA 429 (Bogue, 1999).
[119] 98 LA 519 (McDonald, 1992).

not mention workers compensation hearings. Therefore, the union representative, while they could not be disallowed from attending the meetings, would not do so on paid release time.

CONTRACT INTERPRETATION TABLE

This chart lists what actions have been determined to violate CBAs. It is limited to arbitrators who regularly appear in arbitrations in the Pacific Northwest. It includes arbitration decisions in Washington, Oregon, Alaska and Montana but also decisions rendered by Northwest arbitrators concerning agencies in other states.

BENEFITS

Citation: *Deschutes County*, 104 LA 18 (Downing, 1994)

Issue: Health Insurance For Retired Employees

Holding: The arbitrator held that the Employer did not violate the CBA when it failed to contribute toward the costs of medical insurance premiums for retired deputies.

Explanation: The arbitrator noted that the CBA was silent regarding benefits for retirees. The arbitrator stated that employees were allowed to purchase health insurance coverage through their Employer upon retirement but it was not practice of the Employer to contribute towards the cost of medical insurance premiums for retired employees and therefore the CBA's "Existing Conditions" provision was inapplicable.

Citation: *City of Centralia*, 114 LA 929 (Smith, 2000)

Issue: Tuition Reimbursement

Holding: No CBA violation where employer denied officers' requests for tuition reimbursement.

Explanation: The arbitrator noted the Employer's $440,000 budget shortfall and held that "the [E]mployer had a clear and present ability to suspend the educational reimbursements to police officers for college-level classes" under a contractual waiver, not management rights, theory. "The Arbitrator is . . . persuaded that [the CBA] permitted the employer to deny reimbursement of college tuitions when reasonable and necessary, and in the interests of budget economy."

Citation: *State of Oregon*, 107 LA 138 (Downing, 1996)

Issue: Tuition Reimbursement

Holding: The arbitrator held that the Employer did not violate the CBA with the police officers when it denied tuition reimbursement to an officer.

Explanation: The arbitrator noted that the tuition reimbursement program described in the CBA contained the following features: "1) the subject matter of courses must be reasonably job related . . . ." The arbitrator found that the Employer did not violate the CBA when it failed to reimburse the office for coursework in management because the Employer did not interpret the course work as being directly related to the current job of the police officer.

CONDITIONS OF EMPLOYMENT

Citation: *Klamath Falls Fire Dist.*, 106 LA 789 (Buchanan, 1996)

Issue: Physical Fitness Standards

Holding: The arbitrator held that the Employer violated the CBA with the firefighters when it unilaterally implemented a physical performance test.

Explanation: The arbitrator agreed with the Union that "inclusion of some specific guarantees…in a contract works to exclude those items not listed. In effect that by specifically listing the tests to be used…and failing to include a physical test, the District is precluded from using such tests for the duration of the contract."

Citation: *Town of Ossining*, 114 LA 1761 (Henner, 2000)

Issue: Working Conditions and Work Rules

Holding: No CBA violation when employer required an officer to wear formal clothes.

Explanation: The arbitrator held, "I am unable to conclude that prohibiting casual shirts, running shoes or windbreaker jackets is the kind of imposition of a dress code which must be negotiated." Furthermore, employees were still granted a lot of leeway and the change was ok'd by the Union.

HOURS

Citation: *City of Portland*, 115 LA 164 (Pool, 2000)

Issue: Standby Time or Callback

Holding: Employer did not violate CBA when it assigned employees after-hours call triaging responsibilities.

Explanation: The arbitrator first emphasized that the triaging system was not an "on-call" system, and then determined that the CBA's "Management Rights [provision] clearly sets forth the City's right, absent expressed prohibitions in the CBA or an established past practice, to mandate that supervisory sergeants be included in the rotating after-hours call triaging schedule."

Citation: *Municipality of Anchorage*, 131 LA 1577 (Landau, 2013)

Issue: Shift Schedule

Holding: Employer violated CBA when it unilaterally ended the compressed work schedule.

Explanation: Alaska law requires collective bargaining over "wages, hours and other terms and conditions of employment." The change of working hours was clearly something that should be bargained over. The arbitrator noted the while the parties never bargained over the compressed shifts, they had been used for 10 years which was enough to create a binding past practice.

Citation: *City of Sunnyside*, 123 LA 1217 (Boedecker, 2007)

Issue: Work Schedules

Holding: The arbitrator held that the Employer did not violate the CBA with the firefighters when it unilaterally changed their work schedules because of the plain meaning of the CBA which empowered management to make the changes.

Explanation: The arbitrator found that the plain meaning of the CBA was that the Fire Chief, who is part of management, had the authority to unilaterally change the work schedule. The arbitrator also found that past practice was irrelevant because the language of the CBA was unambiguous.

Citation: *Washington Dep't of Fish and Wildlife*, 123 LA 413 (Henner, 2006)

Issue: Work Schedules

Holding: The arbitrator held that the Employer did not violate the CBA with the Fish and Wildlife employees when it denied the Grievant's request for a different work schedule.

Explanation: The arbitrator found that the CBA's Management Rights clause "specifically retains all rights of management, including establishing or modifying hours and days of work." The arbitrator held that "[t]aking the record as a whole, I find that nothing has been presented that would require me to overrule management's exercise of its discretion in making its determination . . . [that would necessitate] adoption of an alternate workday schedule . . . "

Citation: *City of Fairbanks*, 121 LA 1530 (Coyle, 2005)

Issue: Shift Schedule

Holding: Employer violated CBA when it assigned less senior employee to a shift without first asking for more senior volunteers.

Explanation: The arbitrator emphasized that the CBA explicitly required that "[w]hen a Shift change is necessary, the Fire Chief will *first* ask for qualified volunteers to agree to a change. If more than one Member volunteers, the senior Member shall be transferred."

Citation: *Lincoln County*, 118 LA 1340 (Calhoun, 2003)

Issue: Shift Schedule

Holding: Employer violated CBA when it assigned an employee to a shift not based on seniority.

Explanation: The arbitrator found that the CBA was ambiguous, but that there was no binding past practice of assigning shifts outside of the bidding system. Finally, "The public safety exception to shift bidding by seniority does not allow the Department to exercise unfettered discretion in creating and filling an administrative shift."

Citation: *City of Kalama*, 116 LA 1349 (Henner, 2002)

Issue: Shift Schedule

Holding: Employer violated CBA when it failed to include shifts which were vacant because employees are sick or in training in the vacant shifts it was required to offer to union members as overtime.

Explanation: The CBA describes vacant shifts by saying "regularly scheduled work shift becomes vacant"—the arbitrator determined this phrasing did not limit it to scheduled vacant shifts but also included shifts that were left vacant by sick leave or training. The arbitrator also found nothing in the CBA what would permit employer to not offer shifts to union members it assumed would be unlikely to accept.

Citation: *Town of Ossining*, 114 LA 1761 (Henner, 2000)

Issue: Shift Schedule

Holding: Employer did not violate CBA when it changed employee's schedule with the Union's permission.

Explanation: The arbitrator noted the Employer presented evidence that it consulted with the Union about the shift change, and "[t]he Grievant has offered no testimony or evidence in refutation [that] testimony."

Citation: *City of Helena*, 99 LA 1090 (Calhoun, 1992)

Issue: Shift Schedule

Holding: Employer violated CBA when it gave regular extra shifts to non-Union employee.

Explanation: The CBA required extra shifts to be "filled by combat firefighters assigned to the Fire Prevention Bureau." The arbitrator determined that although this "does not expressly prohibit the assignment of regular extra shifts to non-bargaining unit employees, when read in conjunction with other provisions of the agreement … the integrity of the contract can only be upheld by interpreting the agreement to mean bargaining unit work, more specifically regular extra shifts, cannot be assigned to non-bargaining unit individuals unless there are justifying circumstances."

JOB SECURITY

Citation: *Island County*, 127 LA 1153 (Boedecker, 2010)

Issue: Seniority Protection

Holding: The arbitrator held that the Employer did not violate the CBA when it laid off a deputy prosecuting attorney who had accepted her position before a second deputy prosecuting attorney did. However, the arbitrator found that the CBA calculated seniority as the "date of hire" which meant the first day of work and therefore since the second deputy prosecuting attorney started before the grievant, the layoff was proper.

Explanation: The arbitrator noted that the CBA specified that layoffs were based off an individual's seniority. The CBA stated that seniority was determined by "date of hire." The arbitrator first look at the relevant contract provision and determined that "'date of hire' is the date on which an employee starts work." So the date which an employee accepts a job is not relevant in this circumstance.

Citation: *Port of Portland*, 126 LA 833 (Reeves, 2009)

Issue: Subcontracting

Holding: The arbitrator held that the Employer did not violate the CBA with the Port of Portland security officers when it contracted with a private company to conduct river patrols. The arbitrator found that CBA section 4.01, when read in context of the contract, cannot extend the Union's jurisdiction beyond property owned and managed by the Port.

Explanation: The arbitrator stated that a CBA is "not an ordinary commercial bargain but 'an effort to erect a system of industrial self-government." The arbitrator stated that to ascertain the intent of the parties he would look at (1) purpose of a particular provision; (2) give reasonable meaning to contract terms; and (3) avoid interpreting contractual terms in isolation of the whole agreement.

Citation: *Municipality of Anchorage*, 115 LA 190 (Landau, 2000)

Issue: Subcontracting

Holding: The arbitrator held that the Employer did not violate the CBA with firefighters when it allowed a private ambulance service to transport non-emergency patients because it was legitimate to make ambulances available for actual emergencies.

Explanation: "The arbitrator is limited to determining whether the . . . [Employer's] decision was within its reasonable range of discretion, was not arbitrary or capricious, and was not motivated by anti-Union animus . . . "The arbitrator held that the Employer had a legitimate justification which was to make ambulances more available for emergency calls.

Citation: *Port of Seattle*, 110 LA 753 (Skratek, 1998)

Issue: Subcontracting

Holding: The arbitrator held that the Employer violated the CBA with Port of Seattle police officers when it subcontracted the Research and Development police officer (R&D) position. The arbitrator found that the R&D position was to be negotiated with the Union under the CBA and it was the past practice of the Employer to fill the R&D position with police officers.

Explanation: The arbitrator noted that she could not find a specific restriction against contracting out positions within the CBA but that the contract was limited by the recognition clause which covered police officers. In addition, the arbitrator noted past practice (i.e., for the last two decades), was to fill the R&D position with police officers.

LEAVE

Citation: *Municipality of Anchorage*, 131 LA 84 (Daly, 2012)

Issue: Sick Leave

Holding: The city violated the CBA when it charged an officer 35 hours of comp time rather than 16 hours of comp time and 17 hours of Sick leave. Where the CBA provides that compensatory time must be exhausted before an employee can use "paid leave" and that sick leave can be used on the 3rd day of any illness.

Explanation: The arbitrator found the CBA clearly stated " (comp time must be exhausted before paid leave) to address paid vacation leave and not to address any other kind of paid leave...the mutual intent and purpose was to apply the language to mean "annual/vacation leave" not sick leave...the municipality in good faith misinterpreted the meaning of the words."

Citation: *City of Napavine*, 128 LA 1134 (Romeo, 2011)

Issue: Sick Leave

Holding: The arbitrator held that City's policy under the CBA that required police employees who had used all accumulated sick leave to seek approval prior to receiving approval for more time off was reasonable and a typical policy of most businesses.

Explanation: The arbitrator noted that Policy 7.3 stated that employees who use all their accumulated sick leave must receive prior approval from the Mayor to take further leave without pay. The arbitrator stated that this mandate was "a typical policy or requirement seen in the course of business of most employers . . . [and] was] reasonably to the efficient and safe operation of the employer's business and performance . . . "

Citation: *Kitsap County*, 119 LA 1753 (Gaba, 2004)

Issue: Sick Leave

Holding: The county violated the CBA when it required an officer, who was frequently sick, to provide a doctor's note whenever she called out, where the contract stated that a doctors not would be required for leaves greater than 3 days, and where the county had a past practice of not requiring doctors notes for leave shorter than 3 days.

Explanation: While the CBA was ambiguous, "the past practice of the parties would indicate that the Sheriff's department has contractually limited itself to requiring doctor's certification for using sick leave to the sole situation where an employee has been on sick leave for three or more consecutive days."

Citation: *City of Moses Lake*, 114 LA 744 (Smith, 2000)

Issue: Sick Leave/Paternity

Holding: The City violated the CBA when they denied officer the use of paid sick leave during his wife's pregnancy , even though FMLA did not cover this, the city's past practice had been to grant such requests, thus they were bound by this past practice.

Explanation: "even in August of 1998 after this controversy began to churn, the chief appeared to conceded that sick leave was available…Thus, the arbitrator concludes that the employer changed its policy after the officer relied upon the representations that he would be eligible to use his accumulated sick leave…the grant of sick leave must be interpreted in the context of the MAC and past practices."

Citation: *City of Fairbanks*, 121 LA 693 (Landau, 2005)

Issue: Light Duty; Shift Schedule

Holding: Employer violated CBA when it assigned injured, light-duty employees to a different shift schedule.

Explanation: The arbitrator reasoned that a CBA provision "establishes a general requirement that a fire suppression employee's hours of work may not be changed without the consent of the employee or the Association. The last sentence of [another provision] creates an exception from this requirement for 'light duty which is addressed in Article 8, Section 7.' However, the title of Article 8.7 makes clear that its scope is limited to "Non-work Related Injury or Illness." The arbitrator reasoned that this excluded work-related injuries, such as the grievants'.

Citation: *Federal Bureau of Prisons*, 127 LA 852 (Henner, 2010)

Issue: Annual Leave/Vacation

Holding: Employer did not violate CBA when it reduced the number of employees who could take concurrent leave.

Explanation: The arbitrator reasoned the number of scheduled leave slots was solely in the employer's discretion because the CBA stated "the Employer will determine the maximum number of employees that may be on scheduled annual leave."

Citation: *Port of Portland*, 118 LA 83 (Reeves, 2002)

Issue: Holidays

Holding: The arbitrator held that the Employer violated the CBA with the police officers when it ordered detectives to take a holiday off.

Explanation: The arbitrator found that the CBA was clear that "[e]ach member of the Union employed prior to any of the above stated holidays will be credited with one (1) compensatory day off in lieu of the holiday." The arbitrator found that the Parties' use of the words "each" and "will" in CBA indicate that the Employer did not have discretion to order the detectives to take the holiday off. Since there was clear contractual language the management's rights clause was trumped.

Citation: *City of Duncan*, 106 LA 398 (Cipolla, 1996)

Issue: Annual Leave/Vacation

Holding: The employer did not violate the CBA when it did not permit employees to carry forward more than 520 hours of accumulated leave.

Explanation: The arbitrator noted that the CBA explicitly stated "[v]acation may be carried forward with a maximum of five hundred twenty (520) hours (21 2/3 shifts) throughout the year." The arbitrator found this clearly meant "capped at 520 hours [and not] 520 hours plus the number of hour accumulated in the previous year."

Citation: *Lewis County*, 107 LA 321 (Stuteville, 1996)

Issue: Annual Leave/Vacation

Holding: Employer did not violate CBA when it denied employee's vacation requests when no other employees had scheduled that day off.

Explanation: The CBA stated, "Not more than one (1) employee per squad shall be allowed to be on vacation at the same time. Exceptions to this policy may be granted ..." The arbitrator reasoned "exceptions could be made in either direction," so the employer was free to deny the vacation requests due to operational requirements. The arbitrator emphasized the importance of operational requirements in the instant case because the employer was a jail requiring 24-hour staffing.

Citation: *Municipality of Anchorage*, 131 LA 84 (Daly, 2012)

Issue: Leaves of Absences

Holding: The arbitrator held that the employer violated the CBA when it required an employee to exhaust all compensatory leave before she could use her sick leave.

Explanation: The CBA stated, "An employee's compensatory time off must be exhausted before the employee may use paid leave," but the arbitrator interpreted this to mean "paid vacation leave" because of the intent of the parties, and because to read it to mean all other types of leave would virtually eliminate those leaves.

Citation: *City of Moses Lake*, 114 LA 744 (Smith, 2000)

Issue: Family Leave

Holding: Employer violated CBA when it denied paid sick leave to employee whose wife was on maternity leave.

Explanation: The arbitrator reasoned that the employer's past practice was to allow sick leave to be used for family leave, and the relevant municipal code allowed the practice.

PROMOTIONS & ASSIGNMENTS

Citation: *City of Richland*, 111 LA 872 (ZaneLumbley, 1998)

Issue: Promotion Procedure

Holding: The City did not violate the CBA when it passed over the higher ranking firefighter because they gave reasons and the CBA only required that city give "for informational reasons…valid reasons for not being selected."

Explanation: "I believe the answer lies in according less weight than ordinarily might be given the world 'valid' because of the continuing presence of the words "for informational purposes only" In effect the presence of each requires a reduction of weight given to the other…Accordingly, I am of the view that if the reasons given by the Chief for bypassing the Grievant are found to be lacking in arbitrariness or caprice…they will be considered valid."

UNIFORM & EQUIPMENT

Citation: *Klickitat County*, 109 LA 4 (Bradburn, 1997)

Issue: Cleaning Allowance; Wages

Holding: The County violated the CBA when it refused to give a cleaning allowance to plain clothes deputy where the contract stated that the allowance apples to each deputy.

Explanation: "The parties have approached this grievance as if only the first sentence of the section applied to it, and have given me no basis to do anything else. That sentence states the employer shall give each deputy a cleaning allowance of $15 each winter month. Bond is a deputy; October, November, and December are winter months; therefore, Bond should have received a $45 dollar cleaning allowance for the last quarter of 1996."

WAGES

Citation: *City of Sunnyside*, 123 LA 1217 (Boedecker, 2007)

Issue: Premium Pay; Overtime Work

Holding: The arbitrator held that firefighters must receive overtime pay for any work beyond their scheduled work and that sick or vacation leave is to be calculated into scheduled work.

Explanation: The arbitrator noted that the plain meaning of the CBA would be analyzed; that using the plain meaning of the words sets up an objective standard. The arbitrator found that the CBA stated that time actually worked over the scheduled work was overtime. The arbitrator also found that the CBA did not exclude sick or vacation time in the definition of scheduled work.

Citation: *Washington County, Oregon*, 75 LA 1183 (Knudsen, 1980)

Issue: Premium Pay; Overtime Work

Holding: The arbitrator held that police officers were not entitled to overtime under the CBA for their 15 minute meetings prior to their respective shifts starting because of past practice.

Explanation: The arbitrator agreed with the Employer in that the overtime provision in the CBA was ambiguous however "we find a past practice not only having existed for years, but having existed side by side for some seven years with what would appear to be a fairly clear overtime provision. The evidence was not in dispute that these shift meetings always began 15 minutes before the hour . . . [a]nd, yet, no claim for such overtime compensation was ever made until late

1979."

Citation: *Municipality of Anchorage*, 129 LA 942 (Landau, 2011)

Issue: Performance Pay; Merit Pay

Holding: The City violated the CBA when it clarified a merit pay provision to count annual leave an employee would use before taking sick leave as sick days that count against an officers record for performance pay.

Explanation: "I find this language to be clear and unambiguous on its face. The "sick leave" to be considered for performance pay is expressly limited to "the combination of the employees own sick leave account and the sick leave bank…the foregoing contract provisions make it clear that annual leave and sick leave are two separate and distinct types of leave which are not interchangeable.

Citation: *City of Mill Creek*, 116 LA 101 (Gaba, 2001)

Issue: Merit Pay; Bonuses

Holding: The City did not violate the CBA when it failed to provide bonuses, despite the past practice where the new contract changed the benefit structure of officers.

Explanation: "The contract negotiations were expressly convened to deal with the question of what benefits would be provided to the sergeants in the new agreement; whatever they have been receiving up to that point was subject to negotiation." Thus the past practice of bonuses if irrelevant when viewed in the context of new contractual language.

Citation: *State of Alaska*, 133 LA 1436 (DiFalco 2014)

Issue: Classification Pay

Holding: The arbitrator held that the State did not violate the CBA when it failed to pay CO's who voluntarily demoted at a wage rage equal to that as to if they had not promoted.(essentially they were put in a worse position because they promoted and were being paid less than those who had not promoted).

Explanation: There was no contract provision guaranteeing that those who voluntarily demoted would receive the same pay as if they had never been promoted. While arbitrator agreed this was unfair, he ruled that being unfair was not enough to make up for the lack of contract language. The Union cannot create a breach of contract simple because they did not fully understand the way in which a certain provision could negatively affect members of their bargaining unit.

Citation: *Los Angeles Police Dep't*, 122 LA 1048 (Henner, 2006)

Issue: Classification Pay

Holding: The arbitrator held that the Employer did not violate the CBA with the police officers when it failed to temporarily promote a Sergeant I to Sergeant II.

Explanation: The arbitrator found that there was conflicting testimony regarding whether the Sergeant I had performed enough duties temporarily to be temporary promoted to Sergeant II. ". In many respects it comes down to just the Grievant's testimony against the testimony of Lieutenant Booker. Both are credible witnesses. The documentary evidence is also ambiguous."

Citation: *City of Fairbanks*, 121 LA 978 (Savage, 2005)

Issue: Classification Pay

Holding: The arbitrator held that the Employer violated the CBA with the dispatchers when it decreased the pay for a dispatcher who requested to be permanently reassigned to a front desk clerk duty.

Explanation: The arbitrator noted that the CBA provided that permanently reclassified employees cannot lose pay and that the CBA only allows for lowering the pay of employees who are temporarily reclassified. The arbitrator also noted that the dispatchers were not allowed to make any oral agreements that are inconsistent with the CBA.

Citation: *City of Mukilteo*, 131 LA 1149 (Irvin, 2013)

Issue: Distribution of Overtime

Holding: Employer did not violate CBA when it used mandatory overtime, rather than voluntary overtime, when there were insufficient volunteers.

Explanation: The arbitrator found that "the CBA envisions mandatory overtime as a possibility, insomuch as the article begins with '[i]n the event overtime is required to fill vacancies….'" And while past practice had been to use only volunteers, this "did not prevent the employer from exercising its right to require overtime when the situation warranted."

Citation: *City of Bozeman*, 127 LA 577 (Colhoun, 2010)

Issue: Distribution of Overtime

Holding: Employer violated CBA when it unilaterally classified employee as "exempt" and did not pay him overtime to which he would otherwise have been entitled.

Explanation: FLSA defines non-exempt as primarily management work. But "[t]o conclude [his] primary duty includes the exercise of discretion and independent judgment with respect to matters of significance … is illogical at best and self-serving on the City's part at worst." And although the employee signed a letter stating he was exempt he lacked the authority to enter into that agreement.

Citation: *Federal Bureau of Prisons*, 123 LA 129 (Calhoun, 2006)

Issue: Distribution of Overtime; Grievance Procedures

Holding: Dispute over three years' of overtime calculations is arbitrable.

Explanation: The arbitrator reasoned that although the CBA required grievances to be filed within 40 days of the occurrence, "pay claims invoke a continuing violation theory that holds that each alleged improper payment constitutes a separate violation of the contract that starts anew the grievance filing period."

Citation: *State of Montana*, 114 LA 916 (Prayzich, 2000)

Issue: Distribution of Overtime

Holding: The Employer did not violate CBA when it changed employee's timecard to eliminate overtime hours when employee had been granted leave, so long as the leave did not result in overtime for the period.

Explanation: The CBA states "authorized" leave counts toward overtime computation. The arbitrator noted that an employer memo states "leave requests at the end of the pay period will be disapproved if it results in" overtime. The arbitrator determined it was within the employer's "Management Rights" to authorize the leave only if it did not result in overtime, and to alter the timecard after employee refused to do so.

Citation: *City of Chehalis*, 121 LA 38 (Schwendiman, 2005)

Issue: Wages

Holding: The arbitrator held that the Employer violated the CBA with the police officers when it denied longevity pay to an officer.

Explanation: The arbitrator noted that the CBA stated that "Employees shall receive longevity pay in proportion to their year of service." The arbitrator held that "[i]n the absence of proven bargaining history and past practice to the contrary, the Arbitrator finds the union argument [that years of service should be used for longevity pay and not "continuous" service] . . . persuasive." The arbitrator noted that in other sections of the CBA, the contract had used the language "continuous length of service," but in the longevity provision it used years of service. "Here, the Arbitrator finds that the use of different terms here implies different meanings." The arbitrator held that "the 'years of service' applicable to longevity pay include all [of the Grievant's] . . . employment as a police officer with the [E]mployer since he was first hired . . . exclusive of the eight month and two day absence when he left employment . . . "

Chapter 9

The Civil Rights of Public Safety Employees

A. Introduction

This chapter set forth as a reminder of the principle that public safety employees have constitutional rights too.

Public safety employees are generally subject to departmental rules, often including a "code of ethics," which require the employees to respect the constitutional rights of the citizens they encounter. Public safety personnel who knowingly violate citizens' constitutional rights are subject to discipline. But what happens when it is the *employer* that is violating the constitutional rights of *employees*? This chapter set forth as a reminder of the principle that public safety employees have constitutional rights too.

This principle has not always been well-established. Before a revised jurisprudence concerning the constitutional rights of public employees was developed over the past 50 years, it was commonly assumed that public employment was a "privilege," and that public employees could be compelled to give up their constitutional rights as a condition of maintaining that privilege. This notion was probably most aptly stated by Oliver Wendell Holmes:

> The petitioner may have a constitutional right to talk politics but he has no constitutional right to be a policeman. There are few employments for hire in which the servant does not agree to suspend its constitutional right to free speech, as well as the vitalness, by the implied term of his contract. The servant cannot complain, as he takes the employment on the terms which are offered him. On the same principle, the city may impose any reasonable conditions upon holding offices within its control.[1]

By 1967, when the United States Supreme Court issued its decision in *Garrity v. New Jersey*,[2] it made clear that the old notions, that employees should be compelled to abandon their

---

[1] *McAuliffe v. New Bedford*, 115 Mass. 216, 220, 29 N.E. 517, 517-18 (1902).
[2] 385 U.S. 493 (1967).

constitutional right as a condition of employment, had fallen by the wayside. In *Garrity*, the court stated:

> We conclude that policemen, like teachers and lawyers, are not relegated to a watered-down version of constitutional rights. There are rights of constitutional stature whose exercise the state may not condition by the exaction of a price.[3]

Often these rights are interconnected with the CBA and collective bargaining rights

This chapter addresses a number of civil and constitutional rights held by employees. Some of these have a basis in statute; some have a basis in the Constitution. An effective representative will want to acquire at least a basic understanding of the civil rights concepts set forth here. Often these rights are interconnected with the CBA and collective bargaining rights, which is among the reasons this chapter is included in the book. Sometimes these rights will be pursued in tandem with or as an alternative to labor contract enforcement. The right to speech, association, and nondiscrimination all directly bear on the rights of the union itself as well as its members. Discipline, for example, that turns on infringing on an employee's first amendment rights or is based on discrimination, can be presented as a civil rights issue either in court or raised to an arbitrator.

We will address the right of public safety employees to speak freely both inside and outside the workplace, the right of public safety employees to engage in political activity, and the right to public safety employees to engage in union activity. We will review the rights of public safety employees in their private lives, including what information is to be made public and what is to remain private, where they may live and who they may live with. We also cover issues of unlawful discrimination.

[3] 385 U.S. at 499.

The courts have struggled for some time to find how to apply free speech rights to the public sector employment where the public employer is also the government.

B. The Right to Free Speech

Citizens at large clearly have a right to speak out and freely criticize their government. On the other hand, in private-sector employees (absent the limited protection of a collective bargaining agreement) do not have the right to criticize their employer. The courts have struggled for some time to find how to apply free speech rights to the public sector employment where the public employer is also the government. If public employees could never criticize their employer, they would have fewer rights than citizens as large. If public employees had an unfettered right of criticism, service delivery could slow to a standstill. These competing interests are at the base of public employment free speech issues.

Most of the past 50 years of court decisions have worked towards defining the appropriate balance between the conflicting interests presented by the public employee, who exercises his or her right to speak, and the public employer, who strives for operative efficiently. This section addresses the question the courts have reccurring faced — under what circumstances may public employees express themselves that may be critical or embarrassing to their public employer.

1. The Supreme Court Balancing Test

To make this determination, the Supreme Court has adopted a series of tests.

A public employer may not discharge an employee on a basis that infringes that employee's constitutionally protected interest in freedom of speech.[4] The determination of *whether* a public employer has improperly discharged or disciplined an employee for engaging in speech involves an assessment a balance between the interests of the employee, as a citizen, in commenting upon matters of public concern and the interest of the government, as

[4] *Rankin v. McPherson*, 483 U.S. 378, 383, 107 S.Ct. 2891, 2896 (1987).

an employer, in promoting the efficiency of the public services it performs through its employees.[5] This "balancing" is necessary in order to accommodate the *dual role* of the public employer as a provider of public services and as a government entity operating under the restrictions of the First Amendment.[6]

To make this determination, the Supreme Court has adopted a series of tests. First, does the speech involve a matter of public concern? Second, does the speech involve the employee in the course of their job duties or does it involve an expression in their role as a citizen? Third, does the employee's interest in speaking freely outweigh the government agencies interest in the performance of its functions? The balancing test is reached only after questions 1 and 2 are answered in the affirmative.

Public Concern. The threshold question in applying the balancing test is whether the employee's speech may be "fairly characterized as constituting speech on a matter of public concern."[7] Whether an employee's speech addresses a matter of "public concern" must be determined by the *content, form, and context* of a given statement, as revealed by the *whole record.*[8]

The political, controversial or even inappropriate character of a statement is deemed irrelevant to the question whether the speech relates to a matter of public concern.[9] As the Supreme Court has indicated: "Debate on public issues should be uninhibited, robust, and wide-open, and . . . may well include vehement, caustic, and sometimes unpleasantly sharp attacks on government and public officials."[10] Just as erroneous statements must be protected to give freedom of expression the breathing space it needs to survive, so statements criticizing public policy and the implementation of it must be similarly protected.[11]

[5] *Pickering v. Board of Education*, 391 U.S. 563, 568 (1968); *Connick v. Myers*, 461 U.S. 138, 140 (1983).

[6] *Rankin v. McPherson*, 483 U.S. 378, 383, 107 S.Ct 2891, 2896 (1987).

[7] *Connick*, 461 U.S. at 146.

[8] *Id.* at 147-148; *see, also, Rankin*, 483 U.S. at 383.

[9] *Rankin*, 483 U.S. at 387.

[10] *New York Times Co. v. Sullivan*, 376 U.S. 254, 270 (1964).

[11] *Bond v. Floyd*, 385 U.S. 116, 136 (1966).

The threshold question in applying the balancing test is whether the employee's speech may be "fairly characterized as constituting speech on a matter of public concern.

In *Connick v. Myers,*[12] the Court distinguished between employee speech on matters of "public concern," which it found to be protected, and matters only of personal concern that it found not to be protected. In its decision, it overturned a lower court ruling finding that an assistant district attorney had been unlawfully terminated by the district attorney for circulating a questionnaire which primarily focused on office morale and the office transfer policy. (The employee had been the subject of recent transfer that she had taken issue with). The Court found none of her questions alone were constitutionally protected *except* for one which pertained to whether employees had felt pressure to work on political campaigns for certain candidates. The Court found that this one question did not otherwise change its characterization as being "an employee grievance concerning internal office policy", so her claim was dismissed.

Since *Connick*, the courts have had to determine whether worked related speech was concerning primarily (1) a public concern, or (2) a personal workplace grievance or concern. If an employee's comment does *not* touch a matter of public concern, the speech loses the protection of the First Amendment. *The public concern standard is a threshold test.*

Job Duties. In 2006 the *Connick* test was eventually overshadowed by, but not entirely displaced by, a more restrictive workplace test: the "job duties" standard. In *Garcetti v. Ceballos,*[13] the Supreme Court imposed a more restrictive rule governing speech within the workplace.

Ceballos was a Los Angeles prosecutor who had filed an office complaint about potentially untruthful warrants. He questioned whether the cases associated with the warrants should be pursued. He later claimed that he suffered retaliation as a result of raising those concerns. The Supreme Court concluded that Ceballos complaints were presented in the course of his job duties and were not part of an exercise of a citizen speaking.

[12] 461 U.S. 138 (1983).

[13] 547 U.S. 410, 425, 126 S. Ct. 1951, 1957, 164 L. Ed. 2d 689 (2006).

The Court explained that "speech which owes its existence to an employee's professional responsibilities" is *not* protected by the First Amendment.[14] On the other hand, speech which has 'no official significance and bears similarities to actions taken by numerous citizens everyday'" is not within an employee's job duties and "*would* be protected by the First Amendment."[15]

The operative question is whether the speech is part and parcel of the employee's job or whether it is something else, such as whistleblowing speech. *The lower courts have found it very difficult to implement the distinctions created in Garcetti consistently, and its durability is doubtful.*

In determining whether speech was or was not made pursuant to an official duty, "the listing of a given task in an employee's written job description is neither necessary nor sufficient to demonstrate that conducting the task is within the scope of the employee's professional duties for First Amendment purposes."[16] Rather, determining whether speech is pursuant to one's job duties is context specific and does not turn on one's actual job description.

The *Garcetti* decision has been widely criticized for blocking public employee speech rights within the workplace. In fact, the decision does restrict public employee speech rights significantly beyond the *Connick* standard but does not leave all work related speech unprotected. The operative question is whether the speech is part and parcel of the employee's job *or* whether it is something else, such as whistleblowing speech. *The lower courts have found it very difficult to implement the distinctions created in Garcetti consistently, and its durability is doubtful.*

---

[14] *Garcetti v. Ceballos*, 547 U.S. at 424 (2006).

[15] *Huppert*, 574 F.3d at 703 (9th Cir. 2009) (emphasis added) (*quoting Garcetti,* 547 U.S. at 422); *see also Eng*, 552 F.3d at 1071 (if the speaker is under "no official duty" to make the statements or "if the speech was not the product of performing the tasks the employee was paid to perform," the employee's speech was made as a private citizen).

[16] *Garcetti*, 547 US at 425.

The Ninth Circuit has generally applied the "job duties" exclusion in a narrow manner.

Court decisions are all over the map as to what speech is inside or outside the Garcetti "job duties" standard. One significant (and ironic) factor as to whether speech is part of an employee's duties is whether the employee "complaints up the chain of command, or instead relays his concerns to persons outside the workplace."[17] For example, a police officer's conversation with his superiors about an arrest is "obviously part of" the officer's duties, but his deposition as a witness in a retaliation lawsuit was found to be "clearly" not part of the officer's job.[18] And in *Hernandez v Cook County*, corrections officers who made internal complaints about overcrowding, the lack of supervision, and the need for Plexiglas in the jail to improve their safety were found to be acting pursuant to their official duties and, therefore, were not entitled to First Amendment protection.[19]

The Ninth Circuit has generally applied the "job duties" exclusion in a narrow manner. In a number of times since *Garcetti,* the court has declined to apply the job duties exclusion even for speech that had a connection to workplace concerns:

- In *Karl v. City of Mountlake Terrace,*[20] an Administrative Assistant's deposition supportive of an officer suing the department was protected speech, not part of job duties.
- In *Freitag v. Ayers,*[21] correction officer's complaints about hostile working conditions due to inmate behaviors presented to Inspector General and State Senator was protected speech, but complaints presented to prison managers was deemed part of "job duties" and unprotected speech.

---

[17] *Id.* at 705; *citing Davis v. McKinney*, 518 F.3d 304, 313 (5th Cir. 2008).

[18] *Huppert*, 574. F.3d at 705 (*citing Morales v. Jones*, 494 F.3d at 595).

[19] *Hernandez v. Cook Cnty. Sheriff's Office*, 634 F.3d 906 (7th Cir. 2011); *see also Spiegla v. Hull*, 481 F.3d 961 (7th Cir.) *cert. denied*, 128 S.Ct 441 (2007) (corrections officer's reassignment after she reported suspicious conduct and a possible breach of prison security was not retaliation for First-Amendment-protected speech because the officer was not speaking as a citizen "but as a correctional officer charged with the duty to ensure the prison's safety").

[20] 678 F.3d 1062 (9th Cir. 2012).

[21] 468 F.3d 528 (9th Cir. 2006).

- In *Marable v. Nitchman,*[22] a Washington State Ferry system engineer's complaints outside the chain of command, including to the State Auditor, were found to be protected speech

- In *Eng v. Cooley,*[23] a prosecutor's criticism of supervisor about information leaks and public complaints regarding retaliation found arguably protected speech.

- In *Robinson v. York,*[24] a Police Sergeant denied a promotion to Lieutenant after filing misconduct reports and testifying in a lawsuit about discrimination was found to have undertaken protected speech.

- In *Anthoine v. North Century Counties Consortium,*[25] an employee who skipped chain of command and reported to Chairman about employee misconduct presented protected speech.

- In *Posey v. Lake Pend Oreille School District,*[26] a school security officer that had filed a complaint regarding schools safety and emergency procedures was found to have presented an arguable claim that he acted outside job duties.

- In *Ellins v. City of Sierra Madre,*[27] an officer leading a police union's "vote of no confidence" effort against the chief was found to have spoken on a matter of protected "public concern" and his speech was deemed to be the speech of a private citizen, not duty related speech.

- In *Dahlia v. Rodriguez*[28] an officer that reported fellow officer misconduct to his union and an internal investigator was protected "public concern" speech.

But in some other recent cases the Ninth Circuit as disallowed First Amendment retaliation claims that likely would have survived before *Garcetti*:

---

[22] 511 F.3d 924 (9th Cir. 2007).
[23] 552 F.3d 1062 (9th Cir. 2009).
[24] 566 F.3d 817 (9th Cir. 2010).
[25] 606 F.3d 740 (9th Cir. 2010).
[26] 546 F.3d 1121 (9th Cir. 2008).
[27] 710 F.3d 1049 (9th Cir. 2013).
[28] 735 F.3d 1060 (9th Cir. 2013).

- In *Brownfield v. City of Yakima,*[29] the court found that an officer's complaint about lazy coworkers an unfair supervision was not protected speech.

- In *Hagen v. City of Eugene,*[30] an officer alleged to have suffered retaliation after complaining about the lack of SWAT Team safety standards was found to have engaged in work-related speech unprotected by the First Amendment.

- In *Huppert v. City of Pittsburgh*[31] officers' grand jury testimony about misconduct of fellow officers was not protected speech.

But the ruling in *Huppert* was later overturned by the Ninth Circuit in 2013 by *Dahlia v. Rodriguez.*[32] In *Dahlia*, the court emphasized, contrary to its earlier *Huppert* ruling, that the issue is not whether the "broad job description" requires reporting official misconduct but whether the more narrow "practical" question of whether the job duties are within the employee's "professional duties."

The irony that has been noted about the job duties test is that employees who skipped the chain of command to present complaints are *more likely* to be protected by the First Amendment. Those employees who file complaints with their supervisors or managers are generally found to be presenting the information as part of their job duties and, therefore, outside the protection of the First Amendment when they suffer retaliation for such complaints. The *Garcetti* standard allows protection for whistleblowing speech but generally leaves public employees unprotected if they attempt to address issues at a lower level, such as through the chain of command. The Ninth Circuit in Dahlia and other decisions is clearly attempting to define the *Garcetti* ruling narrowly. Some other Federal courts are doing likewise. Likely the Supreme Court will ultimately have to readdress and clarify its *Garcetti* ruling.

In 2014 the Supreme Court took at least one small step to clarify *Garcetti*, perhaps taking a preliminary step towards a more sweeping modification. In *Lane v. Franks*, the Court rejected the Eleventh Circuits efforts to apply the job duties test in a literal

---

[29] 612 F.3d 1140 (9th Cir. 2010).
[30] 736 F.3d 1251 (9th Cir. 2013).
[31] 574 F.3d 696 (9th Cir. 2009).
[32] 735 F.3d. 1060 (9th Cir. 2013).

manner. In *Franks*, a college administrator alleged retaliation based on his court testimony. The 11th Circuit, attempting to apply Garcetti, found that he had no First Amendment protection because this was part of his job duties.

If the expression is of public concern and is not part of their job duties, the employees' interest in making the statement must then be balanced against the interest of the government, as an employer, in promoting the efficiency of the public services it performs through its employees.

The Court overturned the 11th Circuit and expressly stated that "*Pickering* provides the framework" to analyze public employee speech rights. The Court acknowledged that *Garcetti* removed job protection for speech in furtherance of "job duties," but appeared to reframe the scope of *Garcetti* more in the direction of the 9th Circuit. The Court did not cite to the scope of duties under the official job description but instead references "ordinary job responsibilities."

Though subtle, there is an important difference between "official" job duties and "ordinary" job duties. Such a reframing of the legal standard by the Supreme Court in Franks may well bring back into first amendment protection employee whistleblowing activities that some observers thought *Garcetti* left unprotected.

Balancing Test. If the expression is of public concern and is not part of their job duties, the employees' interest in making the statement must then be balanced against the interest of the government, as an employer, in promoting the efficiency of the public services it performs through its employees.[33] The employer will bear the burden, if an employee is discharged as a result of an expression of speech, of justifying the discharge on legitimate grounds.[34]

In performing the balancing, the speech is not considered in a vacuum but rather the manner, time, and place of the employee's expression are relevant as is the context in which the dispute arose.[35] Relevant factors include whether the statement impairs

[33] *Rankin*, 483 U.S. at 387.
[34] *Connick*, 461 U.S. at 150.
[35] *Givhan v. Western Line Consolidated School Dist.*, 439 U.S. 410, 415 (1979).

discipline by superiors or harmony among co-workers, has a detrimental impact on close working relationships for which personal loyalty and confidence are necessary, or impedes the performance of the employee's duties or otherwise interferes with the regular operation of the enterprise.[36]

In 1968 in *Pickering v. Board of Education*, the Supreme Court established the right of public employees to criticize the policy decision of a government for which they were employed on a matter of public concern at a public forum.[37] Explaining the Pickering balance test, the Washington State Supreme Court identified these factors to be weighed:

> (1) the time, place, and manner of the employee's speech;
>
> (2) whether the statement would create problems in maintaining discipline by immediate supervisors or harmony among co-workers;
>
> (3) whether the employment relationship is one in which personal loyalty and confidence are necessary; and
>
> (4) whether the speech impeded the employee's ability to perform daily responsibilities.[38]

A couple of Supreme Court decisions identify how the Court has balanced the competing factors. In *Rankin v. McPherson*,[39] a noncommissioned member (deputy constable) of a Texas Sheriff's office made comments about the president which, though extreme, were found to be protected. The employee was terminated when, after hearing of an attempt on the President's life, she commented "if they go for him again, I hope they get him."[40] She was not an officer, had no contact with the public in her job duties, did not wear a uniform, and was not authorized to make arrests or permitted to carry a gun. Because she made the statement during a private conversation in a room not readily accessible to the public (thereby shedding no negative light on the employer), and

---

36 *Pickering*, 391 U.S. at 570-573.

37 *Pickering v. Board of Education*, 391 U.S. 563 (1968).

38 *White v. State of Washington*, 131 Wn.2d 1, 15(1997); *see also McEvoy v. Spencer*, 124 F.3d 92 (2nd Cir. 1997); *Pickering*, 391 U.S. at 569-73.

39 483 U.S. 378, (1987).

40 *Rankin*, 483 U.S. at 379.

because her comment was not an actual threat, the employee's was protected under the First Amendment.[41]

In 1995, in United States v. *National Treasury Employees Union*,[42] the Supreme Court addressed the constitutionality of a congressionally enacted "honoraria ban," prohibiting federal employees from accepting compensation for making speeches or writing articles even when the speech has nothing to do with the employee's official duties.[43] The Court concluded that the government could not prohibit *all* federal employees from being paid for speech because the First Amendment protects speech unrelated to their jobs.[44] But federal employees in high ranking positions could be banned from speech – even that which is unrelated to their job – because the balance favored the government's interests in banning compensation that might improperly influence the speaker in his public capacity.[45]

2. Speech That is Clearly Unprotected

There is a whole category of speech outside the protection of the First Amendment. Speech, for example, which is obscene or involving profanity is generally not protected by the First Amendment. Speech that is defamatory — speech which the employee knew or should have known was false — is not protected either. Also, speech involving threats is not even considered "speech" under the First Amendment, but is considered to be unprotected "conduct."[46]

Although freedom of association is generally protected under the First Amendment, as a general rule public employees, especially police officers, must avoid membership in or attendance at meetings of violent or hateful groups. This exception exists because the appearance of a public employee can unduly interfere with the basic function of the employer. For example, the Second

[41] *Rankin*, 483 U.S. at 387; *see also United States v. Bagdasarian*, 652 F.3d 1113, 1116 (9th Cir. 2011) (private individual's post on online message board: "Obama fk the niggar, he will have a 50 cal in the head soon" and "shoot the nig" were not true threats because the speaker did not mean to "communicate a *serious* expression of an intent to commit an act of unlawful violence.").

[42] 513 U.S. 454 (1995)

[43] *Nat'l Treasury Employees Union*, 513 U.S. at 457.

[44] *See Id.*

[45] *Id.*

[46] The *Rankin* case discussed above is distinguishable. No one there had contended the deputy constable had actually threatened the President; she voiced disdain for the President and expressed a hope that someone else would harm him.

Circuit found the termination of a New York City police officer and two firefighters was proper because the three had all appeared on a racially-offensive Labor Day parade float.[47] The City's "interest in maintaining a relationship of trust between the police and fire departments and the communities they serve" outweighed the employees' free speech interests.[48] On the other hand, membership in mere controversial - not harmful or extreme - groups, such as nudists, is generally protected.[49] This protection exists because nudism, while controversial, does not actually interfere with the smooth running of the government or an employee's ability to perform their job.

Several viewpoints and organizations have been routinely excluded from First Amendment protection, including hate groups, such as the Ku Klux Klan,[50] and groups involved in illegal activities, such as the Outlaws Motorcycle Club.[51] Similarly, blackface is generally disallowed unless it is part of an unpaid artistic performance where the individual is not holding himself or herself out as a public employee.[52] However, even in clear-cut cases, the employer must still present evidence against the employee. In one case, an arbitrator reinstated an employee who was terminated for displayed a Nazi flag on his porch because the employer did not provide sufficient evidence that the display was potentially disruptive.[53]

The Supreme Court has identified certain speech to be of such

---

47 *Locurto v. Giuliani*, 447 F.3d 159, 183 (2nd Cir. 2006).

48 *Locurto v. Giuliani*, 447 F.3d 159, 183 (2nd Cir. 2006).

49 *See Bruns v. Pomerleau*, 19 F.Supp. 58 (D.Md. 1970).

50 *See .e.g., State v. Henderson*, 277 Neb. 240, 762 N.W.2d 1 (2009) (State Supreme Court reversed an arbitration award permitting officer's membership in Ku Klux Klan, finding the award to be contrary to public policy); *McMullen v. Carson*, 754 F.2d 936 (11th Cir. 1985) (records clerk for police department terminated for being a recruiter for the Klan); *Young v. McDaniel*, 664 F. Supp. 362 (W.D. Ky. 1986) (officer fired for distributing hate literature and lying about selling tickets to Klan-sponsored functions).

51 *See Piscottano v. Murphy*, 511 F.3d 247 (2d Cir. 2007) (thee officers were appropriately disciplined for membership in Outlaws Motorcycle Club – a drug trafficking and white supremacist group).

52 *Compare Pappas v. Giuliani*, 447 F.3d 159 (2nd Cir. 2006) (blackface of officer and two firefighters on a parade float was appropriate grounds for termination), *with Berger v. Battaglia*, 779 F.2d 992 (4th Cir. 1985) (officer terminated for performing Blackface in artistic performance during a musical act for which he was not compensated and did not hold himself out to be an officer received a $200,000 settlement).

53 *In re Department of Correctional Services [Naponoch, N.Y.] and Council 82, Security Unit Employees AFSCME*, 114 L.A. 1533 (Simmelkjaer, 1997).

"slight social value" that any benefit from the ability to speak openly is "clearly outweighed by the social interest in order and morality."[54] The First Amendment permits "restrictions upon the content of speech in those narrow set of topics which are 'of such slight social value...that any benefit that may be derived from them is clearly outweighed by the social interest in order and morality.'"[55]

In other words, a few limited categories of speech, such as "obscenity, defamation, and fighting words" may not warrant First Amendment coverage "*because of their constitutionally proscribable content.*"[56] Thus, there is no Constitutional protection for words "which by their very utterance inflict injury or tend to incite an immediate breach of the peace."[57] Speech that is defamatory — speech which the employee knew or should have known was false — is not protected either.[58]

But the courts will examine the *purpose* of the action restricting the speech. Even if speech is the type that does not generally warrant First Amendment protection, such speech may nonetheless not be forbidden "based on hostility, or favoritism, towards a nonproscribable message [it] contain[s]."[59]

---

[54] *Virginia v. Black*, 538 U.S. 343, 358-59, 123 S. Ct. 1536, 1547, 155 L. Ed. 2d 535 (2003) (*quoting R.A.V. v. City of St. Paul*, 505 U.S. 377, 382-383 (1992)).

[55] *Virginia v. Black*, 538 U.S. 343, 358-59, 123 S. Ct. 1536, 1547, 155 L. Ed. 2d 535 (2003) (*quoting R.A.V. v. City of St. Paul*, 505 U.S. 377, 382-383 (1992)).

[56] *R.A.V.*, 505 U.S. at 377; *see also Cohen v. California*, 403 U.S. 15, 20, 91 S.Ct. 1780, 29 L.Ed.2d 284 (1971) (Fighting words-"those personally abusive epithets which, when addressed to the ordinary citizen, are, as a matter of common knowledge, inherently likely to provoke violent reaction" proscribable under the First Amendment).

[57] *Virginia v. Black*, 538 U.S. at 358-59 (*citing Chaplinsky v. New Hampshire*, 315 U.S. 568, 572 (1942)); *see also Black v. City of Auburn*, 857 F.Supp. 1540 (M.D.Ala. 1994) (Public use of words such as bitch and whore by a police officer cannot be justified as "rough" language protected by the First Amendment. Rather, words that are derogatory of or offensive to women create a hostile work environment). *But see Minneapolis, City of and Minn. AFSCME Council 14*, 101 LA (BNA) 1006 (Daly, 1993) (Arbitrator annuls punishment of 911 operator who used profanity in the workplace. Remarks were not directed to a coworker, but were used to relieve stress. Also, the agency's standards of speech were vague.).

[58] *See New York Times Co. v. Sullivan*, 376 U.S. 254 (1964); *Greenbelt Co-op. Pub. Ass'n v. Bresler*, 398 U.S. 6 (1970) (holding that the accurate reporting of a public meeting in which a particular position was characterized as "blackmail" was protected under the First Amendment); *Old Dominion Branch No. 496, Nat. Ass'n of Letter Carriers, AFL-CIO v. Austin*, 418 U.S. 264, 94 S. Ct. 2770, 41 L. Ed. 2d 745 (1974) (labeling of nonunion members as "scabs" was not actionable without knowledge of the label's falsity or reckless disregard of truth).

[59] *R.A.V. v. City of St. Paul, Minn.*, 505 U.S. 377, 112 S. Ct. 2538, 120 L. Ed. 2d

Even if it is against the workplace rules, a one-time profane outburst, for example, "might be excused."[60] Similarly, the use of socially devalued speech may be justified in the circumstances.[61] While free speech might be found to trump claims of libel, as seen in the "scab" example, the right to speak does not necessarily extend to cover speech-related crimes, such as harassment.[62] Courts have had difficulty determining the proper course of action when the character of the speech seems to be of slight social value, but may also have a protected purpose.[63]

At least one guiding principle is that "speech" which is essentially "conduct" is not necessarily protected. So, for example, the government has the right to create laws that criminalize threats, harassment and other types of behaviors that harm third parties.

If the speech pertains to a general issue of public policy or a public official, it will generally be protection under the First Amendment. Courts have been particularly protective of the right of public employees to speak in public forums outside the workplace.

---

305 (1992).

60 *Levinsky v. Dept. of Justice*, #06-3046, 161 Fed. Appx. 954, 2006 U.S. App. Lexis 1680 (Fed. Cir. 2006) (unpublished); *see also Batley v. Kendall Co. Sheriff's Merit Cmsn.*, 425 N.E.2d 1201 (Ill.App. 1981) (single utterance of profanity does not warrant termination of officer).

61 *City of Hurst and Individual Grievant*, AAA Case #71-390- 00290 -06, 123 LA (BNA) 302 (Moore, 2006) (arbitrator found department lacked just cause to suspend a police officer for his use of the word *fuck* at a crime scene, in violation of department rules, because the language was not indecent, profane, or harsh, but actually quieted down the suspects.).

62 *See, e.g., State v. Read*, 163 Wn. App. 853, 261 P.3d 207 (2011) *review denied,* 173 Wn. 2d 1021, 272 P.3d 850 (2012) (a man who received a parking ticket was found to have harassed the female ticketing officer because he followed the officer, yelling racial epithets at the her, then – after the officer told him she was not the race he was yelling about – got out of the car, approached the officer - who was half his size - and cursed and screamed at her).

63 *See, e.g., Hunt v. County of Orange*, 672 F.3d 606, 611 (9th Cir. 2012) ("[U]nless the government can demonstrate an overriding interest of vital importance requiring that a person's private beliefs conform to those of the hiring authority, his beliefs cannot be the sole basis for depriving him of continued public employment.") (*quoting Branti v. Finkel,* 445 U.S. 507, 515–16, 100 S.Ct. 1287, 63 L.Ed.2d 574 (1980)).

3. Political Speech

The speech with the greatest protection under the First Amendment is that speech that is considered to be relating to a "public concern." If the speech pertains to a general issue of public policy or a public official, it will generally be protection under the First Amendment. Courts have been particularly protective of the right of public employees to speak in public forums outside the workplace. As the Ninth Circuit has noted: Citizens do not check their First Amendment rights "at the door" when they accept a government job.[64]

The leading case concerning the right to make public statements is the previously identified case of *Pickering v. Board of Education.*[65] In *Pickering,* a school teacher had made public comments criticizing the school board's policy. She was terminated. The Supreme Court adopted a balancing test which balanced the "interest of the employee as a citizen in commenting upon matters of public concern and the interest of the state, as an employer, in promoting the efficiency of public service its performs through its employees." *Pickering* found that the statements by the school teacher were of significant public importance and that the interest in having those statements freely circulated outweighed the "efficiency" interest of the employer.

Pickering has since been applied to extend a high level of protection for political speech. Political participation by unions is extended an even higher degree of first amendment deference. In general, courts have been particularly protective of the right of public employees "to criticize a government official, to support a candidate opposing an elected official, or to run against an elected official."[66] Courts have also overturned on First Amendment Grounds disciplinary action against public safety employees who have raised issues regarding department corruption.[67]

The distinction between what constitutes "workplace speech," which might be subject to a lesser degree of protection, and "political speech," has not always been a clear one. When speech has been deemed "political speech" it has been accorded a high degree of protection in the courts.

In fact, the kind of speech generally given the *highest*

---

[64] *Bardzik v. County of Orange,* 32 IER Cases 13 (9th Cir. 2011); *citing Brainti v. Finkel,* 445 U.S. 507, 513-17 (1980).

[65] 391 U.S. 563 (1968).

[66] *Bardzik,* 635 F.3d at 1144.

[67] *Brawner v. Richardson,* Texas 3 IER Cases 1377 (5th Cir. 1988); *McDonald v. City of Freeport,* 8 IER Cases 1635 (S.D. Tex. 1993).

protection under the First Amendment is "political speech." The Supreme Court has found that disagreement with the content of the speech is not enough of a reason to stifle that speech because "debate on public issues should be uninhibited, robust, and wide-open and....may well include vehement, caustic, and sometimes unpleasantly sharp attacks on government and public officials."[68]

In no place is this truer than in politics. In fact, political speech is listed specifically amongst the types of speech generally deemed to be a matter of "public concern." This list includes:

- Speech on matters relating to the functioning of government;[69]
- Speech that is relevant to the public's evaluation of the performance of governmental agencies;[70]
- Speech that relates to any matter of *political*, social, or other concern to the community;[71]
- Speech reporting unlawful conduct by a government employee;[72]
- Speech reporting unlawful activity by a government agency;[73]
- Speech reporting misuse of public funds, wastefulness, and inefficiency in managing and operating government entities.[74]

---

68 *Rankin*, 583 U.S. at 384; *New York Times*, 376 U.S. at 270.

69 *Eng v. Cooley*, 552 F.3d 1062, 1073 (9th Cir. 2009).

70 *Id.* For example, an employee's complaints about a District Attorney's leak of information to the IRS is "relevant to the public's evaluation of the performance of the District Attorney's office." *Id.* at 1072; *see also Huppert*, 574 F.3d at 703.

71 *Huppert*, 574 F.3d at 703 (*quoting Weeks v. Bayer*, 246 F.3d 1231, 1234 (9th Cir. 2001)).

72 *Huppert*, 574 F.3d at 703.

73 *Id.*

74 *Id.*

Courts have been most likely to find matters to be only of a personal concern when they relate to criticisms of "mismanagement," claims of personal deprivation, or where the employee has been involved in conflicts with supervisors.

While political speech is generally protected, the boundaries of what constitutes "political speech" are not always clear, especially when the speaker works in a government agency. As the Ninth Circuit has explained, the "analysis of public concern is not an exact science,"[75] but is a question of law, considered in light of all the facts and circumstances.[76]

Speech that might on the surface appear to be "political speech" may, on closer examination, actually be a matter of "personal concern" which then becomes removed from First Amendment protection. Courts have been most likely to find matters to be only of a personal concern when they relate to criticisms of "mismanagement," claims of personal deprivation, or where the employee has been involved in conflicts with supervisors.[77]

Because "exposing governmental inefficiency and misconduct is a matter of considerable significance,"[78] speech is more likely to be deemed "a public concern when it focuses on governmental policies and not on any particular person or supervisor."[79] However, where there have been ongoing labor-management disputes that have become publicized, the courts have given labor unions greater leeway in publicly airing what might otherwise be

---

[75] *Salgado v. City of Pittsburg*, 574 F.3d 696 (9th Cir. 2009).

[76] *Eng*, 552 F.3d at 1070 (*citing Johnson v. Multnomah* 48 F.3d 420, 422 (9th Cir. 1995)).

[77] *McEvoy v. Shoemaker*, 882 F.2d 463 (5th Cir. 1989) (letter to city council disagreeing with management of department resulting in officer's failure to receive promotion was not protected speech); *see, also, Terrell v. Univ. of Texas Sys. Police*, 792 F.2d 1360 (5th Cir. 1986) (finding the contents of a diary in which a police captain kept critical commentary about the chief where the captain had himself been under investigation not to be protected speech).

[78] *Garcetti v. Ceballos*, 547 U.S. 410, 425, 126 S. Ct. 1951, 1957, 164 L. Ed. 2d 689 (2006).

[79] *Binkley v. City of Tacoma*, 114 Wn.2d 373, 381 (1990) (*citing Meyer v. UW*, 105 Wn.2d 847, 851 (1986)).

considered to be a personal grievance.[80]

Washington public employees are also protected under the state's particularly strong whistleblower laws.

In general, courts have been particularly protective of the right of public employees "to criticize a government official, to support a candidate opposing an elected official, or to run against an elected official."[81] Courts have also overturned on First Amendment Grounds disciplinary action against public safety employees who have raised issues regarding department corruption.[82]

Washington public employees are also protected under the state's particularly strong whistleblower laws.[83] These laws require local governments to enact whistleblower ordinances under which municipalities and counties must create a procedure by which employees may complain about official misconduct. In short, an elected official ordinarily cannot fire or retaliate against an employee for his political opinions, memberships, activities, or whistleblowing.

The previously discussed Supreme Court decision in *Rankin v. McPherson* demonstrates the extent to which courts will go to protect "political speech." In *Rankin* a Texas Sherriff's Office data-entry employee's negative comments about the president were found to be protected. The employee was terminated when, after hearing of an attempt on the President's life, she commented "if they go for him again, I hope they get him."[84] The court did point out that she was not a commissioned officer, had no contact with

---

[80] *See Gregory v. McDonnell Douglas Corp.*, 17 Cal. 3d 596, 601, 552 P.2d 425 (Cal. Sup. Ct. 1976) (holding that publications otherwise protected under the First Amendment may, without losing such protection, contain statements that attribute improper motives to a public officer or to an active participant in a labor dispute: "where potentially defamatory statements are published in a public debate, a heated labor dispute, or in another setting in which the audience may anticipate efforts by the parties to persuade others to their positions by use of epithets, fiery rhetoric or hyperbole," is permissible).

[81] *Bardzik*, 635 F.3d at 1144.

[82] *Brawner v. Richardson*, Texas 3 IER Cases 1377 (5th Cir. 1988); *McDonald v. City of Freeport*, 8 IER Cases 1635 (S.D. Tex. 1993).

[83] *See*, RCW 42.40.010, *et seq.*; 42.41.010, *et seq.*; 49.60.210. *See also Lane v. Dep't of Homeland Security*, #DC-1221-10-0231-W-1, 2010 MSPB 245 (under the Federal Whistleblower Act, a disclosure will not be protected if it is made as part of an employee's normal duties reported through normal channels or if the disclosure is made to the wrongdoer).

[84] *Rankin*, 483 U.S. at 379.

the public in her job duties, did not wear a uniform, and was not authorized to make arrests or permitted to carry a gun. Because she made the statement during a private conversation in a room not readily accessible to the public (thereby shedding no negative light on the employer), and because her comment was not an actual threat, the employee's was found to be protected under the First Amendment.[85]

The more difficult public employee speech issues for the courts to resolve are those which involve primarily personal matters, but are nonetheless also matters of public importance.[86] Even if public importance is present, the court may still find the predominant personal interest in the employee's speech to tip it outside the protection of the First Amendment. For example, an employee's personally motivated comments regarding lack of enforcement of a smoking ordinance was found not to be protected speech. His complaint was framed only in personal terms because he complained "on his own behalf and in his own interest," speaking "solely in terms of his own sensitivity to smoke."[87]

The Ninth Circuit has generally been more protective of public employee speech, but several other federal circuits have approached public concern speech as exclusive, or something that must meet certain requirements. For example, other jurisdictions find that speech on police misconduct qualifies as a matter of public concern *if* the speech is made as a citizen.[88] Taking the opposite approach, the Ninth Circuit approaches public concern speech as everything that is not totally personal: "*only* speech that deals with 'individual personnel disputes and grievances' and that would be of '*no* relevance to the public's evaluation of the performance of governmental agencies' is generally *not* of 'public

---

[85] *Rankin*, 483 U.S. at 387; *see also United States v. Bagdasarian*, 652 F.3d 1113, 1116 (9th Cir. 2011) (private individual's post on online message board: "Obama fk the niggar, he will have a 50 cal in the head soon" and "shoot the nig" were not true threats because the speaker did not mean to "communicate a *serious* expression of an intent to commit an act of unlawful violence.").

[86] *See Davis v. Ector County, Tex.*, 40 F.3d 777 (5th Cir. 1994) (After his employer told him not to involve the district attorney's office in a sexual harassment claim being made by his wife, the employee, a task force investigator, wrote a letter detailing his wife's allegations and was terminated. His termination violated the First Amendment.); *Wilson v. UT Health Ctr.*, 973 F.2d 1263 (5th Cir. 1992).

[87] *Smith v. Fruin*, 28 F.3d 646 (7th Cir. 1994).

[88] *See Bonn v. City of Omaha*, 623 F.3d 587 (8th Cir. 2010); *Kline v. Valentic*, 283 Fed. Appx 913 (3rd Cir. 2008) (*citing Vose v. Kliment*, 506 F.3d 565, 569 (7th Cir. 2007), *Markos v. City of Atlanta, Texas*, 364 F.3d 567, 570 (5th Cir. 2004)).

concern.'"[89]

4. Speech That Occurs in the Workplace

Speech that occurs in the workplace, or is made regarding work related issues, is very often not found to have the protection of the First Amendment, *even when it involves issues of legitimate "public concern."* For workplace speech to be protected at all, it must satisfy the "public concern" requirement. But, as we have seen from the *Garcetti* decision, work-related speech can fall outside the First Amendment protection if the speech is made as an extension of the employee's normal "job duties."

The newly imposed *Garcetti* "job duties" test effectively removes a wide swath of public employee speech from First Amendment protection. But even before *Garcetti,* based on the *Connick* balancing approach, many forms of work-related speech fell outside the ambit of the First Amendment.

The question posed is whether a public employee's First Amendment interest to speak on matters of public concern is outweighed by any disruption that the speech may cause to the efficiency of the public employer's enterprise.

Connick v. Myers. In *Connick v. Myers,*[90] the Supreme Court drew a distinction between employee speech on matters of "public concern" — which it found to be protected, and matters only of personal concern, such as employee grievances — which it found be unprotected. Since *Connick*, the courts have had to determine whether speech involved primarily (1) a public concern, or (2) a personal grievance. Even in the former category — speech affecting a public concern — speech is *only* protected when it does not unduly disrupt the workplace in the manner in which it is expressed.

The question posed is whether a public employee's First

---

[89] *Robinson v. York*, 566 F.3d at 822 (emphasis added) (*quoting McKingley v. City of Eloy*, 705 F.2d 1110, 1114 (9th Cir. 1983)); *see also Thomas v. City of Beaverton*, 379 F. 3d 802, 808 (9th Cir. 2004) (finding that an employee's misconduct report alleging discrimination was protected even though it addressed personnel matters because "it did not pertain to [the employee's] own job status.").

[90] 1 IER Cases 179 (1983).

Amendment interest to speak on matters of public concern is outweighed by any disruption that the speech may cause to the efficiency of the public employer's enterprise.[91] The result of this balancing test varies, depending upon the nature of the employee's expression.[92] The more central the matter of public concern is to the speech at issue, the stronger the employer's showing of counterbalancing governmental interests must be.[93]

Rankin v. McPherson. The Supreme Court in *Rankin v. McPherson,*[94] listed factors relevant to assessing undue disruption:

> Whether the statement impairs discipline by superiors or harmony among coworkers has a detrimental impact on close working relationships for which personal loyalty and confidence are necessary, or impedes the performance of the speaker's duties, or interferes with the regular operation of the enterprise.[95]

The *Connick* court looked at similar factors, but it stated that a stronger showing by the government agency of disruption may be necessary if the employee's speech is more substantially involved in matters of public concern.[96]

Waters v. Churchill. The 1994 Supreme Court decision in *Waters v. Churchill*[97] seems to strengthen the employer's hand in the balancing test. Prior to *Waters*, evaluating the "disruption factor" required a finding of *actual* disruption.[98] In *Waters*, however, the court found the need to show "likely" disruption, not actual disruption: "The *potential* disruptiveness of the speech as reported was enough to outweigh whatever First Amendment value it might have had...."[99]

---

[91] *See Pickering v. Board of Education*, 391 U.S. 563, 572-73, 20 L. Ed. 2d 811 (1968); *Waters v. Churchill*, 128 L. Ed. 2d 686, 114 S.Ct. 1878 (1994).

[92] *Connick*, 461 U.S. at 150.

[93] *See Caughlin v. Lee*, 946 F.2d 1152, 1157 (5th Cir. 1991). *See, also, United States v. National Treasury Employees Union*, 130 L. Ed. 2d 964, 15 S.Ct. 1003, 1021 (1995) (O'Connor, J., concurring in judgment and dissenting in part) ("As the magnitude of the intrusion on the employee's interest rises, so does the government's burden of justification").

[94] 483 U.S. 378, 97 L. Ed. 2d 315, 107 S.Ct. 2891 (1987).

[95] 483 U.S. at 388, citing *Pickering*, 391 U.S. at 570-73.

[96] *See Connick* 461 U.S. 138 at 151 (The statements in *Connick* were closely related and connected to a personal grievance.).

[97] *511 U.S. 661, 679,* 114 S.Ct. 1878, 128 L. Ed. 2d 686 (1994).

[98] *See Vamboni v. Stamler*, 847 F.2d 73, 78 (3d Cir. 1988) (public criticism of proposed reorganization of prosecutor's office), cert. denied, 488 U.S. 899, 102 L. Ed. 2d 233, 109 S.Ct. 245 (1988).

Waters was the manager of the Philadelphia Police Department EAP manager. Waters was quoted in a newspaper article criticizing aspects of the EAP. He discussed the lack of official policies which caused problems in two areas: One dealing with maintaining confidentiality as to the identity of police officers who sought counseling and the other dealing with reimbursement for services referred to providers by the EAP. He was later terminated and sued for retaliation.

Waters ultimately prevailed in his lawsuit, but the Supreme Court adopted a more lenient test of "disruption" in the process of ruling on his claim. In discussing the balancing of interests, the Court in *Waters* distinguished between the disruption caused by actions independent of the speech at issue and disruption caused by the speech itself. As in the other cases, the "disharmony" and "discontent" appear to be the result of the very problems to which the speech was directed.[100] There was no evidence in the *Waters* case to show that the discontent in the police department was caused by Waters' speech rather than the problems to which Waters' speech was addressed. The *Waters* court found that the city simply did not make the requisite substantial showing that the speech was likely to be disruptive.[101]

Potential Disruption Factor. There are several cases that demonstrate this "potential disruption factor" in the context of law enforcement agencies. In *Glass v. County of Chippewa,*[102] an officer spoke to another officer regarding the possible illegal conduct of a supervisor. The conversation was off-duty and at home. The main issue in the case was whether Glass's speech interfered with the working relationships between coworkers and supervisors in a manner whereby public service is compromised. According to the Seventh Circuit Court of Appeals, the employee's failure to follow the proper chain of command was a factor in the court's decision. The issues of mutual trust and respect among officers and between officers and supervisors, the court explained are particularly important in law enforcement and the risks of disharmony can be grave. This heightened need for trust and harmony was found a permissible consideration when balancing interests.[103]

Tyler v. City of Mt. Home[104] involved a city sergeant who wrote a

---

99 114 S.Ct. at 1890 (emphasis added).

100 *See Monsanto*, 674 F.2d at 999; *Waters*, 55 F.3d at 898.

101 55 F.3d at 899.

102 2 F.3d 733, 742 (7th Cir. 1993).

103 2 F.3d at 743.

104 72 F.3d 568 (8th Cir. 1995).

letter on city letterhead to a sergeant in the county sheriff's department.He complaining about certain deputies of the county who had been violating policy regarding arrest of suspects with blood alcohol levels in excess of legal limits. City police department employees had received prior instruction that letters on official stationery had to be cleared with the chief of police first. The county sergeant wrote a letter to the city chief of police regarding the argumentative manner of the city sergeant's letter and his failure to follow the chain of command. In his letter, the county sergeant stated that the incident could damage the good relationship between the city and the county.

Work-related speech involving traditional union or working condition concerns are more likely to be deemed protected speech.

The Eighth Circuit Court of Appeals in *Tyler* affirmed the District Court's grant of summary judgment in favor of the city, citing *Tindle v. Caudell*:[105]

> Because policy departments function as paramilitary organizations charged with maintaining public safety and order, they are given more latitude in their decisions regarding discipline and personnel regulations than an ordinary government employer.[106]

Working condition speech. Work-related speech involving traditional union or working condition concerns are more likely to be deemed protected speech. For example, comments made by firefighters regarding safety and other staffing level concerns have been found to relate to a "public concern."[107] Also, where there have been ongoing labor-management disputes that have become publicized, the courts have extended union presidents greater

[105] 56 F.3d 966, 971 (8th Cir. 1995) ("The public safety employer's determinations of both the potential for disruption as a result of the speech, as well as the employer's response to the actual or perceived disruption, are entitled to "considerable judicial deference").

[106] *Tyler*, 72 F.3d at 570, citing *Shands v. City of Kennett, 993 F.2d 1337, 1345 (8th Cir. 1993).*

[107] *See, e.g., Moore v. Kilgore*, 4 IER Cases 1175 (5th Cir. 1989) (overturning discipline of firefighter and president of firefighter association who stated at a press conference that the staff reduction had caused the injury and a death of two firefighters at a recent fire).

leeway in publicly airing what might otherwise be considered to be a personal grievance.[108]

On the other hand, courts have been most likely to find matters to be only of a personal concern where they relate to criticisms of "mismanagement" where the employee has been involved in conflicts with supervisors. So, for example, a court found not to be protected a lieutenant's letter to City Council claiming the police department was mismanaged after the lieutenant had been denied a promotion.[109]

courts have been most likely to find matters to be only of a personal concern where they relate to criticisms of "mismanagement" where the employee has been involved in conflicts with supervisors

The more difficult issue for the courts to resolve are those which involve primarily personnel matters, but are nonetheless *also* matters of public importance. This category of cases includes, for example, discrimination cases. Courts have generally allowed employees protection in their speech regarding sexual harassment claims, providing these types of claims greater protection often than other workplace grievances.[110]

Complaints about workplace operations are sometimes but not always found unprotected. At least one court found protected a a prosecutor's complaint about the office's reorganization. It found it to be a matter of public concern — even though the primary motivation of the employee in making the complaint was the adverse manner in which the reorganization affected him personally. This court indicated, nonetheless, that the personal motivation was only *one factor* to look at in determining whether the speech affected a public concern.[111] On the other hand, another court found an employee's comments regarding the lack of

---

108 *See Roberts v. Binkley*, 5 IER Cases 1855 (C.D. Cal., 1990); *Wulf v. City of Wichita*, 1 IER Cases 895 (D.C. Kan., 1986).

109 *McEvoy v. Shoemaker*, 4 IER Cases 1223 (19th Cir. 1989); *see, also, Terrell v. University of Texas System Police*, 1 IER Cases 1455 (5th Cir. 1986) (finding the contents of a diary in which a police captain kept critical commentary about the chief where the captain had himself been under investigation not to be protected speech).

110 *Davis v. Ector County, Texas* 10 IER Cases 225 (5th Cir. 1994); *Wilson v. University of Texas Health Center*, 7 IER Cases 1513 (5th Cir. 1992).

111 *Samboni v. Stamler* 847 F.2d 73 (3rd Cir. 1988).

enforcement of the smoking ordinance not to be protected as he was only advancing his own interest in a smoke-free workplace.[112]

In another case, an Ohio federal court upheld a reprimand of a sheriff's department civilian employee who complained to the FBI about the treatment of her son during an arrest by a deputy sheriff. She was reprimanded for violating a department rule requiring that grievances first be submitted to a supervisor.[113] The court sought to stress that its finding was based on the fact that the only discipline imposed was a written reprimand.

Nonetheless, other courts likely would have reached a different result on these facts *without regard to whether the discipline was minor or not.* The allegations of a civil rights violation had no relationship with her job other than the fact that she happened to be an employee in that department. She was not complaining to the FBI about misconduct that she had discovered through her work, but rather was complaining about something that affected a family member, a complaint which any private citizen would have had a right to file. Consequently, it would be difficult to characterize this has a "workplace concern" as described by the Supreme Court in *Connick v. Myers*.

Policymaker exception. Another issue that the courts have had to deal with is the dilemma of high-ranking officials who speak out on matters of clear public concern, yet have a confidential or "policy-making" relationship to the employer whom they are criticizing. Washington courts have followed the approach of the federal court in adopting a "policymaker" exception to the public concern speech protection doctrine. Therefore, high-ranking officials, those who are involved in the creation or implementation of an employer's policy, are not protected by the First Amendment when they criticize that employer publicly.[114]

Whistleblower speech. The category of speech often referred to a "whistleblower speech" is generally accorded a high degree of protection under the First Amendment. Consequently, courts have overturned on First Amendment Grounds disciplinary action against public-safety employees who have raised issues regarding department corruption.[115] As discussed above, under *Garcetti* employees wishing to present complaints have a strong incentive to present those in the form of a whistleblower complaint rather than

---

[112] *Smith v. Fruin*, 9 IER Cases 1203 (7th Cir. 1994).

[113] *Huber v. Leis*, 4 IER Cases 43 (Southern District of Ohio, 1989).

[114] *Dicomes v. State of Washington*, 4 IER Cases 1635 (1989).

[115] *Brawner v. Richardson*, Texas 3 IER Cases 1377 (5th Cir. 1988); *McDonald v. City of Freeport*, 8 IER Cases 1635 (S.D. Tex. 1993).

utilizing the chain of command.

Washington public employees have the additional protection offered under the state whistleblower law. The law requires local governments to enact whistleblower ordinances. Under these ordinances, municipalities and counties are required to create a procedure by which employees may complain about official misconduct.

It is a fairly common practice for public safety departments to have department regulations purporting to restrict when and how employees may speak. Many of these appear unconstitutional.

5. Validity of Department Rules Regulating Speech

It is a fairly common practice for public safety departments to have department regulations purporting to restrict when and how employees may speak. Many of these appear unconstitutional. The primary problem with many of these rules is they tend to be overbroad in what they regulate, and they require prior notification and sometimes even prior approval before an employee can speak.

The majority of cases that have dealt with the subject of prior restraints in the public employment setting have taken a dim view as to their constitutional validity. It practically goes without saying that government employers will have to provide strong justifications for any prior restraint to pass constitutional muster with the courts.

Generally, public employees who find themselves subject to on-the-job rules restricting their ability to speak with the media have two avenues of First Amendment protection available to challenge the restrictions: First, employees can attack the rules as being facially unconstitutional because of vagueness and/or overbreadth, or second, employees can challenge the rule as applied, thus invoking the use of the *Pickering* balancing test. Employees have been successful using both approaches, and following the United States Supreme Court's decision in *National Treasury Employees Union,*[116] *(NTEU),* courts appear to be more willing to apply the *Pickering* approach to broad forms of prior restraint.

Department "prior restraint" rules have proven especially

[116] 10 IER Cases 452 (U.S. S.Ct 1995).

difficult to sustain. Two Second Circuit cases highlight this difficulty for employers. In *Harman v. City of New York*,[117] the Second Circuit, in 1998, disallowed a city regulation forbidding employees from speaking with media regarding agency policies or activities without first obtaining permission. The court reasoned that the city's interest in preventing the disclosure of confidential information was not enough to outweigh the First Amendment problems of self-censorship, delay, and the lack of objective review criteria.

But the following year in *Latino Officers Ass'n v. Safir*,[118] the Second Circuit permitted a similar pre-speaking ban. In *Latino Officers*, plaintiffs challenged a police department's requirements that all officers notify the department of their intention to speak before a governmental agency or a private organization about department policy and also provide an after-the-fact summary of their comments.[119] In this case, the court found the theoretical possibility of a chilling effect on officers' speech too conjectural and insufficient to establish irreparable harm.[120]

The Third Circuit has also highlighted a particular difficulty in assessing pre-speech regulation. In the *Weaver v. U.S. Information Agency*, a pre-speech regulation was upheld.[121] The statute required employees to submit all speaking, writing, and teaching material on matters of "official concern" for pre-publication review.[122] The court found this rule to be valid because the statute *did not actually prohibit any speech*, i.e. the agency had no power to punish the employees.[123] In fact, the court also implied that it would have ruled differently if the agency had, in fact, been able to punish its employees for the speech itself.[124]

SUMMARY OF PUBLIC EMPLOYEES' FREE SPEECH RIGHTS

- Courts apply a "balancing test" to weigh the extent speech involves public concern against the extent it causes workplace disruption.

[117] *Harman v. City of New York, 140 F.3d 111* (2nd Cir 1998).
[118] *Latino Officers Ass'n v. Safir*, 170 F.3d 167 (2nd Cir. 1999).
[119] *Id.* at 171.
[120] *Id.*
[121] *Weaver v. U.S. Info. Agency*, 87 F.3d 1429 (D.C. Cir. 1996).
[122] *Id* at 1435.
[123] *Id.*
[124] *Id.* at 1436.

- Speech outside the workplace addressing issue of public concern is almost always protected speech.
- Speech that is defamatory or obscene is almost always unprotected speech.
- Workplace speech primarily about personal concerns and workplace conflicts is generally not protected.
- Workplace speech regarding public policy, discrimination, safety, corruption and other issues of interest to the public is generally protected.
- Speech in a paramilitary organization is more likely to be found disruptive than speech in a civilian department.
- Rules that require prior approval before an employee may speak are generally unconstitutional.

Some courts[125] have found the regulations in question to be unconstitutional because the rules failed to provide the "narrow, objective and definitive standards" necessary to guide the reviewing official, something these courts find to be required by the Supreme Court decision in *Shuttlesworth v. City of Birmingham.*[126] Others, such as the Fifth Circuit Court of Appeals in *Barrett v. Thomas,*[127] have struck down prior restraint regulations because they were too overbroad, vague, or both. The regulation at issue in *Barrett* prohibited the unauthorized statements, comments to the news media which could be "controversial," and any discussion of matters pertaining to rules or policies with any elected officials or department heads. The court found these rules to be unconstitutional because they could not be narrowly specified and were both overbroad and vague. A number of other federal courts have also stricken down such regulations.[128]

---

125 *See Fire Fighters Ass'n Dist. of Columbia v. Barry*, 742 F. Supp. 1182 (D.D.C. 1990), (ruling unconstitutional a rule which required that any interview given by a member of the department be pre-approved); *Spain v. City of Mansfield*, 915 F. Supp. 919 (N.D. Ohio 1996), (rules requiring that no member speak without permission of the fire chief and that captains and assistant chiefs not comment publicly on matters concerning department rules and policies without prior written consent found to be unconstitutional).

126 394 U.S. 147 (1969).

127 649 F.2d 1193 (1981).

128 See *Wolf v. City of Aberdeen, S.D.*, 758 F. Supp. 551 (D.S.D. 1991), (Rule requiring firemen to get prior approval before making a speech or granting an interview, or making a comment on department rules or regulations found to be overbroad); *Micilcavage v. Connelie*, 570 F. Supp. 975 (N.D.N.Y. 1983) (rule requiring state trooper to get authorization before making public speech found to be overbroad and vague); *Salerno v. O'Rourke*, 555 F. Supp. 750

Washington courts have not yet ruled on this issue, except to say that when a statute restricts political speech the burden is on the government to justify the restriction.[129] The Ninth Circuit has yet to issue a definitive ruling as to these prior restraint rules. But it would be expected, based on the Ninth Circuit's general approach to public employee speech rights, that it would likely take a dim view of the validity of such rules.

Dress as "speech." Although courts are greatly divided over the extent to which freedom of speech trumps a public employer's dress code, uniform adornments are generally excluded whenever they are a potential source of undue disruption presenting a safety or other legitimate business concern.[130] Because what a public employee wears reflects directly on the department and often involves safety concerns, the public employer has a direct interest in regulating dress codes.[131]

But public employees also have a strong interest in expressing their opinions (political or otherwise). A competition of interests is created when a personal view requires or is advanced by a clothing choice or adornment. While greater leeway is generally given by courts to non-uniformed[132] and off-duty employees,[133] many courts

---

(D.C.N.J. 1983) (rule requiring consent of sheriff before information could be giving to news media or the public found to be overbroad).

[129] *Washington State Republican Party v. Washington State Pub. Disclosure Comm'n*, 141 Wn.2d 245, 254 (2000).

[130] *See e.g., EEOC v. Kelly Services, 598 F.3d 1022* (8th Cir. 2010) (upholds an employer's safety policy prohibiting headwear and loose-fitting clothing for workers at a printing plant because the employer had a "legitimate, nondiscriminatory ... facially neutral, safety-driven dress policy prohibiting all employees ... from wearing loose clothing or headwear of any kind"); *Kalsi v. N.Y. Transit Auth., 62 F. Supp. 2d 745* (E.D.N.Y. 1999) (sustaining the termination of a public employee who refused to wear a protective helmet for religious reasons); *Seabrook v. City of N.Y., 80 Fair Empl. Prac. Cas. (BNA) 1452* (S.D.N.Y. 1999) (Federal court rejects the religious claims of women corrections officers who demanded the right to wear skirts on duty; emergency response vests could not be properly secured unless they wore pants). *See also Jenkins v. New York City Transit Auth., 646 F. Supp. 2d 464* (S.D.N.Y. 2009) (refusing to dismiss a suit brought by a terminated female Pentecostal bus driver challenging a rule requiring all drivers to wear pants had a disparate impact on her religion, which requires women to wear skirts, where she alleged that she was terminated for refusal to comply with policy and that there was no business justification for it).

[131] *See, e.g., Troster v. Pa. Dept. Corr.*, 65 F.3d 1086, 10 IER Cases (BNA) 1714 (3rd Cir. 1995) (employer permitted to require a patriotic flag patch on correction officer uniforms); *Kalsi v. N.Y. Transit Auth., 62 F. Supp. 2d 745* (E.D.N.Y. 1999) (employer could terminate a public employee who refused to wear a protective helmet for religious reasons).

allow employers to disallow pro-union or religious pins[134] and religious clothing or headgear[135] while on duty if the employer's rule is intended to advance employee safety or the smooth functioning of the agency.[136] But this flexibility does not extend to most federally-funded employees who, as a group, are prohibited by the Hatch Act from announcing any *partisan* messages at work.

Courts have found that a public employer may regulate postings to bulletin boards (either physical or electronic) around the office. For example, an employer may require a posting receive a stamp of approval before being posted and may remove all unstamped postings.[137] Employers can generally deny access to a

---

132 *See Miss. Emp. Sec. Cmsn. v. McGlothin*, 556 So.2d 324 (Miss. Sup. Ct. 1990) (upholding the right of non-uniformed public employees to wear religion-inspired headgear at work); *Daniels v. City of Arlington*, 246 F.3d 500 (5th Cir. 2001) (officer was permitted to wear a cross pin in a non-uniformed position but not in a uniformed position); *but see Cooper v. Eugene School Dist. 4J*, 301 Ore. 358, 723 P.2d 298; *appeal dismissed*, 480 U.S. 942, 107 S. Ct. 1597 (1987) (permitting a public employer's prohibition of religious garb at work).

133 *See Leonard v. City of* Columbus, 705 F. 2d 1299, *reh. en banc. denied*, 716 F.2d 914 (11th Cir. 1983) (permitting picketing in uniform); *PBA NY State Troopers and Div. of State Police*, 37 NYPER (LRP) 4533, 2004 NYPER (LRP) Lexis 111 (NY PERB 2004) (holding that off-duty troopers can wear police union pins when they attend a criminal trial, while off-duty and in civilian clothes). *But see Belch v. Jefferson Co.*, 108 F.Supp.2d 143 (N.D.N.Y 2000) (unreported) (reprimand of a deputy sheriff for appearing on TV in uniform without the sheriff's approval did not violate the First Amendment).

134 *Compare Communications Workers of Am. v. Ector County Hosp. Dist.*, 467 F.3d 427 (5th Cir. 2006) (the on-duty uniform non-adornment policy, as content and viewpoint-neutral restriction did not violate free speech rights of employee who was disciplined for refusing to remove pro-union badge.), *and Daniels v. City of Arlington*, 246 F.3d 500 (5th Cir. 2001) (finding that officer's communication of his personal religious views through a cross pin was not speech addressing a "legitimate public concern" and termination for violating the department's "no-pins" policy did not violate the First Amendment), *with Sheriff of Worcester County v. Labor Relations Comm'n*, 60 Mass. App. Ct. 632, 805 N.E.2d 46 (2004) (management must bargain with the union before ordering the removal of union buttons from their uniforms, where the officers wore those buttons for many years without adverse consequences), *and Town of Oxford and Mass. Coalition of Police*, L-173 AFL-CIO, MUP-2659 (Mass. LRC 2004) (absent an actual showing of harm, management cannot prohibit uniformed public employees from wearing a union pin).

135 *Compare EEOC v. GEO Group*, 616 F.3d 265 (3rd Cir. 2010) (panel splits 2-to-1, upholding a regulation barring correctional employees from wearing non-uniform headwear), *with Webb v. City of Philadelphia, 562 F.3d 256 (*3rd Cir. 2009) (upholding a Philadelphia Police Dept. ban on scarves and other religious headgear because prohibiting all religious symbols and attire, helps prevent any divisiveness when officers encounter a diverse population).

136 *See* n.93, *supra*.

group in a neutrally drafted manner,[138] and are sometimes required to exclude content to maintain political neutrality. [139] On the other hand, management is not allowed to limit specific messages because of the nonproscribable content of the messages.[140]

C. The Right to Engage in Political Activities

The right to engage (or not to engage) in political campaigns or parties of one's choosing is fundamental to the rights of an American citizen. Despite the primacy of that right, courts have upheld federal laws (the Hatch Act) and state law which restrict the right of a federal employee to participate in parties and political campaigns. These laws still allow the employees to speak out on other matters of public importance, including non-partisan political issues.

Washington state law. While a number of other states have followed the federal government's lead towards their own employees, Washington State has not. In fact, Washington state law affirmatively *grants* public employees the right to participate fully in all types of elections.[141] And Washington's law has been interpreted by the courts to "preempt" and thereby prohibit local regulation of their employee's right to participate in elections.[142]

Constitutionality of patronage systems. While the Supreme Court has not upheld the public employee's right to participate in partisan political elections, it has, on the other hand, protected public employees as well from their *non-participation* in partisan elections and politics. The Court has ruled that except for top-level "policymaking" employees, an employer may not use a new election as a basis for discharging employees based on their political beliefs or partisan affiliations.[143]

The Court took aim at what prior to 1976 had been a well-established and well-recognized practice, at least in many states, of political patronage. The Court found that while patronage might

---

137 *See Kuchenreuther v. City of Milwaukee*, 221 F.3d 967 (7th Cir. 2000).

138 *See The Guard Publ'g Co. v. NLRB*, 571 F.3d 53 (D.C. 2009).

139 *See Hatch Act*, 5 U.S.C. §§ 7321-7326; *Burrus v. Vegliante*, 336 F.3d 82 (2nd Cir. 2003) (the next memo in chapter 9 will have a political rights section that will discuss the *Hatch Act* more fully).

140 *See e.g., Latino Officers Ass'n v. City of New York*, 1998 U.S. Dist. LEXIS 2018 (S.D.N.Y. 1998) (department could not restrict use of bulletin boards based on political dislike of group).

141 RCW 41.06.250.

142 *Bellevue Firefighters Local 1604 v. City of Bellevue*, 100 Wn.2d 748, 675 P.2d 592 (1984).

143 *Elrod v. Burns*, 1 IER Cases 61 (1976).

have become a "tradition" in many localities, it was not constitutional. The Court holding as to whether an individual was a "policymaker" was not whether state law had accorded the individual civil service protection, but whether the individual actually made policy for the employer. The non-discrimination rule enunciated in *Elrod v. Burns* was later extended by the court to all types of personnel actions including promotions and transfers.[144]

Policymaker exception. On the other hand, courts have recognized a legitimate "policymaker exception" to this rule. The rationale provided for this exception is that someone who is "paid a salary so that she will contribute to an agency's effective operation begins to do or say things that detract from the agency's effective operation, the government employer must have some power to restrain her."[145] This "policymaker exception" recognizes that an elected official must "be able to appoint some high-level personally and politically loyal officials who will help him implement the policies that the public voted for."[146]

Because it would violate this necessary loyalty, employees who are involved in the creation or implementation of an employer's policy, are not protected by the First Amendment when they criticize their employer publicly.[147] The elected official, therefore, may dismiss "policymaking employees" if they are "no longer loyal, if they oppose his reelection, or simply if the official would prefer to work with someone else."[148]

To determine if an employee is a "policymaker" the court considered several factors: "vague or broad responsibilities, relative pay, technical competence, power to control others, authority to speak in the name of policymakers, public perception, influence on programs, contact with elected officials, and responsiveness to partisan politics and political leaders."[149] The Ninth Circuit has held that the "most critical factor" is whether an employee has "influence over programs."[150] In one case, the U.S. Supreme Court ruled that public defenders were not "policymakers" but

---

[144] *Rutan v. Republican Party of Illinois*, 5 IER Cases 673 (1990).

[145] *Borough of Duryea v. Guarnieri*, 131 S. Ct. 2488, *180 L. Ed. 2d 408* (2011) (*citing Waters v. Churchill*, 511 U.S. 661, 675, 114 S. Ct. 1878, 128 L. Ed. 2d 686 (1994) (plurality opinion)).

[146] *Bardzik*, 635 F.3d at 1144.

[147] *Dicomes v. State of Washington*, 113 Wn.2d 612, 625-26, *782 P.2d 1002* (1989).

[148] *Bardzik*, 635 F.3d at 1144.

[149] *Id* at 1151, *citing Fazio v. City of S.F.*, 125 F.3d 1328, 1334 (9th Cir. 1997) *cert. denied, 523 U.S. 1074* (1998).

[150] *Walker v. City of Lakewood*, 272 F.3d 1132 (9th Cir. 2001).

specifically declined to rule as to whether deputy prosecuting attorneys were.[151]

Mid-level law enforcement employees are clearly *not* policymakers. For example, in one case the court found that the head jailer and administrative assistant were not policymakers and could not be discharged due to their political affiliation.[152] While other circuits disagree, the Ninth Circuit Court of Appeals has specifically held that a sheriff's lieutenant cannot be terminated for running against the incumbent sheriff as the lieutenant was not a policymaker.[153] Instead, the employer bears the burden of proving, on a case-by-case basis, that the terminated employee was, in fact, a policymaker. Even "though a private person is perfectly free to uninhibitedly and robustly criticize an elected official's policies," the Ninth Circuit has "never suggested that the Constitution bars the elected official from firing a high-ranking deputy for doing the same thing."[154]

Small employers. Application of the Supreme Court's patronage rules has sometimes proven to be difficult in small counties where there have been contentious elections. In one case involving a small Texas county where the new sheriff failed to retain most of the employees who had supported the incumbent, the court remanded the matter for a factual determination as to whether the employees' conduct during and subsequent to the election was so disruptive as to interfere with the proper functioning of the newly elected sheriff's operations.[155] At least in that court, as it has been with others, it was an open question whether the election conduct might prove to be disqualifying for future employment.

Although these federal cases seem to be in conflict, Washington public safety employees have a much broader right to be free from political patronage by statute.

But the courts are divided on the question. In the Texas case, for example, there was a strong dissenting opinion accompanying

[151] *Branti v. Finkel*, 445 U.S. 507, 100 S.Ct. 1287, 63 L.Ed.2d 574 (1980).

[152] *Dickeson v. Kuarberg*, 844 F.2d 1435 (10th Cir. 1988).

[153] *Walker*, 272 F.3d at 1145; *Thomas v. Carpenter*, 881 F.2d 828 (9th Cir. 1989).

[154] *Bardzik*, 635 F.3d at 1144 (*citing Moran v. Washington*, 147 F.3d 839, 82 (9th Cir. 1998)).

[155] *McBee v. Jim Hogg County*, 1 IER Cases 375 (5th Cir. 1984).

the decision. The dissent argued that their activity was irrelevant because it was constitutionally protected regardless of the specific conduct at issue. The approach of the dissent is the approach most other courts likely would have followed under these circumstances, but this remains a contested issue.

Although these federal cases seem to be in conflict, Washington public safety employees have a much broader right to be free from political patronage by statute. Most public safety employees are covered under civil service, and the entire thrust of the civil service process is to protect employees from such patronage-based personnel actions. But as discussed above, except for those employees covered by a labor agreement, these issues would need to be presented in front of a civil service commission which may or may not view claims of retaliation sympathetically.

On at least two occasions in recent years, incumbent Sheriffs have attempted to keep challengers off the ballot by complaining to the federal Hatch enforcement agency that their opponent's salary had been financed partially by federal grants.

Washington State Hatch Act issues. Despite the unequivocal right of political participation for Washington local government employees, there has arisen in a few recent Sheriff campaigns a technical issue concerning the federal Hatch Act. The Hatch Act is a federal law prohibiting federal employees (with a few notable exceptions) from engaging in partisan political activity.[156] The Hatch Act also extends to individuals employed by a State or local agency whose principal employment is in connection with an activity which is *financed*, in whole or in part, by loans or grants made by the United States or a Federal agency, except for educational and research facilities.[157]

On at least two occasions in recent years, incumbent Sheriffs have attempted to keep challengers off the ballot by complaining to the federal Hatch enforcement agency that their opponent's salary had been financed partially by federal grants. Often the grants at issue are not even direct federal grants, but funds passed through the state, and often for overtime hours for traffic enforcement. The

---

[156] *See* "About the Hatch Act: Federal Employees." *U.S. Office of Special Council,* http://www.osc.gov/hatchact.htm.

[157] *Id.*

federal attorneys actually take this pass through claims very seriously and threaten to block candidacies, but they also apply a de minimis rule and do not object when the grant funds constituted a very minor percentage of the income. The federal standards are not completely clear but usually no objection is made to such candidates when only several hours of pay was federally funded and the candidates indicate they will accept no further overtime.

D. Privacy Rights

Public safety employees have a number of statutory and constitutional protections against an undue invasion of their privacy. The parameters of these rights are still developing, but, in general, there has been an effort by the courts to balance the interests of the public safety employers and the public safety employees.

1. The Right to Privacy in Medical and Psychological Examinations

Police safety employees are in occupations that can take a tremendous physical and mental toll. Public safety employers traditionally have ordered employees to submit to a fitness for duty examinations when they suspect that the employees are having difficulty performing the job because of injury, illness, or emotional difficulty. In the past, courts and arbitrators have been deferential to employers' concern for the welfare of the officers, fellow employees, and the public. The ADA, however, revised many of the past rules.

ADA Guidelines. If an employee can perform the essential functions of the job, the department has no right to request a fitness for duty examination. But if a department has reasonable grounds for believing that an employee cannot perform these essential functions, then it may require the employee to obtain a medical or psychological examination. The examination must be "job related" and "consistent with business necessity."

In the 20 year since the implementation of the ADA, the case law to date remains sparse concerning the justification and evidence needed for an employer to have a sufficient basis to compel a medical or psychological examination. Certainly, if the employee has demonstrable on-the-job problems for which there is no ready explanation, the employer may require a properly focused medical examination to determine if there is a medical cause for the difficulties.

Yin v. California. In its initial case to address this issue the Ninth Circuit decision on this issue released to date, the court indicated some degree of deference to management's claims of business necessity. In *Yin v. California,*[158] the court ruled that an employee's claim — that she had been improperly compelled to submit to a medical examination when there was no demonstrated inability to perform the job — lacked merit. The individual had an attendance record that involved an advanced amount of sick leave usage. There had also been some indications of on-the-job impacts from these illnesses. Under these circumstances, the court reasoned that there was a sufficient business necessity to compel an examination.

Brownfield v. City of Yakima. More recently, in *Brownfield v. City of Yakima,*[159] the Ninth Circuit explained that the business necessity test is not limited to situations where the employee has demonstrated an inability to do the job. The court ruled that business necessity might also apply to "prophylactic" examinations to determine whether fitness, "especially when the employer is engaged in dangerous work."

In *Brownfield,* an officer periodically would become enraged during interactions with management. After several incidents, one of which involved the officer becoming "consumed" with anger and fear about his community service partner, the department referred him for a fitness exam. A psychologist concluded that the officer was unfit for duty. A later examination by his doctor cleared him for duty, after which the department wanted an additional examination. He refused the additional examination and was terminated for insubordination. The Ninth Circuit then addressed the legality of the fitness examination order.

> The court explained the employer's right to request an examination was real but not limitless

The City of Yakima argued that it had a business necessity.[160] The Ninth Circuit agreed, concluding that the department did not violate the ADA because it had a reasonable and legitimate to doubt the officer's ability to perform the duties of a police officer.

The court explained the employer's right to request an examination was real but not limitless:

---

[158] 95 F.3d 864 (9th Cir. 1996).

[159] 612 F.3d 1140 (9th Cir. Wash. 2010).

[160] *Brownfield,* 612 F.3d 1140.

> In interpreting the "business necessity" standard in another ADA context, we have cautioned that it "is quite high, and is not to be confused with mere expediency."

The court explained that an "employee's behavior cannot be merely annoying or inefficient to justify an examination; rather, there must be genuine reason to doubt whether that employee can perform job-related functions."

The court further explained in *Brownfield* that the justification test must be an "objective" one, applying the "reasonable person" standard. It also held, despite granting employers the right to do "prophylactic" examinations that the burden of demonstrating "business necessity" fell upon the employer. It explained that especially in the context of law enforcement work, some deference would be extended to the employer's judgments:

> Brownfield attempts to explain away each incident by providing background facts suggesting his reactions were entirely reasonable and by challenging the third-party reports as factually inaccurate, but he does not dispute that he reacted as described or that the third-party reports were made to the YPD. Although a minor argument with a coworker or isolated instances of lost temper would likely fall short of establishing business necessity, Brownfield's repeated volatile responses are of a different character. Moreover, our consideration of the FFDEs' [Fitness for Duty Examination] legitimacy is heavily colored by the nature of Brownfield's employment. Police officers are likely to encounter extremely stressful and dangerous situations during the course of their work. *See Watson*, 177 F.3d at 935 ("Police departments place armed officers in positions where they can do tremendous harm if they act irrationally."). When a police department has good reason to doubt an officer's ability to respond to these situations in an appropriate manner, an FFDE is consistent with the ADA. Reasonable cause to question Brownfield's ability to serve as a police officer was present here.[161]

Causes triggering a fit for duty examination. There are a

[161] Id. at 1146-47.

number of circumstances under which the employer might have a right to compel a medical examination:

- The employee indicates a disability and requests an accommodation;
- It appears that the employee might have a medical limitation that could interfere with the job;
- There is an unexplained performance deficiency;
- The employer has complied with the EEOC requirements to establish a "periodic physical examination" of the employees — the program must be as established under "federal, state or local law" and be consistent with the ADA.

Often, the employer or the doctor will try to get the employee to sign a "waiver" that would allow the doctor to make unrestricted reports to the employer. The legality of these waivers is doubtful.

Scope of Report. The ADA was drafted with a lack of clarity regarding the role of the doctor and what the doctor can report to the employer. Courts have yet to clarify what those restrictions are, but at least one plausible reading of the statute is that the doctor is only permitted to report to the employer the information narrowly focused on whether the employee can perform the specific job and what accommodations might be needed to assist in performing the job. Although it is a common practice for doctors to release the entire medical report, it appears that this practice might be illegal under the ADA.

Often, the employer or the doctor will try to get the employee to sign a "waiver" that would allow the doctor to make unrestricted reports to the employer. The legality of these waivers is doubtful. Although the employee is obligated to cooperate with valid medical examinations, there is no legal basis for either the employer or the doctor to require employees to waive whatever legal rights they may have under the ADA if the reports are made in contravention of the statute. Employees or union representatives who are presented with the issue of a required waiver form should seek legal counsel concerning their response to the request.

Confidentiality of medical information. The ADA contains strict requirements for maintaining the confidentiality of the medical information once it is disseminated to the employer. Medical reports are to be maintained in separate medical files, and access is restricted to designated individuals. The ADA requires that supervisors and managers may be informed about specific work limitations, but not about the nature of the medical condition.

The ADA does not define who is a "manager." Is the police chief a "manager," in which case, only the doctor the employer contracts with has the right to hold the information? Or is there someone at the top of the employer's management pyramid who has a right to this information? The courts have yet to decide these issues.

Sick leave verification. Another common practice for employers — which is likely in violation of the ADA — is to record specific medical information on sick leave request or verification forms. First, unless there is a history of sick leave abuse, it is unlikely that the employer is entitled to *any* information concerning the reason the employee is sick on a given day. Second, even if there is a business necessity for requiring this information, it *must* be maintained as a separate medical report and cannot be retained in a general personnel file or file of leave records.

2. Right to Privacy in Personnel Files

Disclosure of personal information is an issue of great interest to many law enforcement personnel. As discussed above, the ADA places very strict limits on the disclosure of confidential medical information. In regards to the other type of information a department might collect, the case law is still somewhat underdeveloped.

Constitutional privacy rights in personnel file. In one of the leading cases out of Philadelphia, the Court of Appeals upheld a fairly broad-ranging questionnaire created by the Philadelphia police department for applicants to its anti-corruption unit.[162] The court allowed the City to require a questionnaire for an applicant that sought extensive financial and family information and inquired into employee's gambling and alcohol habits.

In issuing its decision, the court raised two limitations that are noteworthy. First, the court stressed that the ruling was only

[162] *Fraternal Order of Police v. City of Philadelphia*, 1 IER Cases 1497 (3rd Cir. 1987).

applicable to the applicants for the special investigations unit that was essentially an anti-corruption unit intending to attack corruption within the city of Philadelphia itself. Second, the court remanded the matter to a lower court to engage in a fact finding regarding the City's safeguards against disclosure. The court refused to allow the questionnaire to be processed *until* the City had put in place strong safeguards penalizing officials for disclosing any of the information. At least one other court has adopted the approach of the court in the Philadelphia case.[163]

Washington Public Records Act. Under Washington law, third parties sometimes attempted to acquire information regarding the personnel file of law enforcement employees under the public disclosure law. That law allows third parties the right to acquire documents that are considered a "public record," although the statute contained numerous exemptions from this requirement.

Two issues, in particular, have repeatedly arisen in the context of request for law enforcement personnel records: the exemption of personnel records that the disclosure of which would violate the employee's right to privacy and the disclosure of documents whose release would interfere with the "effective functioning" of a law enforcement department.

The State Supreme Court has found open-ended access to the personnel file, including evaluations, does, in fact, violate an employee's right to privacy and, therefore, does not mandate disclosure of such documents. More recently, though public records plaintiffs have developed a work around to obtain some discipline records on public employees.

Washington courts have long held that discipline records for *sustained* acts of misconduct by law enforcement officers do not violate the right to privacy and must be released upon request. When courts had ordered public disclosure under these circumstances, the requests for information had been for a broad range of internal affairs records with the names expunged.

But more recently plaintiffs have figured out how to request the files by name so that expungement of the name is essentially meaningless. Furthermore, the courts have, unfortunately, ruled that these requests are enforceable even in the context of *nonsustained* misconduct allegations.

In a pair of cases,[164] the State Supreme Court has recently

---

[163] *Walls v. City of Petersburg*, 5 IER Cases 455 (4th Cir. 1990).

[164] *Bainbridge Island Police Guild v. City of Puyallup*, 172 Wn.2d 398, 416, 259 P.3d 190 (2011) and *Bellevue John Does v. Bellevue School District*, 164, Wn.2d 199, 189 P.3d 139 (2008).

held that although requestors do not have a right to employee identity, they do have a right to obtain investigative files even on nonsustained allegations. The court reasoned that there is a legitimate public interest in the quality and nature of the public agency investigation procedures. As the court explained in *Bainbridge Island Police Guild v. City of Puyallup*:

> Although lacking a legitimate interest in the name of a police officer who is the subject of an unsubstantiated allegation of sexual misconduct, the public does have a legitimate interest in how a police department responds to and investigates such an allegation against an officer.[165]

Only one Justice dissented explaining the obvious point that "where some investigative records have already been disclosed and information connecting the individual officer to unsubstantiated allegations has already been made public, further disclosure of the investigative records in any form invades and violates the individual officer's right to privacy."[166]

Where a disclosure is made to a third party of personnel files, public employees may have limited legal rights to challenge their disclosure. The public disclosure law gives broad authority to the public employer to release information within the scope of the public disclosure law, but it does not authorize the release of private information to invade the right of privacy. Release of information that was so private that it would be offensive to a person of ordinary toleration and was not justified would constitute a possible tort.

It just turns out now, though, that unsubstantiated allegations, not matter how ordinarily offensive, are not protected from disclosure. The public agency is permitted to redact the employees name but must still release the record. According to the Supreme Court, this extends even to "letters of direction" which are not necessarily "discipline."[167] An apparent loophole in the Public Records Act has been created in which a requestor can ask for otherwise private personnel records, and receive them with the name redacted. The fact that "it is possible that a third party" to

---

[165] *Bainbridge Island Police Guild v. City of Puyallup*, 172 Wn.2d 398, 416, 259 P.3d 190 (2011).

[166] Id. at 431 (Dissenting opinion of Justice James Johnson).

[167] *Bellevue John Does v. Bellevue School District*, 164, Wn.2d 199, 226-227, 189 P.3d 139 (2008).

figure out which public employee is referenced by the redacted record does not exempt the record from disclosure.[168]

3. Right to Off-Duty Employment

Public safety employees have often argued that they have a right to some particular off-duty work. As a matter of constitutional rights, these arguments have *generally* been rejected. The right to work off-duty is not of great constitutional magnitude and, therefore, the employer must only have a "rational" basis to restrict off-duty employment. (Under the collective bargaining statute, as was discussed in Chapter 3 this is a different matter; *it is clear that off-duty employment is a mandatory subject of bargaining.*[169])

Apart from the collective bargaining obligation to negotiate off-duty employment rules, there are some limits on the employer's ability to enforce off-duty employment restrictions. For example, the Fourth Circuit found a free speech interest outweighed the government's interest when an officer was denied permission to have a secondary position lecturing on concealed handgun safety to the public. The chief had denied permission because civilian's ability to carry concealed handguns was a controversial and sensitive subject. But, based on the *Pickering* test, the court held that the officer's interest in speaking upon the proper use and manner of carrying a concealed handgun in North Carolina outweighed the City's interest in providing effective and efficient services to the public.[170]

On the other hand, one notable category of employment generally proscribed as inconsistent with official duties is the production of pornographic works. In *City of San Diego v. Roe*, The Supreme Court upheld an officer's termination for making and selling homemade pornographic tapes.[171] Using a generic name on eBay, the officer sold (1) used underwear, (2) video of himself issuing a warning in a tan uniform then masturbating, and (2) a video of himself stripping off a generic police uniform and masturbating. The officer's "speech" was found not to be "of public concern" because "the debased parody of an officer performing indecent acts while in the course of official duties brought the

---

168 See Predisik v. Spokane School District, 319, P.3d 801, 805 __ P.3d. ___ (2014).

169 See *City of Bellevue*, Decision 893 (PECB 1980)

170 *Edwards v. Goldsboro*, 178 F.3d 231, 15 IER Cases (BNA) 333 (4th Cir. 1999).

171 *City of San Diego v. Roe*, 125 S. Ct. 521 (2004).

mission of the employer and the professionalism of its officers into serious disrepute."[172]

Similarly, in *Thaeter v. Palm Beach County Sheriff's Office*, the termination of three sheriff's deputies who were featured in pornographic photographs and videotapes viewable online for a fee was found not to be "a matter of public concern."[173] Despite having blurred their faces, the officers were recognized as deputy sheriffs with a specific department, and were determined by the court to be portrayed in a light that "undermined public confidence" in that department.[174] But the Tenth Circuit has found that a police department could not prohibit the offering of adult rentals at a video store operated by two officers.[175]

Courts have been especially likely to uphold a restriction on off-duty employment when the industry in which the off-duty employee wishes to work is inconsistent with their government position. For example, because police officers enforce beverage laws, it might be inconsistent for an officer to work in a liquor store, tavern, or liquor-licensed restaurant.[176] Similarly, because officers catch and assist in gathering evidence for the prosecution of criminals, it would likely be inconsistent for an officer to represent a criminal defendant, or operate a law practice where an associate represents a criminal defendant.[177] On the other hand, the Third Circuit Court of Appeals struck down as overbroad the requirement of the Pittsburgh Police Chief that officers, even when uncompensated, acquire his approval to testify.[178] But the court implied that if the rule bar related only to compensated testimony, it might view the restriction differently.

Denial of secondary employment cannot be exercised as retaliation.[179] Even if not retaliatory, denial of off-duty employment as a form of discipline *might* be disallowed. The *extent* of an

---

[172] *Id.* at 524.

[173] *Thaeter v. Palm Beach County Sheriff's Office*, 449 F.3d 1342, 1356 (11th Cir. 2006).

[174] *Id.*

[175] *Flanagan v. Munger*, 890 F.2d 1557 (10th Cir. 1989) (potential dislike for the message was insufficient to show evidence of actual or potential internal disruption caused by plaintiffs' speech).

[176] *Fraternal Order of Police Lodge 73 v. City of Evansville*, 559 N.E.2d 607 (Ind. 1990).

[177] *Holden v. Police board of Chicago,* 55 N.E.2d 67 (2001).

[178] *See Swartzwelder v. McNeilly*, 2002 U.S. App. Lexis 14556 (3rd Cir. 2002).

[179] See *McNamara v. City of Chicago*, 700 F.Supp. 917 (N.D. Ill. 1988) (federal court allowed a civil rights suit for interfering with a police officer's secondary employment for allegedly political reasons).

employer's authority to restrict off-duty employment rights would ordinarily be subject to the restrictions of the CBA and the requirements of just cause. Absent an express provision (or possibly past practice) allowing revocation of secondary employment as discipline, it might be considered impermissible to impose it.

For example, a Maryland police chief gave an officer a three-month ban on secondary employment after the officer engaged in secondary work as a security officer without obtaining the necessary approval.[180] The court found the penalty was improper because it was not among the disciplinary actions allowed under the department's disciplinary regulations.[181] Even if the CBA does allow secondary employment revocation as a form of permitted discipline, as with all discipline, it would be subject to review under the just cause standard both as to justification and to reasonableness.

The courts have consistently rejected claims that uniformed public safety officers have a liberty interest or privacy right in maintaining grooming and appearance standards of their choice.

4. Right to Maintain Personal Appearance

The courts have consistently rejected claims that uniformed public safety officers have a liberty interest or privacy right in maintaining grooming and appearance standards of their choice. In *Kelley v. Johnson,*[182] the Supreme Court ruled that a police department had the right to establish strict hair and grooming standards. The Court cited the paramilitary nature of the organization and gave weight to the employer's determination that the standard was needed for "discipline, *esprit de corps*, and uniformity." Since *Kelley*, courts have generally struck down police officers' challenges to such dress code rules. These have included challenges to including one challenge to a department rule banning mustaches and another prohibiting the wearing of off-duty ear studs.[183]

---

180 *Fraternal Order of Police v. Mehrling*, 343 Md. 155, 680 A.2d 1052 (1996).

181 *Id.*

182 *Kelley v. Johnson*, 1 IER Cases 55 (1976).

183 *Weaver v. Henderson*, 8 IER Cases 431 (1st Cir. 1993) (upholding mustache

Nonetheless, a Department's ability to regulate appearance is not without limits. Like the ability to regulate secondary employment, it is subject to a "rational basis" review by courts. And also like secondary employment rules, personal appearance rules are likely a mandatory subject of bargaining, although PERC has not specifically address this subject yet.[184]

Not without controversy, but courts have imposed limits on employer authority when necessary to accommodate a medical disability or religious concerns. For example, a Maryland court ordered reinstatement and back pay for an officer who had refused to shave because he suffered from pseudofolliculitis barbae (PFB) (a condition where hair follicles grow back into the skin causing inflammation and keloidal scarring.)[185] Similarly, an arbitrator found that a U.S. Border patrol officer with PFB was improperly denied permission to grow a beard because the officer presented satisfactory medical evidence of his skin condition.[186]

If a hair regulation limits a religiously-motivated hair style, exceptions are generally made because the public employer must have a *compelling* interest to trump a religious expression expressed in a *narrowly tailored* and *facially neutral* rule.[187] For

---

ban); *Rathert v. Village of Peotone*, 5 IER Cases 919 (7th Cir. 1990).

184 See *U.S. Bureau of Customs & Border Prot., and N.T.E.U.*, 43 (2133) G.E.R.R. (BNA) 1159 (Vaughn, 2005) (An arbitrator ruled that Customs and Border Protection's new appearance guidelines were improperly implemented without bargaining with the union because bargaining would not impair the agency's mission); *National Gallery of Art and AFGE L-1831*, FLRA #WA-CA-30380, FLRA ALJ Decis. No.117 (FLRA ALJ 1995) (federal Administrative Law Judge found that management had a duty to bargain an appearance and clothing regulations with the union that represented security police officers at the Smithsonian Institution). But see *Law Enforcement Labor Services v. Co. of Hennepin*, 449 N.W.2d 725 (Minn. 1990) (Minnesota Supreme Court held that a county sheriff's grooming policy was a "managerial prerogative" avoiding the necessity of bargaining with the certified union).

185 *Univ. of Maryland v. Boyd*, 93 Md.App. 303, 612 A.2d 305, 3 AD Cases 1471 (1992).

186 *INS Border Patrol and AFGE L-1929*, FMCS #92/16394, 100 LA (BNA) 1084 (Rezler, 1993).

187 *See Church of the Lukumi Babalu Aye, Inc. v. City of Hialeah,* 508 U.S. 520, 531, 113 S.Ct. 2217, 124 L.Ed.2d 472 (1993); *Hines v. S.C. Dep't of Corrections,* 148 F.3d 353, 357 (4th Cir. 1998) (noting that the First Amendment "forbids state governments from adopting laws designed to suppress religious beliefs or practices"). The First Amendment, however, "does not relieve an individual of the obligation to comply with a valid and neutral law of general applicability on the ground that the law proscribes (or prescribes) conduct that his [or her] religion prescribes (or proscribes)." *Booth v. Maryland*, 327 F.3d 377, 380 (4th Cir. 2003).

example, in a Pennsylvania case, the court enjoined the Philadelphia fire department from disciplining a firefighter who grew a beard in accordance with his Muslim faith.[188] Considering all the facts of the case, including uncontradicted expert witness testimony that "[p]ositive-pressure [masks] may be utilized safely by bearded firefighters ... so long as the facepiece-to-face fit is adequate," the court found the city's safety concern was not compelling enough to outweigh the firefighter's interest in conforming to his Muslim religion.[189] In a similar Chicago case, an Islamic detective with a religiously-mandated beard was given injunctive relief against police beard regulations because the city did not establish a nexus between the application of the beard regulation to the police officer and a compelling safety need.[190]

Even if a regulation limiting religious hair styles is facially valid, *it must also be equally applied.* For example, in Maryland, the discipline of a Rastafarian corrections officer for wearing his hair in religiously-mandated dreadlocks in violation of his employer's grooming policy was overturned because the policy was unequally applied.[191] The grooming policy itself – limiting length and style of hair for safety purposes – constituted a compelling government interest, but the application of the policy – allowing exceptions for other similarly-situated corrections officers, but denying the Rastafarian – was improper.[192]

While standards must be equally applied, grooming and dress codes that distinguish between men and women are generally permissible. For example, an ambulance company's "no beard" policy was found to be non-discriminatory because the policy was motivated by the required use of particular pathogen-protecting respirator that beards interfere with.[193] The judge reasoned that, while it is true that only men can usually grow beards, it does not follow that a rule prohibiting beards amount to sex discrimination.[194]

Greater leeway is generally given to non-uniformed[195] and off-

---

188 *Deveaux v. City of Philadelphia*, 75 Pa. D. & C.4th 315 (Com. Pl. 2005) (unreported)

189 *Id.* at *1.

190 *Sharif v. City of Chicago*, 530 F. Supp. 667 (N.D. Ill. 1982).

191 *Booth v. Maryland*, 327 F.3d 377, 378 (4th Cir. 2003)

192 *Id.*

193 *Barrett v. Am. Med. Response N.W., Inc.*, CV-00-1539-ST, 85 Fair Empl.Prac.Cas. (BNA) 1245 (D. Or. Mar. 20, 2001).

194 *Id.* at *4.

195 *See Miss. Emp. Sec. Cmsn. v. McGlothin*, 556 So.2d 324 (Miss. Sup. Ct. 1990) (upholding the right of non-uniformed public employees to wear religion-inspired headgear at work); *Daniels v. City of Arlington*, 246 F.3d 500 (5th Cir.

duty employees.[196] But many courts permit employers to ban pro-union or religious pins[197] and religious clothing or headgear[198] while on duty if the employer's rule is intended to advance employee safety or the smooth functioning of the agency.

E. Public Safety Employees' Right to Maintain Associations

There has been abundant litigation concerning what public safety employees may do in their off-duty time and who they may do it with. These cases are given a high degree of protection to the employees' right to maintain private relationships, but have allowed restrictions where those relationships had a demonstrable negative impact on the workplace.

2001) (officer was permitted to wear a cross pin in a non-uniformed position but not in a uniformed position); *but see Cooper v. Eugene School Dist. 4J*, 301 Ore. 358, 723 P.2d 298; *appeal dismissed*, 480 U.S. 942, 107 S. Ct. 1597 (1987) (permitting a public employer's prohibition of religious garb at work).

[196] *See Leonard v. City of* Columbus, 705 F. 2d 1299, *reh. en banc. denied*, 716 F.2d 914 (11th Cir. 1983) (permitting picketing in uniform); *PBA NY State Troopers and Div. of State Police*, 37 NYPER (LRP) 4533, 2004 NYPER (LRP) Lexis 111 (NY PERB 2004) (holding that off-duty troopers can wear police union pins when they attend a criminal trial, while off-duty and in civilian clothes). *But see Belch v. Jefferson Co.*, 108 F.Supp.2d 143 (N.D.N.Y 2000) (unreported) (reprimand of a deputy sheriff for appearing on TV in uniform without the sheriff's approval did not violate the First Amendment).

[197] *Compare Communications Workers of Am. v. Ector County Hosp. Dist.*, 467 F.3d 427 (5th Cir. 2006) (the on-duty uniform non-adornment policy, as content and viewpoint-neutral restriction did not violate free speech rights of employee who was disciplined for refusing to remove pro-union badge.), *and Daniels v. City of Arlington*, 246 F.3d 500 (5th Cir. 2001) (finding that officer's communication of his personal religious views through a cross pin was not speech addressing a "legitimate public concern" and termination for violating the department's "no-pins" policy did not violate the First Amendment), *with Sheriff of Worcester County v. Labor Relations Comm'n*, 60 Mass. App. Ct. 632, 805 N.E.2d 46 (2004) (management must bargain with the union before ordering the removal of union buttons from their uniforms, where the officers wore those buttons for many years without adverse consequences), *and Town of Oxford and Mass. Coalition of Police*, L-173 AFL-CIO, MUP-2659 (Mass. LRC 2004) (absent an actual showing of harm, management cannot prohibit uniformed public employees from wearing a union pin).

[198] *Compare EEOC v. GEO Group*, 616 F.3d 265 (3rd Cir. 2010) (panel splits 2-to-1, upholding a regulation barring correctional employees from wearing non-uniform headwear), *with Webb v. City of Philadelphia, 562 F.3d 256 (*3rd Cir. 2009) (upholding a Philadelphia Police Dept. ban on scarves and other religious headgear because prohibiting all religious symbols and attire, helps prevent any divisiveness when officers encounter a diverse population).

1. Right to Maintain Private and Familial Relationships

Overview. Courts have found the right to marry and the privacy in the marital relationship to be one of the most fundamental constitutional rights. Efforts have been made to extend these rights to nonmarital relationships. But such claims arise under the category of "privacy rights" for which the Constitution makes no explicit mention. "Privacy rights" initially arose originally in the context of a married couple's right to use birth control. Further attempts to extend this constitutional right to other intimate relationships have resulted in great confusion and controversy, particularly as to the right of individuals to engage in various forms of sexual activities.

Nepotism. Public employers have adopted "anti-nepotism" rules which to a greater or lesser degree regulate when a married couple may work for the same employer. These rules may have a particularly strong impact in public safety departments where marriage between individuals in the same department is not uncommon.

A number of challenges have been brought in courts questioning the constitutionality of such rules. The general thrust of these arguments is that anti-nepotism rules interfere with the constitutional right to maintain a marital relationship. But courts have almost uniformly rejected these constitutional claims. Under Washington law, though, anti-nepotism rules may be unlawful, at least when they are overbroad. But amendments to the marital discrimination statute have cast some uncertainty concerning the status of these anti-nepotism rules.

RCW 49.60.180 states that it is unlawful for an employer to discriminate against "any person because of... marital status...unless based upon a *bona fide* occupational qualification." In a series of cases, the courts have ruled that anti-nepotism policies violated this marital discrimination prohibition if it discriminated against individuals based on the "identity" of an employee's spouse.[199] The term "marital status" includes people in a "civil union" or "domestic partnerships" instead of a "marriage," as people in a civil union or domestic partnership, regardless of sex, are extended the same rights as married couples under Washington State law.[200]

---

[199] *Kastanis v. Educational Employees Credit Union*, 122 Wn.2d 483, 488, 859 P.2d 26, 29 (1993), modified 122 Wn.2d 483, 865 P.2d 507 (1994); *Magula v. Ben Franklin Title Company*, 131 Wn.2d 171, 930 P.2d 307 (1997).

In 1993, the statute was amended to redefine the definition of marital status. In that amendment, "marital status" was redefined to include "the legal status of being married, single, separated, divorced or widowed." In *Magula v. Ben Franklin Title Company,*[201] the court visited again the issue of anti-nepotism policies and found such policies could violate the marital discrimination statute. But the court explicitly decided this issue based on the pre-1993 law and suggested that the 1993 amendment might alter that holding. Since *Magula,* no published Court of Appeals decision has readdressed this issue, so there remains some uncertainty regarding whether anti-nepotism rules are unlawful.

Even then, anti-nepotism rules do not bar all regulations of the working relationship of married persons in the workplace. The statute provides exceptions for "*bona fide* occupational qualifications" (BFOQs). Human Rights Commission regulations recognize several BFOQs that may permit narrowly drafted anti-nepotism policies. First, an employer may enforce a policy addressing a documented conflict of interest,.[202] including situations where one spouse has the power to supervise or discipline another spouse or has the responsibility to audit the work of the other.[203] Also, an employer may regulate in order "to avoid the reality or appearance of improper influence or favor, or to protect its confidentiality."[204]

In short, it is unclear whether there is any statutory prohibition on anti-nepotism policies. And even if overbroad anti-nepotism policies are unlawful, employers may still draft — subject to the obligation to bargain — narrow anti-nepotism policies that are directed at addressing conflict of interest situations.

Heterosexual relations and conduct. Although the Washington Supreme Court has made clear that "marital status" protections under the employment discrimination statute does not apply to "cohabiting, dating, or other social relationships,"[205] court decisions regarding discipline and termination for off-duty employees' sexual conduct have been contentious. One rule of thumb seems to be "when off-duty and out of uniform, [a public

---

200 *See* WA SB 5688-2009-10 (effective 7/26/2009) *available at* http://apps.leg.wa.gov/billinfo/summary.aspx?bill=5688&year=2009#documents.

201 131 Wn.2d 171, 930 P.2d 307 (1997).

202 WAC 163-16-250(2)(b).

203 *Id.*

204 *Id.*

205 *Waggoner v. Ace Hardware Corp.*, 134 Wn. 2d 748, 953 P.2d 88 (1998).

employee] can do privately what he wishes to do until such time as it materially and substantially impairs his usefulness as a [public employee]."[206]

Under this approach, when there is no "rational basis" on which to find an individual's sexual conduct to be work-related, the employer may not terminate or refuse to hire that individual simply because they disapprove of their particular sexual conduct. For example, the Ninth Circuit found a department's failure to hire a police applicant due to the fact she once had an affair with a police officer was improper. It reasoned that the employer had failed to show how the affair would potentially affect the officer's job performance.[207]

But elsewhere, the courts are divided as to whether consensual non-marital heterosexual conduct is entitled to constitutional protection. While some courts have held that public employees retain a fundamental constitutional right to engage in such conduct and may not be disciplined because of it, other courts have found no such constitutional right.[208]

Generally if a private sexual relationship interferes with one's job duties, the employer may have grounds to interrogate or even terminate an employee. For example, the Merit Systems Protection Board found the termination of an FBI officer who videotaped several sexual partners without their consent to be proper because (1) there was a clear nexus between the officer's off-duty conduct and his fitness for duty,[209] and (2) termination was a reasonable response to the "intentional, egregious and clearly dishonest nature of the appellant's misconduct."[210]

Even if there is a legitimate business interest, though, there may be an independent prohibition against certain forms of inquiry, depending on the jurisdiction. For example, the Ninth Circuit Court of Appeals has held that it is unconstitutional for an employer to delve into an employee's off-duty sexual conduct

---

206 *Smith v. Price,* 446 F.Supp. 828, 835-6 (M.D. Ga. 1977) *reversed on other grounds*, 616 F.2d 1371 (5th Cir. 1980).

207 *Thorne*, 726 F.2d at 471 (There was no sexual deviance, the affair was not public, there was no reason to believe the officer would engage in affairs on duty or that the past affair would cause morale problems, having an affair is not grounds for disciplining a police officer).

208 *Briggs v. North Muskegon Police Dept.*, 1 IER Cases 195 (W.D. Mich. 1983) (finding a right); *Shawgo v. Spradlin*, 1 IER Cases 165 (5th Cir. 1983) (finding no right).

209 *Doe v. Dept. of Justice*, #CH-0752—04-0620-I-2, 2006 MSPB 246, 103 MSPR 135 (2006).

210 *Doe v. Dept. of Justice*, #CH-0752-04-0620-B-1, 2007 MSPB 282 (2007).

during a pre-employment polygraph examination.[211] However, another court of appeals has specifically rejected the Ninth Circuit approach, finding no constitutional right to avoid questions regarding sexual practices.[212] And, as discussed a public employee's involvement in a sex business may be a proscribed secondary employment avenue.

The constitutional right to "privacy" in intimate relationships does not extend to criminal conduct. Ninth Circuit Court of Appeals has declined to find a privacy right in on-duty sex with a prostitute,[213] or a police officer's sexual conduct with a 15-year old explorer scout.[214] Other courts have found that even off-duty sex with a prostitute is proscribable due to the illegality of prostitution.[215] Similarly, maintaining a sexual relationship with a criminal or a criminal informant is generally proscribable for the officers enforcing the law.[216] In short, sex that is age inappropriate, paid-for, or involving an inherent conflict with one's job duties is not offered any protection. Illegal sexual relationships are also grounds for criminal charges, not just an employment discipline.

Homosexual relations and conduct. In the early 1990s, following their lead from the U.S. Supreme Court in a different context, some lower courts found that public employees have no privacy right in homosexual conduct and may be disciplined for engaging in homosexual activities.[217] In 1997, the Ninth Circuit held that homosexuals are not a "suspect" or "quasi-suspect class" for equal protection purposes and, therefore, judicial review of a classification based on homosexuality is limited to the "rational basis test."[218]

---

[211] *Thorne v. City of El Segundo*, 726 F.2d at 469.

[212] *Hedge v. Co. of Tippecanoe*, 890 F.2d 4 (7th Cir. 1989).

[213] *Fugate v. Phoenix Civil Service Board*, 791 F.2d 736 (9th Cir. 1986).

[214] *Fleisher v. City of Signal Hill*, 829 F.2d 1491 (9th Cir. 1987).

[215] *Ruiz v. Brown*, 579 N.Y.Supp.2d 47, 179 A.D.2d 543 (N.Y. App. Div. 1, 1992).

[216] *See, e.g., Rackers v. Dept. of Justice*, #CH-0752-97-0218-I-1, 79 MSPR 262 (MSPB, 1998).

[217] *Dawson v. State Law Enforcement Div.*, C/A 3:91-1403-17, 1992 WL 208967 (D.S.C. Apr. 6, 1992) ("Courts, however, have consistently held that homosexual activity is not a fundamental right guaranteed under the Constitution") (*citing Bowers v. Hardwick*, 478 U.S. 186 (1986) (no right of privacy guaranteed under due process clause of the Fourteenth Amendment to engage in consensual homosexual conduct); *Endslee v. Naes*, 3 IER Cases 349 (D. Kan. 1987); *Shahar v. Bowers*, 8 IER Cases 1933 (N.D. Ga. 1993).

[218] *Watson v. Perry*, 918 F. Supp. 1403, 1412 (W.D. Wn. 1996) *aff'd sub nom. Holmes v. California Army Nat. Guard*, 124 F.3d 1126 (9th Cir. 1997) (*citing High Tech Gays v. Defense Indus. Sec. Clearance Office*, 895 F.2d 563, 571 (9th Cir.1990)).

But in 2003, the Supreme Court found a statutory prohibition against same-sex consensual sexual relationships to be unconstitutional.[219] In that case, the Court noted that states lack a legitimate public interest in regulating the private sexual conduct of consenting adults.[220] So, a heightened standard of review for an employer's invasion into sexual relations is now appropriate regardless of an individual's sexual orientation.

2. The Right to Choose a Residency

After abundant litigation in the lower courts, in 1976 the United States Supreme Court finally resolved a long-debated issue of the constitutionality of residency requirements that such requirements were not unconstitutional.[221]

Despite the absence of a constitutional right to choose a residency, there is a statutory right for most Washington public safety employees. Those employees who are covered under municipal civil service systems specifically prohibit residency requirements as it is unlawful for a city to create a rule requiring residency. This limitation does not extend to county sheriff's offices, however. And fire districts are not mandated to follow the state civil service law, but they may opt in on a voluntary basis. If they do opt in they will be subject to the prohibition on residency requirements in the municipal firefighter civil service law.

Even for those who are protected by civil service residency requirement bans, this does not mean that the employer cannot negotiate any geographic limit.

The civil service laws that prohibit residency requirements have been interpreted by the Washington courts to prohibit granting additional privileges to employees based on residency. For example, a civil service rule that recognized residency as a basis for a layoff preference was found to violate the state civil service law.[222]

For those falling outside these civil service protections, it should be noted that residency requirements are nevertheless a mandatory subject of bargaining.[223] Even for those who are

---

[219] *Lawrence v. Texas*, 539 U.S. 558, 562, 123 S. Ct. 2472, 2475, 156 L. Ed. 2d 508 (2003).

[220] *Id.*

[221] *McCarthy v. Philadelphia Civil Service Commission*, 424 U.S. 645 (1976).

[222] *Bjorseth v. City of Seattle*, 15 Wn. App. 797, 551 P.2d 1372 (1976).

protected by civil service residency requirement bans, this does not mean that the employer cannot negotiate any geographic limit. For example, a rule that indicated that an officer had to reside within 45 minutes of the City would not violate the State civil service law but would be mandatorily negotiable.

Those negotiated residency rules are subject to interpretation and the grievance procedure of the CBA. Under those CBA provisions, questions concerning what constitutes the officers actual "residence" sometimes arise but those would be addressed, if necessary, by an arbiter.

3. The Right to Associate with Individuals of One's Choosing

Although marital relations are accorded a high degree of protection and, by some courts, non-marital relations as well, the courts have been less protective of any "right" to affiliate with any and all persons of one's choosing. In particular, courts have often enforced department rules restricting law enforcement personnel from affiliating with "known criminals" or similar regulations.

Originally, such regulations were almost uniformly upheld, but more recent case law indicates that these regulations will be subject to greater scrutiny and these rules have increasingly been set aside. On a more frequent basis, courts are finding these rules to be either vague or overbroad and have denied law enforcement departments the ability to enforce the rules as written.

The existing decisions reflect some balance of competing interests. Although certain relations are accorded a high level of protection, the courts have been less protective of a blanket "right" to affiliate with any and all persons of one's choosing. Courts have often enforced department rules restricting law enforcement personnel from affiliating with "known criminals" or similar regulations.[224] Personal relationships with criminals who are currently, or previously involved in criminal activities are not insulated by the First Amendment.[225] Similarly, maintaining a sexual relationship with a criminal or a criminal informant is generally proscribable for the officers enforcing the law.[226] For an

223 See *Kitsap County Fire District 7*, Decisions 2872 & 2872-A (PECB, 1988).

224 See e.g., Seattle Police Department DP&P, §5.001(VI)(A)(2) ("Employees shall not associate with persons, entities, and organizations where such association reasonably gives the appearance of conflict of interest in employee enforcement decisions or actions").

225 *Rackers v. Dept. of Justice*, #CH-0752-97-0218-I-1, 79 MSPR 262 (MSPB, 1998).

officer to have a relationship with an informant or criminal as it would create a conflict of interest.

Many association-limiting rules have been set aside as vague or overbroad.

However, even the most obvious application of these regulations limiting affiliations must be clearly written and narrowly-tailored. In one instance, an assistant chief of police who had been in contact with a criminal over 30 times in a month avoided punishment by claiming he was developing the criminal as a confidential informant.[227] This defense was successful because there was no written policy on developing confidential informants, and the assistant chief had not been warned that his conduct was improper.[228]

Many association-limiting rules have been set aside as vague or overbroad. For example, a Chicago rule against fraternization, which read "No member or employee of the Department shall associate or fraternize with persons known to have criminal records," was found to be too vague to constitute grounds for terminating an officer who took a trip to Europe with a mafia boss.[229]

The rules that receive the greatest scrutiny involve those directly affecting bona fide personal and familiar relationships. For example, a federal district court in Oregon set aside a Multnomah County Sheriff's Department rule that prohibited any relationship with an ex-felon. The court found that the "intimate relationship" at issue was constitutionally protected and that the department's rule was overbroad.[230] The employee's relationship began before the implication of the rule prohibiting relationships with ex-felons, and the employer did not show sufficient evidence that the relationship had any reasonable connection to the employee's work performance or workplace safety.[231] Therefore, because the

---

226 *See, e.g., Rackers v. Dept. of Justice*, #CH-0752-97-0218-I-1, 79 MSPR 262 (MSPB, 1998).

227 *Flosi v. Board of Fire & Police Cmsnrs. of Rock Falls*, 582 N.E.2d 185 (Ill. App. 1991).

228 *Id.*

229 *DeGrazio v. Civil Service Commission*, 31 Ill.2d 482, 202 N.E.2d 522 (Ill. 1964) (officer was terminated on another provision).

230 *Reuter v. Skipper*, 832 F. Supp. 1420 (D. Ore. 1993), affirmed 4 F.3d 716 (9th Cir. 1993).

231 *Reuter v. Skipper*, 832 F. Supp. 1420 (D. Or. 1993), *affirmed* 4 F.3d 716 (9th Cir. 1993); *See also GEO Group/Wackenhut Corp. and Delaware Co. Prison*

employer relied on "private non-job-related considerations" the termination was found to have violated the employee's "protected constitutional interests and [could not] be upheld under any level of scrutiny."[232]

In general, however, discipline and rules of conduct regarding law enforcement personnel associating with known criminals will be upheld.[233] On the other hand, when existing family relationships are affected, these rules will be scrutinized and are often found to be overbroad.[234]

the rules limiting off-duty conduct cannot be completely arbitrary and capricious. The employer must establish that they have a *rational basis* for adopting a certain regulation

4. Privacy Rights and Off-Duty Conduct

Public safety departments frequently promulgate rules purporting to regulate off-duty conduct. Although these rules will be closely scrutinized by any arbitrator if they become an issue in a disciplinary proceeding, as a general matter there is no broad constitutional right to engage in off-duty conduct of one's choosing. However, the rules limiting off-duty conduct cannot be completely arbitrary and capricious. The employer must establish that they

---

Employees Ind. Union, 120 LA (BNA) 729, FMCS Case #04/05495 (Almenoff, 2004) (arbitrator reduced discharge of a correctional officer for violating a work rule prohibiting the forming of a romantic relationship with a prisoner because the relationship started 14 years prior to the prisoner's incarceration; written reprimand was given because the officer "should have notified the Warden of the relationship as soon as [her boyfriend] was incarcerated and should have sought instruction as to the appropriate course of action").

[232] *Reuter v. Skipper*, 832 F. Supp. at 1423-4.

[233] *See, e.g., Cottingham v. Kelly*, 11 A.D.3d 285, 782 N.Y.S.2d 462 (N.Y. App.Div. 2004) (termination of an officer who associated with a person she had reason to believe was engaged in criminal activity sustained); *James v. Dale*, 355 F.3d 1375 (Fed. Cir. 2004) (arbitration award reinstating a Border Patrol Agent that bailed out a woman who lived at his home arrested on a cocaine possession charge was overturned); *Ortiz v. L.A. Police Relief Assn.*, 98 Cal.App. 4th 1288, 120 Cal.Rptr.2d 670 (Cal.App.2d Dist. 2002).(California Appeals Court upheld the termination of a clerk, at a police association's insurance office, for having an ongoing intimate relationship with a convicted felon because her behavior was incompatible with her access to officers' confidential files).

[234] See, e.g, Via v. Taylor, 224 F. Supp. 753 (D.Del. 2002); Corso v. Fisher, 2013 U.s District Lexis 152336 (SDNY 2013).

have a *rational basis* for adopting a certain regulation. For example, public employees, especially police officers, must avoid membership in or attendance at meetings of violent or hateful groups because the agency has a *rational basis* for limiting conduct that would affect the appearance of a public employee in a way that would unduly interfere with the basic function of the employer.[235]

The City's "interest in maintaining a relationship of trust between the police and fire departments and the communities they serve" can outweigh the employees' free speech interests.[236] Indeed, various viewpoints and organizations have been routinely excluded from First Amendment protection, including hate groups, such as the Ku Klux Klan,[237] and organizations that are involved in illegal activities, such as the Outlaws Motorcycle Club.[238] However, even in clear-cut cases, the employer must still present evidence against the employee. In one case, an arbitrator reinstated an employee who was terminated for displayed a Nazi flag on his porch because the employer did not provide sufficient evidence that the display was potentially disruptive.[239]

F. Right to be Free of Unlawful Discrimination

The United States Constitution, as well as various federal and state statutes, prohibit discrimination on a number of grounds, including race, color, national origin, gender, age and disability. Additionally, collective bargaining agreements often contain clauses prohibiting discrimination.

Those representing labor organizations need to be aware of

---

235 *Locurto v. Giuliani*, 447 F.3d 159, 183 (2nd Cir. 2006) (finding the termination of a New York City police officer and two firefighters to be proper because the three had all appeared on a racially-offensive Labor Day parade float).

236 *See id. But see Bruns v. Pomerleau*, 19 F.Supp. 58 (D.Md. 1970) (membership in nudist colony was merely controversial - not harmful or extreme - and is protected speech).

237 *See .e.g., State v. Henderson*, 277 Neb. 240, 762 N.W.2d 1 (2009) (State Supreme Court reversed an arbitration award permitting officer's membership in Ku Klux Klan, finding the award to be contrary to public policy); *McMullen v. Carson*, 754 F.2d 936 (11th Cir. 1985) (records clerk for police department terminated for being a recruiter for the Klan); *Young v. McDaniel*, 664 F. Supp. 362 (W.D. Ky. 1986) (officer fired for distributing hate literature and lying about selling tickets to Klan-sponsored functions).

238 *See Piscottano v. Murphy*, 511 F.3d 247 (2nd Cir. 2007) (thee officers were appropriately disciplined for membership in Outlaws Motorcycle Club – a drug trafficking and white supremacist group).

239 *In re Department of Correctional Services [Naponoch, N.Y.] and Council 82, Security Unit Employees AFSCME*, 114 L.A. 1533 (Simmelkjaer, 1997).

these requirements because they may affect your role in a number of subtle and unexpected ways. Among the circumstances under which discrimination issues might arise:

1. A grievance relating to the anti-discrimination clause in the collective bargaining agreement;
2. A disciplinary action or disciplinary investigation conducted in a manner contrary to anti-discrimination laws;
3. An order for a physical or mental examination which violates state or federal disability discrimination laws;
4. CBA administration issues regarding accommodation of certain protected classes of individuals; and
5. A union on the receiving end of a duty of fair representation complaint alleging discrimination.

This section discusses the various anti-discrimination rules regarding statutorily protected classes.

1. Racial Discrimination

Laws prohibiting discrimination on the basis of race and ethnicity not only prohibit direct and intentional discrimination, but they also prohibit a class of conduct which is indirect discrimination — that of "disparate impact." Disparate impact discrimination is that discrimination that results from employer practices that have an adverse impact on members of a protected class, *regardless of the employer's actual intent.*

Where members of a protected class can demonstrate that a given employment practice statistically has an adverse impact on members of that class, they have carried their burden of proof, at least initially, on a disparate impact claim. The burden then shifts to the employer to show that, despite that adverse impact, the practice is justified as a valid business practice and relates to actual job performance. If the practice has an insufficient business rationale, it will be deemed to be unlawfully discriminatory.

A common issue in "disparate impact" cases — and the issue when the United State Supreme Court first adopted the disparate impact theory — are employer requirement of minimum education qualifications. These education requirements have often been challenged because, in many communities, there is a statistical showing that certain ethnic groups have lower formal education attainments. Therefore, where the education requirements do not have a strong relationship with actual job performance, they might be found to be discriminatory.

The practical impact of the legal recognition of the disparate impact theory is that employers are obligated to scrutinize closely and validate their minimum qualification requirements. Where those minimum qualifications have not been validated by outside studies a relating to the job at issue, they are very likely to be set aside by courts if those qualifications have a disparate impact on protected classes.

Any question regarding the remedies for unlawful discrimination leads to the subject of affirmative action. Affirmative action has not only led to controversies within legal circles, but has led to even greater controversy within society as a whole.[240] A significant contributing cause to the scope of the controversy is that there are widespread misconceptions regarding the lawful scope of affirmative action programs. In fact, many of these misconceptions are held by those who are responsible for personnel practices.

Affirmative action programs are lawful *only when adopted and administered consistent with the following principles:*

1) An affirmative action program meant to address historical or societal discrimination not directly the fault of the employer are unlawful to the extent they involve any "reverse discrimination," provided that employers may undertake *non-discriminatory* steps to improve the recruitment and retention of protected class members;

2) Affirmative action that might have an adverse or discriminatory impact on a non-protected class is allowed when *that particular employer* has

[240] In 1998, Washington's Law Against Discrimination was amended to prohibit "preferential treatment". *See* RCW 19-60.400. Despite the political heat the Initiative generated, it does not appear to have altered the principles defined here which preexisted the amendment: To the extent the Initiative restricts affirmative action programs which might be legally mandated as a remedy against discrimination, the amendments will likely be held invalid. An Initiative cannot amend the Constitution or federal law.

engaged in a previous course of conduct involving intentional discrimination against a protected class;

3) Employers may also adopt an affirmative action plan when they can statistically demonstrate *their employment practices* have had a disparate impact on protected classes; and

4) Any affirmative action program undertaken involving remedies which might constitute "reverse discrimination" must comply with legal requirements that the plan be *of a limited duration, involve goals rather than specific quotas and that all employees hired or promoted under such a plan must meet minimum qualifications.*

Plans that do not comport with these requirements are themselves discriminatory, and individuals who are harmed by such plans have their own cause of action which they may bring.

Issues regarding entry-level affirmative action are much less likely, if at all likely, to directly involve labor organizations. Generally, labor organizations and their members have a stronger interest in affirmative action plans affecting the promotion of already hired employees.

Consistent with the principles set forth above, employers are allowed to establish affirmative action programs including those with "race-conscious" remedies to the extent that the employer can demonstrate they have a historical pattern of discrimination. Since employees usually do not admit they have intentionally discriminated, generally these issues arise where the employer shows a statistical study demonstrating that their policies *must have had* some disparate impact on protected classes at some time in the past.

The most significant legal issue here and the one that is still unresolved by the courts is what the relevant pool is for determining such a statistical disparity. It is clearly not enough to show a statistical difference between those employees in the higher-ranking positions and the labor pool in the general community. While some courts have held that the statistical test for established promotional affirmative action is comparing those in the higher rankings of the employees at large, courts have generally rejected this broader pool in favor of a narrow pool which looks at those current employees of the employer who are actually qualified. Consequently, qualifications such as experience and education which are required for promotion become the measuring standard in determining whether there is a statistical disparity in the higher ranks.

2. Gender Discrimination

Federal and state statutes likewise prohibit intentional discrimination based on gender. These statutes have also been interpreted to prohibit "disparate impact" discrimination.

Most common issues that have arisen the public safety field regarding gender discrimination and disparate impact are those job requirements related to size and physical strength. Because of the statistical disparity between the genders on size and physical strength, any such standards will necessarily have a disparate impact. Therefore, the employer will be obligated to demonstrate that these requirements relate to business necessity and job performance standards. Many of the requirements established in the past did not conform to the business necessity test and were stricken down by courts.

The most frequent issue that arises in the context of gender discrimination is that of sexual harassment. Sexual harassment is deemed to be a form of gender discrimination and his prohibited both by .state and federal law. Sexual harassment generally arises in one of two forms: (1) *quid pro quo* harassment; or (2) “hostile work environment” harassment.

Quid pro quo harassment involves the conditioning of employment opportunities and benefits on the receipt of sexual favors. A clear example of this type of harassment occurs where a supervisor takes an adverse employment action against an employee who does not consent to a request for sexual activities. It is not a defense to a later sexual harassment charge that the employee consented to the activity, provided there was some actual benefit or threat of a loss of benefit if the employee did not consent.

The law is fairly clear regarding what constitutes unlawful *quid pro quo* sexual harassment. The area that has caused the greatest controversy and confusion is hostile work environment harassment. In general, in order to constitute hostile working environment harassment, the conduct at issue has to be *severe and pervasive.*

Therefore, isolated comments, even of a sexual nature, will not generally be found to constitute hostile work environment harassment. When the harassment rises to the level of being severe and pervasive is a question of fact that turns on all the circumstances of the case.

A Washington Court of Appeals decision makes it clear that sexual harassment need not involve sex to be unlawful. In the case at hand, a supervisor had displayed offensive and discriminatory conduct towards the females in the office, but none of it revolved around sexual requests or sexual comments. The court upheld the harassment complaint, reasoning that the females in the office were mistreated *because* of their gender, and that was all that needed to be established.

There has been some controversy in the courts concerning whether sexual harassment had to be across gender lines in order to be a cause of action. The United States Supreme Court resolved this controversy recently by ruling that "same-sex" harassment is actionable.[241]

3. Religious Discrimination

The prohibition against government interfering in the religious beliefs of individuals is virtually absolute. This prohibition applies equally to public employers and their employees. While public employers may not interfere with discipline or otherwise discriminate for employees based on their beliefs, this does not automatically extend in all cases to the conduct of employees which is based on their beliefs.

When an employee engages in certain conduct that is an extension of their religious faith, the public employer has an obligation to reasonably accommodate that conduct. An accommodation does not constitute a reasonable accommodation, however, where the accommodation would create an "undue hardship" on the employer.

A common issue involving a conflict and the employer's interest and the tenets of the employee's religious faith involve the scheduling of work. The category of religion classified as "Sabbatarian" holds as a tenet of their faith that the designated Sabbath Day is a day that is not to be worked. For those employees adhering to this belief, the practices of their religion are likely to conflict with the needs of any employer who provides 24-hour service.

Where the employer may accommodate such a request for time off, without disrupting the work peace or interfering with the contractual rights of other employees they will be required to do so.[242]

---

[241] Oncale v. Sundowner Offshore Services, 523 U.S. 75 (1998).

[242] *See Dept. of Corrections Services*, 92 LA 459 (Babistin 1989) (overturned

Courts have consistently held, however, that the employer had no obligation to accommodate such leave where it conflicted with the seniority shift bidding requirements of a collective bargaining agreement. These courts reason that violating the collective bargaining agreement was itself an "undue hardship."[243] In fact, one court has held that the employer would not be required to allow employees to voluntarily trade shifts, although this result is questionable in that it is hard to imagine that simply allowing shift trade would constitute an undue hardship.[244]

Even in the absence of a seniority provision, courts have been reluctant to compel rescheduling of work. One court rejected an employee's argument that the employer could simply compel other individuals to work his shift. The court concluded that if the employer so compelled employees, it would violate *their* rights under the First Amendment.[245] Also, employees who could otherwise be accommodated need not be accommodated where they have voluntarily placed themselves in a position where the accommodation was made more difficult.[246]

The courts have also recognized the rights of employees not be compelled to pay union or agency shop fees where membership or support of the union would conflict with their *bona fide* religious beliefs. In fact, in Washington State this constitutional requirement has been expressly acknowledged in the collective bargaining statute,[247] and there have been numerous cases under PERC's jurisdiction defining the respective rights of religious objectors and unions in the collection of such dues.

Dress code issues occasionally arise in the context of public employment where certain employees who wear clothing articles

---

discipline against a corrections officer who had refused to work Friday shift when the officer had offered to reimburse the employer for additional costs incurred); *Vicksburg Community Schools*, 101 LA 771 (Daniel 1993) (overturned school district's disallowance of teacher's use of "business leave day" for religious observation where arbitrator found the employer had liberally construed the application of the business day leave provisions).

243 *Matter of State and Council 82, AFSCME*, 176 A.D. 2d 1009, 575 NYS.2d 175 (A.D. 3 Dept., 1991); *Blair v. Graham Corrections Center*, 782 F. Supp. 411 (C.D.I. 1992).

244 *Blair, supra.*

245 *Pennsylvania State University v. Pennsylvania Human Relations Commission* (505 A.2d 105) (Pa. Commw. 1986).

246 *See Mann v. Frank*, 795 F. Supp. 1438 (W.D. MO, 1992) (employee who requested Sabbath off, but then also placed himself voluntarily on the overtime list which would require her to work the Sabbath could not have it both ways).

247 RCW 41.56.122.

relating to an aspect of their religious faith. Although not precisely on point, in that the case involves the military, a Supreme Court decision provides some definition of rights in that it has rejected a claim of a right to wear a yarmulke while in uniform as an Air Force servicemen.[248] The Court rejected the serviceman's claim concluding that the Armed Services were not required to accommodate a religious practice which would be contrary to the uniformity mandated by its dress code.

The same principle will likely apply to virtually all the uniform divisions of public safety departments. On the other hand, non-uniformed civilian positions would be covered under a different approach which would allow the wearing of such religious items absent other compelling circumstances.

As discussed above, public safety employers have some ability to adopt uniform dress codes and regulations of hair styles. To the extent these rules conflict with bona fide religious expression, the balance of rights might favor the religious adherent.

The right to believe and participate in a religious faith does not extend to the right to proselytize coworkers during duty hours. One court has rejected the claim of an employee who was also a supervisor and who had attempted to conduct prayer sessions during working hour, including quotation of scripture to subordinate employees. The court concluded that the employer had an obligation to maintain a "religiously neutral" atmosphere in the workplace, and it had a right to restrict a supervisor from such activities.

Although the court did not directly rule on one aspect of the case, it criticized the employer's conduct that involving removal of religious artifacts from the employee's workspace. The court concluded that where the items were positioned for the sake of the employee and "not to inundate others with a religious message" the employee had a right to have those items in his space.[249]

Employers will certainly be found to have an undue hardship where the employee's religious conduct directly affects job performance. In one case, the court upheld the termination of an FBI agent who was a Roman Catholic who concluded he was prohibited by his religious faith from investigating certain peace groups. When he refused to proceed with an investigation of one group, he was terminated for insubordination, a decision the court upheld.[250] In another case, the court upheld the suspension of a

---

[248] *Goldman v. Weinberger*, 475 U.S. 501 (1986).

[249] *Brown v. Polk Co., Iowa*, 832 F. Supp. 805 (D.C. Iowa, 1993).

Jewish police officer who had threatened to arrest a citizen who had made an anti-Semitic comment.[251] The Court concluded that there was a strong public interest in requiring police officers to avoid expressing their personal feelings in such situations.

4. Age Discrimination

The Age Discrimination in Employment Act (ADEA) addresses age discrimination. The Act makes it unlawful to discriminate against individuals over the age of 40 *because* of their age. ADEA also recognizes BFOQs, and it does not make it unlawful to discharge employees incapable of performing essential functions of a job.

There has been a long history of the ADEA and public safety employees. At different points in the history of the statute, it either did or did not allow broad protection for police officers and firefighters. Originally, enacted as to police and firefighters, the ADEA provided a limited exemption for employers. That exemption expired in 1993. In 1996, public safety employers were successful in lobbying Congress for reinstatement of the police and firefighter exemption with modifications.

Under the current state of the ADEA, it is not unlawful to discriminate against police officers or firefighters over the age of 55.[252] Presumably, therefore, it would be lawful, or at least under the ADEA, to terminate police officers and firefighters once they reach the age of 55.

The ADEA defines "law enforcement officer" as:

> An employee, the duties of whose position are primarily the investigation, apprehension, or detention of individuals suspected or convicted of offenses against the criminal laws of a state, including an employee engaged in this activity who is transferred to a supervisory or administrative position. For purposes of this subsection, "detention" includes the duties of employees assigned to guard individual incarcerated in any penal institution.

The ADEA does not further define the term "firefighter."

There had been challenges to age discrimination under the

---

250 *Ryan v. U.S. Dept. of Justice*, 950 F.2d 458 (7th Cir. 1991).

251 *Hershinow v. Bonamarte*, 735 F.2d 264 (7th Cir. 1984).

252 And the mandatory retirement age can be even lower if it was in effect when the ADEA was originally enacted in 1983.

United States Constitution prior to the enactment of the ADEA. These challenges were brought to an end by the Supreme Court's ruling in *Massachusetts Board of Retirement v. Murgia.*[253] In *Murgia*, the court ruled that mandatory retirement rules need only have a "rational basis" and that other workers were not a "suspect class" entitled to a higher degree of constitutional protection. The Court then proceeded to uphold a state law forcing Massachusetts police officers to retire at the age of 50.

5. Disability Discrimination

Both state and federal laws prohibit discrimination against individuals with disabilities. Because disability issues are pervasive questions facing collective bargaining representatives, this issue warrants a chapter of its own, which is next.

[253] 427 U.S. 307 (1976).

Chapter 10

The Right to Wages and Overtime

A. Introduction

The Fair Labor Standards Act (FLSA) and the Washington Minimum Wage Act (MWA) both require payment of minimum wages and overtime. Both of these statutes apply to public safety employees in Washington.

As to police officers and firefighters, though, the State MWA contains an especially high overtime threshold so that as a practical matter statutes are rarely invoked for police and firefighter wage and overtime claims. Other than that, for the most part, the MWA provisions are analogous to the FLSA provisions. This chapter will focus primarily on the elements of the FLSA.

The FLSA was enacted by Congress in the 1930s as part of the "New Deal" legislation intended to address the effects of the Depression. The economic theory behind the Act was designed to improve the standard of living by setting a floor on wages. The overtime provisions were also intended to deter long workweeks and simultaneously increase employment. The theory behind the Act was that by creating a disincentive to "overwork," employers would employ more people to do the same amount of work.

The FLSA is a "remedial" statute. As the Ninth Circuit Court of Appeals has indicated: "Exemptions to FLSA are to be narrowly construed in order to further Congress's goal of providing broad federal employment protection."[1] Employers claiming exemptions under the FLSA must carry the burden of proof.[2] That burden must be to "plainly and unmistakably" demonstrate the existence of an exemption.[3]

The remedial purpose of the statute furthers not only to protect the wages of workers, but also to limit the length of the workday. As the Supreme Court indicated in *Barrentine v. Arkansas-Best Freight System, Inc.* "The principal congressional purpose in enacting the Fair Labor Standards Act of 1938 was to protect all covered workers from substandard wages and *oppressive working hours. . . .*"[4] The Court has also indicated that enacting the law

---

1 *Abshire v. County of Kern*, 908 F.2d 483, 485 (9th Cir. 1990) (citing *Mitchell v. Lublin, McGaughy & Assoc.*, 358 U.S. 207, 211 (1959).

2 *Id.* at 485 (citing *Corning Glassworks v. Brennan*, 417 U.S. 188, 196-97 (1974).

3 *Id.* at 486 (quoting *Arnold v. Ben Kanowsky, Inc.*, 361 U.S. 388, 392 (1960).

4 101 450 U.S. 728, 739 (1981) (emphasis added).

Congress was not only concerned about "underpay" but also "overwork."[5]

The Ninth Circuit Court of Appeals has noted that the FLSA was intended to remedy the "strain of long hours" through deterring overtime by making it more expensive for an employer to mandate long hours.[6] And it once noted: "The legislative policy of the overtime provisions of the [Fair Labor Standards] Act is to spread employment throughout the workforce by putting financial pressure on the employer, and to compensate employees for the burden of overtime workweeks."[7]

These policies advanced by the FLSA are considered of sufficient importance that they are nonwaivable. They may not be waived by an employee, and they may also not be waived by unions. Therefore, the Supreme Court rejected an employer argument that its CBA with the union allowed it to deviate from the FLSA.[8] The Ninth Circuit has echoed this viewpoint:

> The Supreme Court's decision in *Barrentine*. . . makes clear that *the rights of employees arising out of the collective bargaining agreement are separate and distinct from those arising out of a statute such as the FLSA*:While courts should defer to an arbitral decision where the employee's claim is based on rights arising out of the collective-bargaining agreement, *different considerations apply where the employee's claim is based on rights arising out of a statute designed to provide minimum substantive guarantees to individual workers.*[9]

B. Scope of Coverage under the FLSA

1. Coverage for Public Employers

There has been a sporadic history under the FLSA for coverage of public employers. Public employers were not initially covered under the FLSA. This apparently was a reflection of the "jurisprudence" in place when the FLSA was initially enacted. "Federalism" principles applied by the court at that time arguably

---

[5] *Id.* (quoting *Overnight Transportation Co. v. Missel*, 316 U.S. 572, 578 (1942).

[6] *Donovan v. Crisostomo*, 689 F.2d 869, 876 (9th Cir. 1982).

[7] *Brennan v. Elmer's Disposal Service, Inc.*, 510 F.2d 84, 87 (1975).

[8] *Barrentine*, 450 U.S. at 740; also see 29 CFR 785.8.

[9] *Albertson's, INC v. United Food & Commer. Workers Union, AFL-CIO & CLC*, 157 F. 3d 758, 760 (1998).

limited the ability of Congress to impose law governing on state and local government employees.

Over time, these "federalism" concerns gave way and Congress extended the reach of the FLSA legislatively to state and local governments. But the Supreme Court struck down these 1974 amendments in *National League of Cities v. Usury.*[10] It did, though, permit the FLSA's extension into "nontraditional" government functions such as the provision of transit service or other supposedly "proprietary" enterprises.

It did not take long before court litigation demonstrated that the court's distinction between "traditional" and "nontraditional" government functions was unworkable. In 1985, the U.S. Supreme Court reversed itself in a 5-4 decision. That decision — *Garcia v. San Antonio Metropolitan Transit Authority*[11] — explicitly overruled *National League of Cities v Usury.*[12]

Immediately after the 1985 *Garcia* decision, Congress again amended the FLSA, this time to clarify the manner in which the FLSA would apply to public sector entities. Some of these amendments were intended to soften the impact of the FLSA as to public safety employers largely based on public employer complaints. The 1985 amendments created a number of special rules applicable to public safety employers, which will be discussed later in this chapter.

The FLSA only applies to police and fire departments with at least five commissioned officers or firefighters. If the department uses part-time employees to fulfill functions, each individual counts toward the requirement of five. Other support personnel such as dispatchers and clerks do not count towards this threshold. These employees would still be covered under the state MWA, although as already indicated the provisions of the MWA have limited protection for police officers and firefighters because of the high overtime threshold — 240 hours in a 28 day cycle.[13]

2. Employees Covered

a. White Collar Exemption

FLSA contains an exemption for certain "executive, administrative, and professional" personnel. There has been abundant litigation regarding the so-called "white collar" coverage

---

10 426 U.S. 833 (1976).
11 469 U.S. 528 (1985).
12 *Id.* at 563.
13 RCW 49.46.130(4).

to public safety managers. The prevailing rule that rises from that litigation is that most mid-level managers will be considered exempt under the FLSA. But the first-line working supervisors, such as sergeants, are not be exempt.

Even though the employees who fit the exemption will still qualify for FLSA coverage if the employer fails to comply with what is called the "salary basis test." Under the "salary basis test" the employer must provide for a guaranteed salary for each day the employee works. In short, it may not treat the employees, as a wage earner, tethering the employee to the desk while the employer obtains the benefit of providing a "salary" with no overtime. The employer may not deduct from wages leave for "partial day absences." Employers may take a deduction from salary, however, when an employee takes off time for personal leave a day or longer.

b. Coverage of Law Enforcement Officers and Firefighters

Law enforcement officers and firefighters are covered under the FLSA, but there are a series of special rules which apply to them. The definitions of police officers and firefighters are set out in the statute and are discussed in the context of the § 207(k) pay exemption.

Under the FLSA, the "hours worked" concept is central.

C. Hours Worked

Under the FLSA, the "hours worked" concept is central. Employers must pay the minimum wage for all "hours worked" up to the overtime threshold on time and one-half for all "hours worked" in excess of that threshold. This section will discuss the types of "work" performed by employees which constitutes "hours worked." A Table summarizing relevant court rulings and DOL interpretations concerning compensable time is attached to the end of this Chapter as an Appendix.

1. Nature of the Work Performed

a. The General Concept of Compensable Work

The terms "work", "workday", and "workweek" are important in determining the scope of compensation, yet are not defined in the statute. The Supreme Court held in *Tennessee Iron and Railroad*

Co. v. Muscado Local 123,[14] that "work" is to be defined broadly. In *Muscado*, the Court rejected the argument that time needs to be "productive" to be compensable:

> Nothing in the statute or in reason demands that every moment of an employee's time devoted to the service of his employer shall be directly productive. Section 3(j) of the Act expressly provides that it is sufficient if an employee is engaged in a process or occupation necessary to production. Hence, employees engaged in such necessary but not directly productive activities as watching and guarding a building, waiting for work, and standing by on call have been held to be engaged in work necessary to production and entitled to the benefits of the Act.[15]

The Court took an even broader view of compensable work in *Mt. Clemens Pottery Co*:

> Since the statutory workweek includes all time during which an employee is necessarily required to be on the employer's premises, on duty, or at a prescribed workplace, the time spent on these activities must be accorded appropriate compensation.[16]

These cases established the principle that employees were to be compensated portal-to-portal.[17]

After the 1948 Mt. *Clemens* decision, the Republican-controlled Congress, under the influence of the business lobby, narrowed the concept of compensable "work." Congress enacted the Portal-to-Portal Act created an exemption for certain types of "preliminary" and "postliminary" work. This exemption is considered next.

b. The Exemption for Preliminary and Postliminary Work

Under the terms of the Portal-to-Portal Act — an amendment to

---

[14] 321 U.S. 590, 599 (1944).

[15] *Id.*

[16] 328 U.S. at 690-91.

[17] *See, e.g., Ballard v. Consolidated Steel Corp.*, 61 F. Supp. 996 (S.D. Cal. 1945) (all time is compensable "from the time [the employees] enter the premises and clocked in even though 10, 15, 20, or 30 minutes intervened between their clocking in or receiving their daily instructions, and their arriving at their post of duty prior to shift change time.").

the FLSA — the following types of work activities are not compensable:

> [W]alking, riding, or traveling to and from the actual place of performance if the principal activity or activities which such employee is employed to perform, and;
> [A]ctivities which are preliminary to or postliminary to said principal activity or activities, which occur either prior to the time of any particular workday at which such employee commences, or subsequent to the time on any particular workday at which he ceases, such principal activity or activities.[18]

if the employee must do certain pre-shift preparation in order to do his principal activity, the employee must be compensated for this work

The key to understanding the Portal Act is that it is not designed to avoid the requirement of employers to pay for work performed as the principle or primary activity of the employee. It only exempts from payment work occur *before* the first "principal activity." "Principle activity" includes not only the job for which the employee is hired for, but it also includes all those activities which are "an integral and indispensable part of the principal activity." Therefore, if the employee must do certain pre-shift preparation in order to do his principal activity, the employee must be compensated for this work.

The Portal Act was primarily designed to remove from the FLSA mandate work which traditionally noncompensable. The Supreme Court's broad initial interpretations of the FLSA appeared to make employers liable for what had been considered ordinary commuting such as walking from the factory gate to the assembly line where the work was to begin. The Portal Act took direct aim at that broad interpretation.

In subsequent Department of Labor (DOL) regulations on how the Portal exemptions apply to the work of public safety employees it stated:

---

[18] 29 U.S.C. §§ 254(a).

> Compensable hours of work generally include all of the time during which an employee is on duty on the employer's premises or at a prescribed workplace, as well as all other time during which the employee is suffered or permitted to work for the employer. Such time includes *all pre-shift and post-shift activities which are an integral part of the employee's principal activity or which are closely related to the principal activity*, such as attending roll call, writing up and completing tickets or reports and washing and re-racking fire hoses. [Emphasis supplied.][19]

As indicated in this DOL opinion, preliminary work such as briefings, must be compensated. The prevailing interpretation of uniform changing for police officers and firefighters is that it is not compensable. This has been the subject of some litigation, and the Ninth Circuit has recently clarified that unless officers are directed to install their uniform and equipment and work, changing into a uniform does not trigger the commencement of the compensable day.[20]

c. *On-Call Time*

The leading cases concerning compensability for "waiting time" are *Armour & Co. v. Wantock*[21] and *Skidmore v. Swift.*[22] In *Armour & Co.*, the court considered compensation for firefighters who stood by waiting to be called to fires. The employer argued that it need not pay the firefighters for all its waiting time including time spent "playing cards and in other amusements, or in idleness."[23] The court rejected that opinion, stating:

> Of course an employer, if he chooses, may hire a man to do nothing, or do nothing but wait for something to happen. Refraining from other activity often is a factor of instant readiness to serve, and idleness plays a part in all employment in a stand-by capacity. Readiness to serve may be hired, quite as much as service itself, and time spent lying in wait for threats to the safety of an employer's property may be treated by the parties

[19] 29 C.F.R. § 553.221(b).
[20] *Bamonte v. City of Mesa*, 598 F.3d 1217 (9th Cir. 2010).
[21] 323 U.S. 126 (1944).
[22] *Armour & Co.*, 323 U.S. 134 (1944).
[23] *Id.* at 132.

> of the benefit to the employer. Whether time is spent predominantly for the employer's benefit or for the employees is a question dependent on all the circumstances of the case.[24]

And in the companion case of *Skidmore v. Swift & Co.*, the Court likewise ruled that firefighters standing by waiting to be called to fires were required to be compensated. The court noted: "The men use their time and sleep for amusement as they saw fit, except that they were required to stay in or close by the fire hall and be ready to respond to alarms."[25] The court concluded that "no principle of law found either in the statute or in court decisions precludes waiting time from also being working time."[26]

The Court explained that whether waiting time was compensable, time was turned on examination of the factual circumstances:

> This involves scrutiny and construction of the agreements between the particular parties, appraisal of their practical construction of the working agreement by conduct, consideration of the nature of the service, and its relation to the waiting time, and all of the surrounding circumstances. *Facts may show that the employee was engaged to wait, or they may show that he waited to be engaged.* His compensation may cover both waiting and tasks, or only the performance of the task itself. Living quarters may in some situations be furnished as a facility of the task and in another as part of the compensation. The law does not impose an arrangement upon the parties. It imposes upon the courts the task of finding what the arrangement was.[27]

---

[24] *Id.*at 133.
[25] *Skidmore* 323 U.S. at 136.
[26] *Id.*
[27] *Id.* at 137 (emphasis added).

> The overwhelming majority of courts have ruled that employees are not entitled to compensation when they are simply required to make themselves available through some type of electronic means and respond within a reasonable period of time.

There has been frequent litigation over the issue of whether police officers and firefighters in a generalized type of on-call arrangement are subject to compensation. The overwhelming majority of courts have ruled that employees are not entitled to compensation when they are simply required to make themselves available through some type of electronic means and respond within a reasonable period of time. This is particularly true where the department has allowed the trading of such duties between employees. On the other hand, where a department expects an employee to be essentially a "call responder," waiting at home to be dispatched through a call, this is likely to be compensable time.

Case precedent indicates the following factors will be considered and balanced by the court in making the determination as to whether the on-call pay is compensable:

- Whether there was an on-premises requirement;
- Other geographic restrictions on the employee's movement;
- The frequency of calls;
- Whether there was a fixed time for response to the calls;
- Whether employees could easily trade such duties;
- The extent to which a pager eased the restrictions;
- Whether the employees had been able to engage in personal activities during on-call time.

d. Meals and Breaks

The *only* exception to the mandate that employees be

compensated for all the workday is for periods in which they are *completely* relieved of duty for a period of sufficiently meaningful duration. Employees who are simply between work assignments must be compensated for their waiting time.[28] An employer cannot impose noncompensable "free time intervals" during the workday simply because of a lull in productive activity.[29]

DOL recognizes this in its regulations. Short breaks are always compensable.[30] Long breaks — longer than 30 minutes — are noncompensable *only* where employees are completely relieved of duty.[31]

Despite the "completely relieved of duty" language of the DOL regulations, some courts have ruled that even if employees are subject to call and must leave on their radios during lunch this time is not compensable. This dispute between the circuit courts will eventually need to be resolved by the Supreme Court. In the meantime, the Ninth Circuit has not made a ruling on this issue, but it seems likely that it will follow the DOL rule which provides that, in general, if an employee must leave on the radio and monitor calls during their lunch periods, they are not being completely relieved of duty. Other courts have skirted the clear language of the DOL regulation by focusing on whether the lunch break was for the primary benefit of the employee.

e. Sleeping Time

A rule with application to firefighters will be FLSA provisions concerning sleeping time. Where an employee has a duty, of 24 hours or more, the employer is allowed to exempt from compensation regularly scheduled sleeping periods to 8 hours. This standard required in the law is unlikely to be met by most fire departments. If the employee's sleep is interrupted so often that a reasonable night's sleep is not possible, the employer may not avail itself of the sleeping time exemption.

f. Training Time

Compensation issues regarding training time for public safety employees are problematic. There are competing interests at stake.

---

[28] *Armour & Co. v. Wantock*, 323 U.S. 126, 133 (1944).

[29] *Willmark Service System, Inc. v. Wirtz*, 317 F.2d 486 (8th Cir. 1963); *see, also, Mireles v. Frio Foods, Inc*, 899 F.2d 1407 (5th Cir. 1990) (production breaks shorter than 45 minutes are compensable because employees could not effectively use the time for their own purposes).

[30] 29 C.F.R. § 785.18.

[31] 29 C.F.R. § 785.19.

Employees wish to enhance their professional development and employers do not want to pay.

Those issues notwithstanding, the FLSA generally require specific training be compensated. The DOL has stated the following four tests determine whether training time is compensable hours worked under the FLSA:

1. Attendance is outside the employee's regular working hours;
2. Attendance is in fact not voluntary;
3. The course, lecture, or meeting is not directly related to the employee's job; and
4. The employee does not perform any productive work during such attendance.[32]

---

job specific training will almost always constitute "hours worked" because it is inherently "directed related to the employee's job"

An unsupported notion public safety administrators often assume is that as long as the training is "voluntary," they need not pay for it. DOL regulations indicate otherwise. An element of the DOL regulation that public safety employee training will almost always fail to fulfill is the requirement that the training "not directly relate to the employee's job."

In short, the DOL requires no compensation for general education. But job specific training will almost always constitute "hours worked" because it is inherently "directed related to the employee's job."

An open and interesting question is whether an employer's policy of disallowing training opportunities for those employees unwilling to waive their FLSA claims to overtime constitutes a form of unlawful retaliation. It would seem that it would, but case law to date has not addressed this issue. Anti-retaliation provisions in the FLSA are discussed later in this chapter.

Another issue that arises from time to time, though with

[32] 29 C.F.R. § 785.27).

limited enforcement action by public safety unions, is the issue of compensation for trainees. It is well known that there are violations at the police academy where officers are required to attend training sessions beyond the normal workday. These additional hours are probably also in violation of the CBA, but most certainly a violation of the FLSA.

DOL has an opinion that training time at the academy is compensable, but has rejected arguments that such work falls under the "apprenticeship" exemption of the Act. In the early 1990s the Washington State Patrol paid dearly for this violation — although they did get away with it for several years.

Questions sometimes have been raised concerning whether training time, as well as physical fitness requirement of the employer, is compensable. Though there was one lower court decision finding this time to be compensable, that reasoning was later overturned by the Court of Appeals. No case in the Ninth Circuit has addressed this issue, but it seems unlikely that federal courts will require compensation for such exercise time given the generalized benefit employees receive from such activities — even where fitness level is mandated by the employer. A different rule would attach, though, if the employer were to specifically mandate a certain number of hours per week be spent in such exercise.

g. *Travel Time*

FLSA has a crazy quilt of rules, regulations, and case law which applies to the question of compensability of travel time. The regulations seem at times to be in conflict, and they have been subject to varied interpretations by the courts. It is important to bear in mind that there are different types of travel time at issue.

Ordinary commuting is not compensable. This is true under current FLSA rules, even if an employee such as a deputy sheriff, is traveling in a marked patrol unit with a requirement that the radio be left on — as long as it is understood the unit is not in service. If the employee is required to respond to an actual call, compensable time starts when the call response starts.

Time beyond that which is commuting is a necessary preliminary to the shift and would be compensable. For example, if an employer required the employees to pick up emergency service vehicles in a remote location and transport it to a different location on a pre-shift basis, this would be compensable time.

DOL regulations concerning emergency callback are somewhat unclear. DOL has given an opinion that if employees required to be called back after the day's work is over to an off-site location, the travel time will be considered compensable time. The DOL has expressly declined to state an opinion on the question of whether compensation would be required when the employee is called back to the employee's "regular place of business . . ."[33]

Rules are likewise somewhat confusing concerning "overnight travel." For an employee required to travel by means of a common carrier, such as a train or other public transportation, time is not compensable, according to the DOL, for overnight travel outside the employee's normal hours of work. Such time is compensable, though, if it corresponds to the normal time of work. But if the employee is expected to drive on the trip, the act of driving is considered "work."

DOL has rules for "special one-day trips." If the travel is for the benefit of the employer, it is compensable.[34] An exception exists, though, as to the time the employee spends traveling from their home to the location of the common carrier. This is considered normal commute time.[35]

Given the conflicting DOL regulations concerning travel time, it is no surprise that there are questions concerning the compensability of travel time to training. A Ninth Circuit decision was issued that partially clarifies this issue — in the direction of the employer — while at the same time leaving a number of questions in its wake. In *Imada v. Hercules,*[36] the court ruled that travel time to distant training sites — what would be an ordinary commute — was not compensable.[37] This opinion directly conflicted with the DOL letter opinion which tended to define compensability around whether or not a "normal" commute was involved.[38]

Nonetheless, there are some limitations in the court's ruling that limits its potential impact:

- The court noted that in this case the officers were compensated whenever they were first required to report to the department when beginning their travel.[39]

---

[33] *See* 29 C.F.R. 785.36.
[34] 29 C.F.R. 785.38.
[35] *Id.*.
[36] 138 F.3d 1294 (9th Cir. 1998).
[37] *Id.* at 1297-1297.
[38] *Id.* at 1297.
[39] *Id.* at 1295.

- The officers were compensated for travel time which cut across their normal workday.[40]

- The court cited the fact that the training was a benefit to the officers were required California POST certification requirements.[41]

The last point in particular raises a question of the applicability of *Imada* to Washington public safety employers. California mandates POST training. It is a condition of state certification. Where the training is required only by the employer and is not in state law, it is questionable whether *Imada* applies. DOL has held in other contexts that training mandated to maintain an occupational license is not compensable.

Also, it is typical that departments provide a vehicle for such travel — and the continuation of this benefit is a mandatory subject of bargaining. All the time traveling from the department to the training site is compensable, and *Imada* is explicit in not altering that requirement.

And, as *Imada* points out, compensation is required when it cuts across the normal employee's work shift and it was provided to the employees in *Imada*. But another often misunderstood element of this rule is that it applies *even on the employee's day off.* For example, if an employee typically works Wednesday through Sunday 8:00 to 4:00 and goes to training on a Monday, the employer must pay for any travel time which occurs between 8:00 and 4:00.

When cases such as *Imada* are released, unions should be aware that when rules are revised in the employer's favor and are in conflict with the parties' past practice, the past practice still controls. Unions should always bear in mind that the FLSA only sets the *floor* and the parties may develop past practices more protective of employees which then become subject to the duty to collectively bargain.

It is well established that time spent in training and care of canines at home is compensable.

---

[40] *Id.*

[41] *Id.* at 1297.

h. Canine Duty

It is well established that time spent in training and care of canines at home is compensable. DOL regulations permit parties to come up with an "agreement" for a fixed sum, provided that agreement reasonably approximates the amount of time spent actually spent on these at-home duties. The agreement should also provide for additional compensation for occasional extraordinary responsibility such as canine health problems necessitating frequent veterinary visits.

Some courts have held that time spent commuting with a canine is compensable, but this is a distinctly minority view. The Ninth Circuit has yet to rule on that issue either.

i. Responsibilities for Vehicle and Equipment

Under both DOL and court cases, employees may claim compensation for certain maintenance of department-assigned vehicles on off-duty hours. Arguably, this could also be compensation required for maintenance of off-duty equipment such as weapons. Some of this is likely to fall under the *de minimis* doctrine which will be discussed later.

j. Union Activities

When no union is in place, and an employer has an informal grievance system established, time spent by an employee addressing these grievances is considered "hours worked." But DOL has stated that where a union is in place, as an "enforcement matter," it will not consider the time compensable.

It is unclear what the legal basis exists for DOL's stated distinction. Even under this interpretation, though, time spent during the normal work shift grievances in preparing for arbitration is compensable. But time which occurs outside the shift is noncompensable.

Often overlooked are requirements which relate to testimony during arbitrations and civil service hearings. Public employers often do not compensate for such testimony, reasoning that the interests are adverse between the employee and the employer. DOL has issued opinion letters to the contrary, however. If an employee is subpoenaed by the union to testify at such a hearing, according to DOL, this time is most likely compensable.

DOL has not recognized employer arguments that a distinction between appearances in court on behalf of the employer or appearances on behalf of third parties. According to DOL, the test is simply whether the testimony arises from the employment. If it does, the time must be compensated. Consequently, DOL has also rejected employer arguments that employees called to testify in civil proceedings need not be compensated.

Another often overlooked requirement for compensation is compulsory medical *examinations*. When an employer sends an employee to a fitness for duty examination this time is compensable, even it falls outside the employee's normal shift.[42] It remains an open question of the compensability time spent on mandatory medical *treatment*. For example, if as a condition of a "last chance agreement" the employer is required to attend patient alcohol treatment, arguably this time could be considered compensatory. There appears to be no DOL ruling or court case addressing this issue, though.

k. "Off-Duty" Work Through the Employer

A potential trap for employers concerns off-duty work contracted through the employer. If the employer contracts with outside third parties for off-duty work coverage, and runs the employee through payroll system, it might have to pay the employees time and one-half. It depends whether the work is simply for the benefit of the third party of whether the Employer also receives some benefit in the off-duty work. The law recognizes that sometimes a public entity is a "joint employer" with another entity in which case the hours count towards the overtime threshold.

The off-duty work would be deemed non-compensable if it is voluntary off-duty work performed for the benefit of the employee. In such circumstances, the public employer may still impose a certain limited degree of oversight:

> The primary employer may facilitate the employment or affect the conditions of employment of such employees. For example, a police department may maintain a roster of officers who wish to perform such work. The department may also select the officers for special details from a list of those wishing to participate, negotiate their pay, and retain a fee for administrative expenses. The department may require that the separate and independent employer pay the fee for such services directly to the department, and establish procedures for the officers to receive their

---

[42] *See* 29 C.F.R. § 785.43.

> pay for the special details through the agency's payroll system. Finally, the department may require that the officers observe their normal standards of conduct during such details and take disciplinary action against those who fail to do so.[43]

If the "third party" is simply another department or agency operated by the public employer, the hours worked will count as overtime. For example, if a public employer owns a stadium and has the officers work at the stadium on an off-duty basis, this is still work for the entity and is considered overtime under the FLSA.

There are possible ways to circumvent this strict mandate, although these may carry some risks. If the type of work performed in the off-duty capacity is truly different from work performed normally, the parties could arguably agree to a lower rate for this work. If the parties agree that the work will be compensated at a rate that is equivalent to two-thirds the employee's normal rate, when the overtime rate is applied, the result is the employee's normal straight time wage.

If the "third party" is simply another department or agency operated by the public employer, the hours worked will count as overtime.

2. Employer Defenses to Hours Worked Claims

In response to employee claims to have performed uncompensated work, employers will interpose a number of defenses.

a. The "Suffer or Permit" Defense

Occasionally, employers will attempt to avoid FLSA liability by claiming that they did not "suffer or permit" the work and they were ignorant it was being done. It is true that in order for work to be compensable, it must be "suffered or permitted" by the employer. But the DOL has placed the responsibility to control such work on the employer:

> Work not requested but suffered or permitted is work time. For example, an employee may voluntarily

[43] 29 C.F.R. § 553.227(d).

> continue to work at the end of the shift. He may be a piece worker, he may desire to finish an assigned task or he may wish to correct errors, past work tickets, prepare time reports or other records. The reason is immaterial. The employer knows or has reason to believe that he is continuing to work and the time is working time.[44]

The DOL views it as management's responsibility to prevent such work if it does not wish to pay for it:

> In all such cases it is the duty of the management to exercise its control and see that the work is not performed if it does not want it to be performed. It cannot sit back and accept the benefits without compensating for them. The mere promulgation of a rule against such work is not enough. Management has the power to enforce the rule and must make every effort to do so.[45]

In *Forrester v. Roth's IGA Foodliner Inc.,*[46] the Ninth Circuit affirmed the DOL standard for "suffer or permit":

> Thus an employer who knows or should have known that an employee is or was working overtime must comply with the provisions of Section 207. An employer who is armed with this knowledge cannot stand idly by and allow an employee to perform overtime work without proper compensation, even if the employee does not submit a claim for the overtime compensation. However, where an employer has no knowledge that an employee is engaged in overtime work and that employee fails to notify the employer or deliberately prevents the employer from acquiring knowledge of the overtime work, the employer's failure to pay for the overtime hours is not a violation of Section 207.[47]

---

[44] 29 C.F.R. § 785.11.
[45] 29 C.F.R. § 785.13.
[46] 646 F.2d 413, (9th Cir. 1981).
[47] *Id.* at 414.

Work performed off the clock before and after a shift is compensable where an employer suffers or permits the work.

In *Forrester*, the court rejected the employee's claim because the employee maintained a dual set of time records—one set that he turned in for his regular pay and another set of additional hours, which he secretly recorded, and for which he later filed a claim.[48] The court noted:

> An employer must have an opportunity to comply with the provisions of the FLSA. This is not to say that an employer may escape responsibility by negligently maintaining records required by the FLSA, or by deliberately turning its back on a situation. However, where the acts of an employee prevent an employer from acquiring knowledge, here of alleged uncompensated overtime hours, the employer cannot be said to have suffered or permitted the employee to work in violation of Section 207(a).[49]

Work performed off the clock before and after a shift is compensable where an employer suffers or permits the work. This is true even though the employee could have performed the work during the shift.[50] As the Ninth Circuit noted in *Lindow v. United States:*

> An employer cannot escape its obligations to pay overtime compensation for necessary and indispensable work that it expects to be performed outside of normal hours or that must be performed prior to a shift simply by instructing employees not to report early.[51]

Additionally, 29 C.F.R. § 785.12 extends the "suffer and permit" doctrine to work away from the workplace:

---

[48] *Id.*
[49] *Id.*
[50] *Lindow v. United States*, 738 F.2d 1057, 1061 (9th Cir. 1984).
[51] *Id.*

> The rule is also applicable to work performed away from the premises on the job site, or even at home. If the employer knows or has reason to believe that the work is being performed, he must count the time as hours worked."[52]

An employer negligent in keeping track of when employees are working is, by definition, deemed to have suffered and permitted work.[53]

b. The De Minimis Defense

The *de minimis* doctrine was validated initially by the Supreme Court in *Anderson v. Mt. Clemens Pottery Co.*[54] There the Court stated:

> We do not, of course, preclude the application of a de minimis rule where the minimum walking time is such as to be negligible. The workweek contemplated by § 7(a) must be computed in light of the realities of the industrial world. When the matter in issue concerns only a few seconds or minutes of work beyond the scheduled working hours, such trifles may be disregarded. Split-second absurdities are not justified by the actualities of working conditions or by the policy of the Fair Labor Standards Act. It is only when an employee is required to give up a substantial measure of his time and effort that compensable working time is involved. The de minimis rule can doubtless be applied to much of the walking time involved in this case, but the precise scope of that application can be determined only after the trier of facts make more definite findings as to the amount of walking time in issue.[55]

DOL's interpretation of the *de minimis* standard is set forth in 29 C.F.R. 785.47:

> In recording working time under the Act, insubstantial

---

[52] 29 C.F.R. § 785.12.
[53] *Sorensen v. Holman Erection Co.*, 141 LRRM 2688, 1 WH Cases 2d 68 (D.C. Or. 1992).
[54] 328 U.S.680 (1945).
[55] *Id.* at 692.

> or insignificant periods of time beyond the scheduled working hours, which cannot as a practical administrative matter be precisely recorded for payroll purposes, may be disregarded. The courts have held that such trifles are de minimis. (*Anderson v. Mt. Clemens Pottery Co.*, 328 U.S. 680 (1946)) This rule applies only where there are uncertain and indefinite periods of time involved of a few seconds or minutes duration, and where the failure to court such time is due to considerations justified by industrial realities. *An employer may not arbitrarily fail to count as hours worked any part, however small, of the employee's fixed or regular working time or practically ascertainable period of time he is regularly required to spend on duties assigned to him.*[56]

The regulation permits the nonpayment for small and uncertain amount of times that *only* "where the failure to count such time is due to considerations justified by industrial realities." Therefore, DOL concludes: "An employer may not arbitrarily fail to count as hours worked any part, *however small*, of the employee's fixed or regular working time or practically ascertainable period of time he is regularly required to spend on duties assigned to him."[57]

A fair reading of both the Department of Labor regulation and the *Mt. Clemens* decision together would seem to point to the following rule as to when work was considered *de minimis*:

> Work which is required on an ongoing, nearly daily basis is not de minimis unless it only involves a matter of seconds or a "few" minutes;
>
> Time involving more than a few minutes should only be considered de minimis if it occurs on an irregular, unpredictable basis such that it is not reasonable to

---

[56] *See Glenn L. Martin Nebraska Co. v. Culkin*, 197 F.2d 981, 987 (C.A. 8, 1952), cert. denied, 344 U.S. 866 1952, rehearing denied, 344 U.S. 888 (1952), holding that working time amount of $1 of additional compensation a week is 'not a trivial matter to a workingman," and was not de minimis; *Addison v. Huron Stevedoring Corp.*, 204 F.2d 88, 95 (C.A. 2, 1953), cert. denied 346 U.S. 877, holding that 'To disregard workweeks for which less than a dollar is due will produce capricious and unfair results.' *Hawkins v. E. I. du Pont de Nemours & Co.*, 12 WH Cases 448, 27 Labor Cases, para. 59, 094 (E.D. Va., 1955), holding that 10 minutes a day is not de minimis. (emphasis added).

[57] *Id.* (emphasis added).

require the employer to keep track of such time.

Nonetheless, a review of the case law does not indicate that the de minimis doctrine has always been consistently applied in this manner. There are a number of court cases seeming to apply some type of 10-minute threshold to when work is de minimis. In some of these cases, work that even appears to be occurring on a regular basis has been found to be de minimis but generally when it does not involve more than 10 minutes.

In *Lindow v. United States*,[58] the Ninth Circuit considered the *de minimis* rule and its application. At issue in *Lindow* was the holding of a district court "that the seven to eight minutes spent by employees reading the log book and exchanging information, even if not preliminary, was *de minimis* and therefore not compensable."[59]

The Ninth Circuit reviewed a number of the cases as well as 785.47 and then set forth a number of the factors involved in evaluating whether a work performed is truly *de minimis*. The court stated:

> An important factor in determining whether a claim is de minimis is the amount of daily time spent on the additional work. There is no precise amount of time that may be denied compensation and de minimis. No rigid rule can be applied with mathematical certainty. Rather, common sense must be applied to the facts of each case.[60]

The Ninth Circuit then observed that "most courts have found daily periods of approximately 10 minutes *de minimis* even though otherwise compensable."[61]

The court then observed:

> The de minimis rule is concerned with the practical administrative difficulty of recording small amounts of time for payroll purposes. Employers, therefore, must compensate employees for even small amounts of daily time unless that time is no miniscule that it cannot, as an administrative matter, be recorded for payroll purposes. Accordingly, the court in *Anderson* reasoned

---

[58] 738 F.2d 1057 (9th Cir. 1984).
[59] *Id.* at 1062.
[60] *Id.*
[61] *Id.*

> that overtime compensation for 'a few seconds of minutes' is de minimis 'in light of the realities of the industrial world.'[62]

And the court added:

> In addition, we will consider the size of the aggregate claim. Courts have granted relief for claims that might have been minimal on a daily basis but, when aggregated, amounted to a substantial claim.[63]

The court also noted: "Moreover, courts in other contexts have applied the *de minimis* rule in relation to the total sum or claim involved in the litigation."[64] The court then also stated:

> Finally, in applying the *de minimis* rule, we will consider whether claimants perform the work on a regular basis. Similarly, the uncertainty of how often employees perform that tasks and of how long a period was required for their performance are also irrelevant.[65]

After reviewing all of the applicable authority, the court then concluded:

> To summarize, in determining whether otherwise compensable time is de minimis, we will consider (1) the practical administrative difficulty of recording the additional time; (2) the aggregate amount of compensable time; and (3) the regularity of additional work.[66]

In sum, for off-duty "work" described above such as care and cleaning of handguns, the *de minimis* defense may provide a defense to the employer. But the *de minimis* defense provides little defense where work is regular and not difficult to measure. It is not intended to provide a defense simply because the work does not take too long where the work is performed on a regular basis and can usually be tracked.

---

[62] *Id.* 1062-1063 (citing 29 C.F.R. § 785.47; *Anderson* 328 U.S. 692).
[63] *Id.* at 1063.
[64] *Id.*
[65] *Id.*
[66] *Id.*

c. *Work Performed Away from Employer's Premises*

DOL recognizes that some work is, by necessity, performed away from the employer's work site and it may be difficult to supervise and monitor. Canine work is a good example. In these circumstances, DOL allows "reasonable agreements" to provide compensation on an estimated basis.[67] In a number of canine cases, courts have upheld these agreements provided they were in the general ballpark of the amount of time it took to perform the off-duty work.

D. Calculating Wages Owed

1. Applicable Overtime Threshold

There is no daily threshold for overtime under the FLSA (even if there is one under the CBA).

For most employees covered by the FLSA, the applicable threshold for determining when overtime owed is 40 hours. In other words, in any week in which employees work hours in excess of 40, they must be paid time and one-half their regular rate of pay for all work beyond the 40-hour threshold.

There is no daily threshold for overtime under the FLSA (even if there is one under the CBA). If an employee works normally an 8-hour day and works 12 hours on one day, yet then works only 4 on another day so that it totals 40 for the week, there is no FLSA overtime due. It is another question, though, whether overtime would be due under the applicable labor agreement. The CBA overtime rules often trump the FLSA — but only to the extent the CBA exceeds FLSA minimums.

a. *The "7(k)" Exemption*

As to firefighters and police and corrections officers, Congress has extended public safety management much more flexibility in paying overtime. After Congress amended the FLSA in the aftermath of the *Garcia* decision, it created a "Section 207(k)" — commonly referred to simply as "7(k)" — variation on the overtime threshold. It permits public safety employers of firefighters and law enforcement officers to create work schedules which have employees work beyond 40 hours in a 7-day week without accruing

---

[67] *See* 29 C.F.R. § 785.23.

overtime.

Fire protection, employees may work up to 212 hours during a 28-day period without overtime. The threshold for law enforcement employees is 171 hours during a 28-day period. Employees may also elect alternative options — they may elect a 7-day cycle, a 28-day cycle, or anywhere between 7 and 28 days. In the event a cycle other than 28 days is selected, a threshold will be that "number of hours which bears the same ratio to the number of consecutive days" in the work period. The DOL has issued the following table which sets forth this ratio: [68]

207K OVERTIME THRESHOLDS		
Days	**Law Enforcement**	**Fire Protection**
7	43	53
8	49	61
9	55	68
10	61	76
11	67	83
12	73	91
13	79	98
14	86	106
15	92	114
16	98	121
17	104	129
18	110	136
19	116	144
20	122	151
21	128	159
22	134	167
23	141	174
24	147	182
25	153	189
26	159	197
27	165	204
28	171	212

b. Scope of Employees Covered by 7(k)

Congress, though, did not fully define "law enforcement" or "fire protection" activities. Instead, ity left it to DOL to issue regulations. Under that authority DOL defined exempt "law

[68] 29 C.F.R. § 553.201.

enforcement activities" to include:

> . . . any employee (1) who is a uniformed or plainclothed member of a body of officers and subordinates who are empowered by State statute or local ordinance to enforce laws designed to maintain public peace and order and to protect both life and property from accidental or willful injury, and to prevent and detect crimes, (2) who has the power to arrest, and (3) who is presently undergoing or has undergone or will undergo on-the-job training and/or a course of instruction and study which typically includes physical training, self-defense, firearm proficiency, criminal and civil law principles, investigation and law enforcement techniques, community relations, medical aid and ethics.[69]

Employees who meet this test are exempt regardless of their "rank" and regardless of their status as permanent or probationary.[70]

The DOL provides an illustration of what work would typically be considered to fall within the scope of "law enforcement activities."

> Typically, employees engaged in law enforcement activities include city police; district or local police, sheriffs, under sheriffs or deputy sheriffs who are regularly employed and paid as such; court marshals or deputy marshals; constables and deputy constables who are regularly employed and paid as such; border control agents; state troopers and highway patrol officers. Other agency employees not specifically mentioned may, depending upon the particular facts and pertinent statutory provisions in that jurisdiction, meet the three tests described above. If so, they will also qualify as law enforcement officers. Such employees might include, for example, fish and game wardens or criminal investigative agents assigned to the office of a district attorney, an attorney general, a solicitor general or any other law enforcement agency concerned with keeping public peace and order and

---

[69] 29 C.F.R. § 553.211(a).
[70] 29 C.F.R. § 553.211(b).

protecting life and property.[71]

DOL regulations also provide examples of personnel who engage in some types of law enforcement work, yet are not within the 7(k) exemption. Code enforcement personnel, such animal control officers and parking enforcement officers, fall outside this exemption.[72]

Certain corrections personnel are also defined as within the scope of "law enforcement":

> The term "any employee in law enforcement activities" also includes, by express reference, "security personnel in correctional institutions." A correctional institution is any government facility maintained as part of a penal system for the incarceration or detention of persons suspected or convicted of having breached the peace or committed some other crime. Typically, such facilities include penitentiaries, prisons, prison farms, county, city and village jails, precinct house lockups and reformatories. Employees of correctional institutions who qualify as security personnel for purposes of the section 7(k) exemption are those who have responsibility for controlling and maintaining custody of inmates and of safeguarding them from other inmates or for supervising such functions, regardless of whether their duties are performed inside the correctional institution or outside the institution (as in the case of road gangs).[73]

This definition has been deemed broad enough to include municipal jailers.[74]

The regulations also specifically do not extend the 207(k) exemption to number of "civilian" law enforcement personnel:

> `Not included in the term "employee in law enforcement activities" are the so-called "civilian" employees of law enforcement agencies or correctional institutions who engage in such support activities as those performed by dispatcher, radio operators,

[71] 29 C.F.R. § 553.211(c).
[72] 29 C.F.R. § 553.211(e).
[73] 29 C.F.R. § 553.211(f).
[74] *Avery v. City of Talladega*, 24 F. 3d 1337 (11th Cir. 1994).

apparatus and equipment maintenance and repair workers, janitors, clerks and stenographers.[75]

The DOL regulations also define what work is or is not deemed exempt firefighting work. Initially some confusion existed as to EMTs and paramedics were exempt when they also performed firefighter duties. After much litigation about dual role fire department personnel, Congress addressed finally by extending the exemption for "paramedics, emergency medical technicians, rescue workers, [and] ambulance personnel." DOL now defines employees engaged in "fire protection activities" to include employees:

> [I]ncluding a firefighter, paramedic, emergency medical technician, rescue worker, ambulance personnel, or hazardous materials worker, who—(1) is trained in fire suppression, has the legal authority and responsibility to engage in fire suppression, and is employed by a fire department of a municipality, county, fire district, or State; and (2) is engaged in the prevention, control, and extinguishment of fires or response to emergency situations where life, property, or the environment is at risk.[76]

This regulation explicitly defines as outside the exemption fire department employees such as "maintenance and office personnel who do not fight fires on a regular basis."[77]

Also excluded from the definition are paramedic personnel uninvolved in fire suppression.[78] The court cited several factors to determine whether "dual function" paramedics meet the test for the 207(k) exemption:

(1) dual-function paramedics do not carry firefighting equipment or breathing apparatuses,

(2) the dispatcher would not know whether he or she was sending a single- or dual-function paramedic to a call,

(3) paramedic ambulances are not regularly

[75] 29 C.F.R. § 553.211(g).
[76] 29 C.F.R. § 553.210(a).
[77] 29 C.F.R. § 553.210(b).
[78] *Haro v City of Los Angeles*, 745 F.3d 1249 (9th Cir. 2014).

dispatched to fire scenes,

(4) dual-function paramedics are not expected to wear fire-protective gear,

(5) dual-function paramedics are only expected to perform medical services, and

(6) no paramedic had ever been ordered to perform fire suppression.[79]

c. *Establishing a 7(k) Exemption*

In order to avail themselves of a 207(k) exemption, public safety employers must affirmatively elect the exemption. But courts have been extremely lenient in how they have allowed employers to make this election. Although this should be — and is — a subject of collective bargaining, often employers have claimed exemption informally, often without even providing formal notice to the union, and these have been held to be valid in court — where it is usually asserted years later, long after the 6 month ULP deadline has passed.

In order to avail themselves of a 207(k) exemption, public safety employers must affirmatively elect the exemption.

The Second Circuit even went so far as to claim that the 7(k) exemption could be selected "retroactively," after employees brought litigation.[80] The DOL, in a somewhat unusual move, issued an opinion letter specifically criticizing this decision and rejecting its holding:

> It continues to be our position that § 7k must be affirmatively claimed to take advance of its provisions. An employer must designate or otherwise objectively establish the work period for each employee (or group of employees) for which § 7k is claimed *and* pay the affected employees in accordance with its provisions. As indicated in 29 C.F.R. §§ 553.50-51, the employer is required to maintain and preserve records which, among other information, show the work period for each employee and which indicates the length of that

[79] Id.

[80] *Martin v. Coventry Fire Dist.*, 981 F.2d 1358 (9th Cir. 1992).

period and its starting time period.

> *It is our view that the claim to the § 7k exemption may not be objectively made retroactively.* Thus, it is our position that an employer is not relieved from § 7a overtime compensation unless § 7k has been claimed and affected employees have actually been paid in accordance with its provisions.[81]

Other courts have followed this DOL opinion and have uniformly ignored the Second Circuit approach.[82]

There has been some litigation, including litigation involving local police departments, about what happens when an employer does not adequately comply with the 207(k) recordkeeping requirements. In a District Court case involving the Washington State Patrol, a federal judge ruled that an employer who fails to comply with the recordkeeping requirements loses the exemption.[83] But this view was later rejected by the Ninth Circuit Court of Appeals in a case involving Kirkland Police officers in which the court held that the recordkeeping violations of the City of Kirkland did not void their 7(k) exemption.[84] Nonetheless, where an employer cannot show that they can track the start and end of their particular 2079(k) cycle, DOL will likely treat the exemption as essentially nonexistent.

2. Calculating the "Regular Rate of Pay"

> Included in the regular rate, then, are not only base wages but also special premiums such as education pay, longevity pay, specialty premiums and shift differentials.

As indicated above, overtime is to be paid at the rate of time and one-half the "regular rate of pay." The "regular rate" is a key concept under the FLSA and has been carefully defined by Congress and DOL to prevent employers from circumventing the overtime requirement to the Act by artificially using an "hourly rate" which did not include all compensation.

The FLSA defines the "regular rate" broadly to include "all

[81] DOL opinion letter January 13, 1994 (emphasis in original).

[82] 1 WH Cases 2d 913 (D.C. Pr. 1993).

[83] *Holmes v. State of Washington*, 3d Wage Hour Cases 1630 (Dist. Wn. 1992).

[84] *Adair v. City of Kirkland*, 185 F.3d 1055 (9th Cir. 1999).

remuneration" except for certain types of pay which are explicitly included. Included in the regular rate, then, are not only base wages but also special premiums such as education pay, longevity pay, specialty premiums and shift differentials. Although FLSA contains a narrow exemption for certain types of "bonuses," the types of bonuses public safety employees would receive would *not* fall under this exemption. For example, pay for such activities as accreditation certification or physical fitness incentive bonuses, do not fall under this exemption and must be included as part of the regular rate used to calculate overtime.

THE "REGULAR RATE"

- Frequently improperly calculated
- Is not just the base rate
- Includes in addition to the base rate "all remuneration," including longevity, education premiums, fitness bonuses, and acting pay
- If significant premiums are paid, impact on overtime rate can be dramatic

A quick, back of the envelope calculation can reveal how dramatically improper calculation of the regular rate shorts employees. For example, if an employee's base wages are $28 an hour and another $4 an hour is paid out in various forms of premiums pay, the employee is being shortchanged $6 (1.5 times the amount of the premiums) for every hour of overtime worked if these premiums are not incorporated into the "regular rate."

3. Exemptions in Calculating FLSA Damages

Hours worked includes only those hours actually *worked.* It does not include various forms of leave, such as sick leave, vacation leave, compensatory time, Kelly time or other leave in which no productive work was assigned.

Despite the numerous ways in which employers can and do violate the FLSA, there are a number of credits and offsets built into the statute which often substantially reduce, or at times even eliminate, FLSA damages. The most significant available exemption is contained in the definition of "hours worked." Hours worked includes only those hours actually *worked*. It does not include various forms of leave, such as sick leave, vacation leave, compensatory time, Kelly time or other leave in which no productive work was assigned. When calculating damages, these paid leaves must be excluded.

As a practical matter, for employees on a 40-hour overtime threshold, application of this exemption does not substantially impact damages. But such employees subject to the 7(k) exemption the impact can be dramatic, especially when the employer has elected the full 28-day cycle. If, for example, an employee has 20 hours of unpaid overtime in a given 28-day cycle, and brings a claim to collect damages, the employer can offset that claim by showing that the employee had, for example, 24 hours of paid leave.

Another form of exemption is the work schedule itself, at least for most departments. Typically, public safety departments, except for firefighters, use an average of a 40-hour work week even if they are using an alternative schedule. This typically produces hours worked in the amount of 160 in a 28-day cycle, but the FLSA permits 171 hours before the employee hits the overtime threshold. There is an 11-hour "gap" that must be closed before the employee even begins to earn the right to FLSA overtime.

There has been some litigation concerning compensation due as a result of this gap. Although there is some division on this point, the majority view is that for the first 11 hours between 160 and 171, there is no obligation to pay *any* time. The reason the courts give for this is that as long as the *average* wage for employees over the entire 28-day cycle exceeds the minimum wage, there is no FLSA violation. And it would be unusual for the average wage of a public safety employee not to exceed the minimum with or without pay for those extra 11 hours.

On the other hand, the view of the Ninth Circuit and most other courts — as well as DOL — is that even if there is no obligation to pay for what has been referred to as "pure gap time," there is still an obligation to pay for what others have called "overtime gap time." If the employee exceeds the overtime threshold, the DOL and the Ninth Circuit have both agreed that the FLSA is violated *unless the employer pays at least the regular rate up to the threshold and the time and one-half rate for all hours in excess of the threshold.*

In short, where unpaid time is worked, but a 7(k) plan is in place, there is likely to be some damages, although they may be limited to those time periods in which officers work significant amounts of overtime. As a practical matter, this may have the impact of reducing the damages available in a case by 75% or more, depending on the nature of the claim.

Yet another type of "credit" arises where unions have developed CBA terms which require payments in excess of the FLSA minimum. Where the labor agreement has required employers to make additional types of overtime payments, the employer is entitled to a "credit" for these contractual payments made in excess of FLSA minimums. For example, if an employer pays overtime for all hours beyond the normal shift, in the case described above where the normal shift is 160 hours in a 28-day period, there are 11 hours of time paid at the overtime rate, but the FLSA only would have required straight time pay for time. The employer, then, is entitled to some credit for that amount against its FLSA overtime liability.

This may have the effect of shortchanging what is earned under the contract, but this "credit" was added to the FLSA generally at the request of the business lobby which persuaded Congress that they should receive some benefit for this. Some employers have argued that the "credit" can be borrowed from other work weeks in which the "hours workedthe "hurs worked" were insufficient to trigger and overtime obligation and apply any "contractual overtime" payments as a credit to other weeks. But the Ninth Circuit recently rejected this interpretation in *Haro v City of Los Angeles*.[85]

4. Shift Trades

The FLSA has created a narrow exemption which allows employees to voluntarily trade shifts. The statute permits employees "with the approval of the public agency and solely at the option of such individual, to substitute during scheduled work hours for another individual who is employed by the same agency in the same capacity."[86] The hours shall not count towards the overtime threshold.[87]

The DOL has issued a regulation to reinforce the requirement that shift trade be truly voluntary:

> The provisions of section 7(p)(3) apply only if employees' decisions to substitute for one another are made freely and without coercion, direct or implied. An employer may suggest that an employee substitute or

[85] 745 F.3d (1249 (9th Cir. 2014).
[86] 29 U.S.C. 207(p)(3).
[87] *Id.*

> "trade time" with another employee working in the same capacity during regularly scheduled hours, but each employee must be free to refuse to perform such work without sanction and without being required to explain or justify the decision. An employee's decision to substitute will be considered to have been made at his/her sole option when it has been made (i) without fear of reprisal or promise of reward by the employer, and (ii) exclusively for the employee's own convenience.[88]

DOL has recognized an exemption to the recordkeeping requirement with this regulation indicating that the traded time need not be recorded.[89] Employees are simply paid their normal hours that they were previously scheduled for. Employers often claim that they can only establish shift trade programs that require that the trade conclude within a particular payroll or work cycle. There is no basis in the law for this belief.

5. Other Issues Concerning Payment of Overtime

Retroactivity is normal on labor agreements when the contract is signed after the expiration of the prior agreement. Where the base wages have agreed to be retroactive (and as indicated earlier there is a presumption of retroactivity), then this retroactive major requirement applies as well to overtime hours.

Also, overtime must be paid promptly. DOL has issued a regulation defining what it means by prompt payment:

> The general rule is that overtime compensation earned in a particular workweek must be paid on the regular payday for the period in which such workweek ends. When the correct amount of overtime compensation cannot be determined until sometime after the regular pay period, however, the requirement of the Act will be satisfied if the employer pays the excess overtime compensation as soon after the regular pay period as is practicable. Payment may not be delayed for a period longer than is reasonably necessary for the employer to compute and arrange for payment of the amount due and in no event may payment be delayed beyond the next payday after such computation can be made. . . [90]

---

[88] 29 C.F.R. § 553.31(b).

[89] 29 C.F.R. § 553.31(c).

An employer which does not make prompt payment on wages for whatever reason is in violation of the FLSA. The Ninth Circuit rejected the State of California's argument in *Biggs v. Wilson* that it does not need to make prompt wage payments because of a fiscal crisis related to a legislative stalemate.[91] Even though the payments were later made, the Ninth Circuit held the State of California fully liable for liquidated damages an amount equal to the initial wages.[92]

E. Compensatory Time

Compensatory time, under the FLSA, is a relatively recent invention. Compensatory time is not allowed in the private sector. Historically, there had been concerns that allowing a compensatory time option would open the statute up to abuse by employers who would coerce employees into "agreeing" to accept compensatory time.

Following the 1986 *Garcia* decision public sector employers voiced their concerns to Congress concerning the impact of the extension of the FLSA on their practices. Congress agreed to allow a compensatory time option strictly for the public sector.

Congress, though, placed a number of strict rules concerning compensatory time. Compensatory time is not something the employer can "order." For there to be a compensatory time scheme, there must be an agreement between the union and the employer that compensatory time is an alternative method of paying for overtime. If there is no union, the employer can reach an agreement with the employee instead.

The maximum amount of compensatory time which can be accrued is 240 hours for most public employees, but 480 hours for public safety employees. Compensatory hours must accrue at the same rate as the overtime — time and one-half.

There has been a lot of confusion and disagreement over the rules concerning use of the compensatory time once it is accrued. A Supreme Court case adds some clarification to this issue, although it largely throws the issue into the collective bargaining arena.

The FLSA requires employees to be able to take the time off within a reasonable amount of time after using it upon request. The employee has the right to use the compensatory time upon

---

[90] 29 C.F.R. § 778.106.

[91] 1 F 3.d 1537 (9th Cir. 1993).

[92] *Id.* at 1541.

request unless it would cause an "undue hardship." The DOL has given an opinion that the undue hardship requirement is very narrow. For example, the employer cannot deny compensatory time for an undue hardship simply because it would have to pay overtime to replace the departing employee. But some federal courts, including the Ninth Circuit, have rejected this protective interpretation.

In 2000 the Supreme Court ruled in *Christensen v. Harris County*[93] that an employer also had rights in connection with scheduling time.[94] According to the Supreme Court, the employer can dictate that employees take compensatory time off at the employer's election.[95]

There had previously been a split in the circuits with some of the courts of appeals holding that the time off could be scheduled solely at the discretion of the employee. The Court rejected that view, noting that: (1) under the FLSA, the employer had a right to schedule the employee off work at any time[96]; and (2) the employer had a right to cash out the compensatory time at any time.[97] Courts reasoned that since the employer could send the employee home at any time and pay him the compensatory time — simultaneously — there should be nothing that prevents the employer from simply assigning the employee off on compensatory time.

This decision does not seem to have broadly impacted practices for units covered by a CBA. Where the prevailing past practice has been that the employees schedule the time off on their own, — Supreme Court decision or not — PECBA requires that the past practice must be maintained absent a new agreement between the parties.

F. Pre-Hire Agreements

Occasionally, public safety employers, especially police departments, will require officers to sign some type of "pre-employment agreement" which requires that they make some type of reimbursement back to the employer if they quit the department within some set period of time. Often, the departments will try to do calculations of what it cost to "train" the employee and sometimes they even include the employee's wages for the period of

---

93 529 U.S. 576 (2000).
94 *Id.* at 588.
95 *Id.* at 586.
96 *Id.*
97 *Id.* at 580.

time they were at the Academy and on FTO status and perhaps other costs such as the salary of the FTO.

These agreements are not merely unconscionable, they may also be unlawful. The author recently acquired an opinion letter from the DOL inquiring about the legality of these agreements. The contention was that in the event an officer left shortly after the initial training phase then they were required to repay the wages, the average wages should be less than the statutory minimum wage. The DOL agreed with this contention and found that to the extent the employee did not earn "free and clear" a wage in excess of the minimum, it violated the FLSA.

G. FLSA Anti-Retaliation Provisions

RCW 49.46.100(2) and 29 U.S.C. § 215(a)(3) both prohibit employers from discharging or taking any discriminatory actions against an employee who files a complaint or participates in a proceeding against the employer. In addition, courts have ruled that raising a complaint at work even without filing an official claim is protected.[98] Whether or not an employee has been discriminated against is determined on a case-by-case basis.

Some cases are clear cut as to when retaliatory action has occurred. The one Washington case addressing the issue of retaliatory discharge under RCW 49.46.100 found a clear violation where the employees of a food mart were discharged after they told their employer they had consulted with the Department of Labor and Industries about overtime wages.[99] This case recognized the wrongful discharge as a public policy exception to the employment at-will doctrine.[100]

Obviously, there are cases where the FLSA claim is not a motivating factor. Violations must be proven by a preponderance of the evidence.[101] In *Bonham* the employees did not sustain their burden of proof, but rather their general complaining behavior in one case, and a heated argument in the other, was the cause of discharge. Thus, whether the assertion of rights is a motivating factor is definitely fact-based.

It is not necessary to show the employee was discharged in order to have a violation of the statutes. Both statutes also prohibit discrimination "in any other manner." It may be more difficult to

---

[98] *See, e.g., Bonham v. Copper Cellar Corp.*, 476 F. Supp. 98, 103 (E.D. Tenn. 1979).

[99] *Hayes v. Trulock*, 51 Wn. App. 795 (1988).

[100] *Id.*at 800.

[101] *Bonham* 476 F. Supp. at 103.

prove the discrimination, however. *Soto v. Adams Elevator Equipment Co.* involved a case where the employee was not discharged, but, after filing a claim under the Equal Pay Act she was treated differently.[102] The employee had more confrontations at work and her co-workers isolated her.[103] The employer argued these things were "minutia," but the court found there was sufficient evidence to support the jury's finding of retaliation.[104]

H. Enforcement

1. Standing

FLSA claims belong to the individual, not the union. A union may have standing to seek certain declaratory relief in some situations, but it does not have standing to attempt to collect back wages owed by the employee. The duty of fair representation does not obligate the union to assist in bringing FLSA claims.

FLSA claims are individual and need to be brought by individuals. In fact, they may not be waived by the labor agreement.[105]

The Washington State Minimum Wage law provides a more lenient standard for filing claims. While the FLSA require individual opt in to any lawsuit, the State MWA may be brought as a class action or even by a union on behalf of its members.[106]

2. Problems in Estimating Hours Worked

Occasionally, there will be a problem in determining exactly how much time was worked. This is usually due to the fact that the employer has failed to comply with the FLSA recordkeeping requirements. In this case, it is clear that it is the *employer*, not the *employee*, who must bear the burden to prove the actual amount of time worked.

The obligation to record *all time* worked by the employees is stated in §§ 106(b) and 211(c) of the FLSA and 29 C.F.R., Part 510. 29 C.F.R. 516.2(c) requires employers "to record hours worked each workday and total hours worked each workweek. . . ."[107]

Early in the history of the FLSA, the Supreme Court resolved the problem of how to provide employees a remedy where they had

---

[102] 941 F.2d 543 (7th Cir. 1991).
[103] *Id.* at 546.
[104] *Id.* at 551-552.
[105] *Barrentine.*, 450 U.S. 728 (1981).
[106] *Teamsters Local 117 v. DOC*, 145 Wn. App.507, 187 P.3d 754 (2008).
[107] 29 C.F.R. 516.2(c).

performed work yet the amounts were unknown because the employer had violated the record-keeping requirements. The Court required the employer to prove the amount of work performed once the employee establishes there was uncompensated work:

> An employee . . . has the burden of proving that he performed work for which he was not properly compensated . . . .it is the employer who has the duty . . . to keep proper records of wages, hours and other conditions and practices of employment . . . .
>
> . . . Where the employer's records are inaccurate or inadequate and the employee cannot offer convincing substitutes, a more difficult problem arises. The solution, however, is not to penalize the employee by denying him any recovery on the grounds that he is unable to prove the precise extent of uncompensated work. Such a result would place a premium on an employer's failure to keep proper records in conformity with their statutory duties; it would allow the employer to keep the benefits of an employees' labors without paying due compensation as contemplated by the Fair Labor Standards Act. *In such a situation we hold that an employee has carried out his burden if he proves that he has in fact performed work for which is was improperly compensated and if he produces sufficient evidence to show the amount and extent of that work as a matter of just and reasonable inference.* The burden then shifts to the employer to come forward with evidence of the precise amount of work performed or with evidence to negative the reasonableness of the inference to be drawn from the employee's evidence. *If the employer fails to produce such evidence, the court may then award damages to the employee even though the result may only be approximate.*[108]

The Ninth Circuit has followed and applied *Mt. Clemens Pottery* in numerous cases.[109] Other courts are in accord.[110]

---

[108] *Mt. Clemens Pottery*, 328 U.S. at 687-688 (emphasis added).

[109] *Brock v. Seto*, 790 F.2d 1146 (9th Cir. 1986); *McLaughlin v. Ho Fat Seto, supra*; *Wirtz v. Dix Box Co.*, 322 F.2d 499 (9th Cir. 1963).

[110] *Fegley v. Higgins*, 19 F.3d 1126 (6th Cir. 1994); *Marine Services Unlimited v. Rakes*, 918 S.W.2d 132 (Ark. S.Ct. 1996); *Mitchell v. Mitchell Truck Line*, 286

3. Liquidated Damages

Liquidated damages are mandatory absent a finding by the trial court that the employer has affirmatively established both a good faith belief in its compliance and evidence of reasonable steps taken toward such compliance.

Under the FLSA, liquidated damages — double damages — are paid in lieu of pre-judgment interest.[111] Liquidated damages are mandatory absent a finding by the trial court that the employer has affirmatively established both a good faith belief in its compliance *and* evidence of reasonable steps taken toward such compliance.[112] But an employer does not act in good faith where it simply remains ignorant and fails to investigate.[113]

When the FLSA was first passed, liquidated damages were mandatory upon a finding that an employer violated the Act.[114] But even though a statutory defense was added in 1947 under the Portal-to-Portal Act to permit employers to sometimes avoid liquidated damages,[115] the employer bears the heavy burden of establishing the unusual circumstances which will support both parts of that defense, subjective good faith and objectively reasonable grounds.[116]

The right to liquidated damages is defined in 29 U.S.C. § 216(b): "Any employer who violates the provisions of § 206 or § 207 of this title shall be liable to the employee or employees

---

F.2d 721 (5th Cir. 1969); *Reich v. Scherer Buick*, 887 F. Supp. 1142 (D.C. C.Ill 1995).

[111] *Brooklyn Savings Bank v. O'Neill*, 324 U.S. 697 (1945).

[112] *Mireles v. Frio*, 889 F.2d 1407 (5th Cir. 1990); *Joiner v. Macon*, 28 WH Cases 268 (11th Cir. 1967).

[113] *Barcelona v. Tiffany English Publis, Inc.*, 24 WH Cases 201 (5th Cir. 1979).

[114] 29 U.S.C. § 216(b); Brooklyn Savings Bank, *supra*, *Biggs v. Wilson*, *supra*, 1 F.3d at 1541-1542 (emphasis added).

[115] *See* 29 U.S.C. § 260 ("[I]f the employer shows to the satisfaction of the court that the act or omission giving rise to such action was in good faith and that he had reasonable grounds for believing that his act or omission was not a violation of the [FLSA], the court may, in its sound discretion, award no liqu*Id.*ated damages or award any amount thereof not to exceed the amount specified in section 216.")

[116] *Local 246*, 83 F.3d at 297; *EEOC v. First Citizens Bank*, 758 F.2d 397, 403 (9th Cir.), cert. denied, 474 U.S. 902 (1985); *Thomas v. Howard University Hospital*, 139 F.3d 370, 372 (D.C. Cir. 1994).

affected in the amount of the unpaid wages and in an additional equal amount in liquidated damages."[117]

The United States Supreme Court had interpreted this position as mandating liquidated damages whenever there was a violation.[118] When enacting the Portal amendments to the Fair Labor Standards Act, Congress also softened the liquidated damages mandate by adding the following provision to 29 U.S.C. § 260(b):

> [I]f the employer shows to the satisfaction of the court that the act or omission giving rise to such action was in good faith and that he had reasonable grounds for believing his act or omission was not a violation of the Fair Labor Standards Act the court may, in its sound discretion, award no liquidated or award any amount thereof not to exceed the amount specified in § 216 of this title.[119]

Even "if the employer carries its burden of establishing subjective and objective good faith, the court is not required to deny all liquidated damages. '[T]he court may, in its sound discretion, award no liquidated damages or award any amount thereof not to exceed the amount specified in section 216 . . . .'"[120] And if no liquidated damages are awarded, the Ninth Circuit has ruled that prejudgment interest is mandatory.

This Court discussed the good faith and reasonable grounds tests in 1990 in *Bratt*[121] as follows:

> . . . To satisfy the subjective 'good faith' component, the [County was] obligated to prove that [it] had 'an honest intention to ascertain what [the FLSA] requires and to act in accordance with it. . . .
>
> . . .
>
> The additional requirement that the employer have reasonable grounds for believing that his conduct complies with the Act imposes an objective standard by which to judge the employer's behavior." . . . Here, determining the reasonableness of the County's belief involves applying the proper interpretation of the FLSA

[117] 29 U.S.C. § 216(b).
[118] *Brooklyn Savings Bank v. O'Neil*, 324 U.S. 697 (1945).
[119] 29 U.S.C. § 260(b).
[120] *Local 246*, 83 F.3d at 298 (quoting 29 CFR § 260).
[121] *Bratt v. County of Los Angeles*, 912 F.2d 1066, (9th Cir. 1990)

> and supporting regulations to uncontested facts, a primarily legal determination which we review de novo.[122]

Just as ignorance of the law is no defense in most civil and criminal contexts, the FLSA is no exception, particularly given the policy that employers are responsible for knowing the applicable requirements. Nor is it an excuse that the employees failed to complain about the FLSA violation. A "head-in-the-sand" ignorance is evidence of the *failure* to meet § 260's subjective good faith test.

4. Willful Violation

Under the FLSA, "willful" violations are subject to a three-year statute of limitations; whereas, non-willful violations are subject to the two-year limitation.[123] A violation is deemed "willful" when the employer intentionally violated the statute or had reckless disregard as to whether its conduct violated the statute.[124] Courts have found violations not to be willful if the employer had taken significant steps to ascertain the legality of its conduct, such as acquiring opinion letters.[125]

The leading case on this issue is *McLaughlin v. Richland Shoe Co.*[126] In *McLaughlin*, the Supreme Court held that a willful violation means something more than merely a negligent violation.[127] It stated: "In common usage the word 'willful' is considered synonymous with such words as 'voluntary' 'deliberate' and 'intentional.'"[128] The Court then adopted the standard of willfulness from a prior decision under the ADEA that "the employer either knew or showed reckless disregard for the matter of whether its conduct was prohibited by the statute."[129] In so doing, it rejected the "in the picture" analysis which a number of the circuit courts, including the Ninth Circuit, had applied.

In *Reich v. Montfort*,[130] the Tenth Circuit upheld a district court's finding that a violation of willful where the defendants' managers had knowledge that uncompensated time was being worked.[131]

---

[122] *Id.* at 1073 (citations omitted).
[123] 29 U.S. C. § 225(a).
[124] *McLaughlin v. Richland Shoe Company*, 486 U.S. 128, 133 (1988).
[125] *See, e.g., Aaron v. Wichita, Ks.*, 1 WH Cases 2d 550 (D.C. Kan. 1993).
[126] 486 U.S. 128(1988).
[127] *Id* at 133
[128] *Id.*
[129] *Id.*
[130] 144 F.3d 1329 (10th Cir. 1998).
[131] *Id.* at 1334.

As a practical matter, it is often difficult to establish that a violation was truly "willful." In the normal case, the court will agree that the employer owes liquidated damages, but not the additional third year damages for a willful violation.

5. Attorney's Fees

Attorney's fees and costs are part of the FLSA enforcement scheme. This provides incentives for private FLSA actions which conserve DOL resources and helps deter FLSA violations.

29 U.S.C. § 216(d) provides in pertinent part: "Court in such actions *shall*, in addition to any judgment awarded to the plaintiff or plaintiffs, allow a reasonable attorney's fee to be paid by the defendant and the costs of the action." (Emphasis supplied.) The district court has wide discretion to determine what constitutes "reasonable attorney's fees."

FLSA TABLE

This chart lists what "work" have been determined to be compensable – that is, hours that employees must be paid for. It includes references to federal law, and court rulings, and DOL interpretations and regulations. Where some decisions say work is compensable and other decisions say it is not, this chart lists both. It is divided by categories of work activities.

PREPARATORY & CONCLUDING ACTIVITIES

Issue: Writing tickets/reports **Compensable: Yes**

Compensable Authority:
29 C.F.R. § 553.221(b) - Compensable hours . . . include[s] all pre-shift and post-shift activities which are an integral part of the employee's principal activity or which are closely related to the performance of the principal activity, such as *attending roll call*, *writing up and completing tickets or reports*, and *washing and re-racking fire hoses*. (Emphasis added)

Issue: Washing and re-racking fire hoses **Compensable: Yes**

Compensable Authority:
29 C.F.R. § 553.221(b) - Compensable hours . . . include[s] all pre-shift and post-shift activities which are an integral part of the employee's principal activity or which are closely related to the performance of the principal activity, such as *attending roll call*, *writing up and completing tickets or reports*, and *washing and re-racking fire hoses*. (Emphasis added)

Issue: Attending roll call/briefing session **Compensable: Yes**

Compensable Authority:
29 C.F.R. §553.221(b) - Compensable hours . . . include[s] all pre-shift and post-shift activities which are an integral part of the employee's principal activity or which are closely related to the performance of the principal activity, such as *attending roll call*, *writing up and completing tickets or reports*, and *washing and re-racking fire hoses*. (Emphasis added)

O'Brien v. Town of Agawam, 9 WH Cases2d 193 (1st Cir. 2003) - City must pay police officers overtime under FLSA for roll-call time expressly made compensable by their CBA if such time pushes officers' weekly hours over 40, even though this scheme has effect that in a given week some officers will be paid for roll-call attendance at their regular rate, while other officers will receive time-and-one-half, depending on how many shifts they happened to work in that week.

AFSCME Local 889 v. Louisiana, 4 WH Cases2d 1355 (5th Cir. 1998) - State prison officers are entitled to overtime compensation for 15-minute pre-shift mandatory roll call, where corrections department regulations provide for payment of overtime for all hours over 40 in each work week.

Issue: Informal briefing between officer going off duty and officer going on duty while commuting **Compensable: No**

Non-Compensable Authority:
Bartholomew v. Burlington, Kansas, 4 WH Cases2d 1156 (D. Kan. 1998) - City patrol officers are not entitled to compensation for time spent in briefings which were conducted on the way to work and after the officer going off duty picked up replacement officer. The time spent commuting in city vehicles is not compensable inasmuch as the city met requirement of Employee Commuting Flexibility Act by having an agreement with employees with respect to use of city vehicles, and informal briefing is non-compensable preliminary activity.

Shepard v. Burlington, Kansas, 4 WH Cases2d 1149 (D. Kan. 1998) - City patrol officer is not entitled to compensation for time spent in briefings that were conducted on way to work after officer going off duty picked up replacement officer, because time spent commuting in city vehicles is not compensable and, even if it were, the *de minimis* doctrine would preclude such compensation.

Issue: Arriving early, picking up equipment, keys, briefing and exchange information **Compensable: Disputed**

Compensable Authority:
Carlsen v. United States, 13 WH Cases2d 985 (Fed. Cir. 2008) - Police officer who worked at federal prison was not entitled to overtime compensation under for the time spent before his shift waiting in line to pick up keys and equipment or time he spent waiting for and exchanging information and equipment with an incoming officer on next shift. An agency memorandum treated the officer's shift as beginning with receipt of equipment, and the time spent waiting and coordinating was *de minimis* because it amounted to less than ten minutes a day.

Non-Compensable Authority:
Brubach v. City of Albuquerque, 19 WH Cases2d 1614 (D.N.M. 2012) - The time security guards spent in pre-shift briefings constitutes compensable "work" that may be included in calculating FLSA overtime threshold of hours worked, even if actual briefing takes less than 5 minutes and no physical or mental exertion is required, where the City actually required the guards to arrive 5 minutes early; it enforced operating procedure recommending early arrival; guards generally arrived early to comply with early-arrival mandate from their supervisors.

Issue: Changing into and out of protective equipment **Compensable: No**

Non-Compensable Authority:
Administrator's Interpretation No. 2010-2 (June 16, 2010) - [I]t is the Administrator's interpretation that the § 203(o) exemption [excluding "changing clothes"] does not extend to protective equipment worn by employees that is required by law, by the employer, or due to the nature of the job.

Issue: Vehicle maintenance **Compensable: Disputed**

Compensable Authority:
Hours Worked (Dec. 30, 1985) - Yes. The cleaning and maintenance of motorcycles, which is specifically required by city rules to be performed by police officers, is considered to be within the term "principal activities" and, consequently, time spent in such activity is compensable.

Mory v. City of Chula Vista, 2010 U.S. Dist. LEXIS 100777, 25-26 (S.D. Cal. 2010)

Non-Compensable Authority:
Aiken v. City of Memphis, 190 F.3d 753, 759 (6th Cir. 1999) - Keeping vehicles clean and scheduling maintenance to be done at the city's expense are hardly arduous and precisely the sort of activities that Congress had in mind when it used the phrase "incidental to the use of [the employer's] vehicle."

Valladon v. City of Oakland, 2009 U.S. Dist. LEXIS 74439, 15 (N.D. Cal. 2009) - The district court in *Aiken* found that the plaintiffs were required only to schedule maintenance on the vehicles and that the plaintiffs had submitted no evidence that "requiring the officers to maintain their vehicles in a clean condition is other than a minor task." *Aiken* does not establish that these activities are incidental even when officers are required to expend considerable effort on them.

Issue: Uniform and equipment maintenance **Compensable: Disputed**

Compensable Authority:
Albanese v. Bergen County, 6 WH Cases2d 399 (D.N.J. 1997) - Sheriff's department must compensate officers for overtime they spent off the clock maintaining their uniforms and guns to extent activities were performed for department's benefit and said time is found not be to *de minimis*, where department requires officers to perform these activities presumably because they enhance *esprit de corps* and ensure that department presents a polished image to the public.

Non-Compensable Authority:
Rogers v. City and County of Denver, 16 WH Cases2d 1153 (D. Colo. 2010) - City is entitled to summary judgment on police officers' claims for unpaid overtime under FLSA for time spent cleaning and maintaining uniforms, equipment, and department vehicles, because their CBA precludes such compensation.

Nolan v. City of Los Angeles, 2009 U.S. Dist. LEXIS 70764, 64-65 (C.D. Cal. 2009) - Plaintiffs are not entitled to compensation for time spent cleaning and maintaining their uniforms and safety equipment.

Issue: Optional donning and doffing of uniforms **Compensable: No**

Non-Compensable Authority:
Bamonte v. City of Mesa, 15 WH Cases2d 1761 (9th Cir. 2010) - Municipal police officers, who were given option of donning and doffing their uniforms and protective gear either at home or at police station, are not entitled under FLSA to compensation for time spent changing.

Wright v. Pulaski County, 17 WH Cases2d 337 (E.D. Ark. 2010) - Officers who are able to don their uniforms at home are not entitled to compensation for such preliminary activities; evidence establishes that most officers at detention facility don their uniforms and utility belts holding safety equipment at home in less than 10 minutes, and time they spent picking up radios and body alarms, which are issued simultaneously with their going on duty, is *de minimis*.

Edwards v. City of New York, 19 WH Cases2d 616 (S.D.N.Y. 2011) - City was granted summary judgment on corrections officers' FLSA overtime claims for the time they spent donning and doffing their uniforms and equipment in a locker room facility. Even though this activity is necessary or "indispensable" to their guard duties, the activity wasn't "integral" to the officers' performance of their principal activity, because the officers choose to don and doff their uniforms/equipment in facility locker room for reasons ranging from convenience to fear of being recognized by former inmate or mistaken for a police officer.

LECTURES, MEETINGS, & TRAINING

Issue: Training time **Compensable: Disputed**

Possibly Compensable Authority:
Atkins v. General Motors Corp., 701 F.2d 1124 (5th Cir. 1983) - Where there was evidence that employees in a required training program were, pursuant to the program, required to perform productive work, the court held that such activity might be subject to the minimum wage and overtime requirements of the FLSA

even though the activity took place before or after regular working hours.

Compensable Authority:
Bienkowski v. Northeastern University, 7 WH Cases2d 1249, 1251 (1st Cir. 2002) - Here there is no question that, during the EMT training sessions, the employees perform no productive work for the employer. Nor is there any question that, rather than providing such training to its employees during their period of probationary employment, Northeastern could simply make the successful attainment of an EMT certificate a precondition of employment. Thus, we will not hold Northeastern liable for overtime pay for time its employees spend as students, rather than as workers, simply because Northeastern has decided to hire its employees on a probationary basis until they complete the training required to hold the job on a permanent basis.

Allen v. City of Texas City, 18 WH Cases2d 1701 (S.D. Tex. 2012) - Summary judgment is inappropriate regarding whether off-duty time spent by firefighters attending specialized training to obtain or maintain certain certifications to continue in their jobs should count as "hours worked," where Portal-to-Portal Act's exemption for preliminary or postliminary activities does not apply to firefighters' training time, and factual disputes exists as to whether firefighters' attendance at training was voluntary.

Non-Compensable Authority:
Wirtz v. Healy, 227 F.Supp. 123 (N.D. Ill. 1964) - Where the training of tour escorts was performed during working hours and for the primary benefit of, and under the instructions, direction, and control of, their employers, the time spent in such training would be considered "hours worked," and thus subject to minimum wage and overtime requirements under the FLSA.

Dade County v. Alvarez, 4 WH Cases2d 225 (11th Cir. 1997) - Off-duty time officers of police department's special response team spend maintaining physical fitness standards mandated by their jobs is not compensable work under FLSA, where (1) training was conducted outside of officers' regular working hours, (2) officers did not perform any productive work while training, (3) training is voluntary inasmuch as officers could exercise where, when, and for any duration they selected, and they were not required to perform certain exercise routines, and (4) training was not directly related to officers' special response team employment.

Issue: <u>Attendance at lectures, meetings, training programs, etc.</u> **Compensable: Disputed**

Possible Compensable Authority:
29 C.F.R § 785.27 - General - Attendance at lectures, meetings, training programs and similar activities need not be counted as working time if the following four

criteria are met:
(a) Attendance is outside of the employee's regular working hours;
(b) Attendance is in fact voluntary;
(c) The course, lecture, or meeting is not directly related to the employee's job; and
(d) The employee does not perform any productive work during such attendance

Mandatory Training as Compensable Hours FLSA2009-15 (Jan. 15, 2009)

Issue: **<u>Attending training when the attending officer has the responsibility to perform the functions learn at the training</u>** **Compensable: Yes**

Compensable Authority:
Training Time/Police Officers (July 29, 1997) - Yes . . . because the training is directly related to the patrol officer's job responsibility.

Issue: **<u>Attending a career development interview by an officer during off-duty hours</u>** **Compensable: No**

Non-Compensable Authority:
Hours Worked/Career Interview (March 19, 1993) - [T]he program is voluntary in nature, and there is nothing in your submission which indicates that the officer's failure to participate would adversely affect his present working conditions or the continuance of his employment by the City. Thus, we conclude that condition (b) is met. Since the purpose of the program is career development in another skill (i.e., traffic control and motorcycle training) rather than to enhance the officer's performance in his present job, we conclude that the condition (c) is also met.

29 C.F.R. § 785.29

Issue: **<u>EMT training during non-working hours, required by law, and necessary to maintain job</u>** **Compensable: No**

Non-Compensable Authority:
Regular Rate/Training (September 30, 1999) - While time spent in attending training required by an employer is normally considered compensable hours of work, attendance outside of regular working hours at specialized or follow-up training which is required by law for certification of employees of a governmental jurisdiction, does not constitute hours of work under the FLSA.

29 C.F.R. § 553

Issue: Firefighters who voluntarily train to upgrade their skills and thereby become eligible for higher salaries **Compensable: No**

Non-Compensable Authority:
Training Program/Hours Worked (April 6, 1992) - No. For the purposes of this response, we have assumed that the firefighters do not perform any services . . . while attending paramedic training.

29 C.R.F. § 553.226(b)(1), (2)

29 C.F.R. § 785.27–785.29

Issue: Certified first responder training imposed by the employer and not mandated by state law **Compensable: Yes**

Compensable Authority:
Police Officers/Training Time (Aug. 29, 1997) - Where an employer (or someone acting in the employer's behalf or interest) either directly or indirectly requires employees to undergo training, the time so spent is clearly compensable. The employer has usurped and controlled employees' time and must pay for it.

29 C.F.R. § 785.27–785.28

Issue: Time spent by officers in the special tactics unit in maintaining the unit's readiness **Compensable: Yes**

Compensable Authority:
Police/Hours Worked (Sept. 12, 1985) - It is our position that an employee cannot be both a paid employee and an unpaid volunteer while performing the same type of work for the same employer. Therefore, the time spent by employees in the special tactics unit in maintaining the unit's readiness would be hours worked under FLSA.

Issue: Downtime spent a residential facility for police cadet training **Compensable: No**

Non-Compensable Authority:
Bank v. City of Springfield, 3 WH Cases2d 1507 (C.D. Ill. 1997) - Police cadets are not entitled to compensation for non-training time spent during 10-week residential training class in which they remained on premises from Sunday evening until Friday afternoon, where they were free to use such time for personal pursuits, including watching television, reading, talking on the phone, and, after

initial week of training, to leave their apartments and go virtually anywhere they wanted to; although cadets were subject to bed checks and their apartments were subject to inspections, few, if any, were performed; requirement that cadets reside at sites of training does not mean that all time spent there becomes time spent predominately for the City's benefit.

Issue: Mandatory typing homework to improve police recruits typing skills **Compensable: Yes**

Compensable Authority:
Police Recruits' Homework/Hours Worked FLSA 2006-2NA (Jan. 17, 2006) - In this case, the typing training program is not voluntary because the recruits are penalized if their notebooks are not submitted typed. . . In addition, the program is, in fact, directly related to the recruits' job as it is meant to improve their typing skills for use in typing police reports. . . For these reasons, based on the information provided, it is our opinion that the time spent by the police recruits typing their notes outside of class constitutes hours worked under the FLSA and must be compensated.

Issue: Training on the use of a firearm that the officers carry voluntarily while off-duty **Compensable: No**

Non-Compensable Authority:
Police Officers' Firearms Training/Hours Worked FLSA2006-19 (June 1, 2006) - [W]e conclude that time spent by the officers training on the use of an off-duty weapon is not hours worked under the FLSA if the training occurs outside the officer's regular working hours.

Issue: Time spent practicing firearms skills **Compensable: No**

Compensable Authority:
Practicing Firearms Skills/Hours Worked (Jan. 9, 1998) - With respect to the time spent by officers practicing their firearms skills, the practice (or training) appears to be the type contemplated by the Regulations 785.31. Thus, we are not prepared to assert that firearms skills practice outside duty hours is compensable under the FLSA.

Issue: "Ride along" police training to gain experience for advancement opportunities **Compensable: Yes**

Compensable Authority:

"Ride Along" Police Training/Hours Worked (Feb. 16, 2001) - [T]ime spent in training programs need not be counted as "hours worked" for FLSA purposes if *all* of the following criteria are met: (a) attendance is outside of the employee's regular working hours; (b) attendance is, in fact, voluntary; (c) the course, lecture or meeting is not directly related to the employee's job; and (d) the employee does not perform any productive work during such attendance...It is our opinion, however, that criterion (d) is not met [in ride along situations] because when a deputy rides with a road deputy and participates in the assignments "in order to gain experience", the corrections deputies undoubtedly are providing hands-on assistance to the patrol deputies. For example, the ride-along deputies would surely help detain an unruly suspect by assisting in searching for weapons, handcuffing, etc. We view such a "ride-along situation" as a form of on-the-job training which would be compensable under the FLSA.

Police Officers' Ride-Along Program/Hours Worked (May 28, 1998)

Issue: Time spent during off-duty hours by police officers in practicing for, and performing in, drill team events — **Compensable: No**

Non-Compensable Authority:
Hours Worked (Dec. 30, 1985) - Time spent voluntarily in motorcycle drill team activities outside of the employee's normal working hours is not considered hours worked for the police department and therefore is not compensable under FLSA. This type of voluntary activity is analogous to civic and charitable work.

WAITING AND ON-CALL TIME

Issue: On-call during breaks or time off — **Compensable: Disputed**

Possible Compensable Authority:
Owens v. Local No. 169, 971 F.2d 347 (9th Cir. 1992) - Courts determine compensability base on a seven factor test:
1) Whether there was an on-premises living requirement;
2) whether there were excessive geographical restrictions on employee movements;
3) whether the frequency of call was unduly restrictive;
4) whether a fixed time limit for response was unduly restrictive;
5) whether the on-call employee could easily trade on-call responsibilities;
6) whether the use of a pager could ease restrictions;
7) whether the employee had actually engaged in personal activities during call-in time.

Compensable Authority:

Armour & Co. v. Wantock, 323 U.S. 126 (1944) - Firefighters must be compensated for their on call time spent at the firehouse.

Brigham v. Eugene Water & Elec. Bd., 357 F.3d 931 (9th Cir. 2004) - Remaining within earshot of their home phones and alarm systems, while stationed at the employer's power-generating facility, meant the employees were subject to strict geographic constraints.

Taylor v. American Guard & Alert, 1998 U.S. App. LEXIS 26934 (9th Cir. 1998) - The court found that the lack of pagers limited the employees' ability to engage in personal pursuits.

Brigham v. Eugene Water & Elec. Bd., 357 F.3d 931 (9th Cir. 2004) - Unduly restrictive because the plaintiffs were required to respond instantaneously to any alerts.

Taylor v. American Guard & Alert, 1998 U.S. App. LEXIS 26934 (9th Cir. 1998) - The court found that the lack of pagers limited the employees' ability to engage in personal pursuits.

Non-Compensable Authority:

Dixon v. King County, 1996 U.S. App. LEXIS 565 (9th Cir. 1996) - The fact that [plaintiffs] seldom are willing to impose upon one another's off-duty time does not mean they cannot easily trade shifts if they seek to trade.

Dixon v. King County, 74 F.3d 1245 (9th Cir. 1996) - Inspectors receive, on average, one call per on-call shift. This does not create a significant restriction on their use of on-call time for personal purposes.

Brigham v. Eugene Water & Elec. Bd., 357 F.3d 931 (9th Cir. 2004) - Calls made on average once or twice a month to be infrequent.

Adair v. Charter County of Wayne, 11 WH Cases2d 985 (6th Cir. 2006) Airport police officers who were required to live within 30-minute range of airport and to carry a pager with them at all times are not entitled to be compensated under FLSA for all of time they spent off duty, despite officers' contention that they were subject to discipline for not responding when paged. The mere threat of discipline does not prevent employees from effectively using their off-duty time for personal pursuits. Moreover, there is no evidence that officers were subject to discipline for failing to respond to a page while off duty.

Taylor v. American Guard & Alert, 1998 U.S. App. LEXIS 26934 (9th Cir. 1998) - The employees were allowed to travel away from the pump station while on call and that the 35-mile restriction was not excessive.

Dixon v. King County, 74 F.3d 1245 (9th Cir. 1996) - Inspectors are required to respond to most calls within forty-five minutes. However, the inspectors are not employed to respond to an emergency in progress, and, moreover, no inspector has ever been disciplined for arriving late (suggesting the 45 minute response time, with no punishment for tardiness, was not unduly restrictive).

Issue: Residing on employer's premises **Compensable: Disputed**

Compensable Authority:
Pabst v. Okla. Gas & Elec. Co., 228 F.3d 1128, 6 WH Cases 2d 609 (10th Cir. 2000) - Employees were required to be on-call to monitor building alarms on weekdays from 4:30 p.m. to 7:30 a.m. and 24 hours a day on weekends. When the technicians were on-call, all alarms were routed to computers located within their homes, as well as to pagers, and the technicians initially had 10 minutes to respond (later the response time was increased to 15 minutes), or they would be subject to discipline. Such an arrangement constitutes work under the FLSA and must be compensated.

Non-Compensable Authority:
29 C.F.R § 785.23 - Employees residing on employer's premises or working at home - An employee who resides on his employer's premises on a permanent basis or for extended periods of time is not considered as working all the time he is on the premises. Ordinarily, he may engage in normal private pursuits and thus have enough time for eating, sleeping, entertaining, and other periods of complete freedom from all duties when he may leave the premises for purposes of his own. It is, of course, difficult to determine the exact hours worked under these circumstances and any reasonable agreement of the parties which takes into consideration all of the pertinent facts will be accepted.

Issue: On-site back-up duty **Compensable: Yes**

Compensable Authority:
SEIU Local 102 v. San Diego County, 2 WH Cases2d 545 (9th Cir. 1994) - Probation officers were working while on standby duty at probation facility from 8 p.m. to 6 a.m., where they must remain at facility, abide by facility rules, and keep their supervisor informed of their whereabouts.

Issue: On-call time waiting to provide medical assistance to inmates **Compensable: Yes**

Compensable Authority:
Casserly v. Colorado, 1 WH Cases2d 103 (Colo. Ct. App. 1992) - Physician assistants were entitled to overtime compensation for time spent waiting for calls to provide emergency medical services to inmates, where they could not use on-call time effectively for their own purposes, inasmuch as they had to respond within 20 minutes to any of seven facilities covering eight mile radius, and they received from 10 to 12 calls per weekday shift and up to 24 calls on a weekend shift.

Issue: <u>Idle time while on duty</u> **Compensable: Yes**

Compensable Authority:
29 C.F.R § 785.15 - A stenographer who reads a book while waiting for dictation, a messenger who works a crossword puzzle while awaiting assignments, fireman who plays checkers while waiting for alarms and a factory worker who talks to his fellow employees while waiting for machinery to be repaired are all working during their periods of inactivity.

REST BREAKS AND MEAL PERIODS

Issue: <u>Multi-hour breaks on weekend long shifts</u> **Compensable: Yes**

Compensable Authority:
Lee v. Coahoma County, 30 WH Cases 764 (5th Cir. 1991) - Deputies' two-hour rest breaks on weekend long-shifts were compensable working time under FLSA, where weekend shifts constituted tours of duty of less than 24 hours, and thus county could not exclude sleep time from compensable hours of work.

Issue: <u>Meal breaks while in uniform and monitoring radio calls</u> **Compensable: Disputed**

Compensable Authority:
29 C.F.R § 785.19 - Meal - (a) Bona fide meal periods. Bona fide meal periods are not work time. Bona fide meal periods do not include coffee breaks or time for snacks. These are rest periods. *The employee must be completely relieved from duty for the purposes of eating regular meals.* Ordinarily 30 minutes or more is long enough for a bona fide meal period. A shorter period may be long enough under special conditions. (Emphasis added)

Lamon v. City of Shawnee, 972 F.2d 1145, 30 WH Cases 1665 (10th Cir. 1992) - police officers who had to either leave a telephone number where they could be reached or monitor a portable radio, stay within city limits, and respond to citizen requests and confront crimes committed in their presence were entitled to be paid for their meal periods.

Non-Compensable Authority:
Henson v. Pulaski Cnty. Sheriff Dep't, 6 F.3d 531, 1 WH Cases2d 1057 (8th Cir. 1993) - Police officers who could go wherever they pleased and could and did attend to personal errands during a 30-minute meal period were not entitled to compensation for mealtime. The break was predominantly for the officers' benefit because the only potential restrictions on the free use of their meal period arose from the possibility that citizens might ask them questions and from monitoring

radios for emergency calls.

Lee v. Coahoma County, 937 F.2d 220, 30 WH Cases 764 (5th Cir. 1991) - deputies who could go where they pleased during their lunch break, would only radio out once they reached the place where they wanted to eat, and were called back only in an occasional emergency were not entitled to compensation for their meal breaks.

Issue: <u>Interrupted meal breaks</u> **Compensable: Yes**

Compensable Authority:

Weeks v. Chief, Washington State Patrol, 25 WH Cases 970 (Wash. 1982) - One-hour lunch period during which Washington State Patrol troopers are required to be on call (remain available by radio or telephone) constitutes "work" despite permission being granted for troopers to engage in personal activities outside the work area during the lunch period.

Aboud v. City of Wildwood, 20 WH Cases2d 1131 (D.N.J. 2013) - Officers who were subject to recall during their 30-minute meal breaks are not completely relieved from duty for the purpose of eating meals, so their meal breaks will, for conditional class-certification purposes, be considered compensable.

Brennan v. Elmer's Disposal Service, Inc., 22 WH Cases 118 (9th Cir. 1975) - An employee cannot be docked for lunch breaks during which he is required to continue with any duties related to his work.

Renfro v. Emporia, 30 WH Cases 1017 (10th Cir. 1991) - Federal district court properly found that sleep and meal times during city firefighters' 24-hour on-call shifts were compensable under FLSA, despite claim that firefighters were not on regular tour of duty as required by Department of Labor regulations. "Tour of duty" is period of time during which employee is considered to be on duty for purposes of determining compensable hours, and court found that on-cFsl shifts were compensable hours.

Issue: <u>Short breaks (bathroom, cigarette)</u> **Compensable: Yes**

Compensable Authority:

29 C.F.R. § 785.18 - Rest - Rest periods of short duration, running from 5 minutes to about 20 minutes, are common in the industry. They promote the efficiency of the employee and are customarily paid for as working time. They must be counted as hours worked. Compensable time of rest periods may not be offset against other working time such as compensable waiting time or on-call time.

Mitchell v. Greinetz, 235 F. 2d 621, 13 W.H. Cases 3 (10th Cir. 1956) - Rest periods of short duration, running from 5 minutes to about 20 minutes, are common. They promote the efficiency of the employee and are customarily paid for as working time. They must be counted as hours worked. Compensable time of rest periods may not be offset against other working time such as compensable waiting time or on-call time.

Issue: <u>Shift splitting breaks</u> **Compensable: No**

Non-Compensable Authority:
UTU Local 1745 v. Albuquerque, 5 WH Cases2d 555 (10th Cir. 1999) - Bus drivers who work a morning shift and late afternoon shift, separated by three-to-five-hour split-shift period, are not entitled to compensation for split-shift period as hours worked under FLSA, where drivers were free to do as they wish during this period, except drink alcohol, and most of them were able to use time effectively for their own purposes without restrictions; while split-shift period is less convenient or less desirable than straight shift, this does not mean drivers are on duty and deserve compensation during that period; fact that the city pays split-shift differential does not constitute acknowledgment that split-shift period is compensable hours worked.

TRAVEL TIME

Issue: <u>Travel that is all in a day's work</u> **Compensable: Yes**

Compensable Authority:
29 C.F.R § 785.38 - Travel that is all in the day's work - Time spent by an employee in travel as part of his principal activity, such as travel from a job site to job site during the workday, must be counted as hours worked. . . If an employee normally finishes his work on the premises at 5 p.m. and is sent to another job which he finishes at 8 p.m. and is required to return to his employer's premises arriving at 9 p.m., all of the time is working time. However, if the employee goes home instead of returning to his employer's premises, the travel after 8 p.m. is home-to-work travel and is not hours worked.

Walling v. Mid-Continent Pipe Line Co., 143 F.2d 308 (10th Cir. 1944)

Issue: <u>Commuting from home to mandatory training when that time exceeds regular commuting time</u> **Compensable: No**

Non-Compensable Authority:
Imada v. Hercules, Calif., 138 F.3d 1294 (9th Cir. 1998) - The officers argued that the travel here was not in the category of ordinary home-to-work travel, since it occurs only a few times a year. They also claimed that the travel was

compensable as an unusual one-day assignment in another city to meet a special need. The court found, however, that mandatory training is a normal incident of the officers' employment and cannot be characterized as either "special" or "unusual." Although the training benefits the city, it is at least equally beneficial to the officers, the court found.

Issue: Travel to mandatory examinations **Compensable: No**

Non-Compensable Authority:
Whalen v. United States, 16 WH Cases2d 648 (Fed. Cl. 2010) - Federal Aviation Administration did not violate FLSA when it failed to provide air-traffic controllers at air force base with overtime compensation for time spent traveling between their homes and off-base medical center for mandatory examinations, even though they were paid for travel time between air-traffic control facility and medical center and for the time spent at required medical examinations, since controllers' work day either began or ended at medical center, and travelling between a medical center and their homes amounted to non-compensable commuting time under Portal-to-Portal Act.

Issue: Travel time and time attending a medical appointment to obtain required medical verification **Compensable: No**

Non-Compensable Authority:
Time Spent Verifying Sick Leave FLSA2005-3NA (May 16, 2005) - If the facts do not suggest that the employer placed any restrictions on the activities of employees who are on sick leave, then the time employees spend obtaining medical verification of their illnesses, so as to comply with the terms of the State's paid sick leave policy, is not "hours worked" and therefore is not compensable.

Issue: Travel in government owned vehicles between fire stations **Compensable: Yes**

Compensable Authority:
McGuire v. Hillsborough County, Fla., 12 WH Cases2d 336 (M.D. Fla. 2007) - Fire inspectors are entitled to compensation under FLSA for time they spent driving county-owned vehicles between fire stations and their first and last worksites, where 11th Circuit case law has upheld such drive time as compensable as a matter of law.

Issue: Travel from principle activity to gym for **Compensable: No**

required physical-fitness training

Compensable Authority:
McLaughlin v. General Electric Co., 28 WH Cases 1519 (N.D.N.Y. 1988) - Travel time from nuclear power plant to local gymnasium by security inspectors who are required to engage in physical-fitness training by federal regulation is not compensable under FLSA overtime provisions as travel from one principal activity to another, where travel is not work itself, is not principal activity, and is not integral and indispensable part of principal workday activity.

Issue: Commuting time in government vehicle **Compensable: No**

Non-Compensable Authority:
Hellmers v. Vestal, 969 F. Supp. 837, 843 (N.D.N.Y 1997) - Nowhere in the [FLSA] does there appear to be an exemption for commuting time spent in marked police cars.

Adams v. United States, 471 F.3d 1321, 12 WH Cases2d 231 (Fed. Cir. 2006) - Time that federal law-enforcement officers for five agencies spent solely in driving to and from work in government vehicles is not compensable work under FLSA.

Wolfen v. United States, 14 WH Cases2d 691 (Fed. Cl. 2008) - Claim of federal law-enforcement officer seeking overtime under FLSA for time solely spent driving government vehicle to and from work is dismissed for failure to state claim for which relief may be granted, inasmuch as *Adams* clearly rejected commuting-time claims under FLSA and Portal-to-Portal Act.

Garner v. United States, 14 WH Cases2d 1768 (Fed. Cl. 2009) - Employees of Drug Enforcement Administration are not entitled to overtime for time spent driving to and from work in government-owned vehicles, where DEA employees did not allege they performed any activities during their commute that would trigger compensability and made only conclusory allegations about the work performed during their commutes.

Hamilton v. United States, 15 WH Cases2d 113 (Fed. Cl. 2008) - Holding the same as *Garner.*

Issue: Commuting time in marked police vehicle and performing job functions **Compensable: Disputed**

Possibly Compensable Authority:
Hertz v. Woodbury County, Iowa, 13 WH Cases2d 1141 (N.D. Iowa 2008) - It is up for a jury to decide whether sheriff's lieutenant and sergeant, commuting to work in marked police cars, are entitled to compensation. Time might be

compensable where the City enjoys the increase police presence, reduce response time, and ability to engage in law and traffic enforcement while commuting to and from the office. Moreover, plaintiff's radio 10-41 (meaning on-duty) when getting into the car and 10-42 (off-duty) when getting out.

Issue: <u>Travel from home to work in emergency situations</u> **Compensable: Yes**

Compensable Authority:
29 C.F.R § 785.36 - Home to work in emergency situations - There may be instances when travel from home to work is overtime. For example, if an employee who has gone home after completing his day's work is subsequently called out at night to travel a substantial distance to perform an emergency job for one of his employer's customers all time spent on such travel is working time.

Issue: <u>Travel from home to work (and vice versa) while being required to respond to calls</u> **Compensable: Yes**

Compensable Authority:
Travel Time in Marked Police Cars (July 28, 1997) - The officer would be considered to be "on-duty" from the moment that he or she responds to the emergency.

29 C.F.R. § 553.221(f) - A police officer, who has completed his or her tour of duty and who is given a patrol car to drive home and use on personal business, is not working during the travel time even where the radio must be left on so that the officer can respond to emergency calls. Of course, the time spent in responding to such calls is compensable.

Issue: <u>Home to work on special one-day assignment in another city</u> **Compensable: Yes**

Compensable Authority:
29 C.F.R § 785.37 - Home to work on special one-day assignment in another city - For example, an employee who works in Washington, D.C., with regular working hours from 9 a.m. to 5 p.m. may be given a special assignment in New York City, with instructions to leave Washington at 8 a.m. He arrives in New York at 12 noon, ready for work. The special assignment is completed at 3 p.m., and the employee arrives back in Washington at 7 p.m. Such travel cannot be regarded as ordinary home-to-work travel occasioned merely by the fact of employment. It was performed for the employer's benefit and at his special request to meet the needs of the particular and unusual assignment. It would thus qualify as an integral part of the "principal" activity which the employee was

hired to perform on the workday in question.

Issue: Picking up other deputies on the way to the academy for training and then back to their homes **Compensable: Yes**

Compensable Authority:
Hours Worked/Travel Time (May 4, 1989) - Any work which an employee is required to perform while traveling must of course be counted as hours worked. The driver of an automobile who is required to pick up other passengers and transport them to a specific location is working while driving.

Issue: Travel away from home **Compensable: Yes**

Compensable Authority:
29 C.F.R § 785.39 - Travel away from home community - Travel that keeps an employee away from home overnight is travel away from home. Travel away from home is clearly work time when it cuts across the employee's workday. The employee is simply substituting travel for other duties.

Issue: Travel time from a deputy's area substation to an assigned location for court appearances or training **Compensable: No**

Non-Compensable Authority:
Travel Time/Hours Worked (April 17, 1998) - An employee who travels from home before his/her regular workday and returns home at the end of the workday is engaged in ordinary home to work travel which is a normal incident of employment. This is true whether the employee works at a fixed location or at different job sites. Normal travel from home to work is not work time.

29 C.F.R. § 785.35

Issue: Travel time to and from the officer's residence when an officer is required to appear in court during off-duty hours **Compensable: Yes**

Compensable Authority:
Police/Hours Worked/Labor Contracts (April 6, 1992) – [Question] When an officer is required to appear in court during off-duty hours, does compensable time include travel time to and from the officer's residence?
[Answer] Yes. As indicated in the opinion letter dated September 10, 1987

(enclosure 6), it is our position that time spent in travel from an officer's home to court and return, as well as time spent in court, is compensable under FLSA when the court appearance involves official duty.

Issue: <u>Transportation of prisoners by police officers</u> **Compensable: Yes**

Compensable Authority:
Police Officers' Time Spent Transporting Prisoners FLSA2006-12NA (June 23, 2006) - Police officers who are guarding prisoners while transporting them and who are responsible for the safety of the prisoners and the public are working while traveling. Consequently, all of the hours an officer spends transporting prisoners are compensable hours and must be compensated in accordance with the provisions of section 6 and 7 of the FLSA.

SLEEP TIME

Issue: <u>Sleep time: less than 24-hour duty</u> **Compensable: Yes**

Compensable Authority:
29 C.F.R § 785.21 - Less than 24-hour duty - An employee who is required to be on duty for less than 24 hours is working even though he is permitted to sleep or engage in other personal activities when not busy. A telephone operator, for example, who is required to be on duty for specified hours is working even though she is permitted to sleep when not busy answering calls. It makes no difference that she is furnished facilities for sleeping. Her time is given to her employer. She is required to be on duty and the time is worktime.

Issue: <u>Sleep time: duty of 24-hours or more, not interrupted</u> **Compensable: No**

Non-Compensable Authority:
Roy v. Lexington County, 4 WH Cases2d 869 (4th Cir. 1998) - County properly excluded sleep time from EMS employees' compensable hours, where majority of EMS employees enjoyed at least five hours of uninterrupted sleep.

Schryvers v. Coulee Cmty. Hosp., 138 Wash. App. 648, 656 (Wash. Ct. App. 2007) - All interruptions to sleep time are compensable, if interruptions prevent a reasonable night of sleep – defined as five hours on a 24 hour shift - entire sleep time is compensable

Hultgren v. County of Lancaster, 913 F.2d 498, 501 (8th Cir. 1990) - If the employee's sleeping period is interrupted by a call to duty, the interruption must be counted as hours worked. If the period is interrupted to such an extent that the employee cannot get a reasonable night's sleep [5 hours], the entire period must be counted.

Bodie v. Columbia, 30 WH Cases 584 (4th Cir. 1991) - City properly excluded sleep time from compensable hours of firefighter who worked a tour of duty of more than 24 hours, where employee impliedly agreed to such exclusion inasmuch as he voluntarily acquiesced in a new schedule, with the exclusion of sleep time, for almost two years without slightest protest.

Issue: Impliedly agreed to sleep time **Compensable: Disputed**

Compensable Authority:
Firefighters Local 349 v. City of Rome, 28 WH Cases 1150 (N.D. Ga. 1988) - Firefighters' continuation in working and accepting paychecks after employer instituted policy of excluding sleep time from compensation, under FLSA overtime regulation excluding sleep time if there is express or implied agreement between employer and firefighters to exclude such time, may not support inference of implied agreement, where there exists contemporaneous protest to employer's policy.

Sleep Time/Hours Worked (April 7, 1995)

Sleep Time/Hours Worked (Jan. 17, 1995)

Non-Compensable Authority:
Bodie v. Columbia, 30 WH Cases 584 (4th Cir. 1991) - City properly excluded sleep time from compensable hours of firefighter who worked a tour of duty of more than 24 hours, where employee impliedly agreed to such exclusion inasmuch as he voluntarily acquiesced in a new schedule, with the exclusion of sleep time, for almost two years without slightest protest.

CANINE & HORSE DUTY

Issue: Canine duty **Compensable: Yes**

Compensable Authority:
Dixon v. City of Forks, 2009 U.S. Dist. LEXIS 44227, 10 (W.D. Wash. 2009) - [T]he law is well-established that law enforcement canine officers like Plaintiff are entitled to compensation for their off-duty time spent feeding, bathing, exercising, training, cleaning up after, and otherwise caring for their police dogs, because such activities benefit their employer and are compensable as "work" under the FLSA.

Leever v. City of Carson, 360 F.3d 1014, 1020 (9th Cir. 2004) - [I]t makes sense for the parties to come to an agreement, to eliminate complicated, repetitious, and hard-to-resolve disputes about exactly how much time it took to take care of the dogs each day.

Holzapfel v. Town of Newburgh, 145 F.3d 516, 527 (2nd Cir. 1998) - Involving both employee and employer representatives in negotiations to decide how many off-duty hours will be compensated is a simple solution benefitting all parties. K-9 officers will know precisely the extent of their responsibilities. Municipalities and their police departments can budget with relative accuracy, and minimize concern that they will be required to defend against an overtime claim involving thousands of dollars.

Lewallen v. Scott County, 16 WH Cases2d 591 (E.D. Tenn. 2010) - Off-duty time that K-9 police officer spent caring for and training narcotics-detection dog is compensable “work”, where officer had to take dog home with him, look after and keep dog in good health, and perform maintenance training to keep dog certified, county was aware that officer cared for and trained dog while off duty.

DOL Opinion Letter: Hours Worked/Canine Care (Aug. 11, 1993)

Issue: <u>Transport of a canine</u> **Compensable: Disputed**

Compensable Authority:
Reich v. New York City Transit Auth., 839 F. Supp. 171, 182 (E.D. N.Y. 1993) - The *Reich* court found the transportation to be integral and thus compensable based on three factors: 1) that transporting the dogs to work in the officers' own vehicles was required by the employer; 2) that transporting the dogs was necessary to facilitate the bonding relationship between dog and owner that is essential to a successful working relationship; and 3) that transporting the dogs "directly benefits the defendant employer" because it facilitates the working relationship between dog and owner and spares the city the expense of a centralized kennel.

Non-Compensable Authority:
Andrews v. DuBois, 888 F. Supp. 213 (D. Mass. 1995) - Time spent by state correction canine handlers transporting dogs between home and correctional facilities is not compensable under FLSA, where act explicitly states ordinary commuting time is not compensable, transportation of dogs benefits corrections department only indirectly and presence of dogs rarely adds even marginal amounts of time to a regular commute, and time spent loading animals in and out of the car is *de minimis*.

Levering v. District of Columbia, 869 F. Supp. 24, 29 (D.D.C. 1994) - This court rejected the *Reich* test and instead found, “[i]n this Court's view, the issue of whether the travel time is compensable as ‘integral’ to a principal activity turns largely on whether plaintiffs are required to provide a significant amount of care to the dogs while travelling.”

Easter v. United States, 15 WH Cases2d 440 (Fed. Cir. 2009) - Border Patrol dog handlers who were required to transport the dogs with them during their commute in special government owned vehicles, and were not allowed to engage in personal business during the commute, are not entitled to compensation because time spent was *de minimis*.

Issue: Laundry for K-9 drug training **Compensable: Yes**

Compensable Authority:
Bull v. United States, 12 WH Cases2d 699 (Fed. Cir. 2007) - Customs officers were entitled to two hours compensation per week for off-duty time they spent laundering towels used in training of drug detector dogs because the officers were "engaged to wait" inasmuch as their activities during downtime were significantly limited by need to monitor running washers and dryers that were capable of overflowing or causing fires.

Issue: Transportation of police horses **Compensable: Yes**

Compensable Authority:
Ketchum v. City of Vallejo, 523 F. Supp. 2d 1150, 1162 (E.D. Cal. 2007) - Plaintiffs' time spent preparing their horses and equipment, including time spent traveling to pick-up their horses prior to events, was sufficiently 'principal' to commence the workday since such activities were integral and indispensable to Plaintiffs law enforcement duties at MPU events and were undertaken necessarily and primarily for the benefit of Defendant.

Issue: Care of police horses used for mounted policing **Compensable: Yes**

Compensable Authority:
Police/Hours Worked (Sept. 12, 1985) - [I]t should be noted that where the cleaning and feeding of the horses is but an adjunct of the animals' principle activity of being used by the mounted patrol unit in law enforcement work, the time so spent would be hours worked under FLSA.

Issue: Care of police horses used strictly for ceremonial purposes **Compensable: No**

Compensable Authority:
Trooper's Care of Horse/Hours Worked (June 15, 1998) - As to whether FLSA compensation is required for time spent by the trooper in caring for his horse, the answer is no. Unlike canine officers who use their police dogs in law enforcement

activities when on-duty and whose duties require them to "care" for their dogs at home, the trooper's horse is not used in law enforcement activities, but only for ceremonial purposes.

TESTIFYING IN COURT, GRIEVANCES & DISCIPLINE

Issue: Time spent in testifying in court or other proceedings **Compensable: Yes**

Compensable Authority:

Disciplinary Hearing Attendance/Hours Worked (Jan. 21, 1997) - [W]e have held that time spent in testifying in court or other proceedings is compensable hours of work under the FLSA if:

1. the time spent is controlled or required by the State or local government; or
2. if attendance is intended to benefit the State or local government; or
3. if attendance is a direct result of official police duties

Hours Worked/Court Time (March 19, 1986) - Time spent by police officers in testifying at court proceedings is compensable hours of work if the time spent testifying (whether voluntary or mandated by the courts) is controlled or required by a State or local government, if the police officers' attendance at the proceedings is intended to benefit the State or local government, or if their attendance at the proceedings is a direct result of the performance of the officers' official police duties.

Issue: Appearing before the Accident Review Board during off- duty hours to explain the accident he or she was involved in **Compensable: Yes**

Compensable Authority:

Hours Worked (Oct. 11, 1985) - It is our opinion that, in all the situations outlined above [including whether appearing before an accident review board is compensable], the time involved would be considered hours worked under FLSA.

Issue: Being called in during off-duty hours for discipline **Compensable: Yes**

Compensable Authority:

Hours Worked (Oct. 11, 1985) - It is our opinion that, in all the situations outlined above [including whether coming in to be disciplined is compensable], the time involved would be considered hours worked under FLSA.

Issue: Time spent outside of normal working hours at a hearing for infractions of the City rules, as well as time spent with an attorney preparing for such a hearing, if voluntary **Compensable: No**

Compensable Authority:
Police/Hours Worked (Aug. 2, 1989) - It is our position that time spent outside working hours on grievance adjustment, and by implication on other matters relating to labor-management disputes, would not be considered hours worked under FLSA where participation in such activities by an employee is voluntary. We would not consider an employee who has been subpoenaed as a voluntary participant.

Issue: Coming in during off-duty hours to be interviewed concerning a citizen's complaint against him or her **Compensable: Yes**

Compensable Authority:
Hours Worked (Oct. 11, 1985) - It is our opinion that, in all the situations outlined above [including whether coming in for an interview concerning a citizen's complaint is compensable], the time involved would be considered hours worked under FLSA.

Issue: Coming in during off-duty hours to be interviewed as a witness concerning a complaint or discipline against another officer **Compensable: Yes**

Compensable Authority:
Hours Worked (Oct. 11, 1985) - It is our opinion that, in all the situations outlined above [including whether coming in to be interviewed as a witness concerning a complaint or discipline against another officer is compensable], the time involved would be considered hours worked under FLSA.

MEDICAL

Issue: Compulsory medical exams **Compensable: Yes**

Compensable Authority:
29 C.F.R § 785.43 - Time spent by an employee in waiting for and receiving medical attention on the premises or at the direction of the employer during the employee's normal working hours on days when he is working constitutes hours worked.

Sehie v. City of Aurora, 8 WH Cases2d 1663 (N.D. Ill. 2003) - City's motion for summary judgment was denied on city dispatcher's claim to overtime for time she spent outside of her normal 40-hour work week scheduling, attending, and traveling to and from psychiatric counseling session that she was required to attend to maintain her employment following fitness-for-duty evaluation after health-related absence from work.

Police/Hours Worked (Aug. 2, 1989) - Time spent in taking such examinations is time during which the employee's freedom of movement is restricted for the purpose of serving the employer and time during which the employee is subject to employer's direction and control. Therefore, such time spent must be counted as hours worked under FLSA.

Issue: Medical certification to return to work **Compensable: No**

Non-Compensable Authority:
Hours Worked/Medical Certificates (March 12, 1987) - Therefore, it is our opinion that the time spent by employees of the Fire Department visiting their private physician outside of normal working hours would not be considered compensable hours of work even if they are instructed to do so by their employer as a condition for return to work after an absence due to illness.

Issue: Required physical examinations **Compensable: Yes**

Compensable Authority:
Required Physical Examinations/Hours Worked (Oct. 7, 1997) - The physical examination is an essential requirement of the job and thus primarily for the benefit of the employer. Therefore, it is our opinion that the time so spent must be counted as hours worked under the FLSA.

Issue: Employer imposed restrictive recuperation time from illness or injury **Compensable: No**

Non-Compensable Authority:
Hours Worked/Recuperation Time (Dec. 19, 1988) - [T]his section makes clear that periods of time during which an employee is completely relieved from duty and which are long enough to enable the employee to use the time effectively for personal purposes are not hours worked under FLSA.

Issue: Mandatory dexterity testing for bus drivers **Compensable: Disputed**

Possibly Compensable Authority:

Physical Examinations/Hours Worked (Nov. 4, 1998) - [If] the requirement appears to be placed on the school bus drivers in order to begin or continue employment with any school district . . . then time spent in submitting to physical examinations and dexterity testing would not be compensable hours of work. It is a condition of employment that must be met to work as a school bus driver in any county in the state. However, if the requirement of physical examination and dexterity testing was placed on the driver . . . in order to work in that school district, then the time would be compensable hours of work. In this situation, it is the employer's condition of employment placed only on its employee(s).

Issue: Medical attention **Compensable: Yes**

Compensable Authority:
9 C.F.R § 785.43 - Medical attention - Time spent by an employee in waiting for and receiving medical attention on the premises or at the direction of the employer during the employee's normal working hours on days when he is working constitutes hours worked.

Issue: Requiring sick or injured time be spent at home unless otherwise given permission **Compensable: No**

Non-Compensable Authority:
DeBraska v. Milwaukee, 5 WH Cases2d 982 (7th Cir. 1999) - Time that police officers on sick or injury leave spent at home under city's policy that requires officers on such leave to remain at home unless they obtain permission, which is readily granted for purposes such as attending doctor's appointment or purchasing food, should not be counted as hours worked under FLSA, despite contention that time at home is like "on call" time for which employees must be compensated if personal activities are severely restricted, where sick and injured officers are not fit to work, are not "engaged to wait" at home, and thus are not working.

Issue: Police peer counseling, during time off, by counselors trained under the supervision of a psychologist assigned to the department **Compensable: Yes**

Compensable Authority:
Hours Worked (Dec. 30, 1985) - Is the time spent by peer counselors in off-duty peer counseling activity hours worked under FLSA? Yes. It is clear that a peer counselor is engaged in "work," in the ordinary sense of that term, when engaged in peer counseling. The term "employ" includes "to suffer or permit to work."

Issue: Mandatory drug and alcohol classes **Compensable: Disputed**

Compensable Authority:
Sehie v. City of Aurora, 11 WH Cases2d 129 (7th Cir. 2005) - Possible Exception- In this case the city of Aurora was short telecommunication officers so there is an inference that the mandatory sessions were done primarily to keep a qualified employee on the job.

Non-Compensable Authority:
Gibbs v City of New York, 24 WH Cases2d 274 (S.D.N.Y 2015) - Is time spend at mandatory drug and alcohol classes compensable under FLS? No because that activity it done primarily for the benefit of Employer. Especially if the Employer has no particular need for the Employee.

CHARITABLE WORK & SEPARATE WORK THROUGH THE EMPLOYER

Issue: Civic or charitable work **Compensable: Disputed**

Possibly Compensable Authority:
29 C.F.R § 785.44 - Civic and Charitable work - Time spent in work for public or charitable purposes at the employer's request, or under his direction or control, or while the employee is required to be on the premises, is working time. However, time spent voluntarily in such activities outside of the employee's normal working hours is not hours worked.

Newspaper Guild v. Republican Pub. Co., 8 WH Cases 140 (D. Mass. 1948) - Time spent by reporter on metropolitan newspaper in attending theater and movie showings for purpose of writing reviews held compensable work time for purpose of Act, despite publisher's contention that such duties were voluntary and thus not compensable for that reason. *The test for working time is not whether the work was voluntary, but whether the employee performed service for the benefit of the employer with knowledge and approval of the* employer.

Issue: City firefighters who volunteer for the County **Compensable: No**

Non-Compensable Authority:
Firefighters Volunteering for County Fire District/Hours Worked

FLSA2006-6NA (April 28, 2006) - [I]t is our opinion that if City firefighters volunteer for the District and perform fire-fighting services within the City's primary service area and areas annexed by the City, the City is not required to treat such volunteer time as compensable hours worked.

Issue: **Performing "same type of services" voluntarily** **Compensable: Yes**

Compensable Authority:
EMTs as Volunteer Firefighters (July 12, 1999) - Under the FLSA, an individual cannot be both a paid employee and an unpaid "volunteer" while performing the same type of services that the individual is employed to perform for his or her employer. The phrase "same type of services" means similar or identical services. Thus, an EMS employee may not volunteer his or her services as a fireman without compensation in accordance with the provisions of the FLSA.

Issue: **Off-duty work through a separate government agency** **Compensable: Disputed**

Possibly Compensable Authority:
Police Officers/Work for Second Public Agency FLSA2006-21NA (Oct. 5, 2006) - Whether the hours officers work must be aggregated for overtime purposes when officers work for two public entities depends on:
(1) whether the employers have separate payroll systems;
(2) whether the employers have separate retirement systems;
(3) whether the employers have separate budgets and funding authorities;
(4) whether the employers are separate legal entities with the power to sue and be sued; (5) whether the employers deal with each other at arm's length concerning the employment of the individuals10 in question;
(6) how the employers' relationship is treated under state law; and
(7) whether one employer controls the appointment of the officers of the other agency.

Issue: **Off-duty security jobs** **Compensable: No**

Non-Compensable Authority:
Police Officers/Off-Duty Security Jobs FLSA 2007-12 (Dec. 31, 2007) – [I]t is our opinion that the City Police Department would not be obligated to include the hours worked by police officers on special assignment to the [private non-profit security corporation organized under state law] in calculating and paying overtime due them.

Issue: **Off-duty work through employer** **Compensable: Yes**

Compensable Authority:
Rutherford Food Corp. v. McComb, 331 U.S. 722, 729, 91 L. Ed. 1772, 67 S. Ct. 1473 (1947) - Where the work is done, in its essence, follows the usual path of an employee, putting on an 'independent contractor' label does not take the worker

from the protection of the Act.

Brennan v. Field, Inc., 21 WH Cases 711 (1st Cir. 1974) - Activity of employee is employment under FLSA if it is done at least in part for the benefit of the employer, even though it may also be beneficial to employee.

Chapter 11

The Rights of Injured and Disabled Public Safety Employees

A. Introduction

This chapter covers the range of laws which apply to employees who are limited in their ability to work due to injury or disability. It includes a discussion of state and federal disability discrimination laws. It also looks at laws relating to pregnancy discrimination, the Family Medical Leave Act, and workers compensation. It considers how each of these laws relate to each other, as well how these laws relate to the obligation to engage in collective bargaining.

Disability laws require employers to "reasonably accommodate" individuals with disabilities. Attached to this chapter, as an Appendix, is a table listing how courts have treated the employer responsibility to accommodate various injuries and illnesses in different public safety occupations.

B. State and Federal Disability Discrimination Laws

1. General Obligations of Employers

Applicable Statutes. Attention has been paid by public safety employers, and unions as well, to the Americans with Disabilities Act (ADA). But the focus on the ADA has often been misplaced. There are *three different* disability discrimination statutes which apply to Washington public safety employers, and, in some respects, the ADA is the least stringent of these three.

The ADA was preceded by another federal law, the Rehabilitation Act of 1973.[1] The Rehabilitation Act prohibits discrimination against disabled persons by federal agencies and all entities receiving federal financial assistance.[2] The ADA broadened the coverage against discrimination to reach most employers, private and public.[3]

Most local governments in Washington are subject to the Rehabilitation Act because they need only receive a nominal amount of federal assistance in order to qualify for the Act's jurisdictional requirements. Separately, Washington State law

[1] 29 U.S.C. § 790, *et seq.*
[2] 29 U.S.C. § 794(a).
[3] 42 U.S.C. § 12111.

RCW 49.60.180 also prohibits discrimination against persons with disabilities.

The state law, as we will discuss below, takes a *more expansive* view of what constitutes a "disability."

Differences Between Statutes. The ADA followed the pattern set forth by the Rehabilitation Act, but it did not totally supplant it. There are some differences between the two statutes and there are circumstances where each offers greater protections to employees than the other statute. Employers must comply with the requirements of both. Most of these differences are technical and do not immediately impact your role as a union representative; you just want to be aware that there are various statutes and to recognize that a court interpretation under one law does not necessarily extend to the other laws.

For those of us involved in Washington labor and employment issues, this point is especially important to remember. The state law, as we will discuss below, takes a *more expansive* view of what constitutes a "disability." Having a qualifying "disability" is what opens the door to the protection of these disabilities statutes. The Washington Law against Discrimination (WLAD) also often, depending on the issue, imposes a higher standard on employers as to the extent of accommodation owed.

The differences between the ADA and the Rehabilitation Act are relatively minor, at least relative to the difference between the federal laws and the state law. By and large, in enacting the ADA, Congress adopted the statutory structure that had been set forth under the Rehabilitation Act. As a result, when the ADA was adopted, federal courts looked at prior Rehabilitation Act cases to help guide their interpretation of the ADA.

Elements of the ADA. It is important to understand first the narrow, carefully crafted language of the statute. First, the statute prohibits discrimination, in a number of forms, against individuals with "disabilities." The statute defines "disability" as a: "(a) a physical or mental impairment that substantially limits one or more of the major life activities of such individual; (b) a record of such an impairment; or (c) being regarded as having such an impairment."[4]

Therefore, an employee need not have an actual current

[4] 42 U.S.C. § 12102(2).

medical limitation to be considered disabled. It is enough that the employee either has had that condition in the past, or that he is *perceived* as having one by an employer. The "perception" element becomes important when the employer discriminates based on stereotypical perceptions of what persons who have had certain disabilities in the past are capable of.

The general statement of prohibition of discrimination under the ADA is that

> [N]o covered entity shall discriminate against a qualified individual with a disability because of the disability if such individual in regard to job application procedures, the hiring, advancement, or discharge of employees, employee compensation, job training, and other terms, conditions and privileges of employment.[5]

Therefore, to be entitled to the protection under the ADA, an employee *must* be a "qualified individual with a disability."

The statute also defines a "qualified individual with a disability":

> The term qualified individual with a disability means an individual with a disability who, with or without reasonable accommodation, can perform the essential functions of the employment position that such individual holds or desires. For purposes of this title, consideration shall be given to the employer's judgment as to what functions of a job are essential, and if an employer has prepared a written job description before advertising or interviewing applicants for the job, the description shall be considered evidence of the essential functions of the job.[6]

Therefore, to be a qualified individual with a disability entitled to protection from the statute, the employee must have:

- A disability; and

---

[5] 42 U.S.C. § 12112(a).
[6] 42 U.S.C. § 12111(8).

- The ability to perform the "essential functions" of the job — with or without a "reasonable accommodation."

Only after employees can demonstrate that they meet this rigorous standard, can they invoke the protections of the ADA. In other words, if they cannot prove that they are qualified individuals with a handicap (or are "perceived" as such) *they have no protection against discrimination under this law*. But if they can meet this test, then they can assert an entitlement to a "reasonable accommodation" of their disability.

The ADA defines "reasonable accommodation":

> The term reasonable accommodation may include (a) making facilities used by employees readily accessible to and usable by individuals with disabilities and (b) job restructuring, part-time or modified work schedules, reassignment to a vacant position, acquisition or modification of equipment or devices, appropriate adjustment or modification of examinations, training materials or policies, the provision of qualified readers or interpreters, and other similar accommodations for individuals with disabilities.[7]

These are the types of accommodations an employer *may* make. But even these identified accommodations are *not* mandated *if* they would not be "reasonable" (as that term is elsewhere defined in the law).[8] That exit door exists due to the "undue burden" test and other related defenses.

The statute defines a reasonable accommodation as one that does not impose "an undue hardship on the operation of the business of such covered entities."[9] In adopting the ADA, Congress defined "undue hardship" as "an action requiring significant difficulty or expense."[10]

Congress identified a number of factors to consider in assessing whether an accommodation involved an undue hardship. The primary factor is "the nature and cost of the accommodation

---

[7] 42 U.S.C. § 12111(9).
[8] 42 U.S.C. § 12111 (5)(a).
[9] 42 U.S.C. § 12112(5)(b).
[10] 42 U.S.C. § 12111(10).

needed."[11] But the nature and cost of accommodation is to be balanced against the "overall financial resources of the 'facility' involved and the 'covered entities.' "[12] It also allows consideration of "the type of operation or operations of the covered entity, including the composition, structure and functions of the workforce of such entity."[13]

There are two major areas where employees lose their coverage of the ADA. First, there is a requirement that the condition "substantially limits one or more of the major life activities of such individual."[14] Although "work" is listed as a major life activity, there is a dispute among the courts about whether work means one particular job, a class of jobs, or the ability to work in general. For example, the courts are split on the question of whether the inability of an employee to work as a police officer or firefighter substantially limits a "major life activity" where an individual can do other work, even within the same department.

The second area where employees lose out on ADA coverage is the "essential functions" requirement. If an employee cannot fulfill the *bona fide* "essential functions" of the position — with or without reasonable accommodation — the individual is not covered under the discrimination protections of the ADA. Often, three leading issues that arise in connection with fulfilling essential functions are:

- Whether the functions claimed as necessary by the employer are truly "essential."
- Whether the employee can perform those functions with or without an accommodation.
- If an individual who could perform the "essential functions" only with accommodation, whether that accommodation is a "reasonable" one.

---

[11] *Id.*
[12] *Id.*
[13] *Id.*
[14] 42 U.S.C. § 12102(1).

Washington law grants employees broader coverage and is almost always the law selected in preference to the federal law when plaintiffs litigate their disability claims. Primarily this is due to a much broader definition of the term "disability."

Elements of Washington Law. For reasons discussed below, the Washington law grants employees broader coverage and is almost always the law selected in preference to the federal law when plaintiffs litigate their disability claims. Primarily this is due to a much broader definition of the term "disability."

The Washington state disability discrimination law (WLAD), like the ADA, starts by making it unlawful to discriminate against individuals based on their "disability." But, oddly, the statute itself does not specifically define "disability." Rather it defines "disability" in almost the most general of terms to mean:

> [T]he presence of a sensory, mental, or physical, impairment that: Is medically cognizable of diagnosable; or exists as a record or history; or is perceived to exist whether or not it exists in fact." [15]

To supplement this broad concept of "disability" as simply a "diagnosable" medical "impairment," the law is further clarified and by the regulations of the Human Rights Commission.

But these regulations still define disability in broad terms. The regulations refer to disability as involving simply a health condition with an "abnormality"[16] which only slightly narrows the definition of "disability." Unlike the ADA, the WLAD does *not* require that to be qualifying the disability must affect a "major life activity." *This difference is key and is why the state disability law offers much greater protection, in most cases, than the federal laws.*

Even though this broad definition of disability might seem to create almost boundless claims of protection, courts have somewhat reigned in the scope of the statute by incorporating some of the federal law concepts. Specifically, and importantly, the courts have redefined "reasonable accommodation" to *exclude*

---

[15] RCW 49.60.040.

[16] *See* WAC 162-22-040.

accommodations which involve maintaining employees in a position for which they cannot perform the "essential functions" of the job.[17]

There are some differences and similarities in how the federal laws and the state law approach the concept of "reasonable accommodation." Both sets of laws agree that an accommodation is not reasonable if it imposes an undue hardship upon the employer. *The primary difference between state and federal law concerns the accommodation of an individual who cannot fulfill the job functions.*

Under the federal laws, if individuals cannot perform the essential functions — with or without reasonable accommodation — they are not entitled to the protection of the disability discrimination portions of the statutes. The state cases, though, have been explicit that even if individuals are unable to perform the essential functions of the job, they are still entitled to protection.

But this liberal protection does not confer on the employee the right to maintain their position. Rather, it obligates the employer to engage in a specific "interactive" process with the employee concerning their availability for alternative positions. In fact, it actually requires the employer to provide *priority consideration* to those individuals for those positions.

Federal cases have been less clear concerning the obligation of employers to accommodate such individuals. A number of cases have held that since the individuals cannot fulfill the essential functions of the job, they are entitled to *no* protection under the statute. But other more recent cases are tending toward the position that there is still an obligation to make a "reasonable accommodation," even with individuals unable to fulfill the job requirements, *and* employers have been held to the obligation to undertake work reassignments to accommodate an individual.

These later decisions explain that since the statute specifically mentions reassignments and job restructuring as a means of making an accommodation, whenever it is possible to assign an employee into a different assignment, that person meets the definition of a "qualified individual" and should, therefore, be accommodated into that different assignment. This more expansive application of the ADA term "qualified individual" would, in these circumstances, grant the individual some protections similar to

[17] *See, e.g., Dedman v. Personnel Appeals Board*, 98 Wn. App. 471, 989 P.2d 1214 (1999).

what is otherwise available under the more liberal WLAD provisions. Regardless, for a variety of reasons mentioned, plaintiffs' employment lawyers virtually always proceed primarily under the WLAD with the ADA no more than an afterthought.

The Appendix at the end of this Chapter identifies a wide range of circumstances in which public safety employees have sought an accommodation and what the responses of the courts have been to those requests.

2. Specific Types of Discrimination Issues

Understanding the nature of the accommodation due is often a fact specific inquiry. The Appendix at the end of this Chapter identifies a wide range of circumstances in which public safety employees have sought an accommodation and what the responses of the courts have been to those requests. The question of whether an accommodation is a "reasonable" one is dependent on a variety of factors. The discussion below also addresses generally how courts have viewed the duty to accommodate in particular situations.

a. Obligation to Create Light Duty Positions

First, the federal laws, at least, do not protect individuals with temporary medical conditions. The right to "light duty" under these circumstances is left to the parties' collective bargaining arrangement (or their established "past practices"). PERC has ruled *City of Wenatchee* that light duty is a mandatory subject of bargaining and that an employer may not unilaterally abandon a light duty program.[18] (This is another example of the important ways in which collective bargaining rights related to disability rights.)

The federal cases have been, for the most part, fairly clear that there is *no* obligation to create a permanent light duty program. The basic rule concerning "light duty" accommodation, is stated by the EEOC:

> The ADA does not require an employer to create a "light duty" position unless the "heavy duty" tasks an injured worker can no longer perform are marginal job

[18] *City of Wenatchee*, Decision 6517-A (PECB, 1999)

> functions which may be reallocated to co-workers as part of the reasonable accommodation of job-restructuring. In most cases, however, "light duty" positions involve a totally different job from the job that a worker performed before the injury. *Creating such positions by job restructuring is not required by the ADA.* However, if an employer already has a vacant light duty position for which an injured worker is qualified, it might be a reasonable accommodation to reassign the worker to that position. *If the position was created as a temporary job, a reassignment to that position need only be for a temporary period.*[19]

In the Ninth Circuit, as in other federal circuits, the "reasonableness" of an accommodation will depend on particular circumstances of each case.[20] But here are the general principles that federal courts have applied:

- The ADA *might* require employers to reassign a disabled employee to a different position as reasonable accommodations when the employee can no longer perform the essential functions of his or her current position;[21]
- On the other hand, employers are *not* required to transform temporary light duty jobs into permanent jobs in order to accommodate a disability;[22]
- Employers are *not* required to create new jobs;[23]
- Employers are *not* bound by earlier "good faith" accommodations of disabled employees;[24] *but*

[19] EEOC Technical Assistance on Title 1 of ADA 8 FEP Manual (BNA) § 9.4 at 405:7057-58 (1992).

[20] *See Lujan v. Pacific Maritime Association*, 165 F.3d 738 (9th Cir. 1999); *Barnett v. U.S. Air Inc*, 196 F.3d 979 (9th Cir. 1998).

[21] *Malabarba v. Chicago Tribune Co.*, 149 F.3d 690 (7th Cir. 1998).

[22] *Mengine v. Runyon*, 114 F.3d 415, 418-419 (3d Cir. 1997); *Staub v. Boeing*, 919 F. Supp. 366 (W.D. Wa. 1996).

[23] *Mengine* (3d); Malabarba (7th); *Benson v. Northwest Airlines*, 62 F.3d 1108 (8th Cir.1995); *Barnett v. U.S. Air Inc.*, (9th Cir. 1998).

[24] *Myers v. Hose*, 50 F.3d 278 (4th Cir. 1995); *Vande Zande v. State of Wisconsin Dept. of Administration*, 44 F.3d 538 (7th Cir. 1995).

employers probably will be bound where such accommodations are part of an existing policy;[25]

- Employers are *not* obligated to provide an employee the singular accommodation he or she requests or prefers;[26]

- Employers are *not* required to 'bump' other employees to create a vacancy just to be able to reassign the disabled employee;[27]

- Employers certainly do *not* have to accommodate a disabled employee by promoting him or her to a higher level;[28]

- Employers do *not* have to make an accommodation that would be inconsistent with an existing CBA or contravene the seniority rights of other employees;[29]

- Reasonable accommodation does *not* require employers to eliminate or reassign "essential" job functions;[30]

- Employers do not have to *alter fundamentally* the nature of a job.[31]

Although the federal courts do not appear willing to *require* an employer to transform a temporary light duty accommodation into a permanent position, some have not entirely ruled out the possibility. The Third Circuit has stated that even though an employer is not required to create new jobs or transform its temporary light duty jobs into permanent jobs to accommodate a disability, the court is:

---

[25] *Carter v. Tisch*, 822 F.2d 465 (4th Cir. 1987) (FRA case citing *dicta* in *Marsh v. Arline*, 480 U.S. 273 (1987)).

[26] *Malabarba* (7th).

[27] *Id.*

[28] *Id.*

[29] *Benson v. Northwest Airlines*, 62 F.3d 1108 (8th Cir.1995); *Lujan v. Pacific Maritime Association*, 165 F.3d 738 (9th Cir. 1999); *Willis v. Pacific Maritime Association*, 162 F.3d 561 (9th Cir. 1998).

[30] *Barnett* (9th).

[31] *Id.*

> [R]eluctant to adopt a per se rule that the conversion of a temporary job to a permanent job can never constitute a "reasonable accommodation". . . . We think that in most cases the imposition of such a requirement will be unreasonable, but there might arise the rare case in which the cost of converting the temporary job into a permanent job is slight and the benefits considerable.[32]

Although the federal courts do not appear willing to *require* an employer to transform a temporary light duty accommodation into a permanent position, some have not entirely ruled out the possibility.

There also has been some litigation about how to assess the employer accommodation obligation once an employee has been transferred into a "temporary" light duty position. The primary cases are *Taylor v. Garnett,*[33] a case arising under the Federal Rehabilitation Act, and *Valdez v. Albuquerque Public Schools,*[34] an ADA case.

In both *Taylor* and *Valdez,* the employees had been accommodated by their employers and transferred to light duty, but eventually both were discharged. The main issue in both cases was how to identify which positions the plaintiffs' abilities should be measured against — *their original positions or the "temporary" light duty positions that they occupied at the time of their discharge.* And in both cases (*Valdez* citing *Taylor*), the courts found that the employers had essentially moved the disabled employees into permanent positions and ruled that, for the purposes of the claims, their abilities should be measured against the light duty positions they held when discharged.

Discussion of these two case has focused on the permanent/temporary nature of the disabled employees' light duty jobs. In *Malabarba v. Chicago Tribune Co.,*[35] the plaintiff cited *Taylor* and *Valdez* for the proposition that an employee alleging an

---

[32] *Mengine v. Runyon,* 114 F.3d 415, 418-19 (3d Cir. 1997).
[33] 820 F. Supp. 933 (E.D. Penn., 1993).
[34] 875 F. Supp. 740 (D. N. Mex., 1994).
[35] 149 F.3d 690 (7th Cir. 1998).

ADA violation need only be qualified to perform the essential functions of the light duty position to which he was reassigned in order to meet the "qualified individual with a disability" requirement.

The Seventh Circuit, however, distinguished the lower court cases by characterizing them as involving *permanent* light duty reassignments, as opposed to a temporary position. In fact, the *Taylor* court appears to acknowledge the relevance of a permanent/temporary distinction so the Seven Circuit characterization may be correct.[36] According to the *Taylor* court, it recognized that the employer could legitimately claim that it had placed the employee into temporary light duty with the belief that the employee would only be temporarily injured and that once the disabilities proved permanent, they reserved the right to discharge the employee because the employee could no longer perform the essential functions of his *original* position.

At least one local federal district court, in a case involving the King County Jail, has commented on *Taylor/Valdez* controversy. In *Kees v. Wallenstein*,[37] fired corrections officers claimed they had been permanently accommodated by the employer. Once again the question was about which position their abilities should be measured against: (1) their *original* position (corrections officer); or (2) their position upon temporary accommodation (reassignment to the control room). The district court ruled against the officers and distinguished *Taylor/Valdez* on the basis that the accommodations made for the corrections officers were temporary, not permanent.[38]

In *Wallenstein*, the employees tried to prove permanency, despite the fact that the employer had a written policy stating that the light duty assignments were temporary. They did this by introducing other evidence showing that the accommodations were permanent (mostly instances of lax enforcement of the policy). The *Kees* court dismissed this evidence by stating that *laxity of policy enforcement would not be enough to rebut the written policy*.[39] The Ninth Circuit later affirmed the District Court.[40]

But in *Cripe v City of San Jose*,[41] the Ninth Circuit ruled that the City was obligated to accommodate officers into special duty assignments despite physical injuries that kept the officers from

---

36 820 F. Supp. at 938 n.9.

37 973 F. Supp. 1191 (1997), *aff'd*, 161 F.3d 1196 (9th Cir. 1998).

38 973 F. Supp. at 1196.

39 *Id.* at 1197.

40 161 F.3d 1196 (9th Cir. 1998).

41 261 F.3d 877 (9th Cir 2001).

being able to execute forcible arrests. Citing the large size of the department (over 1000 officers), the court expressed doubt that the existence of a limited number of special duty officers unable to respond to an emergency situation was an undue hardship on the City. Taking a position at odds with some other court decisions, the Ninth Circuit panel in *Cripe* concluded that because making a forcible arrest was not required for special duty assignments an accommodation by assignment to such a position was required.

Because of the differences between the state and federal laws, there has been some uncertainty as to how state courts would approach the subject of permanent light duty jobs for employees, including public safety employees. There is now at least one Court of Appeals decision which rejects an argument that there is a broader state disability discrimination law right for such an accommodation.

Using similar reasoning under state law, a Washington appeals court held in *Dedman v. Personnel Appeals Board*,[42] that there is no obligation of the State Department of Corrections to accommodate a state corrections officer who could not serve in all of the different correction functions in the prison. The court concluded that the "essential function" requirement was *implicit* in the state law as part of a reasonable accommodation test. It rejected the claim that the officer should be accommodated in positions with limited inmate contact, such as control room operator positions.

In *Dedman*, the court also found persuasive the employer's argument it did not have an obligation to restructure the existing position description and that rotating the corrections officers through each various correction officer post served important operational interests. Consequently, it concluded, being able to make inmate contact was an "essential function" which could not be waived.

It remains unclear whether this will be the final resolution of the light duty question in Washington or the Ninth Circuit. The State Supreme Court will likely eventually have to resolve this question but has not yet addressed this issue squarely.

It remains clear that there is an obligation for employers to accommodate individuals under the state disability law by providing them opportunities to acquire other employment within the employer's workforce. The suggestion arising from the case law is that these employees are entitled to priority consideration before

[42] 98 Wn. App. 471, 989 P.2d 1214 (1999).

other employees. The courts have yet to clarify how those rights of accommodation will interface with civil service rules.

The federal courts are divided as to whether restructuring the hours of work is a reasonable accommodation.

---

b. Scheduling Issues

Often, public safety employees have a disability which impairs their ability to work around-the-clock, or, at least, in frequently rotating shifts. As one example of a common disability, diabetes, at least for some individuals, impedes their ability to rotate back and forth through the 24/7 shifts because of the health implications of such schedule changes. There are a variety of other health issues which can be aggravated by shift work.

The federal courts are divided as to whether restructuring the hours of work is a reasonable accommodation. The majority view is that if an accommodation such as this can be made, it should be made. In some departments, though, especially smaller ones, this type of accommodation can have a much greater negative impact on the department's ability to get the work scheduled and, for that reason alone, could be seen as an "undue hardship." In larger departments, this type of accommodation would not normally involve an undue hardship. But it may be an undue hardship within particular classifications where fewer personnel are assigned, and the impact necessarily be greater.

c. Mental Health Issues

Where an employee has a mental health problem which impedes their ability to recognize and request assistance, courts have imposed a burden *on the employer* to act unilaterally to begin the interactive process of identifying an accommodation.

Public safety employees, like any other employee, can have mental health issues. Constant stress can aggravate these issues and ultimately affect their ability to perform. In such cases, employees will be entitled to the protection of the disability discrimination laws *to the extent that these issues can be reasonably accommodated.*

Mental illness is certainly a protected disability, but so are other forms of less severe mental health problems, such as post-traumatic stress disorder (PTSD). As with other disabilities, courts have wrestled with the extent of an employer's obligation to accommodate these situations.

Typically an employee seeking an accommodation has the burden to come forth, make the request, and identify the circumstances warranting it. But due to the nature of mental health issues, here the burden is different. The case law has been clear in defining a special accommodation obligation for employers in connection with mental health issues: Where an employee has a mental health problem which impedes their ability to recognize and request assistance, courts have imposed a burden *on the employer* to act unilaterally to begin the interactive process of identifying an accommodation.

d. Physical Fitness Tests

Courts are unlikely to find physical fitness tests to be valid under disability discrimination laws. There have been only a handful of cases addressing this issue yet, but it appears unlikely that these plans will be sustained. Courts have already struck down a number of these plans on gender discrimination grounds. The primary deficiency in these plans is that they do not correlate precisely to the essential functions of the job. *If* they did, they would not be age and gender graded the way they typically are. Since everyone in the job classification must perform the same essential functions, there is no justifiable basis, from the perspective of disability law, to age and gender score such tests.

Some of these plans have premium pay attached for successful test takers. Denial of the premium to an individual with a disability might potentially violate disability discrimination laws. An employer might be able to circumvent this requirement by simply automatically paying the premium amount to any individual who could demonstrate their failure to qualify was directly as a result of their disability.

e. Weight Issues

It is unclear the extent to which disability laws will protect individuals with weight problems. The federal laws do not treat normal overweight as a protected disability.[43] Morbid obesity might

---

[43] *EEOC v. Watkins Motor Lines, Inc.*, 463 F.3d 426 (6th Cir. 2006).

qualify as a disability, but federal courts have often looked to whether there is an underlying physiological disability that caused the obesity.[44] Regardless, individuals who are morbidly obese are very unlikely to be able to fulfill the essential functions of most law enforcement and firefighter positions.

The extent to which Washington state disability law may protect overweight individuals is still undefined. Since state law defines disabilities in terms of "abnormalities," it is an open question as to how heavy an individual might be before they are entitled to legal protection.

There has been some conflict between the ADA, the Rehabilitation Act, and the state disability law concerning whether and how alcoholism can be accommodated.

f. Alcoholism

There has been some conflict between the ADA, the Rehabilitation Act, and the state disability law concerning whether and how alcoholism can be accommodated. The Rehabilitation Act and the state law do seem to require some degree of accommodation, even when alcoholism produces on-duty job impacts. The ADA, by contrast, has been primarily interpreted *not* to require accommodation of alcoholism to the extent that it involves a violation of a work rule. The divergence in approaches arises from the different language in each statute.

Duty to Accommodate. Where the disability at issue involves alcoholism behaviors, the prevailing view of courts under the federal Rehabilitation Act is that the employer has an obligation to provide extensive opportunities for treatment, *even to the point of accommodating short-term relapses which are anticipated to occur.*

While the law does not require the employer to tolerate an *indefinite* number of relapses, it does require the employer to acknowledge that certain relapses might occur and this, in turn, imposes upon the employer the duty to offer additional treatment opportunities.

[44] *Id.*

The seminal case defining an employer's obligation to accommodate alcoholism is a Fourth Circuit decision — *Rodgers v. Lehman*,[45] The Ninth Circuit Court of Appeals has approved and adopted the stringent approach of the Fourth Circuit in its leading decision on this issue — *Fuller v. Frank*.[46] In *Fuller*, the Ninth Circuit defined the reasonable accommodation standards of *Rogers* as requiring "that a governmental employer follow a progression of increasingly severe responses to an employee's alcoholism."[47] Under this *Rodgers/Fuller* standard:

> The employer should 1) inform the employee of available counseling services; 2) provide the employee with a "firm choice" between treatment and discipline; 3) afford an opportunity for outpatient treatment, with discipline for continued drinking or failures to participate; 4) afford an opportunity for inpatient treatment, if outpatient treatment fails; and 5) absent special circumstances, discharge the employee for any further relapse.[48]

While the law does not require the employer to tolerate an *indefinite* number of relapses, it does require the employer to acknowledge that certain relapses might occur and this, in turn, imposes upon the employer the duty to offer additional treatment opportunities.

Although, under federal law, alcoholism is clearly established as a "disability" (with primarily the extent of accommodation at controversy), the Washington State Supreme Court has held that whether alcoholism is a disability is case-by-case question. In *Phillips v. City of Seattle*,[49] the court held that ultimately whether alcoholism is a qualifying "disability" is a question of fact for the jury to decide. Citing the varied nature of the alcoholic condition and the policy and medical disputes regarding the nature and cause of alcoholism, the court in *Phillips* concluded that the trier of fact should assess in a given case whether the individual alcohol condition constituted a legal disability.

The ADA also provides certain protection for alcoholics in certain circumstances, but more limited than that under state law

[45] 869 F.2d 243 (4th Cir. 1989).

[46] 916 F.2d 558 (9th Cir. 1990).

[47] *Id.* at 562.

[48] *Id.*

[49] 111 Wn.2d 903, 766 P.2d 1099 (1989).

or under the Federal Rehabilitation Act. The text of the ADA provisions regarding alcohol and drug specifically with the provisions of the Rehabilitation Act. The ADA expressly permits employers to "hold an employee who engages in the illegal use of drugs or who is an alcoholic to the same qualification standards for employment or job performance and behavior that such entity holds other employees, even if any unsatisfactory performance or behavior is related to the drug use or alcoholism of such employee."[50] The meaning of this clause has been the source of on-going litigation.

Both the Rehabilitation Act and the ADA prohibit employers from disciplining employees because of their disability. The laws also require affirmative accommodation of alcoholism including multiple treatment opportunities. This much seems to be undisputed.

The policy of the Rehabilitation Act is aptly stated in *Teahan v. Metro-North Commuter Railroad Co.*:[51]

> This section of the labor law [Section 504 of the Rehabilitation Act] aims to balance the statutory guarantee of equal opportunity for the handicap person so that he or she may become a contributing member of the work force against the rightful concern of an employer that is a recipient of federal funds to preserve the effectiveness of its programs. For an employer to assume that simply because of a handicap an individual is unable to function in a given employment context stereotypes that person, seeing him, as it were, through a glass, darkly. To view a handicapped person in such a simplistic way affects the discrimination forbidden by 504.[52]

At issue in *Teahan* was the termination of an employee who suffered from alcoholism from — which he had since been rehabilitated — after which had an extensive record of absenteeism. The employer had convinced the trial court that by terminating *Teahan* for absenteeism, it was not discriminating against him *because of* his disability, even though it conceded that the absenteeism was caused by the alcoholism. Teahan appealed.

The Second Circuit overturned the district court, holding that

---

[50] ADA § 104(C)(4).

[51] 951 F.2d 511 (2d Cir. 1991).

[52] *Id.* at 513.

the employer's argument would allow *any* employer to "rely" on any conduct as a manifestation or a symptomatic of a disability, and, in so doing, avoid the burden of proving that the disability is relevant to the job qualifications. The court explained:

> An example may help illustrate this point. An employee has one leg shorter than the other, causing him to limp, which we assume is a "handicap" under Section 504. The limp causes the worker to make loud "thump" when he takes a step. He is fired, his employer says, because of the thumping. Under the District Court's analysis, the employee may not maintain a suit under Section 504 because the handicap is the limp, not the thump; hence the worker was not fired "solely by reason of" his handicap, but rather because of the attribute caused by the handicap. . . . Yet the proper analysis is that the causal all connection between the limp (handicap and the thump, symptomatic manifestation of the handicap) is such that the employer did "rely" on the handicap.[53]

The Second Circuit's reasoning in *Teahan* has been adopted by a number of other courts. For example, the Sixth Circuit approved this reasoning in another alcohol disability case in *Ferby v. Runyon.*[54]

Teahan was also cited in a controversial district court decision, within the Ninth Circuit, *Ham v. Nevada.*[55] *Ham* involved the ironic termination of Chief of the State of Nevada "Bureau of Alcohol and Drug Abuse" following a drunk driving arrest. The employer argued that they had terminated Ham for the crime of drunk driving, not his alcoholism.

The court rejected this argument and ordered Ham reinstated, reasoning that "since the drunk driving was a causally connected manifestation of the alleged handicap, defendant's actions were admittedly based upon plaintiff's alcoholism." The court added: "Being fired for behavior caused by one's affliction is the same thing as being fired for one's affliction." But other courts have interpreted the ADA and the Rehabilitation Act to allow employers to impose discipline for misconduct *even if directly related to*

---

[53] 951 F.2d at 515-16.

[54] 1993 Lexis 20705 (6th Cir. 1993) (unpublished).

[55] 788 F. Supp. 455 (D. Nev. 1992).

alcoholism.[56]

The law requires employers to make "reasonable accommodations" of individuals with disabilities and alcoholism is an established disability under federal law. But the duty to accommodate is not endless. In *Rodgers v. Lehman,*[57] the Fourth Circuit Court of Appeals set forth guidelines for determining when the employer has made a "reasonable accommodation" in connection with an alcoholic employee. Those standards — which have frequently been cited by other courts with approval — involve multiple steps and repeat opportunities:

- When the agency suspects that an employee's poor performance results from alcoholism, it should inform the employee of available counseling services.

- If the employee's unsatisfactory work performance continues, the agency must provide the employee with a "firm choice" between treatment and discipline. The agency must clearly unequivocally warn the employee that unsatisfactory work performance caused by drinking will result in discipline, eventually including the termination of employment.

- Unless in a particular case that it is clear that an in-patient treatment is immediately required, the employee must be allowed to participate initially in out-patient treatment of sufficient duration to assure him a reasonable opportunity for cure.

- If the employee continues to drink while participating in that treatment, the agency may impose progressive discipline upon him for any resulting job-related misconduct.

- If the employee ceases to participate in or fails out-patient treatment, discharge is not automatic. Unless the agency can establish that it would suffer an undue hardship from the employee's absence,

---

[56] *See, e.g., Randall v. Port of Portland,* 8 AD Cases 1404 (1998) (citing *Collings v. Tanguien Fibre Co.*, 73 F.3d 828 (9th Cir. 1993)).

[57] 869 F.2d 253 (4th Cir. 1989).

the agency must, before discharging him, afford him an opportunity to participate in an in-patient program using accrued and unpaid leave.

- If the employee completes the program, but thereafter relapses, and thereafter fails to perform his job satisfactorily, a decision by the agency to discharge him will be *presumed* to be reasonable. Only in the rare case, such as where a recovering alcoholic has had a single relapse after a prolonged period of abstinence, can this presumption be rebutted.[58]

The court explained its reasoning for adopting such an elaborate system:

> On the other hand, the nature of the disease of alcoholism requires that there be a continuum of treatment and that the alcoholic be allowed some opportunity for failure in order to come to the acceptance of his disease which is the critical element of his cure. On the other hand, both effective treatment and the needs of the workplace require that an alcoholic employee be firmly confronted with the consequences of his drinking.[59]

In *Fuller v. Frank*,[60] the Ninth Circuit Court of Appeals cited *Rodgers v. Lehman* with approval. The court also adopted as mandatory the multiple accommodation measures defined by the Fourth Circuit in *Lehman*. In *Fuller*, though, the Ninth Circuit concluded, that given the case the employer had more than complied with those steps, including *repeated* treatments and *repeated* leaves of absence, and even ultimately extending a "last chance" agreement. The court stated, "The postal service was not required to provide Fuller with another chance after giving him a 'last chance.' "[61]

ADA and the Workplace Rule Violation. There is a competing set of ADA cases which holds, though, that if the employee engages in a violation of the work rule there is no duty to accommodate the

---

[58] 869 F.2d at 259.
[59] *Id.*
[60] 916 F.2d 558 (9th Cir. 1990).
[61] *Id.* at 562.

individual. If, for example, a police officer incurs a DUI, he may not be entitled to accommodation, even though a direct result of alcoholism. That probable outcome is a result of the fact that the ADA does not require accommodation of work rule violations, and most police departments have a "work rule" which prohibits violation of criminal laws. Such individuals, though, may have other protection under the Rehabilitation Act and the state disability discrimination law so the ADA would not be pled as a cause of action in a resultant lawsuit.

The courts have been fairly clear that to the extent an accommodation would *actually violate* the terms of the CBA, accommodation is not reasonable and need *not* be made.

---

3. Collective Bargaining and Disability Laws

There are a number of issues that arise concerning the interface of disability laws and the collective bargaining law. The courts have been fairly clear that to the extent an accommodation would *actually violate* the terms of the CBA, accommodation is *not* reasonable and need not be made. For example, if the CBA contains a shift bidding process, an individual with a disability seeks an adjustment in the bid process cannot demand that the shift bidding process be altered. But there is also case law that holds an employer violates the ADA when it fails at least to *ask* a union whether it is willing to enter a memorandum of understanding modifying the CBA.

It is an open question under law what the employer's obligations are when the requested accommodation does not violate an explicit term of the CBA, but is contrary to a "past practice" not expressed in the CBA. There is limited case law on this question, but the prevailing view seems to be that such past practices do not impede the ability to make an accommodation.

It is an open question under law what the employer's obligations are when the requested accommodation does not violate an explicit term of the CBA, but is contrary to a "past practice" not expressed in the CBA.

At the very least, it seems the courts would require that an employer would have to seek out the union's position on whether it was willing to alter an existing past practice. If after such a modification is requested, and the union indicates it *is willing* to forego prior practices to make an accommodation, it likely the accommodation is required and that it constitutes unlawful discrimination not to make the accommodation (assuming that it is otherwise reasonable).

Occasionally, employers will seek a broad contractual waiver of the union's bargaining right to allow it to make "whatever changes are required" by the ADA. It is unwise to enter into such a broad waiver because of the unforeseen impact such language may have on the rights of other employees. The better practice is to address the requests for accommodation on a case by case basis as they occur, rather than forfeit the union's rights to participation in a discussion about the scope of the allowed accommodations.

C. Pregnancy Discrimination

1. The ADA and Pregnancy

Pregnant employees have significant protection under the Pregnancy Discrimination Act (PDA) and the Family Medical Leave Act (FMLA). This section considers those rights below. The condition of pregnancy is accorded fewer protections under the ADA than the other statutes.

One major hurdle preventing pregnant employees from invoking the ADA is that *pregnancy is not considered a disability.* Although the ADA does not expressly exclude pregnancy from coverage, the implementing regulations do. The EEOC, in its adoption of the interpretative regulations implementing the ADA, stated that pregnancy is *not* a disability and, as a direct result, is not covered by the ADA.[62] The federal courts have concurred, primarily because they have looked to the EEOC's interpretations for guidance.[63]

---

[62] *Appendix to Part 1630 — Interpretive Guidance on Title I of the Americans with Disabilities Act,* ADA Manual, 70:0109. ("It is important to distinguish between conditions that are impairments and physical, psychological, environmental, cultural and economic characteristics that are not impairments. . . . . Other conditions, such as pregnancy, that are not the result of a physiological disorder are also not impairments.")

[63] *Byerly v. Herr Foods, Inc.*, 2 A.D. Cas. (BNA) 666, 669 (E.D. Pa 1993) (Holding ADA "clearly indicates that pregnancy was not to be considered an impairment covered by the Act."); *Gabriel v. City of Chicago*, 9AD Cas. (BNA) 483, 488 (N.D. Ill. 1998) (holding pregnancy, absent abnormal or unusual

But pregnant employees invoke ADA if they develop pregnancy-related medical complications, assuming that that these complications would themselves be considered disabilities under the ADA. Back pain or high blood pressure are examples of pregnancy related conditions that *may* be covered under the ADA. Both the EEOC[64] and the federal courts[65] specifically agree with this conclusion.

On the other hand, the mere presence of an impairment, however, does not automatically mean that an employee has a "disability" as defined under the ADA. This question, instead, will turn on whether the impairment substantially limits, or is regarded as substantially limiting, a major life activity.[66] For these reasons, a pregnant employee seeking protection of disability law would be far more likely to invoke the more liberal protections of the WLAD.

2. Elements of the PDA

Under the Pregnancy Discrimination Act (PDA),[67] employers are prohibited from discriminating against employees because of or on the basis of pregnancy, childbirth, or related medical conditions. The PDA also requires that pregnant employees be treated the same for *all* employment-related purposes, including receipt of benefits under fringe benefit programs, as other persons not so affected *but similar in their ability or inability to work*. (Emphasis added).

To establish a "prima facie" case of discrimination under Title VII, a plaintiff may prove her claim either through direct evidence, statistical proof, or the test established by the Supreme Court in *McDonnell Douglas Corp. v Green*.[68] Pregnant employees have been

---

circumstances, is not a disability).

[64] *EEOC: Definition of the Term 'Disabilty'*, ADA Manual, 70:1137.

[65] *Cerrato v. Durham*, 5 A.D. Cas. (BNA) 1660 (S.D.N.Y 1996) (applying analysis that distinguishes between normal, uncomplicated pregnancy and complications arising out of pregnancy that, under certain circumstances, can constitute "disability" under ADA); *Patterson v. Xerox Corp.*, 4 Cas. (BNA) 1602 (N.D. Ill. 1995) (holding contention that pregnancy-related severe back pain qualified as disability under the ADA sufficient to withstand motion to dismiss).

[66] ADA Manual, 70:1138.

[67] 42 U.S.C. § 2000e(k).

[68] 411 U.S. 792 (1973). The test requires that the plaintiff show: (1) she was a member of a protected class; (2) she was qualified for the position she lost; (3) she suffered an adverse employment action; and (4) that others similarly situated were more favorably treated. The employer then has an opportunity to offer a non-discriminatory reason for its action. Finally, if the employer offers a reason, the employee has an opportunity to show that the offered

most successful under the PDA when they can show that the employer took an adverse employment action *specifically because* of their pregnancy *or* when they can use the *McDonnell Douglas* test to demonstrate an inconsistency in the employer's actions.[69]

3. The Interplay of the ADA and the PDA

Individually, the ADA and the PDA do not specifically grant pregnant employees the right to on-the-job accommodations. However, when the two acts work in conjunction with each other, they may give pregnant employees extensive protection. The ADA requires employers to accommodate their qualified disabled workers and the PDA requires that pregnant employees be treated the same as those employees similarly situated in their ability or inability to work. Therefore, the PDA allows pregnant employees to tag along with many employees covered by the ADA.

The U.S. Supreme Court held that if an employer "accommodates most nonpregnant employees with lifting limitations while categorically failing to accommodate pregnant employees with lifting limitations," the employer may have violated the PDA.[70]

This does not mean that *any* accommodation in *any circumstance* means that an employer must accommodate pregnant employees – the Court rejected the argument that:

> [a]s long as an employer provides one or two workers with an accommodation—say, those with particularly hazardous jobs, or those whose workplace presence is particularly needed, or those who have worked at the company for many years, or those who are over the age of 55—then it must provide similar accommodations to *all* pregnant workers (with comparable physical limitations), irrespective of the nature of their jobs, the employer's need to keep them working, their ages, or any other criteria.[71]

But where the employer often accommodates injured employees, it

---

reason was a pretext.

[69] *See Adams v. Nolan*, 962 F.2d 791 (1992) (upholding finding in favor of pregnant police officer denied light duty job on grounds pregnancy is non-occupational injury when male officer with non-occupational injury was later given job).

[70] *Young v. United Parcel Service, Inc.*, 575 U.S. ___, 126 FEP Case 765, 775 (2015).

[71] *Id.* at 771.

likely must similarly accommodate pregnant employees.

For example, if an employee has an ADA qualified disability that renders them unable to lift heavy boxes or stand for long periods of time, then the employer would be required to make reasonable accommodations. Once the employer makes the accommodations, it likely will need to make the same accommodation for a pregnant employee who was unable to lift heavy boxes or stand for long periods of time.

4. Pregnancy Accommodation and the Hazardous Workplace

An employer is not required to accommodate a pregnant employee because the employee wants to protect her unborn child. While the U.S. Supreme Court has held that pregnant employees have the right to work in a hazardous environment,[72] there is no inverse rule requiring employers to provide on-the-job accommodations to employees who wish *not* to work in a hazardous environment. Furthermore, employees who have been denied requested accommodations to protect their unborn children have not been successful in court under the PDA.[73]

The leading case on this subject is *Armstrong v. Flowers Hospital, Inc.*[74] In *Armstrong*, a nurse brought a discrimination claim under the PDA because her employer refused to reassign her after she voiced concerns about treating an HIV-positive patient. The nurse, who had been concerned that caring for an HIV-positive patient would put her fetus at risk, claimed that the hospital's decision was unfairly applied to her. She also claimed, based on the U.S. Supreme Court's holding in *Johnson Controls*,[75] that the hospital's policy resulted in a disparate impact because it created a "difficult choice" for pregnant employees. The choice, she argued, between keeping her job or protecting her child, was prohibited by the U.S. Supreme Court.

The Eleventh Circuit rejected this argument. *Johnson Controls*, it stated, stood for the right of a pregnant employee, not the employer, to choose whether or not the employee continued in a particular job. The court further pointed out the limitations of

---

[72] *Auto Workers v. Johnson Controls*, 491 U.S. 197 (1991). (Finding PDA violation where employer, fearful pregnant employee's unborn children will be harmed by exposure to toxins, banned fertile women from certain jobs).

[73] Calloway, Deborah. *Accommodating Pregnancy in the Workplace*, 25 Stetson L. Rev. 1, 36 (1995).

[74] 33 F.3d 1308 (11th Cir. 1994).

[75] Note 78, *supra*.

pregnant employees' rights and the reasons why an employer has no duty to make alternative work available to pregnant employees: The PDA contains no language that addresses "the right of a pregnant employee, fully able to work, to receive benefits that are different from, and arguably superior to, the benefits available to other employees."[76]

Furthermore, "employers can treat pregnant women as badly as they treat similarly affected but non-pregnant employees. Title VII simply does not require employers to treat their employees with kindness."[77]

Finally, a pregnant employee who finds herself facing the possibility of working in a potentially hazardous environment has three alternatives: continue working, seek a work situation with less stringent requirements, or leave the workforce. "In some cases, these alternatives may, indeed, present a difficult choice. But it is a choice that each woman must make."[78]

The court also dismissed the disparate treatment claim because the nurse had been unable to provide evidence that the hospital was treating her differently because of her pregnancy.

Although the case law does not lend support to a woman's desire to protect her fetus, there may be alternative methods of obtaining the desired outcome. One proposal holds that the best way to gain accommodation may be to demonstrate that the workplace hazard in question is harmful to the health of the pregnant woman herself.[79] If the ADA requires accommodations for individuals with disabilities who cannot perform physical labor or whose disabilities make them sensitive to toxins or who require frequent doctors' visits, then pregnant women who are similar in their ability to work and who require similar relief should, under the PDA, be entitled to the same accommodations.

D. Family Medical Leave Act

The Family Medical Leave Act (FMLA)[80] offers additional protection to pregnant employees, and to other individuals who are injured or disabled. In fact, it protects nearly all individuals who may, at some point during their careers, have some family crisis requiring their absence from the workplace.

---

[76] *Armstrong*, 33 F.3d at 1316.

[77] *Id.* at 1317.

[78] *Id.* at 1315.

[79] Calloway, Deborah, *Accommodating Pregnancy in the Workplace*, 25 Stetson L. Rev. 1, 38 (1995).

[80] 29 U.S.C. § 2601.

> The FMLA does not mandate that the leave be paid. But where the employee has paid leave available, the employer *must* allow the employee to draw on those leave banks.

The Federal Family Medical Leave Act is designed to balance the interests of employees and their families alongside the interests of the employer to maintain a productive work force. The FMLA essentially supersedes the earlier enacted state family leave law, in that its terms are more generous than had existed in the state law. The state law, though, remains on the books in the event the federal law is ever repealed or modified.

Under the FMLA, an employee is entitled to up to 12 work weeks of family leave in any 12-month period for family leave purposes. Family leave purposes include care of a newborn child, a newly adopted child, or care of a family member — child, spouse or parent — with a "serious health condition." The FMLA also permits leave for the employee's own "serious health condition."[81]

The FMLA does not mandate that the leave be paid. But where the employee has paid leave available, the employer *must* allow the employee to draw on those leave banks.[82] And once those leave banks are exhausted, the FMLA requires employers to allow employees to go out on unpaid leave status for the balance of the permitted time.

> At the end of the FMLA leave, employees have the right to return to the same position or "an equivalent position with equivalent pay, benefits and working conditions."

Although, as indicated, the FMLA does not require that employees (apart from their access to existing leave banks) be paid their wages, it does mandate the continuation of one important form of compensation. It requires that the employer continue the existing health benefit benefits and maintain its payment of its designated share of the premium for those benefits.[83]

At the end of the FMLA leave, employees have the right to

---

[81] 29 U.S.C. § 2612(a)(1).

[82] 29 C.F.R. § 825.207(a) (2014).

[83] 29 U.S.C. § 2614(c).

return to the same position or "an equivalent position with equivalent pay, benefits and working conditions."[84] An employee's leave may not involve a forfeiture of accrued benefits or seniority that an employee has had prior to taking a leave, but it does not require employers to continue accrual of such seniority-based privileges while out on leave (unless the employer allows such privileges for other forms of leave).[85] In other words, the employee's seniority time will be "tolled" during the leave of absence, but seniority may not be forfeited.

To establish that the leave is *bona fide*, the employer has the right to obtain and seek a "certification" from a health care provider to substantiate the need for the leave. This requirement applies whether the requested leave is for the employee or the employee's family member.[86]

Under the ADA, if the employer has a bona fide reason to question the employee's fitness, it can demand a fitness for duty examination. But under the FMLA it cannot delay returning the employee to pay status *once the employee presents a medical return to work certification.*

According to the FMLA, the employer may also demand a "certification of fitness" upon the employee's return.[87] But often there is confusion as to the distinction between this certification and a fitness certification. There is no confusion in the law itself, but often the employer or the employees incorrectly confuse or even conflate the two separate requirements.

In public safety work, injured employees reentering occurs all the time. An employee is injured, later recovers, indicates an ability to return and the employer, upon learning of this, is unsure whether the employee is fit or not. Under the ADA, if the employer has a bona fide reason to question the employee's fitness, it can demand a fitness for duty examination. But under the FMLA it cannot delay returning the employee to pay status *once the employee presents a medical return to work certification.*

This point is well demonstrated in the 2013 decision from the State Supreme Court in *Chaney v. Providence Health Care.*[88]

---

[84] 29 U.S.C. § 2614(a).
[85] 29 C.F.R. § 825.215(c) (2014).
[86] 29 U.S.C. § 2613.
[87] 29 C.F.R. § 825.312 (2014).

Chaney developed health issues, and the hospital directed him submit to a fitness exam from their selected doctor. He agreed but first went to his own physician. The two physicians provided competing explanations as to his fitness for duty. Later he was released by his doctor to return. The employer declined to accept his doctor's certification, arguing that it was ambiguous. It then fired him when his allowed leave expired.

The Court ruled that Providence Hospital erred by not accepting Chaney return to work certification even though it thought it ambiguous:

> When an employee is placed on leave, the FMLA permits employers to require a note from the employee's doctor stating that the employee is fit to work before reinstating the employee. The note need be only a simple statement that the employee is able to return to work. The only other requirement is that the statement must be made at the same time the employee is able to return to work. *Under the FMLA, if these requirements are met, an employer must reinstate the employee. If the employer is concerned about the adequacy of the fitness for work statement, it may seek a clarification from the employee's health care provider but may not delay returning the employee to work.*[89]

The employer is not without recourse if it genuinely believes the employee may not be fit. The Supreme Court is not saying an unfit employee must be returned to duty. The employee must be returned to *pay status*. The employee does not have to linger on paid or unpaid leave that might not have even been requested in the first place. Once the employee seeks to return to work and has a certification to support the request, they employer cannot delay that return to debate the merits of the certification.

The FMLA benefit does not cover most part-time employees. To be eligible, an employee must have worked at least 1250 hours in the prior 12 month period.[90] FMLA allows exemptions of certain "key employees." Key employees are those included in the highest "10%" of pay on the employer's payroll.[91] This requirement could conceivably impact the FMLA coverage of certain mid-level

---

[88] 176 Wn.2d 757, 295 P.2d 728 (2013).
[89] 176 Wn.2d at 738.
[90] 29 C.F.R. § 825.110 (2014).
[91] 29 U.S.C. § 2614.

managers in a given public safety department.

A common pitfall for employers relates to the duration of the leave. The law permits the employer to count paid leave used while an individual is medically unable to work toward the 12-week FMLA period. But in order to do so, the employer must give *notice* to the employee that their 12 weeks have begun to run, although such notice may be retroactive "provided that the employer's failure to timely designate leave does not cause harm or injury to the employee."[92]

When an employer, for example, allows an employee to use all their paid sick leave and vacation leave without providing the FMLA notice period, a 12-week period of unpaid leave will then commence *following* the exhaustion of the paid leave. Understandably, this has caused some headaches for personnel directors who have difficulty determining when an individual has begun a long-term period of absence from the workplace. For this reason, employees are often placed on FMLA leave status even though they did not specifically invoke the FMLA. The employer is simply trying to "start the clock" for their own benefit.

When the need for the leave is "foreseeable," the statute requires that employees provide advance notice of not less than 30 days.[93] A good example of a "foreseeable" need for leave is in the case of pregnancy-related leave.

Another complication under this statute is addressing medical situations where an employee can work some, but not every day. The FMLA requires the accommodation of these employees, allowing them to take intermittent days off.[94] The statute regulates how employees will get the notice and manage the taking of such intermittent time. These rules grant management a right to transfer such employees into alternative positions with equivalent pay and benefits, if such a transfer would prove less disruptive to the workforce.

The FMLA is essentially an amendment and a separate statute under the Fair Labor Standards Act. As a result, all available FLSA remedies are also generally available under the FMLA.

The FMLA provides an *additional* protection for employees. *It is not designed to remove or limit whatever protections employees otherwise have under the ADA or the CBA.*

This issue is likely to arise in the context of a continued

---

[92] 29 C.F.R. § 825.301(d) (2014).

[93] 29 U.S.C. § 2612 (e)(1).

[94] 29 U.S.C. § 2612 (b)(1).

request for an accommodation of an individual who has a physical limitation and whose condition continues after the expiration of the FMLA period. Some employers are under the misimpression that once the FMLA period expires, they have automatic grounds to discharge an employee. This may be true under some circumstances, but it is certainly not always true.

The FMLA and disability law requirements are separate and distinct. And under the CBA just cause requirement, employers have an ongoing obligation to retain an individual on the payroll *as long as there is a reasonable prospect for the return in a reasonable amount of time.* The FMLA does not alter this "just cause" mandate.

As discussed above, state and federal disability laws may require a leave of absence as a medical accommodation in some circumstances and mere expiration of the FMLA 12 week period does not alter that mandate. And most arbitrators would find these disability law mandates also to be an implied requirement of the CBA.

In short, an employee may have exhausted their statutory FMLA period (and the accompanying paid health insurance benefit), but that does not bar them from requesting continued leave (paid or unpaid) as a medical accommodation. Just as with the FLSA wage and overtime requirements, the FMLA establishes a floor, not a ceiling.

E. Workers Compensation and LEOFF

LEOFF I provided broad protection to public safety employees in the uniformed ranks of police officers and firefighters. LEOFF II significantly alters those protections. That is not a secret to anyone.

But the way the LEOFF II laws interact with workers compensation requirements still seems to be far more mysterious than it ought to over 30 years since the enactment of LEOFF II. There seems to be widespread noncompliance with the requirements of LEOFF II. Specifically, a number of jurisdictions are improperly applying the LEOFF II Supplement mandate.

In 1985, the legislature acted to address at least some of the equity issues that had been identified between LEOFF I and LEOFF II officers as to duty related injuries. They did this through the form of a "LEOFF II Supplement." The LEOFF II Supplement certainly does not entirely close the gap, but it does extend coverage under workers compensation more beneficial for police and firefighters injured at work than the law extends to any other class of employees covered.

The statute requires employers to provide for a period of 6 months, a "disability leave supplement." The supplement places the employee in the position of being able to maintain their wages. That supplement is defined in RCW 41.04.505:

> The disability leave supplement shall be an amount which, when added to the amount under RCW 51.32.090 [L&I Time Loss Payments] will result in the employee receiving the same pay he or she would have received for full time active service, *taking into account that industrial insurance payments are not subject to federal income or social security taxes.*[95]

There are two key aspects of this section that need to be interpreted and understood. First is the notion of "same pay." "Same pay" is not defined in the regulations or elsewhere in the law. Certainly, it means, at a minimum, that employees must be paid the same base wage plus the applicable premiums the employee had before.

There is an extensive misunderstanding and misapplication of the LEOFF II Supplement among public employers and even employees

---

It is an open question about whether it requires continuation of other compensation such as deferred compensation. The statute does elsewhere require the continuation of "insurance benefits." But this clause would not seem to extend to benefits such as deferred compensation.

The second key requirement of this section is that employees are to bring the employee up to the same pay by "taking into account that the industrial insurance payments are not subject to federal income tax or social security taxes." This element seems clear enough, *but it seems to be often ignored by employers.*

There is an extensive misunderstanding and misapplication of the LEOFF II Supplement among public employers and even employees, as well. It has been a practice of employers to take the entire check from L&I and then pay the employee their regular wage. Employees have been persuaded by payroll clerks that this is

[95] (emphasis in original).

a "better way" to do it. It usually is explained to them that there is some type of benefit that they are receiving in this "better way." Although when employees are later asked what the advantage was of this "better way," usually they are unable to point to anything other than that they were able to maintain a regular paycheck and their benefits — to which they are entitled to anyway.

One other enhancement that employees get out of maintaining their position on the payroll is that they continue to accrue contractual leave benefits under the CBA and continued DRS service credit (which can be repurchased by the employee on their own). But whatever advantage this reaps, it is more than offset by the loss incurred by subjecting this to federal payroll tax. These tax consequences that are the most misunderstood and that have led to a misapplication of proper payment procedure. To see how, you have to consider how the disability supplement would be applied if the employer did not convert the L&I check.

Under RCW 41.04.510, employers are required to arrange for a "disability leave supplement." This supplement is to be paid one-half out of the accrued paid leave of the employee, and the other half simply paid by the employer. The purpose of the disability leave supplement is to return the employee to the "same pay."

An example tends to demonstrate why turning over the L&I check to the employer, and receiving a regular paycheck in return which is taxed, is generally not a good idea. Let us say, for example, an employee's net earnings are 75% of the gross. L&I payments — which are not subject to tax — are, for example, 50% of the employee's gross wage. Here the gap to close is not the difference between the 50% and 100% of the gross wage. Rather, it is the gap between the 50% and the 75% — which represents the "net" wage. This gap — which is 25% — is to be made one-half out of accrued leave and one-half paid by the employer. This means that the employee is only contributing out of paid leave banks enough time to equal 12.5% of the total gross about 2 to 2-1/2 days a month.

If done properly, the employee still ends up with the full pay they had before, *but much less is taken out of the leave banks.* By subjecting this amount to a tax, the employer is making the employee pay 25% of their wage out of their leave banks, as opposed to 12.5%.

This is obviously a disadvantage to an injured employee who ends up depleting their leave banks at a much faster rate than if the rules had been properly applied. In fact, in this example, and in many actual cases, the leave banks will deplete at twice the proper rate.

The employers do this, perhaps, for two possible reasons. First, it simply is "easier" for payroll people who do not have to make the painstaking calculations about what the net wage actually is supposed to be. Second, the employee, in fact, does deplete the leave banks quicker, meaning that the employer has less of an obligation to an employee who ends up with a long-term injury from which they cannot return after the LEOFF Supplement expires after 6 months. But from the officers perspective, during the midst of an injury is when you most need to preserve your leave banks.

There is another element of this program employees should be aware of, as well. The statute allows employees who are out on long-term covered by disability supplement to "buy back" their credit so they can keep accruing retirement credit. *Employees must act affirmatively to obtain this benefit.* Employers sometimes sell employees on the notion that they get to continue accruing credit toward retirement when they are on full payroll status by turning over their L&I checks, but this is attainable anyway by the employee making direct arrangements to have the payment made.

PUBLIC SAFETY EMPLOYEES TABLE OF CASES CONCERNING REASONABLE ACCOMMODATIONS

This table lists cases that have examined employee disabilities and determined whether the employee asked for an accommodation, whether the employer granted the accommodation, and whether the accommodation was sufficient to address the disability. It identifies the specific occupation recognizing that different occupations may have different "essential functions" that an employee must qualify to meet. It also lists the relevant statute that protects that disability. The table is divided by type/part of the body and should give you an idea of how similar injuries and disabilities have been treated by employers and the courts.

MUSCULOSKELETAL

Neck and Back

Disability: Spinal injury

Accommodation Requested: Transfer to another position

Accommodation Required: No

Accommodation Adequate: Yes

Citation: *Iverson v. City of Shawnee*, 2008 U.S. Dist. LEXIS 75703 (D. Kan. 2008)

Statute: ADA

Explanation: After a being released for full duty after recovering from a work-related injury, a **police officer** was unable to requalify at the firing range. She inquired into a detective position but was told it was not available. Though she requested a transfer, there were no vacant positions and she could not qualify at the gun range, rendering her unqualified to be a police officer. The court upheld her termination.

Disability: Extreme, constant pain in neck and decreased mobility of left arm

Accommodation Requested: Transfer to computer task force

Accommodation Required: Maybe

Accommodation Adequate: N/A

Citation: *Breitfelder v. Leis*, 151 Fed. Appx. 379 (6th Cir. 2005)

Statute: ADA; Rehabilitation Act

Explanation: After being injured at work, a **detective** experienced ongoing problems with extreme pain. He requested to be transferred to the division investigating computer crime, but this request was denied. The detective could not perform the essential functions of even that position. Even his doctors indicated that he could not perform even a sedentary position.

Disability: Ongoing shoulder problems

Accommodation Requested: Reinstatement, consideration for promotion

Accommodation Required: Yes **Accommodation Adequate:** Yes

Citation: *Kincaid v. City of Omaha,* 378 F.3d 799 (8th Cir. 2004) **Statute:** ADA

Explanation: An employer required a **correctional officer** to provide medical release from their doctor before accommodating the employee. The court held this was reasonable.

Disability: Degenerative disc disease (back pain)

Accommodation Requested: Leave of absence

Accommodation Required: No **Accommodation Adequate:** N/A

Citation: *Epps v. City of Pine Lawn,* 353 F.3d 588 (8th Cir. 2003) **Statute:** ADA

Explanation: City was not required to accommodate a request for a six-month leave of absence from a **police officer** with degenerative disk disease. The court concluded that the officer's excessive absenteeism rendered him unable to perform the essential job function of attendance at work. Also, his accommodation request was not reasonable because the Police Department was small and could not reallocate his duties among staff of 15 to 22 police officers. The City was not required to hire additional officers or assign essential tasks to other employees to make up for his absence.

Disability: Herniated disk, bulging disk in spine

Accommodation Requested: Reassignment/light duty

Accommodation Required: Yes **Accommodation Adequate:** Maybe Not

Citation: *Shapiro v. Twp. of Lakewood,* 292 F.3d 356 (3d Cir. 2002) **Statute:** ADA

Explanation: After injuring his back lifting a patient, an **EMT** requested some form of accommodation numerous times. These requests were essentially ignored. Though it is the employee's responsibility to show that there is a vacant position for which they are qualified, the employer is responsible for engaging with the employee to accommodate them. That might mean it is acceptable to circumvent established job application procedures.

Disability: Permanent back injury

Accommodation Requested: Reassignment

Accommodation Required: Yes

Accommodation Adequate: Yes

Citation: *Pflanz v. City of Cincinnati,* 149 Ohio App.3d 743 (Ohio Ct. App. 2002)

Statute: State Disability Law (R.C. Chapter 4112)

Explanation: A **firefighter** was terminated for his inability to perform his job after he injured himself trying to catch a woman falling from a stretcher. He claimed he had not been offered any accommodations. The court held that employees have to show that there actually are vacancies in certain positions when they request reassignment to that position. If an equivalent is not available, offering a lower position is permissible.

Disability: Neck and back injuries

Accommodation Requested: Reassignment

Accommodation Required: Yes

Accommodation Adequate: No

Citation: *Cripe v. City of San Jose*, 261 F.3d 877 (9th Cir. 2001)

Statute: ADA

Explanation: The court holds that a city policy — that **police officers** whose disabilities prevented them from fulfilling a beat-patrol requirement could not receive specialized assignments and were only eligible for undesirable, degrading non-patrol positions — did not call for reasonable accommodations and, therefore, violated the ADA. Even though the seniority system in the officer union's CBA was applicable, the City's argument that varying contract terms might generate resentment among officers and undermine morale did not constitute an "undue hardship" analysis nor provide a basis for a "business necessity" defense.

Disability: Work-related injury from inmate disturbance, permanent back and knee problems

Accommodation Requested: Reassignment

Accommodation Required: No **Accommodation Adequate:** Yes

Citation: *Johnson v. Otter Tail County,* 2000 U.S. Dist. LEXIS 20671 (D. Minn. 2000) **Statute:** ADA

Explanation: The employer was not subject to an interminable duty to reassign employee. The court believed that the **detention officer** had been fired before she requested accommodation, but even if she had not been properly terminated prior to her request for accommodation, "the duty to reassign exists for finite period of time, and the outer limits of which the EEOC has limned at no more than six months."

Disability: Permanent back injury

Accommodation Requested: Reassignment to light duty

Accommodation Required: Maybe **Accommodation Adequate:** N/A

Citation: *Devine v. City of Dallas,* 2000 U.S. Dist. LEXIS 390 (N.D. Tex. 2000) **Statute:** ADA

Explanation: A **firefighter** with an injured back sued when he was terminated for the inability to do his job. He claimed he should have been accommodated by being placed in a dispatcher or an engine company. "[B]ased on the medical evidence presented, the Court finds that a genuine fact issue exists as to whether Devine was subject to the DFD's restricted duty policy and, therefore, eligible for a transfer to the Communications Department. Accordingly, because fact issues exist as to whether Devine was released to perform full paramedic duties and as to whether he was subject to the DFD's restricted duty policy, a fact issue exists as to whether Devine was qualified for the dispatcher position."

Disability: Back pain

Accommodation Requested: Transfer to a position where he did not have to wear gun belt

Accommodation Required: Yes **Accommodation Adequate:** No

Citation: *Konewko v. Village of Westchester,* 2000 U.S. Dist. LEXIS 11500 (N.D. Ill. 2000) **Statute:** ADA

Explanation: A **patrol officer** sued his police department, claiming the department failed to accommodate him by refusing to let him work without a gun belt, which aggravated his back problems. "An employer has an 'affirmative obligation to seek [plaintiff] out and work with [him] to craft a reasonable accommodation, if possible, that would have permitted [his] return to work.'" If an employer does not seek out an employee after an accommodation request and begin the interactive process of trying to create an accommodation, they may be held liable. This case questions whether being able to apprehend a suspect is an essential function to all police positions.

Disability: Knee and back injuries

Accommodation Requested: Reassignment

Accommodation Required: Yes **Accommodation Adequate:** Yes

Citation: *Dedman v. Wash. Personnel Appeals Bd.*, 98 Wn.App. 471 (Wash. Ct. App. 1999) **Statute:** WLAD

Explanation: Washington State DOC was not required to accommodate disabled **corrections officer** by permanently assigning her to a control booth position. Her requested accommodation was to be assigned to a position that did not involve any inmate contact. The court concluded that the ability to restrain an inmate was an essential function of a corrections officer job and, that by virtue of her disabilities; she was unable to perform essential duties.
The court reasoned that permanently assigning her to the control booth would restrict DOC's staffing flexibility and thereby create an undue hardship on its ability to respond to foreseeable emergency situations. Even though she had not been called from the booth to respond to such emergencies during her previous assignments there, the necessary qualifications of a corrections officer assigned to the control booth still included the ability to have some inmate contact.

Disability: Permanent neck and back injuries

Accommodation Requested: Promotion

Accommodation Required: Maybe

Accommodation Adequate: N/A

Citation: *Roberts v. City of Dallas*, 1999 U.S. Dist. LEXIS 2052 (N.D. Tex. 1999)

Statute: ADA

Explanation: A **police officer** was injured during a riot and placed on desk duty. She applied for a promotion which would have permitted her to continue her work but earn more money. She ranked 3rd of the 600 who took the promotion exam. The department then declared the ability to perform street patrol a prerequisite to the position the officer applied for. She did not receive the promotion.
The court held that there was a material question of fact as to whether or not the ability to do street patrol was an essential function of the position that the officer had applied for. She was permitted to continue her case and summary judgment in favor of the defendants was denied.

Disability: Degenerative disc disease

Accommodation Requested: Reassignment to dispatcher position or other alternative

Accommodation Required: Yes

Accommodation Adequate: Yes

Citation: *Seth v. City of Seattle,* 1999 U.S. App. LEXIS 28046 (9th Cir. 1999)

Statute: ADA

Explanation: A **police officer** was forced to retire due to his back problem. He requested accommodation, but failed the dispatcher exam. He was not qualified for other positions, but the department sent him letters informing him of available positions. The court held this was adequate accommodation.

Disability: Back, neck, shoulder, and leg injuries

Accommodation Requested: Reassignment

Accommodation Required: Yes

Accommodation Adequate: Yes

Citation: *Keever v. City of Middletown*, 145 F.3d 809 (6th Cir. 1998) **Statute:** ADA

Explanation: City's accommodation of **police officer's** work-related injury was found reasonable where it offered him a desk job, even though it was not his preferred accommodation — a transfer to night shift.
An employer has discretion to choose which reasonable accommodation it will provide. The offer to transfer to a desk job with reduced physical and mental responsibilities, in combination with allowing him to take leave as necessary, the court holds, was reasonable given his disability.

Disability: Back injury

Accommodation Requested: Reinstatement

Accommodation Required: Yes **Accommodation Adequate:** Yes

Citation: *Farrell v. Reno,* 983 F. Supp. 1099 (M.D. Fla. 1997) **Statute:** ADA

Explanation: As a **US Marshal** healed from a debilitating back injury, he was not entitled to reinstatement until he was fully recovered. Once he was, there was no proof that he had been offered jobs that were inferior to the one he held before going on leave. He had turned down the positions he was offered and his employer was not obligated to do more.

Disability: Back pain

Accommodation Requested: Ability to use cane during shift

Accommodation Required: No **Accommodation Adequate:** N/A

Citation: *Bennett v. State*, 1996 Mich. App. LEXIS 508 (Mich. Ct. App. 1996) **Statute:** Handicappers Civil Rights Act (HCRA); MCL 37.1202(1)(b); MSA 3.550(202)(1)(b)

Explanation: A **corrections officer** struggled with back pain, which necessitated his use of a cane. However, despite the use of his cane, he still missed work responsibilities, fell over, and dealt with pain as he climbed stairs because of his condition. His employer would not let him use his cane at work and he sued. The court held that they did not fail to accommodate the officer, as even the plaintiff's physician admitted that he may not be able to perform the essential functions of his job with the cane.

Disability: Back injury

Accommodation Requested: Limiting assignments to control room/guard tower where plaintiff would have little chance of having to physically confront an inmate

Accommodation Required: No **Accommodation Adequate:** N/A

Citation: *Allison v. Department of Corrections,* 94 F.3d 494 (8th Cir. 1996) **Statute:** ADA, Rehabilitation Act

Explanation: A **correctional officer** hurt her back while on duty, had to take medical leave, her doctor permitted her to return to work in a limited capacity. However, the department of corrections had a policy of terminating corrections officers who could not perform 100% of the work expected of them. Given the department's knowledge at the time of Allison's termination, which was limited to several instances that were not similar to plaintiff's, the defendants were granted qualified immunity to the claim.

Disability: Neck and back pain

Accommodation Requested: Modification to worksite

Accommodation Required: Yes **Accommodation Adequate:** Yes

Citation: *Stewart v. County of Brown,* 86 F.3d 107 (7th Cir. 1996) **Statute:** ADA; Rehabilitation Act

Explanation: County fulfilled its duty to provide a reasonable accommodation, even though the employee was still unsatisfied with its efforts. **Deputy sheriff** developed back and neck pain after being assigned to courthouse security TV viewing room. The county provided modifications to lighting, layout, an ergonomic chair, and work schedule that were deemed adequate to accommodate.

Disability: Cervicodorsal spinal symptoms (i.e., neck and back pains), headaches, depression

Accommodation Requested: More modifications to courthouse security room

Accommodation Required: Yes **Accommodation Adequate:** Yes

Citation: *Stewart v. County of Brown,* 86 F.3d 107 (7th Cir. 1996) **Statute:** ADA, Rehabilitation Act

Explanation: After being transferred to the courthouse security for improper conduct, a former **deputy** complained that the way the room was structured negatively impacted his health. The employer provided a number of accommodations, including building a platform in the security room, purchasing blinds, placing film on certain windows to reduce glare, and even buying a special ergonomic chair. The employer also modified his work schedule to accommodate his needs. However, the employee remained dissatisfied with his work space. The court held that the employer had made efforts to reasonably accommodate the employee and were not required to provide the employee with every single accommodation he requested.

Disability: Chronic back pain

Accommodation Requested: Continued light duty

Accommodation Required: Yes **Accommodation Adequate:** Yes

Citation: *Dancy v. Kline,* 1987 U.S. Dist. LEXIS 2336 (N.D. Ill. 1987) **Statute:** Rehabilitation Act

Explanation: A **Federal Protective Officer** had developed disabling pain in his back. He was on light duty for several years and was then terminated. The court determined that the employer was not required to make the light duty position they had given the employee was permanent, as they were not obligated to create a new position for the employee.

Limbs and Extremities

Disability: Knee injury with permanent limitations

Accommodation Requested: Reinstatement

Accommodation Required: Yes **Accommodation Adequate:** Yes

Citation: *Perdick v. City of Allentown,* 2014 U.S. Dist. LEXIS 24980 (E.D. Pa. 2014) **Statute:** ADA

Explanation: After a **police officer** returned from leave resulting from his knee injury, he was placed in the records department. He knew officers received light duty upon their return, but that it was only for six months. He was offered a number of positions outside the police department since he was technically an employee of the city and not just the department. He turned them all down, and when his light duty ran out he was terminated. The court upheld his termination, stating that the employer had initiated the accommodation process but the officer had brought that process to a close by failing to respond to any of the job offers he was given.

Disability: Injured heel, pain when she ran, walked, climbed stairs, or stood for long periods of time

Accommodation Requested: Permanent light duty

Accommodation Required: No **Accommodation Adequate:** N/A

Citation: *Feeley v. New York City Police Dep't,* 2001 U.S. Dist. LEXIS 25431 (E.D.N.Y. 2001) **Statute:** ADA

Explanation: **Transit police officer** injured her heel, took two months of leave, and returned to work in a light duty capacity. She was eventually cleared for full duty but was terminated when she failed to report. She claimed she should have been permanently placed on light duty. The court held that the position was only intended to be temporary, and the employer did not have to create a new permanent position to accommodate the officer. Furthermore, the officer admitted that she was not capable of performing the essential functions of her job, so the employer was permitted to terminate her.

Disability: Amputated leg

Accommodation Requested: Reassignment

Accommodation Required: Yes **Accommodation Adequate:** Yes

Citation: *Rehling v. City of Chicago,* 207 F.3d 1009 (7th Cir. 2000) **Statute:** ADA

Explanation: Though a **police officer** wanted to work in the district where he had been assigned before he lost his leg, the department had provided reasonable accommodation by offering two other positions. "It is well-established that an employer is obligated to provide a qualified individual with a reasonable accommodation, not the accommodation he would prefer."

Disability: Partially disabled hand

Accommodation Requested: Reinstatement and permanent assignment to control center

Accommodation Required: Yes **Accommodation Adequate:** No

Citation: *Anglin v. Department of Corrections*, 160 Ore. App. 463 (Or. Ct. App. 1999) **Statute:** Or. Rev. Stat. § 659.410 *et seq.*

Explanation: A **corrections officer** fractured his hand saving the life of another officer. This resulted in permanent pain and damage to his hand. He was deemed unable to perform essential functions of his job and terminated, despite his request to be accommodated by a permanent assignment to the control room. He sued and the jury ruled that the control room assignment was a viable accommodation that the employer had failed to provide. The court upheld the jury's accommodation verdict, holding that the employer could not hold an entire job classification or profession off-limits. As long as he could be accommodated in the control room and perform one corrections officer position, he should not have been terminated.

Disability: Carpal tunnel syndrome

Accommodation Requested: Ergonomically correct desk and keyboard, as well as an assistant to help her with typing

Accommodation Required: Maybe **Accommodation Adequate:** N/A

Citation: *Frazier v. Smith,* 12 F. Supp. 2d 1362 (S.D. Ga. 1998) **Statute:** ADA

Explanation: A **jail administrator** requested accommodations and the request was denied. The court held that there was enough evidence of failure to accommodate to permit the question to go to trial.

Disability: Crohn's disease, necrosis of the tibias in both legs resulting from treatment

Accommodation Requested: Light duty

Accommodation Required: No

Accommodation Adequate: Yes

Citation: *Hardy v. Village of Piermont,* 923 F. Supp. 604 (S.D.N.Y. 1996)

Statute: Rehabilitation Act

Explanation: A **police officer** unable to walk or run wanted to be provided a light duty position, but none existed in the department so she was placed on medical leave when her sick leave ran out. The court held that this was a reasonable accommodation because the employer was not obligated to create a light duty position for the employee.

Disability: Wrist injury

Accommodation Requested: Reinstatement and permission to wear brace

Accommodation Required: No

Accommodation Adequate: N/A

Citation: *Yodice v. Metropolitan Dade County,* 1995 U.S. Dist. LEXIS 21872 (S.D. Fla. 1995)

Statute: ADA

Explanation: The employee **police officer** "suggests that she is able to perform the essential functions of a police officer if she is allowed the reasonable accommodation of wearing a brace." However, the employer already permitted this accommodation. The employee still suffered from hypersensitivity in her wrist, placing herself and others at risk of losing control of her hand if she were hit in that area.

Disability: Completely disabled upper left arm

Accommodation Requested: Permanent light duty

Accommodation Required: No

Accommodation Adequate: Yes

Citation: *Champ v. Baltimore County*, 884 F. Supp. 991 (D. Md. 1995)

Statute: ADA; Rehabilitation Act

Explanation: After a **police officer** was injured in an off-duty motorcycle accident he lost complete use of his upper left arm. He was supposed to be permitted only 251 days of light duty but was given 16 years of light duty. When he was terminated after budget problems because he couldn't perform all of the essential functions of a police officer he held that the department had no accommodated and that he could still fire a gun and drive an emergency vehicle. The court held that he still could not meet the requirement of being able to perform a forcible arrest and that the employee provided no possible accommodation that could help him perform this function. Even though he was engaged in non-patrol work he had to be prepared to address any wrongdoing which he might observe, which could happen at any time.

Disability: Hand tremors

Accommodation Requested: Reinstatement

Accommodation Required: Yes

Accommodation Adequate: Yes

Citation: *Fussell v. Georgia Ports Auth.*, 906 F. Supp. 1561 (S.D. Ga. 1995)

Statute: ADA

Explanation: The employer was not required to permit a **police officer** to stay employed in that position when he continually failed a firearm qualification test." He presented too great of a danger to others because it was not clear that he could shoot straight. The employer was also not required to stay in contact with the employee and inform him when other positions opened up. It is the employee's responsibility to stay in touch and if he cannot be bothered to do so the employer does not need to continually seek the employee out after termination.

Disability: Restricted use of right arm due to blood vessel tumors

Accommodation Requested: Examination

Accommodation Required: Yes

Accommodation Adequate: Yes

Citation: *Ethridge v. State of Alabama*, 860 F. Supp. 808 (M.D. Ala. 1994)

Statute: ADA

Explanation: Police officer applicant with limited use of his right arm due to a blood vessel tumor, failed handgun retest at the police academy, and could not successfully complete handgun course required under state law. The court held that the State provided an acceptable and reasonable accommodation by permitting him to shoot with one hand instead of two. The applicant's other contentions — that his shooting ability deteriorated between the time of original test and the retest because of injuries and because he was out of practice — did not tend to show that State's accommodation was unreasonable. The court cited the testimony of the police academy director and other students stating that the applicant could not shoot safely using only one hand during original test.

The court found that the police academy's handgun test for police officers was job-related and consistent with business necessity. The handgun course curriculum was established by standards and training commission created by state law, and the commission determined that a handgun qualification course was necessary to ensure the safety of police officers and the community.

Disability: Ankle fracture

Accommodation Requested: Policy, transfer

Accommodation Required: Yes

Accommodation Adequate: Yes

Citation: *Molloy v. City of Bellevue*, 71 Wash.App. 382 (Wash. Ct. App. 1993)

Statute: WLAD

Explanation: The City of Bellevue's offer of dispatcher position to a former **police officer** with permanent partial disability in his left ankle was a reasonable accommodation, even though the dispatcher position only paid half his previous patrol officer salary. The officer initially told the City, after he refused the dispatcher position, that he planned to move to another state to obtain his teaching credentials. Later he argued it should have advised him of other openings. But the court ruled the City was under no obligation to continue to offer him other civilian positions that became available where the officer expressed no interest in other such positions.

The police department had a policy that all officers must be able to perform all duties of a police officer in order to adequately protect the public, and the officer conceded that he could no longer carry out the essential functions of a patrol position. The City had no duty to exempt him from this policy or to create a special position for him within the Police Department.

Disability: Myositis of right arm concentrated around the right elbow area, lateral epicondylitis of right elbow requiring a brace, thrombophlebitis lower left foot requiring elastic support, varicose veins, and myasthenia, epicondylitis of the right elbow and hand

Accommodation Requested: Light duty

Accommodation Required: No

Accommodation Adequate: N/A

Citation: *Blissitt v. Chicago,* 1990 U.S. Dist. LEXIS 5132 (N.D. Ill. 1990)

Statute: Rehabilitation Act

Explanation: An officer began experiencing debilitating pain and weakness in her right arm, preventing her from being able to fulfill her duties as a **police officer**. She was placed on medical leave. After healing she requested reinstatement in a light duty assignment, but this request was denied. The court held that this was appropriate. Light duty assignments were for those who had been injured on duty, which the plaintiff was not. They had accommodated her through medical leave. She knew she would only receive one year of medical leave and then be required to return to full duty. However, she could not and the department was not required to grant her light duty.

Disability: Occasional, unpredictable numbness in left arm, headaches

Accommodation Requested: Reinstatement or transfer to a position comparable to that of her former position

Accommodation Required: No

Accommodation Adequate: Yes

Citation: *Blumhagen v. Clackamas County*, 91 Ore. App. 510 (Or. Ct. App. 1988)

Statute: Or. Rev. Stat. §§ 659.415, 659.420, and 659.425

Explanation: After a **police officer** was in a car accident, she began to suffer from permanent problems. She was given light duty for nine months but was ultimately terminated. She was offered and accepted a position that provided less compensation than her previous job. Afterwards, the department created several new positions closer in status to her old job, but she was not hired for any of them. As a result, she sued.

The court held that the department had not failed to accommodate the officer.

They let her stay in a temporary position for far longer than the position was supposed to be given to her. They offered her an open position after she was terminated that met the needs of her disability. Though several positions opened up after she started her new job, after she had accepted the position the department was no longer required to grant her preference in hiring.

Mobility Issues

Disability: Mobility impairment (injuries to knees and right hand)

Accommodation Requested: Parking space

Accommodation Required: Yes

Accommodation Adequate: Maybe

Citation: *Price v. City of New York*, 797 F. Supp. 2d 219 (E.D.N.Y. 2011)

Statute: ADA

Explanation: City **corrections officer** with injuries to both knees and right hand could proceed to trial with a failure-to accommodate claim based on the City's denial of his request for a handicapped parking space. Eventually the City provided him a space, but he then alleged that space provided was insufficient because it was too far away and would require standing at a bus stop. The court found that a triable question arose as to whether the City's offer was reasonable and it allowed to the officer to proceed to trial on his request for a better parking spot.

Disability: Degenerative joint disease

Accommodation Requested: Transfer to computer data entry position

Accommodation Required: No

Accommodation Adequate: N/A

Citation: *Hastings v. Department of Corrections*, 110 Cal. App. 4th 963 (Cal. App. 3d Dist. 2003)

Statute: California Fair Employment and Housing Act (FEHA)

Explanation: During a period of conditional employment during which a **correctional peace officer cadet** was completing Basic Correctional Officer Academy, the cadet injured his knees during training. Doctors discovered a permanent joint disease in his knees, and his ability to walk and stand became very limited. He required a cane to walk more than a few states and could not stand for long. The court held that the employer was not required to accommodate the cadet because he was completely unable to perform the job duties he would need as a correctional officer.

Disability: Unable to walk long distances due to polio

Accommodation Requested: Motorized transportation from her car to her office and for use throughout the work spaces, railing and chairs to help her get around

Accommodation Required: Maybe **Accommodation Adequate:** N/A

Citation: *Bagatti v. Department of Rehabilitation*, 97 Cal. App. 4th 344 (Cal. App. 3d Dist. 2002) **Statute:** Fair Housing and Employment Act (California state law)

Explanation: A **corrections clerk** struggled to walk long distances while at her job, which required her to traverse long distances within the facility. She requested an accommodation involving motorized transportation or the placement of handrails and chairs throughout the building to help her move around. The court held she had a viable claim and permitted her to move forward with her case, contrary to the holding of the lower court.

Disability: Degenerative joint arthritis

Accommodation Requested: Permanent assignment to tower duty

Accommodation Required: No **Accommodation Adequate:** N/A

Citation: *Martin v. Kansas,* 996 F. Supp. 1282 (D. Kan. 1998) **Statute:** ADA

Explanation: A **corrections officer** with mobility issues wanted to be permanently assigned to tower duty, which accommodated his needs. However, this would have constituted permanent light duty, which was not deemed a reasonable accommodation.

Disability: Paraplegia

Accommodation Requested: Reassignment

Accommodation Required: Yes **Accommodation Adequate:** No

Citation: *Stone v. City Of Mount Vernon*, 118 F.3d 92 (2nd Cir. 1997) **Statute:** ADA

Explanation: Paraplegic former **firefighter** was found by the court to have presented sufficient evidence to demonstrate that his permanent assignment to fire department's fire alarm bureau or fire prevention bureau would be a reasonable accommodation. Placement in those bureaus was not unprecedented. Over previous four years, approximately 15-20 firefighters had been assigned to one of those bureaus following their injuries. The fire department had never called on anyone assigned to fire alarm bureau or fire prevention bureau to engage in fire-suppression activities, suggesting to the court it was highly speculative that permanently assigning a former firefighter to one of those bureaus outweighed the concrete benefits of the firefighter's assignment.
The fire commissioner's concern that operations would be hampered if the fire department were forced to hire disabled persons not as well qualified as the paraplegic former firefighter was found irrelevant. The court explained that each reasonable accommodation request must be decided on the basis of then existing circumstances, and recognized that the number of incumbent employees with disabilities could be a material factor to be considered to the extent that an employer needed to hire a certain number of persons without a disability. The court concluded that hiring 5-10 disabled persons would be an undue hardship is not a credible defense when an employer had hired none.

Disability: Difficulty walking

Accommodation Requested: Paved parking spot

Accommodation Required: Yes **Accommodation Adequate:** Yes

Citation: *Martin v. Department of Corrections,* 1996 Mich. App. LEXIS 2092, (Mich. Ct. App. 1996) **Statute:** ADA

Explanation: The correctional facility provided a **maintenance worker** with a graveled-over parking spot close to his workplace. He initially indicated that this accommodation was suitable, but the employee later complained to the EEOC saying it was not. The court affirmed the EEOC's decision that the space was still a reasonable accommodation, especially because the walkway from the parking spot to the building was paved.

Disability: Injured ankle, limits on running, walking, standing, etc.

Accommodation Requested: Assignment to dispatched position at pay rate of police officer

Accommodation Required: No **Accommodation Adequate:** N/A

Citation: *Conklin v. City of Englewood,* 98 F.3d 1341 (6th Cir. 1996) **Statute:** ADA

Explanation: The court held that a **police officer** was not disabled, but even if he were considered disabled the department had not failed to accommodate him. It was not a reasonable accommodation to request that essential functions of the police officer position were transferred to others because the employee could not do them with his injured ankle. Furthermore, requesting reinstatement as a dispatcher at the pay rate of a police officer essentially would have required the employer to create a new position, which they were not obligated to do.

Disability: Paraplegia

Accommodation Requested: Reinstatement

Accommodation Required: No **Accommodation Adequate:** N/A

Citation: *Simon v. St. Louis County,* 735 F.2d 1082 (8th Cir. 1984) **Statute:** Rehabilitation Act

Explanation: Even though the **police officer** could perform four of the positions that officers were expected to rotate through, the department's refusal to reinstate him in only those positions was not unreasonable. He could not perform two of the essential functions of a police officer--forceful arrest and transfer to all positions in the department. These were based on national standards and essential to the job.

Other

Disability: Inflammatory muscle disease (inclusion body myositis)

Accommodation Requested: Reassignment

Accommodation Required: Yes **Accommodation Adequate:** Maybe

Citation: *Reilly v. Upper Darby Township*, 809 F. Supp. 2d 368 (E.D. Penn. 2011) **Statute:** ADA

Explanation: A township **police officer** fired after developing an inflammatory muscle disease could proceed to trial with his failure-to-accommodate claim. He claimed that his denial of a reassignment to non-patrol job violated the ADA. The township argued that his assignment to permanent control-room job would have posed an "undue hardship." It cited the limited budget for officers and the fact that lower-paid civilians staff those jobs. But the court refused to dismiss the officer's claim on summary judgment. It ruled that he could proceed to trial to determine the reasonableness of his proposed accommodations: 1) that active-duty officers already staffed the control room on the night shift; 2) that he would accept night shift position; and 3) that he would move, if necessary, to meet the township's residency requirement in order to qualify for civilian control-room positions.

Disability: Degenerative joint disease (Ehlers Danlos Syndrome)

Accommodation Requested: Work from home, reduced workload, electric door installation, maintain parking lot in winter, assign in-office reports

Accommodation Required: Yes **Accommodation Adequate:** No

Citation: *Sturz v. State of Wisconsin Dep't of Corrections*, 22 AD Cases 825 (W.D. Wis. 2009) **Statute:** Rehabilitation Act

Explanation: State policy prohibiting **parole officer** with degenerative joint condition from working from home was not inherently unreasonable, the court ruled, but it nonetheless allowed the officer to proceed with her other failure-to-accommodate claims. The DOC had denial several other accommodation requests she made. She could only work 30 hours per week, but the DOC had refused to reduce her workload. The State also failed to explain the reasons for its delay in installing an electric door, its failure to maintain the office parking lot in the winter, its failure to review home visit accessibility, and its failure to assign her in-office reports.

Disability: Rheumatoid arthritis, injury that exacerbated this condition

Accommodation Requested: Retraining, reinstatement in a different position

Accommodation Required: Maybe **Accommodation Adequate:** N/A

Citation: *Warren v. Volusia County*, 188 Fed. Appx. 859 (11th Cir. 2006) **Statute:** ADA

Explanation: The burden to request an accommodation is on the employee. While the **corrections officer** stated that she never saw the communication between the County and her attorney, her attorney had not actually requested accommodation when requesting retraining. Furthermore, information provided to the employer by the doctor also did not count as a request for accommodation, as the doctor was not functioning as her representative. Additionally, retraining was not considered a reasonable accommodation by the court.

Disability: Severe arthritis, hip replacement

Accommodation Requested: Alternative method to reach basement dispatcher office such as elevator repair

Accommodation Required: Yes **Accommodation Adequate:** No

Citation: *Littlefield v. York County*, 2000 U.S. Dist. LEXIS 20907, 2000 WL 760959 (D. Me. 2000) **Statute:** ADA

Explanation: A **dispatcher** with arthritis requested an accommodation in order to help her go up and down the stairs to the dispatcher office. A chairlift was eventually installed, but in order for an accommodation to be reasonable, it must be timely. The employer installed chair lift to assist with ascending and descending stairs eleven months after employee resigned because of lack of accommodation. The employer was required to look into other methods of accommodating the employee other than the method the dispatcher initially suggested in order to provide a timely accommodation.

Disability: Restrictions on physical activity due to off-work injury resulting from horse falling on her

Accommodation Requested: Light-duty position, shifting some duties to other employees

Accommodation Required: Yes **Accommodation Adequate:** Yes

Citation: *Hoskins v. Oakland County Sheriff's Dep't,* 227 F.3d 719 (6th Cir. 2000) **Statute:** ADA

Explanation: A **deputy sheriff** was seriously injured outside of work, resulting in limitations in her ability to lift objects and requiring she be kept away from situations where she could be hit in the chest. However, there were no light duty positions available and she was terminated. The employer is not required to accommodate an employee by putting the responsibility for an essential job function on another employer. "[T]he ADA does not require employers to accommodate individuals by shifting an essential job function onto others." Furthermore, making a temporary light-duty position permanent is the equivalent of creating a new position, which the employer is not required to do.

Disability: Artificial hip

Accommodation Requested: Restructuring job, relieve him of responsibility to be able to restrain inmates

Accommodation Required: Maybe **Accommodation Adequate:** N/A

Citation: *Wilson v. County of Bernalillo,* 2000 U.S. App. LEXIS 7752 (10th Cir. 2000) **Statute:** ADA

Explanation: Restraining inmates is an essential duty for a **corrections officer** and an employee cannot be relieved of this responsibility. Not only is it unreasonable under the ADA, but it also places the employee's coworkers in danger.

Disability: Degenerative joint disease

Accommodation Requested: Allow him to remain in DARE program or similar position

Accommodation Required: Maybe **Accommodation Adequate:** N/A

Citation: *Dorris v. City of Kentwood,* 1994 U.S. Dist. LEXIS 15640 (W.D. **Statute:** ADA

Mich. 1994)

Explanation: Because it was unclear whether or not the ability to perform patrol duties was an essential function of the **police officer's** job, the court permitted the plaintiff officer to continue with his suit. He had been a DARE officer and had never performed any duties associated with patrol, but when he requested to be permanently assigned to the DARE position, his employer insisted that he needed to be able to perform at a patrol level.

VISION DISORDERS

Disability: Loss of vision

Accommodation Requested: Driving exemption

Accommodation Required: Maybe

Accommodation Adequate: Maybe

Citation: *Rorrer v. City of Stow*, 29 AD Cases 447 (6th Cir. 2014)

Statute: ADA

Explanation: Vision-impaired city **firefighter's** failure-to-accommodate claim could proceed to trial. Firefighter's request to be exempt from driving emergency vehicles might have been reasonable, the court found, given the evidence that such driving was a marginal rather than an essential job function. Also, the City failed to establish how such an exemption would necessarily impose an undue burden on the department. The court explained that the City's immediate insistence that he was unfit to serve as a firefighter indicates that it failed to adequately determine if his monocular vision could, or could not, have been accommodated.

Disability: Genetic eye condition, scarring of retinas, very poor vision

Accommodation Requested: Alternate vehicle usage

Accommodation Required: No

Accommodation Adequate: N/A

Citation: *Fey v. State*, 174 Wash. App. 435, 447 (Wash. Ct. App. 2013) *review denied*, 179 Wash. 2d 1029 (2014)

Statute: ADA

Explanation: Vision-impaired **grounds keeper** had no failure to accommodate claim as a matter of law when his eyesight prevented him from obtaining a CDL license to drive typical snow-removal vehicles. The grounds keeper applied for a position at another facility and was denied the position because his employers knew that he was unable to obtain CDL licensing due to his eyesight. He claimed that, although snow clearing was an essential job duty, he could perform the duty with equipment that didn't require CDL licensing. The Court found that the licensing was a "bona fide occupational qualification" and required that the case be dismissed.

Disability: Night-blindness

Accommodation Requested: Modification of work schedule

Accommodation Required: Yes **Accommodation Adequate:** Maybe

Citation: *Harrell v. Washington State*, 170 Wn.App. 386 (Wash. Ct. App 2012) **Statute:** WLAD

Explanation: On-call counselor at McNeil Island Special Commitment Center who requested only day shifts to accommodate night blindness after being placed on swing shift schedule was not entitled to summary judgment in his favor where a jury could find that the State's offered reasonable accommodation was adequate. The CBA prevented the State from permanently modifying the work schedule of an on-call employee. The Center argued that it had called and offered the counselor the shifts he had requested when they arose and that the personnel department reached out to him to acquire medical records to establish whether his disability actually existed, but that he did not respond adequately.

Disability: Stargardt's macular dystrophy

Accommodation Requested: Device usage, relief from driving duties

Accommodation Required: Maybe **Accommodation Adequate:** Maybe

Citation: *Eldredge v. City of St. Paul*, 809 F. Supp. 2d 1011 (D. Minn. 2011) **Statute:** ADA

Explanation: Vision-impaired **firefighter's** failure-to-accommodate claim could proceed to trial where the fire department had rejected his requests to be excused from driving department vehicles or to be allowed the use of a magnifying glass for necessary reading. The court noted that the City had not conducted a staffing assessment in order to determine whether the firefighter's requested driving exemption was unreasonable. It also explained that the City apparently misunderstood that he had only requested the use of a magnifying glass as an accommodation for reading fine print reading.

Disability: Tardive dystonia and Blepharospas, psychiatric issues

Accommodation Requested: Relief from obligation to perform courtroom coverage in specific courtrooms

Accommodation Required: Maybe

Accommodation Adequate: N/A

Citation: *Kriegel v. Rhode Island*, 266 F. Supp. 2d 288 (D.R.I. 2003)

Statute: Rhode Island Fair Employment Practices Act ("FEPA"), Rhode Island Civil Rights of Individuals with Handicaps Act ("RICRIHA"), Rhode Island Civil Rights Act ("RICRA")

Explanation: A **probation and parole counselor** requested removal from the obligation to cover specific courtrooms that required rapid eye scanning. His visual problems made doing so difficult. After he requested the accommodation he was informed that his request had been denied. He appealed the request, but was simply told that monitoring the two courtrooms were an essential function of his job. The court concluded that there had been no attempt by the employer to accommodate the counselor, and he was permitted to continue with his failure to accommodate claim.

Disability: Blindness

Accommodation Requested: Braille computer

Accommodation Required: Yes

Accommodation Adequate: Yes

Citation: *Leine v. California Dep't of Rehabilitation*, 1999 U.S. App. LEXIS 32521 (9th Cir. 1999)

Statute: ADA, Rehabilitation Act

Explanation: Though the employer took 19 months to provide the employee with a Braille computer, employers are not required to provide employees with the accommodation they prefer, only reasonable accommodations. Throughout the wait for a Braille computer the employer provided a reader, driver, and other assistants to help the **corrections employee** perform her job. The employer also brought in a specialist who ultimately provided a better computer than the one the employee requested.

Disability: Blindness

Accommodation Requested: Permanent assignment to switchboard and armory, reinstatement or transfer to another position at same rate of pay

Accommodation Required: No

Accommodation Adequate: N/A

Citation: *Miller v. Illinois Dep't of Corrections,* 107 F.3d 483 (7th Cir. 1997)

Statute: ADA

Explanation: After a car accident a **corrections officer** was rendered essentially blind. She asked to be reinstated after taking extensive medical leave but was not permitted to return. She stated that there were limited duties she could still perform and wanted to be limited to those duties or transferred to another position. The officer required a seeing eye dog. She was terminated. The court stated that she could not perform the essential functions of her job, even though she could perform two positions within the officer rotation. She also indicated that she'd work another position in the prison, but wanted to continue to receive her officer salary, which was higher than the salary of any of the positions she could be transferred to. The court held that transferring her to a new position but paying her correction officer salary would have created a new position. The employer wasn't required to create a new position for the employee.

Disability: Blind in one eye, only partial vision in other eye

Accommodation Requested: Assistance in performing some duties, only receiving specific types of cases

Accommodation Required: No

Accommodation Adequate: N/A

Citation: *Holbrook v. City of Alpharetta,* 112 F.3d 1522 (11th Cir. 1997)

Statute: ADA; Rehabilitation Act

Explanation: A **detective** with poor vision had been provided with accommodations, but when they were ceased he claimed that the department was obligated to continue them. The court held that the department did not have to continue providing the accommodations, as they were unreasonable. He had received specific case assignments and assistance collecting certain types of evidence, but this was beyond what the department needed to do and the detective could no longer perform the essential functions of his job.

RESPIRATORY DISORDERS

Disability: Severe allergy to cigarette smoke

Accommodation Requested: Designate police headquarter as non-smoking

Accommodation Required: Yes **Accommodation Adequate:** No

Citation: *Thursby v. City of Scranton*, 18 AD Cases 21 (M.D. Pa. 2006) **Statute:** ADA

Explanation: Police officer with severe allergy to tobacco smoke and odors could proceed to trial with her failure-to-accommodate claim. Even though the City made non-smoking rooms available for her to use, there was evidence that she could not perform many of her job duties from the non-smoking rooms provided by the City. Additionally, although the City asked other officers "as a courtesy" to stop smoking when asked to do so by the officer with allergies, other officers continued to smoke despite her complaints. Further, the City did not address her complaints about smoke in a roll call room and police vehicles.
The court ruled that neither the collective-bargaining agreement with the police union nor its statutory duty to bargain prevented City from implementing a no-smoking policy that could have reasonably accommodated the officer. No provision in the agreement entitled officers to smoke and smoking ban would not necessarily require collective bargaining when implemented to promote a healthy environment. Further, there was no evidence that the City had ever attempted to negotiate a policy with the union, or that negotiating would impose an undue hardship on the city. The City had negotiated non-smoking agreements with other unions, and after the officer with allergies stopped working for the City, it finally implemented a no-smoking policy at police headquarters without negotiating it with the union.

Disability: Asthma

Accommodation Requested: Transfer to a smoke-free environment

Accommodation Required: Yes

Accommodation Adequate: Yes

Citation: *Thorner-Green v. N.Y. City Dep't of Corr.,* 207 F. Supp. 2d 11 (E.D.N.Y. 2002)

Statute: ADA

Explanation: A **corrections officer** with asthma requested several accommodations due to difficulty she was experiencing at work. The employer granted all three accommodation requests submitted by the employee, granting her two extended leaves and transferring her to a smoke-free section of the facility. The employee claimed that the location she was placed in was not truly smoke free. The telecommunications room was the only smoke-free room in the facility but the employee believed she should have been transferred to another building to accommodate her asthma. However, she did not request any further transfers once she was assigned to the telecommunications room and the employer was not obligated to provide further transfers if they weren't requested. They had provided all reasonable accommodations requested and were required to do no more.

Disability: Respiratory limitations resulting from lung cancer treatment

Accommodation Requested: Reinstatement, transfer some duties to other employees

Accommodation Required: No

Accommodation Adequate: N/A

Citation: *Hummel v. County of Saginaw,* 40 Fed. Appx. 965 (6th Cir. 2002)

Statute: ADA

Explanation: Though a lung cancer survivor worked for nine months while she was being treated, after she completed treatment she was no longer qualified for her former position as a **building security officer** through the Sheriff's Department. The employee had 25% of one of her lungs removed and she could no longer tolerate the same physical exertion that she could before surgery. The employee could not require the employer to transfer restraint and other responsibilities to other officers, as that was not a reasonable accommodation since restraint was an essential function of the position.

Disability: Asthma

Accommodation Requested: Use of inhaler

Accommodation Required: Yes **Accommodation Adequate:** N/A

Citation: *Huber v. Howard County.*, 849 F. Supp. 407 (D. Md. 1994) **Statute:** ADA

Explanation: Discharged asthmatic probationary county **firefighter's** case was dismissed because the court found that did not show that the County's refusal to allow him to use his inhaler during endurance testing at firefighting academy was not job related or supported by legitimate safety concerns. Evidence indicated that the firefighter's brand of inhaler could not be used or stored near open flame and exposure to high temperatures could cause the device to burst. The court concluded that the County had reasonably determined that such device would be improper if used at the scene of a fire. In addition, the court ruled, the county was legitimately concerned with how inhaler could be used while the firefighter was wearing personal protective equipment, such as a helmet face guard, and gloves, as well as how long the inhaler would take to work.

CIRCULATORY SYSTEM

Disability: Obesity, hypertension

Accommodation Requested: Steady day shift, swapping shifts

Accommodation Required: Maybe **Accommodation Adequate:** N/A

Citation: *Honey v. County of Rockland,* 200 F. Supp. 2d 311 (S.D.N.Y. 2002) **Statute:** ADA

Explanation: After her doctor determined that her frequently rotating shift aggravated her health problems, a **dispatcher** requested accommodation. She was accommodated for a while, but after bringing suit her accommodations were removed. The court permitted the question of failure to accommodate to continue to trial.

Disability: Blood clot requiring anti-coagulants, physical altercation could cause employee to bleed out

Accommodation Requested: Continue previous light duty

Accommodation Required: No **Accommodation Adequate:** Yes

Citation: *Pickering v. City of Atlanta,* 75 F. Supp. 2d 1374 (N.D. Ga. 1999) **Statute:** ADA

Explanation: A **corrections officer** had to be on anti-coagulants due to a blood clot in her body, which put her at risk of bleeding out if she incurred a physical injury. Her employer placed her on light duty for 2.5 years, essentially creating a new position for her. It was not reasonable to require them to continue to keep the position they created for her. She could not perform the essential functions of her job and was rightfully terminated.

Disability: Coronary artery disease

Accommodation Requested: Excused from emergency response

Accommodation Required: No **Accommodation Adequate:** N/A

Citation: *Lusby v. Metropolitan Wash. Airports Auth.,* 1999 U.S. App. LEXIS 18428 (4th Cir. 1999) **Statute:** ADA

Explanation: A **Firefighter/Assistant Fire Marshal** was diagnosed with coronary artery disease. He requested that he be excused from extreme exertion as an accommodation for his condition. The court held that emergency response is an essential function of the employee's job. Restructuring his responsibilities to excuse him from emergency response would eliminate an essential function of the employee's position. If he could not perform this essential function then he was not qualified for his job and the employer was justified in not providing that accommodation.

Disability: Heart condition

Accommodation Requested: Reinstatement

Accommodation Required: Yes **Accommodation Adequate:** No

Citation: *Hamlin v. Charter Twp. of Flint,* 165 F.3d 426 (6th Cir. 1999) **Statute:** ADA

Explanation: Because front-line firefighting is a non-essential function for the

Assistant Fire Chief position, it was a reasonable accommodation to relieve the employee of that duty.

Disability: Circulatory difficulty

Accommodation Requested: Permanent assignment to control room

Accommodation Required: No **Accommodation Adequate:** Yes

Citation: *Hill v. Harper,* 6 F. Supp. 2d 540 (E.D. Va. 1998) **Statute:** ADA

Explanation: A **deputy sheriff** could not rotate throughout all five of the mandatory positions in the jail due to a circulatory issue. When the ability to rotate throughout various posts at the jail is an essential job function, it is not reasonable to require the employer to permanently station the employee in one location as an accommodation, even when no other accommodations are available. This still holds true even if the employer permitted the employee to be permanently stationed there for three years prior.

Disability: Obesity, heart problems

Accommodation Requested: Limited assignment to "light duty" positions

Accommodation Required: No **Accommodation Adequate:** Yes

Citation: *McDonald v. Department of Corrections,* 880 F. Supp. 1416 (D. Kan. 1995) **Statute:** ADA

Explanation: An overweight **corrections officer** suffered from heart problems. His doctor was not sure when his condition would improve. The court held that the employer was not required to limit him to light duty positions such as watchtower and clothing issue. The defendant made and adequate showing that such an accommodation would be an undue hardship and the employee failed to provide any evidence that the accommodation problem could present an issue of fact.

ENDOCRINE

Disability: Diabetes

Accommodation Requested: Modification of work schedule

Accommodation Required: Maybe **Accommodation Adequate:** Maybe

Citation: *Lee v. District of Columbia*, 920 F. Supp. 2d 127 (D.D.C. 2013) **Statute:** ADA

Explanation: Diabetic city **corrections officer** may proceed with ADA failure-to-accommodate claim after he was fired for sleeping at work. He fell asleep 90 minutes after he was denied regular lunch break. The court cited the evidence that he was substantially limited in his ability to stay alert when he missed meals and that he frequently requested meal breaks because of his diabetes and its impact on his alertness. The court rejected the City's argument that the officer had to formally request accommodation or comply with fixed procedures to provide notice of his need for an accommodation in advance of his citation for the rule violation.

Disability: Diabetes

Accommodation Requested: Altered shifts

Accommodation Required: Maybe **Accommodation Adequate:** No

Citation: *Szarawara v. County of Montgomery,* 2013 U.S. Dist. LEXIS 90386, (E.D. Pa. 2013) **Statute:** ADA

Explanation: A **dispatcher** was experiencing health problems from diabetes, which were exacerbated by his work schedule. He requested and suggested a number of accommodations in order to be able to only work days as his physical suggested, but the employer refused because a better sleep schedule would help anyone, not just the plaintiff. "The Court cannot say that Defendant was relieved of its obligations under the ADA because Plaintiff's doctor suggested alternatives to Plaintiff's requested accommodation that would also mitigate the effects of his medical conditions. Defendant cites no authority, and the Court is aware of none, for its implied proposition that Plaintiff must exhaust all other possible methods of mitigating the effects of his alleged disability before requesting an accommodation under the ADA." Furthermore, just because a particular accommodation would be good for non-disabled people does not mean that the accommodation is not related to the employee's disability.

Disability: Diabetes

Accommodation Requested: Re-hire as permit clerk

Accommodation Required: Yes

Accommodation Adequate: Yes

Citation: *Castellani v. Bucks County Municipality,* 351 Fed. Appx. 774 (3d Cir. 2009)

Statute: ADA

Explanation: After a **dispatcher** failed to return from medical leave, the county terminated her. She requested an accommodation after her termination. However, she had no evidence that there were any open positions at her time of termination and she conceded that she could not return to her dispatcher position.

Disability: Diabetes, kidney disease

Accommodation Requested: Transfer to a position with equal pay to what the employee was making in her current position

Accommodation Required: Yes

Accommodation Adequate: Yes

Citation: *Fry v. Sheahan,* 2009 U.S. Dist. LEXIS 70630 (N.D. Ill. 2009)

Statute: ADA

Explanation: The **jail administrative assistant** couldn't perform the essential functions of her job and was limited in her ability to stand for extended periods of time. The employee was offered a position that was lower than hers and would pay her $7,000 less a year. She initially turned the position down but this was an adequate accommodation. Furthermore, the employer wasn't required to continually give the responsibilities she couldn't do to other employees.

Disability: Hypertension, Diabetes, and chronic obstructive pulmonary disease

Accommodation Requested: Transfer, department vehicle, parking space

Accommodation Required: No

Accommodation Adequate: Yes

Citation: *Raffaele v. City of New York,* 16 AD Cases 62 (E.D.N.Y. 2004)

Statute: ADA

Explanation: The court concluded that the fire department did not fail to reasonably accommodate former **Inspector** with hypertension, diabetes, and chronic obstructive pulmonary disease when it denied his requests for: (1) transfer back to post that was close to home and his physician's office; (2) use of department vehicle; and (3) parking space at department headquarters. It found that there was no evidence supporting his testimony that a co-worker was willing to switch assignments with him such that a position would have been available. A doctor's letter accompanying his transfer request stated only that the employee had health conditions necessitating medical treatment and that transfer from his post made it more difficult to receive treatment.
The Inspector was offered an alternative accommodation of be allowed to use his personal vehicle to travel to appointments instead of a department vehicle. Using a personal vehicle met his job-related needs just as adequately as using department vehicle. Therefore, the availability of department vehicles to other employees was irrelevant to determining whether alternative accommodation was reasonable. Finally, the former employee did not explain how parking space would accommodate his impairments other than stating he was unable to use public transportation.

Disability: Diabetes, severe angina pectoris

Accommodation Requested: Reinstatement as a police officer

Accommodation Required: No

Accommodation Adequate: Yes

Citation: *Muhammad v. New Orleans Police Dep't,* 791 So. 2d 788, 2001 La. App. LEXIS 1792, 2000-1034 (La. Ct. App. 2001)

Statute: ADA

Explanation: The employee was completely unable to function as a **police officer** and the department began termination proceedings. At the same time the department attempted to find the employee work in another position with the city. He was offered the position of truck driver but due to his medication he could not accept the position. They terminated him and the court upheld his termination, determining that the city had made a reasonable effort to accommodate the employee.

Disability: Diabetes

Accommodation Requested: Retesting

Accommodation Required: Yes **Accommodation Adequate:** Yes

Citation: *Gonzales v. City of New Braunfels*, 176 F.3d 834 (5th Cir. 1999) **Statute:** ADA

Explanation: This case involved an insulin-dependent diabetic **police officer**, who was discharged after he failed firearms and driving requalification tests. The court dismissed his action in which he claimed he was entitled to a retest the requalification tests he had failed. The court found this requested accommodation would not have been a reasonable one. It concluded that driving is an essential function of police officer position, and a driver with insulin-dependent diabetes poses a direct threat to health and safety of others as matter of law. The officer could not show that retesting would make him a safer driver. Individualized assessment of his medical condition found that his diabetic neuropathy prevented him from being able to handle a firearm safely or to drive vehicle to police specifications.

The court also found that the City was not liable under ADA for failure to reassign the officer to evidence technician position. It reasoned that he was not qualified to be evidence technician — an evidence technician must be commissioned officer, and in order to be a commissioned officer one must be both firearms and driving certified.

Disability: Diabetes

Accommodation Requested: A “second chance”

Accommodation Required: Yes **Accommodation Adequate:** Yes

Citation: *Siefken v. Village of Arlington Heights,* 65 F.3d 664 (7th Cir. 1995) **Statute:** ADA

Explanation: A **police officer** had a diabetic reaction, causing him to become disoriented, lose his memory, and speed recklessly around in his patrol car. The court determined that the department had already accommodated the officer by permitting him to monitor and control his diabetes. The court upheld his termination, despite the officer's request for another chance, as he failed to monitor his condition.

Disability: Diabetes

Accommodation Requested: Ability to enter police force

Accommodation Required: Yes **Accommodation Adequate:** No

Citation: *Bombrys v. City of Toledo,* 849 F. Supp. 1210 (N.D. Ohio 1993) **Statute:** ADA

Explanation: Permitting diabetics to enter the police force and take a few minutes a day to test their blood sugar levels is reasonable. The police force did not prohibit other **police officers** with potentially dangerous conditions, such as epilepsy, form entering the force. Officers who acquired diabetes while on the force were not required to quit. Allowing an officer to carry testing materials, medicine, and extra food did not disrupt the law enforcement activities of the officers. The court therefore held that there could be no blanket exclusion of diabetics from entering the department.

Disability: Diabetes

Accommodation Requested: Ability to become FBI agent

Accommodation Required: No **Accommodation Adequate:** N/A

Citation: *Davis v. Meese,* 692 F. Supp. 505, (E.D. Pa. 1988) **Statute:** Rehabilitation Act

Explanation: The FBI is not required to create permanent light-duty positions for diabetic **agents**. There is a risk that a diabetic could experience an unexpected hypoglycemic attack, putting themselves and others at risk. It is too dangerous to keep them in the field, but there are no permanent light-duty positions so it is permissible to exclude diabetics from the FBI.

NEUROLOGICAL DISORDERS

Disability: Seizures

Accommodation Requested: Limited duty for five year wait period required after seizures

Accommodation Required: No **Accommodation Adequate:** N/A

Citation: *Coleman v. Pa. State Police,* 2014 U.S. App. LEXIS 5237 (3d Cir. 2014) **Statute:** ADA; Rehabilitation Act

Explanation: The court determined that a **trooper cadet** could not demand five years of limited duty when, pursuant to a department policy, he was required to wait five years after experiencing seizures to return to full duty. The court ultimately held that the fact that he was subject to the wait period and had not completed his training rendered him unqualified for the position of officer and therefore not protected by state statute.

Disability: Multiple sclerosis

Accommodation Requested: Job restructuring

Accommodation Required: Maybe **Accommodation Adequate:** Maybe

Citation: *Miller v. Benton County*, 27 AD Cases 1413 (D. Minn. 2013) **Statute:** ADA

Explanation: Former county **jail sergeant's** failure-to-accommodate claim could proceed to trial. The sergeant had multiple sclerosis and was provided an informal accommodation of control center assignment without inmate contact during MS exacerbations. Eventually, the informal accommodation was discontinued, at which point the sergeant began having attendance problems. The court concluded that such attendance problems alone were not sufficient evidence that she was not entitled to a reasonable accommodation.

Disability: Narcolepsy

Accommodation Requested: Assistance from coworkers in waking him

Accommodation Required: Yes **Accommodation Adequate:** Yes

Citation: *Roetter v. Mich. Dep't of Corr.,* 456 Fed. Appx. 566 (6th Cir. 2012) **Statute:** ADA; Rehabilitation Act

Explanation: The **food service supervisor's** accommodation request was approved and he was granted a specific shift during which he was most alert. He claimed that the employer should have done more to accommodate him, but he submitted no accommodation requests beyond the one that had already been implemented. The employer was not required to take further steps, including requiring the employee's coworkers to shake him awake when he was found sleeping.

Disability: Epilepsy

Accommodation Requested: Non-rotating shift

Accommodation Required: Yes **Accommodation Adequate:** N/A

Citation: *Dicksey v. New Hanover County Sheriff's Dep't*, 522 F. Supp. 2d 742 (E.D.N.C. 2007) **Statute:** ADA

Explanation: Epileptic former **deputy sheriff** could not proceed with his failure-to-accommodate claim because he was not a "qualified individual" under the ADA. Although he argued that he would be qualified for a front desk position *if* the county provided his requested accommodation for a non-rotating day shift assignment, he was unable to meet state standards requiring that he be seizure-free, and was, therefore, unable to perform essential job functions requiring uninterrupted vigilance. Additionally, no non-rotating front desk positions existed at the time, and assigning him to permanent day shift, the court ruled, would unduly burden staff required to work his night shifts. Finally, he could not show that he would be seizure-free even if he were accommodated.

Disability: Multiple sclerosis

Accommodation Requested: Overtime scheduling

Accommodation Required: Yes **Accommodation Adequate:** Yes

Citation: *Cormier v. City of Meriden*, 420 F. Supp. 2d 11 (D. Conn. 2006) **Statute:** ADA

Explanation: City public safety **dispatcher** with multiple sclerosis was medically restricted to work no more than 12 consecutive hours, but could not proceed with her ADA failure-to-accommodate claim. The City forbade her from accepting an eight-hour overtime shift before or after her regular shift. The City's proposed accommodation of allowing her to accept all four-hour overtime shifts and any eight-hour overtime shift on days that she was not scheduled to work did not pose

a risk of violating her 12-hour work restriction.
The dispatcher presented no evidence that City's proposal burdened her ability to earn overtime income, or, on the other hand, that her proposal would have resulted in more overtime opportunities. The fact that the City later offered to allow her to bid on contiguous eight-hour shifts, if she could swap first four hours with co-worker, did not render its first proposal unreasonable. Therefore, the court ruled, that because she refused city's proposal she could show that the City's proposed accommodation would have negatively affected her income or other aspect of the job.

Disability: Limited physical abilities due to stroke

Accommodation Requested: Limited physical responsibilities, no inmate contact

Accommodation Required: No **Accommodation Adequate:** N/A

Citation: *Dargis v. Sheahan,* 2005 U.S. Dist. LEXIS 7468 (N.D. Ill. 2005) **Statute:** ADA

Explanation: A **corrections officer** had a stroke, but was subsequently cleared for light duty without any inmate contact. The prison stated that it could not provide that accommodation. The court held that the prison needs to be able to call on all of its correctional officers in the case of an emergency. Even if the possibility that such a situation would occur is low, it is still a risk that must be prepared for. If the employee cannot handle inmate contact then they are not qualified for the job.

Disability: Multiple sclerosis

Accommodation Requested: Transfer to another position

Accommodation Required: Maybe **Accommodation Adequate:** Yes

Citation: *Doner v. City of Rockford,* 77 Fed. Appx. 898 (7th Cir. 2003) **Statute:** ADA; Rehabilitation Act

Explanation: Multiple sclerosis rendered a **police officer** incapable of apprehending suspects. After learning that the officer would never be able to walk again, the Deputy Chief terminated him. The court determined that, because he could not apprehend suspects, the officer was incapable of performing an essential function of the job. The officer also failed to point out any specific vacant position he could have been moved to.

Disability: Fibromyalgia

Accommodation Requested: Reinstatement

Accommodation Required: No **Accommodation Adequate:** Yes

Citation: *Jackson v. City of Chicago,* 293 F. Supp. 2d 836 (N.D. Ill. 2003) **Statute:** ADA

Explanation: The city was not required to reinstate a **police officer** who could not safely use a gun and often had trouble standing and would collapse. The employee then stated that she had not been accommodated by being informed of potential reassignments. However, the city had informed her repeatedly of opportunities and she had failed to avail herself of these opportunities. The officer did not engage in reassignment procedures and was therefore the party at fault.

Disability: Multiple sclerosis

Accommodation Requested: Job restructuring, assignment to a vacant position

Accommodation Required: Yes **Accommodation Adequate:** Yes

Citation: *Frazier v. Simmons,* 254 F.3d 1247 (10th Cir. 2001) **Statute:** ADA

Explanation: An **investigator** for the department of corrections cannot request that his job be restructured to remove responsibility for arrests, as that is an essential function of his job. Eliminating an essential function of his job would be unreasonable. Also, even though the employee identified a number of available alternative positions, he was not qualified for and could not perform the essential functions of those positions, either, rendering them unreasonable as accommodations, too.

Disability: Brain injury leading to mental, emotional, and physical difficulties

Accommodation Requested: Promotion

Accommodation Required: Yes **Accommodation Adequate:** Yes

Citation: *Land v. Washington County,* 243 F.3d 1093 (8th Cir. 2001) **Statute:** ADA

Explanation: A **corrections officer** twice requested and received accommodations, but was passed over multiple times for promotions. The officer believed that he did not get the promotions because he was not adequately accommodated. He was later terminated for bad behavior. The court found that, because the employer had accommodated the requests that had been made, they had made reasonable accommodations for the employee and he simply was no longer qualified.

Disability: Multiple sclerosis

Accommodation Requested: Transfer, shift some duties to other employees

Accommodation Required: No **Accommodation Adequate:** N/A

Citation: *Frazier v. Simmons,* 90 F. Supp. 2d 1221 (D. Kan. 2000) **Statute:** ADA

Explanation: Due to MS a **corrections investigator** had lost 50% of his vision, had balance problems, and lost strength in his hands. This kept him from being able to restrain prisoners and safely handle a firearm. He sought to have some of the essential functions of his job transferred to others or to be transferred to vacant positions that he was not qualified for. He was terminated. The court held that the employer had acted reasonably, as they were not required to shift essential functions of the job or transfer him to a position that was not qualified and would essentially be a promotion.

Disability: Multiple Sclerosis

Accommodation Requested: Light duty

Accommodation Required: Yes **Accommodation Adequate:** Yes

Citation: *Maynard v. Nygren,* 2000 U.S. Dist. LEXIS 9208 (N.D. Ill. 2000) **Statute:** ADA

Explanation: A **corrections officer** with MS requested light duty in order to continue working despite his condition The employer refused, as no light duty assignments existed. An employer does not have to provide an accommodation in the form of a light duty assignment if no light duty assignments are available.

Disability: Multiple sclerosis

Accommodation Requested: Transfer to civilian position

Accommodation Required: Yes **Accommodation Adequate:** Yes

Citation: *Barzellone v. City of Tulsa,* 2000 U.S. App. LEXIS 5987 (10th Cir. 2000) **Statute:** ADA

Explanation: After being convicted for a number of charges, including reckless driving and violating a protection order, a **police officer** was terminated. She stated that her actions had stemmed from her impairments and provided a doctor's note on the matter. She claimed she had not been accommodated, but the court noted that the city had offered her positions that she turned down and the officer had failed to contribute to the interactive process of determining an accommodation, relieving the city of liability.

Disability: Chronic fatigue syndrome, fibromyalgia

Accommodation Requested: Permanent assignment to day shift

Accommodation Required: Maybe **Accommodation Adequate:** N/A

Citation: *Holt v. Olmsted Twp. Bd. of Trustees,* 43 F. Supp. 2d 812 (N.D. Ohio 1998) **Statute:** ADA

Explanation: A **dispatcher** with numerous health issues requested accommodation in the form of consistent shift assignments. The employer provided these for a while, but became concerned about the feelings of the other employees and ceased the accommodation. The court held that a permanent assignment to the day shift may not be an undue hardship for the employer just because other employees will be disgruntled that they will be forced to work less desired shifts. The employer has to prove more than disapproval by other employees.

Disability: Polyneuropathy

Accommodation Requested: Assignment to court room duty

Accommodation Required: Maybe **Accommodation Adequate:** Yes

Citation: *Shannon v. Cook County Sheriff's Merit Bd.,* 1998 U.S. Dist. LEXIS 4859 (N.D. Ill. 1998) **Statute:** ADA

Explanation: A **deputy sheriff** who required sedentary work but was not pleased with the accommodation she was provided. "Here, Plaintiff pleads herself out of her ADA claim. She alleges that her condition, Polyneuropathy, allows her to perform a sedentary job, but that Defendants did not accommodate her alleged disability. At the same time, she also alleges that she is currently assigned to a sedentary job in which her duties require her to sit at a desk and record information in a notebook. Plaintiff also asserts that her disability can be reasonably accommodated only if she is assigned to a court room as a Deputy Sheriff. The ADA, however, does not require Plaintiff's employer to grant Plaintiff's request for a particular job. Defendants need only reasonably accommodate her requirement for a sedentary job."

Disability: Charcot-Marie-Tooth disease, hand tremors

Accommodation Requested: Limited to assignments not requiring firearm proficiency

Accommodation Required: No **Accommodation Adequate:** N/A

Citation: *Johnson v. Maryland,* 940 F. Supp. 873 (D. Md. 1996) **Statute:** ADA

Explanation: A **corrections officer** suffered from hand tremors which impacted his ability to be firearm certified. He requested that he only be assigned to positions that didn't require firearm proficiency, but the court held that this was an unreasonable accommodation.

Disability: Epilepsy, frequent nausea

Accommodation Requested: Duty limited to specific positions

Accommodation Required: Maybe **Accommodation Adequate:** N/A

Citation: *Vazquez v. Bedsole,* 888 F. Supp. 727 (E.D.N.C. 1995) **Statute:** ADA

Explanation: After sustaining an injury that led to permanent problems and a number of surgeries, the plaintiff was demoted from **deputy sheriff**. The sheriff believed that the employee could no longer perform her duties. Plaintiff identified a number of positions she could hold despite her injury, and the court held that she could proceed with her claim.

MENTAL OR PSYCHOLOGICAL DISORDERS

Disability: Insomnia, severe migraines, depression

Accommodation Requested: Modification of work schedule

Accommodation Required: Yes **Accommodation Adequate:** Maybe

Citation: *Maes v. City of Española*, 29 AD Cases 216 (D.N.M. 2014) **Statute:** ADA

Explanation: Former city **corrections officer**, who was medically restricted from working "graveyard" shift due to insomnia and migraine headaches, could proceed to trial with her ADA failure-to-accommodate claim based on her supervisors' refusal to excuse her from such a shift. The court noted that the officer was able to perform the essential job functions if not required to work after midnight, that supervisors were aware of her restrictions, and that City did not state a valid reason for its refusal to provide reasonable accommodation or otherwise show any undue hardship.

Disability: Depression, perceived mental impairment/fear of fire

Accommodation Requested: Reinstatement to fire suppression unit

Accommodation Required: No **Accommodation Adequate:** N/A

Citation: *City of Houston v. Proler,* 29 AD Cases 1721 (Tex. 2014) **Statute:** ADA

Explanation: The court held that the fire department was not required to provide a **firefighter** with any accommodations, as his disqualification from one job was insufficient to constitute the impairment of a major life activity and he was therefore not disabled.

Disability: Anxiety, depression, insomnia

Accommodation Requested: Reduction of shift length to 8 hours

Accommodation Required: Maybe **Accommodation Adequate:** N/A

Citation: *Williams v. Ala. Dep't of Corr.*, 29 AD Cases 1280 (N.D. Ala. 2014) **Statute:** ADA

Explanation: A **correctional officer** had repeated issues with calling in due to medication he was taking for his problems. He requested his shifts be shortened to accommodate him, but the prison refused. The court permitted the accommodation question to move forward to trial.

Disability: PTSD

Accommodation Requested: Reinstatement

Accommodation Required: Yes **Accommodation Adequate:** Yes

Citation: *Diaz v. City of Philadelphia,* 2014 U.S. App. LEXIS 8299 (3d Cir. 2014) **Statute:** ADA

Explanation: Police officer Diaz had taken leave to treat a number of medical issues. Upon her return, she was accommodated by placement in the CCTV unit. After a physical altercation with a co-worker, Diaz was relocated to a patrol unit. Officer Diaz expressed concern regarding her PTSD medication and its impact on her reaction time. She was placed on "no duty" status and not provided pay or benefits. After six months of "no duty" leave Diaz failed to request further leave and did not come to work. The court held that she was reasonably accommodated by this leave as well as the opportunity to renew that leave.

Disability: Unspecified "psychological problems"

Accommodation Requested: Unclear

Accommodation Required: No **Accommodation Adequate:** N/A

Citation: *Brumfield v. City of Chicago,* 735 F.3d 619 (7th Cir. 2013) **Statute:** ADA; Rehabilitation Act

Explanation: "It follows that an employer need not accommodate a disability that is irrelevant to an employee's ability to perform the essential functions of her job—not because such an accommodation might be unreasonable, but because the employee is fully qualified for the job without accommodation and therefore is not entitled to an accommodation in the first place." The real issue was the **police officer's** attendance and misbehavior, both of which led to her termination.

Disability: PTSD

Accommodation Requested: Indoor duty

Accommodation Required: Yes **Accommodation Adequate:** Yes

Citation: *Diaz v. City of Philadelphia,* 26 AD Cases 697 (E.D. Pa. 2012) **Statute:** ADA

Explanation: Former **police officer's** accommodation request seeking restricted indoor duty, the court found, was not reasonable in view of her poor attendance record and disciplinary suspension during her prior indoor-duty assignment. The officer had been diagnosed with post-traumatic stress disorder (PTSD) directly due to supervisor's sexual harassment. Her physician verified that she was unable to serve in any active duty role, and the court concluded that the officer was reasonably accommodated by the City with a grant of temporary unpaid leave.

Disability: ADD

Accommodation Requested: Return to active duty

Accommodation Required: Maybe **Accommodation Adequate:** Maybe

Citation: *Weaving v. City of Hillsboro,* 26 AD Cases 229 (D. Or. 2012) **Statute:** ADA

Explanation: Hillsboro Oregon **police sergeant** with attention deficit hyperactivity disorder (ADHD) was not entitled to summary judgment in his favor on his failure-to-accommodate claim, nor was the City on its asserted defenses to his suit. The court denied both cross-motions for summary judgment and ruled that matter must proceed to trial on the disputed facts. The City argued that his request for return to active duty was not reasonable and may have posed an undue hardship, citing his alleged misconduct when interacting with his subordinates, "described by numerous individuals . . . as tyrannical, unapproachable, non-communicative, belittling and demeaning, threatening/intimidating, arrogant and vindictive" which had resulted in harassment complaints.

Disability: Depression and anxiety

Accommodation Requested: Additional training, counseling

Accommodation Required: Yes **Accommodation Adequate:** Yes

Citation: *Lucke v. Multnomah County*, 21 AD Cases 538 (D. Or. 2008) **Statute:** ADA

Explanation: The court found that Multnomah County had reasonably accommodated a former county sheriff's **corrections deputy** with depression and anxiety. Within one day of learning of her impairments, the county contacted the deputy regarding her need for accommodation, she received her requested accommodations of additional training, and she was offered counseling.

Disability: Depression

Accommodation Requested: Leave of absence, job transfer

Accommodation Required: Yes **Accommodation Adequate:** Maybe

Citation: *Williams v. Philadelphia Housing Auth. Police Dept.*, 380 F.3d 751 (3d Cir. 2004) **Statute:** ADA

Explanation: A housing authority may have failed to reasonably accommodate a former **police officer** who was restricted from carrying a firearm because of his depression. The court denied the employer's motion for dismissal, finding that a jury might appropriately conclude that the housing authority's failure to transfer him to a job in radio or the training unit was a failure to reasonably accommodate.

Disability: Bipolar disorder

Accommodation Requested: Transfer to another department

Accommodation Required: Maybe **Accommodation Adequate:** N/A

Citation: *Bradford v. City of Chicago,* 308 F. Supp. 2d 895 (N.D. Ill. 2004) **Statute:** ADA

Explanation: "[T]he ADA does not require an employer to transfer an employee to avoid working with certain supervisors or co-workers." The **city administrative assistant** requested to be transferred to another department "because the staff at the DOT viewed him as mentally disturbed, which caused him stress and worsened his condition." The court held that the employer was not required to make such an extensive accommodation.

Disability: Severe depression

Accommodation Requested: Modification of work schedule

Accommodation Required: Yes **Accommodation Adequate:** N/A

Citation: *Brown v. City of Tucson*, 336 F.3d 1181 (9th Cir. 2003) **Statute:** ADA

Explanation: Former **police detective** instructed by supervisor to discontinue prescribed medications had a valid claim for an actionable threat qualifying as "interference" under ADA. The detective had been excused from nighttime call-out duty as an accommodation for her depression. But her supervisor later demanded that she stop taking her medications and instead perform nighttime call-out duty *or* face demotion or forced retirement. The City argued that employers are obligated to make reasonable efforts to determine appropriate accommodations. But the Ninth Circuit ruled that ordering an employee to choose between foregoing previously granted accommodation or face adverse employment consequences cannot be interpreted as a reasonable effort to determine an appropriate accommodation.

Disability: Stress, anxiety

Accommodation Requested: Indefinite leave

Accommodation Required: No **Accommodation Adequate:** Yes

Citation: *Hopkins v. City of Bothell,* 2003 Wash.App. LEXIS 1151 (Wash. Ct. App. 2003) **Statute:** ADA

Explanation: A **police officer** with severe anxiety and stress took leave. He continued to be completely unable to work, and was told to either retire or he would be terminated. The officer could not provide an expected return date. Even though the employee had unused medical leave remaining when he was asked to retire, the employer did not have to let him use the entirely of his leave. His doctor indicated that it was unclear when he would be well enough to return, and the department was not required to grant him indefinite leave.

Disability: Urological condition, claustrophobia

Accommodation Requested: Reassignment

Accommodation Required: Yes **Accommodation Adequate:** No

Citation: *Hall v. Claussen,* 6 Fed. Appx. 655, (10th Cir. 2001) **Statute:** ADA

Explanation: While an employer is not required to promote an employee in order to accommodate them, they must look for positions that would constitute a lateral transfer and determine that none are available before offering a position that would constitute a demotion. Furthermore, even though the court did not ultimately determine that the employee's claustrophobia was a disability, the fact that the employer tried to reassign a **deputy sheriff** to a position that triggered problems with that fear could be evaluated in determining whether or not the accommodation was reasonable.

Disability: Psychotic disorder

Accommodation Requested: Reinstatement

Accommodation Required: Maybe **Accommodation Adequate:** Yes

Citation: *Wilson v. City of Itta Bena,* 1999 U.S. Dist. LEXIS 14493 (N.D. **Statute:** ADA

Miss. 1999)

Explanation: A **police officer** was hospitalized and diagnosed with a psychotic disorder. He was then terminated. He tried to get his job back and provided documentation of his condition. However, he did not request an accommodation until several months after he was terminated. The court held that this was too late to request an accommodation.

Disability: Stress, anxiety, depression

Accommodation Requested: Indefinite leave

Accommodation Required: No **Accommodation Adequate:** N/A

Citation: *Davidson v. Atlantic City Police Dep't,* 1999 U.S. Dist. LEXIS 13553 (D.N.J. 1999) **Statute:** ADA

Explanation: A suspended **police officer** requested extended sick leave to deal with psychological problems he had developed. The request was denied. The court held that demanding the employer provide indefinite leave is not reasonable. The requirements of the ADA focus on the ability of the employee to perform their job in the present with accommodation, not at some unspecified time in the future.

Disability: Depression, mixed personality disorder

Accommodation Requested: Reassignment

Accommodation Required: No **Accommodation Adequate:** N/A

Citation: *Lang v. City of Maplewood,* 574 N.W.2d 451 (Minn. Ct. App. 1998) **Statute:** Minnesota Human Rights Act (MHRA)

Explanation: After he was diagnosed with a mental disorder and brain malformation (which was corrected but did not fully remedy his problems), a **police officer** was terminated. Doctors stated that he was permanently incapable of functioning as an officer. He applied for and received benefits, but challenged his termination on the grounds that he should have be given another position. The court held, "No reasonable accommodation would have permitted Lang to perform his job as a police officer. The City is not required under MHRA to provide alternative employment for Lang."

Disability: Depression, hypertension

Accommodation Requested: Formal notice of why he received his requested shifts

Accommodation Required: No **Accommodation Adequate:** Yes

Citation: *Krocka v. Bransfield,* 969 F. Supp. 1073 (N.D. Ill. 1997) **Statute:** ADA

Explanation: A **police officer** received the shifts he requested as an accommodation. The employer was not required to provide him with formal notice of the accommodation or why he had been receiving the shifts he wanted. The fact that he got the accommodation was enough and he was not entitled to "official" notification.

Disability: Depression

Accommodation Requested: Reinstatement as a police officer

Accommodation Required: Yes **Accommodation Adequate:** No

Citation: *Department of Pub. Safety & Corrections, Office of State Police v. Mensman,* 671 So.2d 319 (La. Ct. App. 1996) **Statute:** Appeal of State Police Commission decision

Explanation: A **police officer** repeatedly took unreported, unauthorized breaks and would fail to report for duty. His superiors would not accommodate his attempts to engage in therapy and they attempted to fire him. The court upheld the Commission's decision to reduce his termination to a suspension.

Disability: Paranoid personality disorder

Accommodation Requested: Reinstatement or to be placed on leave until an administrative position became available

Accommodation Required: No **Accommodation Adequate:** No

Citation: *Lassiter v. Reno,* 1996 U.S. App. LEXIS 13138 (4th Cir. 1996)

Statute: Rehabilitation Act

Explanation: A **U.S. Marshal** believed that he should have been accommodated by "allowing him to return to work and regain the right to carry a weapon after periodic psychiatric evaluations" or "to transfer [him] to an administrative position in which he did not have to carry a firearm, or to place [him] on a leave of absence until an administrative position became available." However, neither were reasonable accommodations because an employee must be able to perform their job at the time during which they would have accommodations, not at some point in the future after accommodations have been provided.

Disability: PTSD

Accommodation Requested: Reinstatement

Accommodation Required: No

Accommodation Adequate: N/A

Citation: *Hughes v. City of Malden,* 1994 Mass. Super. LEXIS 122 (Mass. Super. Ct. 1994)

Statute: Mass. Gen. Laws ch. 151B, § 4(16)

Explanation: A **firefighter** had a traumatic experience at the scene of a fire which led to PTSD that interfered with his work. He was ultimately deemed unfit for duty, and the department attempted to retire him involuntarily. When that failed, he was terminated. He sued for, among other things, reinstatement. However, the court held that the firefighter had offered no possible reasonable accommodation and that he was completely unqualified for the position. His termination was upheld.

Disability: Bipolar disorder

Accommodation Requested: Reinstatement conditioned on medication monitoring

Accommodation Required: No

Accommodation Adequate: N/A

Citation: *Hogarth v. Thornburgh,* 833 F. Supp. 1077 (S.D.N.Y. 1993)

Statute: Rehabilitation Act

Explanation: The FBI did not have to re-hire a former **FBI clerk** who had psychotic episodes due to his bipolar disorder. He had suffered recurring delusions and had at times lost touch with reality. Given the sensitive nature of the information he would be dealing with as a communications operator the FBI was not obligated to give him his job back, and were not obligated to monitor his medication consumption to ensure he was complying with his treatment. The risk that he would lose touch with reality again and potentially bring others into harm was too high to require his reinstatement.

Disability: Depression

Accommodation Requested: Reinstatement, light duty

Accommodation Required: No

Accommodation Adequate: N/A

Citation: *Md. Comm'n on Human Rels. v. Mayor & Balt.,* 86 Md. App. 167 (Md. Ct. Spec. App. 1991)

Statute: Rehabilitation Act

Explanation: A **police officer** expressed suicidal ideation to another officer while off-duty. She was put on leave, evaluated by doctors, and deemed not fit to be an officer. One officer suggested she be placed on the phones, but the court held that such an accommodation would be so drastic as to fundamentally alter the employee's essential duties, which they were not required to do.

SUBSTANCE ABUSE

Disability: Alcoholism

Accommodation Requested: Policies

Accommodation Required: Maybe

Accommodation Adequate: Yes

Citation: *Knowles v. Sheriff,* 460 Fed. Appx. 833 (11th Cir. 2012)

Statute: ADA

Explanation: Alcoholic former **deputy sheriff's** failure-to-accommodate claim was dismissed, despite his allegation that he would have voluntarily sought employee assistance program treatment if not for "communication breakdown" as to whether he was to be directed to enter a program. Such a communication breakdown, the court ruled, was not evidence of bad faith or unwillingness to accommodate on the part of the sheriff's office.

Disability: Alcoholism

Accommodation Requested: Reinstatement

Accommodation Required: No

Accommodation Adequate: Yes

Citation: *Maull v. Div. of State Police,* 141 F. Supp. 2d 463 (D. Del. 2001)

Statute: ADA

Explanation: The employer had granted a **state trooper** leave to complete a treatment program, but was still justified in terminating him due to the risk he posed to the public's safety. He had engaged in extensive misconduct, and even though much of it stemmed from his alcoholism, the department wasn't required to tolerate this behavior. Furthermore, they were not required to monitor an alcoholic officer to ensure he was prepared to respond to calls at any time.

Disability: Alcoholism, drug use

Accommodation Requested: Continued employment

Accommodation Required: Yes

Accommodation Adequate: Yes

Citation: *Van Ever v. New York State Dep't of Correctional Servs.,* 2000 U.S. Dist. LEXIS 16960 (S.D.N.Y. 2000)

Statute: ADA

Explanation: A **corrections officer** was terminated for his abuse of alcohol and mood-altering substances. He requested continued employment that accommodated rehabilitative treatment. "Alcoholism is not a per se disability under the ADA," but employers can provide unpaid leave in order to enter a treatment program. Here, the employer provided the employee with three leaves of absence to complete rehabilitation programs. When the employee continued to have issues the employer was not required to do more than they already had and were permitted to let the employee go.

Disability: Alcoholism

Accommodation Requested: Reassignment to position closer to his treatment facility, rearrange schedule to facilitate treatment

Accommodation Required: No **Accommodation Adequate:** N/A

Citation: *Roberts v. New York State Dep't of Correctional Servs.,* 63 F. Supp. 2d 272 (W.D.N.Y. 1999) **Statute:** ADA

Explanation: Employers are not required to provide accommodation for employees whose lives are not impaired by their illness, as that fails to rise to the status of a disability requiring accommodation. In this case, a **corrections officer** wanted to be transferred to a facility closer to where he received treatment for his alcoholism or to rearrange his schedule to make travelling 60 miles to treatment less burdensome. However, employers don't need to make a situation less burdensome when the alcoholism doesn't rise to the level of a disability.

Disability: Alcoholism, depression

Accommodation Requested: Transfer to another facility within the department of corrections

Accommodation Required: No **Accommodation Adequate:** N/A

Citation: *Wallin v. Minnesota Dep't of Corrections,* 974 F. Supp. 1234 (D. Minn. 1997) **Statute:** ADA

Explanation: A **corrections officer** was almost discharged for attacking his girlfriend, but was required to complete a treatment program and stay chemical-free for three years. He had problems with his coworkers after his return, and held that he was mistreated based on his disability and requested a transfer to accommodate his condition. The court stated that transfer to another facility would not have accommodated the employee's specific disability; he still would have performed the same duties as he had before. A transfer would therefore not have been a reasonable accommodation.

Disability: Alcoholism

Accommodation Requested: Continued employment as police officer

Accommodation Required: No **Accommodation Adequate:** N/A

Citation: *Antoine v. Department of Pub. Safety & Corrections,* 681 So. 2d 1282 (La. Ct. App. 1996)

Statute: ADA

Explanation: A **policer officer** reported for duty under the influence of alcohol, eventually blowing a .191 % BAC. The officer had been warned before about the consequences of showing up to work drunk and had been offered assistance for his drinking problem. "[T]he ADA permits an employer to terminate one under the influence of alcohol at the workplace and provides that an employer may require that employees not be under the influence of alcohol at the workplace."

Disability: Alcoholism

Accommodation Requested: Continued employment, counselling

Accommodation Required: No

Accommodation Adequate: N/A

Citation: *Rollison v. Gwinnett County,* 865 F. Supp. 1564 (N.D. Ga. 1994)

Statute: ADA; Rehabilitation Act

Explanation: **Police officer** repeatedly engaged in fights and other negative conduct while off duty due to alcohol consumption. "While alcohol may have caused the off-duty problems, the ADA expressly provides that an employer may hold an employee to the same standards for employment or job performance as all other employees, even if the unsatisfactory performance is related to the alcoholism of the employee. The facts of this case fall squarely within the ADA's treatment of alcoholic employees who do not perform up to the standards required by their employer. Under the ADA the employer is allowed to terminate and not accommodate an alcoholic employee, if the employee does not perform up to the same standard as all other employees, even if the behavior is related to the employee's alcoholism."

Disability: Alcoholism

Accommodation Requested: Reinstatement

Accommodation Required: No

Accommodation Adequate: Yes

Citation: *Little v. FBI,* 1 F.3d 255, 1993 U.S. App. LEXIS 20371 (4th Cir. 1993)

Statute: Rehabilitation Act

Explanation: A **FBI agent** entered an outpatient rehabilitation program after conviction for a DUI. He later relapsed while on duty and went to an inpatient program. His relapse was a violation of his probation and also constituted misconduct. He was terminated, stating he had recovered. The FBI had already permitted him to go to rehab and was permitted to fire him.

Disability: Alcoholism

Accommodation Requested: Continued employment as police officer

Accommodation Required: No

Accommodation Adequate: N/A

Citation: *Shields v. City of Shreveport,* 579 So. 2d 961 (La. Ct. App. 1991)

Statute: Rehabilitation Act

Explanation: Two **police officers** were dismissed after consuming alcohol on duty while providing security during a high school reunion. They were determined to be alcoholics, but the court upheld their termination as based not on their alcoholism but their misconduct and the fact that they broke numerous rules throughout the event. "It appears from the plain language of the statute that only alcoholics . . . whose problems are under control are protected from discriminatory treatment."

Disability: Drug addiction

Accommodation Requested: Reinstatement

Accommodation Required: No

Accommodation Adequate: N/A

Citation: *Desper v. Montgomery County,* 727 F. Supp. 959 (E.D. Pa. 1990)

Statute: Rehabilitation Act

Explanation: A police department was not required to accommodate a **narcotics officer** who was addicted to drugs. As a drug user he was not qualified for the position. Accommodating him in that particular program would not have been reasonable.

MISCELLANEOUS DISORDERS AND DISEASES

Disability: Sleep Disorder

Accommodation Requested: Excused Tardiness Procedure

Accommodation Required: Maybe **Accommodation Adequate:** Maybe

Citation: *Kuehn v. Snohomish Cnty.*, 2015 AD Cases 180573 (Wash. Ct. App. 2015) **Statute:** WLAD

Explanation: State **Road Maintenance Worker** was accommodated by the County for his sleep disorder by allowing him excused tardiness instances when he could show it was directly related to his sleep disorder. However, after six unexcused tardiness instances, Worker was terminated. Although the parties did not dispute that the accommodation was reasonable, the Court dismissed the complaint on statute of limitations grounds.

Disability: Shy Bladder Syndrome

Accommodation Requested: Unknown

Accommodation Required: Maybe **Accommodation Adequate:** No

Citation: *Oberti v. Pac. Mar. Ass'n, et al.*, 31 AD Cases 1000 (W.D. Wash. 2015) **Statute:** WLAD

Explanation: Longshoreman unable to produce urine during supervised drug test because of "shy bladder syndrome." District Court allowed worker's claim for failure to accommodate to survive summary judgment because "shy bladder syndrome" qualified as a "disability" under WLAD (although not the ADA). The court did not state what would constitute a reasonable accommodation.

Disability: Breast cancer

Accommodation Requested: Leave of absence

Accommodation Required: Yes **Accommodation Adequate:** Yes

Citation: *Moore v. Maryland Dep't of Public Safety & Correctional Services,* **Statute:** Rehabilitation Act

27 AD Cases 849 (D. Md. 2013)

Explanation: State prison **corrections officer**, who was placed on unpaid medical leave during treatment for breast cancer, could not proceed with a failure-to-accommodate claim. The officer had been granted eight-month leave, despite state law requiring payroll separation after six months. She repeatedly stated that she did not know when she could return to work; her request for another leave extension was determined by the court to not be reasonable. It also noted that she had reinstated at new location without reduction in pay or grade.

Disability: Dyslexia

Accommodation Requested: Prove "reader" to help him during entrance exam

Accommodation Required: No

Accommodation Adequate: N/A

Citation: *Bageris v. Brandon Twp.*, 264 Mich. App. 156 (Mich. Ct. App. 2004)

Statute: Michigan's Persons With Disabilities Civil Rights Act

Explanation: A **part-time firefighter** was required to take a written test as part of his application to become a full-time firefighter. He asked to have a reader due to difficulties with test-taking. He was not provided with a reader. The court held that he failed to provide adequate notice of his disability by simply stating that he had difficulty with tests.

Disability: Incontinence

Accommodation Requested: Work specific shifts

Accommodation Required: Yes

Accommodation Adequate: Yes

Citation: *Andrews v. Virginia,* 2000 U.S. App. LEXIS 24264 (4th Cir. 2000)

Statute: ADA

Explanation: Employees are not permitted to limit what options they are provided by employers. Here the **corrections officer** was offered multiple options as accommodations. When she picked one and it did not work out, she was not entitled to demand a specific type of accommodation that she preferred.

Disability: Had previous health problems including passing out, may have been perceived to have a disability

Accommodation Requested: Reassignment/light duty

Accommodation Required: Yes

Accommodation Adequate: No

Citation: *Gilbert v. City of St. Charles,* 1999 U.S. Dist. LEXIS 4095 (N.D. Ill. 1999)

Statute: ADA

Explanation: A **police officer** provided his employer with a note on his doctor's prescription pad requesting light duty, though the officer himself never specifically requested accommodation. An employee does not have to clamor aggressively in requesting an accommodation, the employer needs to meet the employee halfway. It has to see if any light duty positions are available. Furthermore, "[w]hile the City was not required to indefinitely "provide a job, but not require that [he] regularly perform it," it was required to engage in an interactive process to determine whether Gilbert was entitled to a medical leave and, if so, the conditions and length of the leave."

Disability: Not stated

Accommodation Requested: Permanent assignment to light-duty position

Accommodation Required: No

Accommodation Adequate: N/A

Citation: *Fasone v. Clinton Twp.,* 1998 U.S. App. LEXIS 7070 (6th Cir. 1998)

Statute: ADA

Explanation: A **firefighter** incapable of fighting fires requested assignment to the position of Fire Prevention Officer. However, there was no vacant fire prevention position. The employer would have had to create a new position for the employee. The court held that the employer was not obligated to create a new position to accommodate the firefighter, as that would be unreasonable.

Disability: Impaired hearing in left ear

Accommodation Requested: Continued employment as police officer

Accommodation Required: Yes **Accommodation Adequate:** Yes

Citation: *Karbusicky v. City of Park Ridge,* 950 F. Supp. 878 (N.D. Ill. 1997) **Statute:** ADA

Explanation: Plaintiff **police officer** had very poor hearing in one ear which led to difficulty performing his duties. He was offered a series of accommodations, including a hearing aid, before he was transferred to a Community Service Officer position. "While reassignment is to be considered only after other accommodations within the employee's current position are attempted, as mentioned above, defendant has made such attempts in the instant case by providing or offering to provide hearing aids that plaintiff regards as ineffective. Plaintiff has suggested no other method of accommodation that he could be offered in light of the fact, as found by the court in section III above, that plaintiff cannot perform the essential functions of a police officer. Although plaintiff, as a CSO, may not carry a gun or arrest persons as a police officer may, he maintains the same pay scale and benefits that he did as a police officer. Based on these uncontested facts, the court finds that defendant's decision to reassign plaintiff to the position of CSO is a reasonable accommodation as a matter of law."

Disability: Unclear, multiple plaintiffs

Accommodation Requested: Reassignment

Accommodation Required: Yes **Accommodation Adequate:** No

Citation: *United States v. City & County of Denver,* 943 F. Supp. 1304 (D. Colo. 1996) **Statute:** ADA

Explanation: Plaintiff **police officers** were placed in limited duty after being injured with instructions to apply for disability retirement. They sued because the department refused to reassign them. The city countered that reassignment would be an undue hardship on them. The court "stated the term included "an individual with a disability, who, with or without reasonable accommodation, can perform the essential functions of the employment position that such individual holds or desires" and "reasonable accommodation" may include "reassignment to a vacant position." These positions could include "a non-patrol vacant position, not having as an essential function, the power to make a forcible arrest or fire a weapon."

Disability: Chronic fatigue syndrome

Accommodation Requested: Transfer to courthouse position

Accommodation Required: Yes **Accommodation Adequate:** No

Citation: *Woodson v. Cook County Sheriff,* 1996 U.S. Dist. LEXIS 15475 (N.D. Ill. 1996) **Statute:** ADA

Explanation: Instead of providing a deputy sheriff with her requested transfer or any other alternative, the employer increased the employee's workload until she resigned. The employee was permitted to continue to trial on her failure to accommodate claim.

Disability: Pseudofolliculitis barbae ("PFB")

Accommodation Requested: To be free from clean-shaven requirement

Accommodation Required: No **Accommodation Adequate:** N/A

Citation: *Fitzpatrick v. City of Atlanta,* 2 F.3d 1112 (11th Cir. 1993) **Statute:** ADA; Rehabilitation Act

Explanation: The fire department implemented a policy requiring all **firefighters** to be clean shaven in order to ensure that their SCBA gear was properly sealed to their faces. A number of firefighters struggled with PFB, which prevented them from being clean shaven. The court upheld the policy based on the necessity of a proper SCBA seal to the face and the fact that the firefighters challenging the policy provided no reasonable alternative to the requirement.

Disability: Bleeding from nose and mouth every time exposed to smoke

Accommodation Requested: Transfer to another position

Accommodation Required: No **Accommodation Adequate:** N/A

Citation: *Ramie v. Department of Fire,* **Statute:** La. R.S. 46:2254

617 So. 2d 92, (La. Ct. App. 1993)

Explanation: After he was terminated because he was unable to fight fires, a **firefighter** claimed the department had failed to accommodate him when he was not transferred to another position in the fire suppression division or another job with the city. The court upheld his termination and stated that the department had not failed to accommodate him. Everyone in the fire suppression division needed to be able to fight fires and those in charge of the department did not have the authority to transfer him elsewhere in the city. Furthermore, there were no other positions available in the department when he was terminated.

Disability: HIV/AIDS

Accommodation Requested: Unclear

Accommodation Required: Yes

Accommodation Adequate: Yes

Citation: *Severino v. North Ft. Myers Fire Control Dist.,* 935 F.2d 1179 (11th Cir. 1991)

Statute: Rehabilitation Act

Explanation: After being diagnosed with HIV/AIDS a **firefighter** willingly resigned. He was offered "light duty" but complained about the responsibilities he was given, calling them "demeaning." He became confrontational about his position and was fired after he refused to perform his duties. The employer had made reasonable accommodations and upheld the employee's termination for his behavior.

Chapter 12

Corporate and Tax Law Issues Applicable to Public Safety Unions and Their Members

A. Introduction

This chapter addresses corporate issues that apply to labor unions — specifically their rights and responsibilities under the Washington nonprofit corporation law. It also covers tax issues which pertain to the union as an entity. And, finally, it addresses tax law rules that have particular application to public safety employees.

B. The Law of Nonprofit Corporations

Although there is no particular law that says a labor organization must incorporate, there are certainly some strong reasons for doing so. Incorporation limits the liabilities of the members who associate for the purposes of the corporation. If no limited liability corporate entity existed, each of the members of the association could become joint and severally liable. Furthermore, as will be discussed later, the nonprofit corporation statute provides some additional civil law protection.

In order to take advantage of nonprofit corporate status, the entity must incorporate with the Secretary of State and update relevant corporation information annually as required by the Secretary of State. *If those formalities are not addressed, the corporate status may be lost.*

Directors of the corporation owe certain duties to the members and the corporation. Those duties are set forth in RCW 24.03.127:

> A director shall perform the duties of a director, including the duties as a member of any committee of the board upon which the director may serve, in good faith, in a manner such director believes to be in the best interests of the corporation, and with such care, including reasonable inquiry, as an ordinarily prudent person in a like position would use under similar circumstances.
>
> In performing the duties of a director, a director shall be entitled to reply on information, opinions, reports, or statements, including financial statements and

other financial data, in each case prepared or presented by:

(1) On or more officers or employees of the corporation whom the director believes to be reliable and competent in the matter presented;

(2) Counsel, public accountants, or other persons as to matters which the director believes to be within such person's professional or expert competence; or

(3) A committee of the board upon which the director does not serve, duly designated in accordance with a provision in the articles of incorporation or bylaws, as to matters within its designated authority, which committee the director believes to merit confidence; so long as, in any such case, the director acts in good faith, after reasonable inquiry when the need therefore is indicated by circumstances and without knowledge that would cause such reliance to be unwarranted.

In short, this statute requires that directors owe *care*, *loyalty* and *obedience* to the corporation. A breach of these fiduciary duties may be the basis for action by the corporation or its members to compel the director to act consistent with the duties or to have a decision of the board set aside. Third parties not part of the corporation cannot enforce these obligations. Nor are these the types of duties that, if breached, would expose the director to financial liability, except in cases where there was some self-dealing at the entity's expense.

Labor organizations should also be aware that, as a legal entity, they may have tort liability under certain circumstances. If, for example, a labor organization hosts an annual party and overconsumption of alcohol leads to a personal injury, there is a possibility of tort liability — the same as for the sponsor of any such event.

Historically, under the common law, nonprofit corporations were completely immunized from any liability. Over time, the common law immunity doctrine eroded until, eventually, the courts held that nonprofit corporations could be held liable to the same extent as any other person or entity.

This erosion of immunity was finally clarified and addressed in 1986 when the nonprofit corporation statute was amended to add:

> (1) Except as provided in subsection (2) of this section, a member of the board of directors or an officer of any nonprofit corporation is not individually liable for any discretionary decision or failure to make a discretionary decision within his or her official capacity as director or officer unless the decision or failure to decide constitutes gross negligence.
>
> (2) Nothing in this section shall limit or modify in any manner the duties or liabilities of a director of officer of a corporation to the corporation of the corporation's members.[1]

Under state law, members of the board will be automatically entitled to indemnification *unless* the corporation specifically amends its articles of incorporation to not indemnify the officers.

The stated standard of "gross negligence" gives an association and its board of directors a fair degree of immunity from civil lawsuits. But not absolute immunity. A jury could find the "gross negligence" standard to have been breached in certain limited situations.

This raises the subject of indemnification and insurance coverage. Under state law, members of the board will be automatically entitled to indemnification *unless* the corporation specifically amends its articles of incorporation to not indemnify the officers:

> Unless the articles of incorporation provide otherwise, a corporation [or nonprofit corporation] is obligated to indemnify a director "who was wholly successful, on the merits or otherwise, in defense of any proceeding to which the director was a party because of being a director on the corporation . . . ." The scope of

[1] RCW 4.24.264.

indemnification does not cover claims the corporation might have against the director though.

Occasionally insurance companies attempt to sell officer and director indemnification liability policies. There is reason to be skeptical whether these policies are needed. But there are also reasons to consider such policies.

The fundamental question is whether insurance policies would advance the interests of the board. One of the common misconceptions is that such policies protect the entity and the board members whenever the association is sued. But the primary subject of suits against unions, Duty of Fair Representation (DFR) claims, are usually specifically exempted in such policies.

If the labor organization is engaging in some social activities or business activities which might expose it to tort liability, it might be prudent to shop around for an appropriate insurance policy. These policies may or may not be cost effective and for that reason it would also be prudent to shop around for different insurance brokers. But to the extent the union is seeking legal protection for it and its officers for the exercise of its representational duties, it will likely find that offered policies do not include such potential liability coverage.

C. Tax Liability of Labor Organizations

Labor organizations have income. Every time a member pays dues to a labor organization it is considered "income" under the Internal Revenue Code. All income is taxable unless, of course, the Internal Revenue Code says it is not taxable.

Labor organizations should file with the IRS to obtain tax exempt status.

This is where the question of tax exempt status comes in. The Internal Revenue Code allows for "charitable organizations" to obtain a tax exempt status provided they fulfill the paperwork requirements. There is a specific exemption which applies to labor organizations. That provision is Internal Revenue Code 501(c)(5).

Labor organizations should file with the IRS to obtain tax exempt status. Otherwise, there is a risk that the Internal Revenue Service may decide to proceed against your organization as an entity with taxable earnings. As an enforcement policy, the IRS has not been demanding taxes on all noncompliant nonprofit organizations, but they have done random audits and have made demands that groups file for tax-exempt status. Attention to these details, like annual Secretary of State Corporation updates is simply a necessary part managing an association.

There is a filing fee for filing for nonprofit status and it will need to be paid and filed along with the paperwork. It is important, again, to *file under the § 501(c)(3) provisions.* Section 501(c)(3) is a specific provision applying to labor organizations. Most "charitable" organizations are subject to a very restricted right to engage in political lobbying. Labor organizations are one of the nonprofit entities that Congress expressly allows to lobby while still retaining its tax exempt status. This exemption obviously recognizes the political reality of the purposes of labor organizations.

State tax law is a different matter. There is no *per se* exemption of nonprofits from state tax. Instead, the state tax law exempts a number of activities which nonprofits engage in, but it also recognizes that there are certain other activities which may be taxable. If a labor organization is involved in the sale of items on the side, or other business-type activities, it may be subject to B&O tax or sales taxes.

The bottom line on the tax issue is this — a labor organization should make an arrangement with a well-qualified accountant to ensure that it complies with both the Internal Revenue Code and state tax laws. This of course costs money but could save money in the long run. Because a regular audit of the Association's books is a best practice, retention of a qualified accountant is called for in any event.

There are also a number of tax rules which apply when labor organizations engage in fundraising. There are some complex requirements under the Internal Revenue Code, which may mandate distribution of the raised funds at a certain rate. Once again, a well-qualified accountant is necessary to provide guidance on these sometimes complicated distribution rules.

D. Employee Tax Issues

The tax liability of your members does not immediately create tax liability for the union itself, unlike some of the organizational tax issues discussed immediately above. But in the discharge of collective bargaining duties, a bargaining team will want to be versed in the details of how the tax code affects the taxation of various employee benefits. The fine points of tax law could impact your approach to negotiations.

It is a misconception that all benefits are automatically exempt from taxation. As the IRS explains: "Any fringe benefit you provide is taxable and must be included in the recipient's pay unless the law specifically excludes it."[2] In other words, you have to look to the specifics of the tax code and its identified exclusions rather than assuming that anything that might be labeled a "fringe benefit" is automatically exempt from tax.

1. Tuition Reimbursement

Tuition Reimbursement used to be entirely tax free. In 1996, the Internal Revenue Code was amended and this exemption was lost. Subsequently, though, the exemption was reinstated but with a cap of $5250 per year. The IRS describes the scope of the permitted exemption as follows:

> Educational assistance means amounts you pay or incur for your employees' education expenses. These expenses generally include the cost of books, equipment, fees, supplies, and tuition. However, these expenses do not include the cost of a course or other education involving sports, games, or hobbies, unless the education:
>
> - Has a reasonable relationship to your business, or
>
> - Is required as part of a degree program.
>
> Education expenses do not include the cost of tools or supplies (other than textbooks) your employee is allowed to keep at the end of the course. Nor do they include the cost of lodging, meals, or transportation.[3]

2. Union Dues and Work Expenses

Prior to 1986, when the tax code was substantially overhauled, union dues were routinely deductible. While some may believe that this deduction was entirely eliminated in 1986 Tax Reform Act, in fact, it was not entirely eliminated but was greatly limited. The 1986 amendments altered work related deductions so substantially that, for most employees, the ability to make this deduction was practically eliminated.

Prior to 1986, employees who undertook business related

[2] IRS Publication 15-B.

[3] *Id.*

expenses were allowed to freely deduct the expenses regardless of whether or not they were owners of the business in question. Beginning in 1986, however, Congress changed the rules so that such deductions are allowed *only where they exceed 2% of gross income*. As a practical matter, most working people do not make enough work-related expenditures to cross this threshold. Typically, union dues hover close to 1% of most employee's income and other legitimate work-related deductions are uncommon.

If you have other work-related deductions available sufficient to exceed 2% of gross income, bear this provision in mind. The IRS allows deductibility of certain expenses associated with work such as the purchase of work related equipment. In the event that your uniform allowance or quartermaster system does not fully cover reimbursement of all work tools and equipment, these expenses may also be deductible and could be combined with the union dues to reach the 2% threshold

3. Deductibility of Meals

Despite recurrent myths to the contrary, meals are not considered a deductible expense, absent extraordinary circumstances. Despite some buzz about a 1988 Minnesota case allowing deductible of meals, the IRS has clearly indicated an intent to disallow such expenses.

In *Christey v. U.S.*[4] the Eighth Circuit Court of Appeals did hold on the narrow set of circumstances that meals for Minnesota State Troopers were deductible. The IRS has never embraced this ruling and has declined to follow it for taxpayers residing outside the Eighth Circuit. Other observers have also noted the narrow set of circumstances present that led the court to conclude the meals should be deductible. The troopers were subject to orders limiting their meal options:

> The General Order requires that troopers "eat their meals in a public restaurant adjacent to the highway whenever practical" and "report by radio when they eat and ... advise the telephone number or the code number of the restaurant where they are eating." The restaurant must be open to the public and may not serve liquor. The Order prohibits troopers from eating meals at home during working hours and has been interpreted to prohibit troopers from bringing meals from home and eating in their patrol cars. The Order

[4] 841 F.2d 809 (8th Circuit 1988).

also details the time at which troopers may eat, the time allowed for a meal, and the number of troopers who may eat together. Failure to adhere to these instructions renders troopers subject to reprimand.

Later decisions distinguishing *Christey* have emphasized the restricted restaurant choice forced upon the troopers. They have followed a 1977 decision by the US Supreme Court, *Commissioner v. Kowalski,* which held that a meal allowance extended to New Jersey State troopers, with no restriction on their meal location (or any indication the money was actually spent), was taxable income.[5]

The Ninth Circuit has allowed the deduction in another unusual case involve Los Angeles Firefighters. *Sibla v. IRS*[6] is a 1980 involving an order from the LAFD, in an effort to desegregate on-duty firefighters, compelled all meals to be taken together. Firefighters were required to contribute to the meal fund a daily amount deducted from their paychecks. Distinguishing *Kowalski,* the Ninth Circuit explained: "In the case before us the firefighters were required to eat their meals on the employer's premises, and were required to pay for them whether they ate them or not."[7]

4. Take Home Vehicles

This is an area where there likely is some degree of non-compliance. The problem is not in connection with take-home, marked police vehicles. The law recognizes a specific exemption for "non-personal use vehicles" — those vehicles which by design are more or less unavailable for personal use other than in a minimal manner. This exemption would appear to specifically extend to marked emergency vehicles.

The tax law is complex as to *unmarked* department vehicles. As a general rule, the IRS does not allow an exemption for ordinary commuting. Therefore, in a typical situation, employees who commute to and from work in an unmarked, department vehicle might be subject to taxation on the imputed benefit. This would be calculated at the applicable IRS rate for the total distance from work to home.

In *Pollei v. Commissioner,*[8] the Tenth Circuit held that a car

---

[5] 434 U.S. 77 (1977).
[6] 611 F.2d 1260 (1980).
[7] *Id.* at 1265.

allowance extended to Salt Lake City Police Captains was not taxable. The court explained the circumstances:

> Each command-level officer was given a monthly $250 car allowance. By that same order, petitioners' tours of duty were extended to begin and end when the officers left for work or arrived home in their cars, rather than when they actually arrived at or left from police headquarters. SLCPD provided and installed necessary equipment in each officer's privately-owned vehicle to enable its use as an unmarked police car. Officers were required to notify the police dispatcher before leaving, and on arriving home, and were "on call" during their travel time to and from headquarters. While en route to headquarters or their homes, petitioners were expected to monitor the radio channels to be aware of the ongoing police activities, observe their subordinate officers in the field, patrol the streets, and respond to dispatcher calls for assistance. Petitioners were also required to call in any time they used the unmarked cars, whether they were on or off duty at the time.[9]

Unmarked take home cars or a car allowance program subject to similar response requirements, would likely be recognized as tax exempt. An unmarked take home car program in which personnel were not required to monitor the radio or otherwise respond to calls would likely be taxable.

5. Clothing

This is another area where there might be some degree of noncompliance. There are no tax problems raised where the employer directly provides employees a uniform. The issue concerns clothing "allowances."

If not properly administered and accounted for, a uniform allowance, though, can create a taxable situation.

The IRS has addressed this over the past year by cracking down on clothing allowance taxation. The issue largely turns on

[8] 877 F.2d 838 (10th Cir. 1989).

[9] *Id.* at 839.

whether the employer has adopted an "accountable" allowance program. The IRS has clearly indicated that a uniform is not considered income where the uniform is not adaptable to general use. Therefore, if an employer has a quartermaster system, for example, no tax problems are raised.

If not properly administered and accounted for, a uniform allowance, though, can create a taxable situation. In order to qualify as a deduction, an allowance for the provision of uniforms must meet at least two requirements: (1) the employer must verify that all the allowance is actually used only for allowable uniforms and equipment, and (2) the employer must require that any portion of the allowance not used for permissible items be returned. These are the elements of what is referred to as an "accountable" system.

If both of these qualifications are not met, a uniform allowance is likely a taxable benefit. This is true even if employees use 100% of the allowance to purchase actual uniform and equipment items. What matters when the system is not "accountable" is not how the officers expended the monies, but what the requirements were upon them to spend and "account for" the monies.

Despite common beliefs to the contrary, a clothing allowance for plainclothes personnel is not tax exempt.

If a department is not in compliance with these requirements, a union should consider negotiating to establish a quartermaster system, or advise the employer of the requirements of the tax law and negotiate accountable procedures. On the other hand, many employees actually prefer the freedom associated with non-accountable uniforms allowances even recognizing it subjects the income to tax. In such situations, the uniform allowance may also be wages for LEOFF purposes and would be subject to LEOFF deductions and would count toward the "final average salary" calculations. So there are trade-offs in how such allowances are treated.

Allowances for plainclothes personnel, such as detectives, are far more problematic than most people realize. Despite common beliefs to the contrary, a clothing allowance for plainclothes personnel is not tax exempt. A frequent misconception of the law is that if employers create a receipt and reimbursement method for payment of plainclothes, the purchase of plainclothes becomes a tax-free benefit. This is simply not true.

The only instance in which clothing items are considered

deductible is where they are "unsuitable" for personal use. This will generally encompass uniforms, but it would not encompass suits, ties and shirts purchase for a plainclothes position. Whether or not the employer establishes an "accountable" system for a plainclothes allowance, it is almost certainly going to be deemed taxable by the IRS.

As discussed above, other equipment and uniform items which an employee might buy can, under certain circumstances, be deductible when the employer does not pay for the item. For example, if the employee is required to pay for duty weapon or other necessary equipment, this could be considered an allowable business deduction. The same 2% business deduction requirement that applies to union dues, though, would have to be met here. In other words, the value of such expenses would have to exceed 2% of gross income in a given year in order to reach the threshold to allow the deduction.

6. Industrial Insurance and Insurance Premiums

The taxation of disability insurance and benefits is a bit more complicated, and public safety unions and their members should make some thought-out choices on this subject.

Industrial insurance premiums such as workers compensation and LEOFF II supplement are not taxable. This issue was discussed in greater detail in the section on workers compensation. As discussed in that section, there appears to be widespread misapplication of these payments by public employers. The exemption of workers comp payments and the LEOFF II supplement, as discussed previously, raises the question of whether it is wise to simply turn over your tax exempt L and I check to the employer.

The taxation of disability insurance and benefits is a bit more complicated, and public safety unions and their members should make some thought-out choices on this subject. One way of the other the income associated on such a benefit is going to be taxed, and you have to decide the best way to face that tax.

If the employer pays for the premium, the insurance *premium* is a tax free benefit, but in an instance in which an individual disability is later incurred, and benefits are paid out, the *payout* will be then treated as taxable income. On the other hand, if the employees pay for the premium of out their already taxed wages, a later insurance payout is exempt from taxation.

A different rule applies where the employer, as often is the case, pays for only a portion of the disability insurance premium. In that instance, the benefit is taxed on a "pro rata" basis: The proportion of the premium paid by the employee's post-tax contribution is exempt from tax, and the proportion that was paid as a benefit by the employer is subject to tax.

Life insurance premiums by the employer deemed a tax free benefit but only to a $50,000 maximum. Coverage above that level is taxable income. If the employer pays the premium, for example, $100,000 of coverage, one half of such a benefit would be considered taxable income and is subject to be added to your W-2 report as such.

Health insurance premiums are exempt from taxation, whether paid by the employer or employees. So too are employer contributions. This exemption extends to employer paid premiums for the benefit of the employees and their "qualified relatives." This includes a spouse and dependent children but does not cover "domestic partners." Benefits extended to domestic partners are subject to taxation but in 2013 the IRS announced it would recognize same sex marriages as resulting in a "qualified relative."

Contributions to an MSA VEBA or a regular VEBA include some tax benefits. These contributions are not subject to taxation either going in or going out. As opposed to deferred compensation benefits, in which the income is ultimately taken when the compensation is received on a "deferred" basis, VEBA payouts are never taxed.

This tax exempt potential raises a point for bargaining teams to discuss as they discuss their proposals to structure elements of their compensation. This section notes other tax issues that likewise should be considered by every bargaining team as they prepare for negotiations.

Chapter 13

The Rights and Responsibilities of Labor Organizations and Their Members

A. Introduction

This chapter covers the right of both labor organizations and their members to be free from discrimination and interference by the employer. It also discusses the relationship between the union and its members, especially in connection with the union's duty of fair representation and enforcement of union dues provisions. Case tables identifying PERC rulings on discrimination and interference are set forth in the Appendix of this Chapter.

B. The Right to be Free of Discrimination and Interference

1. The General Nature of the Rights

The collective bargaining statute makes it a ULP for the employer to discriminate against employees based on their union activities or to interfere with their collective bargaining rights. It is also an unfair labor practice for a union to discriminate against members.

The right of employees to be free of "discrimination" and "interference" arises directly from the collective bargaining statute. The Public Employees Collective Bargaining Act (PECBA) is patterned after the National Labor Relations Act, especially in how it defines what constitutes an unfair labor practice. RCW 41.56.140 provides:

> It shall be an unfair labor practice for a public employer:
>
> (1) To interfere with, restrain, or coerce public employees in the exercise of their rights guaranteed by this chapter;
> (2) To control, dominate, or interfere with a bargaining representative;
> (3) To discriminate against a public employee who has filed an unfair labor practice charge;
> (4) To refuse to engage in collective bargaining with the certified exclusive bargaining

representative.

As indicated, it is also a ULP for unions to discriminate against their members. RCW 41.56.150 provides:

> It shall be an unfair labor practice for a bargaining representative:
>
> (1) To interfere with, restrain, or coerce public employees in the exercise of their rights guaranteed by this chapter;
>
> (2) To induce the public employer to commit an unfair labor practice;
>
> (3) To discriminate against a public employee who has filed an unfair labor practice charge;
>
> (4) To refuse to engage in collective bargaining.

Similar ULP provisions exist in the other Washington public collective bargaining law, such as those covering State employees.[1] The prohibition on "refusing to bargain" defined in RCW 41.56.140(4) has already been covered in detail in Chapter 3. This section addresses the other prongs of RCW 41.56.140. The primary forms of employer conduct prohibited under these subsections have been labeled as "discrimination" and "interference."

Sometimes there is overlap between these two charges — an attempt to retaliate against an employee might be discrimination but might also interfere with the union's attempts to represent members.

"Discrimination" and "interference" are different forms of unlawful activity with different proof elements. "Discrimination" involves an employer's *intentional* acts of retaliation against an employee based on the employee's "protected activity" which results in an "adverse impact" on the terms of employment. "Interference" occurs when the employer unduly impedes the ability of the union and its members to operate as an effective labor organization. Sometimes there is overlap between these two

[1] *See* RCW 41.80.110.

charges — an attempt to retaliate against an employee might be discrimination but might also interfere with the union's attempts to represent members.

there are some important differences between "discrimination" and "interference." As we will see, "interference" is easier to prove

While commonly these various actions are often lumped together and labelled as "retaliation," in reality there are some important differences between "discrimination" and "interference." As we will see, "interference" is easier to prove. But a successful discrimination charge, while requiring a higher level of proof, offers more far reaching and effective remedies. If a proven adverse impact occurs as a result of discrimination, the normal PERC remedy is to order a rollback of the action and make whole relief. In the case of interference, though, the typical remedies are generally limited to publication orders.

Next we will turn to the specific elements of both "discrimination" and "interference."

Attached to this chapter is a table summarizing cases in which PERC has found discrimination and retaliation, and a table summarizing cases where PERC has found interference.

2. Proving Discrimination and Interference

a. Proving Discrimination

The standard. In the *City of Federal Way,*[2] the Commission set forth the basic elements of a discrimination charge:

> To make out a prima facie case, the complainant claiming unlawful discrimination needs to show:
>
> 1) That the employee exercised a right protected by the collective bargaining statute, or communicated to the employer in an intent to do so;
>
> 2) That the employee was discriminatorily deprived of some ascertainable right, benefit or status; and

[2] Decision 5183-A (PECB, 1996).

3) That there was a causal connection between the exercise of the legal right and discriminatory action.[3]

These elements can be reduced even further. For there to be a valid discrimination charge there must be:

- Engagement in "protected activity";
- An "adverse action" on employment conditions; and
- A demonstrated connection *linking* the "protected activity" with the "adverse impact."

Without proof of all three elements, no unlawful discrimination has been established. Next we will take a closer look at each of these elements of a valid discrimination charge.

Protected activity. PECBA extends collective bargaining rights to public employees and their representatives. To make the exercise of those collective bargaining rights effective, the law makes it a ULP to discriminate against employees for exercising those rights. PERC case law provides many examples of activities that are deemed "protected" from discrimination. PERC has consistently found core union representation activities to constitute "protected activity" including:

- Union organizing[4]
- Filing a grievance[5]

---

[3] *Id.*

[4] *Asotin County Housing Authority*, Decision 2471 (PECB, 1986), *aff'd*, Decision 2471-A (PECB, 1987); *City of Federal Way*, Decision 5183 (PECB, 1995), *aff'd*, Decision 5183-A (PECB, 1996), *rev'd by King County Superior Court*, WPERR CD - 1009 (January 10, 1997), *aff'd by Court of Appeals*, WPERR CD - 1009 (October 19, 1998); *Lewis County*, Decision 4691 (PECB, 1994), *aff'd*, Decision 4691-A (PECB, 1994; *Spokane Transit Authority*, Decision 2078-A (PECB, 1985).

[5] *City of Mill Creek*, Decision 5699 (PECB, 1996); *City of Seattle*, Decision 3066 (PECB, 1987), *aff'd*, Decision 3066-A (PECB, 1989); *Clallam County*, Decision 1405-A (PECB, 1984); Kennewick School District, Decision 5632-A (PECB, 1996) *King County*, Decision 11221-A (PECB, 2012); *King County*, Decision 3178 (PECB, 1989); King County, Decision 3318 (PECB, 1989); *Mukilteo School District*, Decision 5899 (PECB, 1997); Washougal School District,

- Demanding arbitration on a grievance[6]
- Filing ULPs[7]
- Refusing to withdraw a ULP[8]
- Serving as union president[9]
- Serving as union board member or officer[10]
- Serving as shop steward[11]
- Representing employees in discipline interviews[12]
- Serving as a member of bargaining team[13]
- Attending labor management meetings[14]

Union activities furthering union objectives have also been found to be "protected activities" even when not directly arising from collective bargaining or contract enforcement, including:

Decision 2055.

6 *City of Benton City*, Decision 10956 (PECB, 2011).

7 *City of Mill Creek*, Decision 5699 (PECB, 1996); *City of Seattle*, Decision 6326 (PECB, 1998); *Mukilteo School District*, Decision 5899 (PECB, 1997); *Pullman School District*, Decision 2632 (PECB, 1987); *Seattle School District*, Decision 5946 (PECB, 1997); *Toutle Lake School District*, Decision 2659 (PECB, 1987).

8 *City of Yakima*, Decision 9451-B (PECB, 2007).

9 *City of Kalama*, Decision 7448 (PECB, 2001); *City of Vancouver*, Decision 10621-B (PECB, 2012), *aff'g* Decision 10621-A (PECB 2010); *Morton School District*, Decisions 5838 and 5839 (PECB, 1997); *Oroville School District*, Decision 6209-A (PECB, 1998); *Pasco Housing Authority*, Decision 6248 (PECB, 1998), *aff'd* with modification, *Pasco Housing Authority*, Decision 6248-A (PECB, 1998).

10 *Clallam County*, Decision 4011 (PECB, 1992) *King County*, Decision 11221-A (PECB, 2012); *Kiona Benton School District*, Decision 11035 (EDUC, 2011).

11 *Pasco Housing Authority*, Decision 6248 (PECB, 1998), affirmed with modification, *Pasco Housing Authority*, Decision 6248-A (PECB, 1998).

12 *Southwest Snohomish County Public Safety Communications Agency*, Decision 11149 (PECB, 2011), *aff'd*, Decision 11149-C (PECB, 2013).

13 *Pasco Housing Authority*, Decision 6248 (PECB, 1998), affirmed with modification, *Pasco Housing Authority*, Decision 6248-A (PECB, 1998); *Southwest Snohomish County Public Safety Communications Agency*, Decision 11149 (PECB, 2011), *aff'd*, Decision 11149-C (PECB, 2013); *Clallam County*, Decision 4011 (PECB, 1992).

14 *University of Washington*, Decision 11309-C (PSRA, 2013).

- Contacting the employer as a representative regarding the status of discipline investigation.[15]
- Participating in internal union communications[16]
- Speaking to media on internal about negotiations[17]
- Challenging employer policy changes[18]
- Objecting to employer noncompliance with benefit policy[19]
- Complaining to the county executive about labor relations practices[20]
- Criticizing the employer[21]
- Contacting legislators about salary funding[22]
- Assisting another union develop their arbitration case[23]
- Sending union related emails[24]
- Collecting information for an arbitration hearing[25]

PERC has also repeatedly found that the activities of rank and file members that support collective bargaining purposes are also

---

[15] *State - Corrections*, Decision 11747 (PSRA, 2013).

[16] *Southwest Snohomish County Public Safety Communications Agency*, Decision 11149 (PECB, 2011), aff'd Decision 11149-C (PECB, 2013).

[17] *Clallam County*, Decision 4011 (PECB, 1992).

[18] *City of Vancouver*, Decision 10621-B (PECB, 2012), *aff'g* Decision 10621-A (PECB 2010).

[19] *Spokane Transit Authority*, Decision 2078-A (PECB, 1985).

[20] *Snohomish County*, Decision 9834 (PSRA, 2007); *aff'd*, *Snohomish County*, Decision 9834B (PSRA, 2008).

[21] *City of Vancouver*, Decision 10621-B (PECB, 2012), *aff'g* Decision 10621-A (PECB 2010); Educational Service District 114, Decision 4361-A (PECB, 1994).

[22] *Renton Technical College*, Decision 7441-A (CCOL, 2002).

[23] *Southwest Snohomish County Public Safety Communications Agency*, Decision 11149 (PECB, 2011), *aff'd*, Decision 11149-C (PECB, 2013).

[24] State - *Corrections*, Decision 10998-A (PSRA, 2011); *University of Washington*, Decision 11091 (PSRA, 2011).

[25] *Kitsap County*, Decision 9326-A (PECB, 2008).

protected activity even when not undertaken by an official representative of the union, including:

- Supporting union organizing effort[26]
- Serving as lead contact to union[27]
- Complaining to the union[28]
- Testifying at a PERC hearing[29]
- Testifying at an arbitration hearing[30]
- Being "friendly" with employees who file a grievance and work related lawsuit[31]
- Calling PERC regarding delivery of election ballots[32]
- Supporting union organizing efforts[33]
- Reporting skimming of unit work to union[34]
- Attending union meetings[35]
- Vocally dissenting at union meetings[36]
- Objecting to transfer of bargaining unit work[37]

---

[26] *City of Winlock*, Decision 4784-A (PECB, 1995).

[27] *City of Federal Way*, Decision 5183 (PECB, 1995), *aff'd*, Decision 5183-A (PECB, 1996), *rev'd by King County Superior Court*, WPERR CD - 1009 (January 10, 1997), *aff'd by Court of Appeals*, WPERR CD - 1009 (October 19, 1998); *City of Winlock*, Decision 4784-A (PECB, 1995).

[28] *Bethel School District*, Decision 6731 (PECB, 1999).

[29] *Chelan Public Hospital District 2*, Decision 11294 (PECB, 2012); *Northshore Utility District*, Decision 11267 (PECB, 2011), *aff'd*, Decision 11267-A (PECB, 2012); *State - Corrections*, Decision 12002-A (PSRA, 2014).

[30] *Kiona Benton School District*, Decision 11563 (EDUC, 2012), aff'd Decision 11563-A (EDUC, 2013).

[31] *City of Seattle*, Decision 3066 (PECB, 1987), *aff'd*, Decision 3066-A (PECB, 1989).

[32] *North Valley Hospital*, Decision 5809 (PECB, 1997).

[33] *Educational Service District 114*, Decision 4361-A (PECB, 1994).

[34] *Washington State University*, Decision 11749 (PSRA, 2013).

[35] *Cowlitz County*, Decision 7037 (PECB, 2000).

[36] *Port of Tacoma*, Decisions 4626 and 4627 (PECB, 1994), *remedy rev'd in* Port of Tacoma, Decisions 4626-A and 4627-A (PECB, 1995).

- Requesting union representation[38]
- Discussing discipline imposed with co-workers[39]
- Meeting with a union organizer[40]
- Involvement in internal union affairs[41]
- Meeting with a union representative[42]

Even activities that are only indirectly or incidentally related to current union activities have been found to constitute "protected activities" including:

- Being related to a shop steward[43]
- Past union activity with employer[44]

Adverse Impact. The second required element of a successful discrimination claim is that the employer action affecting the employee be of sufficient gravity to constitute an "adverse impact" with tangible employment consequences. Not every employer action that incidentally affects an employee constitutes a recognizable "adverse impact." Rather the complainant must prove "the employer deprived the employee of some ascertainable right, benefit, or status."[45]

Attached to this chapter is a table listing various employer actions and whether they have been deemed to be "adverse actions." A summary is provided here.

Certain actions that threaten the job or income constitute an "adverse action including:

---

[37] *Seattle School District*, Decision 11779-A (PECB, 2014).

[38] *Seattle School District*, Decision 11045 (PECB, 2011), *rev'd in part by on other grounds*, Decision 11045-A (PECB, 2011).

[39] *Southwest Snohomish County Public Safety Communications Agency*, Decision 11149 (PECB, 2011), *aff'd*, Decision 11149-C (PECB, 2013).

[40] *Washington State University*, Decision 11749 (PSRA, 2013).

[41] *Cowlitz County*, Decision 7037 (PECB, 2000).

[42] *King County*, Decision 11223 (PECB, 2011).

[43] *Auburn School District*, Decision 2291 (PECB, 1985); *Port of Seattle*, Decision 11848 (PECB, 2013).

[44] *Clallam County*, Decision 4011 (PECB, 1992).

[45] *Kitsap County*, Decision 12022-A (PECB, 2014); *State-Corrections, Decision 11581-A (PSRA, 2013).*

- Discharge[46]
- Layoff[47]
- Suspension[48]
- Demotion[49]
- Temporary demotion[50]
- Failure to promote[51]
- Refusal to hire[52]
- Refusal to rehire[53]
- Refusal to reinstate after clearing fitness clearance[54]

---

46 *City of Mountlake Terrace, Decision 11831-2 (PECB, 2013), aff'd, Decision 11831-A (PECB, 2014); Washington State Ferries, Decision 11335 (MRNE, 2012), aff'd, Decision 11335-A (MRNE, 2012); Washington State University, Decision 11749 (PSRA, 2013); Chelan Public Hospital District 2, Decision 11294 (PECB, 2012); Kiona Benton School District*, Decision 11563 (EDUC, 2012); *Aberdeen School District*, Decision 6434 (PECB, 1998); *City of Winlock*, Decision 4784-A (PECB, 1995).

47 *Northshore Utility District, Decision 11267 (PECB, 2011), aff'd, Decision 11267-A (PECB, 2012); Pasco Housing Authority*, Decision 6248 (PECB, 1998), *modified, Pasco Housing Authority*, Decision 6248-A (PECB, 1998).

48 *Southwest Snohomish County Public Safety Communications Agency,* Decision 11149 (PECB, 2011), *aff'd*, Decision 11149-C (PECB, 2013); *City of Pullman*, Decision 11148 (PECB, 2011), *aff'd*, Decision 11148-A (PECB, 2012).

49 *Seattle School District*, Decision 11779-A (PECB, 2014); *Spokane Transit Authority*, Decision 2078-A (PECB, 1985).

50 *City of Pullman*, Decision 11148 (PECB, 2011), *aff'd*, Decision 11148-A (PECB, 2012).

51 *City of Seattle*, Decision 10803-B (PECB, 2012), *aff'g* Decision 10803-A (PECB, 2011); *Pierce County,* Decision 7258 (PECB, 2001); *Port of Tacoma*, Decisions 4626 and 4627 (PECB, 1994).

52 *King County,* Decision 11221-A (PECB, 2012); *Morton School District*, Decisions 5838 and 5839 (PECB, 1997); *Auburn School District*, Decision 2291 (PECB, 1985); *City of Centralia*, Decision 2904 (PECB, 1988); *Auburn School District*, Decision 2291 (PECB, 1985).

53 *Educational Service District 114*, Decision 4361-A (PECB, 1994); *Clallam Transit System*, Decision 4597 (PECB, 1994).

54 *King County*, Decision 3178 (PECB, 1989), *aff'd*, Decision 3178-A (PECB, 1989).

- Refusal to extend a contract[55]
- Reduction in work hours[56]
- Reduction in overtime opportunities[57]
- Failure to appoint to specialty assignment[58]
- Refusing to consider resignation and severance package under conditions previously found acceptable[59]

Other discipline or personnel actions, though informal and without economic impact have also been deemed to create an "adverse impact" including:

- Letters of reprimand[60]
- Counseling Memos[61]
- Negative performance evaluation[62]
- Placement of negative materials in personnel file[63]

On the other hand, PERC has, at other times found low level personnel actions insufficient to constitute an "adverse impact," including:

---

[55] *Bethel School District,* Decision 6731 (PECB, 1999).

[56] *Benton City,* Decision 436 (PECB, 1978).

[57] *State – Corrections,* Decision 11571 (PSRA, 2012), *aff'd,* Decision 11571-A (PSRA, 2013).

[58] *City of Vancouver, Decision 10621-A & Decision 10621-B (PECB, 2012).*

[59] *City of Mountlake Terrace, Decision 11831-2 (PECB, 2013), aff'd, Decision 11831-A (PECB, 2014).*

[60] *Southwest Snohomish County Public Safety Communications Agency,* Decision 11149 (PECB, 2011), *aff'd,* Decision 11149-C (PECB, 2013); *Seattle School District,* Decision 11045-A (PECB, 2011), *rev'd in part,* Decision 11045-A (PECB, 2011); *North Valley Hospital,* Decision 5809 (PECB, 1997), *aff'd, North Valley Hospital,* Decision 5809-A (PECB, 1997).

[61] *University of Washington, Decision 11309 (PSRA, 2012); University of Washington,* Decision 11199-B (PSRA, 2013).

[62] *Oroville School District,* Decision 6209-A (PECB, 1998), affirming as amended, *Oroville School District,* Decision 6209-A (PECB, 1998); *Pasco Housing Authority,* Decision 6248 (PECB, 1998), *aff'd with modification, Pasco Housing Authority,* Decision 6248-A (PECB, 1998).

[63] *City of Mill Creek,* Decision 5699 (PECB, 1996).

- Verbal counseling[64]
- Corrective counseling notice[65]
- Verbal admonishment[66]
- Undertaking investigation without imposing discipline[67]
- Threatening discipline[68]
- Coaching on performance[69]
- Administrative transfer[70]

Other administrative actions that might create a future possibility of loss of job or income have been recognized as having an "adverse impact" despite the immediate loss of wages:

- Placement on administrative leave[71]
- Transfer[72]
- Refusal to provide work duties[73]
- Reassignment to lesser duties[74]
- Removal from special project assignments[75]

---

[64] *Kitsap County,* Decision 9326-A (PECB, 2008).
[65] *Snohomish County,* Decision 9799, (PECB, 2007).
[66] *Snohomish County,* Decision 9799, (PECB, 2007).
[67] *State-Corrections, Decision 12002 (PSRA, 2014)*
[68] *City of Port Angeles,* Decision 10445 (PECB, 2009).
[69] *Port of Seattle,* Decision 11848 (PECB, 2013), *aff'd,* Decision 11848-A (PECB, 2014).
[70] *Seattle School District,* Decision 11045 (PECB, 2011), *rev'd in part,* Decision 11045-A (PECB, 2011).
[71] *Southwest Snohomish County Public Safety Communications Agency,* Decision 11149 (PECB, 2011), *aff'd,* Decision 11149-C (PECB, 2013); *Seattle School District,* Decision 11045-A (PECB, 2011), reversed in part by Decision 11045-A (PECB, 2011); *State – Corrections,* Decision 11571 (PSRA, 2012), *aff'd,* Decision 11571-A (PSRA, 2013).
[72] *Kiona Benton School District,* Decision 11035 (EDUC, 2011); *City of Tukwila,* Decision 4968 (PECB, 1995); *City of Seattle,* Decision 6357 (PECB, 1998).
[73] *Pierce County,* Decision 7258 (PECB, 2001).
[74] *State – Corrections,* Decision 11571 (PSRA, 2012), *aff'd,* Decision 11571-A (PSRA, 2013).
[75] *Southwest Snohomish County Public Safety Communications Agency,* Decision

- Refusal to provide a recommendation letter necessary for promotion[76]

Other changes in working conditions have also been recognized as having an "adverse impact" on the employee, including:

- Change in work schedule[77]
- Removal from bid for shift[78]
- Restricting location of work[79]
- Prohibiting union meetings during previously allowed work time[80]
- Restricting access to union representation[81]
- Refusing to prepare a letter of recommendation[82]
- Removing internet privileges[83]

But PERC has ruled that other various changes in working condition or work issues do not rise to the level of an adverse impact, including:

- Delayed internal investigation[84]
- Denial of release time to prepare and testify at ULP hearing[85]
- Change in predisicpline procedures[86]

11149 (PECB, 2011), *aff'd*, Decision 11149-C (PECB, 2013).

[76] *Oroville School District*, Decision 6209-A (PECB, 1998), affirming as amended, *Oroville School District*, Decision 6209-A (PECB, 1998).

[77] *City of Winlock*, Decision 4784-A (PECB, 1995).

[78] *State – Corrections,* Decision 11571 (PSRA, 2012), *aff'd*, Decision 11571-A (PSRA, 2013).

[79] *State – Corrections, Decision 11571 (PSRA, 2012).*

[80] *City of Benton City*, Decision 10956 (PECB, 2011).

[81] *King County,* Decision 11223 (PECB, 2011).

[82] *State-Corrections, Decision 12002-A (PSRA, 2014).*

[83] *State-Corrections, Decision 10998 (PSRA, 2011).*

[84] *Seattle School District,* Decision 10732-A (PECB, 2012).

[85] *City of Mountlake Terrace, Decision 11831-2 (PECB, 2013), aff'd, Decision 11831-A (PECB, 2014).*

[86] *City of Mountlake Terrace,* Decision 11831-2 (PECB, 2013), *aff'd*, Decision

- Confusing or incomplete work assignment orders[87]
- Voluntary employee resignation[88]

Proof of "causation" is generally the most difficult part of a complainant's case.

Proving a causal connection. As indicated above, even proof of protected activity and an adverse impact is insufficient to establish a ULP; there must also be sufficient proof that there is a proven *connection* between the two. Proof of "causation" is generally the most difficult part of a complainant's case. Most discrimination ULPs filed before PERC contain ample evidence of the first two elements. Proving that the adverse impact was "because of" the protected activity can be challenging though.

There are different stages or proving "causation." First, there must be proof of an employer "intent" to discriminate. Proving intent may be challenging but not impossible even when the employer intent goes unstated. The intent requirement can be met — and generally is met — through circumstantial evidence. As the Commission aptly noted:

> Employers are not in the habit of announcing retaliatory motives, so circumstantial evidence of a causal connection can be relied upon [citation omitted]. An employee may establish the requisite causal connection by showing that adverse action followed the employee's known exercise of a protected right, under circumstances from which one can reasonably infer a connection.[89]

Once the complaining employee meets the prima facie case that discrimination has occurred, a "burden of production" shifts to the employer to establish non-discriminatory reasons for the action. As was explained in *Port of Tacoma*:

> While the complainant carries the burden of proof throughout the entire matter, there is a shifting of the

---

11831-A (PECB, 2014).

87 *College District 13*, Decision 9171-A (PSRA, 2007).

88 *Clover Park School District*, Decision 7073-A (EDUC, 2001).

89 *Id.*

> burden of production. Once the employee establishes his/her prima facie case, the employer has the opportunity to articulate legitimate, non-retaliatory reasons for its actions. The employer must produce relevant and admissible evidence of another motivation, but need not do so by the preponderance of evidence necessary to sustain the burden of persuasion. If the employer fails to produce any evidence of other motivation for the discharge, however, the complainant will prevail.[90]

At that point, the complainants have an opportunity to reply back:

> If the employer produces evidence of a legitimate basis for the discharge, the complainant may attempt to establish that the employers articulated reason is pretextual. It is the ultimate burden on the alleged discriminatee to show that the protected activity was 'a substantial motivating factor'. . . .[91]

A challenge arises where a superficially plausible nondiscriminatory reason has been proffered by the employer. Sometimes the reason given will be obviously pretextual. But on many other occasions an articulable legitimate reason may, in fact, be *a part* of what was motivating the employer. This situation is referred to as a "mixed motive" cases.

In PERC's early years, it applied the *Wright Line* mixed motive case doctrine borrowed from the NLRB. Under *Wright Line,*[92] the complainant had to prove that "but for" the discriminatory motive, the action would not have been taken. But when there competing employer motives, both legitimate and unlawful, this "but for" standard created a difficult burden of proof for the complainant to carry.

Changes in the PERC case law in the mid-1990s clarified how to evaluate mixed motive cases and have greatly eased what had been a difficult burden of proof for complainants. In *City of Federal Way,* the Commission rejected *Wright Line* and adopted a more protective "substantial motivating factor" test for "mixed motive" cases. It does so by borrowing the "substantial factor" standard that had just been approved by the State Supreme Court in

[90] *Port of Tacoma*, Decisions 4626 and 4627 (PECB 1994).
[91] *Id.*
[92] 251 NLRB 1083 (1980).

interpreting other discrimination statutes.[93] As the Commission then noted in adopting the "substantial factor" test:

> Cases decided under the previous test based on *Wright Line*, 251 NLRB 1083 (1980), may have given greater consideration to an employer's business reasons for adverse actions against its employees, while the current test may be more favorable to employees.[94]

This revised "substantial factor" test makes it easier to prove the causation link between the union activity and the adverse employment action.

The Washington Court of Appeals in *City of Federal Way v. PERC*[95] affirmed the Commission's use of the "substantial factor" test in a case involving retaliation for union organizing activity. The court cited its use of the substantial factor test which it had adopted in a recent worker's compensation retaliation decision. It then reasoned that this test should be equally applicable, if not more so, to deter retaliatory actions against workers who engage in protected collective bargaining activity.[96]

This revised "substantial factor" test makes it easier to prove the causation link between the union activity and the adverse employment action. Often the employer's discriminatory motives are mixed with some legitimate reasons, such as existing performance concerns. In such situations, the legitimate reasons for the employer action will not create a valid defense whenever the complainant can prove that the unlawful motive effected the decision to any measurable degree.

As a practical matter, if complainants can prove that some degree of anti-union animosity existed, they will

---

[93] *Wilmot v. Kaiser*, 1881 Wn.2d 46 (1991); *Allison v. Seattle Housing Authority*, 118 Wn.2d (1991).

[94] *City of Federal Way, supra.*

[95] 93 Wash. App. 509, 970 P.2d 752 (Wash. App. Div. I 1998) (reversing on other grounds).

[96] *City of Federal Way v. PERC*, 93 Wash. App. 509, 970 P. 2d 752 (Wash App. Div. 1 1998).

generally be able to prove that those motives were at least a "substantial factor" in the personnel action. While this test still generally depends heavily upon circumstantial evidence — except when employers are brazen enough to state their ill-motive — the required link between the intent and the action often can be connected successfully with circumstantial evidence alone. Ultimately, though, this burden of proof rests on the complainant.

As a practical matter, if complainants can prove that some degree of anti-union animosity existed, they will generally be able to prove that those motives were at least a "substantial factor" in the personnel action.

b. Proving Interference

the interference standard is normally framed as to *whether the employees would "reasonably perceive" the statements of actions to threaten their union rights*

The Standard. An interference charge, in many respects, is easier to prove than a discrimination charge. Interference complaints turn more narrowly on nature the management conduct, inquiring if it might have a "chilling effect" on employees' union activities. *There is no requirement to prove discriminatory intent.* There is also no requirement to prove the actual loss of a tangible benefit or other tangible "adverse impact." Rather, the interference standard is normally framed as to *whether the employees would "reasonably perceive" the statements of actions to threaten their union rights.*[97]

An interference violation can be found if complainant shows that the employer's conduct could reasonably be perceived by employees as a threat of reprisal or force, or a promise of benefit, or something that could deter them from pursuing union activity.[98]

---

[97] *Id.* at 8.

[98] *City of Mercer Island*, Decision 1580 (PECB 1983); *City of Seattle*, Decision 2134 (PECB 1985); *King County*, Decision 2955 (PECB 1988).

The complainant is not required to make a showing of intent or motivation on behalf of the employer, nor is it necessary to show that employees were *actually* interfered with or coerced.[99] It is simply enough if the employees could reasonably perceive the employer conduct as an attempt to interfere with their statutory rights.[100]

Examples of Interference. One of the earliest PERC interference cases was *City of Pasco.*[101] In *City of Pasco*, the union alleged that the employer interfered with employees when it had a police officer deliver a termination letter to an employee during a union meeting. The hearing examiner found that this constituted an interference under RCW 41.56.140(1). He wrote that:

> Such conduct unlawfully implies a threat of discharge to other employees in the bargaining unit. Further, it creates the impression among the employees that their union activities are under the surveillance of their employer. As such, it tends to inhibit the [employees'] subsequent union activities.[102]

A similar approach was taken in *City of Mercer Island.*[103] In that case, the city sent demotion and lay-off notices to police officers whose union had a pending case before PERC. The city argued that no interference occurred because it rescinded the notices, and the officers did not miss any work. PERC rejected this "rescission" argument:

> Since a reasonable employee involved in such a situation would tend to pinpoint his/her demotion or impending layoff on the results of actions of two employees seeking their statutory rights under RCW 41.56, the employer's actions tend to discourage the members from joining, participating in or pursuing a union.[104]

---

99 *City of Olympia*, Decision 1208 (PECB 1981); *City of Seattle*, Decision 2134 (PECB 1985); *Metropolitan Park District of Tacoma*, Decision 2272 (PECB 1986); *Spokane County*, Decision 2674 (PECB 1987); *City of Seattle*, Decision 2773 (PECB 1987).

100 *City of Mercer Island, supra.*

101 Decision 504 (PECB 1978).

102 *Id.* at 356-357 (footnotes omitted).

103 Decision 1026 (PECB 1980).

104 *Id.* at 11-12 (footnotes omitted).

In other words, PERC found that the employees reasonably perceived a threat to their rights.

Employer statements that could reasonably be perceived as coercive or critical of the union have been found to be the basis of an interference claim:

- Telling an employee under investigation that he was getting "bad advice from your union representative" by not allowing the investigative interviews to be recorded."[105]

- Telling employees that their union's intended subpoena of management official to testify in PERC proceeding was a "bad idea."[106]

- Sending an email to employees that could be interpreted as "undermining, ridiculing, or disparaging" their union president.[107]

- Following employees showing support of officer's grievance, Police Chief's department-wide email addressed to "all whiners" suggesting that he wanted to "stomp on" them and get them to quit saying "woe is me."[108]

- Telling an employee during a performance review that she hopefully would not see her union "role as that of one stirring the pot or causing problems."[109]

On the other hand, some employer statements have fallen short of being deemed "interference" even with instances that sounded somewhat coercive:

- Making statements to the union officer indicating potential acts that might warrant discipline because "statements made by employer officials are examined differently than statements made by employer officials to rank and file members."[110]

[105] *State – Social and Health Services*, Decision 11033 – A (PSRA, 2011).
[106] *Grant County Public Hospital Dist. 1*, Decision 8378-A (PECB, 2004).
[107] *Grandview School District*, Decision 12047 (EDUC, 2014).
[108] City of Omak, Decisions 5579-A, 5580-A, 5581-A and 5583-A (PECB, 1997).
[109] *University Place School District*, Decision 9341 (PECB, 2006).
[110] *Kiona Benton School District*, Decision 11035 (EDUC, 2011).

- Warning a union official that retaliation actions he might undertake could be grounds for discipline.[111]

- Sending an email to employees mentioning "wolf packs" that the union argued was a reference to it when the examiner found that the union embellished and took the statement out of context.[112]

- Criticizing employee job performance because the statements could not reasonably be seen as threats of reprisal for union activities.[113]

- Statement by Sheriff to Guild President "what has the Guild done for me" following a request for release time request.[114]

- Asking employees to take pay cut as part of "shared sacrifice."

- Making negative statements about unionization to employees during open discussion about unionizing activities.[115]

Restricting union activity has been found to constitute unlawful interference, including such employer actions as:

- Prohibiting union buttons during a representation election when dress code did not specifically prohibit pins on uniforms.[116]

- Ordering union posters removed from office cubicles when non-work related posters had been allowed.[117]

---

111 *City of Pullman*, Decision 11148 (PECB, 2011), *aff'd*, Decision 11148-A (PECB, 2012).

112 *City of Pullman*, Decision 11148 (PECB, 2011), *aff'd*, Decision 11148-A (PECB, 2012).

113 *Moses Lake School District*, Decision 8770-A (PECB, 2005).

114 *Kitsap County*, Decision 8292-A (PECB, 2005); *aff'd*, in part, *Kitsap County*, Decision 8292-B (PECB, 2007).

115 *Brinnon School District*, Decision 7210-A (PECB, 2001), *aff'g* Decision 7210 (2000).

116 *Port of Anacortes*, Decision 12155 (PORT, 2014).

117 *State - Employment Security*, Decision 11962 (PSRA, 2013).

- Ordering employees under investigation not to contact co-workers during the course of discipline investigation, including Association officers.[118]
- Ordering employee not to discuss discipline imposed with co-workers, including Association officers.[119]
- Restricting union access to workplace to one of two competing unions, while allowing other union access.[120]
- Ordering that union meetings previously held during work time would no longer be allowed.[121]
- Employer insistence that the union representative meet with him or resign as representative.[122]
- Refusing to process grievance while PERC unit clarification process over position was pending.[123]
- Deliberately destroying record that the union had requested.[124]
- Imposing public records rate on copying charges for documents request by the union.[125]
- Varying records charges imposed on different unions and by the size of the request.[126]

On the other hand, some employer actions that seemingly impaired a union's ability to operate were nonetheless found to fall short of the interference standard:

---

[118] *Southwest Snohomish County Public Safety Communications Agency*, Decision 11149 (PECB, 2011), *aff'd*, Decision 11149-C (PECB, 2013).
[119] *Southwest Snohomish County Public Safety Communications Agency*, Decision 11149 (PECB, 2011), *aff'd*, Decision 11149-C (PECB, 2013).
[120] *King County*, Decision 11223 (PECB, 2011).
[121] *City of Benton City*, Decision 10956 (PECB, 2011).
[122] *Seattle School District*, Decision 9858 (PECB, 2007); *aff'd*, *Seattle School District*, Decision 9858A (PECB, 2009).
[123] *University of Washington*, Decision 11181-A (PSRA, 2013).
[124] *Seattle School District*, Decision 8976 (PECB, 2005).
[125] *Snohomish County*, Decision 9570 (PECB, 2007).
[126] *Snohomish County*, Decision 9570 (PECB, 2007).

- Disciplining employee for insubordination for delivering grievance using keys to locked space contrary to management directions.[127]

- Laying off union president when it was documented by "legitimate, non-discriminatory reasons."[128]

- Commenting on the lack of merit of a grievance.[129]

- Restricting distribution of union campaign materials to non-working hours.[130]

Management surveillance and of, and questioning about, union activity can, under certain circumstances, be unlawful interference. PERC has found the following surveillance to be unlawful:

- Creating the impression that they were monitoring employees attempting to organize.[131]

- Interrogating employees about union meetings.[132]

- Creating an impression of surveillance following the filing of a grievance, even when not.[133]

- Questioning employee about joining union.[134]

But other employer actions have fallen short of constituting unlawful union surveillance:

- Chief's invited attendance at meeting of Sergeants who were seeking to sever from the Guild.[135]

- Interrogating employees about statements made during guild meeting when those alleged statements included threats of retaliation against other officers for cooperating in internal investigations.[136]

---

127 *University of Washington*, Decision 11091 (PSRA, 2011), *aff'd*, Decision 11091 (PSRA, 2012).
128 *Northshore Utility District*, Decision 10534 (PECB, 2009).
129 *Snohomish County*, Decision 9799 (PECB, 2007).
130 *King County*, Decision 8630-A (PECB, 2005).
131 *Town of Granite Falls,* Decision 2692 (PECB, 1987).
132 *City of Longview*, Decision 4702 (PECB, 1994).
133 *City of Omak*, Decisions 5579-A, 5580-A, 5581-A and 5583-A (PECB, 1997).
134 *Metropolitan Park District of Tacoma*, Decision 2272 (PECB, 1986).
135 *City of Spokane,* Decision 11263 (PECB, 2011).

- City subpoena of internal police guild documents sought in the City's defense of a civil rights lawsuit.[137]

- Requiring Sergeant who served as Guild president to report when his union duties were conflicting with his guild duties when City claimed it wanted to make investigations more efficient.[138]

- Searching for work papers in employees' desk drawers.[139]

- Statement by police manager that he always knows what happens at police guild meeting when statement was found to be made in jest.[140]

- Monitoring ferry workers with commissioned deputies after employer contracting out announced when deputies were instructed to look for misconduct.[141]

- Interviewing employees in order to prepare for arbitration hearing.[142]

Employer threats or promise to change conditions of employment are usually found to constitute unlawful interference, especially when made in the context of union organizing or an election:

- Suggesting that employees would avoid a 3% salary reduction if they decertified the union.[143]

- Expanding Sergeant duties to make them more "supervisory" in nature which furthered an effort to sever them from the guild.[144]

- Informing employee that manager had contacted an attorney to consider defamation lawsuit following union complaints against the manager.[145]

---

[136] *City of Vancouver,* Decision 6732 (PECB, 1999).
[137] *City of Seattle,* Decision 9945 (PECB, 2007); *aff'd, City of Seattle,* Decision 9945A (PECB, 2009).
[138] *City of Longview,* Decision 9884 (PECB, 2007).
[139] *City of Seattle,* Decision 3066 (PECB, 1987), *aff'd,* Decision 3066-A (PECB, 1989).
[140] *City of Bremerton,* Decision 3843-A (PECB, 1994).
[141] *Skagit County,* Decision 6348 (PECB, 1998).
[142] *City of Seattle,* Decision 9526-A (PECB, 2009).
[143] *Columbia Basin College,* Decision 11609 (PSRA, 2012).
[144] *City of Spokane,* Decision 11263 (PECB, 2011).

- Transferring employee following a grievance.[146]
- Curtailing police officer duties following their support of another officer's discipline grievance.[147]
- Restricting officers from informing other local law enforcement officers of internal disputes.[148]

The key test is the employee's "reasonable perception" of the employer action.

Proving Interference. As indicated, proof of interference is not nearly as stringent as the proof required to establish a discrimination charge. The key test is the employee's "reasonable perception" of the employer action.

Inherently this test has both an "objective and "subjective" component. Evidence that the employee subjectively believed that they were subject to coercion or retaliation is admissible and highly relevant. But the employee perception alone will not establish the charge. The "objective" component of the standard requires that the employee's belief be *objectively reasonable.* Employee beliefs or assumptions that are unrealistic or an overreaction will not satisfy the proof requirements.

C. Duty of Fair Representation

The basic doctrine. The collective bargaining statute that provides labor organizations numerous *rights* also imposes upon those labor organizations certain *responsibilities.* First and foremost among these responsibilities is the duty of fair representation (DFR). Labor organizations have a duty to represent their members *fairly, honestly and without discrimination* during both contract negotiations and in the processing of grievances.

---

145 *University Place School District*, Decision 9341 (PECB, 2006).
146 *University Place School District*, Decision 9341 (PECB, 2006).
147 *City of Omak*, Decisions 5579-B, 5580-B, 5581-B and 5583-B (PECB, 1998).
148 *City of Omak*, Decisions 5579-B, 5580-B, 5581-B and 5583-B (PECB, 1998).

The courts have concluded that if the lawmakers intended to give labor organizations broad authority to act conclusively on behalf of their members, they also intended a corollary responsibility that the authority be carried out in good faith.

History of the DFR doctrine. The duty to fairly represent members is not explicitly stated in either the state or national labor law. Instead, it is requirement that the courts have found to be *implied* by the statute. The courts have concluded that if the lawmakers intended to give labor organizations broad authority to act conclusively on behalf of their members, they also intended a corollary responsibility that the authority be carried out in good faith.

The DFR doctrine applies under Washington public sector bargaining law based upon State Courts' application of federal private sector NLRA precedent. The Supreme Court in *Ford Motor Co. v. Huffman*,[149] states that the responsibility of labor negotiators is to weigh the advantages and disadvantages of differing proposals. The bargaining representative is responsible to, and owes complete loyalty to the interests of all whom it represents.[150]

In *Vaca v. Sipes*,[151] the Supreme Court held that this duty requires that the union's conduct toward members of the collective bargaining unit not be arbitrary, discriminatory, or in bad faith. Federal courts have interpreted this standard as follows:

> A union must conform its behavior to each of these three separate standards. First, it must treat all factions and segments of its membership without hostility or discrimination. Next, the broad discretion of the union in asserting the rights of its individual members must be exercised in complete good faith and honesty. Finally. The union must avoid arbitrary conduct.[152]

---

[149] 345 US 330, 73 S.Ct. 681, (1952).

[150] 345 US at 338; *Phillip Charles Allen v Seattle Police Officers' Guild*, Court Decisions 264, No. 48925-4 (WA S.Ct. 1983).

[151] 386 U.S. 171 at 190 (1967).

[152] *Griffin v. International Union of United Automobile Workers*, 469 F2d 181 at 183 (4th Cir. 1974); *Ruzicka v. General Motors*, 523 F2d 306 at 309 (6th Cir.

The source of the duty of fair representation is the union's special status of "exclusive bargaining representative". Under RCW 41.56.080:

> The bargaining representative which has been determined to represent a majority of the employees in a bargaining unit shall be certified by the commission as the exclusive bargaining representative of, and shall be required to represent, all the public employees within the unit without regard to membership in said bargaining representative . . . .

DRF is actually one of the original civil rights laws. In the 1940's and 50's, before employment discrimination laws were adopted, frequent lawsuits were brought by black union members who alleged that white-dominated unions had not fairly considered their contract grievances. The courts adopted the DFR in recognition that union members who grievances were denied by their own union rarely had other recourse.

there is *no* DFR obligation where the labor organization does not exclusively control access to the forum

Based upon "exclusivity." Both in its original justification and its current application, the DFR doctrine was squarely based on the concept of "exclusivity." In creating the DFR doctrine, the courts recognized that most labor contracts contained a grievance procedure that allowed only the signatory parties (the employer and the union) to enforce the terms of the contract in arbitration. The courts held then, and continue to hold now, that when only the union can bring a legal claim on behalf of its members, the union's power of *exclusive control* creates a duty of fair representation.

On the other hand, there is *no* DFR obligation where the labor organization does not exclusively control access to the forum. For example, there is no DFR obligation for representation of civil service claims because these are a right belonging to the individual employee and not the union. While a union may provide a member with an attorney or representative during such a hearing if it wishes, it has no obligation to do so.

1975).

An organization's DFR requires it to fully and fairly consider grievances brought to it by its members.

Contract negotiations versus grievances. While most DFR claims arise in the context of a rejected grievance, labor organizations also have a Duty of Fair Representation in the context of collective bargaining. DFR claims rarely arise in this context, however, because unions are allowed extremely broad leeway during contract negotiations when deciding between the competing interests of their members.

The DFR obligations for processing grievances, however, are more stringent. An organization's DFR requires it to fully and fairly consider grievances brought to it by its members. As a result, unions should conduct a reasonably thorough investigation of each grievance, including at a minimum, reviewing all documents brought forth by the grievant and interviewing the grievant.

While a negligent failure to comply with a filing deadline does not ordinarily state a cause of action for a DFR claim, courts have found upheld DFR claims when the union has been "perfunctory" by completely ignoring the grievances presented to it.

A valid DFR claim does *not* exist when a labor union makes a decision in good faith after considering available information, *even if the conclusion drawn by the union was legally or factually erroneously*. In other words, *decisions that are merely negligent do not provide a basis for a DFR claim*. A DFR claimant must establish that the organization in bad faith, either out of malice or discrimination, or in deliberate disregard of the member's right.

But sometimes the line between "merely" negligent actions and actions made in bad faith is not entirely clear. For example, courts have on numerous occasions upheld DFR claims where they concluded that the union acted in a "perfunctory" manner. While a negligent failure to comply with a filing deadline does not ordinarily state a cause of action for a DFR claim, courts have found upheld DFR claims when the union has been "perfunctory" by completely ignoring the grievances presented to it. Since the difference between negligent failing to file the grievance and completely ignoring may be a fine one, it is better practice to comply with all deadlines.

Practical guidelines. There are some basic points a union should consider and follow in handling grievances. If you follow these practices, you are unlikely to be sued, and if you are, the case will almost certainly be dismissed on summary judgment. Here is a basic "do's and "don'ts" checklist to discharge the duty of fair representation:

- Do review employer's report carefully and thoroughly.
- Do interview grievants and get their side of the story.
- Do ask grievants if there is any additional information or witness to consider.
- Do establish and follow an internal procedure before deciding which grievances to take to arbitration.
- Don't assume the employer's report of a matter is accurate and complete.
- Don't ignore clear contract violations based on your dislike of the individual whosc contract rights were violated.
- Don't ignore grievances or grievance deadlines.

D. Union Dues Clauses

Washington public safety unions have legal rights to dues both on a voluntary basis and a compulsory basis.

Voluntary dues collection. Under the Washington collective bargaining law, public safety unions are allowed to collect dues on a voluntary basis, using the check-off system in the statute. In other words, even if there is no agreement with the employer concerning deduction of union dues, employees have a right to use the employer's payroll system to contribute dues to the union.[153] Beyond that, union dues arrangements are a subject of collective bargaining. Most unions have successfully negotiated to acquire a dues deduction clause that requires payment to the union.

---

[153] RCW 41.56.110.

Compulsory dues. Compulsory dues, though, create some legal issues, including some constitutional rights issues. The issues are easily addressed in labor contract negotiation and its administration, but you need to be aware of a few concepts. While a contract containing a dues clause is enforceable, it must comply with legal exempts based on both religion and the constitutional right to "non-association."

If employees have a *bona fide* religious objection, therefore, do not have to pay dues to the union in any way, shape or form. Religious objectors, though, are nonethless required by RCW 41.56.122 to "pay an amount equivalent to regular union dues and initiation fee to a non-religious charity or to another charitable organization

RCW 41.56.122 expressly allows that Washington public sector agreements may contain a "union security" arrangement. A union security arrangement is essentially an agreement that all members will pay dues to the union.

But this statute, in recognition of First Amendment case law, contains an explicit right of "non-association of public employees based on *bona fide* religious tenets or teaching of a church or religious body of which such public employee is a member." If employees have a *bona fide* religious objection, therefore, do not have to pay dues to the union in any way, shape or form. Religious objectors, though, are nonethless required by RCW 41.56.122 to "pay an amount equivalent to regular union dues and initiation fee to a non-religious charity or to another charitable organization mutually agreed on by the public employee affected and the bargaining representative."

First Amendment requirements. Courts have consistently recognized that you cannot compel union membership or dues payment to individuals that have a bona fide religious objection. PERC provides a hearing process for identified objectors and assesses whether the objection is grounded in a bona fide religious belief or some other type of objection.

Court also have ruled there is another First Amendment right that allows individuals not to be compelled to join the union — the First Amendment right of "freedom of association." Just as public employees have a "freedom of association" right to organize and get involved in a union, courts recognize a constitutional right of public employees to not participate in a union

In a series of cases, the United States Supreme Court has ruled that it is not unconstitutional to have an agency shop clause *provided that members have a clear right to opt-out of union membership.* But in return, unions have a right to demand "fair share" contributions, demanding that those who elect to opt out pay for the costs of representation. But these compulsory "fair share" contributions may not be used to pay for activities except those activities specifically related to collective bargaining and contract enforcement.

This doctrine, which balances the rights of employees to opt out of membership with the unions' rights to be paid for services provided, has been in place for some time. But it is current under legal fire and its continued viability under the Supreme Court as it currently exists has been in question. In fact, at the time of publication, a case is pending in the U.S. Supreme Court concerning whether the existing law allowing public sector dues clauses is still recognized as constitutional. A review of the history of this doctrine explains how.

In a series of cases starting in the 1970s, the U.S. Supreme Court adopted rules that balanced constitutional association opt out rights with union service payment rights. New developments, though, raises questions as to whether the court will continue to recognize the right of unions to collect fees for services rendered.

In 1977 in *Abood v. Detroit Board of Education,*[154] the U.S. Supreme Court ruled that it is not inherently unconstitutional to have an agency shop arrangement. The Court did rule, though, that it was unlawful and unconstitutional to require objecting members to pay funds for ideological purposes *not directly related to collective bargaining.* Since *Abood,* public sector labor organizations have developed procedures to allow for a separate accounting of expenditures whenever members objected to paying full union dues.

The fund segregation rules, though, were complex, requiring further court interpretation. In 1986, in *Chicago Teachers Union v. Hudson,*[155] the Supreme Court further clarified its *Abood* holding. The Court ruled that to have a valid agency shop that was enforceable, a labor organization needs to have certain procedural safeguards in place. Those include:

[154] 95 L.R.R.M. 2511 (1977).

[155] 121 L.R.M. 2793 (1986).

(1) Establishment of an escrow fund to hold disputed monies;

(2) Providing employees adequate notice, including a description of the manner in which funds are allocated; and

(3) Providing an "impartial decision maker" on a prompt basis.

Generally, *Hudson* requires a labor union, when challenged, give an accounting of its expenditures by category. The union must show which expenses relate to general collective bargaining purposes and which do not. Under the Hudson process, the union is allowed to hold in escrow all monies over which it has a plausible claim of entitlement in the event a dispute does occur. The union then must make an arrangement to have an "impartial decision maker" review the issue. This requirement has generally been interpreted to mean allowing for the selection of a neutral arbitrator by both parties through a recognized arbitration source such as the American Arbitration Association.

In 1991, in *Lehnart v. Ferris Faculty Association,*[156] the Supreme Court further clarified the scope of which activities by a union were or were not recoverable. The Court reaffirmed its earlier holdings that union activities of an ideological nature were not recoverable from objecting fair-share members. The Court did find, however, that a union could charge for those political activities directly related to the ratification of the labor agreement. The Court also held that a labor organization could charge for general union building activities even those were not directly related to the negotiation and enforcement of an agreement provided those activities were not ideological in nature.

In 1998, in *Marquez v. Screen Actors Guild,*[157] the Supreme Court held that a union contract need not provide specific notice to members on the procedures for claiming fair share status. The unions owe employees procedural rights when they want to opt out of members, including the right to a hearing, but they are not obligated to teach their members how to quit paying dues.

If dissenting members wished to make life more difficult for the union, the *Hudson* process provides an opening for that. The union is obligated to wholly finance this arbitration process.

[156] 137 L.R.R.M. 2321 (1991).
[157] 159 LRRM 2641 (November 3, 1998).

It is uncommon to have objecting members among public safety labor organizations. When there is an objecting member, the requisite procedures a labor organization must set up are expensive and time consuming for that organization. This procedure requires the union to pay for arbitration to prove its "fair share" amount is justified.

A more recent 2014 ruling from the U.S. Supreme Court raise questions of whether the Court might impose even greater restrictions on the ability of public unions to collect dues income. In *Harris v. Quinn,*[158] the court found unconstitutional an Illinois collective bargaining law that allowed a dues deduction system for home health aides. The Illinois dues clause was found unconstitutional. The facts of the case are distinguishable in that the majority decision turned on a conclusion that the home aides were private citizens and not public employees.

What is concerning though is that the majority of the court took a strong swipe at the validity of the Court's previous *Abood* ruling, which started the framework for allowing unions to compel dues payments. The Court stopped short of actually overturning *Abood*, though. It did not seem as if the required five votes existed on the Court to overturn to *Abood* and its line of cases. However, in the Summer of 2015, the Court announced it was accepting review of a case and revisiting whether public unions retain the right to compel payment even on a reduced "fair share" basis.

E. Union Rights to Engage in Political Activities

As indicated earlier, Washington State public employees have a statutory right to participate in political campaigns. Furthermore, labor organizations have a political participation right at least as broad, if not broader than the rights of their members. Labor organizations have First Amendment rights of their own to participate in political campaigns.

Questions have arisen concerning the use of union dues in political campaigns. Initiative 134 was passed several years ago, with the apparent purpose of, among other things, restricting the ability of unions to make political donations. The drafters of the initiative attempted to do this by curtailing the ability of employees to use the agency shop clause provisions in the CBA to divert money to the unions to be used in political campaigns. But a 1998 Supreme Court case rejected the effort of a group called the "Evergreen Freedom Foundation" to prevent unions from using

---

[158] 134 S. Ct. 2618, 2644 (2014).

their dues as a source of income to participate in political campaigns.

The initiative was codified into RCW 42.17. Specifically, RCW 42.17.680 provides:

> (3) No employer or other person or entity responsible for the disbursement of funds in payment of wages or salaries may withhold or divert a portion of an employee's wages or salaries for contributions to political committees or for use as political contributions except upon the written request of the employee. The request must be made on a form prescribed by the commission informing the employee of the prohibition against employer and labor organization discrimination described in subsection (2) of this section. The employee may revoke the request at any time. At least annually, the employee shall be notified about the right to revoke the request.

Shortly after this initiative was enacted, the Public Disclosure Commission (PDC) issued an opinion, which it codified into WAC 390-17-100, that interpreted this provision to only apply to monies being diverted to political committees or monies being specifically designated by the employee for political contributions. This interpretation excluded, then, from the reach of the statute money diverted to a union which in turn might make use of funds for political campaigns.

Therefore, after the statute and the interpretation of the statute by the Public Disclosure Commission, unions continued operating as they always had in collecting funds and distributing those as they saw fit to political campaigns. It is this practice that the "Evergreen Freedom Foundation" took aim at. In *Evergreen Freedom Foundation v. Washington Education Association*,[159] the State Supreme Court rejected the Evergreen Freedom Foundation's argument and upheld the Public Disclosure Commission's interpretation of the statute.

The court reasoned that RCW 42.17A.610 (formerly RCW 42.17.16) had to be harmonized with the collective bargaining statute. The collective bargaining statute specifically allowed money to be diverted to labor unions by an agreement between the employer and the union or, in the absence of an agreement, by the

---

[159] 200 Wash. Lexis 375 (May 18, 2000).

voluntary action of employees. The potential conflict between the two statutes existed — the collective bargaining statute seemingly allowed open-ended access to guild dues, subject to fair share and religious objector withdrawals of funds, while RCW Chapter 42.17 seemingly required employees to annually update their authorization for the deductions. This annual reauthorization requirement obviously would have a practical impact of restricting the flow of funds to the unions.

But the State Supreme Court concluded that finding a conflict between the two statutes was avoidable. It agreed that PDC's narrow interpretation of the statute was sound. The PDC had concluded that, labor organizations were not "political committees" for purposes of the Public Disclosure Act, and the Supreme Court agreed.

One question remains in the aftermath of the case. That question arises from *dicta* (language not essential to the holding) in the majority opinion that is also cited by the dissenting judges. The Supreme Court majority suggested that "when an employer has notice of the funds deducted are for the use of a political committee or candidate, the employer may not then make that deduction without specific annual authorization." Yet the balance of the opinion makes clear that everyone involved in the case fully recognized that unions were, in fact, using these funds for political purposes. Therefore, the court's use of this *dicta* is puzzling, and it leaves open a possible argument that may be made later in cases where employers know that money is being diverted by unions to political campaigns. If that issue arises, there clearly will be a conflict between the specific terms of the collective bargaining statute and the public disclosure statute.

A separate issue arises where public-sector unions use agency shop fees from *nonmembers* for election related purposes. In Washington State, public-sector unions can charge nonmembers an agency fee equivalent to membership dues and have the employer collect that fee through payroll deductions.[160] However, under RCW 42.17A.500(1), unions must obtain the nonmembers' affirmative authorization before using those fees for election-related purposes.

---

[160] RCW 41.80.100.

If the product of that process is the segregation of union funds that are allocated for collective bargaining purposes (which they can compel nonmembers to contribute to) and political purposes (which they cannot compel nonmembers to contribute to), there should be no fair share funds expended on elections.

In *Davenport v. Washington Education Association*,[161] the U.S. Supreme Court also interprted this law. It ruled that there can be no constitutional requirement that nonmembers affirmatively object to the use of their shop fees for election related purposes. In other words, the affirmative duty rests on unions to obtain affirmative authorization before using such fees for election-related purposes. Otherwise, unions might be liable to nonmembers who pay agency fees for restitution and unjust enrichment damages.[162]

For all practical matters, this should not be an issue. If an objector has already opted out of union membership, they should already be subject to the fair share assessment process. If the product of that process is the segregation of union funds that are allocated for collective bargaining purposes (which they can compel nonmembers to contribute to) and political purposes (which they cannot compel nonmembers to contribute to), there should be no fair share funds expended on elections.

Apart from limitations on the sources of union finances for political activities, different local or state contribution limits and reporting requirements may apply, depending on the candidate that a union seeks to support.[163] These limits are adjusted by the PDC each even numbered calendar year based on changing economic conditions and then rounded off "as judged most convenient for public understanding."[164] Before seeking to support political candidates, unions should look to the updated contribution limits and reporting rules imposed by the PDC.

---

161 551 U.S. 177 (2007).

162 *See Davenport v. Washington Educ. Ass'n*, 147 Wash. App. 704 (2008).

163 *See* RCW 42.17A.405.

164 RCW 42.17A.125.

PERC INTERFERENCE CASE TABLE

This chart lists employer actions that have been determined to have been interfering with union rights. It is divided by employer action.

EMPLOYER STATEMENTS

Citation: *Spokane County*, Decision 12216 (PECB, 2014) **Interference Found: No**

Form of Interference: School District Superintendent made a statement to an experienced union vice president during class time that the employer would find out who was responsible for distributing an anonymous letter regarding a principal's performance and discipline them, including civil action.

Explanation: No interference was found where under the "thicker skin" principle, the longer a union official is involved in representing the interest of bargaining unit employees, the less reasonable are their claimed perceptions of threats and coercion. Examiner found the email communication between the Employer and the Union President as frank and candid that reflected frustration within the context of a continuous relationship but that the overall tone and purpose by the Employer was factual or informational, and not persuasive or coercive.

Citation: *Seattle School District*, Decision 12237 (PECB, 2015) **Interference Found: Yes**

Form of Interference: Employer telling custodial engineer that he would not be providing a positive job reference, stating that it was to him as to whether the custodial engineer would get a job, stating that it was unfair for custodial engineer to seek union assistance regarding issue with Employer, and interrupting a step one grievance.

Explanation: Interference could be found where Employer's actions could be reasonably perceived as a threat of reprisal or force, or promise of benefit. Examiner found that this was particularly true when assessing the overall context of the custodial engineer's interaction with the Employer while the lunch set up issue was pending.

Citation: *Kiona Benton School District*, Decision 11035 (EDUC, 2011) **Interference Found: No**

Form of Interference: Employer official's statements to experienced union official during work time regarding acts the employer believed may warrant discipline.

Explanation: No interference found where superintendent made statements to a union official regarding acts that may warrant discipline because, as an experienced union official, he should have been able to recognize that the statements were "puffery." Examiner Atchison explained, "statements made by employer officials are examined differently than statements made by employer officials to rank and file members."

Citation: *Kiona Benton School District*, Decision 11035 (EDUC, 2011) **Interference Found: No**

Form of Interference: Employer telling teacher that her contract would not be renewed after she filed a grievance.

Explanation: No interference found where employer told a teacher that her teaching contract would not be renewed after she filed a grievance because the teacher was informed that her contract would not be renewed before she filed her grievance.

Citation: *State – Social and Health Services*, Decision 11033-A (PSRA, 2011) **Interference Found: Yes**

Form of Interference: Employer's derogatory statements about the union during disciplinary interviews.

Explanation: Interference found by actions and statements of employer's agents during disciplinary interviews. The examiner determined that the union witnesses credibly testified that the employer's agents made statements including, "I want you to know, you are getting bad advice from your union representative." and "They're [union] doing you a disservice by not getting this recorded." The Examiner found that the employer's agents made these derogatory comments in an attempt to influence the employees explaining that it was coercive in tone and it disparaged and undermined the union. "The impact of the detective's behavior undermined and discredited the advice of the union representatives, which interfered with the union's ability to effectively represent its members."

Citation: *Seattle School District*, Decision 10732 (PECB, 2010), *aff'd,* Decision 10732-A (PECB, 2012) **Interference Found: No**

Form of Interference: Employer's email sent to all staff regarding union member duties.

Explanation: No interference found by employer sending an email to "all staff" regarding the employee's work duties and "summon[ing] him and his supervisor" to meet. The Examiner admitted that the employer "should have used more discretion" when sending the email given the content of the message; however, the employee had already made the issue public when he sent his email to "all staff" as well. Moreover, the Examiner found no evidence that the employee reasonably perceived the email as reprisal for the employee contacting the union.

Citation: *City of Pullman,* Decision 11148 (PECB, 2011), *aff'd,* Decision 11148-A (PECB, 2012) **Interference Found: No**

Form of Interference: Employer's policy against retaliation and the consequences for violating the policy.

Explanation: No interference found that the employer did not interfere with employee rights in violation of RCW 41.56.140(1) when the employer's HR manager sent a letter to a union officer "reminding" the union officer of the employer's policies against retaliation and "cautioning him that targeting those who complained against [another union officer] could be considered retaliation" for which he "may be subjecting" himself to disciplinary action. The examiner explained that the "colorful" letter did not constitute interference because it was sent to an experience union leader. "I do not find that a typical union officer who had served on as an executive board member for over 15 years, could reasonably perceived [the] letter as an attempt to discourage protected activity....Her letter discouraged unprotected [retaliatory] activity."

Citation: *City of Pullman,* Decision 11148 (PECB, 2011), *aff'd,* Decision 11148-A (PECB, 2012) **Interference Found: No**

Form of Interference: Employer's policy against retaliation and the consequences for violating the policy.

Explanation: No interference found that the employer did not interfere with employee rights in violation of RCW 41.56.140(1) when the employer's HR manager sent a letter to a union officer about the employer's policies against retaliation and the consequences for violating its policy. The examiner explained that, with respect to the effect of the letter on rank-and–file bargaining unit members, the union's executive board elected to share "limited information" about the employer's letter and thus it cannot reasonably be perceived as a threat of reprisal or force. "Here, the employer cannot be held responsible for the impact of the union's mischaracterization of the employer's letter."

Citation: *City of Pullman*, Decision 11148 (PECB, 2011), a*ff'd,* Decision 11148-A (PECB, 2012) **Interference Found: No**

Form of Interference: "Wolf packs."

Explanation: No interference found when the employer's Chief issued a disciplinary notice including a statement regarding "wolf packs" allegedly sending a message about what it thought of the union. The examiner explained that the union embellished the description and the context of the words in light of the unit member's prior issues with leadership means that the comment did not constitute interference.

Citation: *City of Pullman*, Decision 11148 (PECB, 2011), *aff'd,* Decision 11148-A (PECB, 2012) **Interference Found: No**

Form of Interference: Employer told certain union members at the end of a "managing change" training session to "back off" following reports that certain employees were snickering and making it obvious that they felt the training was a waste of time.

Explanation: The employer did not interfere with employee rights in violation of RCW 41.56.140(1) by statements the employer made regarding unit members participating in a series of trainings telling them to "back off." The examiner explained that in light of complaints the employer received about the unit members, a typical employee could not reasonably perceive the situation as an employer attempt to discourage protected activity.

Citation: *Moses Lake School District*, Decision 8770-A (PECB, 2005) **Interference Found: No**

Form of Interference: Employer criticizing the way the employee completed an assignment, asking the employee to discuss her job performance, and asking the employee to be more efficient.

Explanation: No interference found where employee alleged threatening conduct involving the employer criticizing the way the employee completed an assignment, asking the employee to discuss her job performance, and asking the employee to be more efficient. Examiner found that although these comments may have made the employee feel uncomfortable and led to a poor performance evaluation, they could not reasonably be perceived as threats of reprisal.

Citation: *City of Wenatchee*, Decision 8802-A (PECB, 2006) **Interference Found: No**

Form of Interference: Employer stated that it "would reduce staffing levels unless the union agreed to contractual concessions" during a labor management meeting regarding budgetary overruns of overtime.

Explanation: No interference found by employer's comments and actions during a negotiations meeting because the comments were lawfully within the context of the collective bargaining agreement, and none of the seven concerns outlined in *Grant County Public Hospital District 1*, Decision 8378-A were present. "The employer's comments may have been bad news, but were not reasonably perceived as threats rising to the level of unlawful interference. The message communicated by the employer to the union was that the employer would reduce staffing levels unless the union agreed to contractual concessions. The union's response was to suggest that the employer should hire more fire fighters and it refused to make contractual concessions. The employer then decided to reduce the minimum staffing levels. We see the November 4 meeting as an appropriate discussion between labor and management. An employer faced with a budget problem appropriately asked the union to discuss the issue. Budget problems can be difficult to manage, and employers must be able to have frank discussions with unions to seek possible courses of action."

Citation: *City of Wenatchee*, Decision 8802-A **Interference Found: No**

(PECB, 2006)

Form of Interference: "Ultimatum of action" statements made during labor management meeting regarding budgetary overruns of overtime and minimum staffing levels.

Explanation: No interference found by employer's comments and actions during a negotiations meeting because the comments were lawfully within the context of the collective bargaining agreement, and none of the seven concerns outlined in *Grant County Public Hospital District 1*, Decision 8378-A were present. "There is no indication that the communication was misleading, disrespectful or attempted to evade the legitimate bargaining process. Although the employer's actions could be characterized as an ultimatum of action if the parties do not agree to changes, this alone does not constitute interference. To do so would impose a gag rule on the parties which would hamper the parties' ability to have appropriate communications."

Citation: *Grant County Public Hospital Dist. 1*, Decision 8378-A (PECB, 2004) **Interference Found: Yes**

Form of Interference: Management' s statement during regular staff meeting that he believed issuing subpoenas of employer officials requiring them to testify in another hearing before the Commission was a "bad idea."

Explanation: Interference found where the assistant administrator for patient care at the hospital made statements, during a regularly-scheduled staff meeting, that he believed issuing subpoenas of employer officials requiring them to testify in another hearing before the Commission was a "bad idea." The Commission explained that "while an employer has free speech rights, its opposition to union activities cannot rise to the level of interference with or discrimination against employees for engaging in protected activities." "Employers must use caution when making statements to rank-and-file bargaining unit members as compared to statements made to union officials."

Citation: *Kitsap County*, Decision 8292-A (PECB, 2005), *aff'd in part*, *Kitsap County*, Decision 8292-B (PECB, 2007) **Interference Found: No**

Form of Interference: Sheriff's comment in response to the guild president asking whether the employer was changing its position on release time: "what has the guild done for me?"

Explanation: No interference found where sheriff's comment "what has the guild done for me?" made in response to the guild president asking whether the employer was changing its position on release time. Examiner found that, considering the context and the fact that the sheriff addressed his comment to the guild president, and not a "novice" employee, the comments could not have reasonably been perceived as interfering with collective bargaining rights.

Citation: *City of Tacoma*, Decision 8031-A (PECB, 2004), *aff'd*, Decision 8031-B (PECB, 2004) **Interference Found: No**

Form of Interference: Employer ordering employee to contact her supervisor prior to contacting her union rep about a hostile work environment claim.

Explanation: No interference found where Examiner determined that an employee could not reasonably feel threatened by an employer ordering the employee to contact her supervisor prior to contacting her union representative about a workplace hostility claim.

Citation: *University of Washington*, Decision 9550 (PRSA, 2007) **Interference Found: No**

Form of Interference: Director of Public Safety told some employees that they could leave if they did not like their jobs and that they could be replaced.

Explanation: No interference found where employee was engaged in concerted, not protected union activity when he signed a letter complaining about unsafe working conditions. Examiner Elinski reiterated that "under Washington law, 'concerted activities for ... mutual aid or protection' are not protected under the collective bargaining statutes."

Citation: *Vancouver School District*, Decision 10561 (EDUC, 2009) **Interference Found: No**

Form of Interference: Superintendent's email asking teachers to take a pay decrease as part of "shared sacrifice."

Explanation: No interference found where the District superintendent sent an e-mail asking teachers to take a pay decrease as part of a "shared sacrifice." Bradley found no evidence of intent to coerce bargaining unit members. Generally, evidence of intent is not necessary.

Citation: *Grandview School District*, Decision 12047 (EDUC, 2014) **Interference Found: Maybe**

Form of Interference: An email sent by an employer official to the bargaining unit members about the union president's actions could be construed as undermining, ridiculing or disparaging" the union president.

Explanation: ULP Manager Gedrose issued a preliminary ruling regarding some of union's interference and discrimination claims and dismissed other claims for failure to state a cause of action. An email sent by an employer official to the bargaining unit members about the union president's actions could be construed as undermining, ridiculing or disparaging" the union president and thus "could be reasonably perceived by the other union members as a threat." In contrast, an email from an employer official to the union president admonishing the union president for her behavior is evaluated based on the higher standard because the communication was directed to a union official. The former email states a cause of action for interference whereas the latter email does not. A third email went beyond admonishing the union president and could be construed as a written reprimand. The third email states a cause of action for discrimination and derivative interference.

Citation: *City of Brier*, Decision 10013 (PECB, 2008), *overturned on this issue*, Decision 10013-A (PECB, 2008) **Interference Found: Maybe**

Form of Interference: Employer statements.

Explanation: Interference found where the police chief told a probationary officer that other probationary officers who had served in union leadership had gotten "the short end of the stick."

Citation: *University Place School District*, Decision 9341 (PECB, 2006) **Interference Found: Yes**

Form of Interference: Employer statements.

Explanation: Interference found where a principal indicated to a teacher/union building representative during a performance review that the principal hoped that the teacher did not see her union "role as that of one stirring the pot or causing problems," the comments constituted efforts to inhibit legitimate protected activity.

Citation: *Brinnon School District*, Decision 7210-A (PECB, 2001), *aff'g* Decision 7210 (2000) **Interference Found: No**

Form of Interference: Employer statements.

Explanation: No interference found where staff was open about unionizing activities and employer made statements regarding cost of unionization and statements opposed to unionization because employer and employees met to discuss communication issues and employer had to reduce staff to deal with continued levy failure and declining student enrollment.

Citation: *Columbia Basin College*, Decision 11609-A (PSRA, 2013), *aff'g* Decision 11609 (PSRA, 2012) **Interference Found: No**

Form of Interference: College President responded via e-mail to a bargaining unit member who expressed a desire to remove the union from campus that, "[s]ince this is about the contract and the union, I can't talk about it really. The one thing I can say is what I said in [a] previous email; namely, non-represented employees don't have to take the cut."

Explanation: The Commission affirmed Examiner Irvin's conclusion that the employer did not interfere with employee rights in an email sent by an employer official to all staff discussing the CBA and the temporary salary reduction. The Commission applied the seven criteria to determine whether employer communications constitute interference under *Grant County Public Hospital District 1*, Decision 8378-A (PECB, 2004). The Commission concluded that in this case, the employer's e-mail "was not coercive, the e-mail was not materially misleading, the employer did not offer a new benefit, the employer did not disparage, discredit, ridicule, or undermine the union, and the e-mail did not place the employer in a position from which it could not retreat." The union argued that the email materially misrepresented the facts. The Commission disagreed concluding that the email contained facts about the temporary salary reduction, the union's request to reopen the CBA, the negotiation of the CBA, and the actions the employer took with respect to other employee groups. The Commission explained, "The union's preference for and interpretation of how the employer could negotiate its contract does not render Cummins' communication materially misleading."

Citation: *Seattle School District*, Decision 10435 (PECB, 2009) **Interference Found: No**

Form of Interference: First-line manager told them that a shop was "going away" and transferring would be good for them.

Explanation: No interference found where manager told employees that a shop was "going away" and transferring would be good for them. Atchison found that it would be unreasonable to perceive statement as a threat because "[Manager] was not in a position to make a decision about whether the union would be around and the statement was not supported."

Citation: *City of Omak*, Decisions 5579-A, 5580-A, 5581-A and 5583-A (PECB, 1997) **Interference Found: Yes**

Form of Interference: Police chief by sending daily E-mail messages to police officers announcing changes of policy or practice, creating an impression of surveillance of employees' daily activity.

Explanation: Interference found after police chief became upset with officer making requests for grievance information on behalf of union, by sending daily E-mail messages to police officers announcing changes of policy or practice, creating an impression of surveillance of employees' daily activity, and by threatening discipline of complainants who supported officer in grievance procedure. Messages that officers could no longer make criminal searches from certain computers; could smoke only in the back of the building; should not answer calls outside of the city despite mutual aid agreements with surrounding areas; and directing officers to refrain from discussing internal affairs with police officers of other departments, to take police dogs into restaurant food-service areas only in emergencies, and criticizing incompetent and unprofessional work in a memo addressed "to all whiners", were designed to "stomp on" employees and were reasonably perceived by employees as related to the filing of an earlier grievance.

DENIAL OF WEINGARTEN RIGHT TO REPRESENTATION

Citation: *Pierce County*, Decision 12195 (PECB, 2014) **Interference Found: No**

Form of Interference: Employer told a deputy that having a union representative was unnecessary because their meeting was not investigatory in nature.

Explanation: No interference found where the claim was untimely filed. The Examiner noted that *Weingarten* rights attach to the individual, not the union and therefore the SOL began to run when the deputy in this case had actual or constructive notice of the *Weingarten* rights violation.

Citation: *City of Tacoma*, Decision 11064 (PECB, 2011), *aff'd*, Decision 11064-A (PECB, 2012) **Interference Found: No**

Form of Interference: Employer denied police officer's first choice of union representative when union representative was witness in investigation.

Explanation: No interference found when the employer excluded the employee's first choice union representative due to "special" or "extenuating" circumstances concerning a conflict of interest. The employer properly advised the employee that he needed to select an available, alternate union representative, which he did. "Clearly an employee's right to the union representative of his/her choice is an important right and absent special or extenuating circumstances, is properly the right of union officials, not employers, to decide."

Citation: *Southwest Snohomish County Public Safety Communications Agency*, Decision 11149 (PECB, 2011), *aff'd*, Decision 11149-C (PECB, 2013) **Interference Found: Yes**

Form of Interference: Denial of *Weingarten* right.

Explanation: Interference with a union member's (Basim) *Weingarten* rights found when an assistant police chief from another employer (Caw) interviewed the unit member. The examiner applied the four elements for *Weingarten* rights explaining, "Caw was acting as an agent of SNOCOM when he interviewed Basim on January 14, 2010. Basim had a reasonable belief that discipline could result from the interview. Basim had the right to have a union representative present who was allowed to alert her to problems with questions, ask clarifying questions and communicate with her during the investigatory interview. Basim made it known to Caw and Grady that she brought Penman to the interview as her union representative. By instructing Penman not to interrupt while the interview was in progress and by prohibiting Penman from engaging in any verbal or non-verbal communication with Basim, the employer, through its agent Caw, interfered with Basim's right to union representation in violation of RCW 41.56.140(1)."

Citation: *Southwest Snohomish County Public Safety Communications Agency*, Decision 11149 (PECB, 2011), *aff'd*, Decision 11149-C (PECB, 2013)

Interference Found: No

Form of Interference: Denial of *Weingarten* right.

Explanation: No interference with unit member's (Penman) *Weingarten* rights found when the employer's information services manager called unit member with follow-up interview questions after and investigatory interview in which Penman exercised her right to union representation. The examiner explained in this case, the employer's agent offered to include the union representative in the call and Penman chose to go ahead and answer the questions without representation. "Just as Penman had the right to request union representation during an investigatory interview, Penman also had the right to choose to answer the employer's follow-up questions without a union representative."

Citation: *Seattle School District*, Decision 10732 (PECB, 2010), *aff'd*, Decision 10732-A (PECB, 2012)

Interference Found: No

Form of Interference: Employer denied union representation when meeting at issue was an interview to investigate a harassment complaint.

Explanation: No interference found when the meeting at issue was not investigatory in nature that might lead to disciplinary action. The examiner concluded that the interview was to investigate a harassment complaint filed by the bargaining unit member. The employer made alternate suggestions for meetings in light of a separate investigation against the union rep. The Examiner concluded that the meeting was "to clear up a misunderstanding regarding [the employee's] work duties". Also, the employee did not request a union representative at the meeting and the employer did not reject the request. Here the employee made the request through his union representative who sent an email requesting representation to the employer, and the employer testified that he did not see the email prior to the meeting. The Examiner noted in a footnote that English was the employee's second language.

Citation: *City of Quincy*, Decision 11103 (PECB, 2011) **Interference Found: Yes**

Form of Interference: Employer denied union representation when at a meeting the employer's questions were related to posts employee made on her Facebook page that and he believed they were derogatory toward him.

Explanation: Interference found when the employer's questions during a meeting were related to posts employee made on her Facebook page that he believed were derogatory toward him. The employer argued that it was a short coaching/counseling session and no discipline arose as a result of the meeting. The examiner concluded that the purpose of the interview was investigatory and the employee reasonably believed that discipline might result from the interview given the circumstances around the workplace before and during the meeting.

Citation: *City of Puyallup,* Decision 6784 (PECB, 1999) **Interference Found: Yes**

Form of Interference: *Weingarten* interference.

Explanation: Interference found where employer dismissed a requested union representative from a meeting with an employee and then proceeded to inquire as to why the employee had not signed a deputization form and then threatened the employee with reassignment and insubordination if the form was not signed.

Citation: *Cowlitz County*, Decision 6832 (PECB, 1999) **Interference Found: Yes**

Form of Interference: *Weingarten* interference.

Explanation: Interference violation found where employer denied employee request for union representation at meeting to discuss allegations that employees were kissing while on duty. Employer inquired into whether employees had engaged in alleged conduct, told them to conduct themselves in professional manner, and warned that further incidents could lead to discipline. Employees had contacted union official, and did not waive their right to representation.

Citation: *City of Seattle*, Decision 3079 (PECB, **Interference Found: Yes**

1988), *aff'd*, Decision 3079-A (PECB, 1989)

Form of Interference: Denial of *Weingarten* rights.

Explanation: Interference found where employer refused to allow agent of exclusive bargaining representative to represent bargaining unit employees in the processing of complaints under the employer's internal procedures for sexual harassment.

Citation: *Cowlitz County,* Decision 6832 (PECB, 1999) **Interference Found: No**

Form of Interference: Inquiry whether union representation was needed.

Explanation: No interference found where employee did not make timely request for union representation regarding meeting with supervisor about employee's error in job performance. Employee was entitled to union representation on request, because supervisor said meeting was to be treated as a coaching/counseling session and further errors could result in discipline, but employee only asked if he needed someone to accompany him. Mere inquiry does not constitute a request for representation.

Citation: *Seattle School District*, Decision 9858 (PECB, 2007), *aff'd*, *Seattle School District*, Decision 9858-A (PECB, 2009) **Interference Found: Maybe**

Form of Interference: The district placed a union representative on unpaid leave as a disciplinary matter, and thus prevented the union from communicating with its membership.

Explanation: Interference may be found where the employer takes otherwise permissible actions against a designated union representative that unnecessarily deprives employees of their union representation. In this case, the employer placed a union member on administrative leave for a disciplinary matter under circumstances that could be considered an interference violation.

RESTRICTIONS ON UNION ACTIVITY

Citation: *Port of Anacortes*, Decision 12155 (PORT, 2014) **Interference Found: Yes**

Form of Interference: Wearing union buttons.

Explanation: The employer interfered with employee rights when it called meetings with three employees within a week of the union filing a representation petition to instruct the employees to remove the union buttons they were wearing in support of the union's organization efforts. The examiner determined that employees could reasonably perceive such actions and statements as a threat of reprisal or force associated with their union activity. Also, the examiner concluded that the employer's dress code policy, which did not specifically prohibit wearing buttons or pins, and its interest in maintaining a certain employee image "do not alter the employees' reasonable perception of the employer's actions."

Citation: *State - Employment Security*, Decision 11962 (PSRA, 2013) **Interference Found: Yes**

Form of Interference: Remove union posters from work cubicles.

Explanation: The employer interfered with employee rights in violation of RCW 41.80.110(1)(a), by directing employees to remove union posters from their work cubicles. The examiner explained that the employer's lack of a written cubicle ornamentation policy, allowance of postings within employees' cubicles of many other non-work related materials, and selective enforcement of which union-related posters or union-bearing insignia could be placed in employees' cubicles interfered with protected employee rights under RCW 41.80.110(1)(a). Also, the examiner determined that the employer's directive to remove the posters had a chilling effect on employees from engaging in protected activity by threat of discipline, up to and including termination.

Citation: *Southwest Snohomish County Public Safety Communications Agency*, Decision 11149 (PECB, 2011), *aff'd*, Decision 11149-C (PECB, 2013) **Interference Found: Yes**

Form of Interference: No contact order.

Explanation: The employer interfered with two unit members' (Basim and Penman's) right to engage in protected union activity by prohibiting them from having any contact with current or former employees of the employer and/or the employees of user agencies while they were on paid administrative leave. The examiner explained that the employer's objective to protect the integrity of the investigation could have been achieved simply by ordering the unit members not to discuss the investigation with other employees, as it had done in the past. Hearing Examiner Bradley found that the employer interfered with two unit member's (Basim and Penman's) right to engage in protected union activity by sending an e-mail to all employees prohibiting them from contacting the union's president and second vice-president (Basim and Penman) while they were on paid administrative leave. The examiner explained that the employer's restrictions "directly interfered with the union's ability to conduct business and represent bargaining unit employees in violation of RCW 41.56.140(1)."

Citation: *Southwest Snohomish County Public Safety Communications Agency*, Decision 11149 (PECB, 2011), *aff'd*, Decision 11149-C (PECB, 2013)

Interference Found: Yes

Form of Interference: Order not to discuss discipline.

Explanation: The employer interfered with a unit member's right to engage in protected union activity by prohibiting her from discussing the discipline they received with their co-workers. The examiner explained, "Employees have the right to discuss discipline they receive and to grieve that discipline through processes outlined in their CBA."

Citation: *King County,* Decision 11223 (PECB, 2011)

Interference Found: Yes

Form of Interference: Denying or limiting access to union representative.

Explanation: Interference found where the employer denied and limited access to bargaining unit employees by Local 117 representatives. In this case, the employer admitted it changed its practice of allowing access to the workplace and bargaining unit employees during a pending representation petition. (Under WAC 391-25-140(2), the employer is prohibited from changing the status quo while a representation petition is pending.) The examiner determined that the employer's actions "could lead a typical employee to reasonably perceive the employer was discouraging the right of employees to organize and designate representatives of their own choosing."

Citation: *King County,* Decision 11223 (PECB, 2011)

Interference Found: Yes

Form of Interference: Employer actions conveyed organizational preference.

Explanation: Interference found where employer indicated a preference between competing organizations seeking to represent its employees during the pendency of a representation petition. In this case, the employer admitted it permitted one union rep to restrict access to the employer's facility by another rep and that its actions conveyed the message that the employer preferred one union over another. "Based on these admissions, the examiner concludes that a typical employee could reasonably perceive the employer's preference for the Security Guild over Local 117 as discouraging the right of employees to organize and designate representatives of their own choosing, in violation of RCW 41.56.140(1) and WAC 391-25-140(3)."

Citation: *University of Washington,* Decision 11091 (PSRA, 2011), *aff'd,* Decision 11091-A (PSRA, 2012) **Interference Found: No**

Form of Interference: Formal counseling letter for insubordination related to the delivery of grievances.

Explanation: No interference found where the employer issued a shop steward, who handled grievances, a formal counseling letter for insubordination for failing to follow management's direction not to use his employer-issued keys to enter locked offices to deliver grievances. The examiner applied the reasonableness test and determined that the shop steward's method of using his employer-issued keys to open locked office doors to deliver grievances after being "repeatedly directed not to" was not reasonable because he had other options.

Citation: *University of Washington,* Decision 11091 (PSRA, 2011), *aff'd,* Decision 11091-A (PSRA, 2012) **Interference Found: No**

Form of Interference: Limiting method to deliver grievances.

Explanation: No interference found where employer limited the method in which the electrician shop steward delivered grievances. The Commission explained that the method of delivery (using employee issued keys to enter locked offices after allegedly being warned not to do so) was not protected activity. The union had argued that the Examiner erred in separating the method of delivering a grievance from filing a grievance, which is protected activity. The Commission explained the distinction stating, "While the act of initiating a grievance for processing is considered protected activity, nothing expressly gives an employee a protected right to use employer equipment to serve those contractual grievances upon the employer. This includes using the employer's equipment to physically prepare or file that grievance. Therefore, it is not reversible error for the Examiner to analyze separately the method by which [the shop steward] served grievances.

Citation: *Washington State Ferries*, Decision 11335 (MRNE, 2012), *aff'd,* Decision 11335-A (MRNE, 2012) **Interference Found: No**

Form of Interference: Termination and denial of ferry worker's post termination grievance.

Explanation: No interference found where the employer terminated a ferry employee who had not worked actively for more than seven years because he was on leave for a sleep condition. There is no evidence in the record that would "lead a typical employee to think that [employee's] union activities were being discouraged by the employer."

Citation: *City of Benton City*, Decision 10956 (PECB, 2011) **Interference Found: Yes**

Form of Interference: Employer no longer allowed union representatives to meet with bargaining unit members during their work time.

Explanation: Interference (and discrimination) found where the employer no longer allowed union representatives to meet with bargaining unit members during their work time after the union had demanded arbitration of a grievance. "The union successfully met its burden of proof to show that a protected activity was a substantial motivating factor for discontinuing the union meetings at City Hall during work hours and the justifications provided by employer were pretextual and retaliatory in nature."

Citation: *Northshore Utility District*, Decision 10534 (PECB, 2009), *aff'd*, Decision 10534-A (PECB, 2010) **Interference Found: No**

Form of Interference: Termination of employee for violation of employee handbook and layoff of union president due to downturn in housing market.

Explanation: No interference found for termination of employee and layoff of union president where the District established it had a legitimate, non-discriminatory business reasons for separating two employees from employment, and those actions did not constitute interference with protected union activity.

Citation: *Seattle School District*, Decision 9858 (PECB, 2007), *aff'd*, *Seattle School District*, Decision 9858-A (PECB, 2009) **Interference Found: Yes**

Form of Interference: Principal insisted that either the union representative meet with him, or that he step down and appoint a new representative.

Explanation: Interference found where District Principal insisted that either the union representative meet with him, or that he step down and appoint a new representative. "Unfortunately, [the principal] cut to the political chase and inferred [sic] quite strongly that the union needed to appoint someone other than Femiano as a building representative. In saying that, [the principal] interfered with SEA/WEA authority to appoint or allow election of building representatives."

Citation: University *of Washington*, Decision 11181-A (PSRA, 2013) **Interference Found: Yes**

Form of Interference: Employer refused to process a grievance filed by the union on behalf of employee.

Explanation: Interference found where the employer refused to process a grievance filed by the union on the employee's behalf. The employee was a unit member pending the resolution of a unit clarification petition. The Commission explained that *status quo* must be maintained until the resolution of pending unit clarification and representation cases and the *status quo* in this case is that the employee was represented by the union.

Citation: *City of Lynnwood*, Decision 10522 (PECB, 2009) **Interference Found: No**

Form of Interference: The Lynnwood Engineers Group (LEG) sought to represent employees in the public works engineering services division who were at the time represented by another union, the WSCCCE. The WSCCCE alleged that the LEG's use of employer contact information on a representation petition inferred with employee rights.

Explanation: No interference found where the City did not act in a manner that that could be perceived as interference, when an employee unilaterally used an employer mailing address for union activity without the employer's knowledge. "An interference violation exists when an employee could reasonably perceive the employer's actions as a threat of reprisal or force, or promise of benefit, associated with the protected union activity of the employee or other employees."

Citation: *Snohomish County*, Decision 9799 (PECB, 2007) **Interference Found: No**

Form of Interference: Employer comments regarding the merits of a grievance.

Explanation: No interference found where a reasonable employee could not perceive the comments of the employer regarding the merits of a grievance as a prohibition on filing a grievance. "Bargaining unit employees are smart enough to know that they may always communicate with a union representative for a balanced opinion about what claims could be filed in a labor law setting. And that was the action here."

Citation: *King County*, Decision 8630-A (PECB, 2005) **Interference Found: No**

Form of Interference: Employer rules restricting the distribution of campaign literature to off-duty hours.

Explanation: No interference where the employer implemented rules restricting the distribution of campaign literature to off-duty hours because the rules reasonably allowed employees to conduct campaign activity during non-working hours and in specified areas. The Commission acknowledged that while the employer could have explicitly defined many of the terms used within the memorandum identifying the restrictions on union distributions, such as "off-duty hours," it found that the rules failed to rise to the level of interfering with protected employee rights because the rules reasonably allowed employees to conduct campaign activity during non-working hours and in specified areas.

Citation: *Seattle School District*, Decision 8976 (PECB, 2005) **Interference Found: Yes**

Form of Interference: Destruction of witness statement requested by the union.

Explanation: Interference found where the school principal intentionally destroyed a written witness statement requested by the union. "A typical employee could reasonably perceive the intentional destruction of a statement as coercive or threatening."

SURVEILLANCE OF UNION ACTIVITY

Citation: *City of Spokane,* Decision 11263 (PECB, 2011) **Interference Found: No**

Form of Interference: Attendance at union meeting.

Explanation: The employer did not interfere with employee rights when dealing with a proposal to sever sergeants from the existing bargaining unit. The chief's attendance, by invitation, at a meeting of the sergeants where severance was discussed did not reasonably create an impression of surveillance by the chief or that the chief was there to spy. The meeting was an information gathering session, and not a "propaganda rally" at which both the chief and the Guild president were invited to speak. In this case, the Guild failed to show that a typical employee, in the same circumstances, could reasonably conclude that the chief was encouraging or discouraging union activities by attending the meeting of the sergeants.

Citation: *City of Seattle*, Decision 9945 (PECB, 2007), *aff'd*, Decision 9945-A (PECB, 2009) **Interference Found: No**

Form of Interference: City subpoenaed internal union documents in a civil rights lawsuit filed against the city by an office.

Explanation: No interference where the City subpoenaed specific and limited internal union documents in a civil rights lawsuit filed against the city by an officer who asserted that events pertinent to his cause involved specific union activities. "The manner in which the employer sought information was appropriate. The employer had a valid purpose for seeking information, it had a narrow focus in the type of information sought, and it responded to the union's initial concerns with offers and suggestions to narrow the information requested for production."

Citation: *City of Longview*, Decision 9884 (PECB, 2007) **Interference Found: No**

Form of Interference: Police sergeant/ union president, directed to notify his superiors where his union duties could conflict with his responsibilities as a sergeant.

Explanation: No interference found where a police sergeant, who was also the union president, perceived a directive letter to be interference. The letter did not specify when he could or could not act in his union capacity, but only requested that he notify his superiors where the duties could conflict with his responsibilities as a sergeant of the small police force.
The City's actions were not unlawful interference with union activities where, after a sergeant had two conflicts between his duty to investigate subordinates misconduct and his duty to represent union members as the union president, the employer proposed a policy designed to clarify when the sergeant was acting in each capacity. The policy was not a directive towards one role or the other, but simply attempted to discern "when it would be appropriate for your union role to be primary over that of LPD sergeant," to achieve more efficient investigations.

Citation: *Town of Granite Falls*, Decision 2692 (PECB, 1987) **Interference Found: Yes**

Form of Interference: Perceived surveillance.

Explanation: Interference found where the employer created the impression that employees engaged in organizing and selecting bargaining representatives were under surveillance.

Citation: *City of Seattle*, Decision 3066 (PECB, 1987), *aff'd*, Decision 3066-A (PECB, 1989) **Interference Found: No**

Form of Interference: Supervisor reviewed papers on top of and in drawers of employees' desks.

Explanation: No interference found where supervisor obtained information necessary for computerized record keeping system from review of papers on top of and in drawers of employees' desks.

Citation: *City of Bremerton*, Decision 3843-A **Interference Found: No**

(PECB, 1994)

Form of Interference: Comments creating impression of surveillance.

Explanation: No interference where union fails to establish unfair labor practice for "surveillance" activity at union meetings held at city hall, where comments by police supervisor that he always knew what happened in union meetings were likely made in jest, and employer did not solicit or have a "spy" at union meetings.

Citation: *City of Vancouver*, Decision 6732 (PECB, 1999) **Interference Found: No**

Form of Interference: Questioning unit members during IA investigation about alleged comments made during union meetings.

Explanation: No interference found where questioned members of police officer bargaining unit during internal affairs investigation about alleged harassing, discriminatory, and retaliatory comments made during union meetings because: internal affairs process not inherently coercive regarding future exercise of union rights; employees had voluntarily told employer about alleged harassing, discriminatory, and retaliatory comments made during union meetings so no implication of surveillance; the alleged harassing, discriminatory, and retaliatory comments were discussed openly and widely in workplace before employer questioned employees; allegations raised legitimate business concerns for employer in areas of integrity of internal affairs process, officer safety, and potential liability; assurances given and scope of questions limited so questioning didn't pose reasonable threat of future employer interference with union activities.

Citation: *City of Bremerton*, Decision 3843 (PECB, 1991) **Interference Found: Maybe**

Form of Interference: Allegations that a supervisor sought attendance at a closed union meeting.

Explanation: Allegations that a supervisor sought attendance at a closed union meeting appears to be an unfair labor practice violation and the matter is remanded to an Examiner. Surveillance of union activities by a supervisor is generally found to be an unlawful "interference" under RCW 41.56.140(1).

Citation: *City of Longview*, Decision 4702 (PECB, 1994) **Interference Found: Yes**

Form of Interference: Employer asked unit members about things discussed at closed union meeting.

Explanation: Interference found where employer gave impression of surveillance of lawful union activities by interrogating employees concerning discussions at closed union meeting.

Citation: *City of Omak*, Decisions 5579-A, 5580-A, 5581-A and 5583-A (PECB, 1997) **Interference Found: Yes**

Form of Interference: Police chief by sending daily E-mail messages to police officers announcing changes of policy or practice, creating an impression of surveillance of employees' daily activity.

Explanation: Interference found after police chief became upset with officer making requests for grievance information on behalf of union, by sending daily E-mail messages to police officers announcing changes of policy or practice, creating an impression of surveillance of employees' daily activity, and by threatening discipline of complainants who supported officer in grievance procedure. Messages that officers could no longer make criminal searches from certain computers; could smoke only in the back of the building; should not answer calls outside of the city despite mutual aid agreements with surrounding areas; and directing officers to refrain from discussing internal affairs with police officers of other departments, to take police dogs into restaurant food-service areas only in emergencies, and criticizing incompetent and unprofessional work in a memo addressed "to all whiners", were designed to "stomp on" employees and were reasonably perceived by employees as related to the filing of an earlier grievance.

Citation: *Skagit County*, Decision 6348 (PECB, 1998) **Interference Found: No**

Form of Interference: Employer's having sheriff deputies monitor a ferry operation and watch for employee misconduct.

Explanation: No interference in employer's having sheriff deputies monitor a ferry operation after announcing its plan to contract out bargaining unit work, where assigned officers were instructed to watch for employee misconduct that would not have been protected activity under chapter 41.56 RCW. Deputies' presence was not reasonably perceived by employees as surveillance or interference with their lawful union activities. The benign monitoring led only to a "no-incident" report filed the next day, no employee was disciplined, and no union meeting, picketing, or other union demonstration was planned.

INTERROGATION CONCERNING UNION ACTIVITY

Citation: *City of Seattle*, Decision 9526-A (PECB, 2009) **Interference Found: No**

Form of Interference: Employer interviewed bargaining unit members in advance of grievance arbitration.

Explanation: No interference found where employer interviewed bargaining unit members in preparation for an arbitration hearing. The Commission found that the union failed to demonstrate by a preponderance of the evidence that the employer violated the *Johnnie's Poultry* requirements because the union failed to prove "[...] that the employer asked employees questions relating to the grievance to be arbitrated and that questions were otherwise coercive."

Citation: *City of Vancouver*, Decision 6732-A (PECB, 1999), *rev'g* Decision 6732 (PECB, 1999) **Interference Found: Yes**

Form of Interference: Employer questioning union members

Explanation: Interference found where employer interrogated members of police officer bargaining unit during internal affairs investigation under threat of discipline about statements or conduct at private union meetings. Employees could reasonably perceive the questioning to be coercive.

Citation: *Port Angeles School District*, Decision 7198 (PECB, 2000) **Interference Found: Maybe**

Form of Interference: Employee questioned without union representative.

Explanation: Complaint charging unfair labor practice found to state cause of action of interference, where employee was questioned regarding his conduct at work during a meeting that was part of an ongoing disciplinary plan of improvement. The complaint also alleged interference by means of a threat to impose harsher discipline if the bargaining unit member contacted the union.

Here, the employer official made a statement about the treatment the bargaining unit member would receive if he did not have union representation.

Citation: *City of Vancouver v. PERC,* 107 Wash. App. 694 (2001), WPERR CD, *rev'g City of Vancouver*, Decision 6732 (PECB, 1999), *aff'g* Decision 6732-A (PECB, 1999)

Interference Found: No

Form of Interference: Interrogation concerning union activity.

Explanation: Court of Appeals overturned Commission's decision and found that employer may ask members of unit about discussions occurring at union executive board meeting or at general membership meeting, if: (1) questioning occurs in course of valid investigation into legitimate employment issue, questions are narrowly tailored to purpose of investigation, and (2) employer avoids questions that would amount to interference with collective bargaining rights protected by Chapter 41.56 RCW. Test is whether, under all the circumstances, questioning reasonably tends to restrain, coerce, or interfere. To determine whether employer' s questioning interferes with statutorily protected collective bargaining rights, court considers totality of circumstances, including (1) history of employers attitude towards employees, (2) type of information sought, (3) rank of questioner, (4) place and manner of conversation, (5) truthfulness of employee's responses, (6) whether employer had valid purpose for obtaining information, (7) whether employer communicated purpose to employee, and (8) whether employer assured employee that no reprisals would be forthcoming if employee is supportive of union. Eight factors do not constitute per se test; court may find coercive questioning to have occurred even if all eight factors weigh in employer's favor. When union alleges that employer has been looking into union meeting activities, thereby interfering with union activity or violating collective bargaining rights under Chapter 41.56 RCW, burden shifts to employer to present evidence demonstrating reasonable justification for actions. Activity cannot be unreasonable, irresponsible or abusive. Conspiracy by union members to retaliate against individual member is not reasonable exercise of union activity.

Citation: *City of Pullman,* Decision 11148 (PECB, 2011), *aff'd,* Decision 11148-A (PECB, 2012)

Interference Found: No

Form of Interference: Investigation in bad faith.

Explanation: The employer did not interfere with employee rights in violation of RCW 41.56.140(1) in the manner in which its HR manager conducted its investigation. The examiner rejected the union's argument that the investigation was conducted "in bad faith for the purpose of seeking some basis for disciplinary action against them." The examiner dismissed the interference complaint because a bargaining unit member would expect an employer to conduct an investigation into the allegations. Also, the charge is dismissed because it is based upon the same set of facts that failed to constitute a discrimination violation.

Citation: *City of Vancouver*, Decision 6732-A (PECB, 1999), *aff'g* Decision 6732 (PECB, 1999) **Interference Found: Yes**

Form of Interference: Interrogation of police during IA.

Explanation: Interference found where employer interrogated members of police officer bargaining unit during internal affairs investigation under threat of discipline about statements or conduct at private union meetings. Employees could reasonably perceive the questioning to be coercive.

Citation: *University of Washington*, Decision 11199-B (PSRA, 2013) **Interference Found: No**

Form of Interference: Investigating unit member.

Explanation: No interference found where employer investigated unit member in connection with his union activities and issued him a final counseling memo because no discrimination was found and under PERC precedent, "an independent interference violation cannot be found under the same set of facts that fails to constitute a discrimination violation."

DIRECT DEALING

Citation: *City of Yakima*, Decision 9062-A (PECB, 2006), *aff'd,* Decision 9062-B (PECB, 2008) **Interference Found: No**

Form of Interference: Direct dealing.

Explanation: In *City of Yakima*, Hearing Examiner Yoshitomi found that the employer did not commit an unfair labor practice by circumventing the union in handling an employee's discipline because the union was involved at all the meetings between the employee and the employer, and there was no other evidence that the employer dealt directly with the employee. "An employer that bypasses the exclusive bargaining representative of its employees and deals directly with the employees themselves on mandatory subjects of bargaining commits an unfair labor practice."

Citation: *Tacoma Pierce County Health Department*, Decision 6929-A (PECB, 2001) **Interference Found: No**

Form of Interference: Direct dealing.

Explanation: No direct dealing, where employer met with employees concerning several reorganization plans. Subjects of discussion were permissive subjects of bargaining, and employer also met with union representatives to inform them of reorganization plans being considered.

THREATS OR PROMISES TO CHANGE TERMS OF EMPLOYMENT

Citation: *City of Spokane,* Decision 11263 (PECB, 2011) **Interference Found: Yes**

Form of Interference: Promise of benefits.

Explanation: Interference found where the employer issued promises of benefit to bargaining unit members that could influence their union activities. "When the chief granted disciplinary authority to the sergeants, both the sergeants and the patrol officers represented by the Guild were to be impacted by the change. They could both see that the employer was encouraging the severance of the sergeants from the Guild bargaining unit. The patrol officers could reasonably perceive that their right to maintain their bargaining unit was being discouraged by the employer. By granting "consequential discipline" to the sergeants, the employer interfered with employee rights protected by the statute."

Citation: *Kiona Benton School District*, Decision 11035 (EDUC, 2011) **Interference Found: Yes**

Form of Interference: Investigation.

Explanation: Interference found where an agent of the employer selected nine teachers for investigation because "a typical employee could reasonably believe that the employer's investigation was centered around union activities, and could reasonably perceive the employer's actions as a threat of reprisal or force, or promise of benefit, associated with the union activity of certain employees." The incidents giving rise to the investigation occurred in an elementary school but the union president and the union vice president (both of which who taught in the middle school) were investigated, along with the teacher who filed a grievance, and others.

Citation: *Columbia Basin College*, Decision 11609 (PSRA, 2012) **Interference Found: Yes**

Form of Interference: Salary.

Explanation: Interference found where employer suggested to bargaining unit members that they would not receive a 3 percent temporary salary reduction if they decertified the union. Both occasions involved communications between employer officials and bargaining unit members whereby an employee could reasonably perceive the employer's action as a promise of benefit associated with union activity.

Citation: *City of Tacoma*, Decision 8031-B (PECB, 2004) **Interference Found: No**

Form of Interference: Punishing employee for insubordination.

Explanation: At the time of the alleged interference, the employer had contracted with an independent company to assist with several computer projects. The contractor's arrangements with the employer called for the contractor's employees to act as the "technical lead" for the contracted for work, meaning they were to assume responsibility for the completion and oversight of the project.
However, the employer and its representative retained all disciplinary and personnel authority. Following a series of incidents involving the complainant and contractor personnel, the complainant was instructed to contact her supervisor first in the event of future conflicts to prevent work problems, including a loss of productivity.
The union asserted that the complainant could reasonably have understood supervisor's statements to mean that complainant was not supposed to contact her union representative, and that she could reasonably perceive that she was punished because she did so.

Citation: *University Place School District*, **Interference Found: Yes**

Decision 9341 (PECB, 2006)

Form of Interference: Threats related to performance evaluation.

Explanation: Interference found where during the teacher/union building representative's performance review, the principal told the teacher that she had consulted an attorney about slander and defamation following union efforts to investigate complaints about the principal. Hearing Examiner Helm found the principal's reference to her conversation with an attorney to be "inherently coercive in nature" and connoted a reasonable inference of adverse impact on the teacher, and therefore constituted unlawful interference with the teacher's union rights.

Citation: *Wenatchee School District*, Decision 8206-A (EDUC, 2005) **Interference Found: No**

Form of Interference: Transfer of employee.

Explanation: No interference found that the employer transferred employee to another school because no reasonable employee could have perceived that the employer's transfer of complainant to another school was based on the complainant's union activity. Here, the employer had taken testimony from more than 30 employees regarding other hostile work environment complaints about the complainant, the typical employee knew of other reasons for the complainant's transfer, and did not see it as connected to his protected union activity.

Citation: *King County*, Decision 3318 (PECB, 1989) **Interference Found: Yes**

Form of Interference: Transfer of employee.

Explanation: Interference found where employer imposed adverse transfer on employee who was pursuing a grievance regarding a previous re-assignment.

Citation: *Pierce County Fire District No. 9*, Decision 3334 (PECB, 1989) **Interference Found: No**

Form of Interference: Threat or promise to change terms of employment.

Explanation: No interference was found where employee's conduct and remarks become adversarial and confrontational (remained standing, conducted himself in an adversarial manner, and became agitated and confrontational while in employer's office), while serving as union representative in meeting called by employer to issue written reprimand to another employee. Employee's role as union representative does not allow him to disregard normally accepted standards of behavior in his dealings with his superiors, or to behave with impunity.

Citation: *Seattle School District*, Decision 11045-A (PECB, 2011) **Interference Found: No**

Form of Interference: Threats to change terms of employment.

Explanation: No interference found where the employer threatened an employee with a negative evaluation in retaliation for his exercise of protected employee rights because the supervisor's comment during an investigatory interview was in response to non-protected activity. The union had requested an additional interference finding on appeal related to a supervisor denying an employee his *Weingarten* right to representation. Without additional analysis, the Commission determined that "because the Commission dismissed the discrimination portion of the complaint, an independent interference violation cannot be found."

Citation: *City of Omak,* Decisions 5579-B, 5580-B, 5581-B and 5583-B (PECB, 1998), *modifying* Decisions 5579-A, 5580-A, 5581-A and 5583-A (PECB, 1997) **Interference Found: Yes**

Form of Interference: Chief sending police officers E-mail messages that had a threatening tone, and that threatened discipline of complainants who supported officer in grievance procedure.

Explanation: Employer interfered with employee rights, after an employee filed a grievance, by sending police officers E-mail messages that had a threatening tone, and that threatened discipline of complainants who supported officer in grievance procedure. Messages that officers could no longer make criminal searches from certain computers; could smoke only in the back of the building; should not answer calls outside of the city despite mutual aid agreements with surrounding areas; and directing officers to refrain from discussing internal affairs with police officers of other departments, to take police dogs into restaurant food-service areas only in emergencies, and criticizing employees as incompetent and unprofessional, were designed to "stomp on" employees and were reasonably perceived by employees as related to the filing of an earlier grievance.

Commission deletes announcement of changes of policy and practice and surveillance of union activity as bases for interference violation.

Citation: *King County*, Decision 6994-A (PECB, 2001) **Interference Found: No**

Form of Interference: FMLA.

Explanation: No interference found where union failed to establish that any bargaining unit member reasonably perceived employer actions which altered FMLA reporting requirements as threats of reprisal or force or promises of benefit associated the exercise of rights under Chapter 41.56 RCW, where no employee was adversely affected by employer, employee continued to hold status as employee on leave under FMLA, and no occasion for filing grievance arose.

OTHER

Citation: *City of Pullman*, Decision 11148 (PECB, 2011), *aff'd*, Decision 11148-A (PECB, 2012) **Interference Found: No**

Form of Interference: Other interference.

Explanation: Employer did not interfere with employee rights in violation of RCW 41.56.140(1) when the bargaining unit members were accused of stealing another unit member's keys and the police investigated them because the record does not show that any employer representative played any part in the unit member's decision to report her missing keys to the police. Also, the issue was not timely.

Citation: *City of Pullman*, Decision 11148 (PECB, 2011), *aff'd*, Decision 11148-A (PECB, 2012) **Interference Found: No**

Form of Interference: Subjected to greater scrutiny, investigations and discipline.

Explanation: No interference found that the employer did not interfere with employee rights in violation of RCW 41.56.140(1) by subjecting those employees who spoke out in favor of the union president to greater scrutiny, investigations and discipline for incidents involving swearing and the proper use of personal protective equipment. The union argued that firefighters who were working on C shift were accused of stealing another firefighter's keys and that the police investigation initiated by the other firefighter constituted employer interference. The examiner recognized that the parties were frustrated and tensions mounted but ultimately found that some of the issues were outside of management's control and/or no disciplinary action resulted and thus a typical employee looking at this situation could not reasonably perceive the employer's action as a threat of reprisal for engaging in protected activity.

Citation: *Snohomish County*, Decision 9570 (PECB, 2007) **Interference Found: No**

Form of Interference: Employer charging union for copies.

Explanation: No interference where employer charged for copies because although it affected the financial resources of the union, it did not rise to the level required to find that the employer controlled, dominated, or interfered with a bargaining representative by "involving itself in the internal affairs or finances of the union, or attempts to create, fund, or control a 'company union.'"

Citation: *Snohomish County*, Decision 9570 (PECB, 2007) **Interference Found: Yes**

Form of Interference: Employer charging difference prices for copies.

Explanation: Interference found where in the context of collective bargaining information requests, the employer imposed different prices for copies for different unions and imposing those charges only for voluminous requests for information because the difference prices could result in the perception that an employer is attempting to discourage the union's exercise of its right to request relevant collective bargaining information.

PERC DISCRIMINATION AND RETALIATION TABLE

This chart shows various employer actions and whether they were found to be unlawful discrimination or retaliation against union members.

Citation: *Aberdeen School District*, Decision 6434 (PECB, 1998) **Discrimination Found: No**

Charge: Visible and aggressive union steward discharged for failing to disclose criminal record in employment application.

Explanation: No discrimination found where employee falsified his employment application and all employees who committed the same offense received the same sanction. No employer union animus was shown at time of discharge, or in connection with an earlier discharge.

Citation: *Asotin County Housing Authority*, Decision 2471 (PECB, 1986), *aff'd*, Decision 2471-A (PECB, 1987) **Discrimination Found: Yes**

Charge: Union organizers were discharged for alleged unsatisfactory work and because the positions were outsourced to cut costs.

Explanation: Discrimination found where two employees who signed union authorization cards were terminated within five days of meeting with a union organizer and signing authorization cards. The employer retained the services of the only individual who didn't sign an authorization card despite his lesser seniority. The personnel records of the terminated individuals did not suggest their performance was poor and the employer's economic justification argument was irrational.

Citation: *Asotin County Housing Authority*, Decision 3241 (PECB, 1989) **Discrimination Found: No**

Charge: Hiring new employees while considering laying off long-term employees who had previously filed ULPs.

Explanation: No discrimination found where union failed to sustain its burden of proof that employer's hiring of an administrative assistant/maintenance supervisor intended to interfere with statutorily protected rights or discrimination against bargaining unit members. Union also failed to show link between its successful ULP charge three years earlier and current budget shortfall which resulted in layoffs.

Citation: *Auburn School District*, Decision 2291 (PECB, 1985) **Discrimination Found: Yes**

Charge: Refusal to hire applicant whose sister was active in union grievances.

Explanation: Discrimination found where employer refused to hire applicant because applicant's sister was an active union shop steward involved in a grievance at the time applicant interviewed for available employment.

Citation: *Benton City*, Decision 436 (PECB, 1978) **Discrimination Found: Yes**

Charge: Discharging employees who had supported union.

Explanation: Discrimination found where employer reduced work hours of an employee because of her union activity, and discharged her and another employee involved with the union. Employer failed to respond to allegation or file an answer so union's allegations were accepted as true and examiner did not discuss underlying claim that discharge was in retaliation for union involvement.

Citation: *Bethel School District*, Decision 6731 (PECB, 1999) **Discrimination Found: Yes**

Charge: Failing to offer continuing contract.

Explanation: Discrimination found where the employer failed to offer employee a continuing contract. Union animus held to be a substantial motivating factor in employer's action, where it followed complainant's contact with the union and employer informing her she was a troublemaker because of the contact. Employer's defense that it hired a better candidate is pretext designed to conceal union animus, where employee had been given excellent work performance evaluations and highly complementary recommendations.

Citation: *Brinnon School District*, Decision 7210 (PECB, 2000), *aff'd*, Decision 7210-A (PECB, 2001) **Discrimination Found: No**

Charge: Reduction in staff.

Explanation: No discrimination found even though employer made statements regarding unionizing cost and statements opposed to unionization, because union failed to demonstrate employer was motivated by anti-union bias. Employer had to reduce staff to deal with continued levy failure and declining student enrollment and "[a] simple statement that the employer would incur costs [from unionizing] is not unlawful."

Citation: *Chelan Public Hospital District 2*, Decision 11294 (PECB, 2012) **Discrimination Found: No**

Charge: Discharge of paramedic.

Explanation: No discrimination found where the union alleged the employer discriminated against a paramedic for giving testimony before the Commission or for union activities when it terminated him. Examiner Aravena determined that the union established a prima facie case for discrimination: terminated paramedic engaged in protected union activities, the employer knew of the paramedic's union activities, paramedic was terminated which deprived him of an ascertainable right, benefit, or status, and the short time in between the employee testifying at the Commission hearing and his termination supports a causal inference. But the examiner determined that the employer had legitimate, non-discriminatory business reasons for termination: paramedic created a hostile work environment and threatened and demeaned female coworkers. Union did not establish that the employer's justifications for termination were pretextual or that its actions were retaliatory in nature.

Citation: *City of Bellevue*, Decision 2096 (PECB, 1984) **Discrimination Found: No**

Charge: Discharging employee.

Explanation: No discrimination found where the employer knew, prior to discharge, that employee was involved in assisting union seeking to represent employees: Record showed that employer discharged employee for reasons unrelated to engaging in protected union activities and employee failed to establish prima facie case of antiunion motivation.

Citation: *City of Benton City*, Decision 10956 (PECB, 2011)	**Discrimination Found: Yes**

Charge: Employer changed policy regarding when and where union meetings can occur.

Explanation: Discrimination found where employer no longer allowed union representatives to meet with bargaining unit members during their work time in reprisal for protected union activity of demanding arbitration of a grievance: "The union successfully met its burden of proof to show that a protected activity was a substantial motivating factor for discontinuing the union meetings at City Hall during work hours and the justifications provided by employer were pretextual and retaliatory in nature."

Citation: *City of Bremerton*, Decision 3843-A, 4738, 4739 (PECB, 1994)	**Discrimination Found: No**

Charge: Employer surveillance at union meetings.

Explanation: No discrimination found where union failed to establish "surveillance" activity at union meetings held at city hall, where comments by police supervisor that he always knew what happened in union meetings were likely made in jest, and employer did not solicit or have a "spy" at union meetings.

Citation: *City of Centralia*, Decision 2904 (PECB, 1988)	**Discrimination Found: No**

Charge: Refusal to hire.

Explanation: No discrimination found where unit member is unable to demonstrate a nexus between his former employer's refusal to rehire him and his filing and processing of a previous unfair labor practice charge against it.

Citation: *City of Federal Way*, Decision 5183 (PECB, 1995), *aff'd*, Decision 5183-A (PECB,	**Discrimination Found: Yes, but overturned**

1996), *rev'd*, King County Superior Court, WPERR CD - 1009 (January 10, 1997), *aff'd*, Court of Appeals, 93 Wn.App. 509, 970 P.2d 752 (Wash. Ct. App. 1998)

Charge: Discharge of union activist due to "lack of work."

Explanation: PERC found discrimination found when employer laid-off visible union activist on one-day notice due to "lack of work." PERC concluded this was pretext and that union activities constituted substantial factor motivating termination because employees with less service were retained and co-worker laid off at same time was rehired within months. However, the King County Superior court and the Court of Appeals disagreed with PERC and held there were not enough facts to support a finding of discrimination.

Citation: *City of Kalama*, Decision 7448 (PECB, 2001) **Discrimination Found: Yes**

Charge: Union president discharged on allegations of misuse of employer's credit card to obtain fuel for his private vehicle despite unwritten policy permitting such use.

Explanation: Discrimination found where employer was substantially motivated by animus against newly certified union and its first president. Employer and union had acrimonious bargaining relationship, with union filing multiple unfair labor practice complaints. Union president (whose union activities were known to employer because he actively represented union in contract negotiation, pay claims, and grievance processing, and testified for union in unfair labor practice hearings) discharged on allegations of misuse of employer's credit card to obtain fuel for his private vehicle. City council member who initiated investigation was motivated by union animus and dislike of union president: he served (with mayor) on employer's bargaining team and took active part in processing numerous pay claims and grievances. City clerk who took part in investigation and discharge decisions was himself the subject of numerous pay claims and grievances and held negative opinion of union president. Mayor had taken casual approach to past employee misconduct allegations but wrote inflammatory letter chastising union president and exhibited dislike for president and union was found to be motivated by union animus in investigating and discharging. Although evidence showed chief of police had unwritten policy (widely known among employees) permitting employees to fuel personal vehicles at employer's expense, and union president claimed to be acting in compliance with that policy, mayor deviated from his own practices in investigation and disregarded that policy.

Citation: *City of Mill Creek*, Decision 5699 (PECB, 1996) **Discrimination Found: Yes**

Charge: Employer placed performance reports in the employee's personnel file after filing grievance.

Explanation: Discrimination found where employer placed performance reports and documents in employee's personnel file shortly after grievance and unfair labor practice complaint were filed, and employee's protected activity was a substantial motivating factor in the employer's decision to place the documents in the file.

Citation: *City of Mill Creek*, Decision 5699 (PECB, 1996) **Discrimination Found: No**

Charge: Employer meeting to discuss performance plan after employee files grievance.

Explanation: No discrimination found where the employer met with the employee pursuant to a "performance plan" and discussed the employee's grievance, which employee had filed without first speaking to employer. The employer believed the CBA required an employee to speak to a supervisor before filing a grievance, and the employee argued the meetings were intended to intimidate him and to punish him for filing the grievance. The Examiner found "the employer interfered with [his] statutory rights, and violated RCW 41.56.140(1). There is not, however, sufficient evidence to determine that [employer's] actions constituted discrimination… [because] a complainant must show that an employee was deprived of some ascertainable right, benefit, or status in order to prove discrimination" and the employee here failed to do so.

Citation: *City of Mountlake Terrace*, Decision 11702 (PECB, 2013), *aff'd on discrimination issue*, Decision 11702-A (PECB, 2014) **Discrimination Found: No**

Charge: Employee received two disciplinary penalties arising from same conduct.

Explanation: No discrimination against an officer involved in collision where the employer imposed two disciplinary penalties. The examiner found that the union failed to establish that the officer engaged in protected activity: "Asking for a Collision Review Board review of one's collision is not the type of activity typically defined as union activity.... It is an action taken by an employee for his own review process which was provided by department policy." Because the union failed to make a prima facie case of discrimination, the employer's double punishments were not discussed.

Citation: *City of Omak*, Decisions 5579-A, 5580-A, 5581-A and 5583-A (PECB, 1997), *aff'd on this issue*, Decisions 5579-B, (PECB, 1998) **Discrimination Found: No**

Charge: Employer discontinuing assigned police cars program.

Explanation: No discrimination found by discontinuing assigned cars program, which allowed some police officers to commute with patrol cars, where the action was consistent with previous criticisms of the program and with program costs estimates, and where the record did not show that program elimination was substantially motivated by employee's exercise of collective bargaining rights. Police chief's dislike of program predated the relevant protected activity.

Citation: *City of Omak*, Decisions 5579-A, 5580-A, 5581-A and 5583-A (PECB, 1997), *aff'd on this issue*, Decisions 5579-B, (PECB, 1998) **Discrimination Found: No**

Charge: Discontinuing "K-9" patrol program.

Explanation: No discrimination found against officer who was also K-9 handler where the eliminating K-9 patrol program was consistent with previous concerns about the dramatic increases in costs and lack of suitable dogs and where the only direct connection to protected activity was from employee's own speculation. The examiner concluded the union failed to prove that the program was eliminated in reprisal for union activity.

Citation: *City of Port Angeles*, Decision 10445 (PECB, 2009) **Discrimination Found: No**

Charge: Employer threatened to discipline employee.

Explanation: Examiner dismissed allegation that employer discriminated against employees because the complaint "does not indicate that employees have been disciplined or actually deprived of other rights, status, or benefits."

Citation: *City of Pullman*, Decision 11148 (PECB, 2011), *aff'd*, Decision 11148-A (PECB, 2012) **Discrimination Found: No**

Charge: Employee who created a hostile work environment was disciplined, demoted, and suspended without pay.

Explanation: No discrimination found where employer disciplined a fire department captain by six-month demotion and one-month suspension without pay for creating a hostile work environment. The union met its prima facie case for discrimination but failed to meet its ultimate burden of proving employer's non-discriminatory reasons were pretextual or that the discipline was substantially motivated by union animus. The examiner explained that "the union raises some legitimate concerns about the employer's investigation and the harsh disciplinary action it imposed on a valuable veteran employee with a very good work record. At the same time, however, the record demonstrates genuine concern on the employer's part about [the employee's] inappropriate conduct and the work environment that he created and sustained."

Citation: *City of Pullman*, Decision 11148 (PECB, 2011), *aff'd*, Decision 11148-A (PECB, 2012) **Discrimination Found: No**

Charge: Employer investigation into retaliation complaints.

Explanation: No discrimination found where employer conducted an investigation into allegations that the employer had retaliated against bargaining unit members who provided the employer with adverse information about a fire fighter accused of hostile work environment. Although the union established a prima facie case, the union did not carry its burden to establish that the employer's actions were either pretextual or substantially motivated by union animus because the employer had an obligation to investigate the retaliation complaints, the employer hired an independent investigator to investigation, and the investigator's findings distinguish between employee union activity and individual actions.

Citation: *City of Seattle*, Decision 1038 (PECB, 1980) **Discrimination Found: No**

Charge: Assignment of work.

Explanation: No discrimination found where record showed that although employer knew or reasonably could have known of complainant's union affiliation, it did not deviate from its normal, legitimate business practices in assigning complainant work, and had in fact assigned him as many hours as other intermittent workers employed in the same type of job at the same work location.

Citation: *City of Seattle*, Decision 10803-B (PECB, 2012), *aff'g* Decision 10803-A (PECB, 2011) **Discrimination Found: No**

Charge: Failure to promote.

Explanation: No discrimination found where employer had legitimate, non-retaliatory business reasons for reprimanding the employee and not promoting him, and the employee's pursuit of a protected right was not a substantial motivating factor causing the employer to not promote him. Also, the named sender of the letter that is the subject of the protected union activity *was* promoted.

Citation: *City of Seattle*, Decision 3066 (PECB, 1987), *aff'd*, Decision 3066-A (PECB, 1989) **Discrimination Found: No**

Charge: Employer adopted different work schedule for represented employees but not non-represented employees.

Explanation: No discrimination found where although complaining employee engaged in protected activities, the union failed to prove the employer intended to discriminate against union members. Employer presented legitimate business reasons for not permitting union employees to work 4/40 schedules (including that the CBA disallowed such a schedule) even though non-union employees were allowed a 4/40 schedule.

Citation: *City of Seattle*, Decision 3419 (PECB, 1990) **Discrimination Found: No**

Charge: Employee discharged in reprisal for filing grievance.

Explanation: No discrimination found where union failed to establish a prima facie showing that the discharge of an employee was motivated in reprisal for his use of the grievance procedure because the employer's decision maker was not aware of the employee's grievance until after the filing of the ULP. "There is simply no cause-and-effect relationship demonstrated in the evidence."

Citation: *City of Seattle*, Decision 6326 (PECB, 1998) **Discrimination Found: No**

Charge: Employee who filed ULP discharged for inappropriate comments.

Explanation: No discrimination found for terminating complainant's employment where complainant did not make prima facie case of discrimination. Complainant did not hold union office, serve in an official capacity, or participate in collective bargaining on behalf of the union; she filed an unfair labor practice prior to recent period of employment and prior to events leading to her termination, but she failed to show causal connection between discharge and that complaint. Employer stated legitimate reasons to discharge complainant for violation of policy because she made inappropriate comments about a client affecting the client's ability to fulfill contracts.

Citation: *City of Seattle*, Decision 6357 (PECB, 1998) **Discrimination Found: No**

Charge: Transfer of employee after evaluation and appeal process of evaluation.

Explanation: No discrimination found in transfer of employee after evaluation and appeal process of evaluation, during which employee was not allowed union representation, where there was no "investigation" of facts at the meeting that might lead to later disciplinary action, and no showing that employee was transferred in reprisal for his appeal or in reprisal for his request for union representation. The evaluation appeal meeting was not an investigatory interview of the type to which *Weingarten* principles are applicable.

Citation: *City of Seattle*, Decision 6852 (PECB, 1999) **Discrimination Found: No**

Charge: Employee discharged in retaliation for filing unfair labor practice.

Explanation: No discrimination found where complainant failed to establish that employer officials were aware of the unfair labor practice complaint filed just days before the employee was discharged. Employee had been warned earlier about failure to conform to a work hours requirement, and employer discharged other employees during the same month for the same reason.

Citation: *City of Tukwila*, Decision 4968 (PECB, 1995) **Discrimination Found: No**

Charge: Employer transferred employee one day after employee filed grievance.

Explanation: No discrimination or interference violation found, where employer transferred employee on for legitimate reasons and without knowledge of grievances filed the day before. Grievances had not been presented to employer prior to transfer decision, union's practice is to maintain confidentiality of grievances until processed internally, and small plant doctrine did not provide basis to infer employer knowledge.

Citation: *City of Vancouver*, Decision 10621-B (PECB, 2012), *aff'g* Decision 10621-A (PECB, 2010) **Discrimination Found: Yes**

Charge: Employee not selected for promotion into specialty unit.

Explanation: Discrimination found where decision-maker simply counted the votes of an interview panel to determine who to select for specialty unit, where one member of the panel was tainted by union animus. The Commission held that this animus tainted the decision maker: "under Chapter 41.56 RCW, a decision maker may be found to have committed a discriminatory act if the decision maker makes a decision that was influenced by the animus of his subordinate. This holds true even if the decision maker displayed no animus on her or his own part."

Citation: *City of Winlock*, Decision 4784-A (PECB, 1995), *review denied*, Lewis County Superior Court, CD 1001 (May 22, 1995) **Discrimination Found: Yes**

Charge: Discharge of union member & sudden change in work schedule.

Explanation: Discrimination found where union member was discharged. Applying the small plant doctrine, the employer knew of the union member's protected activity. Union animus can be inferred where employer vigorously opposed representation case, employer official told union member "you're making [the mayor] crazy with this union thing"; employer complained of "union problems" in discharging another employee; and testimony that the employer was "dealing with the union matter" indicated a negative reaction to employees' exercise of protected activity. Timing of sudden change in work schedules coinciding with union member's presentation at city council meeting is further evidence of union animus. Timing of discharge close to significant events in representation case raised suspicion of discrimination.

Citation: *City of Winlock*, Decision 4784-A (PECB, 1995), *review denied*, Lewis County Superior Court, CD–1001 (May 22, 1995) **Discrimination Found: Yes**

Charge: Discharge of union member.

Explanation: Discrimination found where employee's protected activities were "substantial motivating factor" in employer's decision to discharge him, where employer failed to produce legitimate reasons for discharge. Employer purported to discharge individual for alleged change of position regarding use of phone calls, but record showed employer originally considered discharge for another reason, dishonesty. When an employer resorts to overly severe discipline, Commission can draw negative inferences. Employee had reason to believe phone calls to his father had the full sanction of his employer: some phone calls were business related, other employees made some of the calls, and city had no written policy on phone use. Commission can also draw inferences as to motivation if employer does not follow legal procedures in giving employee *Loudermill* hearing.

Citation: *City of Yakima*, Decision 9451-B (PECB, 2007) **Discrimination Found: No**

Charge: Implementation of a "last-chance" agreement that resulted in officer discharge.

Explanation: Commission found no discrimination found where employer implemented a "last-chance" agreement that resulted in officer's termination because the employer provided compelling non-discriminatory reasons for implementing agreement (employee officer had been charged with a DUI). In response to the DUI, the employer also instituted a general drug testing policy, which was the subject of an unfair labor practice complaint, which the union blamed for employee's termination. Union established its prima facie case, but did not demonstrate with substantial evidence that the employee was terminated in response to the ULP and not because of his numerous bad actions.

Citation: *Clallam County*, Decision 1405 (PECB, 1982), *aff'd*, Decision 1405-A (PECB, 1982) **Discrimination Found: Yes**

Charge: Discharge of employee.

Explanation: Discrimination found where supervisor's comments that discharge due in part to the employee's attempt to process a grievance was sufficient to establish a prima facie case on behalf of the union. The County failed to sustain its burden of proof that the discharge would have occurred regardless of the unlawful motivations indicated by the supervisor. The untimely revival of other incidents is clearly pretextual and actually undermines the county's case.

Citation: *Clallam County*, Decision 4011 (PECB, 1992) **Discrimination Found: No**

Charge: Discharge of union officer who had made negative comments publicly against the administration.

Explanation: No discrimination found where although union established *prima facie* showing under principles of Wright Line to support an inference that protected activity was a motivating factor in the employer's decision to discharge a union officer, the employer has demonstrated that its decision to terminate the deputy sheriff for was motivated by good faith business considerations related to the deputy sheriff's poor performance and safety concerns.

Citation: *Clallam Transit System*, Decision 4597 (PECB, 1994) **Discrimination Found: Yes**

Charge: Refusal to rehire.

Explanation: Discrimination found where employer refused to hire a union activist who had previously worked for employer but had resigned for personal reasons. Examiner found compelling, among other evidence: evidence employer altered applicant's psychological test scores based on his own impressions, (2) evidence interview panel was "stacked" against applicant, and (3) evidence of two "smoking gun" conversations where employer said reapplication was a joke because of the applicant's past union history.

Citation: *College District 13*, Decision 9171-A (PSRA, 2007) **Discrimination Found: No**

Charge: Employee alleges incidents of employer creating a hostile work environment.

Explanation: No discrimination found where the employee cannot prove an employer's intent to deprive the employee of a definable right, benefit, or status, and demonstrate that a loss actually occurred because the employee did not quit, she was not disciplined or terminated, nor did she fail to complete any of the work involved.

Citation: *Cowlitz County*, Decision 7037 (PECB, 2000) **Discrimination Found: No**

Charge: Conducting an investigatory interview of union president on the same day the Commission conducted a hearing concerning another investigatory interview.

Explanation: No discrimination found where, beyond the timing of the investigatory interview, no causal connection was proven between the exercise of the statutory right to access unfair labor practice procedures and the investigatory hearing. First, the subject matter of the investigation had been brought to the employer's attention by bargaining unit employees, without any indication of union animus or misconduct on the part of the employer. Second, the union did not establish when the conversation at issue took place, so it was "impossible to form an opinion about whether the timing of the interview was suspect or just coincidence." Third, the investigatory interview was begun and the subjects of that investigation were broached before that hearing was convened. "The fact that two events occurred on the same day is not, in and of itself, sufficient to meet the union's burden of proof that the resumption/continuation of the earlier meeting was causally connected to the hearing process."

Citation: *C-TRAN*, Decision 4005 (PECB, 1992) **Discrimination Found: No**

Charge: Employee benefits different for non-union employees.

Explanation: No discrimination found where employer made available to non-union employees benefits not made available to represented employees because this does not, alone, constitute a basis for a discrimination claim, as organized employees are not in a position to bargain or dictate the wages, hours or working conditions of persons outside of the bargaining unit represented by the union.

Citation: *Educational Service District 114*, Decision 4361 (PECB, 1993), *aff'd*, Decision 4361-A (PECB, 1994) **Discrimination Found: Yes**

Charge: Failure to rehire qualified employees who were involved in union formation.

Explanation: Discrimination found where union established prima facie showing that protected activity was a "substantial" motivating factor in decision not to re-hire union activities. Employer failed to demonstrate that its decision was motivated by good faith business considerations: the employees in question were deemed to be qualified in both experience and training but the employer deviated from its hiring practice of interviewing qualified candidates, and employees had previously been told they were in danger due to their union involvement.

Citation: *Grant County Hospital*, Decision 6673 (PECB, 1999), *aff'd*, Decision 6673-A (PECB, 1999) **Discrimination Found: No**

Charge: Discharge of an employee, suspension of an employee, and discrimination against bargaining unit employees in filling a position.

Explanation: No discrimination found where union failed to establish prima facie cases that employer's actions were substantially motivated by the employees' exercise of statutorily-protected rights or that employer acted with discriminatory intent. Employer articulated lawful reasons for its actions, namely: (1) employee was discharged for sexual harassment misconduct, (2) employee was suspended for dispute about chain of command and work responsibilities, and (3) bargaining unit employees had no particular seniority rights to position, as parties had not signed their first contract.

Citation: *Highline School District*, Decision 10301 (PECB, 2009) **Discrimination Found: No**

Charge: Failure to place employee in bargaining unit.

Explanation: No discrimination found despite union's contention that District discriminated against an employee when it refused to accept the employee into a bargaining unit. "The employer is not automatically susceptible to a discrimination claim because it declines to place [employee] in the bargaining unit."

Citation: *Intercity Transit*, Decision 2580 (PECB, 1986) **Discrimination Found: No**

Charge: Discipline of union shop steward who broke employer rules.

Explanation: No discrimination found where the complainant failed to sustain its burden of proof that the discipline would have not occurred without an unlawful motivation by the employer. Union acknowledged there were legitimate reasons for discipline, but alleged punishment was overly harsh due to union animus. The examiner noted the "comparable" previous incidents resulting in less severe discipline involved much less blameworthy conduct and were not actually comparable to the instant case.

Citation: *Kennewick School District*, Decision 5632-A (PECB, 1996), *rev'd, Kennewick School District*, Decision 5632 (PECB, 1996) **Discrimination Found: Yes**

Charge: Investigation and reprimand.

Explanation: Discrimination found where employer singled out union activist for investigation relating to ordering and distribution of food products, and reprimanded employee to the exclusion of others. Employer found to have been substantially motivated by anti-union animus, inferred from the timing of the events which occurred soon after employee filed a grievance, and in the case of the reprimand, within a month and a half after the filing of an unfair labor practice complaint.

Citation: *King County Fire District 4*, Decision 3366 (PECB, 1989) **Discrimination Found: No**

Charge: Refusal to accept application.

Explanation: No discrimination found where the employer's refused to accept employment application from the district's maintenance employee and limit applicants to those individuals from the ranks of its reserve fire fighters. Refusal was determined to be an appropriate exercise of management prerogative, consistent with its past practices.

Citation: *King County*, Decision 10500 (PECB, 2009) **Discrimination Found: No**

Charge: Termination and related employer actions.

Explanation: Discrimination complaint was dismissed for failure to state a cause of action where complainant failed to show she had taken protected actions – although she had previously filed a grievance for gender and race discrimination, grievances are not protected actions: "A cause of action for discrimination for filing charges does not apply to grievances. A complaint alleging discrimination for filing charges will be processed only when the facts allege that an employee filed a previous unfair labor practice complaint with the Commission or gave testimony before the Commission." Furthermore, the allegations of the original complaint clearly focused on…allegations that the employer's actions were primarily motivated by gender and race bias, not in retaliation for her grievances."

Citation: *King County*, Decision 11221 (PECB, 2011), *aff'd*, 11221-A (PECB, 2012) **Discrimination Found: No**

Charge: Failure to hire.

Explanation: No discrimination found where more than a year lapsed between the protected activity and the employer's failure to hire the individual. Emails of alleged union animus labeling the complainant as a "troublemaker" and stating "don't hire an insider" were sent too remotely in time to establish a causal connection. The employee had established that he engaged in protected activity as a union officer and filing grievances, and an adverse action had occurred by the employer's failure to hire him for positions.

Citation: *King County,* Decision 11223 (PECB, 2011) **Discrimination Found: Yes**

Charge: Denying/limiting access to union rep.

Explanation: Discrimination found where the employer denied and limited access of bargaining unit employees to Local 117 representatives in reprisal for protected union activities during the pendency of a representation petition. In this case the employer admitted to restricting the union representative's access to the workplace and bargaining unit, which deprived bargaining unit employees of their ability to meet with the representative of their choice, and the employer failed to provide any non-discriminatory reasons for its actions.

Citation: *King County*, Decision 3178 (PECB, 1989), *aff'd*, Decision 3178-A (PECB, 1989) **Discrimination Found: Yes**

Charge: Refusal to reinstate.

Explanation: Discrimination found when employer refused to consider the employee for reinstatement upon her release to return to work and insisted she accept employment in another operation because of her record of filing grievances.

Citation: *King County*, Decision 3318 (PECB, 1989) **Discrimination Found: Yes**

Charge: Reassignment.

Explanation: Discrimination found where employer imposed adverse transfer on employee who was pursuing a grievance regarding a previous re-assignment.

Citation: *Kiona Benton School District*, Decision 11035 (EDUC, 2011) **Discrimination Found: Yes**

Charge: Reassignment.

Explanation: Discrimination found where employer reassigned active union officer and teacher within a month of engaging in protected activity (serving as a union representative). The principal and prior principals had concerns about the teacher's union activities, namely that she challenged their authority, and referred to her at a "union person" during an investigation. "The language used by employer officials when describing [the teacher] leads the Examiner to conclude that the employer officials co-mingled [the teacher's] union activities with her teaching and they were unable to separate the two."

Citation: *Kiona Benton School District*, Decision 11563 (EDUC, 2012), *aff'd*, Decision 11563-A (EDUC, 2013) **Discrimination Found: No**

Charge: Layoff.

Explanation: The Hearing Examiner determined that the union did not meet its burden of showing that the employer's reasons for its decisions to lay-off a provisional employee, even though the union had established a *prima facie* case of discrimination, were not a pretext for discrimination. The employer's nondiscriminatory reason for its actions was a projected budgetary shortfall. The examiner determined that the employee was one of nine employees on the list and the union failed to show that she was singled out for the layoff.

Citation: *Kitsap County*, Decision 9326-A (PECB, 2008)

Discrimination Found: No

Charge: Verbal counseling of employee/union president.

Explanation: No discrimination found where the union did not meet its burden of proof that the employee was deprived of any rights protected by RCW 41.56 when he received supervisory review and verbal counseling in response to a rudeness complaint. Although the employee was engaged in protected activity (picking up documents for the union) when he was rude, "verbal counseling is not considered a form of discipline by the parties' collective bargaining agreement" so the union could not prevail.

Citation: *Lewis County*, Decision 4691 (PECB, 1994), *aff'd*, Decision 4691-A (PECB, 1994), *aff'd*, *Lewis County v. Public Employment Relations Commission and Teamsters Union*, Local 252, WPERR CD - 1235 (Lewis County Superior Court, 1997)

Discrimination Found: Yes

Charge: Discharge.

Explanation: Discrimination found where involvement in union campaign was substantial factor in discharge of principal union organizer, who engaged in protected activity when he solicited employee signatures on authorization cards. Employee's persistent, vocal, and intense campaign activity was protected, since he did not coerce, threaten, show physical hostility, or otherwise violate employees' rights.

Citation: *Morton School District*, Decisions 5838 and 5839 (PECB, 1997)

Discrimination Found: Yes

Charge: Refusal to rehire.

Explanation: Discrimination found where employer was substantially motivated by union animus when it refused to rehire head softball coach who was co-president of the union. The employer demonstrated its ongoing animus against coach's union activity by denying him funding for a trip with senior class which included his child because litigation, including the unfair labor practice, was pending, contrary to past practice of paying the expenses of a teacher/chaperone who had a child in the graduating class. Employer's claims that the community had lost respect for the coach, that the community complained about the coach were insufficient to outweigh the union animus.

Citation: *Morton School District*, Decisions 5838 and 5839 (PECB, 1997)

Discrimination Found: No

Charge: Refusal to hire.

Explanation: No discrimination found where employer's reasons for refusal to hire assistant baseball coach were not pretextual and not substantially motivated by union animus, where the action was in conformity with past practice. Although collective bargaining agreement did not cover the coaches, the parties believed it did, and so the interpretation could be evidence weighing for or against discrimination. Employer's reasons for not replacing one assistant baseball coach who quit (the program declined and two volunteer coaches had joined the baseball program) were not pretextual. Claimed incident of refusal to hire was remote in time from board meeting at which union animus was evident.

Citation: *Mukilteo School District*, Decision 5899 (PECB, 1997), *aff'd*, Decision 5899-A (PECB, 1997)

Discrimination Found: No

Charge: No-hire reference by employer.

Explanation: No discrimination found where an "Agreed Order" which resolved previous unfair labor practice complaint by requiring employer to cease contacting past, present, or future employers of complainant (a past employee) was not violated by telephone call in which school district official gave simple (negative) answer to prospective employer's direct question of whether employee was eligible for rehire. Employees could not reasonably perceive the limited exchange as a threat of reprisal or force associated with union activities, and complainant made no prima facie showing of a causal connection between a previously filed grievance and unfair labor practice complaint and the telephone call for a discrimination charge to prevail.

Citation: *North Valley Hospital*, Decision 5809 (PECB, 1997), *aff'd*, Okanogan County Superior Court, WPERR CD - 965 (September 28, 1998) **Discrimination Found: Yes**

Charge: Employer's reprimand and subsequent resignation of employee.

Explanation: Discrimination found where employee's telephone calls to Commission regarding mail ballots were substantial factor in employer's reprimand, which was an unfair labor practice and proximate cause of employee's resignation. Calls made in response to official election notice totaled three minutes, and were made on employee's own telephone calling card. Discipline had chilling effect on exercise of employee rights, and its assertions as to reasons for reprimand were pretexts designed to conceal a true motivation of anti-union animus.

Citation: *Northshore Utility District*, Decision 10534 (PECB, 2009), *aff'd*, Decision 10534-A (PECB, 2010) **Discrimination Found: No**

Charge: Termination of employee for gross misconduct.

Explanation: No discrimination found where an employee was terminated for gross misconduct. Here, the termination of the clerk was motivated by, among other issues, falsified and miscalculated timecards and misapplied supplier discounts, both of which caused the District significant financial loss.

Citation: *Northshore Utility District*, Decision 11267 (PECB, 2011), *aff'd*, Decision 11267-A (PECB, 2012) **Discrimination Found: No**

Charge: Discharge.

Explanation: No discrimination found where union officer was laid off but the decision-makers did not know that the union officer opposed decertification process. Examiner Atchison found that the union officer did not credibly testify that the employer knew he opposed the decertification process, but the decision-maker credibly testified about why she selected another candidate.

Citation: *Oroville School District*, Decision 6209-A (PECB, 1998), *aff'g as amended*, Decision 6209-A (PECB, 1998) **Discrimination Found: Yes**

Charge: Negative performance evaluation.

Explanation: Discrimination found where employer issued a custodian negative evaluation in the midst of acrimonious negotiations. Employee had recently emerged as union leader and union had been certified as exclusive bargaining representative. Employer's reasons for evaluation were pretextual and employer was substantially motivated by anti-union animus because: Evaluation was ambiguous, comment in evaluation about waxing over dirt had no performance-based reason, claim that other union activists were given satisfactory evaluations was not supported by evidence, employee previously had not received low performance evaluations or been disciplined, there was no evidence of shoddy workmanship, and negative comments on evaluation of other custodian/union activist supports a finding of anti-union animus.

Citation: *Pasco Housing Authority*, Decision 6248 (PECB, 1998), *aff'd with modification*, *Pasco Housing Authority*, Decision 6248-A (PECB, 1998) **Discrimination Found: Yes**

Charge: Poor evaluation, extra evaluation, and layoff of union activist.

Explanation: Discrimination found where employer gave highly visible union activist low evaluation, subjecting her to an extra evaluation, informing her that it wished to retain only "team players," and laying her off. Reasons given by the employer for selecting employee for layoff, including a budget deficit and poor performance, were pretexts designed to conceal anti-union animus, and union activities were a substantial motivating factor in the layoff decision. Employee was most senior in classification and personnel policy required consideration of length of service in any layoff. Anti-union animus was evidenced by a memo that resulted in a finding of an unfair labor practice in another case. An employee with an evaluation point total similar to the employee's was not subjected to an extra evaluation, and one case manager was not evaluated before the layoff.

Citation: *Pierce County Fire District 2*, Decision 4307 (PECB, 1993) **Discrimination Found: No**

Charge: Verbal admonishment.

Explanation: No discrimination found where fire dispatch employee apparently failed to establish a prima facie showing sufficient to support an inference that protected activity was a motivating factor in the employer's decision to admonish her. The examiner determined the admonishment was appropriate in light of complainant's actions, and so would not support a retaliation claim (or presumably, a discrimination claim).

Citation: *Pierce County*, Decision 7258 (PECB, 2001) **Discrimination Found: Yes**

Charge: Denying employee promotion and by failing or refusing to assign work opportunities to employee.

Explanation: Discrimination found where employer denied employee promotion and failed or refused to assign work opportunities to employee, to avoid possibility of employee exercising his rights under RCW 41.56.040. Employer was on notice of employee's union activity and harbored anti-union animus, where employee attempted to obtain wage increase, filed grievance, attempted to have position reclassified, and ran for shop steward. Causal connection between protected activity and deprivation found, where employer criticized employee for "raising eyebrows" in attempt to increase wage; denied grievance for out-of-class work and subsequently was reluctant to make assignments for fear employee might seek out-of-class pay for assigned work; and denied promotion, in part, because employee was not "team player" regarding union activities. Pretext or unlawful motivation found, where selection of candidates was not foregone conclusion; employer engaged in structured avoidance of employee after denial of promotion by refusing to assign out-of-class work that might lead to grievance; interview panel had antiunion animus; denials by employer not credited; employer evaluations of employee denied promotion showed work, skills and ability as attributes; and employer showed pattern of adverse actions following protected activity.

Citation: *Pierce County*, Decision 12195 (PECB, 2014) **Discrimination Found: No**

Charge: Termination.

Explanation: The Examiner held that the Union failed to show a causal connection between the deputy's request for Union representation and his termination. The Examiner found that the Union did not present any evidence, circumstantial or otherwise, to prove a discriminatory motivation for the employer's actions. The Examiner determined deputy was terminated because he violated a number of the employer's policies, not because he requested a union representative.

Citation: *Port of Anacortes*, Decision 12160 (PORT, 2014) **Discrimination Found: No**

Charge: Injured employee's light duty work discontinued; employee required to exhaust leave donated to him.

Explanation: No discrimination found where union did not establish that the employer's reasons for discontinuing the employee's light duty assignment were a pretext to retaliate against him for his union activities or substantially motivated by union animus. Employer credibly testified it eliminated light-duty work because L&I would no longer subsidize it, there was a lack of light duty work, and employer had concerns that employee would not timely report injuries.

Citation: *Port of Seattle*, Decision 11848 (PECB, 2013), *aff'd*, Decision 11848-A (PECB, 2014) **Discrimination Found: No**

Charge: Coaching officer on customer service.

Explanation: No discrimination against found where employer documented an incident where the employee's customer service could be improved. Although employee was engaged in protected activity by serving as a shop steward, the officer could not show that he was "deprived of an ascertainable right or benefit" when the Port's sole adverse action was to "coach" him on "providing better customer service." Non-disciplinary documentation of incidents that are meant to coach or educate an employee do not rise to the level of "depriving an employee of a right, benefit, or status" and dismissed the discrimination allegation.

Citation: *Port of Seattle*, Decision 4042 (PECB, 1992) **Discrimination Found: No**

Charge: Layoff.

Explanation: No discrimination found where the union failed to establish a prima facie showing under Wright Line to support an inference that protected activity was a motivating factor in laying off union member. Examiner concluded: relationship between union and employer did not rise to the level of animus, employee's union activities did not rise to the level of union activism, and because the employee's actions that allegedly led to retaliation occurred after he was selected for layoff.

Citation: *Port of Seattle*, Decision 6854 (PECB, 2001), *aff'd*, Decision 6854-A (PECB, 2001) **Discrimination Found: No**

Charge: Discipline.

Explanation: No discrimination found where (1) employee failed to establish, by preponderance of evidence, prima facie case that personnel actions taken against him were in reprisal for employee's exercise of protected rights; (2) employer articulated lawful reasons for personnel actions it took against employee, including requiring employee to punctually report for work, to follow employee parking rules, to refrain from using work time for personal business, to obtain approval for shift trades from foreman, and to hold state license like all other electricians employed in same department; and (3) employee failed to establish, by preponderance of evidence, that employer has committed or is committing any unfair labor practice.

Citation: *Port of Tacoma*, Decisions 4626 and 4627 (PECB, 1994), *remedy rev'd*, Decisions 4626-A and 4627-A (PECB, 1995) **Discrimination Found: Yes**

Charge: Denying promotions and limiting work opportunities of union activists.

Explanation: Unfair labor practice found where union activities were substantial factor in denial of promotion. Employer's proffered reasons (appearance at promotional interview, tendency to run down other employees, or complainant's statement that he was applying for the job for economic reasons) did not justify refusing to promote a long-time employee who, one year earlier, had a higher promotional score by 25%. Employee had been very vocal in union activity during that year, and employer told him he was not selected because he was "iconoclastic" or "argumentative."

Citation: *Pullman School District*, Decision 2632 (PECB, 1987) **Discrimination Found: Yes**

Charge: Threatened termination, written reprimand, termination.

Explanation: Discrimination found where complainant established threat of termination was in response to employee's filing of a grievance, in part because employee had positive work reviews and superintendent, not principal, issued warning. Employer's argument that written reprimand and termination were in response to employee's poor work performance was not supported by evidence.

Citation: *Reardan-Edwall School District*, Decision 6205 (PECB, 1998), *aff'd*, Decision 6205-A (PECB, 1998) **Discrimination Found: No**

Charge: Discharge.

Explanation: No discrimination found where union failed to make a prima facie showing of causal connection between exercise of protected rights and the employer's discharge of bus driver, where evidence of anti-union animus was lacking, circumstantial evidence of a causal connection on basis of timing could not be found, and other union activists had not been subjected to actionable deprivation.

Citation: *Seattle School District*, Decision 11045-A (PECB, 2011) *rev'g in part* Decision 11045 (PECB, 2011) **Discrimination Found: No**

Charge: Written reprimand of security specialist.

Explanation: The Commission reversed the Examiner's findings and conclusions that the employer discriminated against an employee by subjecting him to heightened scrutiny and by issuing a letter of reprimand regarding his attendance in retaliation for the employee's exercise of protected employee rights (invoking his *Weingarten* rights). The Commission explained that by challenging his supervisor about the search policy, being insubordinate, and for disobeying his supervisor's directions, the employee's conduct was not protected activity. Rather, the Commission stated, he should have aired his concerns through bargaining or the contract's grievance procedure. "Because [the employee's] conduct was argumentative and disruptive, it was not protected by Chapter 41.56 RCW. Thus, while the act of invoking one's *Weingarten* rights is a protected activity, the fact that employee misconduct occurs in a *Weingarten* meeting does not excuse the misconduct. The evidence ...demonstrates that the letters of reprimand were not issued for ... union activity; rather, the employer issued the letters in response to his non-protected conduct."

Citation: *Seattle School District*, Decision 11045 (PECB, 2011), *rev'd on other issues*, Decision 11045-A (PECB, 2011) **Discrimination Found: No**

Charge: Placing employee on administrative leave and later transferring him.

Explanation: No discrimination found where employer placed employee on administrative leave during investigation and later transferred him where evidence suggested employee himself wanted transfer and the union failed to show that transfer caused particular harm or loss of prestige.

Citation: *Seattle School District*, Decision 11779-A (PECB, 2014) **Discrimination Found: No**

Charge: Temporary demotion.

Explanation: No discrimination found where the employer temporarily demoted a unit member in a sheet metal shop after temporarily laying off two other employees. Here, the union established a *prima facie* case of discrimination by proving the employees participated in protected activity (expressing concern about possible skimming of bargaining unit work), the employer deprived the employees of a right (demotion from foreperson position is a deprivation of status and pay), and a causal connection existed between the two (timing). The employer responded by presenting a legitimate, non-discriminatory reason for its actions. Specifically, the employer argued that the layoffs and demotion were related to the lack of work and funding. Ultimately, the examiner determined that the union failed to produce evidence showing that the employer's stated reason was pretextual or that the union activity was a substantial motivating factor in the employer's actions. The examiner determined that this was sufficient to demonstrate that the employer's action "was prompted by an unrelated monetary and workload issue."

Citation: *Seattle School District*, Decision 5946 (PECB, 1997) **Discrimination Found: No**

Charge: Refusal to hire.

Explanation: No discrimination found where the complainant did not make prima facie showing of causal connection between two previously filed unfair labor practices complaints and employer's refusal to hire her for a summer school position.

Citation: *Snohomish County*, Decision 9799 (PECB, 2007) **Discrimination Found: No**

Charge: Corrective counseling letter and verbal admonishment.

Explanation: No discrimination found where there was little evidence that a disciplinary action had taken place, or that it was targeted towards union activity. The petitioner guild did not make prima facie case because, although it showed that guild members were engaged in protected activity, it did not show that they were deprived of any ascertainable right or benefit. Neither the corrective counseling letter nor verbal admonishment rose to that level. "To prevail on a discrimination claim, it is critical that the complainant show a disciplinary action was taken in reprisal for union activity."

Citation: *Snohomish County*, Decision 9834 (PECB, 2007), *aff'd*, Decision 9834-B (PECB, 2008) **Discrimination Found: No**

Charge: Conversation at hockey game about negotiations.

Explanation: No discrimination found where employee representative was engaged in protected activity when she approached a county executive at a hockey game and asked him about his knowledge and participation in negotiations, but the union did not present any evidence that the employee representative was deprived of an ascertainable right, status or benefit due to that conversation. The union argued that the county executive interacted professionally and socially with employee representatives from other unions. Here, there was no evidence that this conversation had any ascertainable effect on the bargaining process. Thus, the union failed to establish a prima facie case of discrimination.

Citation: *Southwest Snohomish County Public Safety Communications Agency*, Decision 11149 **Discrimination Found: Yes**

(PECB, 2011), *aff'd*, Decision 11149-C (PECB, 2013)

Charge: Disciplinary letter and five-day unpaid suspension.

Explanation: Discrimination found where employer issued a unit member a disciplinary letter and five-day unpaid suspension. The examiner explained that the union established its prima facie case of discrimination, and the non-discriminatory reasons offered by the employer were pretextual because of the timing of the employer's investigation with the unit member's participation in contract negotiations. The employer argued that the discipline was warranted for a supervisor who exhibits "poor judgment" and damages the reputation of the employer. Ultimately, the examiner found that the unit member's protected union activity was a substantial motiving factor in the employer's disciplinary decision.

Citation: *Southwest Snohomish County Public Safety Communications Agency*, Decision 11149 (PECB, 2011), *aff'd*, Decision 11149-C (PECB, 2013)	**Discrimination Found: Yes**

Charge: Placing employees on paid administrative leave.

Explanation: Discrimination found where employer placed two unit members on paid administrative leave because their union activities were a substantial motivating factor in the employer's disciplinary decision. The examiner found numerous factors supporting conclusion that employer violated RCW 41.56.140(1): (1) the timing of the investigation corresponded directly with the union's denial of the employer's request for an extension of the disciplinary timeline in the CBA; (2) The employer's decision to place them on administrative leave for over a month was inconsistent with the employer's past pattern of use of paid administrative leave; (3) The coinciding prohibition against having contact with any current employees directly interfered with their union activity, and supports the conclusion that the employer had a desire to punish them and prevent them from engaging in union activity; and (4) the nature of the complaint against them regarding union-related discussions in the workplace, does not appear to be so serious as to necessitate complete removal of the unit members from the workplace.

Citation: *Southwest Snohomish County Public Safety Communications Agency*, Decision 11149 (PECB, 2011), *aff'd*, Decision 11149-C (PECB,	**Discrimination Found: Yes**

2013)

Charge: Withdrawal of endorsement for position.

Explanation: Discrimination found where employer withdrew endorsement for unit member to work as a dispatch instructor. The employer's actions deprived the unit member of an ascertainable right because it directly caused her to lose her employment as the dispatch instructor and the loss of that position caused her to lose the teaching contract. The examiner concluded that the unit member's union activity was a substantial motivating factor in the employer's decision to issue a written reprimand and to withdraw endorsement for her to teach.

Citation: *Southwest Snohomish County Public Safety Communications Agency,* Decision 11149 (PECB, 2011), *aff'd,* Decision 11149-C (PECB, 2013)

Discrimination Found: Yes

Charge: Removal from special project committee.

Explanation: Discrimination found where employer removed a unit member as a representative on a special project committee. The employer's actions deprived the unit member of an ascertainable right because serving on the committee gave her additional opportunities to earn overtime pay.

Citation: *Spokane County Fire Protection District No. 9*, Decision 2860 (PECB, 1988)

Discrimination Found: No

Charge: Discipline and nonrenewal.

Explanation: No discrimination found where no causal connection was found between teacher's participation in a grievance and his later nonrenewal, where record showed no employer union animus, teacher's union activity was limited, grievance occurred after at least two meetings concerning teacher's performance, and none of the other participants to grievance were not renewed. General "animus" of employer against employee, without connection to protected union activity, does not form basis for causal connection.

Citation: *Spokane Transit Authority*, Decision 2078-A (PECB, 1984), *aff'd*, Decision 2078-A (PECB, 1985), *aff'd*, *Spokane Transit Authority v.*

Discrimination Found: Yes

Public Employment Relations Commission v. Michael L. Closson, WPERR CD - 1173 (Spokane County Superior Court, 1987)

Charge: Union leader demoted after objecting to employer's attempts to dictate bargaining terms.

Explanation: Discrimination found where employee with known history of union leadership was demoted after engaging in protected activity. Protected activity was objecting to employer's attempt to dictate terms of mandatory subject of bargaining at employer-called meeting during union organizational drive while representation case was pending.

Citation: *State - Corrections*, Decision 10998-A (PSRA, 2011) **Discrimination Found: No**

Charge: Discipline for sending out union related emails.

Explanation: Commission reversed Examiner's finding of discrimination because although employer could not have disciplined employee for underlying conduct (sending two non-work related emails using employer's email system), nothing in those emails was related to union activity and therefore employee did not engage in protected activity by sending them.

Citation: *State - Corrections*, Decision 11747 (PSRA, 2013) **Discrimination Found: No**

Charge: Reassigning shop steward.

Explanation: No discrimination found where employer reassigned a shop steward out of his bid position because he was not engaged in protected activities. The Examiner evaluated two related incidents: a telephone call made by the shop steward to the employer to investigate a union member's termination; and a subsequent meeting between the shop steward and the employer regarding what occurred during the telephone call. The Examiner found that the shop steward was engaged in union duties when he called the employer; however, the activity was not protected because it was not reasonable. Likewise, the Examiner found that the conduct was not reasonable during the subsequent meeting because the shop steward used excessive profanity and personal attacks; intended to intimidate the employer by using multiple confrontational statements; and ignored requests to stop.

Citation: *State - Corrections*, Decision 12002-A (PSRA, 2014), *aff'g in part and rev'g in part* Decision 12002 (PSRA, 2014)

Discrimination Found: No

Charge: Investigation.

Explanation: No discrimination found where employer investigated corrections sergeant in reprisal for union activities because the union was unable to establish a prima facie case of discrimination. In this case, although the union established that the corrections sergeant engaged in protected activity by testifying in a separate PERC hearing, it nevertheless failed to prove that the corrections sergeant was deprived of an ascertainable right, benefit or status when it investigated the employee. The union argued that the investigation affected the employee's "status" because it makes him "more vulnerable for future corrective disciplinary action." The examiner determined that there was no evidence to show that any discriminatory action was taken against the corrections sergeant because he was not actually disciplined. She explained, "Discriminatory action by an employer may be found when an employee is disciplined, but not as a result of an investigation without discipline... The belief that this could lead to future deprivation does not rise to the level of discrimination because the action has not yet occurred."

Citation: *State - Corrections*, Decision 12002-A (PSRA, 2014), *aff'g in part and rev'g in part* Decision 12002 (PSRA, 2014)

Discrimination Found: Yes

Charge: Failure to promote – denial of letter of recommendation.

Explanation: The Commission reversed the Examiner's decision regarding whether the employer discriminated against a correctional sergeant when a lieutenant denied the sergeant a letter of recommendation that was required for an application for a promotional opportunity. The Commission concluded that the union had proved by a preponderance of the evidence that lieutenant's reason for denying the Correctional sergeant a letter of recommendation was pretextual. In this case, the lieutenant's reason was that the correctional sergeant did not meet a performance standard related to the completion rate of performance evaluations. The Commission concluded that the lieutenant's expectations were not communicated and were inconsistent with the performance standard established in writing for the facility. "While the record does not contain evidence of [the employee's] actual completion rate, it is clear that the completion rate [the lieutenant] held [the employee] to was inconsistent with what the employer actually required of employees." Additionally, based upon an email and the lieutenant's testimony, the Commission inferred that the lieutenant had decided to deny the letter of recommendation and was gathering facts to support a decision he had already made. The Commission also pointed to the lack of evidence that other factors were considered in the decision to deny the letter of recommendation.

Citation: *State - Social and Health Services*, Decision 11411 (PSRA, 2012) **Discrimination Found: No**

Charge: Failure to hire.

Explanation: No discrimination found where employer refused to hire applicant who had previously worked for DOC and served as union secretary/treasurer and lead negotiator. But union failed to establish employer's non-discriminatory reasons for not hiring were pretextual: Employer's stated reason for not hiring applicant was his performance during the interview and his lack of professionalism.

Citation: *Toutle Lake School District*, Decision 2659 (PECB, 1987) **Discrimination Found: Yes**

Charge: Failure to assign work.

Explanation: Discrimination found where school district employer failed to employ complainant for any substitute bus driving assignments for the remainder of the school year after it learned that complainant had filed a complaint of unfair labor practices. The employer also prohibited the employee from accessing the worksite and passed her over for a promotion to a full-time position.

Citation: *Town of Steilacoom*, Decision 6213 (PECB, 1998) **Discrimination Found: No**

Charge: Discharge.

Explanation: No discrimination found where employee was discharged for inability to meet long-term, but unwritten standards, and no anti-union hostility or reprisal was shown. Past practices do not have to be embodied in written policies to constitute the status quo. Employer imposed no different standards on employee than on other employees, and complainant failed to establish a prima facie case of discrimination.

Citation: *University of Washington*, Decision 11091 (PSRA, 2011), *aff'd*, Decision 11091 (PSRA, 2012) **Discrimination Found: No**

Charge: Denial of release time.

Explanation: No discrimination found where employer denied shop steward release time to attend a negotiation session, initially denying him overtime to attend a safety meeting, and issued him a final counseling. The examiner determined that the employer's reason that it needed two electricians on duty was a sufficiently legitimate reason and the employer did not have to prove those reasons by a preponderance of the evidence.

Citation: *University of Washington*, Decision 11091 (PSRA, 2011), *aff'd*, Decision 11091 (PSRA, 2012) **Discrimination Found: No**

Charge: Discipline.

Explanation: No discrimination found where employer issued final counseling memo as a form of discipline to union shop steward who attended negotiation meeting after being denied time off to attend it. The union established a prima facie case of discrimination but the employer articulated non-discriminatory reasons for its actions and the complainant failed to prove that the employer's reasons were either pretextual or substantially motivated by union animus. The examiner determined that the employer disciplined the shop steward for "insubordination for attending the negotiation session in spite of having been denied release time" and the employer had legitimate reasons to deny the time off.

Citation: *University of Washington*, Decision 11199-B (PSRA, 2013) **Discrimination Found: No**

Charge: Discipline.

Explanation: On remand from the Commission, Examiner Greene concluded that the employer did not discriminate again a shop steward under Chapter 41.80 RCW by issuing him a final counseling in reprisal for union activities. While the union established a prima facie case of discrimination, the length of time between protected activity and discipline (including intervening incidents of misconduct) demonstrated that although the protected activity may have been a factor in the employer's discipline, it was not a substantial factor.

Citation: *University of Washington*, Decision 11309 (PSRA, 2012), *aff'd*, Decision 11309-C (PSRA, 2013) **Discrimination Found: Yes**

Charge: Discipline.

Explanation: Examiner found that the employer discriminated when it disciplined union steward with a Final Counseling Memorandum; employee was chosen by union to attend meeting with other University of Washington unions, and employer agreed to time off. Employee called in sick that morning, but by 2 pm felt better and attended union meeting. Examiner noted: (1) employer had offered no evidence that employee had not been sick in the morning; and (2) employee's time off was unpaid anyway.

Citation: *University of Washington*, Decision 11309-C (PSRA, 2013) **Discrimination Found: Yes**

Charge: Discipline.

Explanation: On remand from the Commission, Examiner found that the union established its prima facie case of discrimination: the unit member participated in protected activity when she attended the union-management meeting; the employer deprived her of an ascertainable right, benefit or status by issuing her a final counseling disciplinary memorandum; and the timing of the two events provided circumstantial evidence of a causal connection between the protected activity and the discipline.

Citation: *University of Washington*, Decision 8216-A (PSRA, 2004) **Discrimination Found: No**

Charge: Inclusion in a bargaining unit.

Explanation: No discrimination found where complaint failed to prove that she was discriminated against because her position was the only union-represented research technician on the employer's campus. The Examiner explained that she must demonstrate "not only that the inclusion or exclusion [of her position in the union] was improper, but that the employer or union separately or in collusion had unlawfully aligned themselves against the interest of the employee and restricted the employee's collective bargaining rights." The complainant failed to do so since the bargaining unit status of her position had been determined years prior to her acceptance of the job, and therefore, the employer and union's interests in including the complainant's position in the bargaining unit could not have been based on conspiracy against the complainant.

Citation: *Vancouver School District v. Service Employees International Union, Local 92*, 79 Wn. App. 905 (Wash. Ct. App. 1995)

Discrimination Found: No

Charge: Discharge of employee.

Explanation: No discrimination found where union failed to show terminated employee engaged in protected activity. Court applied Wright Line test and reasonableness test. Employee, a school bus driver, was accused of grabbing a child's neck and was suspended without pay. The union sent the school district a letter stating that it was investigating the incident and that if the school interfered, the union would bring an unfair labor practice claim. As part of the investigation, the suspended driver approached young children at their bus stop and questioned them, a process which terrified the children. The school terminated driver for scaring children. The Court reasoned that the driver's questioning of young children was not reasonable and was therefore not protected activity. Secondly, the Court concluded the union failed to show that its letter to the school about the union investigation was a substantial factor in the school's termination decision.

Citation: *Washington State Ferries*, Decision 11335 (MRNE, 2012), *aff'd* Decision 11335-A (MRNE, 2012)

Discrimination Found: No

Charge: Discharge.

Explanation: Discrimination not found where ferry employee, who had not worked actively for more than seven years, was terminated. There was no causal link between his protected collective bargaining activity of filing a grievance and his termination. Examiner Martin noted that "[the employee's] grievance was a result of his termination and not its cause."

Citation: *Washington State University*, Decision 11749 (PSRA, 2013), *aff'd*, Decision 11749-A (PRSA, 2013)

Discrimination Found: No

Charge: Discharge while probationary employee.

Explanation: No discrimination found where employer discharged employee during his probationary work period. Although union established prima facie case based on employee's reporting of skimming and meeting with union organizer, the employer demonstrated it terminated the employee for poor work performance. The union was unable to show that this was pretextual or that union animus was a substantial factor.

Citation: *Washougal School District*, Decision 2055 (PECB, 1984), *aff'd*, Decision 2055-A (PECB, 1985)

Discrimination Found: No

Charge: Transfer to less desirable shift.

Explanation: No discrimination found where transfer and schedule change of complainant found not to be in reprisal for successful prosecution of a grievance even though transfer was three days after grievance resolution. Timing of employer's actions was deemed "very poor management" but ultimately, the employer established a legitimate non-discriminatory reason for its actions because the employee was engaged in intimidating behavior. "Washougal School District has established that its transfer of [employee] was actually based on legitimate business reasons of the employer, including [his] misconduct following his reinstatement and, by such transfer, has not committed unfair labor practices within the meaning of RCW 41.56.140(1)."

Citation: *Wellpinit School District*, Decision 4083 (PECB, 1992)

Discrimination Found: Maybe

Charge: Suspension of union activist.

Explanation: Discrimination may be found where employer suspended union activist for alleged conduct at grievance meeting and reprimanded same employee for attempts to convey grievances on behalf of bargaining unit employees. The PERC Executive Director states, "While their immunity is not absolute, union officials do enjoy some protections under the statute when presenting grievances in their capacity as union officials." Therefore allegations of discrimination not dismissed.

Citation: *Yakima County*, Decision 11621 (PECB, 2013), *aff'd*, Decision 11621-A (PECB, 2013) **Discrimination Found: No**

Charge: Lay-offs and discharges.

Explanation: No discrimination found where employer laid off and demoted members of the bargaining unit following union whistleblowing. The Examiner noted: (1) the union's act of filing a complaint with the State Auditor is not the type of activity typically protected as "union activity," and even if it were, (2) the union failed to demonstrate a causal connection between whistleblowing and the layoffs. The Examiner found credible the employer's stated reason for the layoffs: underfunding.

PERC EMPLOYER ADVERSE ACTION TABLE

Under Washington state labor laws, one of the requirements for **unlawful discrimination** is that the employer's action must be an "adverse action" before it is grounds for an unfair labor practice charge. Specifically, the complainant must prove "**the employer deprived the employee of some ascertainable right, benefit, or status.**" This chart lists employer actions which PERC found to rise to the level of "adverse actions" and what actions fell short of constituting "adverse actions."

Forms of Adverse Actions:

Discharge
Discipline
Demotion
Failure to promote
Assignments
Refusal to hire
Discriminatory working conditions
Other discrimination

Form of Adverse Action	Adverse Action Found?	Case Citation
DISCHARGE		

Form of Adverse Action	Adverse Action Found?	Case Citation
Discharge	Yes	*Pierce County, Decision 12195 (PECB, 2014).* *City of Mountlake Terrace, Decision 11831-2 (PECB, 2013), aff'd, Decision 11831-A (PECB, 2014).* *Washington State Ferries, Decision 11335 (MRNE, 2012), aff'd, Decision 11335-A (MRNE, 2012).* *Washington State University, Decision 11749 (PSRA, 2013).* *Chelan Public Hospital District 2, Decision 11294 (PECB, 2012).* *Kiona Benton School District*, Decision 11563 (EDUC, 2012). *City of Kalama*, Decision 7448 (PECB, 2001). *Aberdeen School District,* Decision 6434 (PECB, 1998). *City of Winlock*, Decision 4784-A (PECB, 1995), *petition for judicial review dismissed*, Lewis County Superior Court, CD - 1001 (May 22, 1995). *Lewis County*, Decision 4691 (PECB, 1994), *aff'd*, Decision 4691-A (PECB, 1994), *Lewis County v. Public Employment Relations Commission and Teamsters Union*, Local 252, WPERR CD – 1235 (Lewis County Superior Court, 1997). *Pullman School District*,

Form of Adverse Action	Adverse Action Found?	Case Citation
		Decision 2632 (PECB, 1987). *Asotin County Housing Authority,* Decision 2471 (PECB, 1986), *aff'd*, Decision 2471-A (PECB, 1987). *Clallam County*, Decision 1405-A (PECB, 1984). *City of Bellevue*, Decision 2096 (PECB, 1984). *Benton City*, Decision 436 (PECB, 1978). *Clallam County*, 43 Wn. App. 589, 719 P.2d 140, CD-319 (Wash. Ct. App. 1986). *Town of Steilacoom*, Decision 6213 (PECB, 1998).
Layoff	Yes	*Northshore Utility District, Decision 11267 (PECB, 2011), aff'd, Decision 11267-A (PECB, 2012).* *Pasco Housing Authority*, Decision 6248 (PECB, 1998), *aff'd with modification*, *Pasco Housing Authority*, Decision 6248-A (PECB, 1998).
	Maybe	*Yakima County,* Decision 11621 (PECB, 2013), *aff'd*, Decision 11621-A (PECB, 2013).
Failing to offer continuing contract	Yes	*Bethel School District*, Decision 6731 (PECB, 1999).

Form of Adverse Action	Adverse Action Found?	Case Citation
Discharge	Yes	*City of Federal Way*, Decision 5183 (PECB, 1995), *aff'd*, Decision 5183-A (PECB, 1996), *rev'd*, WPERR CD - 1009 (King County Superior Court, January 10, 1997), *aff'd*, WPERR CD - 1009 (Wash. Ct. App., October 19, 1998)
Denying police guild member's request to resign and receive a severance settlement	Yes	*City of Mountlake Terrace, Decision 11831-2 (PECB, 2013), aff'd, Decision 11831-A (PECB, 2014).*
DISCIPLINE		
Final counseling memo	Yes	*University of Washington, Decision 11309 (PSRA, 2012).*
Final counseling memo	Yes	*University of Washington*, Decision 11199-B (PSRA, 2013).
Disciplinary letter that remained in employee's personnel file and suspension for 5 days	Yes	*Southwest Snohomish County Public Safety Communications Agency*, Decision 11149 (PECB, 2011), *aff'd*, Decision 11149-C (PECB, 2013).
Paid administrative leave	Yes	*Southwest Snohomish County Public Safety Communications Agency*, Decision 11149 (PECB, 2011), *aff'd*, Decision 11149-C (PECB, 2013).
Written letters of reprimands	Yes	*Southwest Snohomish County Public Safety Communications Agency*, Decision 11149 (PECB,

Form of Adverse Action	Adverse Action Found?	Case Citation
		2011), *aff'd*, Decision 11149-C (PECB, 2013).
Denying release time to attend negotiations and Disciplining the employee	Yes	*University of Washington*, Decision 11091 (PSRA, 2011), *aff'd*, Decision 11091 (PSRA, 2012).
Written reprimands and administrative leave	Yes	*Seattle School District*, Decision 11045-A (PECB, 2011), *rev'd in part*, Decision 11045-A (PECB, 2011).
Letter of reprimand & removal of internet/intranet access	Maybe	*State-Corrections, Decision 10998 (PSRA, 2011), rev'd, Decision 10998-A (PSRA, 2011).*
Supervisory review and verbal counseling	No	*Kitsap County*, Decision 9326-A (PECB, 2008).
Corrective counseling letter and verbal admonishment	No	*Snohomish County*, Decision 9799, (PECB, 2007).
Investigation and reprimand	Yes	*Kennewick School District*, Decision 5632-A (PECB, 1996) *rev'g Kennewick School District*, Decision 5632 (PECB, 1996).
Employer investigation without discipline	No	*State-Corrections, Decision 12002 (PSRA, 2014).*
Threat of discipline	No	*City of Port Angeles*, Decision 10445 (PECB, 2009).
Poor evaluation, extra evaluation	Yes	*Pasco Housing Authority*, Decision 6248 (PECB, 1998), *aff'd with modification*, Pasco Housing Authority, Decision 6248-A (PECB, 1998).
Employer's reprimand and subsequent resignation of employee	Yes	*North Valley Hospital*, Decision 5809 (PECB,

Form of Adverse Action	Adverse Action Found?	Case Citation
		1997), *aff'd, North Valley Hospital*, Decision 5809-A (PECB, 1997), *aff'd*, Okanogan County Superior Court, WPERR CD - 965 (September 28, 1998).
Coaching officer on customer service	No	*Port of Seattle*, Decision 11848 (PECB, 2013), *aff'd*, Decision 11848-A (PECB, 2014).
Negative performance evaluation	Yes	*Oroville School District*, Decision 6209-A (PECB, 1998), *aff'g as amended*, *Oroville School District*, Decision 6209-A (PECB, 1998).
DEMOTION		
Demotion	Yes	*Seattle School District*, Decision 11779-A (PECB, 2014). *Spokane Transit Authority*, Decision 2078-A (PECB, 1985), *aff'd, Spokane Transit Authority v. Public Employment Relations Commission v. Michael L. Closson*, WPERR CD - 1173 (Spokane County Superior Court, 1987).
Six-month demotion & suspension without pay	Yes	*City of Pullman*, Decision 11148 (PECB, 2011), *aff'd*, Decision 11148-A (PECB, 2012).
FAILURE TO PROMOTE		
Denial of recommendation letter needed for promotion	Yes	*State - Corrections*, Decision 12002-A (PSRA, 2014), *aff'g in part and rev'g in part*, Decision 12002 (PSRA, 2014).

Form of Adverse Action	Adverse Action Found?	Case Citation
Selection process for specialty positions: Employer declined to offer police officer a position in the Motors Unit	Yes	*City of Vancouver, Decision 10621-A & Decision 10621-B (PECB, 2012).*
Removal from a division chair position and loss of associated compensation	Yes	*Wenatchee Valley Community College*, Decision 10951 (CCOL, 2010).
Denial of promotion	Yes	*Pierce County*, Decision 7258 (PECB, 2001).
Denial of promotions and limiting work opportunities	Yes	*Port of Tacoma*, Decisions 4626 and 4627 (PECB, 1994).
ASSIGNMENTS		
Placed on home assignment	Yes	*State – Corrections*, Decision 11571 (PSRA, 2012), *aff'd*, Decision 11571-A (PSRA, 2013).
Reassignment to mailroom while he was under investigation for excessive use of force against an inmate	Yes	*State – Corrections*, Decision 11571 (PSRA, 2012), *aff'd*, Decision 11571-A (PSRA, 2013).
Reassigning shop steward out of bid position	Maybe	*State - Corrections*, Decision 11747 (PSRA, 2013).
Failed to assign driving assignments to substitute bus driver	Yes	*Toutle Lake School District*, Decision 2659 (PECB, 1987).
Employee was given no work, or given work with an incomplete work assignment form, or given work without any assignment form and that work was transferred from her to another employee	No	*Community College District 13*, Decision 9171-A (PSRA, 2007).
Removal from special project committee	Yes	*Southwest Snohomish County Public Safety Communications Agency*, Decision 11149 (PECB,

Form of Adverse Action	Adverse Action Found?	Case Citation
		2011), *aff'd*, Decision 11149-C (PECB, 2013).
Administrative transfer	No	*Seattle School District*, Decision 11045 (PECB, 2011), *rev'd in part*, Decision 11045-A (PECB, 2011).
Transfer/Reassignment	Yes	*King County*, Decision 3318 (PECB, 1989).
Reassignment – removed from a division chair position	Yes	*Wenatchee Valley Community College*, Decision 10951 (CCOL, 2010).
Transfer	Yes	*Kiona Benton School District*, Decision 11035 (EDUC, 2011). *City of Tukwila*, Decision 4968 (PECB, 1995).
Transfer of employee after evaluation and appeal process of evaluation	Yes	*City of Seattle*, Decision 6357 (PECB, 1998).
Transfer and schedule change	No	*Washougal School District*, Decision 2055-A (PECB, 1985).
REFUSAL TO HIRE		
Failure to hire	Yes	*King County*, Decision 11221-A (PECB, 2012).
Refusal to hire	Yes	*Auburn School District*, Decision 2291 (PECB, 1985). *Morton School District*, Decisions 5838 and 5839 (PECB, 1997). *City of Centralia*, Decision 2904 (PECB, 1988).
Refusal to hire; limit candidate pool	Yes	*King County Fire District 4*, Decision 3366 (PECB, 1989).
Refusal to reinstate following release to return to work	Yes	*King County*, Decision 3178 (PECB, 1989), *aff'd*, Decision 3178-A (PECB,

Form of Adverse Action	Adverse Action Found?	Case Citation
		1989).
Failure to rehire	Yes	*Educational Service District 114*, Decision 4361-A (PECB, 1994). *Clallam Transit System*, Decision 4597 (PECB, 1994).
DISCRIMINATORY WORKING CONDITIONS		
Temporarily restricting what work areas unit member could work in on certain days	Yes	*State – Corrections, Decision 11571 (PSRA, 2012).*
Union reps no longer allowed to meet with bargaining unit members during their work time	Yes	*City of Benton City*, Decision 10956 (PECB, 2011).
Employer denial of a letter of recommendation	Yes	*State-Corrections, Decision 12002-A (PSRA, 2014).*
Removal of internet/intranet access and letter of reprimand	Yes	*State-Corrections, Decision 10998 (PSRA, 2011).*
Change in work schedules	Yes	*City of Winlock*, Decision 4784-A (PECB, 1995), *petition for judicial review dismissed*, CD - 1001 (Lewis County Superior Court, May 22, 1995).
Discontinuing "K-9" patrol program		*City of Omak*, Decisions 5579-A, 5580-A, 5581-A and 5583-A (PECB, 1997), *aff'd on this issue*, Decisions 5579-B, 5580-B, 5581-B and 5583-B (PECB, 1998).

Form of Adverse Action	Adverse Action Found?	Case Citation
Employer placed performance reports and documents in employee's personnel file shortly after grievance	Yes	*City of Mill Creek*, Decision 5699 (PECB, 1996).
Reducing work hours	Yes	*Benton City*, Decision 436 (PECB, 1978).
Assigning complainant work, and had in fact assigned him as many hours as other intermittent workers employed in the same type of job at the same work location.	No	*City of Seattle*, Decision 1038 (PECB, 1980).
OTHER DISCRIMINATION		
Investigation into retaliation complaints	Yes	*City of Pullman*, Decision 11148 (PECB, 2011), *aff'd*, Decision 11148-A (PECB, 2012).
Delay in investigation	No	*Seattle School District*, Decision 10732-A (PECB, 2012).
Denying/limiting access to union representative	Yes	*King County*, Decision 11223 (PECB, 2011).
Withdrawal of endorsement for a dispatcher to work as an instructor at the Criminal Justice Training Commission	Yes	*Southwest Snohomish County Public Safety Communications Agency*, Decision 11149 (PECB, 2011), *aff'd*, Decision 11149-C (PECB, 2013).
Removal from seniority bid position	Yes	*State – Corrections*, Decision 11571 (PSRA, 2012), *aff'd*, Decision 11571-A (PSRA, 2013).
Employee's position was the only union-represented research technician on the employer's campus	No	*University of Washington*, Decision 8216-A (PSRA, 2004).

Form of Adverse Action	Adverse Action Found?	Case Citation
Personnel actions taken against employee (include Employer's refusal to allow him to complete the overtime work trade, the unpaid leave of absence imposed upon him, and his eventual discharge).	No	*Port of Seattle*, Decision 6854-A (PECB, 2001).
Employee who claimed constructive discharge	No	*Clover Park School District*, Decision 7073-A (EDUC, 2001).
33 incidents creating hostile job atmosphere and pattern of discrimination including: she was given no work, or given work with an incomplete work assignment form, or given work without any assignment form; that she was given work with short deadlines; that work was transferred from her to another employee; that she was blamed for mistakes, that her work was micro-managed; and she was excluded from decision-making and meetings, and that meetings she was called to were cancelled	No	*Community College District 13 (Lower Columbia)*, Decision 9171-A (PSRA, 2007).
Employee resignation following reprimand that created hostile work environment	Yes	*North Valley Hospital*, Decision 5809 (PECB, 1997), *aff'd, North Valley Hospital*, Decision 5809-A (PECB, 1997), *aff'd*, Okanogan County Superior Court, WPERR CD - 965 (September 28, 1998).
Conversation at hockey game about negotiations	No	*Snohomish County*, Decision 9834 (PSRA, 2007), *aff'd*, *Snohomish County*, Decision 9834B (PSRA, 2008).
Limiting overtime while under investigation for excessive use of	Yes	*State – Corrections*, Decision 11571 (PSRA,

Form of Adverse Action	Adverse Action Found?	Case Citation
force against an inmate		2012), *aff'd*, Decision 11571-A (PSRA, 2013).
Denying release time to police guild members to testify at ULP hearing	No	*City of Mountlake Terrace, Decision 11831-2 (PECB, 2013), aff'd, Decision 11831-A (PECB, 2014).*
Denying release time to police guild members to prepare for a ULP hearing	No	*City of Mountlake Terrace, Decision 11831-2 (PECB, 2013), aff'd, Decision 11831-A (PECB, 2014).*
Denying leave requests to take civil service test	Maybe	*City of Mountlake Terrace, Decision 11831-2 (PECB, 2013), aff'd, Decision 11831-A (PECB, 2014).*

ABOUT THE AUTHOR

Jim Cline received his B.A. with distinction in Political Science from the University of Washington in 1980, and an M.A. in Political Science from the University of Washington in 1982. He enrolled in a joint Law/Economics program at the University of Notre Dame and received an M.A. in Economics and J.D. from Notre Dame, both in 1986.

After graduating from law school, Jim served as a Deputy Prosecuting Attorney for the King County Prosecutor's Office.

Since 1990, he has represented public safety labor organizations throughout the State of Washington. He is also the author of "The Rights of Washington Public Safety employees: Members Handbook."

Jim resides in Issaquah with his family. When he is not busy practicing law and writing, he enjoys bicycling and travel.

Made in the USA
Columbia, SC
09 May 2024

35389493R00426